013971945

KT-148-326

Withdrawn from stock

The Companion to Development Studies

Edited by

Vandana Desai

Department of Geography, Royal Holloway,
University of London

and

Robert B. Potter

Department of Geography, University of Reading

ARNOLD

A member of the Hodder Headline Group
LONDON
Distributed in the United States of America by
Oxford University Press Inc., New York

First published in Great Britain in 2002 by
Arnold, a member of the Hodder Headline Group,
338 Euston Road, London NW1 3BH

http://www.arnoldpublishers.com

Distributed in the United States of America by
Oxford University Press Inc.,
198 Madison Avenue, New York, NY10016

© 2002 Arnold, except for the entry 'The social and economic impact
of AIDS/HIV on development', © 2000 Tony Barnett

All rights reserved. No part of this publication may be reproduced or
transmitted in any form or by any means, electronically or mechanically,
including photocopying, recording or any information storage or retrieval
system, without either prior permission in writing from the publisher or a
licence permitting restricted copying. In the United Kingdom such licences
are issued by the Copyright Licensing Agency: 90 Tottenham Court Road,
London W1T 4LP.

The advice and information in this book are believed to be true and
accurate at the date of going to press, neither the author[s] nor the publisher
can accept any legal responsibility or liability for any errors or omissions.

British Library Cataloguing in Publication Data
A catalogue record for this book is available from the British Library

Library of Congress Cataloging-in-Publication Data
A catalog record for this book is available from the Library of Congress

ISBN 0 340 76050 8 (hb)
ISBN 0 340 76051 6 (pb)

6 7 8 9 10

Typeset in 10 on 13 pt Minion by Cambrian Typesetters, Frimley, Surrey
Printed and bound in Malta by Gutenberg Press Ltd

What do you think about this book? Or any other Arnold title?
Please send your comments to feedback.arnold@hodder.co.uk

Contents

Contributors

Dr Bama Athreya, Deputy Director, International Labor Rights Fund, USA

Professor Donald W. Attwood, Professor of Anthropology, McGill University, Canada

Professor Richard M. Auty, Professor in Economic Geography, University of Lancaster, UK

Professor Tony Barnett, Professor of Development Studies, University of East Anglia, UK

Leo Bashyam, Head of Asia Team, Christian Aid, UK

Professor Richard Batley, Professor of Development Administration, School of Public Policy, University of Birmingham, UK

Professor B.S. Baviskar, Formerly Professor of Sociology, University of Delhi, India

Dr Richard Black, Co-Director, Sussex Centre for Migration Research, University of Sussex, UK

Dr Tony Binns, Reader in Geography, University of Sussex, UK

Professor Piers Blaikie, Professor of Development Studies, University of East Anglia, UK

Rob Bowden, Consultant, Environment and Society International – Educational Resourcing (EASI–ER), Staffordshire, UK

Dr Lynne Brydon, Senior Lecturer, Centre of West African Studies, University of Birmingham, UK

Professor Peter Burnell, Professor of Politics, University of Warwick, UK

Dr Raff Carmen, Senior Lecturer, Vocational, Professional and Lifelong Learning Group, University of Manchester, UK

Professor Michael M. Cernea, Senior Social Development Adviser, Middle East and North Africa Region, World Bank, Washington DC, USA

Dr Sylvia Chant, Reader in Geography, London School of Economics, UK

Professor Graham P. Chapman, Professor of Geography, Lancaster University, UK

John D. Clark, Lead Social Development Specialist, World Bank and currently Visiting Fellow, Centre for Civil Society, London School of Economics, UK

Professor Colin Clarke, Professor of Urban and Social Geography, Oxford University, UK

Dr Ernestina Coast, Lecturer in Population Studies, London School of Economics, UK

Stephen J. Connor, Senior Research Fellow, Liverpool School of Tropical Medicine, UK

Professor Dennis Conway, Professor of Geography, Indiana University, USA

Professor Stuart Corbridge, Professor of Geography, London School of Economics, UK, and Professor of International Studies, University of Miami, USA

Sonia Corrêa, DAWN Coordinator for Sexual and Reproductive Rights and Health Researcher at the Brazilian Institute of Social and Economic Analysis, and Member of the Brazilian National Commission on Population and Development, Brazil

Professor Graham M.S. Dann, Professor of Tourism, University of Luton, UK

Dr Rick Davies, Research Fellow, Centre for Development Studies, University of Wales Swansea, UK

Professor Delia Davin, Professor of Chinese Studies, University of Leeds, UK

Ms Elsa L. Dawson, Adviser, Policy Department, Oxfam, UK

Dr Vandana Desai, Lecturer in Development Geography, Royal Holloway, University of London, UK

Professor Jean Drèze, Honorary Professor of Economics, Delhi School of Economics, India

Dr Klaus Dodds, Senior Lecturer in Geography, Royal Holloway, University of London, UK

Professor Denis Dwyer, Visiting Professor of Geography, University of Liverpool, UK

Dr Caroline Dyer, Senior Research Fellow in International Education, University of Manchester, UK

Dr Jennifer A. Elliott, Principal Lecturer in Geography, University of Brighton, UK

Dr Tim Forsyth, Lecturer in Geography, London School of Economics, UK

Dr Margaret Foster, Intermediate Technology Development Group, Schumacher Centre for Technology Development, UK

Dr Alan F. Fowler, Vice-President of the International Society for Third Sector Research (ISTR), and Visiting Research Fellow, Oxford Brookes University, UK

Professor Alan Gilbert, Professor of Geography, UCL (University College London), UK

Dr Alan Grainger, Lecturer in Geography, University of Leeds, UK

Professor David Greenaway, Professor of Economics, University of Nottingham, UK

Professor R.D. Grillo, Professor of Social Anthropology, University of Sussex, UK

Dr Robert N. Gwynne, Reader in Latin American Development, University of Birmingham, UK

Professor Barbara Harriss-White, Professor of Development Studies, University of Oxford, UK

Professor Björn Hettne, Department of Peace and Development Research, Gothenburg University, Sweden

Nikolas Heynen, doctoral student in Geography, Indiana University, USA

Dr David Hilling, Honorary Research Fellow, Royal Holloway, University of London, UK

Yassir Islam, Program Associate, Agricultural Container Research Council, USA

Professor Rob Jenkins, Professor of Political Science, Birkbeck College, University of London, UK

Dr Ray Kiely, Senior Lecturer in Development Studies, University of East London, UK

Professor Tony Killick, Senior Research Associate, Overseas Development Institute, UK

Professor Thomas Klak, Associate Professor of Geography, Miami University, Ohio, and Adjunct Associate Professor of Geography, Ohio State University, USA

Dr David Lewis, Lecturer in Social Policy, London School of Economics, UK

Dr Sally Lloyd-Evans, Lecturer in Geography, University of Reading, UK

Dr Kenneth Lynch, Senior Lecturer in Geography, Kingston University, UK

Dr Don D. Marshall, Research Fellow, Sir Arthur Lewis Institute of Social and Economic Studies, University of the West Indies, West Indies

Dr Emma Mawdsley, Lecturer in Geography, University of Durham, UK

Dr Cheryl McEwan, Lecturer in Human Geography, University of Birmingham, UK

Dr Erika McAslan, Research Assistant, Social Development Direct, UK

Dr Duncan McGregor, Senior Lecturer in Geography, Royal Holloway, University of London, UK

Dr Cathy McIlwaine, Lecturer in Human Geography, Queen Mary, University of London, UK

Professor Chris Milner, Professor of International Economics, University of Nottingham, UK

Dr Jayalaxshmi Mistry, Lecturer in Geography, University of London, UK

Dr Giles Mohan, Lecturer in Development Studies, Open University, UK

Dr Joe Mullen, Senior Lecturer in Rural Development/Poverty, Institute for Development Policy and Management, University of Manchester, UK

Professor Barry Munslow, Professor of Politics, University of Liverpool, UK

Professor Colin Murray, Professor of African Sociology, University of Manchester, UK

Professor Paul J. Nelson, Assistant Professor, Graduate School of Public and International Affairs, University of Pittsburgh, USA

Dr Anthony O'Connor, Reader in Geography, UCL (University College London), UK

Dr Michael J.G. Parnwell, Reader in South-East Asian Geography, University of Hull, UK

Professor Jane Parpart, Professor of History, International Development Studies and Women's Studies, Dalhousie University, Halifax, Canada, and Visiting Professor in Political Science at Stellenbosch University, South Africa

Professor Tulsi Patel, Professor of Sociology, Delhi School of Economics, University of Delhi, India

Professor Linda Peake, Associate Professor, York University, Canada

Dr Mark Pelling, Lecturer in Geography, University of Liverpool, UK

Dr Gina Porter, Research Fellow, Department of Anthropology, University of Durham, UK

Professor Robert B. Potter, Professor of Human Geography, University of Reading, UK

Dr Marcus Power, Lecturer in Human Geography, University of Leeds, UK

Professor Jules Pretty, Professor in Environment and Society, University of Essex, UK

Jonathan Pugh, doctoral student in Geography, Royal Holloway, University of London, UK

Professor Carole Rakodi, Professor of International Urban Development Planning, Cardiff University, UK

Dr Shirin M. Rai, Reader in Politics, University of Warwick, UK

Professor Michael Redclift, Professor of International Environmental Policy, Kings College, London, UK

Professor B. Sudhakara Reddy, Dean, Indira Gandhi Institute of Development Research, Mumbai, India

Dr Jonathan Rigg, Reader in Geography, University of Durham, UK

Professor Paul Rogers, Professor of Peace Studies, Bradford University, UK

Professor David Sapsford, Professor of Economics, Lancaster University, UK

Dr David Satterthwaite, Human Settlements Programme, International Institute for Environment and Development (IIED), UK

Dr Frans J. Schuurman, Senior Lecturer in Development Studies, University of Nijmegen, The Netherlands

Andrew Scott, International Programmes and Policy Director, Intermediate Technology Development Group, Schumacher Centre for Technology Development, UK

Professor Timothy M. Shaw, Director, Institute of Commonwealth Studies, University of London, UK, on leave as Professor of Political Science and International Development Studies, Dalhousie University, Halifax, Canada

Professor Prakash Shetty, Professor of Human Nutrition, London School of Hygiene and Tropical Medicine, UK

John Shotton Senior Education Specialist, ARCADIS BMB Management Consultants, The Netherlands

Dr James D. Sidaway, Associate Professor, Department of Geography, National University of Singapore, Singapore

Professor David Simon, Professor of Development Geography, Royal Holloway, University of London, UK

Professor David M. Smith, Professor of Geography, Queen Mary, University of London, UK

Dr Kathleen Staudt, Professor of Political Science, University of Texas at El Paso, USA

Dr Ramya Subrahmanian, Research Fellow, Institute of Development Studies, University of Sussex, UK

Keith Sutton, Senior Lecturer in Geography, University of Manchester, UK

Professor Anthony P. Thirlwall, Professor of Applied Economics, University of Kent, UK

Dr Janet G. Townsend, Reader in Geography, University of Durham, UK

Dr D. Alissa Trotz, Assistant Professor in Women's and Gender Studies, Ontario Institute of Education, and Sociology and Equity Studies, University of Toronto, Canada

Dr Maya Unnithan-Kumar, Senior Lecturer in Social Anthropology, University of Sussex, UK

Professor Tim Unwin, Professor of Geography, Royal Holloway, University of London, UK

Dr Alison Van Rooy, Deputy Director, Governance and Social Policies Division, Canadian International Development Agency; formerly Senior Researcher, The North-South Institute, Ottawa, Canada

Dr Ann Varley, Reader in Geography, UCL (University College London), UK

Dr Sudhir Wanmali, Consultant, Rural Development and Planning, Rockville, USA

Dr Howard White, Fellow, Institute of Development Studies, University of Sussex, UK

Dr Jim Whitman, Lecturer in Peace Studies, Bradford University, UK

Dr Gordon Wilson, Senior Lecturer in Technology and Development, Open University, UK

Dr Kate Young, Vice-Chair, National Alliance of Women's Organisations, UK

Dr Salah E. Zaimeche, Honorary Visiting Research Fellow in Geography, University of Manchester, UK

Preface

Our intention as the editors of *The Companion to Development Studies* was to bring together leading scholars from throughout the world in order to provide a truly international and interdisciplinary overview of the major issues surrounding development theory and practice in the twenty-first century. From the outset, it was envisaged that the volume would offer a one-stop reference guide for anyone with a practical, professional or academic interest in development studies. The volume will be of particular relevance to those in the fields of development studies, sociology and social policy, geography, anthropology, economics and politics, along with NGO practitioners and those in donor agencies.

The *Companion to Development Studies* recognizes the existence of numerous good general texts on development studies, including selected readers. However, this volume performs a unique function in bringing together between two covers, a wide range of concisely written overviews of the most important issues in the field. As such, the volume can effectively be used as a course textbook, whilst by the exercise of selective judgement, it could be treated as a source of key course readings and discussion pieces in connection with higher level options and training courses, for example, at the Masters degree level. In order to guide both interested students and general readers who want to pursue particular topics, each contribution is followed by an annotated summary of key items for further reading, plus a full listing of the references cited in the text. It is also our hope that students on certain programmes may be able to use the volume over the duration of their studies, and not just for one or two units or modules.

The *Companion* contains authoritative overviews covering a wide range of issues, from colonial to postcolonial strategies of development, neo-liberalism, non-governmental organizations, agents of development such as the World Bank and United Nations, as well as alternative forms of development, thereby providing a history of over half a century of development planning and change. In so doing, the volume also deals with the changing nature of development and development studies as a discipline over the decades. The linkages that exist between the so-called 'North' and 'South' are likewise dealt with, covering topics such as foreign aid and grassroots development.

The contributions are divided into ten principal sections, dealing respectively with: the nature of development and development studies; theories and strategies of development; rural development; industrialization and employment; urbanization; the environment; gender, population and development; health and education; the political economy of violence and insecurity; and agents of development.

One of the major strengths of the volume is that it has been written by well-known and respected personalities from the development community, both from the so-called 'South' and the 'North'. Indeed, we specifically targeted authors from around the world. We have been surprised and heartened that our invitations to take part in this project were so overwhelmingly greeted with positive responses. More than one hundred contributions to the *Companion* were received and edited ready for publication in little more than 12 months. There is no doubting the fact that e-mail and the internet greatly facilitated the completion of this project ahead of schedule. We feel sure that this excellent response from our contributors reflects the fact that there was a real gap in the development studies literature, which will be filled by *The Companion to Development Studies.*

Vandana Desai and Rob Potter
Englefield Green
November 2000

The nature of development and of development studies

EDITORIAL INTRODUCTION

The chapters included in this first section of the book explore and comment on two closely linked themes: first, the nature and progress of development studies as a distinct avenue of enquiry; and second, how development itself can be defined and conceptualized. In respect of the first of these two topics, it is important to stress the origins of the First, Second and Third Worlds in the politics of the Cold War, and the later transition to a North–South dichotomy following the Brandt Commission. With the collapse of the Berlin Wall and the near total demise of the socialist Third World, it is now best to talk in terms of 'developing countries', and even more so perhaps, 'poor nations'.

Early views of development within the field of development studies, undoubtedly stressed catching up with, and generally imitating, the 'West'. The failure of development in so-called Third World countries, together with the postmodern critique and trends of globalization, are customarily regarded as having given rise to a major impasse in development studies in the 1980s. Recent approaches have been somewhat more liberating in terms of the worldviews promulgated, and there are trends to link development studies with cultural studies, for example, in respect of the condition of postmodernity and the vital nature of issues of peace and security. Further, the trend of globalization, the reduction in the importance of the state, and the associated alienation of the state from civil society, all mean that development studies face a battery of problems, not least whether these trends are real and inescapable phenomena, or are constructs designed to legitimize the logic of the neo-liberal market.

Stemming from these various trends, in the last ten years, it has become increasingly fashionable to criticize 'Western' development imperatives, and this has given rise to a variety of what can be referred to as 'postist-stances', including post-development, anti-development and beyond development. In truth, these positions should not be seen as new, but rather as joining earlier Marxist and feminist critiques of the status quo nature of development. Further, some would argue that whatever its sins, the 'development project' has brought financial aid and technological assistance, which have sought to raise standards of living in the South, even if they have only been successful locally. Accepted concepts and theories have also been challenged by the collapse of state socialism and the Asian crisis from mid-1997, characterized by a rush of investment capital out of the region.

If development is defined in terms of poor countries, an enduring problem remains the need to measure and understand poverty. This is especially so today, with poverty 'alleviation' and 'elimination' programmes, and the difficulties of Highly Indebted Poor Countries (HIPCs) being stressed by the international development agencies. Poverty means that in spite of global trends, it still matters where you live, especially if you fall into the poorest third or so of people, living in tropical Africa and Asia. Addressing poverty requires political will, and many would maintain that this remains the real obstacle to development.

The issues on which a growing consensus appears to be emerging include the fact that economic growth is a necessary, but not sufficient condition for development. Without redistribution of income and wealth, inequalities are not going to be reduced, and there is mounting evidence that it is inequalities that hurt. Thus, development must be regarded as synonymous with enhancing human rights and welfare, so that self-esteem, self-respect and improving entitlements become central concerns. In such a guise, participatory planning is a vital prerequisite, reflecting the salience of anthropological perspectives, in particular, in coming to appreciate the value of indigenous knowledge.

1.1 The Third World, developing countries, the South, poor countries

Klaus Dodds

THE POWER OF WORDS

In his fluent and polemical analysis of development, Arturo Escobar, makes a salient point concerning the discursive power of geographical description (see Escobar, 1995: 1–20). With reference to post-war Western development discourse he notes that it:

> inevitably contained a geopolitical imagination that has shaped the meaning of development for more than four decades. For some, this will to spatial power is one of the essential features of development (Slater, 1993). It is implicit in expressions such as First and Third World, North and South, centre and periphery. The social production of space implicit in these terms is bound with the production of differences, subjectivities and social orders.
>
> (Escobar, 1995: 9)

The origins of this geopolitical imagination lay in the uncertain aftermath of the Second World War when the allies, led by the United States, attempted to rebuild shattered wartime economies and invent international institutions capable of restoring order to world politics. While these developments were unfolding, US–Soviet relations were transformed, as wartime co-operation gave way to a dangerous rivalry that rapidly overturned the political geography of the European continent. By the late 1940s, the American journalist, Walter Lippman, had coined the term 'Cold War' in order to describe the culture of hostility and suspicion that had developed between the two superpowers and their rival blocs (the North Atlantic Treaty Organization and the Warsaw Pact).

In the process of economic and political reconstruction, the Truman administration had taken a particular interest in the condition of the 'underdeveloped' areas. In his inaugural address as President of the United States on 20 January 1949, Truman announced his plan for a 'fair deal' for the rest of the world, based on 'Greater production [as] the key to prosperity and peace' (Truman, 1949, cited in Escobar, 1995: 1). While this intent was undeniably ambitious, the significance of this address lies in the manner in which Truman's geographical imagination transformed the post-war world into 'underdeveloped' and 'prosperous' areas. In doing so, critics have argued that the American administration prepared the foundation for a programme of active and sometimes aggressive intervention in these 'underdeveloped' regions (Dodds, 1999).

The power of geographical description lies, therefore, in the manner in which America's post-war policies were justified with reference to 'underdevelopment' and the needs of the less fortunate areas of the planet. Truman's vision of development rested on an assumption that Western capital, knowledge and technological capability was essential for the transformation of 'underdeveloped' areas and consequently, the less fortunate should then seek to emulate American-style democracy, prosperity and peace (Rist, 1997; Agnew, 1998). In subsequent years, this appeal for improvement and progress was to be nourished not only by countless United Nations' programmes concerned with development, but also by Cold War rivalries with the Soviet Union which were intent on encouraging these 'underdeveloped' areas to follow a socialist path to development. Regardless of their ideological positions, both superpowers were actively seeking to influence and shape the political and economic complexion of the post-war world.

THE INVENTION OF THE THIRD WORLD

In the aftermath of the Korean crisis (1950–53), a new geopolitical imagination began to emerge as the conflict between the Soviet Union and the United States spread across the globe. Key geographical designations such as 'First World' and 'Third World' were deployed by Western social scientists in an attempt to highlight the profound social and political differences between the advanced industrialized countries and the recently decolonized states in Africa, Asia and the Middle East. According to one critic:

> This term [the Third World] is itself a product of the Cold War. Although it was first coined in France in the late 1940s to refer to a possible Third Estate or Third Way, it soon began to refer to those parts of the world outside the settled spheres of influence of the 'superpowers', the First and Second Worlds.

> (Agnew, 1998: 111–12).

In this simplified geopolitical setting, the systemic–ideological conflict with the Soviet Union and the Second World was then used by the United States to justify either armed and/or economic intervention in the Third World (Yoon Yung, 1997). Successive administrations in Washington DC justified such actions on the basis that the Third World needed to be protected from the evils of communism and totalitarianism.

During the Cold War, the experiences of the developing countries of the Third World were never uniform as some regions such as Latin America and Southeast Asia attracted active American intervention. In Taiwan and South Korea, for instance, the Americans provided substantial amounts of financial and military aid (amounting to up to 10 per cent of total national income in the 1950s), because they were regarded as significant elements in the geopolitical struggle against the Soviet Union. In Latin America, US administrations invaded and destabilized countries thought to be vulnerable to socialism and anti-capitalist sentiment within the Catholic Church and the trade unions. In 1965, for example, 20,000 marines were sent by President Johnson to the Dominican Republic in order to suppress the emergence of a socialist government (Dunkerley, 1994). In 1973, the Central Intelligence Agency (CIA) co-operated with General Augusto Pinochet in a *golpe de estado*, which witnessed the violent dissolution of the socialist government of President Salvador Allende. Oppressive military rule was then to dominate Chile and other parts of Latin America for well over a decade (Phillips, 1985). Despite occasional outbursts of concern relating to widespread human rights violations, American administrations were prepared to over-look this issue in favour of their Cold War strategy of restraining communism in the Third World.

Not surprisingly, the 'hotting up' of the Cold War in Latin America and Southeast Asia provoked some members of the Third World to create a Non-Aligned Movement (NAM) in 1961. The latter was intended to be an international organization composed, in the main, of recently decolonized states such as India and Indonesia which sought not only to avoid the dangerous politics of the Cold War but also to articulate alternatives to modern development. Three years later, these non-aligned states had been joined by other Third World states in a movement called the 'Group of 77' in order to pressurize 'Northern' states to acknowledge the linkages between welfare, war, external debt and poverty (Willetts, 1978). While those demands for fundamental reforms in the world economy and international political structures were ignored by Northern states, the superpowers were deeply involved in bloody conflicts such as that in Southeast Asia, which was to leave over 600,000 people dead by the mid-1970s.

By the early 1970s, the developing countries had been shaped by a combination of circumstances and it would be mistaken to imply that superpower intervention determined the fate of this diverse set of states and societies. In some cases, economic development appeared to have brought unprecedented wealth and opportunity to so-called newly industrialized countries (NICs) such as Taiwan, Singapore and Malaysia. Alternatively, the emergence of oil economies such as Saudi Arabia, Venezuela and Nigeria offered another vision of political and economic change in the developing world even though the social cost was often great in terms of corruption, human rights abuses and environmental degradation (see, for instance, Watts, 1994, on Nigeria). Finally, some states in sub-Saharan Africa and Central America (such as Nicaragua and Mozambique) simply became poorer as a consequence of bitter civil wars, massive corruption, and persistent and violent intervention by the superpowers.

THE SOUTH

Amidst a general feeling of despair and pessimism following the onset of the so-called Second Cold War, the United Nations-sponsored Brandt Commission reported on the state of the world in 1980 and 1983 (Brandt Commission, 1980, 1983). Significantly, the Commission depicted a world divided between North and South rather than First, Second and Third Worlds. These reports not only called into question the notion of separate worlds but also maintained that it was in the interest of the 'North' to aid the development of the 'South' because increased levels of economic activity and interaction would benefit all states, regardless of their geographical and ideological locations. Moreover, the political message from the Brandt Commission also touched upon the interdependence of the human race and suggested that mutual dependence (rather than rigid separation) was likely to become an inevitable feature of global political life.

As the 1980s unfolded, the distinction between the First and Second Worlds began to fragment further as state socialisms in Eastern Europe and elsewhere collapsed as a consequence of popular movements demanding radical political and economic change. For many observers, the fall of the Berlin Wall in November 1989 signalled the formal ending of a socialist Second World and provoked an intellectual crisis for those analysts who had become reassuringly familiar with the political geographies of the Cold War. John Mearsheimer, for instance, argued that the uncertain future of the post-Cold War world would provoke considerable anxieties and produce a longing for the return of the certainties of a divided world (Mearsheimer, 1990). While his argument is more sophisticated than one might initially imagine, it did touch upon a sentiment in the North that the ending of the Cold War had led to the dissolution of a specific period of international political order. For those living in the South, the ending of the Cold War was greeted with a mixture of relief and a hope that renewed attention would be given to the hundreds of millions living in poverty and hardship in many parts of the Third World.

POOR COUNTRIES

Despite the arguments relating to the intellectual validity of terms such as the 'South' 'Third World', there is good reason to persist with these descriptions in the sense that attention to the profound inequalities that endure in the post-Cold War world. The for example, recognized in the 1990s that the poorest countries in the world are South. Indeed, it is commonly accepted that the 25 poorest countries such as B

Laos effectively constitute a 'Fourth World' that is quite distinct from other nations within the South. Oil exporting countries such as Saudi Arabia and industrialized economies such as Brazil have more in common, economically and politically, with their northern counterparts such as the United States and Germany in terms of concerns relating to market access and world economic trends. However, there can be little doubt that abject poverty is geographically concentrated in Central America, sub-Saharan Africa and parts of South, Southeast and Northeast Asia.

Notwithstanding those observations relating to the poorest countries in the world, the geographical distribution of poverty defies simple categories such as North and South. It is increasingly evident that there are some parts of the South (such as Singapore and Mumbai) which have a degree of affluence more akin to the northern industrialized cities of London, New York and Paris. Alternatively, there are parts of Europe such as Albania and the former Yugoslavia that are undoubtedly poor as assessed by all the traditional criteria relating to income levels, childhood mortality, healthcare and other measures of human development. Put simply, there are parts of the Third World in the First World and vice versa. It is no longer appropriate or simply accurate to describe global poverty in terms of a North–South division.

CONCLUSIONS

This short essay has attempted to account for the Cold War origins of development and its subsequent connections with North–South relations. While it is becoming increasingly fashionable to criticize Western development, it must be recognized that financial aid and technological assistance have played their part in raising the living standards of millions of people in the South. In many parts of the world, people are enjoying unprecedented levels of health and prosperity. Development, in all its complex variations, has not been (and never was) a singular Western project hell-bent on the subjugation of the South. This does not mean that economic inequalities and the legacies of colonialism and imperialism have been overwhelmed by widespread social and cultural improvement. At the very least, it has to be acknowledged that categories such as 'developing' deserve careful analysis because *inter alia* there are substantial pockets of wealth which are to be found throughout the South. And it is the task of geographers and other social scientists to investigate and imagine mechanisms and institutions capable of spreading wealth and well-being in a way that is environmentally and politically sustainable. This is a daunting, but pressing task.

GUIDE TO FURTHER READING

For a powerful critique of post-war Western development, see Escobar, A. (1995) *Encountering Development*, Princeton: Princeton University Press.

‎ ‎ *History of Development*, London: Zed Books, is a masterly overview of the history of development... kes the point that concern for the condition of the Third World predates Truman's speech

‎ ‎ ...as of Development: Reflections on the Counter-Revolution in Development Theory and ...kwell, is very helpful when considering the dilemmas posed by development in

on: Routledge.

...h–South: A Programme for Survival, London: Pan.

Brandt Commission (1983) *Common Crisis: North–South Cooperation for World Recovery*, London: Pan.

Dodds, K. (1999) 'Taking the Cold War to the Third World', in D. Slater and P. Taylor (eds) *The American Century*, Oxford: Blackwell, pp. 163–80.

Dunkerley, J. (1994) *The Pacification of Central America*, London: Verso.

Mearsheimer, J. (1990) 'Back to the future: instability in Europe after the Cold War', *International Security* 15: 5–56.

Phillips, G. (1985) *The Military in South American Politics*, Beckenham: Croom Helm.

Watts, M. (1994) 'Oil as money: the devil's excrement and the spectacle of gold', in S. Corbridge, R. Martin and N. Thrift (eds) *Money, Power and Space*, Oxford: Blackwell, pp. 406–45.

Willetts, P. (1978) *The Non-Aligned Movement*, London: Pinter.

Yung, Yoon M. (1997) 'Explaining US intervention in Third World internal wars 1945–1989', *Journal of Conflict Resolution* 41: 580–602.

1.2 Current trends and future options in development studies

Björn Hettne

DEVELOPMENT STUDIES IN RETROSPECT

At the beginning of the twenty-first century we are in an era which, rather depressingly for development theorists, has been described as 'post-development' (Escobar, 1995). There is a need to reconsider purpose, content, agency and context in a reconstituted field of development studies. The classical discourse, which had its roots in the late 1940s and was institutionalized in the 1950s and 1960s, assumed the possibility of an autonomous, (inter)disciplinary field, containing a set of theoretical cores with development economics as a respected member of the family. The relevant theoretical schools, competing but yet in dialogue, were: *modernization, structuralism, dependency* and '*another development*', all normatively concerned with the specific problem of national development in the so-called 'Third World'.

The reconstruction of war-torn Europe provided the model for state-directed *modernization* of the 'new nations'. In this model, development was largely sociological and political in nature, and under-development was defined in terms of differences between rich and poor nations. Development implied the bridging of the gap by means of an imitative process, in which the less developed countries gradually assumed the qualities of the developed. Marxist theory essentially shared this perspective. For *structuralism,* which dominated the early phase of development economics (still influenced by Keynesianism), a certain amount of intervention was considered necessary, due to institutional conditions which made growth in the poor areas less automatic than it was assumed to be in the so-called developed countries. From the late 1960s modernization theory and structuralism were challenged by the Latin American *dependencia school,* which together with the more global *world system theory* articulated the weak structural position of Third World countries in the world system. The 'dependentistas' or 'neo-Marxists' asked for a radical political transformation within these countries, as well as a 'delinking' of their economies from the world market (Blomström and Hettne, 1984; Kay, 1989). With its focus on state-driven industrialization, dependency theory did not differ much from the modernization and structuralist schools with respect to the content of development. In contrast, *another development*, a counterpoint to this modernist view, was defined as need-oriented, endogenous, self-reliant, ecologically sound and based on structural transformation (Nerfin, 1977). However, the main concern for this and subsequent 'alternative' approaches was the many problems created in the course of mainstream development, and what to do with people who were excluded from development. Here the imperative of intervention reached a high degree of utopianism, but still it can be argued that the normative basis, against inequality and for emancipation, remains significant for development studies (Schuurman, 2000).

DEVELOPMENT AND GLOBALIZATION

The interventionist approach was challenged by the rise of neo-liberalism in the 1980s, a theoretical shift associated with a deepening of internationalization (globalization) and referred to as the 'counter-revolution' in development economics (Toye, 1987). This was a purified neo-classical discourse, according to which development was an inherently universal and increasingly global economic process. Development economics was thus deprived of its autonomous status and removed from the interdisciplinary family. The development problem was seen as primarily domestic, created by 'rent-seeking' bureaucrats and corrupt politicians, with no blame at all put on the 'world system'. Another problem with the old interventionist approach was that in a 'globalized' world, the nation-state no longer constituted the dominant framework for analysis and action. Development theory found itself at an impasse, and the subsequent debate was about escaping it (Booth, 1985).

Much of what is new is summarized in the rather elusive concept of *globalization*. This is clearly a long-term historical process, but at the same time a qualitatively new one in the sense that it is tooled by new information and communication technologies and a new organizational logic: networking (Castells, 1996). The global and the local are enmeshed in a shrinking world. A related dimension of importance is the rise of supraterritoriality (Scholte, 2000).

Globalization, as influenced by neo-liberal economic policies, has become the new word for mainstream development. *Globalism* as development ideology implies the growth of a world market, increasingly penetrating and dominating 'national' economies. In contrast with the interventionist bias of the classical discourse (ideological) globalists consider 'too much government' as a systemic fault. Good governance is thus defined as less government. In accepting this ideology the state becomes the disciplining spokesperson of global economic forces, rather than the protector against these forces. It is not much of an exaggeration to say that, whereas a five-year plan was previously a must for a developing country expecting international assistance, after the 'counter-revolution' it would have disqualified that country from receiving aid.

From this perspective classical development studies stands out as a non-starter, and as the new discourse reached a hegemonic position, the classical one ebbed away. Postmodern critics even claimed that what they referred to as 'the modern project' had collapsed. Others wanted to save it, arguing for a return of the political in some transnational form. According to this approach development must be analysed within a larger space than the nation and merged with international political economy (IPE). This could amount to a 'counter counter-revolution' (Krugman, 1992) and a revival of the modern project. Many doubts remain, however.

DEVELOPMENT AND SECURITY

The classical discourse on development and security viewed global poverty and 'underdevelopment' as a threat to the liberal world order in the context of the emerging Cold War (Hettne, 2001).

This was a hierarchical world order of centres and peripheries, which, together with bipolarity, shaped the general pattern of conflict, a struggle for power and at the same time a competition between different socioeconomic systems. None of the theories constituting this discourse, summarized above, proved to be of much instrumental value for development in the poor countries. They were ultimately replaced by the policy of *structural adjustment*, a purified modernization paradigm of disciplined economic development, completely divorced from security concerns. These concerns reappeared soon enough in the form of food riots (the 'IMF riots') but also in more traumatic forms of societal stress and violence. This disturbing reality has been referred to as 'postmodern conflict', 'neo-mediaevalism' or 'durable disorder' (Cerny, 1998; Duffield, 1998), a multitude of concepts which could indicate a 'paradigm shift' in the making, reflecting an emerging globalized, chaotic world. The new 'political economy of warlordism' can be found in most parts of the world.

What could be the meaning of development in a world where the nation-state is abdicating, people act in a vacuum, where global inequalities are increasing, where 'new wars' multiply and the poverty problem in development aid has been reduced to a civil form of intervention in 'complex humanitarian emergencies'? According to the conventional view, disintegration of the state leads to chaos and, consequently, non-development. The typical reaction among donors is that development aid also has to include conflict management and efforts to 'normalize' the situation. But non state-centric analyses of 'real' substantive economies suggest a more complex picture of emerging 'local' (or rather 'glocalized') economies, delinked from state control, run by new entrepreneurs, supported by private military protection and drawing on international connections. This is only the most obvious example of increasing global chaos, contradicting everything that the concept of development represented.

DEVELOPMENT AND CULTURE

One theoretical way of accommodating the new uncertainties is postmodernism. Development thinking is undoubtedly a child of the Enlightenment or the 'modern project', i.e. the increasing capacity to design societies in accordance with rationalist principles. The credit for having deconstructed this magnificent myth or Grand Narrative is shared between feminism, postmodernism and cultural studies, emerging trends with a great deal of overlap.

The introduction of cultural studies to the study of development is a significant change going far beyond the 'cultural factor' in development (Tucker, 1996). The cultural approach also implied a deconstruction of 'development' and the 'Third World'. Postmodern theory, which dominates cultural studies, is relativizing the whole business of development theorizing, thus making the project of 'development' rather senseless. Other theorists reject the relativism of postmodern thinking and look for a combination of political economy and cultural studies in order to get rid of the bathwater but keep the baby. The significance of culture and identity in development has to do not so much with the cultural factor in the process of development as with abandoning Eurocentric development thinking, i.e. development as catching up and imitation, and instead conceiving and conceptualizing development as an inclusive, liberating process, in which different worldviews are accommodated and constitute a dialogical process (Munck and O'Hearn, 1999). The new emphasis on culture has far-reaching implications, and may constitute the greatest challenge to the rethinking of development. The early development theorists were not self-critical enough on this issue, *inter alia* neglecting the fact that development necessarily is culture and context specific and that the specificity concerns the observer as well. Today, however, few social scientists would dispute that social theorizing will be significantly marked by the particular intellectual and practical context from which it emerges.

DEVELOPMENT AND WORLD ORDERS

Globalization implies the 'unbundling' of traditional state functions and a changed relationship between the state and civil society, and in particular a tendency for the state to become increasingly alienated from civil society. In this process of change, legitimacy, loyalty, identity and even sovereignty are transferred up or down in the system, to political entities other than the state – i.e. to macro-polities or micro-polities, at present with the latter predominating. Taking these diverging trends as a point of departure, one can think of three major routes towards a new world order. They do not determine content, but provide different global contexts, enabling some and excluding other solutions. Each of them thus contains variations on the main theme.

The first route is some sort of regression into pre-Westphalianism (which in most of the Third World corresponds to 'pre-colonial') – a world order with a drastically reduced role for the nation-state as we know it, and little to compensate for this defect at the global level. It thus does not permit effective global regulation. This route can be divided into two contrasting forms: one malevolent, implying a diffuse and turbulent system of changing authority structures in some-times violent competition; and one benevolent, implying a more well-functioning multilevel order with a strong local base. The mode of development possible in the first context may be some sort of 'primitive accumulation' at best promising development in a distant future. In contrast the benevolent decentralized model would give more room for 'alternative' forms of development, including protection of local resources, indigenous groups and other subnational regional interests risking exclusion in mainstream development.

The second is a neo-Westphalian order, reformed and stabilized either by a reconstituted UN system or by a more loosely organized 'concert' of dominant powers, assuming the privilege of intervention by reference to a shared value system focused on order. Here most of us would consider the former as the more benevolent form, since the latter lacks legitimacy. Furthermore an assertive multilateralism would facilitate participation of the marginalized regions of the world.

The third is a post-Westphalian alternative, where the locus of power lies more firmly at the transnational level. The state can either be substituted by a regionalized order of political blocs, or by a strengthened global civil society, in both cases representing a step towards supranational governance either on a regional or a global level (Hettne *et al.*, 1999; Nederveen Pieterse, 2000). The regional approach contains both negative and positive communitarian forms, the cosmopolitan, certainly an attractive model, so far lacks both supportive institutions and emotional underpinnings. Could the two meet and merge?

A NEW START?

One problem in understanding qualitative/structural change in the globalized condition is a lack of appropriate social science terminology. The nation-state system and the establishment of capitalism gave rise to a conceptual framework devoted to the analysis of national space and – rather as an addition – 'international (interstate) relations', creating the great debate between 'statist' and 'transnational' approaches to the international system. The recent popularity of the word 'globalization' illustrates the disturbing lacuna with regard to appropriate concepts relevant for understanding contemporary structural change and providing a scientific basis for grasping a future order beyond the current turbulence. This conceptual poverty also implies a lack of political solutions to problems in the real world 'out there', since the novelty of the situation is not even grasped.

This is a challenge for all social sciences, but development studies in particular. This field has changed in everything except its normative concern with emancipation from inequality and poverty. The emerging approach can be described as transcendence: development studies as a precursor of a comprehensive and universally valid historical social science, devoted to the contextual study of different types of societies in different phases of development, struggling to improve their structural position within the constraints of one world economy and one, albeit multilayered, world order. Furthermore, development theory needs to be reconstructed in terms of content as well. Some of the building blocks for a reconstitution, ultimately contributing to a unified historical and comprehensive social science, or 'global social theory' discussed above are: certain strands of international political economy (IPE) theory, a theory of the new development-related conflicts (and the links between peace and development), a new emphasis on cultural studies and (reflecting the relevance of alternative thinking) a continuing concern for the excluded (including the difficult question of what the excluded shall then be included in). The question of development must, finally, be related to the issue of world order, since the framework within which development is analysed and acted on will no longer be the nation-state only. The nature of this larger framework is still open, but undoubtedly of great importance for the future of development.

GUIDE TO FURTHER READING AND REFERENCES

The following text references provide the basis for further reading.

Blomström, Magnus and Hettne, Björn (1984) *Development Theory in Transition. The Dependency Debate and Beyond: Third World Responses*, London: Zed Books.

Booth, D. (1985) 'Marxism and development sociology: interpreting the impasse', *World Development*, 13(7): 761–87.

Castells, Manuel (1996) *The Rise of the Network Society*, Vol. 1 *The Information Age*, Oxford: Blackwell.

Cerny, Philip G. (1998) 'Neomedievalism, civil war and the new security dilemma: globalization as durable disorder', *Civil Wars* 1(1): 36–64.

Duffield, Mark (1998) 'Post-modern conflict: warlords, post-adjustment states and Private Protection', *Civil Wars* 1(1): 65–102.

Escobar, A. (1995) *Encountering Development: The Making and Unmaking of the Third World*, Princeton, NJ: Princeton University Press.

Hettne, Björn (2001) 'Discourses on peace and development', *Progress in Development Studies* 1(1).

Hettne, Björn, Inotai, Andras and Sunkel, Osvaldo (eds) (1999) *Globalism and the New Regionalism*, London: Macmillan.

Kay, C. (1989) *Latin American Theories of Development and Underdevelopment*, London: Routledge.

Krugman, Paul (1992) *Toward a Counter Counter-revolution in Development Theory*, Washington: World Bank.

Munck, Ronaldo and O'Hearn, Denis (eds) (1999) *Critical Development Theory: Contributions to a New Paradigm*, London: Zed Books.

Nederveen Pieterse, Jan (2000) *Global Futures: Shaping Globalization*, London: Zed Books.

Nerfin, Marc (ed.) (1977) *Another Development: Approaches and Strategies*, Uppsala: Dag Hammarsköld Foundation.

Scholte, Jan Aart (2000) *Globalization: A Critical Introduction*, London: Macmillan.

Schuurman, Frans J. (2000) 'Paradigms lost, paradigms regained? Development studies in the twenty-first century', *Third World Quarterly* 21(1): 7–20.

Toye, John (1987) *Dilemmas of Development: Reflections on the Counterrevolution in Development Theory and Policy*, Oxford: Basil Blackwell.

Tucker, Vincent (1996) 'Introduction: a cultural perspective on development', *European Journal of Development Research* 8(2): 1–21.

1.3 The impasse in development studies

Frans J. Schuurman

INTRODUCTION

Development studies is a relatively new branch of the social sciences. Coming into being in the late 1960s and early 1970s, it inherited many features of post-Second World War developments within the social sciences. Modernization theory contributed to its developmental orientation and its comparative methodology. From dependency theory it inherited its normative and progressive political character and its interdisciplinary conceptual frameworks.

In the 1970s, with dependency theory denouncing modernization theory as crypto-imperialist and modernization theorists hitting back by accusing dependency authors of being populist pseudo-scientists, development studies found fertile ground and grew into an increasingly accepted new discipline of the social sciences. Universities – often under pressure from leftist professors and students – created Third World Centres. Debates about the nature and impact of development assistance became popular, and the existence of many dictatorial regimes in the South led to numerous solidarity committees in the North. In the 1980s, things started to change for development studies. A number of occurrences in that decade, which will be dealt with in the following paragraphs, led to an increasingly uneasy feeling within the discipline that old certainties were fading away. It was felt that development theories in the sense of a related set of propositions of the 'if . . . then' kind, could ever less adequately explain experiences of development and underdevelopment. Whether it concerned modernization theories or neo-Marxist dependency theories, both sets of development theories were losing out in terms of their explanatory power. From the mid-1980s onwards, the so-called 'impasse in development studies' was talked about. The contours of this impasse were sketched for the first time in a seminal article by David Booth in 1985. In the years which followed other authors continued the discussion, which took on new dimensions with the end of the Cold War and the debate on globalization.

REASONS FOR THE IMPASSE

Three reasons can be held responsible for having changed the panorama for development studies to such an extent that it created this theoretical impasse. Chronologically they were: (i) the failure of development in the South and the growing diversity of (under)development experiences; (ii) the postmodernist critique on the social sciences in general and on the normative characteristics of development studies in particular and, finally (iii) the rise of globalization in its discursive as well as in its ontological appearance. Each of these issues is considered in the account that follows.

The failure of development in the South

Although until the 1980s developing countries realized average improvements in life expectancy, child mortality and literacy rates, more recent statistics have shown, however, that these improvements were less valid for the poorest of these countries and, more specifically, for the lowest income groups. In fact, in the 1980s there was a reversal in some of the development indicators. It was realized that given the growth rates of that time, it would take another 150 years for Third World countries to achieve even half the per capita income of Western countries. Modernization theories failed to account for these figures and trends. Instead of a self-sustained growth (a much favoured concept of modernization), many developing countries were up to their ears in debt, which served to paralyse development initiatives.

Problems such as unemployment, poor housing, human rights offences, poverty and landlessness were increasing at alarming rates. UNICEF estimated a fall of 10–15 per cent in the income of the poor in the Third World between 1983 and 1987. In 1978, the Third World received 5.5 per cent of the world's income; in 1984 this had fallen to 4.5 per cent. The 'trickle-down' process (another favoured concept of modernization) had failed miserably. In 1960, the income ratio between the world's rich and poor countries was 20:1, in 1980 it increased to 46:1, and in 1989, the ratio was as high as 60:1.

Although dependency theory could certainly not be accused of an over-optimistic view concerning the developmental potentials of developing countries, it could not really account for the growing difference between Third World countries, nor were the developmental experiences of so-called socialist countries particularly enviable. In addition, Marxist and neo-Marxist development theories were dealt a heavy blow when the fall of the Berlin Wall meant the delegitimization of socialism as a political project of solving the problem of underdevelopment.

The postmodernist critique of the social sciences

The 1980s witnessed the advancement of postmodernism within the social sciences, bringing with it a tendency to undermine the 'great narratives' of capitalism, socialism, communism and so forth. The basic argument was that there is no common reality outside the individual. As such, political alternatives, which always exist by the grace of a minimum of common perception, were manoeuvred out of sight. Development theories based on meta-discourses or on the role of a collective emancipatory agency lacked, according to the postmodern logic, a sound basis. The Enlightenment ideal of the emancipation of humanity (shared by modernization and dependency theory alike) had not been achieved nor could it be achieved. In addition, in its quest for hidden metaphors, the postmodern method of deconstruction revealed that the notion of development contained a number of hidden and unwarranted evolutionist, universalist and reductionist dimensions which would definitely lead anyone working with this notion down the wrong path. As such, development studies became a direct target for a wide range of views furthering the notion of 'alternative development'. Under postmodernist, or perhaps better put, anti-modernist pressures, the central object of development studies – unequal access to power, to resources, to a humane existence – became increasingly substituted by something like 'socioeconomic diversity'. Apparently, the notion of diversity was considered to avoid the hidden universalist (read: Western or imperialist) and reductionist dimensions which inequality brought with it. At the same time, others considered this switch to a voluntarist and pluralist approach to the development problem not only as anathema, but also as inferior to a universalistic emancipation discourse.

Globalization

In the 1990s, the forces which had led to the impasse in development theories, were joined by the discourse on globalization. Although the most recent factor, it probably represents the most important positive challenge to development studies. Whether globalization is a real phenomenon (cf. Hirst and Thompson, 1996), or nothing more than a discourse to legitimize neo-liberal market logic, it is undeniable that it has had a major influence on development studies in the 1990s. To understand why this is so, it is important to realize the significance of the (nation-)state for social science theories in general, and for development studies in particular.

It is the declining, or at least changing, position and status of the (nation-)state which has been, and still is, at the core of the literature on globalization. As an interdisciplinary branch of the social sciences, theories within development studies try to connect economic, political and cultural aspects of inequality and development trajectories. The connection between these aspects is realized by using the (nation-)state as a linchpin. As such, theories of economic development became focused upon the workings of the national market and on economic relations between countries. In theories of political development the role of the state and the process of nation-building were central objects of study. In more culturalistic development theories, the notion of a national identity was crucial in understanding the differences between development trajectories. This importance of the (nation-)state became visible in modernization theories, in both neo-Marxist and Marxist development theories alike. Globalization changed all that. Many authors writing about globalization agree on the decreasing, or at least the changing, economic, political and cultural importance of (nation-)states. The central role of the state, it is said, is being hollowed out from above as well as from below. In a political sense there is the increasing importance of international political organizations which interfere politically and also militarily in particular states. In this way, they relegate to the past the Westphalian principles about the sovereignty of (nation-)states and their monopoly on the use of institutionalized violence within their borders. The national state is hollowed out from below by the growing phenomenon of decentralization and local government.

Economically, the state is seen as disappearing as an economic actor through privatization supported by deregulation. Also, there is the growing importance of the global financial market where about $1,500 billion is shifted daily around the globe. Culturally, the idea of national identity as the central element in identity construction for individuals or groups is quickly eroding, in favour of cosmopolitanism on the one hand and/or the fortification of ethnic, regional and religious identities on the other.

It is not only that the globalization debate gives reason to suppose that the role of the (nation-)state has been, and still is, declining but also that, as a consequence, the former conjunctive dynamic (i.e. following the same spatial and time paths) of economy, polity and culture – upon which the interdisciplinary character of many a development theory was based – has been replaced by a disjunctive dynamic (cf. Appadurai, 1990). Development studies has yet to redefine its object and its subject as, in fact, the other social sciences, *vis-à-vis* globalization but this quest presents much more of a challenge than the former impasse ever did.

CONCLUSION

The impasse in development studies can in fact be traced back to a crisis of paradigms. The three reasons which were mentioned as being responsible for the impasse and its deepening – the lack of development and increasing diversity in the South, the postmodernist critique on 'grand narratives', and globalization – challenged, respectively, three post-Second World War developmental paradigms. These were:

1 The essentialization of the Third World and its inhabitants as homogeneous entities
2 The unconditional belief in the enlightenment concepts of progress and the 'makeability' of society
3 The importance of the (nation-)state as an analytical frame of reference and a political and scientific confidence in the state to realize progress.

Each of these paradigms came in for criticism, one after the other. Development theories related to these paradigms (such as modernization and dependency theories) became automatically tainted as well, initiating the so-called impasse in development studies.

However, in spite of this impasse, an important number of authors in the field of development studies have continued their work, some using more grounded theories, others trying to elaborate upon new concepts like civil society, global governance and global social movements. Many feel that the growing inequality between, as well as within, North and South is enough of a reason to continue with development studies. To fit this effort in with the new reality shaped by globalization presents a new and exciting challenge, and one which relegates the impasse to a past period.

GUIDE TO FURTHER READING

Corbridge, S. (1989) 'Marxism, post-Marxism and the geography of development', in R. Peet and N. Thrift (eds) *New Models in Geography*, Vol. 1, London: Unwin Hyman, pp. 224–54, identifies and elaborates upon three dimensions in Booth's critique of neo-Marxist development theories, i.e. essentialism, economism and epistemology.

Edwards, M. (1989) 'The irrelevance of development studies', *Third World Quarterly* 11(1): 116–36 approaches development theories from the point of view of the practitioner.

Schuurman, Frans J. (ed.) (1993) *Beyond the Impasse: New Directions in Development Theory*, London: Zed Books provides a general overview of the dimensions of the impasse and the attempts to develop new theories as well as the problems and possibilities of these attempts.

Vandergeest, P. and Buttel, F. (1998): 'Marx, Weber, and development sociology: beyond the impasse', *World Development* 16(6): 683–95 focuses upon Booth's critique upon the underlying meta-theoretical assumptions of Marxism, pointing out the necessity of looking within the heterogeneity of developing countries for common denominators.

REFERENCES

Appadurai, A. (1990) 'Disjuncture and difference in the global cultural economy', in M. Featherstone (ed.) *Global Culture, Nationalism, Globalization and Modernity*, London: Sage, pp. 295–311.

Booth, D. (1985) 'Marxism and development sociology: interpreting the impasse', *World Development* 13: 761–87.

Hirst, P. and Thompson, G. (1996) *Globalization in Question*, Cambridge: Polity Press.

1.4 Post-development

James D. Sidaway

Instead of the kingdom of abundance promised by theorists and politicians in the 1950s, the discourse and strategy of development produced its opposite: massive underdevelopment and impoverishment, untold exploitation and repression. The debt crisis, the Sahelian famine, increasing poverty, malnutrition, and violence are only the most pathetic signs of the failure of forty years of development.

(Escobar, 1995: 4)

Development occupies the centre of an incredibly powerful semantic constellation . . . at the same time, very few words are as feeble, as fragile and as incapable of giving substance and meaning to thought and behavior.

(Esteva, 1992: 8)

Along with 'anti-development' and 'beyond development', post-development is a radical reaction to the dilemmas of development. Perplexity and extreme dissatisfaction with business-as-usual and standard development rhetoric and practice, and disillusionment with alternative development are keynotes of this perspective. Development is rejected because it is the 'new religion of the West . . . it is the imposition of science as power . . . it does not work . . . it means cultural Westernisation and homogenisation . . . and it brings environmental destruction. It is rejected not merely on account of its results but because of its intentions, its world-view and mindset. The economic mindset implies a reductionist view of existence. Thus, according to Sachs, 'it is not the failure of development which has to be feared, but its success' (1992: 3).

(Nederveen Pieterse, 2000: 175)

Jan Nederveen Pieterse goes on to explain that amongst the starting points and basic assumptions of post-development is the idea that a middle-class, 'Western style' of life and all that goes with it (which might include the nuclear family, mass consumption, suburbanization and extensive private space), is not a realistic or desirable goal for the majority of the world's population. In this sense, development is seen as requiring the loss of 'indigenous' culture, or environmentally and psychologically rich and rewarding modes of life. Development is also seen as a particular vision and one that is neither benign nor innocent. It is a set of knowledges, interventions and world-views (in short a 'discourse') which are also powers – to intervene, to transform and to rule. It embodies a geopolitics, in that its origins are bound up with Western power and strategy for the Third World, enacted and implemented through local Third World elites (see Slater, 1993). Western agencies, charities and consultants (see Stirrat, 2000) often dominate the agendas. Related to concepts of anti-development and post-colonial criticisms, post-development is above all a critique of the standard assumptions about progress, who possesses the keys to it and how it may be implemented.

Of course, as a number of people have pointed out, many of these critiques represent reformulations of scepticisms and alternatives that have long been evident. According to Marshall Berman (1983) an example is the myth of Faust, which crops up repeatedly in European cultures. Faust is a man who would develop the world and himself, but must also destroy all that lies in his path to this goal and all who would resist. The myth of Faust, who sells his soul for the earthly power to develop, bears witness to a very long history of critics of progress and modernity. Throughout the twentieth century, populist ideas of self-reliance and fulfilling 'basic needs' have also been sceptical of many of the claims of development; particularly when the latter takes the forms of industrialization and urbanization (see Kitching, 1989). Subsequently, the history of ideas of dependency has been, in part, a rejection of Western claims of development as a universal panacea to be implemented in a grateful Third World. From Latin American roots (see Kay, 1989), dependency ideas were disseminated very widely and sometimes took the form of a rejection of Western modernization/development as corrupting and destructive (see Blomstrom and Hettne, 1984; Leys, 1996; Rist, 1997) or as a continuation of colonial forms of domination (Rodney, 1972). In particular, writers from predominately Islamic countries (most notably Iran) saw the obsession with development as part of a misplaced 'intoxification' with the West (see Dabashi, 1993). Likewise, more conventional Marxist accounts have long pointed to the 'combined and uneven' character of development and its highly contradictory consequences (see Cammack, 1988; Lowy, 1980). Feminist writings have also criticized the ways in which the so-called 'Third World woman' is represented as needing 'development' and Western-style 'liberation' (Mohanty, 1988).

Some critics have therefore complained that 'post-development' is not really beyond, outside or subsequent to development discourse. According to Kiely (1999) for example, 'post-development' is merely the latest version of a set of criticisms that have long been evident *within* writing and thinking about development. Development has always been about choices, with losers, winners, dilemmas and destruction as well as creative possibility. Gavin Kitching (1989: 195) who is concerned to put post-Second World War debates about development into a longer historical perspective (stressing how they also reproduce even older narratives from the nineteenth century) reminds us:

> It is my view that the hardest and clearest thinking about development always reveals that there are no easy answers, no panaceas whether these be 'de-linking', 'industrialization', 'rural development', 'appropriate technology', 'popular participation', 'basic needs', 'socialism' or whatever. As I have had occasion to say repeatedly in speaking on and about this book, development is an awful process. It varies only, and importantly, in its awfulness. And that is perhaps why my most indulgent judgements are reserved for those, whether they be Marxist-Leninists, Korean generals, or IMF officials, who, whatever else they may do, recognize this and are prepared to accept its moral implications. My most critical reflections are reserved for those, whether they be western liberal-radicals or African bureaucratic elites, who do not, and therefore avoid or evade such implications and with them their own responsibilities.

In this sense, perhaps post-development is chiefly novel not for its scepticism towards grand narratives about development, but for the theoretical frames (the analysis of discourse) it brings to bear in problematizing these. For post-development writers not only are there 'no easy answers', but the whole question of 'development' should be problematized and/or rejected.

There are a number of more fundamental objections to post-development. The first is that it overstates the case. Such arguments usually accept that development is contradictory (that it has winners and losers), but refuse to reject all that goes under its name. For, to reject all development is also seen as rejection of the possibility for progressive material advancement and transformation. Or it is to ignore the tangible transformations, in life chances, health, wealth and material well-being that have been evident in parts of the Third World, notably East Asia (Rigg, 1997). Moreover, development itself is so varied and carries so many meanings (see Williams, 1976) that critiques need to be specific about what they mean when they claim to be anti- or 'post-development'.

In this context, Escobar's (1995) work, in particular, is often criticized. One objection is that he understates the potential for change within development discourse (see Brown, 1996; Gardner and Lewis, 2000). Escobar's work reflects his experiences as an anthropologist in the country of Colombia. As a rendition of Colombia, a society of ongoing violent civil war and foreign intervention, whose main export (by value) is cocaine, Escobar's critique of development would seem suggestive. But perhaps there is a risk that it obscures the diversity of experiences of development, not all of which are as problematic and contradictory as the Colombian experience.

The second objection involves rejecting post-development as yet another intellectual fad, of limited (or no) relevance to the poor in the Third World. Sometimes this objection draws attention to the fact that many of those who write about or disseminate post-development ideas live precisely the cosmopolitan, middle-class, relatively affluent lives that development promises to deliver. Such questions parallel the critique of *post-colonialism* as an intellectual fashion most useful to the careers of Western-based intellectuals.

However a few counter-points are in order here. First a whole set of writings and ideas are grouped together under the rubric of post-development. Michael Watts (2000: 170) explains:

> There is of course a polyphony of voices within this post-development community – Vandana Shiva, Wolfgang Sachs, Arturo Escobar, Gustavo Esteva and Ashish Nandy, for example, occupy quite different intellectual and political locations. But it is striking how intellectuals, activists, practitioners and academics within this diverse community participated in a global debate.

Moreover, it is important to point out that for Escobar (1995) and others (for example Blaikie, 2000; Ferguson, 1999), to criticize development is not necessarily to reject change and possibility. Rather, it is to make us aware of the consequences of framing this as 'development'. Alternative visions considering, for example, democracy, popular culture, resourcefulness and environmental impacts would transform the imagined map of more or less developed countries. Recognition that development is but one way of seeing the world (and one which carries certain consequences and assumptions) can open up other perspectives. What happens, for example, to the perception of Africa when it is seen as *rich* in cultures and lives whose diversity, wealth and worth are not adequately captured by being imagined as more or less *developed*? Alternatively, why are poverty and deprivation (or for that matter, excessive consumption amongst the affluent), in countries like the United States or the United Kingdom not issues of 'development' (see Jones, 2000)? What is taken for granted when the term 'development' is used? For it often seems that, in Escobar's (1995: 39) words, development has 'created a space in which only certain things could be said or even imagined'. ❧

GUIDE TO FURTHER READING

Crush, J. (ed.) (1995) *Power of Development*, London and New York: Routledge. An introduction and collection of 14 essays that examine the 'power' of development discourses. The essays show how claims of development to be a solution to problems of national and global poverty, disorder and environmental degradation are often illusions.

Escobar, A. (1995) *Encountering Development: The Making and Unmaking of the Third World*, Princeton, NJ: Princeton University Press. Written by a Colombian anthropologist and drawing on the trajectory of that country (whilst making more general claims), this critique uses the ideas of Michel Foucault to understand 'development' as a discourse and therefore as a particular (Western) regime of truth, power and knowledge. Challenging but stimulating.

Ferguson, J. (1990) *The Anti-Politics Machine: 'Development', Depoliticization and Bureaucratic Power in Lesotho*, Cambridge: Cambridge University Press. Like Escobar another book-length critique of the discourse of development written by an anthropologist. Less sweeping in its claims than Escobar, but no less persuasive in its arguments.

Rahnema, M. and Bawtree, V. (eds) (1997) *The Post-Development Reader*, London: Zed Books. An introduction plus 440 pages comprising of 37 short extracts (and an afterword) from thinkers, politicians and activists who problematize development. Each reading has a short introduction that helps to contextualize it (written by the editors). This is probably the best place to start a course of further reading and/or to get a flavour of 'post-development'.

REFERENCES

Berman, M. (1983) *All That Is Solid Melts Into Air: The Experience of Modernity*, London: Verso.

Blaikie, P. (2000) 'Development, post-, anti-, and populist: a critical view', *Environment and Planning A* 32: 1033–50.

Blomstrom, H. and Hettne, B. (1984) *Development Theory in Transition: The Dependency Debate and Beyond: Third World Responses*, London: Zed Books.

Brown, E. (1996) 'Deconstructing development: alternative perspectives on the history of an idea', *Journal of Historical Geography* 22(3): 333–9.

Cammack, P. (1988) 'Dependency and the politics of development', in P.F. Leeson and M.M. Minogue (eds) *Perspectives on Development: Cross-disciplinary Themes in Development*, Manchester: Manchester University Press, pp. 89–125.

Dabashi, H. (1993) *Theology of Discontent: The Ideological Foundation of the Islamic Revolution in Iran*, New York and London: New York University Press.

Esteva, G. (1992) 'Development', in W. Sachs (ed.) *The Development Dictionary: A Guide to Knowledge as Power*, London: Zed Books.

Ferguson, J. (1999) *Expectations of Modernity: Myths and Meanings of Urban Life on the Zambian Copperbelt*, Berkeley: University of California Press.

Gardner, K. and Lewis, D. (2000) 'Dominant paradigms overturned or "Business as Usual"? Development discourse and the White Paper on International Development', *Critique of Anthropology* 20(1): 15–29.

Jones, P.S. (2000) 'Why is it alright to do development "over there" but not "here"? Changing vocabularies and common strategies of inclusion across the "First" and "Third" Worlds', *Area* 32(2): 237–41.

Kay, C. (1989) *Latin American Theories of Development and Underdevelopment*, London and New York: Routledge.

Kiely, R. (1999) 'The last refuge of the noble savage? A critical account of post-development', *European Journal of Development Research* 11(1): 30–55.

Kitching, G. (1989) *Development and Underdevelopment in Historical Perspective: Populism, Nationalism and Industrialization* (revised edition), London and New York: Routledge.

Leys, C. (1996) *The Rise and Fall of Development Theory*, London: James Currey.

Lowy, M. (1980) *The Politics of Combined and Uneven Development: The Theory of Permanent Revolution*, London: New Left Books.

Mohanty, C.P. (1988) 'Under western eyes: feminist scholarship and colonial discourses.' *Feminist Review* 30: 61–88.

Nederveen Pieterse, J. (2000) 'After post-development', *Third World Quarterly* 21(2): 175–91.

Rigg, J. (1997) *Southeast Asia: The Human Landscape of Modernization and Development*, London and New York: Routledge.

Rist, G. (1997) *The History of Development: from Western Origins to Global Faith*, London: Zed Books.

Rodney, W. (1972) *How Europe Underdeveloped Africa*, London: Bogle L'Ouveture.

Slater, D. (1993) 'The geopolitical imagination and the enframing of development theory', *Transactions of the Institute of British Geographers NS* 18: 419–37.

Stirrat, R.L. (2000) 'Cultures of consultancy', *Critique of Anthropology* 20(1): 31–46.

Watts, M. (2000) 'Development', in R.J. Johnson, D. Gregory, G. Pratt and M. Watts (eds) *The Dictionary of Human Geography*, Oxford: Blackwell, 167–71.

Williams, R. (1976) *Keywords*, London: Fontana.

1.5 The collapse of state socialism in the socialist Third World

Keith Sutton and Salah E. Zaimeche

The pre-1990 Cold War division between the capitalist West and the communist East was paralleled by a related division of the Third World into socialist and market-economy countries. Late 1980s studies of this 'Socialist Third World' could separate off over 25 socialist-orientated countries tied to the USSR to varying degrees (Forbes and Thrift, 1987; Drakakis-Smith *et al.*, 1987). Some were long-established socialist countries such as China and some even members of COMECON such as Cuba and Vietnam. Others were recent 1980s additions to the socialist world such as Surinam and Burkina Faso. Yet other countries, such as Chile and Grenada, briefly flirted with a socialist approach before pro-West military interventions. Egypt was also socialist in the 1950s and 1960s after the ultimate nationalization, that of the Suez Canal.

Disagreements over defining 'socialism' obfuscate the issue. Clapham (1992: 14) defines socialism as both an ideology and a set of institutional practices derived from it. These treat the state as the key agency of direct economic planning and management whereby resources are allocated according to priorities decided by the state rather than through market mechanisms. Thus, Forbes and Thrift (1987) offered a working set of criteria to identify socialist countries:

- one-party rule
- egalitarian goals within the constitution
- high or increasing degree of state ownership of industry and agriculture
- collectivization of agriculture
- centralized economic control.

Some would dispute that without democratic/participatory mechanisms such a system was not socialist, preferring the terms 'command economy' or 'state capitalism'. Certainly the sample of countries in Table 1 is far from homogeneous though having certain things in common. By the 1980s they were all intent on doing away with most capitalist structures and ending the control over resources by private capital. The role of the state was high, especially in production and planning, and most such countries had opted for the direct path to socialism without first achieving capitalist development. While several aimed for rural mobilization, most aimed to transform society and achieve economic growth through industrialization. Together, the development strategies of these socialist developing countries provided in the late 1980s 'an important counterpoint to the orthodoxy of much of the development literature' (Forbes and Thrift, 1987: 1). Then in the late 1980s/early 1990s Europe's Cold War division ended with the collapse of the Soviet Union and its Eastern Europe hegemony. Poland's Solidarity movement, the USSR's draining Afghan War, Gorbachev's policy of perestroika, all contributed to the end of communism in the USSR and its break-up into its constituent republics. This left the Socialist Third World without its prime model and its main source of monetary and material aid, and even trade. Whereas the First World's systems of support such as the IMF remained, the Second World could now offer little and the related collapse of Third World Socialism seemed inevitable. Indeed, the changes in Russia and Eastern Europe may, ironically, may have diverted to the former Second World capital and market opportunities which would otherwise have gone to the Third World (Clapham, 1992: 20).

BACKGROUND TO THE CRISIS OF COMMAND ECONOMIES

Without debating whether it is important to grow first and then redistribute, or vice versa, it is generally recognized that in terms of economic competitiveness the socialist system failed compared with the capitalist system. However, socialism often provided much employment and a good level of social services, even in some of the poorest Third World countries. Furthermore, as well as weaknesses inherent in the system, local conditions in each socialist country compounded the problems. In Southern African countries Paulson (1999) recognized that countries that embraced state-led development have shown symptoms of state monopoly over production, resource allocation and distribution, together with distorted prices, an absence of foreign competition and the neglect and/or suppression of the private sector. The consequences have been poor economic performances, a bloated and inefficient public sector, weak governance and a lack of accountability. However, market-led economies in Africa have often fared little better. The problems of African countries are probably beyond ideology alone and result from factors as divergent as the debt burden and the incidence of drought.

In Algeria, which pursued a socialist development strategy from the mid-1960s based on considerable oil and gas wealth, the ruling elite appropriated considerable privileges. Moreover, this hydrocarbons wealth created a rentier mentality and once such oil wealth began to fall in the mid-1980s, Algeria plunged into crisis. The Algerian socialist state of the 1970s was compared to a milch cow. Overmanning within the sector of light industry affected a third of the labour force. Public enterprises found pseudo-employment for people in offices, as drivers and lift watchers, etc. Following the collapse of oil revenues Algeria's media conceded that the milch cow could no longer feed the population.

IMF-LED RESTRUCTURING PROGRAMMES

An important driving force behind economic liberalization and privatization, especially during the 1980s, was the World Bank through the conditions attached to its Structural Adjustment Loans.

Table 1 Sample of changing socialist Third World countries

1980s situation	IMF/World Bank involvement (SAF – structural adjustment facility ESAF – enhanced adjustment facility)	1990s socioeconomic changes	Political aspects	Remaining socialist features	1998 Population: GDP/head: Socialist/non-socialist:
Ethiopia • Military government • 1987 New Marxist-Leninist constitution	• 1992 World Bank programme • 1992 IMF SAF • 1996 IMF ESAF • 1998 IMF restores 1996 ESAF	1995 privatization begins Slow but steady privatization 1999 115 state-owned enterprises being prepared for sale	Mid-1995 elections and federal republic declared	State farms and agro-industrial plants	58 million $102 **Socialist**
Nicaragua • Sandanista socialist government • Agrarian reform	• 1994 IMF SAF • 1998 IMF ESAF	1995 Central bank begins open-market operations Trade liberalization Sold state banks Security offered to agrarian reform beneficiaries 1998 Hurricane Mitch devastation	1990 Sandanistas lost elections 1996 Multi-party elections, right-wing Alianza Liberal won		4.78 million $445 **Non-socialist**

Country					
Vietnam • Communist government	• Dec 1997 agreement with London Club of creditors to reschedule and halve Vietnam's commercial debt	1989 abolished most subsidies and price controls 1992 constitution: 'multisector economy in accordance with the market'	1997 new 450-member National Assembly elected • controlled assembly without political parties	1996 state enterprises still at core of economy Privatization resisted State enterprises re-organized, but they remain	78.9 million $300 **Socialist**
Mozambique • Marxist FRELIMO party from 1975 • Central planning and nationalization of abandoned Portuguese businesses and farms • Civil War in mid-1980s	• 1987 first SAP for IMF market reforms	1993 and 1995 riots in Maputo over price rises 1996 main state bank privatized; privatized over 900 public companies Feb. 2000 major floods and related aid programme	1992 civil war ended 1994 multiparty elections 1995 joined British Commonwealth 1999 second multiparty elections; FRELIMO wins slim majority		16.8 million $256 **Non-socialist**
Yemen • South Yemen nationalized large companies in 1970s	• 1996 IMF SAP • 1997 3-year IMF financing programme • 1998 rioting over price controls	Privatization targets are main banks, industries, airline, etc.; not sold off by late 1999 Reluctant to incur redundancies, and reforms limited by lack of bureaucracy to implement them	1990 North and South Yemen united 1993 multiparty elections 1994 civil war between North and South – North's forces won 1997 multiparty elections 1999 first direct presidential elections		17.06 million $328 **Economically socialist** **Politically non-socialist**

Source: Economist Intelligence Unit, *Country Profiles, 1999–2000*

These were increasingly required by Third World countries to reschedule their spiralling debt commitments. The IMF's stock 'cure' has involved drastic reductions in state spending and in state involvement in the economy, an all-out effort to expand exports, reductions in 'human capital' expenditure, formal sector job losses, and a severe shrinkage of consumption (Wallace, 1990: 271). Furthermore, the World Bank has actively assisted privatization in many countries, especially in sub-Saharan Africa where countries like Tanzania and Mozambique have received several Structural Adjustment Facilities (SAF), and even Enhanced SAFs (Table 1). Related privatization of industries, banks and agricultural organizations has even included Mozambique's customs and excise department.

Egypt underwent restructuring reforms in 1986 with a programme which overhauled the price system and the exchange rate, so markedly shifting away from socialist policies dating from the mid-1960s. Arrangements with the IMF, World Bank and the Club of Paris were made in 1991. Parity in exchange rates and the liberalization of foreign exchange were central to Egypt's subsequent policy reforms. Trade was also liberalized, subsidies were suppressed on a large scale and steps undertaken for the privatization of 314 Egyptian state corporations. At the same time public expenditure was cut, whilst the Egyptian pound was devalued. Private foreign investment was successfully encouraged rising from US$141 million in 1991 to US$850 million in 1997–98. By 1992 the World Bank declared its satisfaction with Egypt's economic reforms (Den Hartog, 2000). Foreign investment was also encouraged by allowing 100 per cent foreign ownership of Egyptian companies, guaranteeing the right to repatriate capital and earnings, and establishing free trade zones in Cairo, Suez and Port Said. By the late 1990s large banking, telecommunications, insurance and electricity companies were scheduled for privatization. Nasserist socialism in Egypt had evidently collapsed.

SOCIALIST FORMS OF AGRICULTURE

Centralized approaches to running agriculture have rarely succeeded. State farms require considerable subsidization and then invariably prove inefficient and exploit their labour force. Co-operative farming is often a charade, with decision-making being centralized or technocratic, with participatory co-operative mechanisms largely theoretical and little used. With centralized marketing structures, co-operatives appear more like collective farms. Only China perhaps achieved a balance of socialist agricultural communes with a market-orientated structure of agricultural production (Clapham, 1992: 23). Having eliminated private plots and having closed rural markets during China's Fourth 5-Year Plan, 1968–72, both were restored during the Fifth Plan, 1976–80 (Chung-Tong Wu, 1987). The next plan, 1981–85, saw production quotas introduced as part of a 'contract system' and surplus produced above that quota could be sold off, heralding the end of China's rural communes. Their formal abandonment came in 1984 (Dickenson et al., 1996: 148). Now there is much more response to market forces, but with this has come a growing problem of surplus labour.

Production co-operatives featured strongly in Algeria's reform of its colonial agricultural structures. Self-management (autogestion) estates replaced French settler farms and a major agrarian reform during the 1970s created production co-operatives which were grouped into service co-operatives. Despite the socialist nomenclature this self-management rarely functioned properly and state-appointed directors took most decisions. Two waves of restructuring in the 1980s largely converted Algeria's agriculture into private holdings plus 22,356 smaller and more manageable collective holdings (Sutton and Aghrout, 1992).

Communal agriculture and communal (*ujamaa*) villages were central to Tanzania's socialist approach (Doherty, 1987). From 1973, the programme descended into a programme of 'villagization' largely through coercion. Some 10 million peasants were concentrated in 7,000 larger villages. The self-reliant collective production resulted in a declining food and cash crop situation and so the collective approach was abandoned. Population concentration in Tanzania also increased environmental degradation through the over-use of land. The improved delivery of educational and health services in rural areas was some compensation.

Vietnam has probably switched to the market-orientated model more than other socialist countries. Through joint ventures its move to a market economy has been successful, especially in rice production. Moreover, Vietnam has introduced democratic elections and representative bodies. Elliott (1992: 138) argues that the collapse of the USSR had little impact on economic reform in Vietnam, but it did slow down political reforms there.

THE SOCIAL COSTS OF RESTRUCTURING SOCIALIST ECONOMIES: CHINA'S EXPERIENCE

Along with other state-controlled economies, China suffered problems, including shortages of basic goods and bottlenecks in the supply of inputs constraining production. China began reforming its economy from 1978 onwards seeking to maintain economic growth and to improve living standards. One approach was to decentralize power, giving more autonomy to managers, as well as introducing profit-sharing and freeing prices. Joint stock companies were created and property rights established. This boosted the significance of the private sector, which doubled its share of economic activity 1985 to 1990. The number of private industrial companies also doubled, eradicating shortages in many sectors of the Chinese economy. So successful was this that the government sought to put a brake on the liberalization process fearing that it was escaping state control. However, China's capitalist 'economic miracle' was in full swing and government decrees were sometimes completely ignored.

This shift away from state control reduced state expenditure and state budgetary deficits. A rise in productivity, efficiency and resource management has also occurred. However, such restructuring can reverse earlier subsidized employment schemes from the socialist era. Even after strong growth, exceeding 8 per cent until 1996, China faced rising unemployment (Kaplinsky, 1999). Estimates of workers laid off range from 8 to 11 millions in 1998. Unemployment results in the migration of rural labour into the cities (Kaplinsky, 1999). In all, 20 per cent of China's workforce is unemployed, a high social cost, and 60 million rural people have moved to the cities.

CONCLUSIONS: STATE SOCIALISM INTO THE TWENTY-FIRST CENTURY

Following the economic and political events of the 1980s and 1990s, the Socialist Third World has changed and has shrunk. Several countries appear to have changed from a socialist to a market economy, namely: Mozambique, Tanzania, Nicaragua, Benin, Mongolia, Burkina Faso, Guinea-Bissau, Afghanistan, Albania and Madagascar. Others while fast transforming, still retain elements of their earlier socialist economies, namely: Guinea, Zimbabwe, Cambodia (Kampuchea), Laos and Algeria. A third group have signs of either economic or political change but are largely still socialist, namely: Yemen, Guyana, Ethiopia, Angola, Congo-Brazzaville and Myanmar (Burma). Finally, China, Cuba, Vietnam, Libya, Iraq, Syria and North Korea are essentially still socialist, especially politically, though even in these cases the first shoots of market economy trends are perhaps evident.

The active mechanisms of change can be regarded as IMF debt restructuring, which leads to economic liberalization and privatization, together with pressures of democratization and globalization. More passively, the end of Soviet aid and assistance following the collapse of the USSR engendered trade and economic restructuring even if more closely linked countries like Cuba and Vietnam are slow to change. The role of the World Trade Organization in continuing the pressures of the IMF for economic liberalization can be anticipated as likely to increase.

While no countries have moved counter to this trend and become additions to the 1980s group of Socialist Third World nations, the designation of several Asian ex-USSR countries as separate nations and economies has certainly extended the possible list of Third World countries. Some of these 'new' countries, such as Turkmenistan and Uzbekistan, retain elements of Soviet 'socialism', others are largely still socialist, including Azerbaijan, Tajikstan and Kazakhstan. Only the Kyrgyz Republic has changed substantially while retaining some elements of its former socialist command economy.

GUIDE TO FURTHER READING

Clapham, C. (1992) 'The collapse of socialist development in the Third World', *Third World Quarterly* 13(1): 13–26. Prefaces a group of country studies. Takes a more political approach, stressing the centralized state systems prevailing in many Socialist countries.

Drakakis-Smith, D., Doherty, J. and Thrift, N. (1987) 'Introduction: what is a socialist developing country?', *Geography* 72: 333–5. Introduces short articles on Socialist Third World countries such as Tanzania and China.

Forbes, D. and Thrift, N. (1987) *The Socialist Third World*, Oxford: Basil Blackwell. This edited work provides an overview of the situation in the mid-1980s with chapters on several Socialist Third World countries.

REFERENCES

Clapham, C. (1992) 'The collapse of socialist development in the Third World', *Third World Quarterly* 13(1): pp. 13–26.

Chung-Tong Wu (1987) 'Chinese socialism and uneven development', in D. Forbes and N. Thrift (eds) *The Socialist Third World*, Oxford: Basil Blackwell, pp. 53–97.

Den Hartog, M.J. (2000) 'Egypt: economy', in *The Middle East and North Africa 2000* (46th edn), London: Europa Publications, pp. 430–9.

Dickenson, J., Gould, B., Clarke, C., Mather, S., Prothero, M., Siddle, D., Smith, C. and Thomas-Hope, E. (1996) *Geography of the Third World* (2nd edn) London: Routledge.

Doherty, J. (1987) 'Tanzania: twenty years of African socialism, 1967–1987', *Geography* 72: 344–8.

Drakakis-Smith, D., Doherty, J. and Thrift, N. (1987) 'Introduction: what is a socialist developing country?', *Geography* 72: 333–5.

Economist Intelligence Unit, *Country Profiles, 1999–2000*, London: Economist Intelligence Unit.

Elliott, J. (1992) 'The future of socialism: Vietnam, the way ahead', *Third World Quarterly* 13(1): 131–42.

Forbes, D. and Thrift, N. (1987) *The Socialist Third World*, Oxford: Basil Blackwell.

Kaplinsky, R. (1999) 'Is globalisation all it is cracked up to be?', *IDS Bulletin*, 30(4): 106–16.

Paulson, J.A. (1999) *African Economies in Transition*, 2 vols, Basingstoke: Macmillan.

Sutton, K. and Aghrout, A. (1992) 'Agricultural policy in Algeria in the 1980s: progress towards liberalization', *Canadian Journal of African Studies* 26(2): 250–73.

Wallace, I. (1990) *The Global Economic System*, London: Unwin Hyman.

1.6 The Asian crisis

Jonathan Rigg

FROM GROWTH TO CRISIS

The Asian crisis has gone by many terms: the Asian malaise, the Asian contagion, the Asian debacle and the Asian crash. After achieving perhaps the most rapid period of economic growth in human history, a group of countries in the East and Southeast Asian regions experienced one of history's most precipitous declines in economic fortune (Table 1). Moreover, while the Asian crisis began as a regional financial crisis, it quickly became a political and human crisis.

That there was a crisis in Asia dating from mid-1997 is not seriously in doubt. But what triggered the crisis, how it was manifested and what lessons can be learnt continue to be subjects of vociferous debate. Furthermore, there can be few topics that have generated such a mass of literature so quickly. Nouriel Roubini's website has hundreds of listed documents and the site's 'chronology' for 1997 and 1998 alone runs to 147,490 words – not far off the length of this book.

THE DIARY OF A CRISIS

The Asian crisis is usually dated from 2 July 1997 when the central Bank of Thailand, after spending some US$9 billion, gave up its futile attempts to support the baht and protect its peg to the US$. The newly 'floating' baht promptly collapsed, losing about a fifth of its value. Fairly quickly the 'contagion' spread to other Asian economies that investors and speculators felt shared some of Thailand's problems (Table 2). These included Indonesia, Malaysia, the Philippines and South Korea. Companies that had not hedged their foreign currency exposure were bankrupted and the associated fall in asset values further accentuated the problem. As a result, the proportion of non-performing loans held by local banks – already high – rose still

Table 1 Growth and decline in Asia, 1996–1999

| | GDP growth | | | |
	1996	1997	1998	1999
Crisis countries				
Indonesia	8.0	5.0	−13.2	0.2
Malaysia	8.6	8.0	−7.5	5.4
Philippines	5.5	5.1	−0.5	3.2
South Korea	7.1	5.5	−6.7	10.7
Thailand	5.5	−0.4	−10.4	4.2
Wider Asia				
China	9.5	8.8	7.8	7.1
Hong Kong	4.7	5.0	−5.1	2.9
Japan	3.8	−0.7	−2.5	0.5
Lao PDR	7.1	6.9	4.0	4.0
Singapore	6.9	7.8	0.3	5.4
Taiwan	5.4	6.8	4.6	5.4
Vietnam	–	8.1	5.8	4.0

Sources: various

Table 2 The diary of a crisis, July–December 1997

2 July	Thai baht collapses under speculative pressure
11 July	Philippine peso allowed to float
14 July	Philippines permitted to extend by US$1.1 billion an existing IMF standby agreement
24 July	Malaysian ringgit hits a three-year low
28 July	Thailand calls in the IMF
20 August	IMF-led rescue package of US$17.1 billion approved for Thailand
2 September	Philippine peso falls to historic low against the US$
8 October	Indonesia announces its intention to call on the IMF for assistance
17 October	New Taiwan dollar allowed to float
20–23 October	Hong Kong stock market loses a quarter of its value over four days
5 November	Standby credit of US$43 billion approved by the IMF for Indonesia
7 November	The government of PM Chaovalit Yongchaiyut in Thailand falls; the first political casualty of the crisis
21 November	South Korea, wracked by economic instability, states it will seek IMF assistance
4 December	IMF-led rescue package of US$58.2 billion approved for South Korea
18 December	Former dissident Kim Dae-jung is elected President of South Korea

further. A currency crisis in Thailand was transformed into a wider, regional, banking, financial and economic crisis. The IMF stepped in to rescue Asia's ailing economies (see Table 2). Malaysia, significantly, turned down the IMF's offer of assistance.

The crisis was particularly acute in Thailand, Indonesia, South Korea, the Philippines and Malaysia. But Hong Kong, Taiwan and Singapore were also infected, as were transitional economies like the Lao PDR and Vietnam. In the 'acute' cases, economic growth of between 5.5 per cent and 8.6 per cent in 1996 was transformed into negative 'growth' of between –0.5 per cent and –13.2 per cent in 1998 (Table 1). However, the 'Asian financial crisis' is a misnomer in so far as the great bulk of Asia (in population terms) was only marginally affected. China may have been touched by the malaise but it did not face a meltdown, while the countries of South Asia were largely immune to the contagion.

DID ANYONE PREDICT THE CRISIS?

Many people have been wise after the event, but scarcely anyone predicted the collapse of Asia. The closest we get to prescience is the Bank for International Settlements' austere 1996–97 annual report with its section on 'Financial fragility in Asia'. With hindsight we can point, as warnings and precursors of the crisis, to the fall in Thailand's (and South Korea's) stock market from early 1996, the weakness in the global semi-conductor industry, the strong dollar (to which many currencies were pegged) and a general loss of competitiveness in the region.

THE INTERPRETATION

> Curiously many of the factors identified as contributors to East Asian economies' current problems are strikingly similar to the explanations previously put forward for their success.
> (Joseph Stiglitz, Chief Economist at the World Bank, in a speech in the Philippines, March 1998)

In 1996 there was a net inflow of private capital to Thailand, Malaysia, South Korea and the Philippines of US$93 billion. In 1997 there was an outflow of US$12 billion. The crisis began life as a classic liquidity crunch.

Initially, mainstream commentators linked the crisis to the nature of Asian capitalism. They stressed the degree of 'crony capitalism' and corruption in the region, the guiding role of the state, the implicit guarantees offered (especially) to government-linked businesses, the tendency to create special interest groups, the lack of banking supervision and the role that 'moral hazard' played in the collapse (see Krugman, 1998). Taken together, this led to inefficient and often excessively risky investment decisions, and the misallocation of resources.

The irony, of course, was that for several years before the crisis it was the developmental state that was identified by some scholars as a critical ingredient in Asia's success. It has also been pointed out that the crisis came at a time when the role of the state, and the degree of cronyism, was actually falling. Some analysts reconciled these positions by arguing that while an activist state may be important in promoting growth during the early stages of development, over time it tends to become transformed into economically destructive rent-seeking.

Radical scholars highlighted integration into the global economy as the root cause of the crisis. Global integration, in this explanatory schema, created dependency and vulnerability. Others, while they also highlight the role of global integration, see the issue as one of inadequate preparation. It is not that global integration is necessarily detrimental to the interests of developing countries but that, in the crisis, Asia's institutional, regulatory and supervisory frameworks were poorly prepared to deal with the enormous increase in international capital mobility brought on by capital account liberalization.

Just one crisis, or many?

Was this a regional crisis, or a coincidence of different crises all with their own special characteristics? It was a bit of both. Just as scholars and institutions tried to identify a 'recipe' for the success of Asia pre-crisis, so the crisis led them to a search for common characteristics to explain Asia's crash. There were elements of 'panic', 'psychological contagion' and 'herd mentality', particularly when it came to the response of foreign investors. There was, therefore, a systemic risk because the contagion created a climate where loss of confidence undermined even sound institutions and businesses. There were also some similarities between the crisis countries: pegged exchange rates and a lack of transparency in their financial systems, for example. Yet it is easy to push these similarities too far: the countries were more different than they were alike and, just as there was no single 'miracle', so there was no single 'crisis'. Indeed, all crises are *sui generis*.

THE SOCIAL AND POLITICAL IMPACTS OF THE CRISIS

A striking feature of many of the initial analyses of the crisis was the absence of people, or at least ordinary people, from the discussion. The so-called 'real' economy rarely got a look-in. Even those publications that claimed to examine the social effects of the crisis did so in a rather disengaged fashion. Unemployment rates rose to record levels during 1998 (Table 3). Most of those being laid off had to fend for themselves. Not only were state-woven social safety nets non-existent or inadequate, but the traditional 'moral' economy had been fractured by years of modernization. With limited savings and modest (if any) severance payments, there were reports of households selling their assets, pawning consumer goods acquired during the years of plenty, even resorting to crime and prostitution. Familiar coping mechanisms from resorting to cheaper non-rice staples, foregoing luxuries like soap, and turning to informal activities from garbage picking to gathering non-timber forest products were all noted. Analysts predicted that increasing numbers of children

Table 3 Unemployment and GNP/capita

	Unemployment (% of labour force)					GNP/capita ($)			GNP/capita (PPP)		
	1990–96 (av.)	1996	1997	1998	1999	1997	1998	1999	1997	1998	1999
Crisis countries											
Indonesia	2.2	–	4.7	15–20	28.5	1,110	680	580	3,450	2,790	2,439
Malaysia	–	2.6	2.6	3.9	3.0	4,680	3,600	3,400	10,920	6,990	7,963
Philippines	–	7.6	–	8.0	–	1,220	1,050	1,020	3,670	3,540	3,815
South Korea	2.1	2.3	2.5	9.7	7.4	10,550	7,970	8,490	13,500	12,270	14,637
Thailand	2.5	1.5	1.0	6.1	5.9	2,800	2,200	1,960	6,590	5,840	5,599

Sources: various

Note: the unemployment data are drawn from various sources and should only be regarded as indicative of trends. The figures for Indonesia are particularly problematic.

would be taken out of school to save on fees, undermining
while the old, infirm and sickly would be denied medical care. T
millions would return to their rural villages.

On balance, the worst social effects did not materialize, partly be
consumption patterns, and partly because NGOs and the state stepped in
risk. In Thailand scholarships were made available to children from the poo
Indonesia primary-level fees were waived and scholarships extended. Local com
to keep children in school. Even in Indonesia, the worst-afflicted country, some of t
tions proved not to have been realized.

The Asian economic crisis was, for several countries, also a political crisis. Governm
had based their political legitimacy on economic growth found this undermined. Theref
necessary reforms had to be political as much as economic. Changes of government in Thaila
South Korea and, most spectacularly, in Indonesia can all be directly linked to the crisis as can
indirectly, the arrest, trial and imprisonment of former Deputy Prime Minister Anwar Ibrahim in
Malaysia. Likewise it is possible to argue that the 'secession' of the Indonesian province of East
Timor and movements for independence or autonomy in Aceh and Irian Jaya have been fuelled by
the crisis. Most tragically, the communal violence in Indonesia is a direct result of the loss of political control arising from President Suharto's resignation in May 1998.

THE SOLUTIONS

The IMF's reform programmes for Thailand, South Korea and Indonesia were founded on the
belief that each country suffered from structural distortions that needed to be rectified. This
particularly applied to financial institutions which were regarded as weak, lacking in regulation
and supervision, and non-transparent. The IMF's approach to solving the crisis was sharply criticized. The main area of criticism centred on the deflationary effects of the IMF's prescription of
fiscal austerity and budget cuts. This accentuated the crisis by further undermining confidence in
national banking systems just at a time when rebuilding confidence was key to stimulating recovery. Critics accused the IMF of treating the Asian economic crisis like earlier crises in Latin
America where the IMF was rescuing bankrupt governments. In the case of the Asian economies,
governments were in surplus. The problem, instead, lay with the private sector and with the institutions in place to supervise and manage the financial system. Paradoxically, the 'fundamentals'
were good: high savings rates, government surpluses or small deficits, low inflation and low levels
of external debt.

For more radical scholars the debate between the IMF and its critics missed the point. The crisis
was used to impose an authoritarian liberal global order on Asia where the state protects the
market from social and political pressures through, for example, creating truly independent central
banks. It was, in this sense, just another part of the Washington Consensus. For radicals, to put an
end to global economic crises it is necessary to put an end to global economic integration.

'BLIP' OR PROFOUND CHANGE?

The crisis has been used to argue many – and often diametrically opposed – things: to challenge
the Asian miracle; to suggest that there is some Occidental conspiracy at root; to argue the case for
farm-based, traditional economic systems; to highlight the dangers of dependent development; to
further the case for globalization; to emphasize the weaknesses in Asia's crony capitalist tendencies;

 highlight the dangers of integration into the
as offering an opportunity to move away from
track industrialization (Bullard *et al.*, 1998: 22),
lihood strategies, and to base development on
1998: 440–1). For others the crisis has empha-
ulatory supervision and transparency, and cut
crisis a need for Asia to establish its own finan-
h a more global perspective have argued for a
urveillance to anticipate and pre-empt crises.
ng point in Asia's economic history.

ES

e *Far Eastern Economic Review* or *The Economist*.
u.edu/~nroubini/asia/AsiaHomepage.html; also
. ... sites of the World Bank and the Asian Development Bank, http://www.worldbank.org/ and
http://www.adb.org/. There are numerous papers in journals such as *World Development*, and in more
radical outlets such as the *Journal of Contemporary Asia*, *Third World Quarterly* and the *Bulletin of
Concerned Asian Scholars* (the latter now retitled as *Critical Asian Studies*).

The following text references provide the basis for further reading.

Bello, Walden (1998) 'East Asia: on the eve of the great transformation?', *Review of International Political Economy* 5(3): 424–44.

Bullard, Nicola, Bello, Walden and Malhotra, Kamal (1998) 'Taming the tigers: the IMF and the Asian crisis', *Third World Quarterly* 19(3): 505–55.

Griffith-Jones, Stephany (1998) *The East Asian financial crisis: a reflection on its causes, consequences and policy implications*, IDS Discussion Paper 367, Sussex: Institute of Development Studies (http://www.ids.ac.uk).

Haggard, Stephen and MacIntyre, Andrew (1998) 'The political economy of the Asian economic crisis', *Review of International Political Economy* 5(3): 381–92.

Krugman, Paul (1998) 'What happened to Asia?', http://www.mit.edu/krugman/www/DISINTER.html.

Masina, Pietro (ed.) (2001) *Rethinking Development in East Asia: From Illusory Miracle to Economic Crisis*, Copenhagen: NIAS.

McLeod, Ross H. and Garnaut, Ross (eds) (1998) *East Asia in Crisis: From Being a Miracle to Needing One?*, London: Routledge.

Roubini, Nouriel (accessed 2000) http://www.stern.nyu.edu/~nroubini/asia/AsiaHomepage.html.

1.7 The measurement of poverty

Howard White

INTRODUCTION

The importance of the task of poverty reduction means that we must be clear as to what we mean
by poverty, who the poor are and the best way to help them escape poverty. This chapter is

concerned with the first of these points – the meaning and measurement of poverty. The next section outlines key concepts which underpin the various poverty measurements discussed in the subsequent section. Finally, some data on poverty trends are presented.

POVERTY CONCEPTS

In everyday usage the term 'poverty' is synonymous with a shortage of income. But the development literature stresses the multi-dimensionality of poverty. In addition to material consumption, health, education, social life, environmental quality, spiritual and political freedom all matter. Deprivation with respect to any one of these can be called poverty.

Some dispute the use of multi-dimensionality, arguing that income-poverty (i.e. lack of material well-being) is what really matters. Arguments supporting this view include the high correlation between income and other measures of well-being such as health and education status and the view that governments can do something about income (i.e. support growth) but are less able to enhance spiritual well-being.

But there are good arguments in defence of multi-dimensionality. First, the correlation with income is not that strong for some indicators. Second, poor people themselves often rank other dimensions as being more important than income. Most famously, Jodha (1988) showed with Indian data that the welfare of the poor had risen by measures they considered important – such as wearing shoes and separate accommodation for people and livestock – whereas surveys showed their income to have fallen. Participatory approaches to poverty measurement seek to identify the things that matter to poor people. Different perceptions matter since the poverty concept adopted will influence policy. When poverty is defined solely in terms of income, then it is unsurprising that economic growth is found to be the most effective way to reduce poverty. But if basic needs such as health and education are valued then the development strategy is likely to put more emphasis on social policy.

Two further conceptual issues are: absolute versus relative poverty; and temporary versus permanent poverty. Absolute poverty is measured against some benchmark – such as the cost of getting enough food to eat or being able to write your own name for literacy. Relative poverty is measured against societal standards; in developing countries the basket of 'essentials' comprises food and a few items of clothing, whereas in developed countries it includes Christmas presents and going out once a month.

The distinction between the temporarily and the permanently poor is linked to the notion of vulnerability. The vulnerable are those at risk of falling into poverty. If there are poverty traps – such that once someone falls into poverty they cannot get out again – then there is a good case for anti-poverty interventions to prevent this happening.

POVERTY MEASURES

National-level measures

The most commonly reported development statistic is a country's GNP per capita. Whilst a case may be made for using GNP as an overall development measure it is not a good measure of poverty for two reasons. First, as an average, the statistic takes no account of distribution. Hence two countries can have the same level of GNP per capita, but in one of the two a far greater proportion of the population fall below the poverty line if income is less equally distributed. Second, GNP is of course an income measure which ignores other dimensions of poverty.

The most common income-poverty measure is the headcount, i.e. the percentage of the population falling below the poverty line. However, this measure takes no account of how far people are below the poverty line – so that a rise in the income of the poor which leaves them in poverty appears to have no effect. Hence another measure, the poverty gap, is often used, which can be variously interpreted as the product of the headcount and the average distance of the poor below the poverty line (expressed as a percentage of the poverty line) and the benefit of perfect targeting. The poverty severity index is a similar measure which puts greater weight on those furthest below the poverty line. These three measures – the headcount, the poverty gap and the poverty severity index – are known collectively as the Foster-Greer-Thorbecke poverty measures and labelled P_0, P_1 and P_2 respectively.

Over the years a number of composite measures of development have been proposed; a composite being an average of a number of different measures. A previous measure, the Physical Quality of Life Index (PQLI), has been superseded in recent years by the UNDP's Human Development Index (HDI). The HDI is a composite of GDP per capita, life expectancy and a measure of educational attainment (which is an average of literacy and mean years of schooling). However, just as income per capita takes no account of distribution neither does the HDI: mean years of schooling can increase by the already well-educated extending their university education rather than expanding access amongst those with little or no education. However, UNDP has also proposed a Human Poverty Index (HPI) which focuses on deprivation. Specifically, the HPI is calculated as the average of the percentage of the population not expected to live to 40, the percentage who are illiterate and what is called the 'deprivation in living standard' (the average of those without access to water and healthcare, and the percentage of under-5s who are underweight).

Although the HDI is widely used there have been criticisms of its construction (which are summarized in a technical appendix to the 1996 *Human Development Report*), one of which concerns problems in using a composite. There are three main problems: which variables to put in the index; the necessarily arbitrary choice of weights in constructing the average; and that information is lost by combining three or four pieces of data into a single number. Thus it may be preferable to report a small range of social indicators, such as life expectancy, infant and child mortality and literacy, rather than attempt to combine these to an overall poverty index.

THE MEASUREMENT OF INCOME-POVERTY

The income-poverty headcount is the percentage of the population whose income is below the poverty line. This calculation is fraught with difficulties.

First, poverty lines must be defined (it is common practice to use two lines), which is done either absolutely with reference to the cost of a basket of goods or relatively to mean income or a certain share of the population. In the former case the basket can be calculated either as the cost of acquiring a certain number of calories or of a basket of goods and services. In the former case the resulting poverty line (food poverty line) is often used as the line for the extreme poor. It is then divided by the share of food in the budget of the poor (or the population as a whole, though strictly defined it should be that of a person on the poverty line) to get the upper poverty line.

In applying the poverty line, consumption (expenditure) is commonly used rather than income. First, because survey respondents will have a far clearer idea of their expenditure than their income. Second, when income is uneven households will smooth consumption (i.e. even it out over time) so that at any point in time current consumption is likely to be a more accurate measure of well-being than current income.

In practice, data are collected at the level of the household rather than the individual. Doing so ignores problems of intra-household allocation. There are no data on the number of women or children living in poverty (despite the tendency of some international organizations to report such figures), only data on the percentage of women and children living in households whose income is below the poverty line. The use of household-level data introduces problems of household composition and size. Household composition matters since the consumption requirements of different individuals varies – specifically children consume less than adults and, more controversially, women may need to consume less than men. This problem is catered for by the use of an adult equivalents scale which expresses the consumption needs of women and children as a fraction of those of an adult male. Household size matters as there are economies of scale in household consumption – that is, two can live together more cheaply than they could apart as there are shared expenses (living space, utilities and many household items). Failure to take account of these economies will overstate poverty in large households.

Finally, prices vary across time and space. Allowance must be made for these price differences in order for the poverty line to be comparable. There are even greater difficulties in comparing between countries, partly since market exchange rates do not reflect differences in purchasing power. Rather, purchasing power parity (PPP) exchange rates should be used, which are not uniformly available.

Comparisons across time and space also require that consumption is measured in a comparable way. If survey designs differ greatly then 'aggregate consumption' may mean quite different things. It is commonly recognized that own-production should be measured as this is an important part of total consumption. But 'wild foods' (collected in nature) and festivals can also form an important source of food and are commonly overlooked. Similarly sources of income from common property or the provision of free social services varies between countries and so introduces another source of incomparability.

It may seem from this discussion that measurement of income-poverty is so difficult that it may be better to stick to some other measure. Certainly a small survey should stick to a proxy for income, such as housing quality and ownership of a few household items. But other indicators are not without problems; indeed data quality is far worse for many social indicators than it is for income/expenditure.

SOME DATA

The World Bank produces data on income-poverty using poverty lines of one and two PPP dollars. Table 1 shows the headcount and absolute numbers of poor people in developing countries by the dollar a day criterion. Table 2 shows data on undernourishment.

The absolute number of poor has risen in all but two regions – East Asia and the Middle East – with the largest absolute rise in Africa and the greatest percentage increase in Eastern Europe. The headcount, at close to half, is highest in South Asia and Africa, with Africa moving ahead as there has been a slight fall in the proportion of people who are poor in South Asia. Although reliable data are not readily available, the data for East Asia seem to reflect a long-run trend of substantial poverty reduction in that region. Latin America also achieved large reductions (from a headcount of around 50 to 20 per cent on a dollar a day) from the 1950s to the late 1970s, though progress has been somewhat uneven since then.

The nutrition data tell a different story, partly reflecting the fact that there have been substantial long-run improvements in social indicators such as life expectancy in all regions of the world.

Table 1 Income poverty in developing countries using dollar a day poverty line

	East Asia and the Pacific	Eastern Europe and Central Asia	Latin America and the Caribbean	Middle East and North Africa	South Asia	Sub-Saharan Africa	**Total**
Absolute numbers (millions)							
1987	415.1	1.1	63.7	25.0	474.4	217.2	1,196.5
1993	431.9	18.3	70.8	21.5	505.1	273.3	1,320.9
1998	278.3	24.0	78.2	20.9	522.0	290.9	1,214.3
Headcount (per cent of population)							
1987	26.6	0.2	15.3	11.5	44.9	46.6	28.7
1993	25.2	4.0	15.3	8.4	42.4	49.6	28.5
1998	15.3	5.1	15.6	7.3	40.0	46.3	24.3

Source: www.worldbank.org/poverty

Table 2 The prevalence of undernourishment in developing countries (per cent of population)

	1979/81	1990/92	1995/97
Asia and Pacific	32	21	17
Oceania	31	27	24
Southeast Asia	27	17	13
South Asia	38	26	23
Latin America and Caribbean	13	13	11
Caribbean	19	25	31
Central America	20	17	17
South America	14	14	10
Near East and North Africa	9	8	9
Near East	10	10	12
North Africa	8	4	4
Sub-Saharan Africa	37	35	33
Central Africa	36	37	48
East Africa	35	45	42
Southern Africa	32	45	44
West Africa	40	21	16
All developing countries	29	20	18

Source: FAO, *The State of Food Insecurity in the World 1999*, Table 1

The overall picture is of a reduction in undernourishment of around one-third from the late 1970s to mid-1990s. Most regions have seen falls, the main exceptions being in Africa and the Caribbean. Improvements in South Asia mean that, having had comparable levels to Africa in the 1970s, the situation in the former is now considerably better than the latter.

GUIDE TO FURTHER READING AND REFERENCES

Most of the literature on poverty measurement concerns income-poverty, the most comprehensive, though technical, treatment being Ravallion (1992). A critique of income measures is given by Jodha (1988) and a discussion of alternatives in Chambers (1995). More general analysis of both concepts and measurement is available

in Baulch (1996) and White (1999). For a broader co¹
briefings produced by ODI, including 'The meaning ar
are available from www.odi.org/briefing. Finally, Gordc
The main data sources are the UNDP's *Human Developm*
Indicators, both of which are published annually (with
HDR contain discussions of the various indices pre
contains useful information on data sources. The
www.worldbank.org/poverty, which includes many us

The following text references provide the basis for furthe
Baulch, B. (1996) 'The new poverty agenda: a disputed cc
Chambers, Robert (1995) 'Poverty and livelihoods: whose
 Studies, *Discussion paper 347*.
Gordon, David and Spicker, Paul (eds) (1999) *Internation*
Jodha, N.S. (1988) 'Poverty debate in India: a minority ....., *Economic and Political Weekly* 22(45–47):
 2421–8.
Ravallion, M. (1992) 'Poverty comparisons: a guide to concepts and methods', *LSLS Working Paper 88*,
 Washington DC: World Bank.
White, Howard (1999) 'Global poverty reduction: are we heading in the right direction?', *Journal of
 International Development* 11: 503–19.

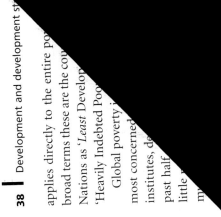

1.8 Poverty in global terms

Anthony O'Connor

The justification for an entry on poverty in this volume is that it is commonly seen as broadly the antithesis of development. They are, of course, not exact opposites, since poverty is a condition while development is a process or set of processes. Like 'development', the word 'poverty' can be used in relation to a wide range of phenomena, generally meaning lack or deficiency; but here attention will be confined to material poverty in respect of money, goods and services. This chapter is concerned with people who are poor in contrast with others who are rich or affluent.

Both in academic social science and in more popular usage the term 'poverty' is sometimes employed in a wholly relative sense to refer to the condition of the poorest within a given society. It is notable that the entry under 'poverty' in the fourth edition of the *Dictionary of Human Geography* (Johnston *et al.*, 2000) is written largely from this perspective, and is much concerned with poverty within the UK. The same applies to Pacione's (1999) essay on 'The geography of poverty and deprivation' in his edited compendium on *Applied Geography*. A fundamentally different approach is to consider poverty in global terms, focusing on the poorest quarter or third of humanity – which includes very few indeed in any part of Europe or North America. This corresponds closely to poverty in an absolute sense of severe deprivation in respect of, for example, food, shelter, education and healthcare.

It is such absolute poverty in global terms that is discussed here. The concept can be applied to individuals, to families, to communities, or to entire countries. In respect of countries, it never

pulation, but in many cases it does apply to a large majority. In
ntries, nearly all in Africa or Asia, which are designated by the United
ed'. Since the early 1990s a sub-set has been officially recognized as the
Countries'.

certainly not a fashionable subject for academic study, either in the countries
or in the richer parts of the world. There is nothing to match the proliferation of
gree programmes and journals of 'development studies' which have sprung up in the
century (and which are exemplified by the publication of this book). One can point to
more than isolated books, such as *The Nature of Poverty* by Margaret Haswell (1975) or the
ch more renowned *Poverty and Famines* by Amartya Sen (1981), and articles tucked away in the
development studies journals.

Similarly, there is no United Nations agency explicitly concerned primarily with poverty, though it is of profound relevance to the work of many of them, from the FAO to the WHO and UNICEF. In terms of published material it is the UNDP which has done the most in recent years to address poverty in all its dimensions, not least within the annual *Human Development Report*. Likewise, most of the prosperous countries have what is labelled an 'international development' government department or agency, within which direct concern for poverty may be more or less evident. In the UK the change from ODA to DFID was quickly followed in late 1997 by the publication of the optimistically titled White Paper *Eliminating World Poverty*. Strangely, while we might assume that, chronologically, poverty normally precedes development, in respect of both study and action the order is often reversed.

One further distinction that might be made between poverty and development relates to the recent debates about the latter as a normative term. While the vast majority of work on development, whether in academia or in the corridors of power, has assumed that it is beneficial and to be actively promoted, there has been a substantial reaction against this both from self-declared radical academics and within some non-governmental organizations (NGOs). There is no equivalent 'school' declaring that poverty is something to be welcomed and preserved, though of course there is much debate on how great a priority its reduction should receive and on what aspects most urgently demand attention. We seem to be in the age of post-almost everything, but not post-poverty.

With respect to various human rights issues, and matters such as gender equality, it is sometimes suggested that 'Western' values are being imposed on other parts of the world. With respect to hunger or high child mortality, however, there is no such cultural confrontation: nowhere are they thought desirable or defensible.

THE GEOGRAPHICAL DISTRIBUTION OF ABSOLUTE POVERTY

The conceptual problems outlined above are such that no attempt at precision is made here: the picture is presented in terms of the broad orders of magnitude in which we can have some confidence. It is clear, for instance, that whatever criteria are employed, and whatever intensity of poverty is under consideration, the majority of the world's poor people live in Asia (Table 1). That majority is reduced, however, if attention is focused on the poorest quarter rather than the poorest one-third, for vast numbers in China and India and many in Southeast Asia lie between these two. It is also reduced if we are concerned with social welfare as well as income, largely because of the levels of education and life expectancy now attained in much of China. On a continental basis, most of the remainder of the world's poor people live in Africa, and the great majority of these within Tropical Africa.

Table 1 Under-5 mortality: absolute numbers, 1998

World	10,000,000
Sub-Saharan Africa	4,000,000
South Asia	4,000,000
East Asia	1,600,000
India	2,600,000
China	950,000
Nigeria	770,000
Pakistan	720,000
Congo	470,000
Ethiopia	460,000
Bangladesh	370,000
Afghanistan	290,000
Indonesia	260,000

Source: UNICEF, *State of the World's Children 2000*

Table 2 Poverty trends, 1970s–1990s

	China	SE Asia	South Asia	Sub-Saharan Africa
GNP per capita annual growth rate 1975–98 (%)	7.5	3.7	2.3	–0.7
Daily supply of calories per capita % change 1970–97	+45	+35	+18	–2
Daily supply of protein per capita % change 1970–97	+62	+40	+13	–4
Under-5 mortality per 1000				
1970	120	150	210	230
1998	50	60	110	170

Source: Main source of data: UNDP, *Human Development Report 2000*

Conversely, the great majority of the countries in which more than half the population live in poverty are in Africa, whatever criteria are used to determine this. Of the 65 countries designated by the World Bank as 'low income', 40 are in Tropical Africa; while of the 50 countries regarded by many UN bodies as 'least developed', Tropical Africa accounts for more than 30. When attention is focused on, say, the 20 poorest, most international tables place between 16 and 18 African countries in the list, while in the UNDP Human Development Index for 1998 all the 24 lowest-ranked countries are African.

In so far as the paragraph above merely reflects the co-existence of two huge Asian countries and many far smaller African countries, it is of limited significance. Of far greater importance is the *trend* over recent decades, which clearly differentiates much of South and East Asia from most of Tropical Africa (Table 2). While no clear trend to either intensification or alleviation of poverty can be determined for most parts of Tropical Africa over the past 30 years, there is very clear evidence of alleviation in many parts of East and South Asia. In India, for example, not only have average incomes risen, but also the proportion of households below any given income level has fallen. There has been similar improvement in almost all aspects of social welfare.

This poverty alleviation in Asia has, of course, occurred in a context of rising total population numbers; and so the absolute numbers of poor people, and hence the absolute amount of poverty, have remained fairly constant. They can be shown to have either increased or decreased depending on the criteria adopted and the particular countries in question. However, the rate of population increase has been even greater throughout Tropical Africa, so that there the absolute amount of poverty has increased massively, and continues to increase, whatever methods of measurement or estimation are adopted.

Contrasts among individual countries are indicated in widely available tables, but even these, of course, mask great regional variations within countries, as well as differences between urban and rural situations. When we move in this way to sub-national units there is increased need to broaden the scope of our analysis of global poverty beyond Asia and Africa to parts of countries such as Brazil.

CAUSES AND CONSEQUENCES

No attempt can be made here to explain the existence of absolute poverty. Indeed, it might be argued that low levels of material consumption, high death rates and so on have been the norm for humanity throughout most of its existence, and that it is only the move towards prosperity which needs to be explained. However, even this leaves questions regarding the *persistence* into the twenty-first century of mass poverty in certain parts of the world.

The only assertion to be made here is that there is no single primary cause of the persistence or the distribution of material poverty today. Explanations lie partly in the past and partly in present-day conditions, partly within the countries or localities concerned and partly far beyond. The legacy of colonialism is undoubtedly highly relevant, but so is the present global distribution of power and present structures of global relationships, including for many countries a crushing burden of debt. The physical environment of most poverty-stricken regions is highly relevant, especially through the agency of disease, but so are many components of each region's culture.

Two elements which are certainly part cause and part consequence of material poverty and its persistence are rapid population growth associated with high fertility, and weak, unstable political structures. In both cases the existence of a vicious circle operating within such countries as Afghanistan, Ethiopia and Congo can be readily demonstrated.

Vicious circles also operate on a global scale, however. The global distribution of power mentioned above as a cause of persisting poverty is also to a large extent a consequence of it. The poverty of most African countries, and even of India, plays a very large part in ensuring that they have an extremely small influence in global affairs in relation to their population size. We are constantly told that the start of the twenty-first century is the age of globalization, and that as a result of *The Death of Distance* (Cairncross, 1997) it matters less and less where in the world you are. Yet these processes are to some extent by-passing large parts of the world, so that these are becoming increasingly more marginalized – economically, politically and culturally. One consequence of poverty for millions of people is that geography does still matter: the place in which you live makes a great deal of difference to your life chances if that place is in rural Cambodia or Chad. The process of globalization is so labelled by the world's rich; but from the perspective of the world's poor it is far from 'global'.

GUIDE TO FURTHER READING

The widest-ranging academic discussion of poverty, both absolute and relative, is Townsend, P. (1993), *The International Analysis of Poverty*, Hemel Hempstead: Harvester Wheatsheaf.

Elaboration of many aspects is provided in Gordon, D. and Spicker, P. (eds) (1999), *The International Glossary on Poverty*, London: Zed Books.

Three 'classics', all of which deal with very specific aspects of poverty, are: Lewis, O. (1959) *Five Families: Mexican Case Studies in the Culture of Poverty*, New York: Basic Books; Lipton, M. (1977) *Why Poor People Stay Poor: A Study of Urban Bias in World Development*, London: Temple Smith; and Sen, A. (1981) *Poverty and Famines: An Essay on Entitlement and Deprivation*, Oxford: Clarendon Press.

Two major annual publications have each devoted one issue explicitly to poverty: UNDP, *Human Development Report 1997*, New York: OUP; and World Bank, *World Development Report 2000–2001: Attacking Poverty*, New York: OUP.

A very readable and decidedly optimistic book following up the UK White Paper referenced above is Marris, R. (1999) *Ending Poverty*, London: Thames and Hudson.

A useful overview from an Indian perspective is provided in Khusro, A.M. (1999) *The Poverty of Nations*, London: Macmillan.

BACKGROUND MATERIAL AND REFERENCES

Cairncross, F. (1997) *The Death of Distance*, London: Orion.

Haswell, M. (1975) *The Nature of Poverty*, London: Macmillan.

Johnston, R.J., Gregory, D., Pratt, G. and Watts, M. (eds) (2000), *The Dictionary of Human Geography* (4th edn), Oxford: Blackwell.

Pacione, M. (ed.) (1999) *Applied Geography*, London: Routledge.

Sen, A. (1981) *Poverty and Famines*, Oxford: Clarendon Press.

UNDP (2000) *Human Development Report 2000*, New York: OUP.

UNICEF (2000) *State of the World's Children 2000*, New York: UNICEF.

White Paper (1997) *Eliminating World Poverty: A Challenge for the 21st Century*, White Paper on International Development, Cmd 3789, London: The Stationery Office.

1.9 Development as economic growth

A.P. Thirlwall

The economic and social development of the world's poorest countries is perhaps the greatest challenge facing mankind at the beginning of this new millennium. Over one billion of the world's six billion population live in absolute poverty; the same number suffer various degrees of malnutrition, and millions have no access to safe water, healthcare or education. This poverty is concentrated largely in countries described as 'developing', and co-exists with the affluence enjoyed by the vast majority of people in countries described as 'developed'.

The standard of living of people is commonly measured by the total amount of goods and services produced per head of the population, or what is called Gross Domestic Product (GDP) per capita (or Gross National Product (GNP) per capita if net income from abroad is added). This, in turn, is determined by the number of people who work, and their productivity. The basic proximate cause of the poverty of nations is the low productivity of labour associated with low levels of physical and human capital (education) accumulation, and low levels of technology.

Income per head in a country is naturally measured in units of its own currency, but if international comparisons of living standards are to be made, each country's per capita income has to be converted into a common unit of account at some rate of exchange. The convention is to take the US dollar as the unit of account and convert each country's per capita income into dollars at the official exchange rate. A country's official exchange rate, however, is not necessarily a good measure of the relative purchasing power of currencies, because it only reflects the relative prices of goods that enter into international trade. But many goods that people buy are not traded, and the relative price of these non-traded goods tends to be lower the poorer the country, reflecting much lower relative labour costs. An exchange rate is required which reflects the purchasing power parity (PPP) of countries' currencies, and this is now provided by various international organizations, such as the World Bank, which uses US$1 per day measured at PPP to define the level of absolute poverty.

The economic growth of countries refers to the increase in output of goods and services that a country produces over an accounting period, normally 1 year. If a country is said to be growing at 5 per cent per annum, it means that the total volume of its domestic output (GDP) is increasing at this rate. If population is growing at 2 per cent per annum, this means that output per head (or the average standard of living) is growing at 3 per cent per annum.

Economic growth, however, is not the same as economic development. The process of economic (and social) development must imply a growth in living standards, but it is a much wider concept than the growth of per capita income alone. Growth, it might be said, is a necessary condition for the economic and social development of nations, but it is not a sufficient condition because an aggregate measure of growth or per capita income pays no attention to how that output is distributed amongst the population; it says nothing about the composition of output (whether the goods are consumption goods, investment goods or public goods such as education and health provision), and it gives no indication of the physical, social and economic environment in which the output is produced. In short, the growth rates of nations cannot be taken as measures of the increase in the welfare of societies because the well-being of people is a much more inclusive concept than the level of income alone.

If the process of economic and social development is defined in terms of an increase in society's welfare, a concept of development is required which embraces not only economic variables and objectives, but also social objectives and values for which societies strive. Many economists and other social scientists have attempted to address this issue, and here we mention the ideas of two prominent thinkers in the field: Denis Goulet and Amartya Sen (who in 1998 won the Nobel Prize for Economics for his work on the interface between welfare and development economics).

Goulet (1971) distinguishes three basic components or core values that he argues must be included in any true meaning of development which he calls life sustenance, self-esteem and freedom. Life sustenance is concerned with the provision of basic needs. No country can be regarded as fully developed if it cannot provide all its people with such basic needs as housing, clothing, food and minimal education. A country may have a relatively high average standard of living and an impressive growth performance over several years, but still have a poor provision of basic needs, leaving large sections of the population in an underdeveloped state. This issue is closely related to the distribution of income in societies measured by the share of total income going to the richest and poorest sections of society. The distribution of income is much more unequal in poorer developing countries than in richer developed countries, and it is perfectly possible for a poor country to be growing fast, yet its distribution of income to be worsening because the fruits of growth accrue to the rich. Such a country would have grown, but it would not have developed if the provision of basic needs for the poorest groups in the community had not improved.

Self-esteem is concerned with the feeling of self-respect and independence. A country cannot be regarded as fully developed if it is exploited by others, or cannot conduct economic relations on equal terms. In this sense, the colonization of large parts of Africa, Asia and South America kept the countries in these regions of the world in an underdeveloped state. Colonialism has now virtually ended, but some would argue that there are modern equivalents of colonialism, equally insidious and anti-developmental. For example, the International Monetary Fund (IMF) and World Bank dominate economic policy-making in many developing countries, and many of the policies that the countries are forced to pursue are detrimental to development. Also, multinational corporations that operate in many developing countries often introduce consumption patterns and techniques of production which are inappropriate to the stage of development of the countries concerned, and to that extent impair welfare. In international trade, poor and rich countries do not operate on a level playing field, and the strong may gain at the expense of the weak. The distribution of the gains from trade are not equitably distributed, not the least because the terms of trade of primary producing developing countries (i.e. the price of their exports relative to the price of imports) tends to deteriorate through time (at an average rate of about 0.5 per cent per annum for at least the last century).

Freedom refers to the ability of people to determine their own destiny. No person is free if they are imprisoned on the margin of subsistence with no education and no skills. The great benefit of material development is that it expands the range of choice open to individuals and to societies at large. For the economic and social development of a country, however, all must participate and benefit from the process of growth, not just the richest few. If the majority are left untouched, their choices remain limited; and no person is free if they cannot choose.

Sen (1983, 1999) argues in a similar vein to Goulet that economic growth should not be viewed as an end in itself, but as the means to the achievement of a much wider set of objectives by which economic and social development should be measured. Development should focus on, and be judged by, the expansion of people's 'entitlements', and the 'capabilities' that these entitlements generate, and income is not always a good measure of entitlements. Sen defines entitlements as 'the set of alternative commodity bundles that a person can command in a society using the totality of rights and opportunities that he or she faces'. For most people, the crucial determinants of their entitlements depend on their ability to sell their labour and on the price of commodities. Employment opportunity, and the level of unemployment, must therefore be included in any meaningful definition of development. Entitlements also depend on such factors as what individuals can extract from the state (in the form of welfare provision); the spatial distribution of resources and opportunities, and power relations in society. Sen (1984) has analysed major world famines using the concept of entitlements and finds that several famines have not been associated with a shortage of food, but rather with a lack of entitlements because the food supply has been withdrawn from certain parts of the country or sections of society, or food prices have risen.

The thinking of Goulet, Sen and others has led to the construction of alternative measures of economic and social development to supplement statistics on growth rates and levels of per capita income of countries. The most notable of these measures are the Human Development Index (HDI) and the Human Poverty Index (HPI) compiled by the United Nations Development Programme (UNDP) and published in its annual *Human Development Report*. These alternative indices of the economic well-being of nations do not always correlate well with per capita income. The same growth rate and per capita income of countries can be associated with very different levels of achievement in other spheres such as life expectancy, death rates, literacy and education. As the UNDP says in its 1997 *Report* that 'although GNP growth is absolutely necessary to meet all essential human objectives, countries differ in the way that they translate growth into human development'.

The UNDP's Human Development Index is based on three variables: life expectancy at birth; educational attainment, measured by a combination of adult literacy and combined primary, secondary and tertiary school enrolment rates; and the standard of living measured by real per capita income measured at PPP (see earlier). These variables are combined in a composite index that ranges from 0 to 1 (see Thirlwall, 1999, for details). Comparing the ranking of developing countries by their HDI and per capita income show some interesting divergences. Many oil-producing countries, for example, have much lower HDI rankings than their per capita income rank, while some poor countries rank relatively high by their HDI because they have deliberately devoted scarce resources to human development. Countries such as Cuba, Costa Rica, Vietnam, Zaire, Tanzania and Sri Lanka fall into this category.

The UNDP's Human Poverty Index is also based on three main indices: the percentage of the population not expected to survive beyond the age of 40; the adult illiteracy rate; and a deprivation index based on an average of three variables – the percentage of the population without access to safe water, the percentage of the population without access to health services, and the percentage of children under the age of 5 years who are underweight through malnourishment. The ranking of countries by their HPI also shows some striking contrasts with their ranking by per capita income. The UNDP has calculated that the cost of eradicating poverty across the world is relatively small compared to global income – not more than 0.3 per cent of world GDP – and that political commitment, not financial resources, is the real obstacle to poverty eradication.

To conclude, economic growth is not the same as economic development. The annual growth rate of a country is a very precise measure of the growth of the total volume of goods and services produced in a country during a year but says nothing about its composition or distribution. Growth is a necessary condition for real income per head to rise, but it is not a sufficient condition for economic development to take place because development is a multi-dimensional concept which embraces multifarious economic and social objectives concerned with the distribution of income, the provision of basic needs, and the real and psychological well-being of people. Many poor countries in the last 30 years have experienced quite a respectable rate of growth in living standards – averaging 2–3 per cent per annum – but the absolute number in poverty has continued to rise, and the distribution of income has become more unequal. Equally, at the global level, there is little evidence of the convergence of per capita incomes across nations. The poor countries have been growing, but the rich countries have been growing as fast, if not faster in per capita terms. While the eradication of poverty, and the narrowing of the rich–poor country divide, remains one of the great challenges of the new millennium, economic growth in poor countries is not enough by itself for development to take place when viewed in a broader perspective.

GUIDE TO FURTHER READING AND REFERENCES

The topics covered here can be taken further by recourse to the following texts.

Goulet, D. (1971) *The Cruel Choice: A New Concept on the Theory of Development*, New York: Atheneum.

Sen, A. (1983) 'Development: which way now?', *Economic Journal*, December.

Sen, A. (1984) *Poverty and Famines: An Essay in Entitlement and Deprivation*, Oxford: Clarendon Press.

Sen, A. (1999) *Development as Freedom: Human Capability and Global Need*, New York: Knopf.

Thirlwall, A.P. (1999) *Growth and Development: With Special Reference to Developing Economies* (6th edn), London: Macmillan.

United Nations Development Programme (1997 and 1999) *Human Development Report*, New York: Oxford University Press.

1.10 Development as improving human welfare and human rights

Jennifer A. Elliott

CRITICAL DEVELOPMENT STUDIES

At the turn of the twenty-first century, human well-being, including individual civil and political liberties, as well as meeting the physical and material needs of human society, are accepted concerns for development, both as outcomes and conditions for sustained progress. Issues of egalitarian development, democracy, participation, ethics and human rights suffuse development theory, the pronouncements of major development institutions such as the United Nations and the World Bank, and the activities of new social movements alike. In short, the practice and discourses of development have become more morally informed particularly over the last decade.

In part, the 'insertion of a critical sensibility' (Radcliffe, 1999: 84) into development studies is a product of the recognition that many of the world's citizens continue to lack even the most fundamental goods and opportunities. Integral to this understanding has been the expansion in tools and measures for monitoring deprivation and progress worldwide, such as those developed and reported annually by the United Nations Development Programme (UNDP).

Theoretical developments have also been important in prompting the current emphasis on human welfare and human rights concerns. The legitimacy and universal acceptance of the 'big ideas' of progress and development, for example, that characterized the modernist tradition in development theory for so long, have to a degree been overturned by the postmodern movement over recent years (Simon, 1999). In so doing, various theories (Radcliffe, 1999: 84) and alternative developments are now influencing development agendas (Potter *et al.*, 1999).

In short, whilst a concern for human dignity and well-being in development studies is not entirely new, it is only recently that 'many new problems *as well as* old ones' (Sen, 1999: xi, emphases added) are being so widely conceptualized in terms of human rights and freedoms.

RIGHTS AND DEVELOPMENT AS SEPARATE CONCERNS

Although human rights and well-being were undoubtedly concerns in the 1940s and 1950s within international institutions, amongst governments of newly independent countries and in the emergent discipline of development studies, it has been argued that the predominant ideas and practices of development at that time were often devoid of ethical considerations and separate from those 'marked out for development' (Corbridge, 1999: 69). For example, ideas of progress during that period were generally synonymous with economic growth and the modernization of traditional societies. In so far as welfare and rights issues were considered, it was assumed that these would follow as outcomes of the linear process of economic development. In turn, development and underdevelopment were quantified (and as reported by the World Bank and United Nation's reports) in terms of the level of Gross National Product (GNP) per capita.

During this period, the traditional view of human rights centred on civil and political (CP) rights (the right to life, liberty and security, for example; the right to vote, to a free press and freedom of speech) and on legal rights such as to due process of law and the presumption of innocence until proven guilty. In short, the debates were led by the West, emphasized material well-being, and took place alongside, rather than being integrated with, the agendas of international development. Although two key International Covenants were adopted by the United Nations in 1966 (on CP Rights and on Economic, Social and Cultural (ESC) Rights), work focused on the ratification and inscription of CP rights into constitutional and legal frameworks. ESC rights, such as the right to an adequate standard of living, the right to education, to work and equal pay, and the right of minorities to enjoy their own culture, religion and language, were less prominent and tended to be considered separately to CP rights (Maxwell, 1999).

THE BASIC NEEDS APPROACH

By the end of the 1960s, however, there was growing disillusionment with the practice of development and with indicators of development that took no account of the distribution of national wealth. It became widely agreed that the economic growth that actually took place in most developing countries seemed to go together with increases in absolute and relative poverty. In response to this dilemma, it was argued that a *direct* approach was required to the delivery of welfare outcomes. In due course, what became known as the Basic Needs Approach (BNA) drew together theorists and practitioners from a range of traditions, academic centres and institutions of development, that searched for more human-centred and locally relevant processes and patterns of development (see for example, Stohr's (1981) 'development from below'). In short under the Basic Needs Approach, development was redefined as a broad-based, people-oriented or endogenous process, as a critique of modernization and as a break with past development theory.

As a result of the influence of the BNA, the 1970s saw a 'vast array' (Escobar, 1995) of programmes focused on households and covering aspects of health, education, farming and reproduction practices designed to create a minimum level of welfare for the weakest groups in society. Development practice became characterized by district and regional planning (supported by major international donor institutions), by proliferating field bureaucracies and by development solutions through targeting (of social groups – particularly women and children, of sectors and of regions) to overcome the recognized inadequacies of the 'planning fantasies of the 1960s' (Chambers, 1993: 108). Concurrently, a series of social indicators for development appeared, most notably within annual reports of the World Bank and the UNDP, as concepts of absolute and relative poverty were redefined to include the distribution of access to education and clean water, for example, in addition to income.

BUYING AND SELLING WELFARE

The BNA did much to put poverty, human needs and rights back on official development agendas in the 1970s. However, many assert that the decade of the 1980s was one of development 'reversals' rather than achievements with evidence, particularly in Africa, of falling school enrolments and literacy levels, for example (Simon, 1999). Similarly, development theory was proposed to have reached an 'impasse' (Schuurman, 1993) through the predominance and power of neo-liberal development ideas.

Progressively throughout the decade, basic human rights such as access to safe water and sanitation, which had been identified in the early 1980s as essential to bringing marginal groups into dominant cultures, became 'commodities subject to the rigours of the market' (Bell, 1992: 85). Donors, for example, came under increasing pressure to find new methods of financing and providing welfare both 'at home' and abroad. Governments of developing nations were also required to cut state expenditures under conditions for access to multi-lateral development finance. Whilst these pressures opened up spaces for new project types, processes and programmes in development, it has been suggested that the more radical aspects of the original BNA philosophies were often devalued in practice, 'reducing them from agendas for change and empowerment into little more than shopping lists that are hawked to donors for implementation, commonly more in line with donors' than recipients priorities' (Simon, 1999: 27).

CONVERGING AGENDAS THROUGH THE 1990s

If the 1980s were an impasse in development thinking, it could be suggested that the 1990s made up for it with a whole set of theoretical 'turns' that generated much debate and (often divergent) ideas on how development could be achieved and indeed, on the meaning of development itself. Smith (2000: 2), however, is cautious regarding the prospects for change in practice; 'while the affluent endure post-modern ambiguity and uncertainty in comfort, for those at the coal-face of human misery what constitutes progress is still likely to be self-evident'.

Throughout the 1990s, the UNDP made a number of changes in its annual reporting of development progress, which have made important contributions to changing ideas on the meaning and goals of development and particularly in relation to non-income indicators of human well-being. In 1990, for example, it introduced the Human Development Index (HDI), a composite index designed to reflect achievements in the most basic human capabilities defined as leading a long life, being knowledgeable and enjoying a decent standard of living. Subsequently, in 1995, the Gender-Related Human Development Index (GDI) and Gender Empowerment Measure (GEM) were introduced encompassing the recognition that gender equality is a measure of and means for human and national development. In 1997, the Human Poverty Index (HPI) was introduced to measure deprivation, in terms of the percentage of population not expected to live until aged 40, illiteracy rates, the percentage of people lacking access to health services and safe water, and the percentage of children under 5 who are moderately or severely underweight. These developments are clear evidence of how, increasingly, 'development' is conceived in terms of human rights and freedoms and of the recognition of the interconnectedness and multi-dimensional nature of these component issues. Table 1 displays a number of quotations that further illustrate the converging agendas of welfare and human rights issues in international development into the twenty-first century.

CONCLUSION

In this short chapter, it has not been possible to do justice to the decades of work done in the fields of poverty, participation, gender and democracy, for example, that have all been extremely important in bringing about a much more holistic and moral agenda for development. However, this brief analysis has highlighted how such an agenda has shifted the focus away from determining any *particular* means or 'specially chosen list of instruments' (Sen, 1999: 3) for development, towards more concern for the overarching ends of development. Critically, these ends are plural and fluid in the sense that different societies at any particular time may assign varied importance within conceptions of human rights, for example, to the obligations of individuals to self and other, or to material well-being over personal liberty. But rather than debating the primacy of one right, good, opportunity or resource over another, the debates are now more regularly focused on questions of

Table 1 The multi-dimensional and interdependent nature of human rights and human development

- Political freedoms (in the form of free speech and elections) help to promote economic security. Social opportunities (in the form of education and health facilities) facilitate economic participation. Economic facilities (in the form of opportunities for participation in trade and production) can help to generate personal abundance as well as public resources for social facilities. Freedoms of different kinds can strengthen one another. (Sen, 1999: 11).

- Civil and social education will help people better understand their rights and increase their choices and income-earning capacity. At the same time, developing and implementing equal opportunity laws will empower people to gain more equitable access to productive resources. (UNDP, 1998: 10).

- Sustainable human development and human rights will be undone in a repressive environment where threat or disease prevails, and both are better able to promote human choices in a peaceful and pluralistic society. (UNDP, 1998: 6)

- The levels of ill-health experienced by most of the world's people threatens their country's economic and political viability and this in turn affects economic and political interests of all other countries. (Brundtland, 2000: 3)

- A fundamental human freedom is freedom from want. Poverty is a human rights violation, and freedom from poverty is an integral and inalienable right. (UN Declaration on the Right to Development, 1986).

- Every step taken towards reducing poverty and achieving broad-based economic growth is a step towards conflict prevention. (Annan, 2000: 45)

appropriate entry points or sequencing in development interventions in recognition of the reinforcing and interdependent nature of these issues. As Sen has recently highlighted, the (inter-related) sources of people's 'unfreedoms' may be extremely varied. Development involves expanding these freedoms, as liberties to be valued in their own right and as the principal means (free agency, capability and choice) through which the overarching goals of development, for individuals to 'lead the kinds of lives they have reason to value' (1999: 10), will be achieved.

GUIDE TO FURTHER READING

Bell, M. (1992) 'The water decade valedictory, New Delhi 1990: where pre- and post-modern met', Area 24(1): 82–9. This paper gives a nice review of the thinking behind, and outputs from, the International Drinking Water Supply and Sanitation Decade.

Hausermann, J. (1998) *A Human Rights Approach to Development*, London: Rights and Humanity. Prepared for the Department for International Development as part of the consultation process behind the first White Paper, this text provides a very clear and comprehensive source of information and ideas on human rights, evolving approaches to development and the opportunities of greater integration of these areas.

Simon, D. (1999) 'Development revisited', in D. Simon and A. Narman (eds) *Development as Theory and Practice*, Harlow: Longman, pp. 17–54. A nice starting point to put the explicit issues of welfare and human rights into a wider context. The overview chapter gives a challenging account of changes in development thinking and practice.

Smith, D.M. (2000) 'Moral progress in human geography: transcending the place of good fortune', *Progress in Human Geography* 24(1): 1–18. A recent paper from an author well known for his contributions over time in this area, that raises many questions for individual researchers, disciplines and institutions of development if 'gaps are to be narrowed'.

Wolfe, M. (1996) *Elusive Development*, London: Zed Books. A readable book that reflects in some detail on the successes and failures of the Basic Needs Approach to development.

REFERENCES

Annan, K. (2000) 'We the Peoples': The role of the United Nations in the twenty-first century, Washington: United Nations.

Bell, M. (1992) 'The water decade valedictory, New Delhi 1990: where pre- and post-modern met', *Area* 24(1): 82–9.

Brundtland, G.H. (2000) *Health and Population*, Reith Lecture http://news.bbc.co.uk/hi/english/static/events/reith_2000

Chambers, R. (1993) *Challenging the Professions: Frontiers for Rural Development*, London: Intermediate Technology Publications.

Corbridge, S. (1999) 'Development, post-development and the global political-economy', in P. Cloke, P. Crang and M. Goodwin (eds) *Introducing Human Geographies*, London: Edward Arnold, pp. 67–75.

Escobar, A. (1995) 'Development Planning' in S. Corbridge (ed.) *Development Studies: A Reader*, London: Edward Arnold, pp. 64–78.

Hausermann, J. (1998) *A Human Rights Approach to Development*, London: Rights and Humanity.

Maxwell, S. (1999) *What Can We Do with a Rights-based Approach to Development?* Briefing Paper 1993 (3) September, London: Overseas Development Institute.

Potter, R.B., Binns, T., Elliott, J.A. and Smith, D. (1999) *Geographies of Development*, Harlow: Longman.

Radcliffe, S.A. (1999) 'Re-thinking development', in P. Cloke, P. Crang and M. Goodwin (eds) *Introducing Human Geographies*, London: Edward Arnold, pp. 84–92.

Schuurman, F. (ed.) (1993) *Beyond the Impasse: New Directions in Development Theory*, London: Zed Books.

Sen, A. (1999) *Development as Freedom*, Oxford: Oxford University Press.

Simon, D. (1999) 'Development revisited', in D. Simon and A. Narman (eds) *Development as Theory and Practice*, Harlow: Longman, pp. 17–54.

Smith, D.M. (2000) 'Moral progress in human geography: transcending the place of good fortune', *Progress in Human Geography* 24(1): 1–18.

Stohr, W.B. (1981) 'Development from below: the bottom-up and periphery-inward development paradigm', in W.B. Stohr and D.R.F. Taylor (eds) *Development from Above or Below?*, Chichester: John Wiley, pp. 39–72.

United Nations Development Programme (UNDP) (1998) *Integrating Human Rights with Sustainable Human Development*, New York: UNDP.

1.11 Participatory development

Giles Mohan

> People today have an urge – an impatient urge – to participate in the events and processes that shape their lives. And that impatience brings many dangers and opportunities.
>
> (UNDP, 1993: 1)

INTRODUCTION

Over the past 20 years a wide range of organizations, with different agendas, have started involving local people in their own development (Mohan and Stokke, 2000). This chapter begins by looking at different definitions of participatory development and examines through what sorts of organizations it is achieved. As there are many possible approaches I have included case studies which demonstrate different facets of participation. This brings us on to a critique and an overview of where things might go in the future.

PARTICIPATORY DEVELOPMENT IN THEORY

The emergence of participatory development (PD) is tied into critiques of both theory and practice.

The emergence of participation

According to the strongest advocates of PD, 'normal' development is characterized by biases – Eurocentrism, positivism, and top-downism – which are disempowering (Chambers, 1997). The tendency is to equate development with the modernity achieved by 'Western' societies and to copy 'advanced' countries through planning by experts. The flipside is that 'non-expert', local people were sidelined and their only role was as the objects of grandiose schemes.

As it became apparent that programmes had yielded limited benefits, the volume of criticism grew. In the 1970s, radicals such as Paulo Freire (1970) advocated Participatory Action Research which created new learning environments for people to express their needs and achieve development. Even mainstream organizations like the World Bank argued for Basic Needs Approaches which targeted marginalized groups. Added to this were academics, most notably Robert Chambers, who argued that 'putting the last first' was the only way to achieve rural development. Since then the acceptance of participation has widened.

Contested definitions

In order to judge how successful a PD programme is you must be clear what *others* mean by 'participation' as well as having a conception of what *you* understand by it. This means that there are no universal definitions of PD and we must appreciate the goals that participation might achieve. If people participate, what are they aiming to gain by participating? One view is *instrumental* whereby participation increases the efficiency of 'formal' development programmes (Mayo and Craig, 1995). The goals of development are valid although the institutions are malfunctioning, but can be improved by involving the beneficiaries. For example, the Women in Development initiatives of the 1970s aimed at incorporating women into the planning process. Others see participation as more *transformative* (Esteva and Prakash, 1998). That is, 'development' is flawed and only by valorizing other voices can meaningful social change occur. For example, Esteva and Prakash (1998) see the Mexican Zapatistas as an anti-developmental movement par excellence. Despite these differences, there has been a growing acceptance regarding the importance of local involvement. Underlying this 'consensus' is the belief in not relying on the state. So, it might not be coincidental that PD gained popularity around the same time as the neo-liberal counter-revolution of the 1980s with its discourse of self-help and individualism.

While I want to avoid cementing one definition of PD, it will be useful to look at some of the major approaches. The German agency, GTZ, defined participation as 'co-determination and power sharing throughout the . . . programme cycle' (1991: 5, cited in Nelson and Wright, 1995: 4). Here, participation involves external and local agencies working together on a project basis;

the implication being that the project was reasonably circumscribed. The World Bank soon established a Learning Group on Participation. For them, participation involved stakeholders who 'influence and share control over development initiatives, decisions and resources which affect them' (World Bank, 1994: 6, cited in Nelson and Wright, 1995: 5). Such a recognition fed into the 'good governance' agenda which sought to share responsibility for project implementation with the donors.

These useful conceptualizations are still rather general. Rahnema (1992) suggests that PD involves the following elements:

- *cognitive* in generating a 'different mode of understanding the realities to be addressed' (1992: 121)
- *political* in 'empowering the voiceless' (1992: 121)
- *instrumental* in order to 'propose new alternatives' (1992: 121).

In a similar vein, the United Nations Development Programme (1993) sub-divided participation into four key forms – household, economic, social-cultural and political – and stressed that all forms overlap and interact.

Powerful processes

It needs emphasizing that whichever definition we use, PD is fundamentally about power (Nelson and Wright, 1995). Participation involves struggle whereby the powerful fight to retain their privileges. Even many supposedly pro-participation development agencies show a marked reluctance to release control. Participation is conflictual whereby the less powerful must struggle for increased control over their lives.

PARTICIPATORY DEVELOPMENT IN PRACTICE

In this section I discuss the institutional arrangements involved in PD and the processes through which it attempts to change power relations.

Grassroots civil society

In rejecting the statism and top-downism of 'normal' development, the focus for PD has become the grassroots level which permits a plurality of developmental goals to be realized as well as giving communities the self-determination they need (Mohan and Stokke, 2000). Hence, PD has become associated with civil society. If state structures are inflexible, bureaucratic, urban-biased and unaccountable, then civil society organizations are believed to be smaller, more accountable, locally aware and hands-on. Although civil society has multiple meanings, it has largely been interpreted as the realm of non-governmental organizations (NGOs). NGOs are incredibly diverse, with many of the Southern-based ones relying on funding and institutional support from Northern partners.

New knowledges

The first step in reversing the biases marginalizing the poor concerns rethinking knowledge generation. The expert systems of modernity relied upon scientific approaches where planners worked from normative social models so that the recipients of development were treated as passive or, more often, conservative and obstructive. PD reverses this. The research methods for accessing local knowledges were inspired by Paulo Freire and have grown into a veritable industry (Chambers, 1997), but all centre upon trying to see the world from the point of view of those directly affected by the developmental intervention.

The most widely used methodology is Participatory Rural Appraisal (PRA). As Chambers (1997: 103) explains:

> The essence of PRA is change and reversals – of role, behaviour, relationship and learn-ing. Outsiders do not dominate and lecture; they facilitate, sit down, listen and learn. Outsiders do not transfer technology; they share methods which local people can use for their own appraisal, analysis, planning, action, monitoring and evaluation. Outsiders do not impose their reality; they encourage and enable local people to express their own.

PRA relies on many visual and oral techniques for generating knowledge because it is felt that the medium of written language is prejudicial to free expression. Methods such as mapping, ranking of preferences and oral histories are all part of the PRA toolkit. So, PD seeks out the diversity which allows the differences between people and between communities to be realized rather than treat-ing everybody as uniform objects of development.

Participation in action

So far I have outlined the theory of PD, but what happens when it is practised in the 'real' world? These brief case studies demonstrate different facets of PD. The Aga Khan Rural Support Programme (India) has used participation to 'smooth' the implementation of pre-determined projects. The approach relates to 'consensus-building' whereby the role of participatory approaches was to 'to find a meeting ground to negotiate terms of collaboration' (Shah, 1997: 75). In a dam scheme the farmers were not given an option regarding water payments, but the partic-ipatory exercise helped reach mutually agreeable solutions. As Shah (1997: 77) concludes, 'What has this exercise achieved? Certainly not true empowerment where villagers decide and prioritise development proposals with minimal external support and facilitation'. Shah suggests that while transformatory participation might be desirable it is rarely viable where external agents are time-bound and accountable to funders. But that is not to say they are dictatorial and that the lack of true empowerment detracts from real benefits.

By contrast, Village Aid, a small UK-based NGO working in West Africa, has been trying to promote deeper participation which leaves the development trajectories more open-ended. It became aware 'that a particular project undertaken in the past had not been a high priority for the village, but was undertaken at the suggestion of an NGO' (Village Aid, 1996: 7). Instead, it seeks to develop a situation where 'village communities set the agenda and outside agencies become responsive . . . this whole capacity building process is about confidence in the village in order to say "No" to organizations that do not meet the village's requirements' (Village Aid, 1996: 8 and 14). This process moves beyond a rigid PRA framework which is based upon the values and communication capacities of outsiders. Instead, through a programme called *Arizama* (a Dagbani word roughly translating as 'dialogue'), Village Aid identifies, adopts and adapts (if necessary) indigenous communication methods, such as dance and story-telling.

THE PROBLEMS OF PARTICIPATORY DEVELOPMENT

Having looked at these case studies it will be worth drawing together some of the major problems that have emerged with PD.

The first is tokenism. As PD has become popular, some agencies use the rhetoric of participation with limited empowerment. Although PRA started as a challenge to expert elitism it has become so routinized that many agencies use it uncritically and treat it as a 'rubber stamp' to prove their participatory credentials. As the Village Aid study showed, some NGOs have grown sceptical about the abuse of PRA as it still relies on methods (e.g. voting) which are non-local (Goebel, 1998).

Second, much PD has treated communities as socially homogeneous. While community empowerment might be an improvement on unresponsive bureaucracies, there have been cases where support for 'the community' has meant that resources have passed to elites. More sensitive PRA picks up on heterogeneity. In particular, gender differences at the household and community level have become key factors (Mosse, 1994).

Third, the emphasis on civil society can create competition between local organizations. As greater quantities of aid are channelled through such organizations it is the better organized, more acceptable or least scrupulous which capture resources. The result is that weaker organizations are further undermined. Allied to this is that many 'partnerships' between Northern and Southern NGOs are heavily loaded in favour of the former. Not only does the Northern NGO usually control the bulk of finances, but it often retains de facto veto power over its counterpart. Financially, intellectually and politically many partnerships are anything but participatory with the Southern NGO acting as a delivery mechanism for a pre-determined agenda.

The final problem is broader and relates to the causes of underdevelopment. PD seeks to give local people control, but many processes affecting their (or our own) lives are often not readily tackled at the local level. For example, it is very hard for a small co-operative in Africa to change the rules governing international trade when the World Trade Organization is dominated by the developed economies. Robert Chambers (1997), while aware of this, takes a rather optimistic view that once organizations see the value of PD it will spread through them like a 'benign virus'. Some organizations appear participatory, but are as exclusionary as the agents of normal development that Chambers derides. The emphasis on grassroots civil society can leave important structures untouched and do nothing to strengthen states and make them more effective and accountable to their citizens.

THE FUTURE OF PARTICIPATORY DEVELOPMENT

It becomes clear that while PD has brought benefits to some communities it has been abused and does little to address extra-local processes. As more development agencies realize that development will involve broader questions of citizenship, sovereignty and globalization, the focus of some has changed. A growing number are seeking to build the capacity of the state rather than by-passing it in their eagerness to empower civil society. This involves state–society 'synergy' whereby partnerships aim to produce more lasting development by bolstering citizenship.

Other NGOs have moved, or expanded, into advocacy and lobbying. The Jubilee 2000 Coalition for debt relief is a case in point. Given that 'local' problems have global causes, the most useful thing that a relatively powerful, non-local organization can do is use its political weight to raise awareness and campaign for reform of global institutions. This sees ever more complex networking between NGOs which generates new forms of participation which are not rooted in place, but stretched across space where 'community' may only exist in a 'virtual' sense. In all these cases the challenges for participatory development multiply.

GUIDE TO FURTHER READING AND REFERENCES

The following text references provide the basis for further reading.

Chambers, R. (1997) *Whose Reality Counts? Putting the First Last*, London: Intermediate Technology Publications.

Esteva, G. and Prakash, M. (1998) *Grassroots Post-modernism: Remaking the Soil of Cultures*, London: Zed Books.

Freire, P. (1970) *The Pedagogy of the Oppressed*, New York: The Seabury Press.

Goebel, A. (1998) 'Process, perception and power: notes from "participatory" research in a Zimbabwean Resettlement Area', *Development and Change* 29: 277–305.

GTZ (1991) *Where There is no Participation*, Eschborn: Deutsche Gessellschaft für Technische Zusammenarbeit.

Mayo, M. and Craig, G. (1995) 'Community participation and empowerment: the human face of structural adjustment or tools for democratic transformation?', in G. Craig and M. Mayo (eds) *Community Empowerment: A Reader in Participation and Development*, London: Zed Books, pp. 1–11.

Mohan, G. and Stokke, K. (2000) 'Participatory development and empowerment: the dangers of localism', *Third World Quarterly* 21(2): 247–68.

Mosse, D. (1994) 'Authority, gender and knowledge: theoretical reflections on the practice of participatory rural appraisal', *Development and Change* 25: 497–526.

Nelson, N. and Wright, S. (1995) 'Participation and power', in N. Nelson and S. Wright (eds) *Power and Participatory Development: Theory and Practice*, London: Intermediate Technology Publications, pp. 1–18.

Rahnema, M. (1992) 'Participation', in W. Sachs (ed.) *The Development Dictionary: a Guide to Knowledge as Power*, London: Zed Books, pp. 116–31.

Shah, A. (1997) 'Developing participation', *PLA Notes*, No. 30: 75–8.

United Nations Development Programme (1993) *Human Development Report*, Oxford: Oxford University Press.

Village Aid (1996) *Beyond PRA: A New Approach to Village-led Development*, unpublished business plan, Village Aid.

World Bank (1994) *The World Bank and Participation* (4th draft), Washington DC: World Bank.

1.12 Anthropologists and development

R.D. Grillo

A DIFFICULT RELATIONSHIP

The relationship between anthropology and development has always been difficult. If by 'development' (many anthropologists put the word in inverted commas) is meant directed social and economic change mainly in a North–South context, anthropologists worldwide, including those based in Britain and continental Europe, the United States and the British Commonwealth, have been engaged with development for about a century. During the colonial period, for example, Bronislaw Malinowski (1884–1942), one of the founding fathers of the modern subject, believed that anthropology had a key part to play advising the 'practical men' (*sic*) administering British colonies under the system of 'Indirect Rule' (i.e. exercising control through the use of local institutions). In the 1930s important work in sub-Saharan Africa, some of it highly critical, on indigenous systems of politics, law and government, land tenure, family and marriage, the agricultural division of labour, and labour migration informed colonial governments about their impact on the societies they were administering. The 'practical men' themselves, however, were often sceptical of the contribution that anthropologists might make, and anthropologists rarely delivered as much useful advice as they appeared to promise.

At the same time, for a mixture of intellectual and political reasons, anthropologists like Evans-Pritchard and Firth, highly influential in British anthropology after the Second World War, sought to distance themselves from 'applied anthropology', as it was called. Thus for some 35 years, *c.*1945–*c.*1980, work in the anthropology of development, as it became known, was relegated to the margins of the subject or seen as a form of neo-colonialism. (In some parts of the world anthropology itself still carries the taint of colonialism.) Thus not a single anthropologist was involved in the creation of the UK's Overseas Development Administration in 1964. In the United States, too, where applied anthropology had a much longer history, especially in research on Native Americans, anthropologists took an increasingly jaundiced view of collaboration with government, a distrust that the involvement of some anthropologists with counter-insurgency schemes in Latin America ('Project Camelot') and in Southeast Asia during the 1960s served only to increase (Eddy and Partridge, 1987).

By the late 1970s, however, attitudes began to change. During a period of growing disillusionment with orthodox economic development policies, and in the light of the apparent failure of large-scale, top-down projects, and the fact that, like it or not, development was a reality in the places they studied, a number of anthropologists (though by no means all) concluded once again that the discipline had something to offer both the study of development and its practice. Anthropology's ethnographically grounded methodology, which emphasizes local and subjective realties and acknowledges the micro-political effects of large events, including within the household, presents insights into how development actually works, which policy-makers could not and should not ignore. Anthropological work on gender and on health, including medical anthropology, has been particularly influential in this regard. In the 1980s and 1990s, with the emergence of new or alternative paradigms, often elaborated outside government in the expanding 'third sector' of local and international NGOs, emphasizing notions such as 'empowerment', 'participation' and the 'indigenous', and the creation of innovative occupational categories such as 'social development adviser', many believed the subject had finally come into its own.

THE 'UNCOMFORTABLE SCIENCE'

A distinction is sometimes made between the 'anthropology of development' and 'development anthropology', one primarily concerned with the socio-scientific analysis of development as an economic, political, social and cultural process, the other engaged directly in application (for example, evaluating a project or offering policy advice). The same individual can, of course, do both at different times and in different contexts, but whereas the anthropology of development is now a well-established branch of the discipline, to which important theoretical and empirical contributions have been made by scholars in many parts of the world, development anthropology remains a contested activity, both inside and outside the discipline. Certainly, so far as development experts are concerned, anthropology is often seen as the 'uncomfortable science', as Firth called it.

The critical stance that anthropologists frequently take on development, often echoed in their policy advice, is illustrated by the considerable body of literature in the 1990s which examined 'development discourse'. Based on the ideas of the French philosopher Michel Foucault, this perspective (in different ways: Escobar, 1995 and Ferguson, 1994) shows how certain economic and political ideas and practices, which have emerged in the North and been applied in and to the South in Northern interests, are embedded in and enacted through powerful institutions such as the World Bank. Development discourse constructs both problems (for example 'The Third World') and their solution (for example 'Modernity'). The importance of the 'development gaze' has been well demonstrated in work dealing with the environment. In a wide-ranging analysis drawing on ethnography and oral and written histories, colonial and post-colonial government records, geographical surveys, aerial photographs and travellers' tales, Fairhead and Leach's (1996) study of deforestation in West Africa reveals how long-held official 'narratives' of deforestation and savannization, the idea that local people's agricultural activities destroy forests, simply 'misread' the landscape. Forest patches have been created by villagers themselves through their everyday agricultural and domestic practices based on their own practical ecological knowledge.

Although powerful and persuasive, discourse analysis has been criticized for seeing development as a monolithic enterprise, heavily controlled from the top, convinced of the superiority of its own wisdom, impervious to local knowledge, or indeed common-sense experience: a single gaze/voice which is all-powerful and beyond influence (Grillo and Stirrat, 1997.) Although studies of development discourse have been very important in the deconstruction of development processes, there is a danger that the subjects of development are perceived as having little voice or power. In fact, anthropologists stress that development involves a highly complex set of institutions in which a diversity of voices is engaged in a multiplicity of sites of struggle. Development processes operate at many different levels simultaneously, and this means that their analysis must be actor-oriented, multi-sited, multi-vocal and sensitive to the multi-layered nature of power relations (Crewe and Harrison, 1998; Arce and Long, 2000).

INDIGENOUS KNOWLEDGE

Fairhead and Leach's work on West African forests also illustrates the importance of a concept which anthropologists often regard as their own, though it has been taken up extensively in the third sector: indigenous knowledge. In colonial and post-colonial development institutions (e.g. departments of agriculture) local people's knowledge, experience and practices have often been considered at best irrelevant, at worst positively harmful to the evolution of a 'modern' society: the widespread condemnation of agricultural techniques such as shifting cultivation is a case in point. To anthropologists it is obvious that an awareness of 'indigenous technical knowledge' (ITK) must be an integral part of development practice, and during the 1980s the value of such knowledge was slowly, but increasingly, accepted (Sillitoe, 1998). Anthropologists have also drawn attention to indigenous, sometimes alternative, conceptions of development and modernity, and made important contributions to understanding how development itself is perceived by supposed beneficiaries.

At the same time, however, anthropologists and development practitioners attracted by the notion of indigenous knowledge need to guard against romanticism. It should not be assumed that indigenous thought and practice (e.g. on the environment) is inherently wise; nor, despite what some still seem to think, should indigenous cultures be seen as finite, bounded and unchanging.

Indigenous knowledge is not perfect, neither is it homogeneous, nor does it exist in a vacuum, sealed off from the outside. This was never true in the past, and is certainly not the case in an increasingly globalized, transnational world.

PARTICIPATION AND EMPOWERMENT

Anthropology's focus on the indigenous and on the multi-vocal character of social relations, chimes with recent shifts in development paradigms towards empowering local people, or at any rate engaging them in the development process.

Like it or not, and many dislike being thrust into this role, anthropologists have often found themselves in the position of speaking for their informants, or advocating their cause with the powers-that-be, simply because as the educated outsider they seem best placed to do so. Against this, they have long sought means to enable local people to voice their concerns directly, without anthropological or other mediation.

In the United States, such ideas were pioneered in what is known as 'action anthropology', originated by Sol Tax in the 1950s, and later in 'participatory action research' or 'PAR' associated with W.F. Whyte. Anthropologists in Britain, South Asia and sub-Saharan Africa have drawn inspiration principally from the work of Robert Chambers whose approach, generally known as 'participatory rural appraisal' or 'PRA' was itself influenced by anthropology. Although anthropologists share many of the aims of PRA, they are not uncritical of it, and indeed there is a danger, as ethnographies of PRA are beginning to show, that PRA methods (and PRA places a great emphasis on method) are sometimes adopted and implemented mechanically and uncritically with practitioners frequently impervious to the complex ways in which systems of power relations operate, especially in small groups and meetings, often to the detriment of women or others whose voices may be muted by both traditional and innovative social practices.

ETHICS AND POLITICS

Although development is no longer in the margins of anthropology, it remains controversial, with anthropologists often finding themselves interrogating the political and moral implications of the development intervention for anthropologists, for development practitioners generally and for presumed beneficiaries. It is not surprising, therefore, that there appears to be greater sensitivity to ethical questions (including, for example, human rights) among anthropologists than among other development-oriented disciplines.

By contrast with the UK's Development Studies Association, professional anthropological associations in Britain and the United States have extensive 'ethical guidelines': those of the Association of Social Anthropologists of the Commonwealth may be consulted at http://www.asa.anthropology.ac.uk/ethics2.html; those of the American Anthropological Association are at http://www.aaanet.org/committees/ethics/ethcode.html. These guidelines, of course, cover all research, and are not confined to those working in or on development. Nevertheless, they are especially pertinent to those engaged in the application of the subject and in fact originated from controversies arising from activities in that sector. Anthropology does not shy away from recognizing development's inherent difficulties and complexities (analytical as well as political and ethical), and perhaps for that reason its perspective is an especially challenging one for all those concerned with the relationship between North and South.

GUIDE TO FURTHER READING AND REFERENCES

Arce, A. and Long, N. (eds) (2000) *Anthropology, Development, and Modernities*, London: Routledge. Surveys counter-tendencies to modernity from an ethnographic perspective.

Crewe, E. and Harrison, E. (1998) *Whose Development? An Ethnography of Aid*, London: Zed Books. Compares two projects, analysing how development is constructed in practice.

Eddy, E. and Partridge, W.L. (eds) (1987) *Applied Anthropology in America* (2nd edn), New York: Columbia University Press. A standard work.

Escobar, A. (1995) *Encountering Development: The Making and Unmaking of the Third World*, Princeton: Princeton University Press. Strongly argued, controversial account of the 'development gaze'.

Fairhead, J. and Leach, M. (1996) *Misreading the African Landscape*: *Society and Ecology in a Forest-savanna Mosaic*, Cambridge: Cambridge University Press. Re-evaluation of environment and development orthodoxies in light of detailed evidence.

Ferguson, J. (1994) *The Anti-politics Machine*: '*Development*', *Depoliticization, and Bureaucratic Power in Lesotho*, London: University of Minnesota Press. Detailed scrutiny of World Bank plans for a small sub-Saharan African country.

Gardner, K. and Lewis, D. (1996) *Anthropology, Development and the Post-modern Challenge*, London: Pluto Press. Critical evaluation of development by two anthropologists with practical experience.

Grillo, R.D. and Stirrat, R.L. (eds) (1997) *Discourses of Development: Anthropological Perspectives*, Oxford: Berg. Explores politics, power, ideology and rhetoric in the institutional practice of development.

Long, N. and Long, A. (eds) (1992) *Battlefields of Knowledge: The Interlocking of Theory and Practice in Social Research and Development*, London: Routledge. An integration of actor-oriented approaches with critical perspectives on development.

Moore, H.L. (1988) *Feminism and Anthropology: Feminist Perspectives*, Cambridge: Polity Press. Remains an influential theoretical source for the anthropology of gender and development.

Sillitoe, P. (1998) 'The development of indigenous knowledge: a new applied anthropology', *Current Anthropology* 39(2): 223–52. Wide-ranging survey of the debate.

PART 2

Theories and strategies of development

EDITORIAL INTRODUCTION

It is generally appreciated that ideas about how development can be effected have long been both controversial and highly contested. Development involves a range of actors, from international agencies, through the state, down to the individual, all of whom have a vested interest in how change and development are to proceed. Thus, all facets of development not only depend on political ideology, but on moral and ethical prescriptions too. Thus, ideas about development over time have tended to accumulate and accrue, and not fade away. These sorts of ideas are considered at the outset in this part of the book, before turning to some of the major theories and strategies of development which have been followed and popularized.

Right-wing stances on development can be regarded as having their origins in the Enlightenment and the era of modernity which followed. The eighteenth-century Enlightenment saw an increasing emphasis placed on science, rationality and detailed empiricism. It also witnessed the establishment of the 'West' and 'Europe' as the ideal. It was during this period that the classical economists, Adam Smith and David Ricardo, writing in the 1700s, developed ideas surrounding the concept of comparative advantage, which stressed the economic efficacy of global free trade and, in many senses, gave rise to the earliest capitalist strategies of economic development. These were followed by a plethora of dualistic and linear conceptualizations of the development process, including modernization theory, unbalanced and unequal growth, and top-down and hierarchical formulations. Together, such approaches are generally referred to as 'neo-classical'. Whatever one's critical view of modernization, the approach usefully pinpointed the salience of transport as a necessary (although not sufficient) factor in the development equation. Such approaches are, of course, still alive and kicking, in the form of the 'new right' orthodoxy, involving the 'magic of the market' and the neo-liberal policies of structural adjustment, and very recently, poverty reduction strategies. All of these approaches can be traced back directly to the works of Smith and Ricardo.

The antithesis to classical and neo-classical views was provided by radical-dependency approaches in the 1960s. It is a reflection of the Eurocentricity of development theory that Andre Gunder Frank has become the name most closely associated with dependency. This is despite the fact that the approach essentially stemmed from the writings of structuralists in Latin America and the Caribbean. In respect of process, dependency theory was couched in terms of inverted cascading global chains of surplus extraction, and it was again all too easy to reduce this to simple dichotomous terms, involving polar opposites such as 'core–periphery', 'rich–poor' and 'developed–underdeveloped'. It was left to world systems theory to stress that contemporary development has involved the emergence of a substantial semi-periphery, consisting of the newly industrializing countries (NICs) of East Asia and Latin America.

The era of postmodernity may not be regarded as fitting the realities of the developing world or poor countries in all respects, but the existence of these notions cannot be ignored in the analysis of the conditions faced by such nations. Early standpoints taking a less generic, less monumental and less linear view of the development process included what are referred to under the headings 'bottom-up' and 'agropolitan' approaches, which have come to include ideas of 'another' development. More recently, the 'postist' stance afforded by postcolonialism has been added to the critique. This argues that the production of Western knowledge has been inseparable from the exercise of Western power. Ethical and moral considerations surface once more, this time in terms of the responsibilities which we carry for so-called 'distant others'. Most of us have been trained to favour people close to home, our so-called 'nearest and dearest', as opposed to those strangers who may be deemed more deserving, but who live far away. Many of the practical problems that are to be faced in the field of humanitarian assistance stem from this basic but enduring conundrum of development. Finally, it is notable that evolving conceptualizations of the roles of the state, civil society and social capital underpin continuing debates concerning development theory.

2.1 Theories, strategies and ideologies of development

Robert B. Potter

A major characteristic of the multi- and inter-disciplinary field of development studies since its establishment in the 1940s has been a series of sea-level changes in thinking about the process of development itself. This search for new theoretical conceptualizations of development has been mirrored by changes in the practice of development in the field. Thus, there has been much debate and controversy about development, with many changing views as to its definition, and the strategies by means of which, however development is defined, it may be pursued. In short, the period since the 1950s has seen the promotion and application of many varied views of development. And the literature on development theory and practice appears to have burgeoned, particularly since the mid-1980s (see, for example, Apter, 1987; Preston, 1987, 1996; Lesson and Minogue, 1988; Schuurman, 1993; Crush, 1995; Escobar, 1995; Hettne, 1995; Streeten, 1995; Brohman, 1996; Cowen and Shenton, 1996; Leys, 1996; Rapley, 1996; Potter *et al.*, 1999; Simon and Narman, 1999). A major theme is that ideas about development have long been controversial and highly contested.

It is also necessary to stress that development covers both theory and practice, that is both ideas about how development should or might occur, and real world efforts to put various aspects of development into practice. This is conveniently mapped into the nomenclature suggested by Hettne in his overview of *Development Theory and the Three Worlds* (1995). In reviewing the history of development thinking, he suggested that 'development' involves three things: *development theories*, *development strategies* and *development ideologies*. Before going any further, these three basic terms can usefully be defined and clarified.

Following the general definition of a theory as a set of logical propositions about how the real world is structured, or the way in which it operates, *development theories* may be regarded as sets of ostensibly logical propositions, which aim to explain how development has occurred in the past, and/or how it should occur in the future. Development theories can either be *normative*, that is they can generalize about what should happen or be the case in an ideal world; or *positive* in the sense of dealing with what has generally been the case in the past. This important distinction is broadly exemplified in the figure that accompanies this account (see figure overleaf). Hettne (1995) remarks that 'development studies is explicitly normative', and that teachers, researchers and practitioners in the field 'want to change the world, not only analyse it' (Hettne, 1995: 12). The arena of development theory is primarily, although by no means exclusively, to be encountered in the academic literature, that is in writing about development. It is, therefore, inherently controversial and contested.

On the other hand, *development strategies* can be defined as the practical paths to development which may be pursued by international agencies, states in both the so-called developing and developed worlds, non-government organizations and community-based organizations, or indeed individuals, in an effort to stimulate change within particular nations, regions and continents. Thus, Hettne (1995) provides a definition of development strategies as efforts to change existing economic and social structures and institutions in order to find enduring solutions to the problems facing decision-makers. As such, Hettne argues that the term 'development strategy' implies an actor, normally the state. In order to sound less top-down, it is necessary to think in terms of a wider set of development-oriented actors, including all those listed above.

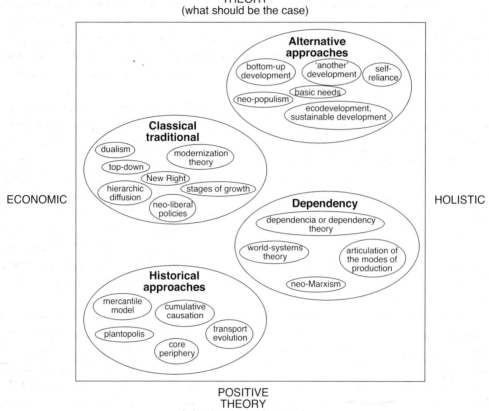

NORMATIVE
THEORY
(what should be the case)

ECONOMIC

HOLISTIC

POSITIVE
THEORY
(what has been the case)

A framework for considering development theories

Source: Potter *et al.*, 1999, Figure 3.2

Different development agendas will reflect different goals and objectives. These goals will reflect social, economic, political, cultural, ethical, moral and even religious influences. Thus, what may be referred to as different *development ideologies* may be recognized. For example, both in theory and in practice, early perspectives on development were almost exclusively concerned with promoting economic growth. Subsequently, however, the predominant ideology within the academic literature changed to emphasize political, social, ethnic, cultural, ecological and other dimensions of the wider process of development and change. Theories in development are distinctive by virtue of the fact that they involve the intention to change society in some defined manner. One of the classic examples is the age-old battle between economic policies which increase growth but widen income disparities, and those wider policy imperatives which seek primarily to reduce inequalities within society.

Perhaps the only sensible approach is to follow Hettne (1995) and to employ the overarching concept of *development thinking* in our general deliberations. The expression 'development thinking' may be used as a catch-all phrase indicating the sum total of ideas about development, that is, including pertinent aspects of development theory, strategy and ideology. Such an all-encompassing definition is necessary due to the nature of thinking about development itself. As noted at the outset, development thinking has shown many sharp twists and turns during the twentieth century. The various theories that have been produced have not commanded attention in a strictly sequential-temporal manner. In other words, as a new set of ideas about development has come into favour, earlier theories and strategies have not been totally discarded and replaced. Rather, theories and strategies have tended to stack up, one upon another, co-existing, sometimes in what can only be described as very convoluted and contradictory manners. Thus, in discussing development theory, Hettne (1995: 64) has drawn attention to the 'tendency of social science paradigms to accumulate rather than fade away'.

This characteristic of development studies as a distinct field of enquiry can be considered in a more sophisticated manner by referring to Thomas Kuhn's ideas on the *structure of scientific revolutions*. Kuhn (1962) argued that academic disciplines are dominated at particular points in time by communities of researchers and their associated methods, and they thereby define the subjects and the issues deemed to be of importance within them. He referred to these as 'invisible colleges', and he noted that these serve to define and perpetuate research which confirms the validity of the existing paradigm or 'supra-model', as he referred to it. Kuhn called this 'normal science'. Kuhn noted that only when the number of observations and questions confronting the *status quo* of normal science becomes too large to be dealt with by means of small changes to it, will there be a fundamental shift. However, if the proposed changes are major and a new paradigm is adopted, a scientific revolution can be said to have occurred, linked to a period of what Kuhn referred to as 'extraordinary research'.

In this model, therefore, scientific disciplines basically advance by means of revolutions in which the prevailing normal science is replaced by extraordinary science and, ultimately, a new form of normal science develops. In dealing with social scientific discourses, it is inevitable that the field of development theory is characterized by evolutionary, rather than revolutionary change. Evidence of the persistence of ideas in some quarters, years after they have been discarded elsewhere, will be encountered throughout the development literature. Given that development thinking is not just about the theoretical interpretation of facts, but rather about values, aspirations, social goals, and ultimately that which is moral, ethical and just, it is understandable that change in development studies leads to the parallel *evolution* of ideas, rather than *revolution*. Hence, conflict, debate, contention, positionality and even moral outrage are all inherent in the discussion of development strategies, and associated plural and diverse theories of development.

There are many ways to categorize development thinking through time. Broadly speaking, it is suggested here that four major approaches to the examination of development thinking can be recognized, and these are shown in the figure opposite. This framework follows that recently suggested by Potter and Lloyd-Evans (1998), and was rendered more concrete in Potter *et al.* (1999). The framework first maps in the distinction previously made between *normative development theories* (those focusing on what should be the case), and *positive theories* (which ponder what has actually been so). Another axis of difference between theories is seen as relating to whether they are *holistic*, or *partial*, and most partial theories emphasize the economic dimension. This is also intimated in the figure.

These two axes can be superimposed on one another to yield a simple matrix or framework for the consideration of development theories, as shown. Following Potter *et al.* (1999: Chapter 3), as noted, four distinct groupings of development theory can be recognized by virtue of their characteristics with regard to the dimensions of holistic–economic and normative–positive. The approaches are referred to as: (i) the classical–traditional approach; (ii) the historical–empirical approach; (iii) the radical political economy–dependency approach; and finally, (iv) bottom-up and alternative approaches. Following the argument presented in the last section, each of these approaches may be regarded as expressing a particular ideological standpoint, and can also be identified by virtue of having occupied the centre stage of the development debate at particular points in time. Classical–traditional theory, embracing dualism, modernization theory, top-down conceptualizations, the new right and neo-liberal imperatives, is seen as stressing the economic and, collectively, existing mid-way between the normative and positive poles. In direct contrast, according to this framework, radical–dependency approaches, embracing neo-Marxism, and the articulation of the modes of production, are seen as being more holistic. At the positive end of the spectrum exist those theories which are basically historical in their formulation, and which purport to build upon what has happened in the past. These include core–periphery frameworks, cumulative causation and models of transport evolution, especially the mercantile model. In contrast, once again, are theories which stress the ideal, or what should be the case. These are referred to as 'alternative approaches', and basic needs, neo-populism, 'another development', ecodevelopment and sustainable development may be included in this category.

However, each approach still retains currency in particular quarters. Hence, in development theory and academic writing, left-of-centre socialist views may well be more popular than classical and neo-classical formulations, but in the area of practical development strategies, the 1980s and 1990s have seen the implementation of neo-liberal interpretations of classical theory, stressing the liberalization of trade, along with public-sector cut-backs, as a part of structural adjustment programmes (SAPs), aimed at reducing the involvement of the state in the economy (Pugh and Potter, 2000). Such plurality and contestation are an everyday part of the field of development studies. In the words of Hettne (1995: 15), 'theorizing about development is therefore a never-ending task'.

GUIDE TO FURTHER READING

Hettne, B. (1995) *Development Theory and the Three Worlds: Towards an International Political Economy of Development* (2nd edn), Harlow: Longman. Briefly introduces the concepts of development theories, strategies and ideologies (see pp. 15–16), before presenting an overview of Eurocentric development thinking, the voice of the 'other', globalization and development theory, and 'another development'.

Potter, R.B., Binns, T., Elliott, J. and Smith, D. (1999) *Geographies of Development*, Harlow: Prentice Hall. An introductory textbook on development, designed mainly for undergraduates. In terms of overall remit, the book seeks to stress the plural and contested nature of development theory and practice. As part of this approach, Chapter 3 overviews theories and strategies of development, stressing their diversity and value-laden character. The structure of the account is based on the figure employed in the present account.

Preston, P.W. (1996) *Development Theory: An Introduction*, Oxford: Blackwell. Sets out to provide an overview of the intellectual resources available to developmentalists working with reference to the classical European tradition of social theorizing. Accordingly, the first part of the book treats social theory in general terms. Thereafter, contemporary theories of development are summarized followed by what are referred to as new analyses of complex change.

REFERENCES

Apter, D. (1987) *Rethinking Development: Modernization, Dependency and Postmodern Politics*, Newbury Park, USA: Sage.

Brohman, J. (1996) *Popular Development: Rethinking the Theory and Practice of Development*, Oxford: Blackwell.

Crush, J. (1995) *Power of Development*, London: Routledge.

Cowen, M.P. and Shenton, R. (1996) *Doctrines of Development*, London: Routledge.

Escobar, A. (1995) *Encountering Development*, Princeton, NJ: Princeton University Press.

Hettne, B. (1995) *Development Theory and the Three Worlds: Towards an International Political Economy of Development* (2nd edn), Harlow: Longman.

Kuhn, T. (1962) *The Structure of Scientific Revolutions*, Chicago: University of Chicago Press.

Lesson, P.E. and Minogue, M.M. (1988) (eds) *Perspectives on Development: Cross-Disciplinary Themes in Development*, Manchester: Manchester University Press.

Leys, D. (1996) *The Rise and Fall of Development Theory*, Oxford: James Currey.

Preston, P.W. (1987) *Making Sense of Development: An Introduction to Classical and Contemporary Theories of Development and their Application to Southeast Asia*, London: Routledge.

Preston, P.W. (1996) *Development Theory: An Introduction*, Oxford: Blackwell.

Potter, R.B. and Lloyd-Evans, S. (1998) *The City in the Developing World*, Harlow: Prentice Hall.

Potter, R.B., Binns, T., Elliott, J. and Smith, D. (1999) *Geographies of Development*, Harlow: Prentice Hall.

Pugh, J. and Potter, R.B. (2000) 'Rolling back the state and physical development planning: the case of Barbados', *Singapore Journal of Tropical Geography* 21: 183–99.

Rapley, J. (1996) *Understanding Development: Theory and Practice in the Third World*, London: UCL Press.

Schuurman, F. (1993) *Beyond the Impasse: New Directions in Development Theory*, London: Zed Books.

Streeten, P. (1995) *Thinking About Development*, Cambridge: Cambridge University Press.

Simon, D. and Narman, A. (1999) *Development as Theory and Practice*, Harlow: Longman.

2.2 Enlightenment and the era of modernity

Marcus Power

In the century of the enlightenment, educated Europeans . . . experienced an expansive sense of power over nature and themselves: the pitiless cycles of epidemics, famines, risky life and early death, devastating war and uneasy peace – the treadmill of human existence – seemed to be yielding at last to the application of critical intelligence.

(Gay, 1973: 3)

INTRODUCTION: KNOWLEDGE, CRITICISM AND POWER

When we use the term 'the Enlightenment' a reference is generally being made to a period in European intellectual history which continued through most of the eighteenth century. It was a century of commitment to enquiry and criticism, of a decline in mysticism, of growing hope for life and trust in effort (Hampson, 1968). One of the primary interests was social reform, and the progression and development of societies built around an increasing secularism and a growing willingness to take risks (Gay, 1973). Enlightenment ideas and writings comprise a fairly hetero-geneous group but did form a set of interconnected ideas, values, principles and facts which provided both an image of the natural and social world and a way of thinking about it. In its simplest sense, the Enlightenment was the creation of a new framework of ideas and secure 'truths' about the relationships between humanity, society and nature which sought to challenge tradi-tional worldviews dominated by Christianity.

New cultural innovations in writing, painting, printing, music, sculpture and architecture, and new technological innovations in warfare, agriculture and manufacture had a major impact on the *philosophes*, the free-thinking 'men of letters' that had brokered this enlightened awakening. Geographically centred in France but with foundations in many European states, 'the Enlightenment' was thus a sort of intellectual fashion which held the attention of many European intellectuals. According to Black (1990: 208) the Enlightenment is more 'a tendency towards critical inquiry and the application of reason' than a coherent intellectual movement or institutional project. Thus the beginnings of the idea of development can be traced not to some movement or project, but rather to this tendency to form critical enquiries about the organization and structure of societies and to apply reason to these social scientific investigations.

The metaphor of the 'light of reason' shining brightly into all the dark recesses of ignorance and superstition in 'traditional' societies was a powerful and influential one at this time. During the Enlightenment a secular intelligentsia had emerged across Europe that was powerful enough to challenge the clergy (Porter, 1990). The *philosophes* sought to redefine what was considered as socially important knowledge, to bring it outside the sphere of religion and to provide it with a new meaning and relevance. In this sense, as Hall and Gieben (1992: 36) point out, there are four main areas which distinguish the thought of the *philosophes* from earlier and existing intellectual approaches:

- anti-clericalism
- a belief in the pre-eminence of empirical, materialist knowledge
- an enthusiasm for technological and medical progress
- a desire for legal and constitutional reform.

There is clearly a risk of applying the term 'the Enlightenment' too loosely or too widely, as if it had touched every intellectual society and every intellectual elite of this period equally. The Enlightenment is thus best considered as an amorphous, hard-to-pin-down and constantly shifting entity (Porter, 1990). There were however many common threads to this patchwork of enlightenment thinking: the primacy of reason/rationalism, a belief in empiricism, the concept of universal science and reason, the idea of progress, the championing of new freedoms, the ethic of secularism and the notion of all human beings as essentially the same (Hall and Gieben, 1992: 21–2). The idea of development arguably emerged from the crucible of these early debates, particularly the Scottish Enlightenment and the work of Adam Smith, which had postulated a 'theory' of development embodying a series of 'natural' or 'normal' stages of human activity and development. Cowen and Shenton (1996: 13) remind us however that the beginnings of the modern 'subdiscipline' of development economics are located as much in the 'rough and tumble of early industrialism' as in the work of Scottish enlightenment writers like Adam Smith.

Thinkers such as Voltaire, Montesquieu, Diderot, Hume, Smith, Ferguson, Rousseau and Condorcet found a receptive audience in many European cities for their 'new style of life' (Hampson, 1968). They produced a large collection of novels, plays, books, pamphlets and essays for the consumption of nobles, professionals (especially lawyers), academics and the clergy. It is important to remember however that this new style of life was in the main reserved for the wellborn, the articulate and the lucky – the rural and urban masses had little share. It was not until the eve of the French Revolution in the 1780s that a new social group emerged concerned with popularizing enlightenment ideas. Similarly, though many women played a major part in the development and diffusion of enlightenment ideas, applying such ideas to their social conditions meant negotiating a number of contradictory positions within patriarchal societies.

The *philosophes* took a very clear position on some of the important transitions under way within European societies at the time, particularly the transition from the tradition and mysticism of the past. This past traditional social order was often counterposed to the bright progressive future promised by scientific understanding. As Peter Gay points out, this meant that '[t]he enlightenment's concentration on the future as a realm of unrealised possibilities invited a corresponding depreciation of the past' (Gay, 1973: 92). These new writings and ideas thus profoundly challenged the traditional role of the clergy as the keepers and transmitters of knowledge, constructing distinctively 'modern' ways of knowing the world. The emancipatory potential of this knowledge turned out to be limited, however, in that it was conceived of as abstract and utilitarian, as a mastery over nature which thus becomes characterized by power. As Doherty (1993: 6) has argued:

> Knowledge is reduced to technology, a technology which enables the *illusion* of power and of domination over nature. It is important to stress that this is an illusion. This kind of knowledge does not give actual power over nature. . . . What it does give in the way of power is, of course, a power over the consciousness of others who may be less fluent in the language of reason. . . . Knowledge thus becomes caught up in a dialectic of mastery and slavery.
>
> (Emphasis in original)

Many enlightenment thinkers were concerned with the changing social orders brought about by the transition from feudal to capitalist modes of social organization and in the formation of modernity. In eighteenth-century France, these social orders were represented as three 'Estates' – Clergy, Nobility and the 'Third Estate', which comprised everyone else, from wealthiest bourgeois to poorest peasant (Hall, 1992). This gap between the *philosophes* (who were often members of the second Estate) and the peasantries of European eighteenth-century societies is an important part of the historical context of enlightenment thinking. Although they appeared to represent a threat to the established order, these ideas and writings sought evolutionary rather than revolutionary change, arguing that progress and development could come about within the existing social order through the dissemination of ideas among 'men of influence' (Hall and Gieben, 1992).

'MODERNITY' AND THE RISE OF THE SOCIAL SCIENCES

The foundations of many social sciences were therefore intimately bound up with the Enlightenment's concept of progress and the idea that development could be created through the application of reasoned and empirically based knowledge. Science would ameliorate the negative effects of modernity and improve the practice of agriculture and industrial organization by harnessing natural forces for human interests and unburdening the 'treadmill of human existence'. The Enlightenment had forged the intellectual conditions in which the application of reason to practical issues could flourish through such 'modern' institutions as the academy, the learned journal and the conference. In turn, a 'modern' audience was constituted for the dissemination of social and political ideas alongside a class of intellectuals that could live from writing about them (Hall, 1992).

The emergence of an idea of 'the West' was also important to the Enlightenment in that it was a very European affair which put Europe and European intellectuals at the very pinnacle of human achievement. This view sees 'the West' as the result of forces largely internal to Europe's history and formation (Hall, 1992) rather than as a 'global story' involving other cultural worlds. In the making of nineteenth-century European 'modernity', Europeans had a sense of difference from other worlds which shaped the ways in which they were viewed as distant, uncivilized and immature stages in the progress of humanity. The establishment of modern modes of scientific enquiry, of modern institutions and the modern 'development' of societies in nineteenth-century Europe thus partly incorporated a contrast with the 'savage' and 'uncivilized' spaces of the non-Western world.

When thinking about the links between the legacies of enlightenment ideas and the making of European 'modernity' it is important to recognize that the history of the era of modernity doesn't have a clear periodization or a simple geography. The paradigms and philosophies of 'the Enlightenment' influenced Hegel's nineteenth-century writings, for example, on the history of human civilization and progress. Hegel was also particularly interested in the question of mastery over nature, depicting European civilization as the furthest advanced along a scale of world historical development. Africa for Hegel was a dark, 'unhistorical and undeveloped land', far removed from the awakenings of self-consciousness amongst 'learned' Europeans. Like the philosophers of the Enlightenment, Hegel subscribed to the view that there was an underlying unity or direction to human history (Doherty, 1993). For Hegel, this underlying unity was related to the 'principle of development' which ran through his philosophy of world history leading to truth and freedom in self-determination.

Karl Marx disagreed with the fundamental premises of Hegel's approach to world history but nonetheless drew upon the Hegelian 'principle of development' to explain the genesis from feudalism to capitalism and his notion of historical materialism. Marx was interested in the 'rough and tumble of early industrialism' in Europe and began to raise important questions about the structure of societies and the organization of industry and agriculture. Marx's narrative of emancipation of the working classes, oppressed by the extraction of value from their labour, also operated like enlightenment reason in abstracting meaning from diverging local histories and traditions and translating them into the terms of a meta-narrative or 'master code'. Marx's attitude toward the bourgeoisie was on the one hand full of admiration for its civilizing energies and on the other critical of its 'incipient barbarous tendencies' (Doherty, 1993: 11).

The civilized face of modernity is thus attended constantly by a barbarism which is its other side. Modernist reason was not as inherently good as the 'enlightened' thinkers believed and has been used for a wide variety of purposes. Reason can be imperialist and racist (as in the making of the idea of 'the West'), taking a specific form of consciousness for a universal, a standard that all must aspire to reach. Reason was also a potent weapon in the production of social normativity during 'the Enlightenment', driving people toward a conformity with a dominant and centred 'norm' of behaviour (Doherty, 1993). Modernist reason was therefore dependent on the 'othering' of non-conformists, of cultures and societies that were not informed by this reason and social norms and were thus banished to the lower echelons of humanity, defined as 'undeveloped' or 'uncivilized'. The emergence of new ideas about social, political and economic development was therefore bound up with these pressures to conform to particular notions of knowledge, reason and progress, and with the making of a 'Third Estate' or 'Third World' of non-conformity as the alter ego of a developed 'West'.

CONCLUSIONS: HISTORY, GEOGRAPHY AND MODERNITY

> There is a relation among history, geography and modernity that resists disintegration as far as the Third World is concerned, despite the changes that have given rise to postmodern geographies.
>
> (Escobar, 1995: 10)

Arturo Escobar (1995) writes of the need for an 'Anthropology of Modernity' as it relates to the constituency of the 'Third World', produced by discourses of modernization and development.

Escobar (1995) neglects the beginnings of the idea of 'development' before 1945 however and also rather problematically his work proposes to speak of development as a historically singular experience or as the creation of a single domain of thought and action. 'Development' represents more than a singular post-war historical experience and has complex roots in the emergence of 'the Enlightenment', in the emergence of European industrial capitalism and the rise of European modernity. It is also important to remember that European and Western identities have been formed by contrasting modernity with the tradition and backwardness of the 'Third World'.

Marx's interpretation of capitalist modernity has continued to be relevant to the theorization of 'development' well beyond 1945 and ideologies of Marxism have been drawn upon in development strategies in a wide variety of historical and geographical settings. At the other end of the ideological spectrum, Adam Smith's free market economics also remains relevant for some observers:

> My conclusion therefore, must be that, in principle, Adam Smith [and his] later disciples were right. Trade, specialization and comparative advantage have always led to growth, not to underdevelopment and immiseration.
>
> (Fieldhouse, 1999: 355)

Here, resurfacing once again, then, is the problematic idea of there being a right or wrong path to 'development', which is highly reminiscent of the secure truths postulated by enlightenment reasoning. For some (even today), people and places can become developed simply though acquiring scientific knowledges and conclusions about the 'normal' or correct series of developmental stages.

GUIDE TO FURTHER READING

For an excellent introduction and overview to early development discourses and ideas see Rist (1997) *History of Development*, London: Routledge.

Cowen and Shenton (1996) *Doctrines of Development* provides an accessible discussion of enlightenment ideas, exploring their bearing on the construction of particular development approaches and doctrines.

Doherty (1993) *Postmodernism: An Introduction* offers clear and accessible definitions of modernism and postmodernism, and also interrogates the links between knowledge and power in the construction of modern Europe.

Hall and Gieben (1992) *Formations of Modernity* focuses on the making of modernity in the non-Western world.

Also useful are Crush, J. (1995) (ed.) *Power of Development*, London: Routledge; Hettne, B. (1995) *Development Theory and the Three Worlds*, London: Longman; and Spybey, T. (1992) *Social Change, Development and Dependency: Modernity, Colonialism and the Development of the West*, London: Polity Press.

REFERENCES

Black, J. (1990) *Eighteenth-century Europe 1700–1789*, London: Macmillan.

Cowen, M.P. and Shenton, R.W. (1996) *Doctrines of Development*, London: Routledge.

Doherty, T. (1993) 'Postmodernism: an introduction', in T. Doherty (ed.) *Modernism/Postmodernism*, Hemel Hempstead: Harvester Wheatsheaf, pp. 1–31.

Escobar, A. (1995) *Encountering Development: The Making and Unmaking of the Third World*, Princeton, NJ: Princeton University Press.

Fieldhouse, D.K. (1999) *The West and the Third World: Trade, Colonialism, Dependence and Development*, London: Blackwell.

Gay, P. (1973) *The Enlightenment: An Interpretation. Volume 2: The Science of Freedom*, London: Wildwood House.

Hall, S. (1992) 'The West and the rest: discourse and power', in S. Hall, and B. Gieben (eds) *Formations of Modernity*, Cambridge: Open University/Polity, pp. 275–331, chapter 6.

Hall, S. and Gieben, B. (1992) *Formations of Modernity*, Cambridge: Open University/Polity.

Hampson, N. (1968) *The Enlightenment*, London: Penguin.

Porter, R. (1990) *The Enlightenment*, London: Macmillan.

Rist, T. (1997) *History of Development*, London: Routledge.

2.3 Smith, Ricardo and the world marketplace

David Sapsford

INTRODUCTION

Why do countries trade with one another? What determines the terms on which trade between countries is conducted in the world marketplace? These two questions are perhaps the most fundamental to be considered in any analysis of international trade, be it trade *between* developed and developing countries or trade *amongst* countries in either the developing or the developed world. These questions are of especial importance in the context of economic development, since if there are 'gains from trade' to be had, the distribution of such gains between trading partners carries important implications for living standards and economic welfare within the participating countries.

The classical economists, most notably Adam Smith (1723–90) and David Ricardo (1772–1823) considered these two questions, and their analyses are outlined in the following section. Subsequent sections consider the available evidence regarding the changes that have occurred over the long run in the terms on which trade between developed and developing nations has been conducted, and explore the implications of this for economic development in the Third World.

ABSOLUTE AND COMPARATIVE ADVANTAGE

The foundations of the economic theory of international trade were laid by Adam Smith in *The Wealth of Nations* (1776). Smith's analysis of division of labour is well known and to a large extent he saw the phenomenon of international trade as a logical extension of this process, with particular regions or countries (rather than particular individuals) specializing in the production of particular commodities. Smith's view is clearly demonstrated by the following quotation:

> It is the maxim of every prudent master of a family, never to attempt to make at home what it will cost him more to make than buy. . . . What is prudence in the conduct of every private family, can scarce be folly in that of a great kingdom. If a foreign country can supply us with a commodity cheaper than we ourselves can make it, better buy of them with some part of the produce of our own industry, employed in a way in which we have some advantage.

> (1776: 424)

Thus, according to Smith, countries engage in trade with one another in order to acquire goods more cheaply than they could produce them domestically, paying for them with some proportion of the output that they produce domestically by specializing according to their own 'advantage'. Central to this view is the notion that relative prices determine trade patterns, with countries buying abroad when foreign prices are below domestic ones. In addition, Smith argued that by expanding the size of the market, international trade permits greater specialization and division of labour than would otherwise have been possible. This is perhaps one of the earliest arguments in favour of globalization as a process by which the size of the world marketplace is increased.

Economics textbooks abound with simple two-country/two-good examples that illustrate Smith's argument. Suppose that the world consists of only two countries (say, Britain and the USA) and only two goods (say, food and clothing). Within this (over)simplified framework let us assume that the USA is more efficient than Britain at producing food (in the sense that fewer resources are needed to produce a unit of food in the USA than in Britain) and (in the same least resource-cost sense) that Britain is more efficient than the USA at producing clothing. In economists' terminology this example represents the case where Britain possesses *absolute advantage* in the production of clothing, while the USA possesses absolute advantage in the production of food. To further simplify, let us assume that labour is the only factor of production and that within each country it is mobile between the two industries. Assume also that wages are the same in both countries and that transport costs are zero. On the basis of this battery of assumptions, the USA will be the cheaper source of food and Britain of clothing. It is a matter of simple arithmetic to show that if both countries are initially producing some of each good, it is always possible to increase output of both goods if each country specialises in the production of that good for which it possesses absolute advantage. It also follows that by trading, each country can consume the bundle of clothing and food that it consumed in the absence of trade (that is, under *autarky*) whilst still leaving some of each product over! Each country thus has the potential to increase its consumption of both goods and, assuming that more of each good is preferable to less, trade can, in principle, allow both trading partners to increase their *economic welfare*. As already noted, the distribution of this surplus (that is, the distribution of the *gains from trade*) between the two countries is an important matter, especially in the context of economic development. We return to this issue in the following section.

The case analysed by Adam Smith considered, quite naturally at the time he was writing, the situation where one country possesses absolute advantage in the production of one good, while the other country possesses it in the production of the other good. Writing four decades later, David Ricardo considered the rather more tricky analytical case in which one of the two countries (say Britain) is more efficient at producing *both* goods. According to Adam Smith's absolute advantage argument both goods should be produced by Britain. However, this situation can clearly not represent a feasible state of affairs in the long run since although the USA will seek to purchase both goods from Britain, Britain will not wish to buy anything from the USA in return. Ricardo (1817) was the first economist to provide a formal analysis of this case and by so doing he derived his famous *Law of Comparative Advantage*.

According to Ricardo's Law of Comparative Advantage, which encompasses Adam Smith's analysis of absolute advantage as a special case, world output and therefore (on the basis of the assumption discussed above) world economic welfare will be increased if each country specializes in the production of that good for which it possesses *comparative* advantage. The concept of comparative advantage is basically concerned with comparative efficiency and Ricardo's law follows from recognizing the fact that differences in the relative prices of the two goods as between

Table 1 Labour requirements matrix

	Labour per unit of output	
	Britain	USA
Food	5	6
Clothing	2	12

the two countries opens up the possibility of mutually beneficial trade. To take a concrete example, suppose that the labour required to produce 1 unit of each good in each country is as set out in Table 1. Notice that Britain requires less labour than the USA in both industries.

On the basis of these figures (and assuming that labour productivity in each industry does not alter with the level of output) we can see that in the absence of trade each unit of food within Britain trades for 2.5 units of clothing since each is equivalent to the output of five people. Likewise in the USA 1 unit of food trades for 0.5 unit of clothing, each being the output of six people. It is the difference between these two relative prices (or internal terms of trade) that opens up the possibility for mutually beneficial trade. For example, if US prices prevail in the world outside Britain, a British person in possession of 1 unit of food can exchange this within Britain for 2.5 units of clothing, which could then be sold in the USA for 5 units of food; thereby providing a gain equal to 4 units of food. Likewise, if British relative prices prevail, an American producer employing 12 people to make 1 unit of clothing could switch to the food industry and thereby produce 2 units of food, which could then be sold in Britain for 5 units of clothing; thus realizing a gain of 4 units of clothing. At intermediate relative prices (or terms of trade) both countries can gain from trade, although not to the extent shown in the respective examples given above.

In a nutshell, according to Ricardo's analysis each country shifts its production mix towards the good for which it possesses comparative advantage. In our example, Britain has comparative advantage in the production of clothing, whereas the USA's comparative advantage is in food, where it is *less inefficient*. Reading across the rows in Table 1 we see that this follows because Britain requires five-sixths of US unit inputs in food, but only one-sixth in clothing.

WHO GAINS FROM TRADE?

While the elegance of Ricardo's analysis and its correctness within the confines of its own assumptions can not be faulted, it does beg a question that is vitally important in the context of trade that takes place between countries of the developed/industrialized world and countries of the Third World. While the analysis demonstrates quite clearly the *potential* benefits to trading partners from engaging in international trade in the world marketplace, it has nothing whatsoever to say about the division of these potential gains between them. As we saw in the preceding example, if relative prices in the world marketplace were equal to US relative prices then Britain would effectively appropriate all of the gains from trade for herself whereas, at the opposite end of the spectrum, the USA would scoop all of the gains if British relative prices prevailed.

In order to focus ideas let us consider trade between the countries of the developed/industrialized world and those of the developing world and, for simplicity, assume that the former produce manufactured goods while the latter produce primary commodities. The fact that Ricardo's analysis did not shed any light on the issue of how the potential gains from trade are shared out in practice did not seem to constitute a problem in the minds of classical economists since in a related context Ricardo, like Smith before him, had argued that as an inevitable consequence of the twin forces of diminishing returns in the production of primary commodities from a fixed stock of land (including mineral resources) as population increased, and the downward pressures on production costs in manufacturing generated by the moderating influences of surplus population and urbanization upon wages, the price of primary products would rise over the long run in relation to the price of manufactured goods, thereby giving rise to an upward drift in the net barter terms of trade between primary commodities and manufactured goods.[1] On the above assumptions this movement will translate into an improvement in the terms of trade of developing countries *vis-à-vis* the developed countries. On the basis of this argument there was little, if any, reason to be concerned about the plight of developing countries in the context of their trading relations with the industrialized world since it predicted that over the long run, the terms of trade would shift steadily in their favour, with the result that they would enjoy an increasing proportion of the potential gains from trade.

However, in the early 1950s the classical prediction of a secular improvement was challenged by both Prebisch (1950) and Singer (1950). Both argued forcefully that in direct contravention of the then still prevailing classical prediction, the terms of trade had actually, as a matter of statistical fact, been historically subject to, and could be expected to continue to be subject to, a declining trend. Both analyses therefore implied that contrary to the classical view, developing countries were actually obtaining a falling proportion of the potential gains from their trade with the countries of the developed world.

A number of theoretical explanations have been put forward in the literature to account for the observed downward trend in the terms of trade of developing countries, relative to developed countries, and these can be conveniently summarized under the following four headings:

- *differing elasticities of demand for primary commodities and manufactured goods* (with the inelastic nature of the former resulting in a tendency for increases in the conditions of commodity supply to be felt more strongly in price decreases than in quantity increases);
- *differing rates of growth in the demands for primary commodities and manufactured goods* (with the demand for primaries expanding less rapidly than the demand for manufactures due to their lower income elasticity of demand – especially so in the case of agricultural commodities due to the operation of Engel's Law – plus the development of synthetic substitutes and the occurrence in manufacturing of technical progress of the raw materials-saving sort);
- *technological superiority* (the argument being that the prices of manufactured goods rise relative to those of primaries because they embody both a so-called Schumpeterian rent element for innovation, plus an element of monopolistic profit arising from the monopoly power of multinational producers);
- *asymmetries in market structure* (the argument here is that differences in market structure – with primary commodities typically being produced and sold under competitive conditions, while manufacturing in industrialized countries is often characterized by a high degree of monopoly by organized labour and monopoly producers – mean that while technical progress in the production of primary commodities results in lower prices, technical progress in manufacturing leads to increased factor incomes as opposed to lower prices).

---

[1] For brevity, I refer hereafter to the net barter terms of trade between primary commodities and manufactured goods (i.e. to the ratio of the price of primary commodities to the price of manufactured goods) as simply their terms of trade.

POLICY IMPLICATIONS

Although space constraints do not allow the discussion in any detail of the policy implications of the observed worsening trend in the terms on which trade is conducted in the world marketplace between primary commodity-producing countries and manufacturing countries, it is important to note that the Prebisch–Singer hypothesis is sometimes advanced as one argument in favour of development policies of the import-substituting industrialization as opposed to export promotion variety (Sapsford and Balasubramanyam, 1994). However, the policy issues here are not clear-cut and the fact that all four of the above explanations relate as much, if not more, to the characteristics of different types of countries as to the characteristics of different types of traded goods highlights the need to devise and implement policies that address differences and imbalances of the former as opposed to the latter sort.

It is now the case that at least some of the international agencies involved in the world trading system have come to accept that primary commodity producers in developing countries do face real and significant uncertainties and risks regarding the prices that they will actually receive for their products when they come to the world market. At the time of writing, a task force set up under the auspices of the World Bank is investigating a range of possible 'market-based' approaches for dealing with the price risks faced by primary commodity producers in developing countries. As pointed out by Morgan (2001) these approaches appear to represent an attempt to confront price risk by modifying the financial environment within which primary producers in less developed countries operate. However, it remains to be seen whether such approaches will prove any more, or less, successful than the various policies which have preceded them.

GUIDE TO FURTHER READING

Detailed discussion of both the theoretical arguments and statistical evidence underlying the declining trend in terms of trade hypothesis can be found in the following texts.

Sapsford, D., Sarkar, P. and Singer, H. (1992) 'The Prebisch–Singer terms of trade controversy revisited', *Journal of International Development* 4(3): 315–32.

Singer, H. (1987) 'Terms of trade and economic development' in J. Eatwell, M. Milgate and P. Newman (eds) *The New Palgrave: A Dictionary of Economics*, London: Macmillan, pp. 626–8.

Spraos, J. (1983) *Inequalizing Trade?*, Oxford: Oxford University Press.

Comprehensive discussion of a wide range of issues relating to the relationship between economic development and international trade may be found in the following.

Greenaway, D. (ed.) (1988) *Economic Development and International Trade*, London: Macmillan.

REFERENCES

Morgan, W. (2001) 'Commodity Futures markets in LDCs: a review and prospects', *Progress in Development Studies* 1(2): 139–50.

Prebisch, R. (1950) 'The economic development of Latin America and its principal problem', UN ECLA; also published in *Economic Bulletin for Latin America* 7(1) (1962): 1–22.

Ricardo, D. (1817) *On the Principles of Political Economy and Taxation*, London: Penguin (reprinted 1971).

Sapsford, D. and Balasubramanyam, V.N. (1994) 'The long-run behavior of the relative price of primary commodities: statistical evidence and policy implications', *World Development* 22(11): 1737–45.

Singer, H. (1950) 'The distribution of gains between investing and borrowing countries', *American Economic Review, Papers and Proceedings* 40: 473–85.

Smith, A. (1776) *The Wealth of Nations*, London: Penguin (reprinted 1961).

2.4 Dualistic and unilinear concepts of development

Tony Binns

THE DEVELOPMENT IMPERATIVE

After the Second World War, Europe embarked on a massive programme of reconstruction, instrumental to which was the Marshall Plan, launched by the US government on 5 June 1947. Whilst the Marshall Plan was heralded as US financial help to the devastated economies and infrastructures of Western Europe, this 'goodwill gesture' was also designed to stimulate markets for America's burgeoning manufacturing sector. The Marshall Plan, which injected US$17 billion mainly into the UK, France, West Germany and Italy between 1948 and 1952, generated much confidence in the role of overseas economic aid (Hunt, 1989; Rapley, 1996). Another landmark in the recognition of the need for richer countries to play an active role in the development of poorer countries came less than two years later, on 20 January 1949, when US President Truman in 'Point Four' of his Inaugural Address proclaimed:

> we must embark on a bold new program for making the benefits of our scientific advances and industrial progress available for the improvement and growth of underdeveloped areas. More than half the people of the world are living in conditions approaching misery. Their food is inadequate. They are victims of disease. Their economic life is primitive and stagnant. Their poverty is a handicap and a threat both to them and to more prosperous areas. For the first time in history, humanity possesses the knowledge and skill to relieve the suffering of these people . . . I believe that we should make available to peace-loving peoples the benefits of our store of technical knowledge in order to help them realize their aspirations for a better life.
>
> (Public Papers of the Presidents of the United States, 1964: 114–15)

'Point Four' probably inaugurated the 'development age' and 'represents a minor masterpiece . . . in that it puts forward a new way of conceiving international relations' (Rist, 1997: 71–2).

THE NEO-CLASSICAL PARADIGM

The so-called 'neo-classical paradigm' dominated much thinking about development in the two or three decades after the Second World War. Adam Smith, the founding father of the classical school, writing in his *Wealth of Nations* (1776) in the early years of the Industrial Revolution, saw manufacturing as capable of achieving greater increases in productivity than agriculture. He emphasized the expansion of markets as an inducement for greater productivity which would, he believed, lead to greater labour specialization and productivity. A century later in 1890, Alfred Marshall, in his influential book, *Principles of Economics*, spelt out the 'neo-classical perspective', emphasizing the desirability of maximizing aggregate economic welfare, whilst recognizing that this was dependent on maximizing the value of production and raising labour productivity (Marshall, 1890). Technological change was recognized as being vital to raising productivity and meeting the demands for food and raw materials from a growing population. There was also a strong belief that free trade and the unimpeded operation of the market were necessary for maximizing efficiency and economic welfare (Hunt, 1989).

D▊▊▊▊▊▊

Another theme that emerged in the post-war period was that underdeveloped economies were characterized by a 'dichotomous' or 'dualistic' nature, where advanced and modern sectors of the economy co-existed alongside traditional and backward sectors. A strong proponent of the dualistic structure of underdeveloped economies was the West Indian economist Arthur Lewis, whose seminal paper 'Economic development with unlimited supplies of labour' was published in 1954 (Lewis, 1954). Like others who followed him, Lewis did not differentiate between economic growth and development. The paper, which significantly opens with the statement, 'This essay is written in the classical tradition', envisages a division of the economic system into two distinct sectors, the capitalist and the subsistence. The subsistence sector, according to Lewis, consists predominantly of small-scale family agriculture and has a much lower per capita output than the capitalist sector, where manufacturing industry and estate agriculture, either private or state-owned, are important elements. The process of development, Lewis suggested, involves an increase in the capitalists' share of the national income due to growth of the capitalist sector at the expense of the subsistence sector, with the ultimate goal of absorption of the latter by the former. Since most labour for the capitalist sector would come from underemployed labour in subsistence agriculture, changes within the latter sector were seen as essential for the process of overall economic development.

The Lewis model had a significant influence on development thinking in the 1950s and 1960s, but it has been criticized for failing to appreciate the positive role of small-scale agriculture in the development process. With such agronomic successes as the Green Revolution, it was realized that raising the productivity of the rural subsistence sector could actually be an important objective rather than a constraint in development policy.

The concept of dualism is also apparent in some early spatial development models, focusing on the different qualities and potential of contrasting regions, rather than economic sectors as in the Lewis model. Whilst some would argue that the development of certain areas at the expense of others is likely to inhibit the growth of the economy as a whole, others regarded initial regional inequality as a prerequisite for eventual overall development. Both Gunnar Myrdal and Albert Hirschman, for example, advocated strategies of 'unbalanced growth'. Myrdal's 'cumulative causation' principle (Myrdal, 1957) suggested that once particular regions have by virtue of some initial advantage moved ahead of others, new increments of activity and growth will tend to be concentrated in already-expanding regions because of their derived advantages, rather than in other areas of the country. Thus, labour, capital and commodities move to growing regions, setting up so-called 'backwash effects' in the remaining regions which may lose their skilled and enterprising workers and much of their locally generated capital. However, Myrdal recognized that such less dynamic areas may benefit from centrifugal 'spread effects', in that by stimulating demand in other, particularly neighbouring regions, expansion in the growing areas may initiate economic growth elsewhere.

Hirschman (1958), working independently of Myrdal, followed similar thinking, proposing a strategy of 'unbalanced growth' and suggesting that the development of one or more regional centres of economic strength is essential for an economy to lift itself to higher income levels. He envisaged spatial interaction between growing 'Northern' and lagging 'Southern' regions in the shape of 'trickle-down' and 'polarization' effects, similar to Myrdal's spread and backwash effects. Keeble (1967) argued that Hirschman's model,

> far from assuming a cumulative causation mechanism, implies that if an imbalance between regions resulting from the dominance of polarization effects develops during earlier stages of growth, counter-balancing forces will in time come into operation to restore the situation to an equilibrium position. Such forces, chief of which is government economic policy, are not to be thought of as intensified trickling-down effects, but as a new element in the model, arising only at a late stage in development. Their inclusion, together with the exclusion of any cumulative mechanism, represents the model's chief structural differences from that of Myrdal.
>
> (Keeble, 1967: 260)

A significant policy implication of Hirschman's unbalanced growth model is that governments should not necessarily intervene to reduce inequalities, since the inevitable search for greater profits will lead to 'a spontaneous spin-off of growth-inducing industries to backward regions' (Potter et al., 1999: 46).

The spatial models of Myrdal and Hirschman have strong parallels with the work of François Perroux and other French economists in the 1940s and 1950s, who pointed out that growth did not appear everywhere simultaneously, but instead is frequently located in a 'growth centre or pole' (pôle de croissance). In essence, the growth centre model depicts the transmission of economic prosperity from a centre, most commonly an urban-industrial area, as a result of the interplay of spread and backwash effects. The model singles out crucial variables in the development of spatial variation in economic prosperity within a region and specifies how they operate. A particular 'growth industry', such as motor manufacturing, is likely to attract other linked industries, such as those which supply it with inputs and/or derive their inputs from it. Other agglomeration economies may encourage further growth, whilst technological change is encouraged through close proximity and interaction between the various industrial enterprises.

UNILINEAR MODELS

Much post-war development thinking was strongly 'Eurocentric' in that, often inappropriately, 'theories and models [were] rooted in Western economic history and consequently structured by that unique, although historically important, experience' (Hettne, 1995: 21). Walt Rostow's 'unilinear' model (1960) (see figure on page 78) is probably the best-known attempt to show how a country's economy and society progress through a series of stages, and is firmly based on the Euro-American experience. It was undoubtedly the most influential modernization theory to emerge in the early 1960s. It is interesting to note that Rostow entitled his book *The Stages of Economic Growth: A Non-Communist Manifesto* and, '[his] perception of the purpose of the United States' promotion of economic development in the Third World was governed by a strongly anti-communist stance' (Hunt, 1989: 96). Indeed, early in his book Rostow asserts that he is aiming to provide 'an alternative to Karl Marx's theory of modern history' (Rostow, 1960: 2). The key element in Rostow's thinking was the process of capital formation, represented by five stages through which all countries pass in the process of economic growth.

Stage 1: Traditional society   Characterized by primitive technology, hierarchical social structures, production and trade based on custom and barter, as in pre-seventeenth-century Britain.

Stage 2: Pre-conditions for take-off   With improved technology and transport, increased trade and investment, economically based elites and more centralized national states gradually emerged. Economic progress was assisted by education, entrepreneurship and institutions capable of mobilizing capital. Often traditional society persisted side by side with modern economic activities, as in seventeenth- and eighteenth-century Britain, when the so-called 'agricultural revolution' and world exploration (leading to increased trade) were gaining momentum. Whilst the preconditions for take-off were actually endogenous in Britain, elsewhere they were probably the result of 'external intrusion by more advanced societies' (Rostow, 1960: 6).

Stage 3: Take-off   The most important stage, covering a few decades, when the last obstacles to economic growth are removed. 'Take-off' is characterized by rapid economic growth, more sophisticated technology and considerable investment, particularly in manufacturing industry. The share of net investment and saving in national income rise from 5 per cent to 10 per cent or more, resulting in a process of industrialization, as in early nineteenth-century Britain. Agriculture becomes increasingly commercialized and more productive with increasing demand from growing urban centres.

Stage 4: Drive to maturity   A period of self-sustaining growth, with increasing investment of between 10 and 20 per cent of national income. Technology becomes more sophisticated, there is greater diversification in the industrial and agricultural sectors and falling imports, as in late nineteenth- and early twentieth-century Britain.

Stage 5: Age of high mass consumption   The final stage, characterized by the increasing importance of consumer goods and services, and the rise of the welfare state. In Britain and Western Europe, this stage was not reached until after the Second World War (post-1945), but in the USA mass production and consumption of consumer goods, such as cars, fridges and washing machines, came earlier, during the 1920s and 1930s.

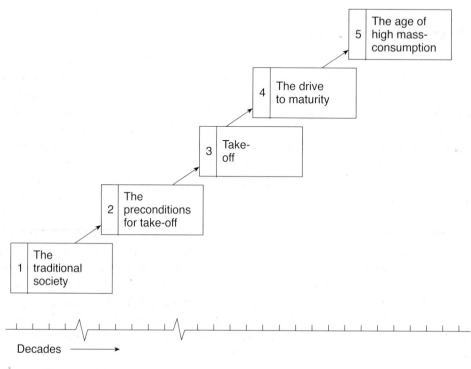

Rostow's unilinear model

Despite its considerable influence on development planning at the time, Rostow's model has been strongly criticized for a number of reasons. First, it is a 'unilinear' model, implying that 'things get better' over time, which is by no means always true as, for example, the experience of many sub-Saharan African countries indicates. Increases in per capita income have scarcely kept pace with world trends and the AIDS pandemic has had a devastating effect on mortality and life expectancy rates. Most sub-Saharan African countries are relatively worse off in the early twenty-first century than in the 1960s when many gained their independence. Second, it is a 'Eurocentric' model, suggesting that all countries will imitate the experience of Europe and America. It is quite inappropriate to apply such a model to countries which have been subjected to colonial rule and whose economies (and societies) have been manipulated to serve the demand for agricultural and mineral resources from the growing manufacturing sectors in the metropolitan countries. Third, the model suggests that all countries progress through these stages in the same sequence as happened in Europe and North America. But in some developing countries the sequence of events has not been so straightforward, with for example, rapid change in the agricultural, industrial and service sectors happening at the same time, rather than sequentially. Whilst modern consumer goods, schools and hospitals, may be present in towns and cities, in remote rural areas these facilities are frequently absent, and poor farmers still use simple technology to produce food for their families. Finally, it is often wrongly seen as a 'development' model, whereas it is actually an 'economic growth' model. Rostow was concerned more with economic progress and increasing industrial investment, rather than human welfare and other non-economic indicators of development. Some countries have experienced periods of rapid economic growth, yet much of the population has felt little benefit from this – what might be called 'growth without development' (Binns, 1994). The real significance of the Rostow model was that it seemed to offer every country an equal chance to develop.

FROM DUALISM TO BASIC NEEDS

The lack of distinction and explanation drawn by Rostow and others between the processes of 'growth' and 'development' led some writers to try to clarify the situation. There was also growing concern that economic growth, which had been the main preoccupation of Lewis, Hirschman, Myrdal and Rostow did not necessarily eliminate poverty and that the so-called 'trickle-down' effects of growth generally failed to benefit the poor in both spatial and social terms. Dudley Seers provided much-needed clarification on the meaning of development, suggesting that poverty, unemployment and inequality should be key foci in the development debate and that there should be greater concern for the fulfilment of basic needs (notably food, health and education) through the development process (Seers, 1969, 1972). The basic needs approach gained momentum in the mid-1970s. The International Labour Organization's 1976 conference on World Employment adopted the 'Declaration of Principles and Programme of Action for a Basic Needs Strategy of Development', highlighting poverty alleviation as a key objective for all countries in the period up to the year 2000. Possibly the main weakness of the basic needs strategy was its 'top-down' approach, 'which made it vulnerable to changing fashions in the international aid bureaucracy' (Hettne, 1995: 180). In spite of such limitations, the debates surrounding the meaning and process of development and the question of basic needs did much to move development thinking and policy away from earlier dualistic, unilinear, and essentially Eurocentric, approaches of the 1950s and 1960s.

GUIDE TO FURTHER READING

For detailed consideration of development theory, see Hettne (1995) and Hunt (1989). Keeble's chapter (1967) in Chorley and Haggett's *Socio-economic Models in Geography*, though written over 30 years ago, is still helpful. A more recently written overview is provided in Chapter 3 of Potter *et al*.'s *Geographies of Development* (1999). Hirschman (1958), Lewis (1954), Rostow (1960) and Smith (1961) are justifiably regarded as 'classic' texts, whilst Alfred Marshall's *Principles of Economics* was a key undergraduate text-book for over 50 years.

REFERENCES

Binns, T. (1994) *Tropical Africa*, London: Routledge.

Hettne, B. (1995) *Development Theory and the Three Worlds: Towards an International Political Economy of Development*, London: Longman.

Hirschman, A.O. (1958) *The Strategy of Economic Development*, Yale: Yale University Press.

Hunt, D. (1989) *Economic Theories of Development*, London: Harvester Wheatsheaf.

Keeble, D.E. (1967) 'Models of economic development', in R.J. Chorley and P. Haggett (eds) *Socio-economic Models in Geography*, London: Methuen, pp. 243–305.

Lewis, W.A. (1954) 'Economic development with unlimited supplies of labour', *The Manchester School of Economic and Social Studies* 22(2), May; reprinted in A. Agarwala and S. Singh (eds) (1958) *The Economics of Underdevelopment*, Oxford: Oxford University Press, pp. 400–49.

Marshall, A. (1890) *Principles of Economics* (8th edn), London: Macmillan (reprinted 1920).

Myrdal, G. (1957) *Economic Theory and Underdeveloped Regions*, London: Duckworth.

Potter, R.B., Binns, T., Elliott, J.A. and Smith, D. (1999) *Geographies of Development*, London: Longman.

Public Papers of the Presidents of the United States (1964) *Harry S. Truman, Year 1949*, 5, Washington DC: United States Government Printing Office.

Rapley, J. (1996) *Understanding Development: Theory and Practice in the Third World*, London: UCL Press.

Rist, G. (1997) *The History of Development*, London: Zed Books.

Rostow, W. (1960) *The Stages of Economic Growth: A Non-communist Manifesto*, Cambridge: Cambridge University Press.

Seers, D. (1969) 'The meaning of development', *International Development Review*, 11(4): 2–6.

Seers, D. (1972) 'What are we trying to measure?', *Journal of Development Studies* 8(3): 21–36.

Smith, A. (1776) *The Wealth of Nations*, London: Methuen (2 vols) (reprinted 1961).

2.5 Transport and development

David Hilling

THE TRANSPORT GAP

There is considerable statistical evidence to confirm that there are vast differences between countries and also between regions within countries with respect to availability of transport provision and levels of development. In the figure opposite (Hilling, 1996) the Index of Transport is based on various measures of transport provision – rail route per km², rail route per 1,000 population, ton-km per capita by road, commercial vehicles per capita, passenger km and cars per capita. When compared with per capita GDP, there emerges a sharp contrast between the richer,

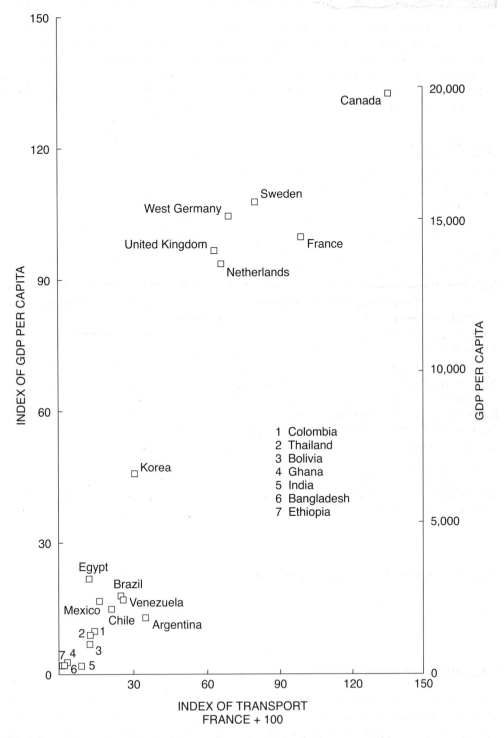

Indices of transport

Source: Calculated from *UN Statistical Yearbook*, 1990

'advanced' countries with high levels of transport provision and the poorer countries with low levels of provision.

In the former there are sophisticated, high-quality services with consumer choice and rapidly rising levels of personal mobility based on car ownership and mass air travel. In the latter there is heavy dependence on traditional, labour-intensive forms of transport (human porterage, hand carts, pedal vehicles) and many of the inhabitants live in localized, spatially circumscribed, static, socio-economic systems in which immobility and poverty are clearly related (Owen, 1987). Further, in poor countries it is often the case that the technical, financial and managerial resources are not available for proper maintenance of existing transport services which deteriorate, often hastened by climatic conditions, so that they are seriously inadequate for present requirements without the complication of accommodating growth in demand.

THE TRANSPORT AND DEVELOPMENT DEBATE

The supply-led model

At a number of points in history great expansion of economic activity appears to follow technological changes which result in the increased range and capacity of transport often associated with reduced cost. Obvious examples include the ship design improvements and the Age of Discoveries of the fifteenth and sixteenth centuries, canal and then rail transport and the industrialization of Western Europe and North America and the steamship and empire in the nineteenth century. In the Gold Coast, now Ghana, there was a dramatic expansion of cocoa cultivation and in Northern Nigeria of groundnuts with the construction of the first railway lines (Mabogunje, 1980). In Malaysia, Leinbach (1975) showed the significance of transport in stimulating rubber cultivation and tin mining, and Kleinpenning (1978) showed how, for better and for worse, road construction in Amazonia allowed the expansion of commercial farming, forest exploitation and mining.

From the demonstration of a relationship between the capacity and sophistication of the transport infrastructure and development it was but a short step to suggest a causal relationship with transport having a special role in the development process. Indeed, through to the 1970s, there was a widely held belief amongst development planners that transport provision would itself lead to development and much investment went into transport projects – during the 1960s, 40 per cent of all World Bank loans and an even higher proportion of capital investment in some countries.

In many developing countries the inadequacy of transport to satisfy both day-to-day needs and exceptional demand at times of drought, flood and famine relief is all too apparent, yet there has been growing concern at the number of transport projects which have seemingly failed to spark development – the extension of rail lines into northern Nigeria and Cameroon and Ghana's short stretch of motorway are often cited. Transport may be an essential element in the development process but of itself it is clearly not a sufficient factor – development certainly depends on transport, but transport will not necessarily ensure development.

The demand-led model

An alternative view is that transport is most likely to stimulate development where there is a demonstrable demand or prior dynamism (Pawson, 1979) – an environment in which economic opportunity will be exploited. In the cases already cited of Ghana, Nigeria and Malaysia there was an insatiable demand for their produce in Europe and entrepreneurs ready to satisfy that demand once suitable transport was in place.

Demand for transport takes several forms. Revealed demand is movement that actually takes place on the existing network, but at any time and in most places there will be an element of latent demand. This may be existing demand that cannot be satisfied because of inadequate capacity or high cost, but which would be revealed if infrastructure were to be improved. Also, it is possible that improved infrastructure will result in the generation of completely new demand, but there is no guarantee that this will happen – this is where prior dynamism assumes significance. However, even where there is demand and prior dynamism, transport is but one of many inputs into development, the lack of any one of which may impede the process. Ideally therefore, transport should be an element in a planned package of inputs.

Transport: the facilitating role

Undoubtedly, transport has an important facilitating role in the development process. In cases, and possibly as part of a package of inputs, transport may have a direct impact on economic activity – what has been called the positive impact (Gauthier, 1970). The opening of iron ore mines in Liberia in the 1960s and Brazil in the 1970s are examples. More often transport is permissive – because it is available, it does not inhibit development when other requirements are satisfied. For footloose development to take place there must be some surplus capacity in the transport system and very often this is just what developing countries do not have.

Transport influences development by stimulating both forward and backward linkages with multiplier effects. A forward linkage would be where farmers change to cash cropping alongside a new or improved road, and a backward linkage would be where the road stimulates maintenance services, quarrying and bitumen production.

By increasing range and capacity, transport improvement makes it easier to move goods and people in greater volumes and over longer distances at reduced cost. While human porterage of goods may appear to be cheap transport, for anything other than the smallest quantity over very short distances it is in fact very expensive. By providing positive changes in mobility and accessibility, improved transport potentially enhances economic and social opportunity, but it does not follow that individuals or communities will respond to such opportunities, and evidence suggests considerable variations in the manner and the extent to which they do so and the unpredictability of their reactions (Howe and Richards, 1984).

The impact of transport

The complex interrelationship between transport and development may be debated but it is not difficult to identify some of the ways in which transport may widen productive and social opportunities (Table 1). Initially, it will be the providers and users of transport who will benefit through increased capacity, greater speed and reliability, and changed costs; and goods and passenger flows – volume and routeing – will be affected.

The indirect impact of changed mobility and accessibility will be reflected in the cost of providing a wide range of public services (health, education), possible changes in the value of land and natural resources and consequent changes in both rural and urban land uses. Wider again will be the impact on patterns of investment, employment opportunity and income distribution, changes in the balance and terms of trade (for example, local goods may become more competitive in distant markets) and the spread of the money economy.

Table 1 Transport and development

Market consequences	Extra-market consequences
1 *For users of transport*	
Vehicle size, character	Tourism
Transport operating costs	Recreational amenity
Cost of time	Improved safety
Financial position of transport firms	Integration
Reliability, speed of transport	Improved information
Commodities that can be carried	
Freight flows – volumes, directions	
Passenger flows – numbers, direction	
Improved distribution channels	
Commodity price changes	
2 *For non-users in zone of influence of transport facility*	
Changes in cost of public services	Impact on community/region well-being
Changes in value of land	Sequent occupance – intensification
Changes in value of crops/natural resources	Emergence of entrepreneurial capacity
Changes in rural land use	
Changes in urban land use	
3 *Wider regional/national impact*	
New patterns of investment	Changing pattern of internal/external
Changed employment opportunity	linkages
Changed income levels/distribution	Changed relative significance of
Changed balance/terms of trade	settlements
Spread of money economy	Demographic change – migration,
Changing patterns of public finance –	structure
taxation, revenue, expenditure	

Source: After Hilling, 1996

Some of the consequences may be termed extra-market. These would include regional integration, improved information flow, safety and recreational opportunities. Community welfare may be enhanced, patterns of occupance altered (production may beome more specialized or intensive), and entrepreneurial enterprise may be encouraged. At the widest level there may be new patterns of regional linkage, the relative significance of different settlements may be altered, demographic patterns may change, and political structures and alliances may be affected.

Much development planning is based on the assumption that improved transport will stimulate just such a chain of consequences and that this will be beneficial. However, we now know that in practice, the impact, far from being wholly beneficial, may be restricted and even harmful.

The negative impact of transport

In purely financial terms, the impact of a particular transport project may be considered negative if the capital it consumed would have produced higher returns invested in an alternative way – perhaps some directly productive activity, education or health.

Improved transport, during construction and in operation, often replaces labour-intensive, informal technology with capital and equipment and reduces the overall demand for labour (Rimmer, 1984) with undesirable economic and social consequences. Increased cash cropping, a usual consequence of transport improvement, may lead to differential land values, increased income inequality and may favour some groups at the expense of others. Arguably the Indian groups in Amazonia have been disadvantaged, and in Nepal it has been noted that the road improvements tended to favour the already advantaged who were often 'outsiders' rather than local people (Blaikie *et al.*, 1977).

While railway construction in Southern Africa certainly stimulated capital investment, and the expansion of commercial farming and mining activity, it also facilitated migrant labour with consequent problems of greater dependency and indebtedness in source areas (Pirie, 1982). Colonial exploitation, usually dependent on transport provision, produced economies that were dangerously dependent on a limited range of primary products and stifled traditional economic activity – textile industries in India and parts of Africa being obvious examples.

The development of transport networks is fundamentally hierarchical in nature and, of necessity, transport improvement is highly selective spatially – rail networks are usually of very low density, only a few roads will be upgraded to motorway standard. Inevitably, regional contrasts will be sharpened in a way which may be undesirable from economic, social and even political points of view.

We are increasingly made aware of the undesirable environmental implications of transport development and some of the economic activities generated. At the local scale this may be impeded drainage, soil creep on bared slopes and ground, and atmospheric pollution; at the regional scale, as in Amazonia and parts of South Asia, it may be large-scale forest clearance and environmental degradation; at the global scale it may mean increased global warming and climate change.

Transport planning

It follows that if transport is to have a maximum beneficial and least harmful effect on the development process and is to be sustainable both economically and environmentally, it must be carefully planned. At its simplest this requires the fullest consideration of five related questions (Hilling, 1996).

The first of these is *when?* Is the time right, does the demand exist to justify the upgrading of the road or the construction of a new one, is a rail line now needed, must the port or airport now be expanded? The second question is *where?* Which roads are to be improved, what should be the route of the new road or rail line, where shall we locate the new port or airport? Third is the question *what?* This is the critical question regarding the technology to be adopted – what type of road surface, which railway gauge, in urban areas will we go for sophisticated rail mass transit, express bus lanes or paratransit? In construction, will labour- or capital-intensive methods be used? In operation will we emphasize formal or informal organization?

It can also be argued that it is important *who* makes the decisions – are the local people involved in the process, are external consultants or contractors the driving force, what is the relative importance of politicians and planners? Finally, *why* are the decisions made – what are the determining factors, is the motivation profit, social welfare, employment generation, avoidance of environmental degradation, sustainability, energy conservation? In many respects this should perhaps be the first question to be posed because all too many transport projects have had little or no relationship to the identifiable needs of local people nor to the broader development objectives of particular regions or groups. Possible negative effects are invariably ignored and it is hardly surprising that the development effect has often been limited and scarce capital has been wasted.

In practical terms it is not a question of which should come first – the demand for, or the supply of, transport infrastructure – but rather that transport provision should be related to clearly defined development objectives, whether of an economic or social nature. This should determine the timing, location and technology, and ensure that transport improvements are appropriate, either in the sense of general suitability for the purpose in mind, or in the sense that intermediate technology is adopted. It is now recognized that there are many situations where less sophisticated, more labour- and less capital-intensive, informal rather than formal, technology will provide the appropriate way forward.

GUIDE TO FURTHER READING

Wilfred Owen's *Transportation and World Development* (1987, London: Hutchinson) provides a useful global overview of transport and development. The arguments are elaborated with modal and regional examples in *Transport and Developing Countries* (Hilling, D. 1996, London: Routledge) and in *Transport and Development in the Third World* (Simon, D. 1996, London: Routledge). Conceptual frameworks for, and case studies of, transport and the development process will also be found in *Modern Transport Geography* (Hoyle, B.S. and Knowles, R. (eds), 1998, Chichester: Wiley). A useful survey of the literature and illuminating case studies will be found in *Rural Roads and Poverty Alleviation* (Howe, J. and Richards, P. (eds) 1984, London: Intermediate Technology Publications).

REFERENCES

Blaikie, P., Cameron, J. and Seddon, D. (1977) *The Effect of Roads in West Central Nepal*, London: Report to the Ministry of Overseas Development.

Gauthier, H. (1970) 'Geography, transportation and regional development', *Economic Geography* 46: 612–19.

Kleinpenning, J.M.G. (1978) 'Further evaluation of the policy for the integration of the Amazon region', *Tijdschrift voor Economische en Sociale Geografie* 62: 285–9.

Leinbach, T.R. (1975) 'Transport and the development of Malaya', *Annals of the Association of American Geographers* 65(2): 270–82.

Mabogunje, A. (1980) *The Development Process: A Spatial Perspective*, London: Hutchinson.

Pawson, E. (1979) 'Transport and development: perspectives from historical geography', *International Journal of Transport Economics* 6(2): 125–37.

Pirie, G.H. (1982) 'The de-civilizing rails: railways and underdevelopment in Southern Africa', *Tijdschrift voor Economische en Sociale Geografie* 73(4): 221–8.

Rimmer, P.J. (1984) 'The role of paratransit in South East Asian cities', *Singapore Journal of Tropical Geography* 5(1): 45–62.

2.6 Neo-liberalism, structural adjustment and poverty reduction strategies

David Simon

THE RISE OF NEO-LIBERALISM

The dramatic oil price increases of 1973 and 1979 triggered a slowdown and then severe recession in the North and the world economy as a whole, and precipitated the so-called 'debt crisis' in the South in 1981–82.

Profound disillusionment in the North with the record of state involvement in economic and social life led to a simplistic and rather naïve belief in 'the magic of the market' as the most efficient economic regulator. State involvement in the economy was held to be inefficient, bureaucratic and an unnecessary drain on public coffers. Hence, by selling off loss-making and inefficient public enterprises and parastatal corporations, and restricting the role of the state to regulation and economic facilitation, taxes could be cut substantially.

This is the essence of neo-liberalism, an economic creed that seeks to deregulate markets as much as possible to promote 'free' trade. It harks back to the ideas of Adam Smith and David Ricardo, in other words, to the very historical roots of neo-classical economics – hence neo (new) liberalism. This ideology rapidly became the economic orthodoxy in the North and was exported to the global South via aid policies and the measures formulated to address the debt crisis.

STRUCTURAL ADJUSTMENT AND ECONOMIC RECOVERY PROGRAMMES

Initial responses to the debt crisis

In late 1981, Brazil and Mexico – soon followed by Poland – announced that they could no longer service their official debts, triggering panic among Northern creditor governments and the transnational banks that had advanced the enormous commercial loans to the debtor countries. They feared that if rapid counter-measures were not taken and strict penalties imposed, there could be a domino effect among debt-ridden countries that would drive individual banks into bankruptcy and undermine the entire international financial system.

The International Monetary Fund (IMF) assumed the lead role in addressing the debt crisis. Its analysis – which was echoed by the multilateral banks and leading creditor governments – hinged on Northern self-interest and a determination to protect the international financial system. The problem of default was diagnosed as entirely the fault of the debtor countries, as a result of their governments being corrupt, interventionist, bloated by bureaucracy and weighed down by inefficient, often loss-making state enterprises; they had also pursued inappropriate policies. The dramatic interest rate increase was noted but was not regarded as sufficient explanation; nor was the fact that the loans in question had been willingly contracted by both parties. The banks, which had actively sought to lend out their surplus petrodollars, were not in any sense held liable for their own misfortune or lack of foresight. They were even able to write off their losses of up to £1 billion annually against tax.

Indeed, the IMF's policy response was geared to maximizing the prospects for, and amounts of repayment by, debtor countries. For many years there was accordingly an almost total unwillingness to consider writing off the debts of even the most impoverished and debt-ridden countries for fear of evoking a chorus of 'can't pay, won't pay'.

The anatomy of structural adjustment programmes

These new policies, known as structural adjustment programmes (SAPs), were designed to cut government expenditure, reduce the extent of state intervention in the economy, and promote liberalization and international trade. SAPs were explicit about the necessity of export promotion based on the Ricardian notion of comparative advantage. Accordingly, each country should specialize in and export those commodities that it can produce more cheaply in real terms than its competitors. However, international trade is often unbalanced and inequitable in its impacts; this depends on many factors, not least market share and power, and the terms of trade.

SAPs comprised four main elements:

- the mobilization of domestic resources;
- policy reforms to increase economic efficiency;
- the generation of foreign exchange revenue from non-traditional sources through diversification, as well as through increased exports of traditional commodities;
- reducing the active economic role of the state and ensuring that this is non-inflationary.

The specific measures designed to achieve these objectives were generally divided into two categories (Simon, 1995: 5), as follows.

Stabilization measures: these were immediate, short-term steps designed to arrest the deterioration in conditions and to provide a foundation on which longer-term measures could act:

- a public-sector wage freeze – to reduce wage inflation and the government's salary bill;
- reduced subsidies on basic foods and other commodities, and on health and education – to reduce government expenditure;
- devaluation of the currency – to make exports cheaper and hence more competitive, and to deter imports.

Adjustment measures: these were generally to be implemented as a second phase, and would take longer to have an impact; their objective was to promote economic structural adjustment (restructuring) and economic competitiveness:

- export promotion – through incentives (including easier access to foreign exchange and retention of some of hard currency obtained from export revenues) and diversification;
- downsizing the civil service – through retrenchments following a consolidation and rationalization of the public sector, in order to reduce 'overstaffing', duplication, inefficiency and cronyism in job allocation;
- economic liberalization – relaxing and eventually removing many regulations and restrictions on economic activity, both domestic and international, in the name of efficiency. Examples include import quotas and tariffs, import licences, state monopolies, price fixing, implicit or hidden subsidies, restrictions on the repatriation of profits by foreign-owned firms;
- privatization – the selling-off of state enterprises and parastatal corporations, especially loss-making ones, in order to reduce direct economic activity and resource use by the state, and to reduce the size of the civil service;
- tax reductions – to create incentives for individuals and businesses (both local and foreign) to save and invest.

Adoption and implementation of an IMF-approved SAP became a prerequisite for obtaining financial support. The World Bank (WB), regional development banks and most major Northern bilateral donors followed suit, so that it became impossible for an indebted country to borrow from them without a SAP. This *economic conditionality* was complemented in 1990 by *political conditionality*, the prerequisite imposed by the British and other donor governments for so-called 'good governance' as well as approved economic policies.

Refining SAPs and economic recovery programmes

SAPs were refined in the late 1980s and 1990s, taking better account of local circumstances, social development needs, seeking to soften the negative impacts of specific measures, and by supporting continuity of policies and funding. To this end, a distinction emerged between SAPs, which became the initial 3–4 year programme implemented by a country, and follow-up economic recovery programmes (ERPs) of similar duration, and which were designed to promote broader economic restructuring. The principal funding mechanism became the Enhanced Structural Adjustment Facility (ESAF) (Wood, 1997).

Some countries have sought, often with only short-lived success, to avoid the pain of formal SAPs and to retain more sovereignty over economic policy by implementing home-grown equivalents. South Africa remains exceptional in not having any structural adjustment loans.

Particularly with respect to Southeast Asia, the analyses offered by the international financial institutions (IFIs) have changed contradictorily: during the economic boom the rapidly industrializing countries were held up as models of market-led development; as soon as the crisis struck, the problems were blamed on interventionist states, cronyism and inappropriate policies (Dixon, 1999; Mohan et al., 1999).

The take-up of SAPs and ERPs

Despite their unpopularity with debtor countries, the rapid take-up rate of SAPs reflected the dire straits in which an increasing number of countries found themselves and the perceived (and often real) lack of alternatives. By 1987 the World Bank had approved 52 structural adjustment loans and 70 sectoral adjustment loans. During the period 1980–89, 171 SAPs were introduced in sub-Saharan Africa; a further 57 had been initiated by the end of 1996.

Evaluating SAPs and ERPs

The impacts of SAPs were frequently harsh. Many ordinary people rather than the elites or the state bore the brunt of the adjustment burden, although some did benefit. Even the IMF has acknowledged that the early SAPs were excessively economistic and neglected or retarded social development. Initially, packages of palliative measures were hastily created (for example, the Ghanaian Programme of Actions to Mitigate the Social Costs of Adjustment (PAMSCAD) in the mid-1980s), and later SAPs were redesigned to contain a social development component.

The initial presumption, which provided a powerful lever for the IFIs, was that successful adjustment would lead to rapidly increasing foreign direct investment; in practice this has not occurred in most countries (Simon, 1995; Wood, 1997).

Many of the adjustment measures took far longer to have a tangible impact, whereas the pain of stabilization measures, often implemented too hastily and in one fell swoop rather than in stages, was immediate. Until the early 1990s, research found little difference in economic performance between strong and weak reformers in Africa. However, more recent evaluations of ERPs tend to be less critical overall, and to discern some marked benefits (but compare Bracking, 1999; Mohan et al., 1999).

One indirect – and arguably desirable – effect has been to adjust the rural–urban terms of trade substantially, by eliminating much of the urban bias implicit in traditional policies of infrastructural provision and price subsidization. Economists have evaluated SAPs and ERPs almost exclusively on a sector-by-sector basis at the national scale. However, this is inadequate and precludes assessment of the impacts upon different social groups and subnational spaces (such as urban, rural, regional) in a situation where there is no reason to believe the effects to be socially and geographically neutral (Simon, 1995).

Among the worst affected groups have been the urban poor and – predominantly – urban-based civil servants, who have lost jobs, suffered severe salary erosion, and faced steep commodity price increases as commodity subsidies have been slashed, and transport fares and utility prices have been commercialized.

Conversely, the principal beneficiaries have been large traders and import–export merchants (as a result of liberalization and improved foreign exchange availability), and rural agricultural producers, including peasants who have a saleable surplus, on account of higher producer prices for their crops.

However, in some countries, food security has been undermined as a result of IMF insistence that food crop production be switched to cash crops for export if comparative advantage existed. For example, in the late 1970s, the Sudanese government promoted food security through maize cultivation. This achieved its objective by 1981, but the process was reversed in favour of cotton production under the country's first SAP. By 1984, world cotton prices fell as Sudan and several other countries increased exports under SAPs, so the revenue was inadequate to pay for needed cereal imports, yet people could not eat the cotton. Famine threatened, causing much suffering and bitterness. Similarly, Zimbabwe was pressurized into selling its maize surplus from the bumper 1991–92 harvest rather than retaining it as a buffer stock. When the rains failed over the following two years, massive maize imports became necessary at a price far higher than that obtained for exporting the previous surplus. Zimbabweans, not the IMF, bore the cost.

The environment has suffered in different ways, as a result of marginal land being brought into cultivation or fallow periods being squeezed in order to grow more food to compensate for lost subsidies or to yield a surplus for export. Tropical forests have been logged at a faster rate to generate export earnings (Reed, 1992).

Finally, economic and political conditionalities attached to SAPs and ERPs represent an unprecedented invasion of the hitherto sacrosanct right of sovereign states to determine their own economic and political policies (Helleiner, 1992; Bracking, 1999; Mohan *et al.*, 1999). This argument has been exploited by many government leaders seeking to deflect the hostility of protesters against food price increases and other measures.

THE NEW INCARNATION: POVERTY REDUCTION STRATEGIES

During 1999, image management and changing fashion led to the introduction of a new vocabulary and objective. Out went SAPs and ERPs in favour of an apparently more positive and co-operative façade, known as poverty reduction strategies (PRSs). This fits well with the major donors' reinvention of development assistance (previously aid) as 'partnerships' since the late 1990s (Kifle *et al.*, 1997; Närman, 1999), and also the adoption of poverty reduction or elimination as *leitmotif* of development policies by several donors, most notably the British Labour Party government that took office in 1997 (Burnell, 1998).

Inevitably under such circumstances, poverty reduction means different things in different contexts. However, the IMF and WB have adopted PRSs as the successor to SAPs. Kenya became one of the first countries to experience the effects of the shift. IMF budgetary support lending was suspended in 1998 because of the government's failure to adhere to the terms of its SAP. Negotiations on a resumption have now become conditional on the production by the government and approval by the IFIs of a poverty reduction strategy paper (PRSP). This document was redrafted and negotiated during 2000. Only after agreement thereon will negotiations on a poverty reduction and growth facility (as the ESAF has been renamed) commence. However, the veneer is rather thin, since poverty is only indirectly the concern, via SAP-type economic reforms.

The rather tenuous assumption is that neo-liberal macro-economic reform will promote a reduction in poverty as a result of leaner, fitter and more efficient economic management and political governance. During preparation of the PRSP's predecessor, the National Poverty Eradication Plan for 1999–2000, civil society NGOs lobbied hard for an approach in which poverty reduction would get priority, in turn promoting economic development. The WB failed to support it. Hence, the current cynicism and scathing criticisms of the PRS on the part of NGO activists, civil society and the media are easy to appreciate.

A tour of the WB's website in early April 2000 was most revealing: the language of SAPs and ERPs had been purged, and replaced by extensive and attractive coverage of the highly indebted poor country (HIPC) debt reduction initiative and the new PRSs, complete with a section on 'what the poor say', based on consultations in several countries (see http://www.worldbank.org/poverty).

CONCLUSION

The resurgence of the conservative doctrine of neo-liberalism at the end of the 1970s was rapidly translated into development and aid policies by the Northern donors and IFIs at the onset of the debt crisis. This amounted to blaming the victims and requiring them to bear the full costs of adjustment and recovery. These market-oriented and trade-integrationist policies were embodied in SAPs and then ERPs, comprising a mixture of short-term stabilization and longer-term adjustment measures. Much hardship has been caused, often to some of the most vulnerable people, although many rural producers have benefited from agricultural and marketing reforms. The environmental costs have sometimes been substantial too. However, urban bias has been reduced; for a short period in the mid- to late 1980s, it appears even to have been reversed in some African countries like Ghana and Tanzania. The initially crude and economistic policies were gradually refined and more carefully targeted. Evaluations need to be more comprehensive and disaggregated than has usually been the case. Very recently, the language and presentation of macro-economic reform programmes have been transformed under the guise of PRSs, but there has been little substantive change.

GUIDE TO FURTHER READING

The literature on SAPs and ERPs is vast but the following texts represent a selection of useful surveys of particular issues or perspectives.

Husain, I. and Faruqee, R. (eds) (1996) *Adjustment in Africa: Lessons from Country Case Studies*, Aldershot: Avebury for the World Bank. One of the most useful World Bank outputs, covering Burundi, Côte d'Ivoire, Ghana, Kenya, Nigeria, Senegal and Tanzania.

Mahjoub, A. (ed.) (1990) *Adjustment or Delinking? The African Experience*, London: Zed Books and Tokyo: United Nations University. A collection of radical essays examining the issues of delinking from the world economy as an alternative to SAPs.

Mohan, G., Brown, E., Millward, B. and Zack-Williams, A. (eds) (1999) *Structural Adjustment: Theory, Practice and Impacts*, London: Routledge. A recent collection addressing the origins, evolution and especially the negative impacts of SAPs; provides examples, careful critiques and suggested alternatives.

Reed, D. (ed.) (1992) *Structural Adjustment and the Environment*, London: Earthscan. This is probably still the only book-length treatment of the environmental consequences of SAPs.

Simon, D., Van Spengen, W., Dixon, C. and Närman, A. (eds) (1995) *Structurally Adjusted Africa: Poverty, Debt and Basic Needs*, London and Boulder: Pluto. Studies the implications of SAPs on different parts of Africa at different scales, from the supranational to the regional and local.

REFERENCES

Bracking, S. (1999) 'Structural adjustment: why it wasn't necessary and why it didn't work', *Review of African Political Economy* 26(80): 207–26.

Burnell, P. (1998) 'Britain's new government, new White Paper, new aid? Eliminating world poverty: a challenge for the 21st century', *Third World Quarterly* 19(4): 787–802.

Dixon, C. (1999) 'The Pacific Asian challenge to neoliberalism', in D. Simon, and A. Närman, (eds) *Development as Theory and Practice: Current Perspectives on Development and Development Co-operation*, Harlow: Longman.

Helleiner, G. (1992) 'The IMF, the World Bank and Africa's adjustment and external debt problems: an unofficial view', *World Development* 20(6): 779–92.

Kifle, H., Olukoshi, A.O. and Wohlgemuth, L. (eds) (1997) *A New Partnership for African Development: Issues and Parameters*, Uppsala: Nordiska Afrikainstitutet.

Närman, A. (1999) 'Getting towards the beginning of the end for traditional development aid: major trends in development thinking and its practical application over the last fifty years', in D. Simon, and A. Närman, (eds) *Development as Theory and Practice: Current Perspectives on Development and Development co-Operation*, Harlow: Longman.

Simon, D. (1995) 'Debt, democracy and development in Africa in the 1990s', in D. Simon, W. Van Spengen, C. Dixon, and A. Närman, (eds) *Structurally Adjusted Africa: Poverty, Debt and Basic Needs*, London and Boulder: Pluto.

Wood, A. (1997) *The International Monetary Fund's Enhanced Structural Adjustment Facility: What Role for Development?*, Briefing Paper, Bretton Woods Project (available on the Project's website at http://www.brettonwoodsproject.org/brief/esaf.html).

2.7 The Latin American structuralists

Colin Clarke

Structuralism is a critique of development economics that was initiated by Latin American social scientists during the 1950s. It has much in common with marginality, internal colonialism and dependency, all of which are predicated on the idea that the countries of Latin America – and, by extrapolation, other Third World countries – are structurally disadvantaged. All four themes are discussed together here, and the linkages and parallels between them are explored. In essence, the Latin American countries are unlikely to follow the stages of economic growth mapped out by the advanced or early capitalist countries. The very existence of a capitalist core (in the Northern Hemisphere) places peripheral countries (and peripheral regions *vis-à-vis* developed regions within countries) at a perpetual, perhaps even an increasing, competitive disadvantage.

Structuralist tenets were first advanced by a group of Latin American economists working for the Economic Commission for Latin America (ECLA), a United Nations agency established in 1947 in Santiago, Chile. Under its Executive Secretary, Raúl Prebisch, the ECLA school of thought, or the ECLA theory of development, was initiated, the main thrust of which was to construe the international economic order as polarized between an industrial centre and an agrarian periphery. Moreover, ECLA argued that the disparities between the core and periphery were reproduced through world trade and the terms of trade; in short, the world economy was competitive and the colonial or ex-colonial periphery, as producer and exporter of primary products, was disadvantaged. So, Latin American countries had to industrialize, but to do so they had to protect themselves from competition (Kay, 1989).

The ECLA school, drawing on evidence from Chile and Argentina during the 1920s and 1930s, advocated a policy of import-substitution industrialization (ISI) to enable peripheral countries to switch from 'outward-looking development' to an 'inward-directed' one. The role of the state was crucial in this, because it was required to raise tariff barriers against imported manufactured goods, and even to embark upon land reform. The placing of land, and other resources, in the hands of social groups that had previously been excluded, became a vital step in expanding the consumption capacity of the rural population, thus countering the inelastic demand for durable manufactured goods among the urban middle classes (Prebisch, 1950).

These ideas were sufficiently accepted by the early 1960s for many of them to be embraced by the US Alliance for Progress and a number of reformist, democratic governments in Latin America. Within a decade, however, the development paradigm was shifting. The easy phase of ISI had passed, so it was argued, and as the need to substitute intermediate and capital goods arose, so the shortage of investment funds and foreign exchange produced stasis. A widening gap appeared between the 'formally' and 'informally' employed, particularly in the urban areas – Furtado's stagnating underdevelopment (Furtado, 1964) – given that there was no mass market.

Marginality was the term initially used to refer to dwellings on the periphery of the city generated by the rapid process of urbanization experienced in Latin America during the 1950s and 1960s. Later it came to be applied to shanty-town dwellers who had poor working and living conditions, particularly those who were marginal to the process of capital-intensive industrialization associated with ISI. Two theoretical interpretations of marginality have dominated the literature: one argued that marginality reflected a lack of integration into capitalist society, which was achievable; the other interpreted marginality as a product of capitalism and argued that the solution depended on the introduction of socialism (Kay, 1989).

Germani argued that marginality was made up of several distinct forms, which individuals and groups experienced in different combinations. Typically, marginality might affect the productive sub-system (from total unemployment to low productive self-employment), the consumption sub-system (degree of access to goods and services), the cultural and political sub-systems, and so on. Only when an individual or a group experienced high rates of exclusion was it possible to speak of absolute marginality (Germani, 1981). Incorporation, on the other hand, might have involved shanty-town dwellers setting up neighbourhood committees to promote improved access to building materials, education or health.

This interpretation of marginality as an aspect of modernization has been criticized by Quijano. Rather than reflecting non-integration, marginality implied for him a particular manner of integration. Marginal workers sought refuge in the marginal pole of the economy where they formed a marginal petty bourgeoisie or a marginal proletariat (Quijano, 1977). Nun (1969), in a similar vein, used the term 'marginal mass' to parallel Marx's ideas about relative surplus labour and the industrial reserve army. For Nun, marginality reflected the failure of Latin American industrialization to absorb urban labour, whether migrant or not.

Internal colonialism, likewise, was developed to challenge the conventional wisdom of *indigenismo* in Latin America, namely that the 'Indian' population should be subjected to enlightened, planned, non-coercive integration into the mainstream of society. Stavenhagen (1963) and González-Casanova (1965), published criticisms of official *indigenismo* in the early 1960s, the former deploying the term 'colonialism', the latter 'internal colonialsim' in their analyses of Indians in Mexico. Their main concern was to shift from the sphere of the Indian community to that of the inter-cultural region where Indians and *mestizos* co-existed. For both authors, the emphasis was on dominating and dominated blocks that are culturally different. Modally, *mestizos* were urban and exploited rural Indians through the market mechanism via profit.

In the appendix to his paper, González-Casanova set out a check-list of the forms of internal colonialism: (a) monopoly and dependence, which examined unequal exchange via trade and credit, and the use of the internal colony as a labour reserve; (b) relations of production and social control, which provided an inventory of different types of exploitation – such as through language – in trade, at law, and in wages; (c) culture and living standards, in which the impoverishment of the Indians was highlighted.

Internal colonialism has been criticized on many grounds: that it overemphasized culture; that economic exploitation of Indians at the marketplace was not inevitable; and that it stressed opposition of *mestizos* to Indian-language speakers in situations that were becoming increasingly fluid, given both bilinguilism and economic development. Moreover, indigenous language speakers were ever more self-confident, partly through the migratory experiences that have enabled them to transcend the isolation of their rural communities. Finally, Indians were not homogeneous; they were often ranked, by language group, in terms of power; by no means were they universally subservient to *mestizos* (Clarke, 1996).

The model of internal colonialism was attractive because it brought peasantry, class, culture and race into a clear set of interrelationships that were characterized as spatial (urban–rural) dichotomies reminiscent of core and periphery. But it was too simple and deterministic a set of linkages; while powerfully suggestive, it was unlikely that the complex social variables being investigated would in all places fall out in this way.

Dependency theory developed after internal colonialism, and Frank's *Capitalism and Underdevelopment in Latin America* (1967) contains a chapter on the Indian Problem that cites Stavenhagen's work. Dependency, like internal colonialism, uses the notions of core and periphery, extraction of surplus value and exploitation. Indeed, the metropolis–satellite relationship of internal colonialism appears as a local-level system of exploitation nesting within the more global First World–Third World opposition. Frank used Marxism to re-write ECLA's structuralism: economic development and underdevelopment were the opposite faces of the same coin. Both were the necessary result and contemporary manifestation of the world capitalist system.

Although dependency theory in the English-speaking world focused on the work of Frank, the main body of contributors was Latin American. They may be divided into two groups, as in the case of marginality theory: Marxists and reformists. The former found their solution to dependence and underdevelopment in a socialist revolution, while reformist *dependentistas* viewed this as utopian, preferring to argue for the reform of the international economic system (also utopian). The reformists were essentially a branch of the ECLA school. Nevertheless, both dependency traditions concurred that developed countries had an endogenous capacity for growth and were dominant, while underdeveloped countries lacked that dynamic and were dependent on foreign investment and technology (Kay, 1989).

For Sunkel, one of the reformist writers, capitalist development was seen as a process of creative destruction. ISI led to greater foreign indebtedness and foreign ownership, as export earnings failed to grow and sustain development (Sunkel, 1967). Lack of an independent capacity for technological innovation, coupled with the transplantation to Latin American countries of developed world consumption patterns, were seen as flaws in dependent development by Furtado (1973). Cardoso and Faletto married ECLA's economic structuralism to social and political analysis. Paying particular attention to the middle class, they showed how internal developments were linked to external changes in the world system. Dependency, in their view, was not inimical to development, but it did involve an association between the national bourgeoisie and international capitalism and led to increased impoverishment and marginalization (Cardoso and Faletto, 1979).

Marxist *dependentistas* agreed that underdevelopment was rooted in the capitalist development of the imperialist countries, and that underdevelopment and development were the common outcome of a worldwide process of capital accumulation. Marini, for example, argued that the basis for dependence was the over-exploitation of labour in the subordinate nations (1973). An outgrowth of this situation was sub-imperialism, a situation experienced in Brazil under the military in the 1960s and 1970s. It involved industrial exports; concentration of income in the hands of the middle class to stimulate consumption; and an increase in the state's demand for consumer durables and capital goods.

According to Marini, this project involved an alliance between the bourgoisie and foreign capitalists. The former offered the prospects of investment and profits in Brazil in return for access to advanced technology and the world market controlled by multinational corporations (Marini, 1971). For Dos Santos, however, dependence was firmly rooted in technological dependency, and ISI was flawed as a national project because industry was controlled by foreign capital. The only way forward was via socialism, or harking back to Brazil, via unacceptable 'fascist barbarism' (Dos Santos, 1978).

Dependence or underdevelopment, for Frank, was based on the central idea that it was the capitalist development of the now developed countries that had engendered underdeveloped structures in the Third World and continued to reproduce them. Dependence was not a condition that lay between Latin America and world capitalism, but was part and parcel of Latin American society itself. So for Frank, too, national liberation hinged on a socialist revolution (1972).

These variegated structuralist approaches by Latin American social scientists have been marginalized by the hegemony of the economic orthodoxy emanating from the World Bank since the 1970s, though neo-liberalism has been widely adopted as policy throughout Latin America only since the 1980s. Tariff-protected ISI, so beloved of ECLA, has been turned inside out. Now trade liberalization accompanied by export-orientated industrialization is the model to be emulated. It is argued that ISI foundered, as some ECLA advocates feared, on the rocks of inelastic national demand for consumer durables and other goods.

Structural adjustment packages, funded by the World Bank to enable Latin American countries to manage their debt, have involved not only tariff reduction and outward-orientated development, but also cuts in public-sector funding and investment, coupled with privatization. As the state has retreated, the changing nature of urban economies has increased the reliance of the labour force on precarious employment, and has limited access to formal employment opportunities, particularly for workers with low skill levels. Structuralism, dependence and exploitation are banned from the neo-liberal vocabulary, though free trade has neo-colonial overtones. The vast urban populations in Latin America are currently more marginal from the formal economy than at any time for half a century (Gwynne and Kay, 1999).

GUIDE TO FURTHER READING

An excellent review of the use of structuralism by Latin American social scientists is provided in Cristóbal Kay's *Latin American Theories of Development and Underdevelopment*. For a recent evaluation of Latin

American development in the context of neo-liberalism, but with a reference back to the structuralists see Robert N. Gwynne and Cristóbal Kay, *Latin America Transformed: Globalization and Modernity*, 1999.

REFERENCES

Cardoso, Fernando Henrique and Faletto, Ernesto (1979) *Dependency and Devlopment in Latin America*, Berkeley and Los Angeles: University of California Press.

Clarke, Colin (1996) 'Cultural pluralism and economic development: perspectives from 20th-century Mexico and the Caribbean', in Denis Dwyer and David Drakakis-Smith (eds) *Ethnicity and Development: Geographical Perspectives*, London: John Wiley.

Dos Santos, Theotonio (1978) *Imperialismo y Dependencia*, Mexico: Ediciones Era.

Frank, André Gunder (1967) *Capitalism and Underdevelopment in Latin America*, London and New York: Monthly Review Press.

Frank, André Gunder (1972) 'Economic dependence, class structure and underdevelopment policy', in J.D. Cockroft, André Gunder Frank and D.L. Johnson (eds) *Dependence and Underdevelopment: Latin America's Political Economy*, New York: Doubleday.

Furtado, Celso (1964) *Development and Underdevelopment: a Structural View of the Problems of Developed and Underdeveloped Countries*, Berkeley: University of California Press.

Furtado, Celso (1973) 'The concept of external dependence in the study of underdevelopment', in C.K. Wilber (ed.) *The Political Economy of Development and Underdevelopment*, New York: Random House.

Germani, G. (1981) *The Sociology of Modernization: Studies in its Historical Aspects with Special Regard to the Latin American Case*, New Brunswick: Transaction Books.

González-Casanova, Pablo (1965) 'Internal colonialism and national development', *Studies in Comparative International Development* 1(4); reprinted in 1969 in Irving L. Horowiz, J. de Castro and John Gerassi (eds), *Latin American Radicalism*, London: Johnathan Cape, pp. 118–39.

Gwynne, Robert N. and Kay, Cristóbal (1999) (eds) *Latin America Transformed: Globalization and Modernity*, London: Arnold.

Kay, Cristóbal (1989) *Latin American Theories of Development and Underdevelopment*, London and New York: Routledge.

Marini, R.M. (1971) 'El Subimperialismo Brasileño', *Documento de Trabajo*, CESO, Universidad de Chile; re-issued in 1972 as 'Brazilian Subimperialism', *Monthly Review* 23(9).

Marini, R.M. (1973) *Dialéctica de la Dependencia*, Mexico: Ediciones Era.

Nun, J. (1969) 'Superpoblación Relativa, Ejército Industrial de Reserva y Masa Marginal', *Revista LatinoAmericana de Sociología* 5(2).

Prebisch, Raúl (1950) *The Economic Development of Latin America and its Principal Problems*, New York: United Nations.

Quijano, A. (1977) *Imperialismo y 'Marginalidad' en América Latina*, Lima: Mosca Azul Editores.

Stavenhagen, Rodolfo (1963) 'Clases, Colonialism y Aculturación: Ensayo Sobre un Sistema de Relaciones Interétnicas en Mesoamérica', *America Latina*, 6(4); reprinted in 1970 as 'Classes, colonialism and aculturation: a system of inter-ethnic relations in Mesoamerica', in Irving Horowitz (ed.) *Masses in Latin America*, London: Oxford University Press, pp. 235–88.

Sunkel, Osvaldo (1967) 'Política Nacional de Desarrollo y Dependencia Externa', *Estudios Internacionales* 1(1).

2.8 Classical dependency theories: from ECLA to André Gunder Frank

Dennis Conway and Nikolas Heynen

Dependency Theory, more than a theoretical construct, is a way of understanding historically embedded, political-economic relations of peripheral capitalist countries, especially Latin American countries, within the broader context of the global economy. It is, essentially, a *critique* of the development paths, policies and strategies followed in Latin America (Palma, 1981), and elsewhere in the periphery. *Dependency Theory* emerged as a critical lens through which the history of Latin American development, marginalized as it was by Western hegemony, could be better understood; the 'development of underdevelopment', no less. The initial theorization was a *structuralist* perspective by economists associated with the United Nations Economic Commission for Latin America (ECLA). This was soon transformed, and informed, by more critical *dependency* notions and the spread of Marxist critiques of imperialism (Palma, 1978).

Perhaps one of *Dependency Theory*'s most important characteristics is that it was a product of Latin American scholarship (much of it written in Spanish) rather than Western or North American/European scholars. These authorities theorized on the Latin American condition as 'insiders', as erstwhile, often passionate, native sons. This gave rise to a more informed, and more involved, appreciation of the reasons for Latin American underdevelopment as *Dependentistas* dealt with the context of various countries' specific national circumstances, and theorized about Latin America's structures of social organization and localized behaviours. For Caribbean (and English-speaking) readers, Norman Girvan (1973) edited a special edition of *Social and Economic Studies* in 1973, with contributions translated from the Spanish. More widely, it was the publication of the writings of André Gunder Frank (and the collection and translation of other Latin American original contributions by North American Latin Americanists), that brought the *Dependency School*'s ideas to the notice of North American and European development studies.

Baran's influential (1957) *Political Economy of Growth* described the reasons for Latin America's underdevelopment within a Marxist framework as being a consequence of advanced nations' forming special partnerships with powerful elite classes in less developed, or pre-capitalist countries (see figure overleaf). Such alliances were, of course, detrimental to the capitalist development of such 'backward' economies, since they benefited the minority class of Latin American elites rather than advancing economic development at large. Such 'partnerships', according to Baran, perpetuated the ability of core countries to maintain traditional systems of surplus extraction, thereby making domestic resources continuously available and making economic development of Latin American counties unlikely, since any surplus generated was appropriated by the elites. This would then enable core countries to keep Latin American counties subordinated and thus ensure their monopoly-power to maintain a steady flow of cheap primary resources.

André Gunder Frank (1967, 1969, 1970) then further developed Baran's ideas, focusing upon the dependent character of peripheral Latin American economies. In Frank's prognosis, the 'development of underdevelopment' was the concept which best characterized the capitalist dynamics that both developed the core countries and at the same time caused greater levels of underdevelopment and dependency within Latin American countries. Frank used this conceptual framework to explain the dualistic capitalist relations which had occurred, and which he felt would continue

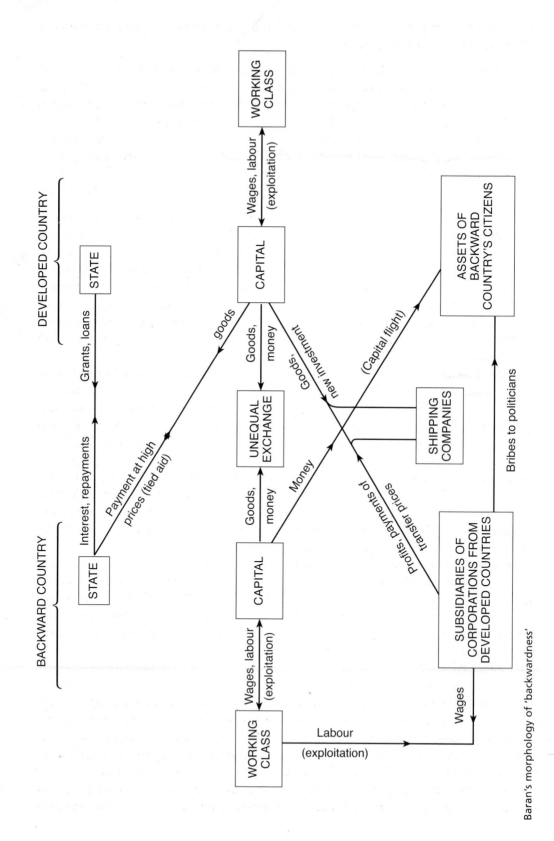

Baran's morphology of 'backwardness'

to occur between Latin American and core counties, as a result of the continued domination of Latin America by the core. He proposed:

> A mounting body of evidence suggests, and I am confident that future historical research will confirm, that the expansion of the capitalist system over the past centuries effectively and entirely penetrated even the apparently most isolated sectors of the underdeveloped world. Therefore, the economic, political, social, and cultural institutions and relations we now observe there are the products of the historical development of the capitalist system no less than are the seemingly more modern or capitalist features of the national metropoles of these underdeveloped countries.
>
> (Frank, 1966: 18)

Although there was a popular perception that Third World countries regained some sense of self-determination following the decolonization of their national lands, Frank argued that this was a fallacy. Exploitation by the core of many Third World counties intensified following decolonization, further contributing to greater unequal relations. Thus, given the class-based stratification of Latin American society, which Baran blamed for the development of ties between Latin American elites, and capitalist and political leaders from core countries, revolutionary action to remove such elites from power would be needed to forge a reformulation of international capitalist relations. Frank (1969) suggested this was only possible through revolutionary action which strove to install socialist ideals within the political systems of the dependent countries.

Besides arguing that the dependent core–periphery relationship was best articulated at the national scale, Frank also posited that a similar metropolis–satellite relationship occurred at smaller (regional) scales. In particular, he described similar dependent circumstances occurring between cities in Latin American countries and colonies and their non-urban peripheries. He illustrates this relationship within the context of the privilege that has always existed for colonial Latin American cities. As the place of administration for colonial powers, the city has always been the power-base from which the expansion of capitalism has spread. Within this more localized scenario, the city and its peripheral hinterland becomes increasingly polarized as a result of the capitalist relations between them, namely the metropolis exploiting its satellites. Given the localized nature of this relationship, dense networks of metropolis–satellite combinations form what Frank referred to as 'constellations across national space' (Frank, 1967).

Frank used various historical Latin American examples to illustrate the dependent relationships he theorizes, albeit strictly non-Andean Latin American cases. The two most notable cases he examines are the Chilean and Brazilian contexts. Concerning Chile, Frank (1967) suggests that not only did the country's conquest lead Chile to be incorporated into the mercantile and industrial capitalist systems, but it also introduced the monopolistic core–periphery, or metropolis–satellite, structure into Chilean economy, polity and society.

Presenting the Brazilian context as the clearest case of national and regional underdevelopment, Frank explains how the expansion of capitalism, beginning in the sixteenth century, sequentially incorporated vast hinterlands and their cores into the global economy by transforming them into export nodes. Such cities as Rio de Janeiro, São Paulo, and Paraná figured most prominently in this capitalist expansion. Although the initial impact of exportation seemed to develop the concerned nodes, Frank (1967) shows how this process led to underdeveloped development that significantly, and negatively, impacted on the regions' economy, polity and society in the long term.

Frank's notions of *dependencia* as perpetuated through global capitalism ran counter to dualist notions that sought to explain Latin America's peripheral position in terms of modern versus traditional structures. Frank contended that by conceptualizing Latin America's position as a function of feudal or traditional structures, the dualist perspective failed to truly comprehend the historical significance and transformative impact capitalism's introduction had upon the continent's economic, political and social structures. The dependent relationship Frank posited as a counter-explanation to such dualist notions drew sharp criticism from many, however. Laclau's (1971) analysis of Frank's theorization is perhaps the most notable.

Laclau asserted that Frank's analytical method has significant shortcomings because it is based on an erroneous characterization of Marx's notion of modes of production. Instead of basing the construction of a mode of production on social or class relations, as Marx did, Laclau claims that Frank's reliance on market relations as the defining quality of the processes under which production occurs is inherently flawed. To Laclau, Frank constructs a circular concept of capitalism which has an inherent imbalance. Although profitable production as a result of exchange value is dominant in such a capitalist system, the opposite may not always be true; i.e. profitable production in the market is not necessarily a signal of capitalist production. Hence the imbalance in global levels and patterns of development results from the expansion of a global capitalist market as opposed to the exploitation of free labour.

Frank's focus on the market as opposed to class relations creates an uneasy tension within his analysis, given his proclamation of the necessity for class-based revolution as the only means of ending dependency upon the core. Laclau concludes that as a result of the flawed interpretation of the mode of production, Frank's analysis offers little more than a historical account of a history that is well reported; in effect, he contributes nothing to theoretical explanation.

Another notable critique of Frank's *Dependency* notions is offered by Lall (1975), who suggests that those characteristics which exist within underdeveloped dependent countries, and which thereby explain such dependency, not only exist in such contexts, but also in other non-dependent countries. According to Lall, this suggests that many characteristics attributed to dependent capitalism are really just a consequence of capitalism more generally. Too often, he suggests, *dependency* analysts selectively choose unfavourable characteristics that exist in underdeveloped countries, and categorize them as results of dependent relations, without establishing their generalizability elsewhere.

The resultant tensions within Frank's analytical framework as a result of arguably incorrect, or less than accurate, usage of Marxist ideology, led the way to other neo-Marxist investigations of the linkages and possible reconciliation between *Dependency Theory* and Marxism. Chilcote's (1982) collection interrogates this seemingly uneasy relationship most stringently. Seeking to 'end the debate', Chilcote's contributors examine many of the linkages between dependency and Marxism, ranging from modes of production and class analysis to the differences between historical-materialist methods of inquiry and those utilized within the dependency framework. A later synthesis by Chilcote (1984), also effectively situates the various capitalist and socialist approaches to the 'development of underdevelopment' – *structuralism, dependencia, internal colonialism, neo-Marxism, even Trotskyism* – as a full set of alternative theories and perspectives on development and underdevelopment. He also finds a place for Wallerstein's more worldly focus in the collection.

Using notions of dependency as an impetus, Wallerstein (1974, 1979, 1980) adapted *dependency* notions to not only comment on the commercial relations between the core countries and Latin America, but rather examined world historiography in terms of the dominant and subordinate relations, successive emerging cores, their peripheries and semi-peripheries have experienced, from the 'long sixteenth century', through eras of capitalism to the present globalizing era. Wallerstein's 'World Systems Theory' complements and expands upon Frank's ideas, providing a larger global scale which is useful for understanding global commercial capitalist relations more completely. Another important authority in development studies who has utilized and expanded upon the notion of *Dependency* is Samir Amin (1974, 1976). Amin critically examined the dependant economic relations of Africa since European colonization, and found them destructive and disastrous consequences of that continent's peripheral capitalist condition. Equally persuasive, and also in line with Frank's assessment of Latin American underdevelopment, Guyana's Walter Rodney (1972) depicted the historical underdevelopment of the African continent and its peoples as a consequence of capitalism, colonialism and imperialism. All three 'voices from the periphery' – Frank, Amin and Rodney – brought a passion and an urgency to their arguments, which adds substantially to the lasting legacy of the *Dependency School* as a critique of neo-classical economic development formulations.

GUIDE TO FURTHER READING AND REFERENCES

*Items marked with an asterisk provide key introductory readings to the concept of dependency.

Amin, S. (1974) *Accumulation on a World Scale: A Critique of the Theory of Underdevelopment*, 2 vols, New York: Monthly Review Press.

*Amin, S. (1976) *Unequal Development: An Essay on the Social Formation of Peripheral Capitalism*, New York: Monthly Review Press.

Baran, P. (1957) *The Political Economy of Growth*, New York: Monthly Review Press.

Chilcote, R.H. (1982) *Dependency and Marxism: Toward a Resolution of the Debate*, Boulder, CO: Westview Press.

*Chilcote, R.H. (1984) *Theories of Development and Underdevelopment*, Boulder and London: Westview Press.

*Frank, A.G. (1966) 'The development of underdevelopment', *Monthly Review* 18(4): 17–31.

Frank, A.G. (1967) *Capitalism and Underdevelopment in Latin America: Historical Studies of Chile and Brazil*, New York and London: Monthly Review Press.

Frank, A.G. (1969) *Latin America: Underdevelopment or Revolution*, New York: Monthly Review Press.

Frank, A.G. (1970) *Lumpen-Bourgoisie: Lumpen-Development, Dependency, Class, and Politics in Latin America*, New York and London: Monthly Review Press.

*Girvan, N. (1973) 'Dependence and underdevelopment in the New World and the Old', Special Issue, Social and Economic Studies 22(1).

Laclau, E. (1971) 'Feudalism and capitalism in Latin America', *New Left Review*, May–June: 19–38.

Lall, S. (1975) 'Is dependence a useful concept in analyzing underdevelopment?', *World Development* 3(11): 799–810.

*Palma, G. (1978) 'Dependency: a formal theory of underdevelopment or a methodology for the analysis of concrete situations of underdevelopment?', *World Development* 14(3): 881–924.

Palma, G. (1981) 'Dependency and development: a critical overview', in D. Seers (ed.) *Dependency Theory: A Critical Assessment*, London: Frances Pinter, pp. 20–78.

Rodney, W. (1972) *How Europe Underdeveloped Africa*, London: Bogle-L'Ouverture.

Wallerstein, I. (1974) *The Modern World System. Volume 1: Capitalist Agriculture and the Origins of the European World-Economy in the Sixteenth Century*, New York: Academic Press.

Wallerstein, I. (1979) *The Capitalist World Economy: Essays,* New York: Cambridge University Press.

Wallerstein, I. (1980) *The Modern World System. Volume 2: Mercantilism and Consolidation of the European World-Economy, 1600–1750,* New York: Academic Press.

2.9 The New World Group of dependency scholars: reflections on a Caribbean avant-garde movement

Don D. Marshall

This chapter neither aspires to a chronology nor historical sequencing of events. Instead it retrospectively examines the rise and demise of an intellectual movement in the Anglophone Caribbean under the animating force of decolonization. Allowance is made for a foray into the reasons behind the thwarted impulses of that age and the present decline of radical critique in the modern neo-liberal period.

INTRODUCTION: POST-NEW WORLD INTELLECTUAL CURRENTS

Some 40 years since the emergence of the New World movement, it might be reasonable to expect that gathering forces in the international system – shaped by the imperatives of globalization – would present the spectre of the emergence once more of vital new political forces. Then, as now, the region was thrown back into contemplation of the relevance of its development strategy. With the benefit of the backward glance, 'New World' was first founded in Georgetown towards the end of 1962 against the backdrop of a long general strike and growing racial conflict between African-Guyanese and Indian-Guyanese. The early founders aspired to invent an indigenous view of the region, convinced that the modernization ideologies very much in vogue neither inhered a strategy for real, independent development nor understanding of the economic legacy of the Caribbean, of which more later.

Currently, Caribbean intellectuals in the main, particularly its social scientists, take on the colour of their historical environs: if neo-liberal capitalism cannot be successfully challenged, then to all intents and purposes it does not exist; all that remains is the challenge of massaging a link between market liberalization and populist-statism. To be sure, this concern among Caribbean scholars and commentators does not preclude expression of despair in some quarters over the sustainability of the island-national project of the Caribbean. This forecast is based on an understanding of the export-impetus girding contemporary capitalism and the difficulties associated with making the transition in political economies dominated by merchant capital.

DECOLONIZATION AND THE RISE OF NEW WORLD

The New World movement in the Anglophone Caribbean was marked by an optimism of will and intellect. Newly independent governments were seen to be in pursuit of development guideposts to chart a self-reliant future. At the popular level, claims for social equality through redistribution became intensely salient as an expression of justice. And knowledge producers both within the academic and literary community, no longer under the heel of colonial power, focused energies either on transformative or ameliorative development agendas. Social dialogue and action seemed governed by an impulse towards West Indian self-definition manifested in discussions on race, class and culture, and the question of ownership and control of the region's resources. The general decolonization horizon within which such mood and thought moved was also marked by raging debates occurring in the academic world between modernization theorists and neo-

Marxist scholars. The New World group of, largely, historians and social scientists would come to draw from, and intervene in, these debates, combining serious inquiry into the development possibilities under capitalism, with integrative, normative and programmatic thinking on nation-building.

Considered by their pragmatic counterparts in government, media and academy as 'radicals', this cluster of writers and debaters across the Caribbean came to be known as the New World Group (NWG). Their thoughts and ideas on socialism, national self-determination and the delimiting horizons of capitalism reached a West Indian mass audience through public lecture series, national forums, and newspapers and newsletters of their creation. The *New World*, a Jamaica-based magazine, first appeared in 1963 and was published fortnightly under the editorship of Lloyd Best with assistance from a host of University of the West Indies (UWI, Mona Campus) scholars: George Beckford, Owen Jefferson, Roy Augier, Derek Gordon, Don Robotham and Trevor Munroe, to list a few. From 1965, *New World* was published as a quarterly (NWQ). Bearing the imprint of the UWI, the 'New World' would serve as a loose association attaching its name to anti-imperialist, consciousness-raising activity across the region. Indeed NWGs were said to be formed in St Vincent, St Lucia, Washington DC, Montreal, St Kitts, Trinidad, Barbados, Anguilla, Jamaica and Guyana. Other publications that appeared either as complements to, or refinements of, *New World*'s mission included *Moko* and *Tapia*, Trinidad-based weekly newspapers appearing in 1969, *Abeng*, a Jamaican newsletter launched in the same year, and the 1970 St Lucia-based *Forum*.

The first issue of NWQ focused on Guyana's development dilemma. The analysis therein moved beyond conventional state-centric explanations about the country's savings gap, low technologies, unskilled, undifferentiated labour markets and inadequate infrastructure. Guyana's and indeed the Caribbean's limited development, it was argued, was a function of the region's structural dependent linkages with Europe in terms of its value system and its economic relations. This point of view resonated with the dependency perspective first advanced by Paul Baran and subsequently extended by others who specialized in Latin American area studies. It was certainly a more assimilable 'angle' for Norman Girvan and Owen Jefferson to deploy in their doctoral theses explaining Jamaican underdevelopment (*circa* 1972), than the market-deficiency arguments of neo-classical proponents. As Girvan and Jefferson saw it, the move towards self-government and independence could not arrest the process of underdevelopment so long as the domestic economies remained dependent on foreign capital and terms of trade set under colonial rule.

Principally, the path of resistance for New World associates was forged out of opposition to Arthur Lewis's (1955) import substitution industrialization (ISI) model, favoured by Caribbean governments in the 1960s. Briefly, the ISI programme required state provision of incentives to transnational enterprises in order to attract offshore industrial operations. The various budgetary and fiscal preparatory statements placed emphasis on the prospects for increased employment and technology transfer, and stimulated markets for local inputs.

Beckford (1972), and Best and Levitt (1968) levelled a critique of Lewis's model that was representative of the dominant positions New World associates adopted on the question of Caribbean capitalist development. With epistemic insights drawn from orthodox Marxists and Latin American structuralists, their research fitted the growing canon of work seeking to establish dependency as the source of persistent underdevelopment. Beckford and others in the NWG would enrich this stock argument by anchoring the dependency concept within the plantation experience of Caribbean societies.

DEPENDENCY THEORY AND PLANTATION ECONOMY

Beckford's (1972) *Persistent Poverty* defined the historic plantation slave economy as a quintessential dependent economy, the units of which included Caribbean land, African unfree labour and European capital. This is Best and Levitt's (1968) 'pure plantation economy', as no other economic activity occurred outside the sugar plantation. Beckford's work was as much a repudiation of Caribbean development strategies as it was a paradigmatic challenge to the liberal fallacy of 'progress'. For him, the mode of accumulation in the region remained a modified plantation economy variant, as dependent investment and aid ties with London and other metropolitan cities persisted. After lamenting the dis-articulation between branch-plant production and the rest of the host economy, and the general mono-product character of local economies, Beckford and, later, Best and Levitt outlined other structural features of plantation economy which generated underdevelopment:

- land requirements of plantation production tended to restrict domestic food production;
- terms of trade often deteriorated as rising food and other imports presented balance of payments difficulties; and
- stagnant educational levels tended to foreclose on product diversification options and improvements.

Havelock Brewster (1973), seized by the plantation economy argument, argued that foreign capital could not possibly champion industrialization in accordance with common needs and the utilization of the internal market. This was so, he surmised, because the gridlocked nature of a plantation economy with its lack of an internal dynamic, its reliance on outdated technologies and hierarchical management practices guaranteed for the region a subordinate role in its relationships with core firms and countries.

From the foregoing we may gather that unlike their dependency counterparts in Latin America, most New World associates relied less on external-determinist theories to explain Caribbean underdevelopment; they focused on the *internal* workings of Caribbean economies to account for the region's structural dependency, even as they were careful to note that the characteristics of these economies extended back to colonial relations between Britain and the West Indies. *Dependentistas* and structuralists, on the other hand, placed the centre–periphery relations they depict within the context of macro-historical forces intent on locking peripheral societies into an unyielding spiral of exploitation and poverty.

Interestingly enough, Walter Rodney, a Guyanese historian, and Jamaican political scientist, Trevor Munroe, could be said to have framed Caribbean development in such deterministic terms except that they singled out the social legacy of the plantation experience as especially debilitating for non-white races. Both were inspired by Marx's historical materialist method but Rodney was inclined to argue that nation-building in the region had to be about renewing spirits, constructing grounds for black liberation and pursuing self-reliance. Trevor Munroe's perspective was expressed in more classical but nuanced terms as he was mindful of the plantation slavery experience. As he would frame it, underdevelopment in the region was the predictable outcome of undeveloped class formation – itself partly perpetuated by that mix of domestic policies which threw the territories back on traditional activity and on traditional metropolitan dependence. The extent of the lag in technological, market, infrastructural and resource development will pose a challenge to aspirant Caribbean societies committed to constructing a capitalist economy.

Of the New World group, however, Best's dependency perspective evinced a deep-seated ambivalence toward Western discourses on development. Perhaps he was self-conscious of the postcolonial scholar's place in such literary transactions, of the dangers of succumbing to the neo-classical association between open economies and automatic economic growth. In the context of plantation economies, such assumptions muddled an already complex situation, Best argued. His dependency perspective was consistently embedded in extended and detailed analyses of ruling circles. Apart from addressing the aforementioned features of neo-colonial dependency in the region, he singled out the shared outlook of Caribbean elites and Western development planners as a major brake against effecting meaningful socioeconomic transformation. Not surprisingly, his appeal was for a shift in the register of social consciousness on the part of the ruling elite. The colonial hangover apart, Best failed to draw sufficient attention to the degree of class conflict decolonization inheres as new class forces move to reorient the social system and the values that define that system.

THE DEMISE OF NEW WORLD

As the 1970s dawned, the New World movement shuffled to a halt as division arose over strategies, tactics and modes of resistance to neo-colonialism. By this time, Best was especially critical of the group, decrying what he saw as New World's fatal attraction for governments, and a tendency to substitute policy-oriented research for contemplative scholarship. Increasingly, such knowledge products, he argued, amounted to exercises in self-justification, and as such were quite explicit disclosures of governmental discourse in action. He was also resistant to the idea that New World could move towards the formation of a political party or organization contending for power. In a polemic entitled 'Whither New World', Best (1968) spoke of the tensions of the group, offering the following observation: 'There is among us, much unwitting intolerance, little cool formulation, hardly any attentive listening and even less effective communication.' Munroe would come to lament their facetious pursuit of class unity and vowed to distance himself from what he termed the 'bourgeois idealism' of the New World.

The disintegration of the New World Group was in part a result of the attention given by many to the immediate realms of the policy process. Mona-based economists, in particular, played key advisory roles in the Michael Manley Administration of the 1970s, while others across the region responded to appeals from governments for technical and project management assistance. But there are some scholars that instead place emphasis on the internal arguments between Best and others on the question of New World's relevance and its activist orientation. Their analysis, in my view, falls short precisely because they insufficiently recognize that New World, as any avant-garde movement, became compromised not so much by bourgeois acceptance *as by absorption into the intelligentsia*. Attendance to career, administration and public service would spawn a culture marked by keynote address, cocktail attendance and doctoral authority. Consequently, the new radicals were to be found on the outskirts of Black Power movements, drawn less to its ideology as to the struggle for worker freedom and justice.

On a wider intellectual plane, New World could be said to suffer the slump it did largely because the dependency concept itself lacked lasting explanatory power. Overall, there was a circularity in the dependency argument: dependent countries are those which lack the capacity for autonomous growth and they lack this because their structures are dependent ones. Other scholars have also made the point about development in the world economy being in fact *dependent* development, pointing to foreign investment relationships between core states and firms. By the late 1970s, the emphasis among neo-Marxists shifted away from an independent weight placed on 'dependency' as undesirable, towards either a normative condemnation of state capitalism or an appeal to Third World states to *negotiate* the scope of their dependency.

SUMMARY: BACK TO THE FUTURE

If we posit that openings for dissent are as necessary to democracy as the securing of consent, then Caribbean civil society can continue to offer sites for objection and challenge. But there has been no New World equivalent emerging out of the tensions of the present neo-liberal period. True the rise and influence of non-governmental organizations (NGOs) under the Caribbean Policy Development Centre have served to exert pressure on increasing public transparency and inclusion but it is not at all clear that NGOs constitute an intrinsically virtuous force for the collective good. These can run a similar course to that of the New World. Beyond a certain point NGOs may lose the critical element that brought them into existence as they render services to governance agencies, take funds from them or 'cross over' to work for government institutions and organizations that they previously challenged. Currently market-mentalities predominate in government bureaucracies, business firms and in academy. From various nostrums, academicians from the UWI, particularly social scientists, are exhorted by media, business and government commentators to give advice and attention to the technicality of social control or constitutional and other reforms. In most issue-spaces, ruling discourses of technocratic expertise seem to arbitrarily suppress alternative perspectives. The UWI's role in this is not entirely surprising as the university's struggle for relevance and its sensitivity to budget efficiency do make for a climate where conformity to the prevailing common sense seem the best course for research programming. Hegemony-affirming research thus continues to triumph. Political and intellectual challenges are foreclosed in the prevailing environment where priority of survival continues to be asserted both as an operating principle and as a rationale for the absence of radical critique. This is the 'bourgeois villainy' Best would speak of when the case was hardly self-evident among intellectuals of New World. The associates then at least managed a discussion of Caribbean dependency that was enriched by site characteristics of plantation production relations. This added colour to parallel debates in Latin America. For New World associates, the dependency concept had operative power; it encouraged an interesting entry-point for challenging the colonial mode of accumulation. It also fashioned an intellectual *cachet* of dissent in the region, illuminating history and social fact as economic paradigms came under challenge.

GUIDE TO FURTHER READING AND REFERENCES

The following text references provide the basis for further reading.

Beckford, G. (1972) *Persistent Poverty: Underdevelopment in Plantation Economies of the Third World*, Morant Bay and London: Maroon Publishing House and Zed Books.

Best, L. (1968) 'Forum: Whither New World', in *New World* 4(1): 1–6.

Best, L. and Levitt, K. (1968) 'Outlines of a model of pure plantation economy', *Social and Economic Studies* 17(3), September: 283–326.

Blomstrom, M. and Hettne, B. (1984) *Development Theory in Transition*, London: Zed Books.

Brewster, H. (1973) 'Economic dependence: a quantitative interpretation', *Social and Economic Studies* 22(1): 90–5.

Dookeran, W. (ed.) (1996) *Choices and Change: Reflections on the Caribbean*, Washington DC: Inter-American Bank.

Lewis, R.C. (1998) *Walter Rodney's Intellectual and Political Thought*, Kingston and Detroit: The Press, University of the West Indies and Wayne State University Press.

Lewis, W.A. (1955) *The Theory of Economic Growth*, London: Allen and Unwin.

Marshall, D.D. (2000) 'Academic travails and a crisis-of-mission of UWI Social Sciences: from history and critique to anti-politics' (Chapter 4), in G. Howe (ed.) *Higher Education in the Anglophone Caribbean: Past, Present, and Future Directions*, Mona: University of the West Indies Press, pp. 59–84.

Munroe, T. (1990) *Jamaican Politics: A Marxist Perspective in Transition*, Kingston and Boulder, CO: Heinemann (Caribbean Limited) and Lynne Rienner.

Rodney, W. (1972) *How Europe Underdeveloped Africa*, London: Penguin Books.

2.10 World-systems theory: centres, peripheries and semi-peripheries

Thomas Klak

DEFINITION

World-systems theory (WST) argues that any country's development conditions and prospects are primarily shaped by economic processes and interrelationships operating at the global scale. Advocates claim that the world has been encompassed by a single economic system since at least the start of European industrialization around 1780–90. According to Immanuel Wallerstein and others, the global system dates back even further, to at least 1450, when international trade began to grow, and when Europe embarked on the 'age of discovery' and colonization (Frank and Gills, 1993). Contrary to much social science thinking, WST stresses that it is futile to attempt to analyse or shape development by focusing at the level of individual countries, each of which is deeply ingrained in the world system.

WST has identified a number of regularly occurring historical cycles associated with the level and quality of business activity. These cycles account for economic booms and busts of various durations (Knox and Agnew, 1998: 11). The main economic periods for WST are *Kondratieff cycles*, named after the Russian economist who discovered them in the 1920s. Each cycle or *long wave* lasts about 50–60 years and represents a qualitatively different phase of global capitalism, not just an adjustment from the previous order. Kondratieff cycles are themselves divided into a period of expansion and stagnation. There is first an A-phase of upswing, economic expansion and profitability, based on certain technological innovations and within established rules. Price inflation increases during the A-phase. This then leads into a B-phase of economic downturn, stagnation, price deflation and profit decline (Knox and Agnew, 1998: 72). The profit squeeze toward the end of the B-phase pushes capitalists and policy-makers to seek new and innovative ways to accumulate capital for the future. They work to shift investment out of established economic sectors, regulated environments, and production locations, and thereby create the conditions for a new Kondratieff cycle (Lee, 1994).

The most recent Kondratieff cycle began in the 1940s, expanded until 1967–73 (A-phase), and then contracted through the 1980s (B-phase). Each cycle's organizing institutions and rules are both economic and political. For this recent cycle, key economic rules and structures included the

US dollar as the global currency, and supranational bodies such as the World Bank, the IMF and the G-7. Political structures include the United Nations, and the geopolitical arrangements made at the Yalta conference. It divided Europe into US- and USSR-dominated zones, and initiated the Cold War pitting capitalism against communism. The turn of the century finds the world in an inter-cycle transition phase. Institutions and rules such as the WTO and free trade, that are designed to stabilize and ensure continued profitability and global power for core countries in a new Kondratieff cycle, are being contested and established.

SCHOLARS AND DISCIPLINES INFLUENCING, AND INFLUENCED BY, WST

WST is almost synonymous with its principal architect, Immanuel Wallerstein. Indeed, few influential theoretical perspectives are so closely linked to one contemporary scholar. WST's conceptual roots are largely in Marxism. Wallerstein (1979) says that WST follows 'the spirit of Marx if not the letter'. Evidence of Marx's 'spirit' can be found in WST's emphasis on class, the state, imperialism, and control over the means of production and labour power. WST's objections to classical Marxism primarily concern a theoretical component known as *developmentalism*. This is the idea that societies move sequentially through feudalism, capitalism and socialism to communism, and that they can be analysed and transformed individually and separately from the world system. WST's alternative view – that there has been for centuries but one world economy driven by capital accumulation – employs a concept of mode of production closer to that of Karl Polanyi than to Marx.

WST's perspective and claims have much interdisciplinary relevance, and it has therefore attracted both supporters and detractors from across the social sciences. WST complements political-economic analysis in the traditions of *dependency theory* (Frank, 1966; Cardoso and Faletto, 1979), *uneven development* (Smith, 1984) and *dependent development* (Evans, 1979). A conceptually overlapping but perhaps less economistic and highly influential alternative to WST is *the regulation school*. Usually applied at a more local level than WST (i.e., to national or subnational systems), regulation theory seeks to identify historical phases of capitalism based on relations between a particular prevailing method of accumulating capital, and an associated set of state regulations and behavioural norms (Boyer, 1990; Tickell and Peck, 1992).

THE GEOGRAPHY OF WST: THREE GROUPS OF NATION-STATES

The temporal cycles of systemic integration, order, turbulence, transition and reconstitution of the global economy play out variably across geographical space. The world system is very unequal. Despite (or, world system theorists argue, *because of*) several centuries of worldwide economic integration and trade, and a half-century of World Bank-led international development, global inequalities continue to rise. The difference in per capita income separating the richest and poorest countries was 3:1 in 1820, 35:1 in 1950 and 72:1 in 1992 (UNDP, 1999). Within this highly unequal world order, however, are some place-specific dynamics. At times, regions rise and fall in terms of power, development and economic potential. WST has mainly described this globally differentiated space with reference to nation-states and regional groupings thereof. These fall into three categories (see figure).

Compared to long waves, the geographical components of the world system are much less conceptually refined and empirically specified. With that caveat in mind, general geographical

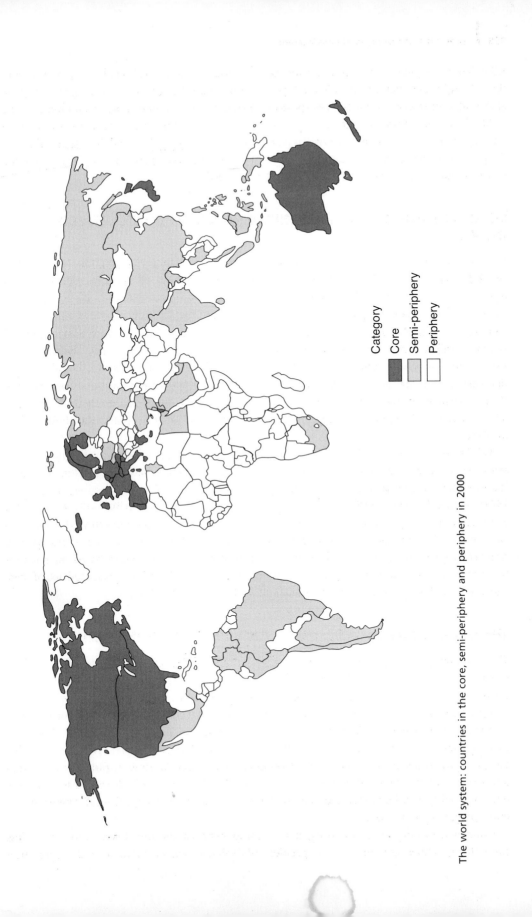

The world system: countries in the core, semi-periphery and periphery in 2000

Category

Core

Semi-periphery

Periphery

features can be described. Countries of the *centre* or *core* are the sites of global economic (and especially industrial) power and wealth, and the associated political influence. Core countries make most key decisions and collectively establish and enforce the rules of the global order. The *semi-periphery* is a mix of characteristics of the core (for example, industry, export power, prosperity) and the periphery (for example, poverty, primary product reliance, vulnerability to outside decision-making). The semi-periphery is the most turbulent category, in that its members most frequently rise or fall in the global hierarchy. In semi-peripheral countries, there is much hope for development and joining the core countries, and narrow windows of opportunity to do so. But there are also intense interactions with core countries bent on fostering their own development while maintaining the hierarchical status quo. The *periphery* is the backwater of the world system. It does little but provide raw materials for industries elsewhere. It has poor living conditions and bleak development prospects. The semi-periphery versus periphery distinction for non-core regions is important. It avoids grouping such a heterogeneous set of countries with respect to development, industrialization, trade and resource control. Still, putting the world's 200 countries into just three groups inevitably glosses over much intra-group heterogeneity. Note the regional clustering of countries in the three categories in the figure. At present the core is mainly North America, Western Europe and Japan. The semi-periphery is essentially East Asia, Latin America and most of the former Soviet realm. The periphery is everything else, but is mostly Africa.

A nation-state's position in the world system is historically *path dependent*, but not deterministically so. Nation-states can move between categories over time, depending on their development success, international aid and alliances, and the nature of the current accumulation regime. Indeed, WST is quite useful for analysing the upward and downward movement of countries over time. But there is not agreement over each country's categorization, which depends on the characteristics used and how they are interpreted. In addition, relative positions *within* each of the three categories can also shift over time.

For example, East Asia illustrates the semi-periphery's potential and turbulence. Following massive US aid and industrial export growth in recent decades, South Korea has recently been knocking on the core's gate, although it has been set back considerably by the 1997 Asian financial crisis. Indonesia has traditionally been peripheral, but in recent decades it has arguably joined the semi-periphery. Its increased clout derives from economic growth based on industrial exports for Nike and others, large resource endowments including oil exports, and its status as the world's fourth most populous country (see figure).

CRITICISMS OF WST

One capitalist world economy, divided by Kondratieff cycles, since at least 1450?

Need we subscribe to WST's totalizing global history to employ it effectively to understand recent development? Compared to Wallerstein, few writers employing a WST framework are as deeply historical, and few treat economic activities during previous centuries in such a globally holistic way. Much work, for example, has been done to identify the evolving features of capitalism associated with five Kondratieff cycles extending back only to 1789 (Lee, 1994). Other WST-borrowing scholars are primarily concerned with the dynamics of contemporary capitalism. WST purists may reject these approaches as insufficiently historical.

While Kondratieff cycles have considerable historical and empirical support (Mandel, 1980), they remain controversial. Others have assembled evidence to cast doubt on the existence and significance of long waves, and to instead suggest that capitalism moves through phases of differing lengths, problems, and features (e.g., Maddison, 1991). As mentioned earlier, the regulation school can be seen as one alternative conceptualization of capitalism's evolution.

Metatheory?

Beyond the considerable empirical analysis of Kondratieff cycles and their associated production and technological features, WST scholarship says much about the world that remains untested, and is perhaps untestable. Most WST-influenced scholarship focuses on the contemporary global political economy, and the lack of time series data limits testing. Further, how could the three-category spatial division of the world system be tested? WST-inspired writing tends to read like an open-ended analysis of unfolding world events. Critics can claim that this method allows one to find and fit the data anecdotally to the theory. Perhaps it is better to think of a world-system *analysis* or *perspective* rather than a fully-fledged world-system *theory*.

Neglect of the local?

Operating at the global level and concerned with economic cycles over decades if not centuries, WST is too holistic to account for local dynamics. Indeed, WST downplays the role of local activities, initiatives and people.

CONCLUSION

World-systems theory, with its keen sense of historical, cyclical, technological and geographical patterns, has undoubtedly deepened our understanding of the global political economy. It is also a satisfying antidote to the reductionism, ahistoricism and superficiality in most popular interpretations of economic change. WST's historical and holistic perspective and level-headedness serves to counter the recent hyperbole about the uniqueness of globalization and inevitability of neo-liberalism (Wallerstein, 2000).

In practice, most scholars employing a WST perspective tend to be murky about the details and measurement of the cycles of upswing and downswing in the global economy. Instead they usually focus primarily on contemporary trends, and adopt a qualitative approach to understanding business cycles, global systemic change, and the associated realignments of economic power and potential. Many economists and some WST purists would judge this more qualitative version of WST to be insufficiently quantitatively rigorous and therefore theoretically deficient. Defenders would counter that a more qualitative approach is most suitable, given their aim to see the 'big picture' and to decipher and rectify contemporary economic and political institutions and options.

GUIDE TO FURTHER READING

Gwynne, R., Klak, T. and Shaw, D. (forthcoming) *The Geography of Emerging Regions*, London: Arnold. Employs WST to examine the recent reconfiguration of countries in the semi-periphery of the global economy.

Knox, P. and Agnew, J. (1998) *The Geography of the World Economy* (3rd edn), London: Arnold. Employs WST within an overview of the field of economic geography, and uses it to explore the workings of the contemporary global economy.

Shannon, T.R. (1996) *An Introduction to the World-System Perspective* (2nd edn), Boulder: Westview Press. Useful overview of WST, endorsed by Wallerstein.

Wallerstein, I. (1976) *The Modern World-System: Capitalist Agriculture and the Origins of the European World-Economy in the Sixteenth Century*, New York: Academic Press.

Wallerstein, I. (1980) *The Modern World-System II: Mercantilism and the Consolidation of the European World-Economy, 1600–1750*, New York: Academic Press.

Wallerstein, I. (1989) *The Second Era of Great Expansion of the Capitalist World-Economy, 1730–1840s*, San Diego: Academic Press.

Historically organized trilogy of Wallerstein classics on the rise and development of the Europe-centered world system.

REFERENCES

Boyer, R. (1990) *The Regulation School: A Critical Introduction*, New York: Columbia University Press.

Cardoso, F. and Faletto, E. (1979) *Dependency and Development in Latin America*, Berkeley: University of California Press.

Evans, P. (1979) *Dependent Development: The Alliance of Multinational, State, and Local Capital in Brazil*, Princeton: Princeton University Press.

Frank, A.G. (1966) 'The development of underdevelopment', *Monthly Review* 18(4); reprinted in Stuart Corbridge (ed.) (1995) *Development Studies: A Reader*, London: Edward Arnold, pp. 27–37.

Frank, A.G. and Gills, B. (eds) (1993) *The World System: Five Hundred Years or Five Thousand?* London: Routledge.

Johnston, R.J., Gregory, D. and Smith, D.M. (eds) (1994) *Dictionary of Human Geography* (3rd edn), Oxford: Blackwell, pp. 677–9.

Lee, R. (1994) 'Kondratieff cycles' in R.J. Johnston *et al.* (1994) *Dictionary of Human Geography* (3rd edn), Oxford: Blackwell, pp. 305–8.

Maddison, A. (1991) *Dynamic Forces in Capitalist Development*, Oxford: Oxford University Press.

Mandel, E. (1980) *Long Waves of Capitalist Development*, Cambridge: Cambridge University Press.

Smith, N. (1984) *Uneven Development: Nature, Capital, and the Production of Space*, New York: Blackwell.

Tickell, A. and Peck, J. (1992) 'Accumulation, regulation and the geographies of post-Fordism: missing links in regulationist research', *Progress in Human Geography* 16: 190–218.

UNDP (1999) *Human Development Report*, New York: Oxford University Press.

Wallerstein, I. (1979) *The Capitalist World-Economy*. Cambridge: Cambridge University Press.

Wallerstein, I. (2000) 'Globalization or the age of transition?: A long-term view of the trajectory of the world system', *International Sociology* 15: 249–65.

2.11 Agropolitan and bottom-up development

Michael J.G. Parnwell

One of the greatest development challenges during the last 50 years has been to find effective means of confronting *uneven development*. Although a perfectly even development may be found only in Utopian visions of the world, it is generally the case that most serious development problems tend to be associated with the downside of uneven development – e.g.

peripherality, marginality, exclusion and powerlessness. Accordingly, ever since Dudley Seers' (1969) influential reinterpretation of the meaning of 'development', in which inequality (as well as poverty and unemployment) should decline for development to occur, scholars and practitioners have paid increasing attention to distributional criteria (spatial, economic, social) in the theory and praxis of development.

There is a strong body of thought which points to alternative forms of development being necessary if inequality is seriously to be confronted. Uneven development is claimed in part to be a by-product of an orthodox capitalist development process which places emphasis on rapid and efficient economic growth, privileges the industrial sector and urban areas, and tends to support the first foremost. Left behind in this process are a host of areas, sectors and social groups which possess neither the means nor the power to keep up with the pace of progress and change. A series of binary descriptors of the *phenomenon* of uneven development has entered common usage – e.g. core and periphery, rich and poor, mainstream and marginal, dynamic and backward, powerful and powerless, and so on. Analysts point also to the *process* of uneven development, with the nature of relationships across these (albeit artificially created) binaries tending disproportionately to serve the interests of the advanced, and work against the neglected or excluded. Given such a situation, the prospects for a reduction in inequality within orthodox capitalist development would appear to be quite weak.

Alternative models of development have tended to opt for the antithesis of the orthodox approach. Thus an urban and industrial bias is replaced with an emphasis on the rural and the agricultural; the top-down directionality and centralized character of development policy is challenged by decentralized, devolved and bottom-up initiatives; capitalism is superseded by socialist ideals; small-scale and particularistic development is seen as preferable to large-scale and universalistic approaches; and so on. In essence, we are presented with another binary, between the orthodox and the alternative. One danger of this, as we shall see below, is that the very real gains from orthodox development are seriously downplayed in favour of sometimes idealistic and neo-populist alternative visions of the future.

Initial efforts to confront the spatial manifestations of uneven development centred on 'growth centre' strategies, and drew heavily on the relatively successful western European experiment with 'growth poles'. The aim was to facilitate economic development in peripheral regions of the developing world (and at the same time ease some of the pressures of over-rapid metropolitan growth) by encouraging firms to locate in or relocate to designated growth centres. The strategy manifestly failed to achieve a significant reversal in the process of uneven development – indeed, some analysts claim that it may have worsened the situation by intensifying the 'trickle-up' process wherein the resources and resourcefulness of the periphery became sequestered by the core. This 'alternative' strategy was, in reality, no such thing: it was quite simply a scaled-down version of the orthodox model, with capitalism, cities, industries, growth and economic efficiency at its heart. Little wonder, then, that its outcome was little different from its orthodox precursors. Something more radical was clearly needed (Stöhr and Fraser Taylor, 1981).

Agropolitan development formed part of the radical critique of development, and centred on the premise (elaborated above) that the functional integration of peripheral and marginal areas into national and supranational systems in a weak and dependent manner contributes fundamentally to their relative economic backwardness. To overcome this, the local must thus be privileged over the national. By selectively closing localities to external domination and competition, it was argued that a self-reliant form of development may ensue which could deliver basic needs, social equality and a solid foundation for future growth and progress. The strategy centred around seemingly contradictory concepts such as 'rural urbanization' and 'rural industrialization', with absolute priority being given to agriculture and small-scale artisanal activities, rural settlement, labour-intensive activities and appropriate technology, local democracy and popular participation in the decision-making process. It was strongly based on socialist principles of access to the means of production (e.g. collective ownership of land) and to the locus of power, and drew on what the principal architect of the concept, John Friedmann (Friedmann and Douglass, 1978), called 'collective consciousness'.

The essential building block of the agropolitan approach was the 'agropolitan district' – a territorial unit with a population of 40,000–60,000 people which was small enough to be self-contained, self-reliant and conducive to face-to-face contact in the process of development, but large enough to bestow certain economies in the provision of essential services, infrastructure, and both agricultural and industrial production. In line with basic democratic principles, the community itself would determine the allocation of productive resources and the utilization of any generated surplus. Human needs were to be placed first and foremost, and where necessary ahead of economic growth per se. The aim was not to create isolated 'mini republics', but instead to afford localities the opportunity to 'get the basics right' and be protected from external competition during their embryonic stage before (if at all) venturing back into the wider competitive world. Large-scale heavy industry was to be set aside in 'enclaves' with which the agropolitan districts would be functionally integrated but fundamentally protected. The *ujamaa* villagization programme in Tanzania, introduced in the late 1960s, provides the closest (not altogether successful) working example of agropolitan development in practice (Lea and Chaudhri, 1983).

This ideal world model was not without its shortcomings. Resource endowments and development potential are not evenly distributed to start with, and thus it was accepted that some agropolitan districts would inevitably be more successful than others, the latter perhaps struggling to satisfy even a minimum acceptable level of human needs. Strong state intervention was thus required in order to influence the allocation of resources and support according to need rather than potential, and to restrict migration between agropolitan districts. However, the required controlling hand of the state ran contrary to one of the fundamental principles of agropolitan development: namely the devolution of political power and control to the communities themselves. State-initiated bottom-up development remains an oxymoron.

Other criticisms levelled at this radical model of alternative development include its highly idealistic, neo-populist, eurocentric, even utopian nature. The romantic visions of egalitarian and corporate rural communities of the past which were to be recreated through agropolitan development – a form of 'back to the future' – often had little foundation in reality. The notion that local power holders would readily and altruistically cede power and influence in the interests of the wider community was also somewhat naïve. The sacrificing of orthodox development (narrowly defined as modernization and economic growth) in the interests of 'distributive justice', as determined by external visionaries, also sometimes ran counter to the aspirations of the communities themselves, and may well have led to everyone becoming equally poor. Analysts have also criticized the overemphasis on the spatial dimension in the agropolitan model, and the consequent downplaying of class, gender, ethnicity, ecology and history, and the important role of human agency. John Friedmann has countered the criticism of agropolitan development as a utopian concept by suggesting that the world will never change unless there is a vision to provide guidance for future action.

The notion of *bottom-up development* goes a stage further than the agropolitan model by fundamentally challenging the directionality of development decision-making. It is argued that large-scale, universal, government-driven national programmes of (especially rural) development frequently fail to meet the particular needs and wants of local communities, and are only rarely tailored to local conditions and contexts. Centralized development decision-making, often involving city-based 'experts', is generally too detached from local contextual realities. It is frequently encumbered by a 'planning arrogance' where technocrats think they know best what is in the interests of people at the grassroots level. State-driven development initiatives may also reflect the prevailing orthodox development paradigm, and may be strongly influenced by misconceptions and stereotypes of life in the countryside. Their paternalistic nature engenders a culture of dependence in local communities, stifling initiative, innovation and self-reliance. Finally, the top-down channelling of commands and support fails to provide a mechanism for evaluating the effectiveness of development initiatives, and for ascertaining to what extent they match local people's needs, expectations and aspirations. Local people are thus seen as passive recipients of development who are powerless to control their own destinies.

What is thus required is another antithetical development which is localized and contextually rooted, small in scale, flexible, culturally sensitive, democratic and participatory, and which centres on the empowerment of the poor. Bottom-up development is thus centred on, and emerges from, the communities themselves. Conscientization enables the poor to understand the root causes of their problems, and to design appropriate solutions. The decision-making role of the community yields a greater sense of ownership and identity with the process of development, and people are thus more likely to contribute the enthusiasm, commitment and endeavour that it requires to succeed. Examples of bottom-up/grassroots development activities include the Grameen Bank, which was established in 1976 to provide much-needed credit facilities to the rural poor in Bangladesh; the Appropriate Technology Association in Thailand, which sought to promote agro-ecology in rural areas; various rural industrialization schemes, which have attempted to strengthen the non-farm sector and thus provide alternatives to out-migration; small-scale irrigation schemes; AIDS/HIV support; housing associations; ethnic and human rights organizations; environmental movements; and so on (see Holloway, 1989; ODI Non-Governmental Organizations Series, 1993).

Bottom-up development has gained in momentum and prominence since the 1970s to the extent that it now challenges orthodox approaches as the mainstream paradigm in many parts of the developing world. Central to the role and function of bottom-up development has been the explosive growth of *non-governmental organizations* (NGOs). NGOs initially took the shape of charitable, often religious bodies from the countries of the North which were targeted at particular development problems such as destitution, persecution, hunger, homelessness and disaster. Some were diametrically opposed to governments and state institutions, most particularly in authoritarian and dictatorial regimes, and were often mirrored by, or linked to, locally-based political movements. Through the 1980s, political space started to open up for Southern NGOs to form and flourish. Initially these relied on alliances with, and support from, the organizations of the North, including the international development agencies, but more recently the NGOs of the South have come to predominate, and in some instances are so numerous, diverse and effective that they are challenging the state's historical prominence and legitimacy. Meanwhile, many governments have started to relax their initial suspicion of, and antagonism towards, the non-governmental movement, and increasingly partnerships are being forged between the state and certain grassroots organizations.

NGOs have many theoretical advantages over the cumbersome and amorphous institutions of the state in terms of delivering development at the grassroots level. They are seen to be more flexible, adaptable and nimble, have shallower decision-making hierarchies and shorter lines of communication, are largely autonomous, and are typically less costly to run because of a high contribution of voluntary inputs into their activities. Their philosophy centres around altruism, democracy, popular participation (learning together rather than the simple transfer of knowledge), empowerment, conscientization, contextual groundedness, responsiveness rather than prescriptiveness, and the promotion of self-reliance.

There are also several weaknesses which again serve to undermine the ideal of bottom-up development when set in real-world situations. Whatever the theoretical advantages of grassroots organizations, as embodied in their philosophical approach, critics have claimed that they simply represent a new form of top-down, paternalistic development occurring further down the development hierarchy. Participation emerges more prominently in words than in tokenistic deeds, and is often coerced rather than natural. There is often a considerable level of rivalry within the non-governmental sector, as organizations vie for funds, prestige and space, and this may draw energy and commitment away from the underlying mission. Pre-existing structures, such as in the distribution of political power, economic and asset wealth or in gender relations, are very difficult to wish away by the best intentions of grassroots activists, and indeed may become reinforced by their activities. Meanwhile, recognizing the dynamism and potential power of the bottom-up movement, governments have attempted to re-style themselves as grassroots-aware, liberally incorporating the rhetoric of participation and self-reliance in their revamped policy statements. However, we again return to the fundamental contradiction of state-driven bottom-up development, not least when developing countries, and the world economy into which they are increasingly being incorporated, are still driven by a narrow development orthodoxy. There is little doubt that the bottom-up philosophy is beginning to have a profound effect on development praxis, but it is unrealistic to suggest that 'alternative development' is set to become the mainstream paradigm. A pragmatic articulation of orthodox and alternative development, with strengthening linkages between the governmental and non-governmental sectors, would appear to be the most realistic way forward.

REFERENCES AND GUIDE TO FURTHER READING

The following few items should prove of interest to readers wanting to go further.

Friedmann, John and Douglass, Mike (1978) 'Agropolitan development: towards a new strategy for regional planning in Asia', in F.C. Lo and K. Salih (eds) *Growth Pole Strategy and Regional Development Policy*, Oxford: Pergamon, pp. 163–92.

Holloway, Richard (ed.) (1989) *Doing Development: Governments, NGOs and the Rural Poor in Asia*, London: Earthscan.

Lea, David A.M. and Chaudhri, D.P. (1983) *Rural Development and the State*, London: Methuen.

ODI, Non-Governmental Organizations Series (1993): John Farringdon and David J. Lewis (eds) *Non-Governmental Organizations and the State in Asia: Rethinking Roles in Sustainable Agricultural Development*; Anthony Bebbington and Graham Thiele (eds) *Non-Governmental Organizations and the State in Latin America: Rethinking Roles in Sustainable Agricultural Development*; Kate Wellard and James G. Copestake (eds) *Non-Governmental Organizations and the State in Africa: Rethinking Roles in Sustainable Agricultural Development*, London: Routledge.

Seers, Dudley (1969) 'The meaning of development', *International Development Review* 4(3).

Stöhr, Walter B. and Fraser Taylor, D.R. (eds) (1981) *Development from Above or Below? The Dialectics of Regional Planning in Developing Countries*, Chichester: John Wiley.

2.12 Community participation in development

Vandana Desai

INTRODUCTION

Community participation (CP) is an indispensable part of any programme or project encouraged by national governments, World Bank, UN agencies and non-governmental organizations. Despite the differing perspectives of these various agencies, all agree that CP should be encouraged. Actions by the poor to influence decision-making through direct and informal means have emerged as an alternative way by which they can gain admission to decision-making and access to resources and thereby improve their well-being.

This chapter aims to analyse the nature and role of the participants in CP. The most critical issue is whether or not CP can achieve real improvements in social conditions. A major gulf exists between reality and the way in which community participation is supposed to operate, particularly in the light of the resource cutbacks experienced by most developing countries as they cope with debt and structural adjustment policies.

There are various reasons why CP is deemed desirable from the point of view of development agencies and governments. These include the following.

- People have a right to participate in decision-making which directly affects their living conditions.
- Social development can be promoted by increasing local self-reliance. Since people themselves know best what they need, what they want and what they can afford, only close co-operation between project implementers and the community can lead to project effectiveness. The project area continues to develop even after the withdrawal of the development agency staff.
- Demonstrating that the people and the government can work together and make political capital.
- Co-opting a strong but manipulable community leadership can increase political or social control.

DEFINITION OF COMMUNITY PARTICIPATION

Participation is defined in a United Nations report (1979: 225) to mean 'sharing by people in the benefits of development, active contribution by people to development and involvement of people in decision making at all levels of society'. Clearly, much more information is needed, if we are to know who participates, what participation entails and how it is to be promoted.

The arguments on participation seem to converge on the relationship between three key concepts, namely 'taking part', 'influence' and 'power' in CP. Moreover, any participation process seems to have two components irrespective of the context, situation or objective: a decision-making process and an action process to realize the objective decided upon. When participants are unequal in their endowments, participation means the less endowed taking part and influencing the decision-making process in their favour. Stiefel (1981: 1–2) defines participation in terms of 'organised efforts to increase control over resources and regulative institutions in given social situations on the part of the groups and movements hitherto excluded from such control'.

People having different perspectives assume very different virtues of CP. Consequently, opinions on who should participate, in what, and how, vary widely between and among development agencies and residents. Literature from non-governmental sources tends to emphasize the need for 'true' participation, (i.e. bottom-up approach, grassroots development). CP can also be distinguished between state-initiated and grassroots-initiated.

The shift in the participation argument, is however, towards the empowerment of the less powerful. In developing countries, resources for development have always been very scarce, but pressures for their allocation from various interested groups have progressively increased. The poor, since they have neither socioeconomic nor political power, do not generally gain access to the decision-making processes and hence are unable to influence them. Therefore the poor have not benefited from economic growth but in fact have become worse off. Oakley and Marsden (1984: 88) state in this regard: 'meaningful participation is concerned with achieving power: that is the power to influence the decisions that affect one's livelihood'.

COMMUNITY ORGANIZATIONS AND COMMUNITY LEADERS

The purpose of community organizations (COs) is to increase unity and solidarity. Mobilization is a key input in the process of empowerment. The collective nature of the community could increase poor people's bargaining power, including their input into the local decision-making process. The question that arises is, to what extent do COs succeed in their demand-making, and what is the degree to which COs are linked into the wider partisan-political system?

Considerable attention is given to the role of COs in articulating demands and in mobilizing resources. Mobilization is intended for capital formation and to relieve scarce government resources. Many COs are issue based. There is usually an interplay of many forces – local, linguistic, regional and even religious – in the functioning of the COs. In all these set-ups, political forces may creep in. They defend rights and win some concessions, and they politicize some individuals. The existence of an organization does not guarantee that it represents the entire community. Men, for example, tend to be over-represented in such organizations, but there are also exclusively women's groups within communities.

Those high in social and economic stratification hierarchies possess greater resources and motivation and, therefore, take greater advantage of the opportunities than those lower on the hierarchy of socioeconomic stratification. The only persons who can afford to be active in COs are perhaps the richer among the poor: businessmen, shopkeepers and landlords. Consequently, community leaders are often not representative of the population but rather represent particular interest groups (see Desai, 1995).

Community leadership is an important ingredient in the level and form of CP and in successful demand-making. Some key issues in the nature of leadership need to be analysed; the first relates to the sources of leaders' power within each community. Do leaders maintain power through force, through charisma and popularity in the community, or because they have influential friends outside the community or are linked into a political-party apparatus? Do patterns of leadership vary with the circumstances of the settlement; do strong authoritarian leaders emerge at times of crisis and for the achievement of major services? Over what time period do they lead the community?

ROLE OF THE STATE IN COMMUNITY PARTICIPATION

Few systematic attempts have been made to examine the relationship between the state and community initiatives. This is partly because CP theorists are implacably opposed to the idea that the state can contribute effectively to the promotion of CP. State responses to CP in development have often been haphazard and poorly formulated, and there are substantial variations in the extent to which these ideals have been applied in different countries. They have also enjoyed greater or lesser popularity depending on the preferences of senior administrators, politicians and planners.

A number of observers have argued that CP in urban development invariably results in a concerted effort by the state to subvert and manipulate local people. Gilbert and Ward (1984: 239) argue on the basis of the study of three Latin American cities (Bogota, Mexico City and Valencia) that the state effectively uses the mechanisms of CP as a means of social control. They found that, in each of the three cities, the state had been successful in deflecting opposition by making concessions, by providing services, by co-opting leaders or, in the last resort, through repression. Such tactics can also make the state stronger.

For the role of the state/government to become one of a facilitator, a supporter, an interpreter and a constructive critic within CP, it has to recognize that it will have to implement substantial structural changes in its administration, bureaucracy and operational style. This is reflected in the lack of suitable personnel (e.g. social workers and community organizers), and the working approaches of professional staff who have been trained in conventional techniques which involve little, if any, CP, and who have little idea how to incorporate it in their planning. Usually the poor are expected to participate actively in project implementation and maintenance, but are often left out of the design stage – obviously the most critical phase from the point of view of ensuring that programmes meet 'real' needs. It must restructure itself (and its field branches) to create a more responsive, public service-oriented administration which involves beneficiaries more directly in organizational control.

The fact that COs are the common level of social organization above that of the household means that inevitably they act as a magnet for supra-local political parties which seek to gain an advantage by working through them (Nelson, 1979: 292). However, the issue is whether communities are likely to enhance their chances of securing outside help or servicing if they use party-political linkages.

There are two important mechanisms used by the governments to gain support from these COs and leaders. These are co-optation and clientelism. Co-optation plays a key role in maintaining a small elite in power, and its manifestations vary widely. Clientelism takes different forms, but it has a long tradition in many societies. The clients are expected to offer in exchange consistent political loyalty.

Co-optation may occur when the leader believes, often mistakenly, that formal affiliation will further the interests of those whom they represent by providing better access to the agencies distributing resources. Political parties and government departments may be eager to co-opt leaders as a means of extending their influence over local constituencies. The community may lose its autonomy and become subject to the orthodoxy of the co-opting body. In some cases, co-optation to the governing party may well reduce the chances of successful demand-making, see Eckstein (1977) with regard to Mexico. It may also provide an important foothold for successful negotiation where political support is exchanged for urban services as in Brazil (Leeds and Leeds, 1976).

The other form of support is based on clientelism. A patron–client relationship is an enduring dyadic bond based upon informally arranged personal exchanges of resources between actors of unequal status. In the case of the poor communities, the leader, or 'broker', maintains a personal relationship with the politicians or administrators who control limited resources required by the community or members of that community. This is the principal form of linkage between aspirant politicians and high-ranking government officials, and the poor. The leader or patron benefits in so far as he is able to demand the loyalty of those dependants upon him and to mobilize that loyalty on behalf of his superiors. Clients benefit as long as they gain access to influential people who may intercede on their behalf and increase the chances of a successful outcome to their demand-making. It must be said that *all* political systems depend on a degree of co-optation and clientelism. The crucial irony is that 'participation by representation' is a contradiction in terms, because the represented perceive of their representatives as unique and distinct from themselves.

THE ROLE OF NGOs IN COMMUNITY PARTICIPATION

Through non-governmental organizations (NGOs), existing community organizations can be guided to exert pressure on the government in order to encompass joint decision-making. It is argued that NGOs provide effective opportunities for the implementation of CP ideals and that these organizations are more likely to promote authentic forms of participation than the state. While it is true that NGOs have played a major role in the promotion of CP, it cannot be claimed that their involvement has been faultless.

Many NGOs, especially the larger ones, function bureaucratically and use formal procedural rules to carry out their tasks. Non-government organizations are prone to ossification, particularly if they are dominated and controlled by charismatic leaders who are unresponsive to new ideas and view innovation as a threat to their authority. Middle-class individuals whose views are liberal and paternalistic rather than radically egalitarian run many NGOs. The assumption that they are usually politically progressive also needs to be questioned.

CONCLUSION

Although the idea of CP is exceedingly popular in development circles, it raises difficult issues. Most governments appear to have a limited view of participation; there is a lack of political will to implement participation because of its implications for the distribution of power and resources. Popular initiatives towards participation are often co-opted by, and in the end serve, the interests of the high-income groups, rather than those of the poor.

The basic problem is that many of the ideologists of participation want politics without politics. *All* organizations bigger than a handful of people necessarily and inevitably involve:

- a degree of delegated power to leaders – even if leaders are replaceable democratically; the representation of interests is always indirect;
- the organization itself having interests different from the perceived interests of some/all of its members.

Participation is often treated as if it could be implemented in a vacuum, with all actors agreeing on its precise meaning and goals. Any discussion of participation is discussion of politics and the exercise of power. CP has been treated as a technical issue, or as a social project component. Too often it is forgotten that CP as 'citizens' control' or 'people's power' is little short of very significant social and political changes.

While the arguments covered here may be depressing, it would be wrong to conclude that nothing can be achieved through CP. Participatory programmes, whether sponsored by the state or the NGO sector, have brought tangible benefits to people in many parts of the world, but have also experienced a great many difficulties that belie the idealism of their advocates. These conclusions suggest that the limits of participation need to be recognized and accommodated. As governments move away from the role of provider to that of facilitator, new management skills need to be developed and more flexible planning tools devised.

GUIDE TO FURTHER READING

Craig, G. and Mayo, M. (eds) (1995) *Community Empowerment: A Reader in Participation and Development*, London: Zed Books.

Desai, V. (1995) *Community Participation and Slum Housing: A Study of Bombay*, New Delhi/London/Thousand Oaks, California: Sage Publications. This book deals with the meaning and scope of community participation. The case study of Bombay deals with the slum dwellers' needs for housing and basic services.

Nelson, N. and Wright, S. (1995) *Power and Participatory Development: Theory and Practice*, London: Intermediate Technology Publications.

White, S. (2000) 'Depoliticising development: the uses and abuses of participation', in Deborah Eade (ed.) *Development, NGOs, and Civil Society*, Oxford: Oxfam, or in *Development in Practice* (1996), 6(1). This chapter elaborates on the various types of participation and its dynamics.

REFERENCES

Eckstein, S.E. (1977) *The Poverty of Revolution: The State and the Urban Poor in Mexico*, Princeton: Princeton Univerty Press.

Gilbert, A. and Ward, P. (1984) 'Community action by the urban poor: democratic involvement, community self-help or a means of social control?', *World Development* 12, 8–20.

Leeds, A. and Leeds, E. (1976) 'Accounting for behavioural differences: three political systems and the responses of squatters in Brazil, Peru and Chile', in J. Walton and L.H. Masotti (eds) *The City In Comparative Perspective*, Halsted Press, 193–248.

Nelson, J.M. (1979) *Access to Power: Politics and the Urban Poor in Developing Nations*, Princeton: Princeton University Press.

Oakley, P. and Marsden, D. (1984) *Approaches to Participation in Rural Development*, Geneva: International Labour Office.

Stiefel, M. (1981) editorial in *Dialogue About Participation* No.1, Geneva: United Nations Research Institute for Social Development.

United Nations (1979) *1978 Report on the World Social Situation*, New York: United Nations.

2.13 Postmodernism and development

David Simon

POSTMODERNISM: PANACEA, PLACEBO OR PERVERSITY?

Postmodernism became a major social scientific theoretical paradigm during the 1990s. Geography and development studies have felt its impact as keenly as any other discipline, not least because of its sharply divisive impact on academic opinion. In development studies it has gained prominence as one of the routes for transcending the so-called theoretical 'impasse' that emerged in the mid- to late 1980s. However, the concept has assumed diverse meanings, a factor contributing substantially to the often heated but unenlightening debates over its usefulness in the context of development. This chapter offers an overview of these issues.

The alliterative heading on the previous page aptly synthesizes the divergent positions on the relevance of postmodernism to development studies. Few theoretical propositions have elicited such strongly polarized views: those who have embraced it enthusiastically are matched by bitter opponents who argue that it is irrelevant and/or pernicious for reasons that will be explained below. Yet, a substantial proportion of academics and practitioners profess no interest in or understanding of the issues. While such apologism is regrettable and has probably attended most theoretical innovations over time, the peculiarly disparate, even amorphous, nature of postmodernism and therefore the lack of clarity to 'outsiders' about its central tenets and mode of explanation, has undoubtedly prompted much lack of interest.

Perhaps as a reflection of such attitudes, the raft of new development theory textbooks appearing during the late 1990s revealed a surprising paucity of attention to postmodernism (Simon, 1999: 38–43). Some make no mention of it and other 'post-' or 'anti-developmentalist' approaches at all, while others include only a few pages or single chapter, almost as an afterthought. Only a handful give fuller coverage. This may change in time, but does mean that most students over the next few years will continue to have little exposure to these debates.

Postmodernism first emerged in art, architecture and literature in the mid-1970s, where it found expression as a rejection of the then-dominant modernist schools. The concepts of ideals, absolutes, order and harmonization, which had given rise to increasing alienation of the individual, were challenged by architects such as Charles Jencks and Vincent Scully. The objective became a celebration of diverse forms and sharp contrasts, in order to rupture conventional expectations (Ellin, 1996). This is generally achieved through the juxtaposition of radically different styles in street façades, something that was and remains anathema to most urban planners and local authority planning codes, or the literal turning inside out of a building, in terms of which its previously hidden infrastructure is boldly displayed as an art form. Perhaps the best-known exemplars of this style are the Pompidou Exhibition Centre in Paris and the Lloyd's Building in the City of London, although the positioning of glass-walled lifts in the atrium of multistorey buildings for dramatic panoramic effect has now become a common architectural feature of even 'establishment' buildings.

In literature, Latin American writers like Gabriel García Márquez and Carlos Fuentes pioneered a literary style that broke with the established tradition of a single, chronological flow to novels, and replaced it with multiple, cross-cutting strands, flashbacks, forward leaps and previews in structurally much more complex forms.

In the social sciences, postmodernism gained a foothold as part of the ferment that included post-structuralist rejection of meta-theories and grand narratives; critical social theory; concern with the deconstruction of ideology and official discourses; a growing cynicism about established orders and vested power; concern at increasing alienation within Northern societies and, partly as a result, the so-called 'cultural turn' in terms of which renewed attention has been paid to the explanatory value of cultural factors, rather than the political and economic. The work of Michel Foucault, Henri Lefebvre, Jacques Derrida and Jean Baudrillard looms large in the foundations of postmodernism. Among the most widely reputed social scientific accounts of postmodernism are those of Frederic Jameson (1984), Jean-François Lyotard (1984), David Harvey

(1989) and Ed Soja (1991). Most situate it explicitly within the (cultural) logic of late capitalism, as part of the search for profit accumulation in a context of globalized production and consumption. As such they are critical and see it as having limited social explanatory value, serving mainly to justify conspicuous self-expression, rather than representing a profound new paradigm.

Significantly, several leading advocates of postmodernism and postcolonialism in cultural studies, sociology and allied disciplines, including Homi Bhabha, Trin Minha and Gyatri Spivak, hail from countries of the global South, even though generally now working in Northern universities. Among geographers, sociologists and development specialists, and especially those working in Latin America, some of the most trenchant critics of conventional development have espoused postmodernism as the way forward – in particular, Santiago Colás, Arturo Escobar, Gustavo Esteva and David Slater. However, Escobar's major work (1995) is principally a critique of 'the development project', offering little insight into a revisioned future beyond an invocation of new social movements. By contrast, Colás (1994) interprets postmodern developments in different spheres of Argentinian society, while Esteva and Prakash (1998) provide one of the very few detailed expositions of regional and local-level postmodernism in practice as social action. Slater (1992, 1997) has taken forward geopolitical and development debates across the North–South divide. Other authors, notably Corbridge (1994), have been cautious about the relevance of postmodernism relative to postcolonialism.

Nevertheless, most social scientists working in, or concerned with, the developing world have tended to ignore postmodernism or to dismiss it as an irrelevance. The latter sentiment is based on one or both of two main considerations.

- Postmodernism literally means 'after the modern'; however, in the global South, the majority of people are still poor and struggling to meet basic needs and to enjoy the fruits of modernization so powerfully held up to them as the outcome of development. In such situations, modernity has yet to be widely achieved, so that which follows on from the modern can have little relevance (e.g. King, 1995).
- Postmodernism is yet another Northern paradigm, which finds expression mainly in aesthetic/architectural terms and as playful, leisured heterodoxes and new forms of consumption centred on individualism which can best be described as self-indulgence by the well-off. Again, such preoccupations are irrelevant to the global South, if not actually harmful in terms of distracting attention from survival and 'development' agendas and the macro-processes which impact upon them.

These positions are understandable but do reveal misunderstandings or confusions among the diverse meanings and applications of postmodernism which, in turn, reflect the diversity of usage.

A CONCEPTUAL SCHEMA

The following schema, which distinguishes the different connotations of the postmodern, is designed to facilitate understanding. At the outset, though, it is apposite to highlight the distinction between the terms postmodernity, which best describes a condition or manifestation, and postmodernism, which is the ideology or intellectual practice.

At least three broad interpretations of the postmodern can be distinguished in the vast and multidisciplinary literatures.

The chronological approach

This is the most literal interpretation, in terms of which the postmodern necessarily follows the modern. This is usually taken to apply to time periods or epochs, but could also refer to artistic and architectural styles. In practice, however, no clean break between eras can be distinguished: there was no dramatic event to act as signifier, and there has been no agreement on the basis of transition. At best, one might be able to conceptualize a transitional phase of many years' duration, the precise timing and length of which reflects the sphere of interest or discipline(s) involved.

In terms of globalization and mass consumption, for instance, Fordist assembly lines would be regarded as characteristic of high modernity; whereas post-Fordist flexible specialization and mobility, or customized and/or team-built vehicles and other high-specification products geared to individualized whim, might be postmodern. Similarly, the traditional mass-market air package holiday would be modern, whereas the more differentiated and personalized small-group luxury tour, complete with ecotourist credentials and/or sanitized versions of conflictual local histories in distant countries for the benefit of international tourists, might be conceived of as postmodern.

As explained above, this chronological approach underlies much of the rejection of postmodernism by development specialists, as they consider the struggle for modernity to be ongoing and important; only when basic needs and other necessities of modern development have been met would it make any sense to consider a transition to a putative era of postmodern development.

The aesthetic approach

The second basic understanding of postmodernism is as a form of expression in the creative and aesthetic disciplines like art, architecture and literature. This perspective reflects the considerations – and is exemplified by the authors and buildings – cited in the introduction. Inevitably, perhaps, most such attention has been centred on elite and middle-class consumption, especially in terms of leisure activities but also increasingly in the working environment and public spaces. Terms most frequently associated with this movement include pastiche, mélange, playfulness, commodity-signs, imaginaries, and spectacles. Theme parks, pleasure domes and other purpose-built leisure complexes which offer decontextualized time–space representations of various places and experiences (Featherstone, 1995; Watson and Gibson, 1995), often in sanitized form, are characteristic of this approach in much the same way as great exhibitions of global exploration, scientific discoveries and industrial achievements were hallmarks of Victorian modernity and prowess.

Postmodernism as intellectual practice

The final approach, of postmodernism as *problematique* or intellectual practice, is also the most relevant from the perspective of development studies. Here, the postmodern supposedly represents fundamentally different ways of seeing, knowing and representing the world. The modern approach, rooted in Enlightenment thinking about rationality, is concerned with a search for universal truths, linked to positivist scientific methodology and neo-classical economics. Proponents of different theories held them to be superior to all their competitors, to have global relevance even if based on limited empirical evidence from specific contexts, and ultimately to represent *the* truth. Hence, for example, the debates between modernization theorists and adherents of *dependencia* and other neo-Marxist variants, were often ideologically driven contests for supremacy against a background of Cold War geopolitics. These were also often debates of the deaf, in which adherents talked at or past one another, rather than engaging in meaningful dialogue. Such universalizing, globalizing approaches are often referred to as meta-narratives.

In theory, at least, postmodern practice rejects such singular explanations in favour of multiple, divergent and overlapping interpretations and views. Simplicity should give way to complexity and pluralism, in terms of which these different accounts are all accorded legitimacy. The privileging of official and formal discourses should be replaced by approaches lending credence to both official and unofficial, formal and informal, dominant and subordinate, central and marginal groups, and to their discourses and agendas. Top-down development, so closely associated with official national and international agendas, has been discredited over a long period; instead bottom-up or some hybrid of the two should be encouraged.

As such, postmodernism can become a fruitful approach for addressing conflictual and divergent agendas of social groups in the global South, be it in relation to access to productive resources and/or the bases for accumulating social power, mediating the impacts of large development schemes, evolving complementary medical services that harness the most appropriate elements from both Western and indigenous systems, or addressing longstanding conflicts between statutory and customary legal systems (Esteva and Prakash, 1998; Simon, 1998, 1999). Empowerment of the poor and powerless should be the objective.

Such discourses have much in common with earlier, liberal pluralism, basic needs and grassroots development paradigms, although the emphasis on co-existence and multiple modes of explanation is different. Equally, there are considerable areas of overlap with some strands of postcolonialism, which is centrally concerned with the cultural politics and identities of previously subordinated groups.

In practice, postmodernists often fail to adhere to these ideals, falling into familiar exclusivist modes of argument, and deprecating those who fail to share their propositions. On the other hand, extreme postmodernism can become almost indistinguishable from anarchism, in that all forms of social or collective action become impossible due to the inability to agree – or conceive of agreeing – on any shared rationality or even basic rules of what is and is not acceptable behaviour. Extreme relativism means that everyone's views are equally valid; without some decision-making rules, any social action not gaining unanimity or consensus becomes impossible.

For this reason and because of the emphasis by some authors on playful, leisured self-fulfilment, postmodernism is sometimes regarded with justification as a conservative ideology – another reason for its rejection by many critics.

CONCLUSION

Postmodern discourses arose within changing intellectual and geopolitical circumstances. An important problem has been the multiple uses and meanings of postmodernism, with resultant confusion and misinterpretation. Although a Northern intellectual toolkit in origin, it has found favour among some leading artistic and intellectual voices, who have contributed greatly to its refinement and prominence. However, it is also true that many Northern writers linking postmodernism to globalization and other politico-economic changes have, either implicitly or explicitly, assumed their Northern research and arguments to have global relevance.

I have argued that 'moderate' forms of postmodern intellectual practice do indeed have global relevance in the cause of problem analysis, development promotion and empowerment. This may be a radically different agenda from that of official agencies as it lends legitimacy to different social groups and their voices rather than merely seeking a compatible mouthpiece to support external interventions in the name of 'development'. However, therein lie the prospects to transcend the shortcomings of discredited official 'rapid modernization as development' and to facilitate local communities to develop according to their own conceptions, governed by acceptable rules of conduct. Of course such processes are not free from conflict, nor can there be room for any nostalgia for long-dead traditions and heritages. What is required is an adaptation to dynamic realities.

Extreme postmodernism is unduly relativistic and permissive; it may preclude any social contract or action and should rightly be rejected.

GUIDE TO FURTHER READING

The following sources provide a useful range of perspectives, with particular reference to development studies.

Esteva, G. and Prakash, M.S. (1998) *Grassroots Postmodernism: Remaking the Soil of Cultures*, London: Zed Books. One of the few book-length treatments of postmodern practice, linking new social movements, grassroots organizations and regionally based rebellions against inequitable and oppressive national governments in Latin America and Asia.

Harvey, D. (1989) *The Condition of Postmodernity*, Oxford: Blackwell. This remains an important reference guide to postmodernity as a function of late capitalism. Although focused on the North, it does have an implied global salience.

Pieterse, J.N. (2000) 'After post-development', *Third World Quarterly* 21(2): 175–91. Addresses the limitations and oversimplifications of the numerous critiques of 'the development project'. Argues that discourse analysis has been turned unhelpfully from a methodological tool into an ideology in itself.

Simon, D. (1998) 'Rethinking (post)modernism, postcolonialism and posttraditionalism: South–North perspectives', *Environment and Planning D: Society and Space* 16(2): 219–45. A detailed exposition of much of the ground covered in this chapter.

Slater, D. (1997) 'Spatialities of power and postmodern ethics – rethinking geopolitical encounters', *Environment and Planning D: Society and Space* 15(1): 55–72. Develops themes of post-Cold War geopolitical change and its implications across the North–South divide, including postmodern concerns for distant strangers.

Watson, S. and Gibson, K. (eds) (1995) *Postmodern Cities and Spaces*, Oxford: Blackwell. An innovative and important collection of essays, both conceptual and applied, addressing different approaches to postmodernism in a range of diverse urban contexts both North and South.

REFERENCES

Colás, S. (1994) *Postmodernity in Latin America: the Argentine Paradigm*, Durham, NC: Duke University Press.

Corbridge, S. (1994) 'Post-Marxism and post-colonialism: the needs and rights of distant strangers', in D. Booth (ed.) *Rethinking Social Development: Theory, Research and Practice*, Harlow: Longman.

Ellin, N. (1996) *Postmodern Urbanism*, Oxford: Blackwell.

Escobar, A. (1995) *Encountering Development: the Making and Unmaking of the Third World*, Princeton: Princeton University Press.

Featherstone, M. (1995) *Undoing Culture: Globalization, Postmodernism and Identity*, London: Sage.

Jameson, F. (1984) 'Postmodernism, or the cultural logic of late capitalism', *New Left Review* 146: 152–92.

King, A.D. (1995) 'The times and spaces of modernity (or who needs postmodernism?)', in M. Featherstone, S. Lash and R. Robertson (eds) *Global Modernities*, London: Sage.

Lyotard, J-F. (1984) *The Postmodern Condition: a Report on Knowledge*, Minneapolis: University of Minnesota Press.

Simon, D. (1999) 'Development revisited: thinking about, practising and teaching development after the Cold War', in D. Simon and A. Närman (eds) *Development as Theory and Practice: Current Perspectives on Development and Development Co-operation*, Harlow: Longman.

Slater, D. (1992) 'Theories of development and politics of the post-modern – exploring a border zone', *Development and Change* 23(3): 283–319.

Soja, E. (1991) *Postmodern Geographies: the Reassertion of Space in Critical Social Theory*, London: Verso.

2.14 Postcolonialism

Cheryl McEwan

WHAT IS POSTCOLONIALISM?

Postcolonialism is a difficult and contested term not least because it is far from clear that colonialism has been relegated to the past. Its meaning is not limited to 'after-colonialism' or 'after-independence'. (Ashcroft *et al.*, 1995: 2). Rather, as Radcliffe (1999: 84) argues, postcolonialism refers to ways of criticizing the material and discursive legacies of colonialism. Broadly speaking, therefore, postcolonial perspectives can be said to be *anti-colonial*. They have become increasingly important across a range of disciplines over the last 20 years.

A number of core issues underpin postcolonial approaches. First, postcolonial critiques stress the need to destabilize the dominant discourses of imperial Europe, such as history, philosophy, linguistics and 'development'. These discourses are unconsciously ethnocentric, rooted in European cultures and reflective of a dominant Western worldview. Postcolonial studies problematize the very ways in which the world is known, challenging the unacknowledged and unexamined assumptions at the heart of European and American disciplines that are profoundly insensitive to the meanings, values and practices of other cultures.

Second, postcolonial critiques challenge the experiences of speaking and writing by which dominant discourses come into being. For example, a term such as 'the Third World' homogenizes peoples and countries and carries other associations – economic backwardness, the failure to develop economic and political order, and connotations of a binary contest between 'us' and 'them', 'self' and 'other' (Darby, 1997: 2–3) – which are often inscribed in development writings. These practices of naming are not innocent. Rather they are part of the process of 'worlding' (Spivak, 1990), or setting apart certain parts of the world from others. Said (1978) has shown how knowledge is a form of power, and by implication violence; it gives authority to the possessor of knowledge. Knowledge has been, and to large extent still is, controlled and produced in 'the West'. The power to name, represent and theorize is still located here, a fact which postcolonialism seeks to disrupt.

Third, postcolonialism invokes an explicit critique of the spatial metaphors and temporality employed in Western discourses. Whereas previous designations of the Third World signalled both spatial and temporal distance – 'out there' and 'back there' – the postcolonial perspective insists that the 'other' world is 'in here' (Chambers, 1996: 209). The Third World is integral to what 'the West' refers to as 'modernity' and 'progress'. It contributes directly to the economic wealth of Western countries through its labour and through being exploited. In addition, the modalities and aesthetics of the Third World have partially constituted Western languages and cultures. Postcolonialism, therefore, attempts to rewrite the hegemonic accounting of time (history) and the spatial distribution of knowledge (power) that constructs the Third World.

Finally, postcolonialism attempts to recover the lost historical and contemporary voices of the marginalized, the oppressed and the dominated, through a radical reconstruction of history and knowledge production (Guha, 1982). Postcolonial theory has developed this radical edge through the works of political and literary critics such as Spivak, Said and Bhabha who, in various ways, have sought to recover the agency and resistance of peoples subjugated by both colonialism and neo-colonialism.

These core issues form the fabric of the complex field of inquiry of postcolonial studies, based in the 'historical fact' of European colonialism and the diverse material effects to which this phenomenon has given rise.

POSTCOLONIALISM AND DEVELOPMENT

The possibility of producing a truly decolonized, postcolonial knowledge in development studies became a subject of considerable debate during the 1990s. In theoretical terms, postcolonialism has been greatly influenced by Marxism and poststructuralism (Blunt and Wills, 2000), drawing on both the political-economy approaches of the former and the cultural and linguistic analyses of the latter. The politics of postcolonialism diverge sharply from other discourses and, although it shares similarities with dependency theories, its radicalism rejects established agendas and accustomed ways of seeing. This means that postcolonialism is a powerful critique of 'development' and an increasingly important challenge to dominant ways of apprehending North–South relations.

Critiquing discourses of development

Postcolonialism challenges the very meaning of development as rooted in colonial discourse depicting the North as advanced and progressive and the South as backward, degenerate and primitive. Early postcolonial writers, such as van der Post, challenged this assumption by referring to hunter-gatherers as the first affluent peoples. Postcolonialism has prompted questions about whether such indigenous systems of equity, reciprocity and communalism are more advantageous to peoples of the South than the pursuit of capitalism, with its emphasis on individual wealth and incorporation into the global economy. The superiority of modern industrialization and technological progress is increasingly questioned, creating alternative knowledges to reshape our views of non-Western societies and their environments.

Crush (1995: 4) suggests that to subject development to postcolonial critique might be considered a form of intellectual faddism. Some would argue that while ever there are pressing material issues such as poverty in the world, concerns with the *language* of development are esoteric. However, language is fundamental to the way we order, understand, intervene and justify those interventions (Escobar, 1995). As Crush argues, postcolonialism offers new ways of understanding what development is and does, and why it is so difficult to think beyond it. The texts of development are written in a representational language – metaphors, images, allusion, fantasy and rhetoric – the imagined worlds bearing little resemblance to the real world. Development writing often produces and reproduces misrepresentation. Postcolonialism seeks to remove Western negative stereotypes about people and places from such discourses (Simon, 1997). It challenges us to rethink categories such as 'Third World' and 'Third World women', and to understand how location, economic role, social dimensions of identity and the global political economy differentiate between groups and their opportunities for development.

As Crush suggests, the texts of development are 'avowedly strategic and tactical', promoting and justifying certain interventions and delegitimizing and excluding others. Power relations are clearly implied in this process; certain forms of knowledge are dominant and others are excluded. The texts of development contain silences. It is important to ask who is silenced, and why. Ideas about development are not produced in a social, institutional or literary vacuum (Crush, 1995). A postcolonial approach to development literature, therefore, can say a great deal about the apparatuses of power and domination within which those texts are produced, circulated and consumed.

Development discourse promotes and justifies very real interventions with very real consequences. It is, therefore, imperative to explore the links between the words, practices and institutional expressions of development, and between the relations of power that order the world and the words and images that represent the world. Otherwise, postcolonial approaches risk a 'descent into discourse', where the effects of development languages are confined to the text and the possibilities of effecting change are denied.

Agency in development

Postcolonialism challenges the notion of a single path to development and demands acknowledgement of a diversity of perspectives and priorities. The politics of defining and satisfying needs is a crucial dimension of current development thought, to which the concept of agency is central. Who voices the development concern, what power relations are played out, how do participants' identities and structural roles in local and global societies shape their priorities, and which voices are excluded as a result? Postcolonialism attempts to overcome inequality by opening up spaces for the agency of non-Western peoples. However, poverty and a lack of technology make this increasingly difficult; non-Western academics, for example, rarely have the same access to books and technologies of communication as their Western counterparts.

Despite this, the work of Third World academics has led to a questioning of authorization and authority. By what right and on whose authority does one claim to speak on behalf of others? On whose terms is space created in which they are allowed to speak? Are we merely trying to incorporate and subsume non-Western voices into our own canons? It is no longer feasible to represent the peoples of the Third World as passive, helpless victims. Their voices are now being heard, and their ideas are increasingly being incorporated into grassroots development policies, if not at the level of the World Bank. Third World critics have also had impacts on development studies, particularly within gender and development. They have forced a move away from totalizing discourses and a singular feminism (based upon the vantage point of white, middle-class Western feminists, which failed to acknowledge the differences between women) towards the creation of spaces where the voices of black women and women from the South can be heard (see, for example, Mohanty's (1988) devastating critique of the concept of the 'Third World Woman' inscribed in feminist development writing and planning). Postcolonial feminisms allow for competing and disparate voices among women, rather than reproducing colonialist power relations where knowledge is produced and received in the West, and white, middle-class women have the power to speak for their 'silenced sisters' in the South.

THE DILEMMAS OF POSTCOLONIALISM

One of the major dilemmas for postcolonialism is the charge that it has become institutionalized, representing the interests of a Western-based intellectual elite who speak the language of the contemporary western academy, perpetuating the exclusion of the colonized and oppressed (Loomba, 1998). Moreover, critics suggest that greater theoretical sophistication has created greater obfuscation; postcolonialism is too theoretical and not rooted enough in material concerns. Emphasis on discourse detracts from an assessment of material ways in which colonial power relations persist. Debates about postcolonialism and globalization have largely proceeded in relative isolation from one another, and to their mutual cost. Economic relations and their effects elude representation in much of postcolonial studies.

Some critics berate postcolonial theory for ignoring urgent life-or-death questions (San Juan, 1998). To have greater immediacy in critical development studies, postcolonial approaches might consider questions of inequality of power and control of resources, human rights, global exploitation of labour, child prostitution and genocide. With some exceptions, postcolonialism cannot easily be translated into action on the ground and its oppositional stance has not had much impact on the power imbalances between North and South. It also tends to be preoccupied with the past and has failed to say much about postcolonial futures (Spivak's (1999) attempt to describe a responsible role for the postcolonial critic in her critique of transnational globalization is one exception). Meanwhile, new forms of orientalism continue to disadvantage the Third World.

Despite criticism, postcolonialism is a significant advancement in development studies. It demonstrates how the production of Western knowledge forms is inseparable from the exercise of Western power (Said, 1978; Spivak, 1990). It also attempts to loosen the power of Western knowledge and reassert the value of alternative experiences and ways of knowing (Thiong'o, 1986; Bhabha, 1994). It articulates clearly some difficult questions about writing the history of 'development', about imperialist representations and discourses surrounding 'the Third World', and about the institutional practices of development itself. As Darby (1997: 30) argues, postcolonialism has an expansive understanding of the potentialities of agency. It shares a social optimism with other discourses, such as gender and sexuality in Western countries, and rethinking here has helped generate substantial changes in political practice. Therefore, despite the seeming impossibility of transforming North–South relations by the politics of difference and agency alone, postcolonialism is a much-needed corrective to the Eurocentrism and conservatism of much writing on development.

GUIDE TO FURTHER READING

Ashcroft, B., Griffiths, G. and Tiffin, H. (eds) (1995) *The Post-Colonial Studies Reader*, London: Routledge. A comprehensive selection of writings in postcolonial theory and criticism.

Crush, J. (ed.) (1995) *Power of Development*, London: Routledge. A collection of essays exploring the language of development, its rhetoric and meaning within different political and institutional contexts.

Escobar, A. (1995) *Encountering Development: the Making and Unmaking of the Third World*, Princeton: Princeton University Press. A provocative analysis of development discourse and practice.

Marchand, M. and Parpart, J. (eds) (1995) *Feminism/Postmodernism/Development*, London: Routledge. A collection of essays that question established development practices and suggest the need to incorporate issues such as identity, representation, indigenous knowledge and political action.

Schech, S. and Haggis, J. (2000) *Culture and Development*, Oxford: Blackwell. This book examines critically how development institutions, processes and practices are based in cultural presuppositions, values and meanings.

Simon, D. (1997) 'Development reconsidered: new directions in development thinking', *Geografiska Annaler* 79B(4): 183–201. An accessible account of recent advances in development studies.

REFERENCES

Bhabha, H. (1994) *The Location of Culture*, London: Routledge.

Blunt, A. and Wills, J. (2000) *Dissident Geographies*, London: Prentice Hall.

Chambers, I. (1996) 'Waiting on the end of the world?', in D. Morley and H.K. Chen (eds) *Stuart Hall: Critical dialogues in Cultural Studies*, London: Routledge, pp. 210–11.

Darby, P. (ed.) (1997) *At the Edge of International Relations: Postcolonialism, Gender and Dependency*, London: Pinter.

Escobar, A. (1995), 'Imagining a post-development era', in J. Crush, (ed.) *Power of Development*, London: Routledge, pp. 211–27.

Guha, R. (ed.) (1982) *Subaltern Studies*, New Delhi: Oxford University Press.

Loomba, A. (1998) *Colonialism/Postcolonialism*, London: Routledge.

Mohanty, C. (1988), 'Under western eyes: feminist scholarship and colonial discourses', *Feminist Review* 30: 61–88.

Radcliffe, S. (1999), 'Re-thinking development', in P. Cloke, P. Crang and M. Goodwin (eds) *Introducing Human Geographies*, London: Arnold, pp. 84–91.

Said, E. (1978) *Orientalism*, London: Routledge and Kegan Paul.

San Juan, E. (1998) *Beyond Postcolonial Theory*, London: Macmillan.

Spivak, G. (1990) *The Postcolonial Critic: Interviews, Strategies, Dialogue*, London: Routledge.

Spivak, G. (1999) *A Critique of Postcolonial Reason*, Cambridge, MA: Harvard University Press.

Thiong'o, Ngugi wa (1986) *Decolonising the Mind*, London: James Curry.

2.15 Responsibility to distant others

David M. Smith

INTRODUCTION

The question of responsibility to distant others is at the heart of the notion of development as the deliberate improvement of life in the world's deprived regions. It is implicitly a perspective of the more affluent ('North') towards the less developed ('South'), raising the role of beneficence in the transfer of resources from rich to poor. Beneficence is the process of active kindness or actually doing good, implied by the acceptance of a moral responsibility, as opposed to benevolence as merely charitable feelings or the desire to do good. A major ethical and practical issue is how benevolence can be turned into beneficence, requiring sacrifices on the part of those in affluent parts of the world for the sake of less fortunate persons elsewhere.

The use of the term 'others' is indicative of differences, with respect to culture or way of life, on the part of those for whom a responsibility may be thought to exist. The term 'strangers' is sometimes adopted in the literature, to emphasize lack of the familiarity which often provides a basis for beneficence. While 'distance' is usually thought of in a geographical sense, it can also signify emotional or psychological separation: hence the coupling of 'nearest and dearest' in some accounts of what might be regarded as the convention of favouring people who are close in both senses. Sentiments of localized partiality are challenged by those who deploy the moral power of impartiality and universality in support of the more spatially extensive or global reach of responsibility for others.

Some versions of the argument for responsibility to distant others include future generations. This adds intergenerational justice to the territorial social justice invoked by the case for promoting more even development by transfers of resources across geographical space. The time dimension raises issues of sustainable development, arising from the question of what natural resources and other production possibilities the present generation should bequeath to its successors.

The question of responsibility to distant others has been debated in moral and political philosophy, as well as in development ethics (see below). There have also been contributions from geographers working in development studies (Corbridge, 1993, 1998), and by others interested in the spatial scope of caring or supportive relationships (Silk, 1998; Smith, 1994, 1998, 2000).

THEORETICAL ISSUES

Responsibility to distant others raises important theoretical issues. The central question is that of how spatially extensive beneficence can be justified by moral argument, given what might appear to be the natural human tendency to favour our nearest and dearest over more needy strangers farther away.

An influential early discussion was provided by Peter Singer (1972), who called for a change in the way people in relatively affluent countries react to a situation like famine elsewhere. He began with the proposition that, if it is in our power to prevent something bad from happening, without thereby sacrificing anything of comparable moral importance, we ought to do it. This takes no account of proximity or distance:

> The fact that a person is physically near to us, so that we have personal contact with him [sic], may make it more likely that we *shall* assist him, but this does not show that we *ought* to help him rather than another who happens to be further away. If we accept any principle of impartiality, universalizability, equality, or whatever, we cannot discriminate against someone merely because he is far away from us.
>
> (Singer, 1972: 24)

Thus, we ought to give as much as possible to famine relief, perhaps to the point at which, by giving more, we would cause ourselves more suffering than we would prevent.

This formulation reflects the general perspective of utilitarianism, under which greatest aggregate good can be achieved by satisfying the more intense needs of the poor at the expense of the less intensive needs of those better-off. Ideally, resources would continue to be transferred (from 'North' to 'South') until need satisfaction or living standards were equalized. According to Singer (1972: 29), redistribution should not be constrained by ownership: 'From the moral point of view, the prevention of the starvation of millions of people outside our society must be considered at least as pressing as the upholding of property norms within our society.'

Another influential contribution was by James Sterba (1981). He suggested that, of the various moral grounds for justifying the welfare rights of distant peoples (and future generations), the most evident are those which appeal to either a right to life or a right to fair treatment. A right to life involves a positive right to the satisfaction of a person's basic needs: those which must be satisfied in order not to seriously endanger health or sanity, preserving life in the fullest sense (such as for food, shelter, medical care, protection, companionship and self-development). It also involves a negative right which requires persons not to interfere with attempts by others to meet their basic needs, which raises the question of whether persons with goods and resources surplus to basic needs are justified in keeping them if this prohibits others from satisfying their basic needs. He echoes Singer in concluding that, in the view of most people, 'their right to acquire the goods and resources necessary to satisfy their basic needs would have priority over any other person's property rights to surplus possessions' (Sterba, 1981: 102). A right to fairness involves the argument that, from a position of disinterest (i.e. not knowing who or where they might be), people would endorse limitations to a right to accumulate goods and resources, so as to guarantee a minimum sufficient to provide each person with the requirements to satisfy their basic needs.

More recent years have seen the emergence of an ethic of care (e.g. Clement, 1996), as a challenge or supplement to the prevailing ethic of justice with its emphasis on human rights and on rules governing redistribution. It has been argued that all persons need care, from cradle to grave, and that the meaning and practice of care should be given greater moral priority. The ethic of care has become an important framework for discussion of responsibility to others, well beyond the feminist ethics within which it was initially promoted (Smith, 1998, 2000).

Some proponents of an ethic of care stress the importance of knowing the other for whom we care. They may be sceptical about the possibility of caring for distant others, claiming that we cannot truly care for people we do not know. Feminist writers often applauded the special quality of caring that requires knowing people in their concrete particularity, rather than as representatives of such disadvantaged groups as the distant poor. However, there is a risk of over-prioritizing the mutuality of face-to-face relations. Critics of parochial interpretations of an ethic of care have argued for the construction of ever-widening circles of care, out to those far distant others in need. This is part of a process of increasing moral sensibility: 'we learn to care for distant others by first developing close relationships to nearby others, and then recognizing the similarities between close and distant others' (Clement, 1996: 85).

Marilyn Friedman (1991) has drawn special attention to the unequal distribution of resources required for caring. If the better-off have greater capacity to care for their own nearest and dearest, and if the less well-off lack the means to care, inequality in need satisfaction will be perpetuated and even exacerbated. Thus, the ethics of care and justice have to be brought together, to combine the sympathy customarily expressed in partiality towards our nearest and dearest with the institutions required for impartiality in the (re)distribution of capacity to care according to need.

Stuart Corbridge (1993, 1998) grounds responsibility to distant others in recognition that our lives are entwined with those of distant strangers, through flows of capital and commodities, modern communications and so on. Various processes subsumed under the concept of globalization are creating a more interdependent world, in ways largely beyond individual control. Our own position of advantage on what may be an increasingly uneven development surface is very much a matter of good fortune, rather than something we deserve. Thus 'the needs and rights of strangers could easily – and but for the "accident" of birth – be the needs and rights of ourselves' (Corbridge, 1993: 464).

PRACTICAL ISSUES

More practical issues may be considered briefly. It is obvious that some persons may be better placed than others (literally, in a geographical sense) to care for those in need, arising from an ongoing and necessarily local relationship. This was recognized by Singer (1972: 24):

> it is possible that we are in a better position to judge what needs to be done to help a person near to us than one far away, and perhaps also to provide the assistance we judge to be necessary. If this were the case, it would be a reason for helping those near to us first.

However, he went on to point out that instant communication and swift transportation enable aid to be disseminated, with the assistance of expert observers and supervisors, concluding: 'There would seem, therefore, to be no possible justification for discriminating on geographical grounds.' While everyday experience confirms that the needs of family or local community members may be first identified by those closest to them, and that some kinds of response may depend on such proximity, the diagnosis of need and the provision of effective care can seldom be so confined. However, the danger of outside agencies or professionals imposing inappropriate remedies suggests that some local, insider knowledge of the situation is helpful.

Both theory and practical experience suggest that, while benevolent sentiments may be a necessary condition for the recognition of responsibility for others, they are not in themselves sufficient to guarantee spatially extensive beneficence. And, like personal voluntarism, organized charity is an uncertain basis for ensuring the assistance required, on a scale likely to make a difference to large numbers of persons in great need. For justice to be done, in the sense of reliably meeting responsibilities to distant others, the process has to be institutionalized, at an international scale, and with a far greater commitment of resources than those currently deployed by individual or supposedly united nations.

GUIDE TO FURTHER READING

Responsibility to distant others, or strangers, is related to various issues at the interface of political philosophy and development studies in two important papers by Corbridge (1993, 1998). A general review of debates concerning the spatial scope of beneficence is provided by Smith (1998), and linked to other concerns about community, development and the environment in Smith (2000). More practical implications of the problem of caring at a distance are covered by Silk (1998).

REFERENCES

Clement, C. (1996) *Care, Autonomy, and Justice: Feminism and the Ethic of Care,* Oxford: Westview Press.

Corbridge, S. (1993) 'Marxisms, modernities and moralities: development praxis and the claims of distant strangers', *Environment and Planning D: Society and Space* 11: 449–72.

Corbridge, S. (1998) 'Development ethics: distance, difference, plausibility', *Ethics, Place and Environment* 1: 35–53.

Friedman, M. (1991) 'The practice of partiality', *Ethics* 101: 818–35.

Silk, J. (1998) 'Caring at a distance', *Ethics, Place and Environment* 1: 165–82.

Singer, P. (1972) 'Famine, affluence and morality', *Philosophy and Public Affairs* 1: 229–43, reprinted in P. Laslett and J. Fishkin, (eds) *Philosophy, Politics and Society* (5th series), Oxford: Blackwell Publishers, pp. 21–35.

Smith, D.M. (1994) 'On professional responsibility to distant others', *Area* 26: 359–67.

Smith, D.M. (1998) 'How far should we care? On the spatial scope of beneficence', *Progress in Human Geography* 22: 15–38.

Smith, D.M. (2000) *Moral Geographies: Ethics in a World of Difference,* Edinburgh: Edinburgh University Press.

Sterba, J.P. (1981) 'The welfare rights of distant peoples and future generations: moral side-constraints on social policy', *Social Theory and Practice* 7: 99–119.

2.16 The changing role of the state in development

Richard Batley

The history of the first three-quarters of the twentieth century can be seen as one where states held clear authority within their borders, acquired growing functions and tended to perform them on their own. The latter part of the twentieth century and early twenty-first century see a more porous view of the nation-state, fewer directly performed functions and more partnership with other actors.

'MODERNIZATION' AND THE EXTENSION OF THE STATE IN DEVELOPING COUNTRIES

The point of reference for the countries which became independent after the Second World War was of an extensive state, whether in the form of the socialist or of the advanced capitalist nations. This was partly a matter of policy transfer from the more developed capitalist and socialist countries in their race to fill the postcolonial 'vacuum'. In the 1950s and 1960s, aid programmes and academic advisers propagated the idea of the state bureaucracy as the lead agent for the transition to what was then known as 'modernization'. Aid agencies favoured large-scale projects of industrial and agricultural development which required the guarantee of government involvement (Esman, 1988). On the side of the new political elites, the idea of state-led development was attractive: it apparently offered a way of satisfying popular expectations and demonstrating a concern with social justice and development.

The case for state-led development was not only imitative but also built on a response to local circumstances. Where market institutions and indigenous entrepreneurs were weak, often only state enterprises were capable of investing or taking over foreign-owned plant. In the case of developing countries linked to the international economy through primary good exports, the case was made for the state to take the lead in restructuring the economy towards 'inward directed' industrial development on the basis of import substitution (Todaro, 1994).

However, the extension of the state and employment in the public sector of developing countries has not generally reached the levels of the advanced countries. By 1985, the proportion of GDP spent by central governments in the rich OECD countries was on average 47 per cent, compared with less than 25 per cent in all developing countries outside the Middle East (World Bank, 1997: 22).

CRITICISMS OF STATE ACTIVISM IN DEVELOPING COUNTRIES

The 'statist' model was quickly subject to criticism. An extensive literature will here be reduced to three themes. The first came from the early (1950s and 1960s) experience of operating aid programmes across a wide geographical spectrum but particularly in Africa, South and Southeast Asia. Critics challenged the view that public administration could act as an agent of development. They argued that bureaucracies were biased to stability or only incremental change, were anti-developmental and suppressed entrepreneurial interests. Moreover, public-sector agencies, which on the surface looked like rational bureaucracies, in practice often served particular interests (Hyden, 1983).

The second theme has been applied particularly, but not only, in sub-Saharan Africa. It refers to the 'softness' or 'weakness' (Migdal, 1988) of the state, in which the state apparatus maintains only a tenuous hold over society, lacking legitimacy and therefore the capacity to enforce policy. This is often associated with personal rule where leaders exercise their own interests through the official apparatus and patron–client networks, or resort to control through 'hard' militaristic regimes.

The third theme, which emerged from neo-Marxism and dependency theory, saw the apparatus of the state (the bureaucracy and military) as being subordinated to non-national interests, particularly international capital. This approach was used to explain the rise of various forms of authoritarian rule in the 1970s – bureaucratic authoritarianism in Latin America (Collier, 1979) and the postcolonial 'over-developed' state in South Asia. Far from being an agent of development the state was seen as an agent of underdevelopment or distorted development.

By the end of the 1970s, with international recession, growing national debt in Latin America and Africa, and widespread military regimes, there was deep pessimism about the scope for development and scepticism about the state's role. Two ways forward became evident in the 1980s – the example of the newly industrializing countries of East Asia and the neo-liberal model developed originally in Britain and the United States.

THE DEVELOPMENTAL STATES OF EAST ASIA

The East Asian 'newly industrializing countries' (NICs) demonstrated, contrary to Left radical thinking of the 1970s, that it was possible for poor nations to develop in a sustained and inclusive way whilst engaging with the international economy. Contrary to Right liberal thinking of the 1980s, they also showed that governments could play a positive role in achieving development.

The NICs showed that it was possible to break with import substitution industrialization, and shift to export-oriented industrialization. They pursued varied policies, ranging from the more state-managed approaches of Korea and Malaysia to the liberal economic policies of Hong Kong and Thailand. However, there was a core in common: they avoided the 'heavy state' traps of India and Latin America. State administrations had authority and capacity to give direction to market development, respond flexibly to private-sector needs, develop technology and human resources, while controlling labour. Wade (1990) describes this approach as one of a 'governed market' rather than either a free market or a command economy.

There have been numerous studies of the conditions of the NICs' success and their replicability in other countries. Among conditions which seem to be rather specific are the external trade conditions at the time of their industrialization, the availability of Japanese investment and American defence, early land reform, ethnic homogeneity, and cultures valuing both material success and mutual obligation. There are other conditions relating to the nature of state administration which are in principle more replicable. Evans (1995) describes the 'embedded autonomy' of the best functioning developmental states: they keep strong contacts with social groups crucial to development, while having sufficient authority and unity to retain a distance from social pressures.

In the case of the East Asian NICs, this delicate balance rested more on public–private understandings than on transparent systems of democratic accountability and regulation. While these arrangements were adequate for the management of relatively closed economies, they could not cope with rapid financial and capital market liberalization in the 1990s (Flynn, 1999).

NEO-LIBERALISM AND ADJUSTMENT

Earlier criticisms of the state's role in development questioned whether the conditions existed for 'third world' states to operate effectively. In the absence of these conditions, the tendency was for state agents to become self-serving, patrimonial and linked to powerful, often foreign, interests. The new liberal view held a deeper scepticism about the capacity of state administration to play a developmental role under *any* circumstances (Friedman, 1962). The bias was now against state expansion and for the market: the motto was 'public provision, the exception not the rule' (World Bank, 1996).

The immediate roots of the neo-liberal revival lay in the financial crises which followed the massive rise in oil prices in the early 1970s. The UK and USA, with histories of low investment and high trade deficits, were particularly badly affected by economic recession. The United Kingdom, in effect, experienced the first 'structural adjustment' programme when, in 1976, it negotiated a loan from the International Monetary Fund. In return it had had to accept public expenditure cuts, divestiture of public enterprises, a floating exchange rate and restraints on money supply. These became the principal elements of the structural adjustment programmes which were later applied globally.

Many countries, particularly in Latin America but also in central Europe and Africa, were slow to adjust to the new economic order and got themselves into deep difficulties of debt and inflation. They eventually had to resort to the International Monetary Fund and World Bank for loans. These two international financial institutions (IFIs) became the main propagators of the 'Washington consensus', a panoply of precepts to do with the liberalization, privatization and stabilization of economies.

Some broad critical points can be made about the experience of adjusting the role of the state in developing countries (Mosley *et al.*, 1995; Turner and Hulme, 1997). First is the question of 'ownership'. Advanced countries were able to mould the pace and nature of their responses and did so with the compliance of their electorates. Developing and post-socialist transitional countries, on the other hand, have usually made their adjustment under strong external pressure ('conditionality') from the IFIs.

Second is the question of uniformity of application. The main tenets of state withdrawal and adjustment were applied to countries with very different circumstances whose only common features were debt and poor economic management: post-socialist central and east European states, post-authoritarian Latin American states, weak states in Africa and bureaucratic states in South Asia. Variations in programmes have resulted less from design and more from failures to honour loan conditions.

Following from this, the third point is that adjustment has often been implemented in an unbalanced way, leading to deeper crisis and poverty, at least in the short term. Cuts in consumption and changes in the distribution of income have often been quickly made, but structural changes to boost the efficiency of private production and public administration have stalled or taken longer.

WHERE ARE WE NOW?

The 1990s and first decade of the twenty-first century have seen a shift from simple commitment to market liberalization. Free markets and liberal economic policies are seen now to be important but not enough on their own – markets depend on effective states (World Bank, 1997). Failures in structural adjustment have contributed to a renewed concern with the capacity of states and their support of the institutional conditions within which markets and citizens can flourish. These conditions include: clear property rights, the rule of law, financial systems, active civil society, 'good government' and effective public administration.

This does not constitute a simple return to previous conceptions of the state's role as the lead agent in development. Government and public administration will perform their own direct functions but they will also interact with and support private and community actors. The term 'governance' is often used to describe this broader view of the way that government should function. Similarly, the term 'public management' is used to differentiate a new more open and entrepreneurial style from bureaucratic public administration (Minogue, 1998).

However, there is also now wide recognition of the importance of a professional rule-based bureaucracy to provide the basic services and the conditions of predictability and honest-dealing within which businesses and citizens can flourish. How far particular states have the capacity to move beyond this to the more interventionist and managerial roles of partnering, promoting and regulating other actors is the question (Grindle, 1997; Larbi, 1999; Batley, 1999).

GUIDE TO FURTHER READING

Smith (1996) provides a survey of changing theories and practices in developing countries since 1945. Turner and Hulme (1997) give more attention to recent issues in public policy and management. The World Bank is an important source of current thinking and practice; see particularly its *World Development Reports* for 1991, 1996, 1997 and 1999.

REFERENCES

Batley, R.A. (1999) 'Introduction' and 'The new public management in developing countries', *Public Administration and Development* 11: 755–65.

Collier, D. (ed.) (1979) *The New Authoritarianism in Latin America*, Princeton: Princeton University Press.

Esman, M.J. (1988) 'The maturing of development administration', *Public Administration and Development* 8(2): 125–34.

Evans, P. (1995) *Embedded Autonomy: States and Industrial Transformation*, Princeton: Princeton University Press.

Friedman, M. (1962) *Capitalism and Freedom*, Chicago: University of Chicago Press.

Flynn, N. (1999) *Miracle to Meltdown in Asia: Business, Government and Society*, Oxford: Oxford University Press.

Grindle, M.S. (ed.) (1997) *Getting Good Government*, Cambridge: Harvard University Press.

Hyden, G. (1983) *No Shortcuts to Progress: African Development Management in Perspective*, London: Heinemann.

Larbi, G.A. (1999) 'The new public management approach and crisis states', Discussion Paper No. 112, Geneva: United Nations Research Institute for Social Development.

Migdal, J.S. (1988) *Strong Societies and Weak States: State–Society Relations and State Capabilities in the Third World*, Princeton: Princeton University Press.

Minogue, M. (1998) 'Changing the state: concepts and practices in the reform of the public sector', in M. Minogue, C. Polidano and D. Hulme (eds) *Beyond the New Public Management: Changing Ideas and Practices in Governance*, Cheltenham: Edward Elgar, pp. 17–37.

Mosley, P., Harrigan, J. and Toye, J. (1995) *Aid and Power: The World Bank and Policy-Based Lending* (2nd edn), London: Routledge.

Smith, B.C. (1996) *Understanding Third World Politics: Theories of Political Change and Development*, London: Macmillan.

Todaro, Michael (1994) *Economic Development* (5th edn), London: Longman.

Turner, M. and Hulme, D. (1997) *Governance, Administration and Development: Making the State Work*, London: Macmillan.

Wade, R. (1990) *Governing the Market: Economic Theory and the Role of Government in East Asian Industrialization*, Princeton: Princeton University Press.

World Bank (1996) *World Development Report 1996: From Plan to Market*, New York: Oxford University Press.

World Bank (1997) *World Development Report 1997: The State in a Changing World*, New York: Oxford University Press.

2.17 Social capital and development

Erika McAslan

INTRODUCTION

The World Bank (1997a) considers social capital to be the 'missing link' in the development equation. The expression 'social capital' first emerged in the early 1990s, and soon became 'one of the key terms of the development lexicon, adopted enthusiastically by international organisations, national governments and NGOs alike' (Harriss and De Renzio, 1997: 920). The emergence of social capital as a useful policy tool began in earnest with the formation of the 'Satellite Group on Social Capital' within the World Bank's Task Force on Social Development. By 1997, the concept was being widely cited in the *World Development Report*, and a number of influential documents had been produced exploring the way in which social capital impacts on development (see in particular, Moser, 1996; Narayan and Pritchett, 1997). Recently, a Social Capital Website has been developed, offering access to hundreds of abstracts of articles and papers on social capital. In addition, the World Bank produces a bi-monthly newsletter on social capital (*Nexus*), an electronic discussion group (*Let's Talk!*) and an electronic bulletin board (*Tell Us!*). In the opinion of the World Bank (1999), social capital has very important implications for development theory, practice and policy. It is, in short, 'the glue that holds societies together and without which there can be no economic growth or human well-being' (Serageldin, 1999: i).

DEFINITION

Definitions of social capital vary substantially. The World Bank (1997a: 114) has defined social capital as 'the informal rules, norms and long-term relationships that facilitate co-ordinated action and enable people to undertake co-operative ventures for mutual advantage'. Who coined the term social capital is uncertain, although what is clear is that the idea of social cohesion as a kind of resource with multiple functions has been implicit in much of sociology and anthropology for a long time. Indeed, Wall *et al.* (1998: 303) have suggested that social capital is merely 'a new term for an old idea'.

Current usage of the term has been classified into three different approaches within the social sciences. Firstly, Pierre Bourdieu (1985) regards it as a social resource that enables individuals to navigate their position within a hierarchical social structure, through the exchange of symbols within an established group boundary. In other words, 'it is what ordinary language calls "connections" ' (Bourdieu, 1993: 32). Secondly, James Coleman (1988) considers social capital within the context of the family in school–community collaboration. In this way, social capital is intimately connected with 'human capital' and the accumulation of education and various skills. Both Bourdieu and Coleman emphasize the importance of 'the potential benefit accruing to actors because of their insertion into networks or broader social structures' (Portes, 1998: 18). The third approach, however, regards social capital as a property of communities and nations, rather than individuals. The political scientist Robert Putnam is the most vocal supporter of this third approach and deserves much of the credit for the popularization of the term, 'social capital'. According to Putnam (1993: 35), social capital can be defined as the 'features of social organisations, such as networks, norms, and trust that facilitate action and co-operation for mutual benefit'. Each of these three perspectives involves a distinct series of assumptions and values, and therefore different methods, scales of analysis, and interpretations of social capital (Wall *et al.*, 1998).

MEASUREMENT

Social capital is a highly complex resource, with multiple strands. Clearly, this presents some difficulties in terms of measurement. However, Solow (1995) has argued that if social capital is to be more than just a 'buzzword', then some form of quantification needs to be proposed. Perhaps the most meaningful way to reflect the multi-dimensional nature of social capital is through the use of a composite index of various social indicators, similar to the UNDP's Human Development Index (HDI). For example, using data collected from household surveys, Narayan and Pritchett (1997) composed an index to measure levels of social capital in several villages. They asked respondents about the extent and characteristics of their associational activity, and their trust in various institutions and individuals. The study concluded that villages with higher levels of social capital had higher levels of income, even after allowing for household education, physical assets and village attributes.

Nevertheless, it is questionable whether social capital can, or even should, be quantified. Some critics have suggested that social capital does not exist as a clear unproblematic phenomenon (Legge, 1999). Instead, they have argued that the value of social capital lies in its use as a metaphor. In short, while it may be possible to determine the various ways that social capital is manipulated, it is doubtful whether the amount of social capital in the 'system' can be usefully gauged.

TYPES OF SOCIAL CAPITAL

Confusion about social capital often arises from a failure to distinguish between the multiple *sources* (the social networks and norms in which social capital are embedded), and *consequences* (the costs and benefits accrued through social capital). Based on empirical research in Italy, Putnam *et al.* (1993) differentiate between two types of social capital: (i) *'horizontal capital'* (also known as *'bonding capital'* and *'localized social capital'*) which unites people across a community; and (ii) *'vertical capital'* (also known as *'bridging capital'* and *'generalized social capital'*) which connects people to others outside of their immediate group.

It is important to distinguish between these two types of social capital, because the differentiation helps explain why a community may participate regularly in informal social interactions, yet still be socially isolated from the valuable resources of the wider city or region. In a case such as this, the community may be rich in localized or bonding social capital, but lack the necessary bridging capital to gain access to important economic opportunities. As Narayan (1999: 13) has stated, 'when power between groups is asymmetrically distributed, it is cross-cutting ties, the linkages between social groups, that become critical to both economic opportunity and social cohesion'. In other words, it is this 'bridging' social capital which is most important in connecting the poor to mainstream resources, for it can improve access to wider markets and formal credit systems and mobilize more funding and better services from the state (World Bank, 1999).

CONSEQUENCES OF SOCIAL CAPITAL

Social capital is a potential source of highly valuable resources and assets, and the literature has tended to focus primarily on these *benefits*, of which there are many. Indeed, social capital has been celebrated as a panacea for a number of development issues from environmental management to healthcare. Empirical research has uncovered many instances whereby social capital has had a positive impact on development. For example, in one of the most comprehensive examinations of vulnerability and development in urban communities, Moser (1996) found that social capital (in the form of reciprocal relationships and social networks) was a fundamental element in the alleviation of vulnerability and the expansion of opportunities. Reciprocity formed the basis for trust and co-operation within the four study communities, leading in turn to the formation of successful community-based organizations (CBOs). In short, stocks of social capital acted as an extremely important asset, in the absence of abundant human and physical capital.

Another area where social capital has had positive consequences is in the field of public healthcare. For example, Kawachi et al. (1997) found that residents of Almeda County, California, who had fewer social ties, were two or three times more likely to die from a variety of causes than those with extensive social networks. Social capital can also promote sustainable development and environmental management. Indeed, using case studies from rural communities in the Andes, Bebbington (1997) clearly demonstrated that social capital tangibly improves economic conditions and promotes the sustainable intensification of agriculture. Social capital is also a fundamental element in informal entrepreneurship. For example, in her exploratory study of gender and ethnicity in Trinidad, Lloyd Evans (1997: 3) has argued that 'as parts of the informal sector are built on local salient networks, supported by community loyalty, trust and patronage, it provides a salient starting point from which to study how social capital underpins the living standards of the poor'.

However, social capital does not only have positive consequences, it also has negative effects. Portes (1998) has identified at least four negative consequences of social capital. First, social capital can exclude outsiders, as in the case of the domination of certain ethnic groups over a particular occupation. For example, Friedman and Krackhardt (1997) have shown how Asian Chinese and Asian Indians generally do not get promoted to positions of power within the American computer industry, in spite of high educational achievements. This is a result of exclusion from the social networks of the majority group of European Americans. Second, social capital can limit personal freedom particularly in small towns or villages. Third, social capital often imposes crippling obligations as in the case of Geertz's (1963) finding that successful entrepreneurs in Bali were constantly bombarded by pleas for assistance from job- and loan-seeking kinsmen. Fourth, social capital sometimes creates significant 'downward levelling norms' (Portes, 1998: 17). For example, Bourgois (1995) has shown how ambitious Puerto Ricans in the Bronx are ridiculed within the local community for trying to be 'white' and ignoring their roots.

CONCLUSION

Social capital has become a fashionable topic within the development community. As Harriss and De Renzio (1997: 920) have argued, the concept of social capital grew in popularity precisely because it could be interpreted in several different ways; 'the idea of social capital has seemed to promise answers which are attractive both to the neoliberal right – still sceptical about the role of the state – and to those committed to ideas about participation and grassroots empowerment'. However, the term 'social capital' is now in danger of becoming a victim of its own success, having been applied in such a wide variety of different contexts that it may soon cease to have any real value. Admittedly, social capital is difficult to define and even more complex to measure, but it is still a relatively new tool for analysis. As Foley and Edwards (1997: 550) have argued, the current priority should be to increase clarity about the notion of social capital by working on building 'theoretical depth and empirical substance'.

The term 'social capital' offers tremendous potential to 'do' development differently (Rose, 1999). For as Wallis et al. (1998: 253) have argued, 'its strength lies in its ability to mobilise diverse interests in a common dialogue and ultimately around a shared action agenda'. In other words, social capital presents the rare possibility of providing an integrating framework, which will in turn facilitate dialogue about development between disciplines and across national and regional boundaries.

A GUIDE TO FURTHER READING

For a useful introduction to social capital, see the World Bank's 'Social Capital for Development' website: http://www.worldbank.org/poverty/scapital.

The following volume contains papers from a 1997 multi-disciplinary workshop on social capital held by the World Bank: Dasgupta, P. and Serageldin, I. (2000) *Social Capital: A Multifaceted Perspective*, Washington DC: World Bank.

For a more critical approach, see Portes, A. (1998) 'Social capital: its origins and applications in modern sociology', *Annual Review of Sociology* 22: 1–24.

One of the first empirical studies of social capital and vulnerability was by Moser, C.O.N. (1996) 'Confronting crisis: a comparative study of household responses to poverty and vulnerability in four poor urban communities', *Environmental Sustainable Development Studies and Monographs Series No. 8*, Washington DC: World Bank.

Also useful are Knack and Keefer (1997) and World Bank (1997b).

REFERENCES

Bebbington, A. (1997) 'Social capital and rural intensification: local organisations and islands of sustainability in the rural Andes', *The Geographical Journal* 163(2): 189–97.

Bourdieu, P. (1985) 'The forms of capital', in J.G. Richardson, (ed.) *Handbook of Theory and Research for the Sociology of Education*, New York: Greenwood, pp. 241–58.

Bourdieu, P. (1993) *Sociology in Question*, London: Sage Publications.

Bourgois, P. (1995) *In Search of Respect: Selling Crack in El Barrio*, New York: Cambridge University Press.

Coleman, J. (1988) 'Social capital in the creation of human capital', *American Journal of Sociology* 94: 95–120.

Foley, M.W. and Edwards, B. (1997) 'Editors' introduction: escape from politics? Social theory and the social capital debate', *American Behavioural Scientist* 40(5): 550–61.

Friedman, R. and Krackhardt, D. (1997) 'Social capital and career mobility: a structural theory of lower returns to education for Asian employees', *The Journal of Applied Behavioural Science* 33(3): 316–34.

Geertz, C. (1963) *Peddlers and Princes*, Chicago: University of Chicago Press.

Harriss, J. and De Renzio, P. (1997) 'Missing link or analytically missing?: The concept of social capital', *Journal of International Development* 9(7): 919–37.

Kawachi, I., Kennedy, B.P. and Lochner, K. (1997) 'Long live community: social capital as public health', *The American Prospect* 35: 56–9.

Knack, S. and Keefer, P. (1997) 'Does social capital have an economic payoff? A cross-country investigation', *Quarterly Journal of Economics* 112: 1251–88.

Legge, D. (1999) 'Comments', *Social Capital 'Let's Talk': The World Bank's Email Discussion Group*, Posting No. 8, 12 January.

Lloyd Evans, S. (1997) *Gender, Ethnicity and Social Capital in Trinidad's Informal Sector*, paper presented at the Annual Conference of the Society for Latin American Studies, 4–6 April 1997, St Andrews University.

Moser, C.O.N. (1996) 'Confronting crisis: a comparative study of household responses to poverty and vulnerability in four poor urban communities', *Environmental Sustainable Development Studies and Monographs Series No. 8*, Washington DC: World Bank.

Narayan, D. (1999) *Bonds and Bridges: Social Capital and Poverty*, Washington DC: World Bank.

Narayan, D. and Pritchett, L. (1997) *Cents and Sociability: Household Income and Social Capital in Rural Tanzania*, Washington DC: World Bank.

Portes, A. (1998) 'Social capital: its origins and applications in modern sociology', *Annual Review of Sociology* 24: 1–24.

Putnam, R. (1993) 'The prosperous community: social capital and public life', *American Prospect* 13: 35–42.

Putnam, R., Leonardi, R. and Nanetti, R. (1993) *Making Democracy Work: Civic Traditions in Modern Italy*, Princeton: Princeton University Press.

Rose, T. (1999) 'Comments', *Social Capital 'Let's Talk': The World Bank's Email Discussion Group*, Posting No. 17, 15 April.

Serageldin, I. (1999) 'Foreword', in T. Van Bastelaer (ed.) *Does Social Capital Facilitate the Poor's Access to Credit? A Review of the Microeconomic Literature*, Social Capital Initiative Working Paper No. 8, Washington DC: World Bank.

Solow, R. (1995) 'But verify', *The New Republic*, 11 September: 36.

Wall, E., Ferrazzi, G. and Schryer, F. (1998) 'Getting the goods on social capital', *Rural Sociology*, 63(2): 300–22.

Wallis, A., Crocker, J.P. and Schechter, B. (1998) 'Social capital and community building: part one', *National Civic Review*, 87(3): 253–71.

World Bank (1997a) 'Social capital: the missing link', *Monitoring Environmental Progress: Expanding the Measure of Wealth*, The World Bank: Indicators and Environmental Valuation Unit, Environment Department (draft, revised January) Chapter 6.

World Bank (1997b) *World Development Report 1997: The State in a Changing World*, New York: Oxford University Press for the World Bank.

World Bank (1999) 'PovertyNet: Social Capital for Development', http://www.worldbank.org/poverty/scapital.

Rural development

EDITORIAL INTRODUCTION

Food security in the developing countries must not come to be dependent on surpluses from the industrialized countries or, worse, food aid. Priority must be given to the future nutritional needs of their people and to ways and means of meeting those needs locally. The term 'Green Revolution' refers to the development of high yielding varieties (HYVs) in the 1960s. This high yield depends upon the use of agrochemicals, irrigation and other purchased inputs. Farmers were persuaded to apply often inappropriate innovations – for example, irrigation and pesticides. These intensive methods degrade agricultural resources. This leads to accelerated deforestation, soil degradation, and vulnerability to pest attacks and extreme weather conditions.

To understand environmental degradation, we need to consider people's livelihoods, for these establish the relationship between economic activity and environment. Characteristically, forms of environmental degradation are generated by livelihoods based on primary commodity production, such as those of wage labourers in agriculture, or petty commodity producers, sometimes degraded to subsistence producers. The vulnerability of rural people, created by shifting seasonal constraints, short-term economic shocks and longer-term trends of change, influence institutional structures and processes which encourage them to pursue diverse livelihood strategies to combat rural poverty.

In order to survive many farmers are exploiting the land beyond its carrying capacity. For these reasons critics argue that yield benefits cannot be extended or even sustained. An alternative system advocates integrated management. Input use can be cut substantially if farmers substitute knowledge, labour and management skills. It is important to explore how different means have affected farmer's livelihoods and whether or not they are likely to deliver food security for hungry people.

Green Revolution-type agriculture is capital intensive and tends to be highly mechanized and used by rich farmers, as these external inputs have become more expensive and fewer farmers can afford them. Rich farmers have become dominant social groups and classes; their intensive capital investment is expanding production and/or increasing its efficiency by improving productivity. This can be used for accumulation.

Sustainable development and poverty alleviation in rural areas depend on effective common resources management, which hinges on adaptations to local agro-ecological and social conditions. Varied types of co-operatives have helped people cope with various economic, social and environmental problems.

3.1 Rural poverty

Joe Mullen

It is currently estimated that 1.3 billion people live below the poverty line (World Bank, 2000a), of which 939 million or 72.2 per cent live in rural areas (IFAD, 1992). Asia has the highest proportion of the rural poor with some 633 million, followed by 204 million in sub-Saharan Africa, 76 million in Latin America and the Caribbean, with the balance in the Near East and North Africa. Although the statistics and methods of computation are often open to debate, what these figures suggest is that a substantial proportion of the world's poor live in and depend upon the rural environment for their livelihoods.

Apart from the geographical concentration of poverty in rural areas there are also regional characteristics. Asia experienced rapid economic growth until the financial crisis in 1998, but it is primarily in East Asia that export-led growth has contributed to poverty reduction. However, while proportionately there is a percentage decline of rural poverty in Asia, numbers overall have increased. Sub-Saharan Africa presents a more pessimistic profile: overall numbers of the poor have increased both absolutely and proportionately, the depth of poverty or the distance below the poverty line has also intensified and economic growth has been weak in many countries. In Latin America and the Caribbean, political instability, currency movements and international market fluctuations have adversely affected the rural poor.

Although the proportion of the poor in relation to the total population below the poverty line has decreased over the last 20 years, despite an increase numerically, this aggregate assumption masks two important facts: one, that poverty has substantially increased in Africa; two, the bottom two quintiles (40 per cent) of the population have not benefited from overall growth and, certainly in Africa and probably in Asia, poverty may have become deeper and more intense in this group. Further, the potential for poor groups within countries to be drawn into ethnic strife, violence and activities that threaten national and international stability is indeed great. Poverty could indeed become a major threat to a safe and investment-oriented national and international environment.

An external variable impacting upon the rural poor has been structural reform, trade liberalization and globalization, particularly of commodity markets, which in turn has led to increased indebtedness. It is widely acknowledged that the poor – and particularly the rural poor – have been adversely affected in terms of their weaker purchasing power, removal of concessional credit schemes, lack of quality inputs, collapse of extension systems and risk aversion in relation to export cropping opportunities (see Mullen and Pearce, 1993). There have been powerful vectors of rural differentiation, erosion of livelihood systems, marginalization, and disempowerment of men and women. Worsening socioeconomic profiles between rural and urban areas, particularly in terms of public goods, such as healthcare and education, and income-earning opportunities are in evidence. Table 1 illustrates the characteristics of the rural poor in terms of population below the poverty line, labour force participation, food security and rural–urban differentiation in service provision, with particular reference to East and Central Africa.

Table 1 Profile of the rural poor in East African countries with rural–urban disparities

Country	Rural pop. as % of total	% of rural pop. below poverty line (1988)	% of labour force in agric. (1990)	Agric. as % of GDP (1993)	Food prod. PC index 1980 = 100 (1993)	Rural-urban disparity in services 100 = parity		
						Health	Safe H²O	Sanitation
Kenya	74	55	84	29	83	–	75	56
Malawi	87	86	87	39	70	–	46	72
Mozambique	69	65	83	33	77	30	235	18
Tanzania	77	60	84	56	76	78	69	84
Uganda	88	80	85	53	109	42	68	55
Average	79	69.2	84.6	42	83			

Source: Commonwealth Secretariat (1996)

Who are the rural poor? Behind the statistics there lies a constellation of tragic trajectories of livelihood decline of families who typically belong to the group of small or marginal farmers, landless labourers, nomadic pastoralists or artisan fisherman. Two country profiles follow, one from Africa and the other from Asia, to illustrate the realities of rural poverty at national level.

BOX 1

Rural poverty in Africa: the case of Tanzania

A typical case of poverty in Africa is Tanzania. The World Bank (1993) specified two poverty lines: one relative, referring to households with less than 50 per cent of the mean adult equivalent income; the other absolute, which applied to households that were unable to afford a basic diet and essential needs and were classified as the hard-core poor. On the basis of these assumptions about 50 per cent of the population overall were deemed to be poor or absolute poor. But poverty is predominantly a rural phenomenon with 90 per cent of the hard-core poor living in rural areas, where 59 per cent of the population overall are relatively poor, as against 39 per cent in urban areas. The discrepancy between urban and rural income is also significant with average rural income being 63 per cent of that in provincial urban areas and only 44 per cent of average income in the capital city, Dar-es-Salaam. The Tanzania case reflects Africa as a whole, where average per capita incomes are lower than at the end of the 1980s, two-thirds of rural people lack adequate water supplies and three-quarters live without proper sanitation (World Bank, 2000b).

Two other factors contributing to rural poverty aggravation are indebtedness and AIDS. Exports from rural areas, whether agricultural products or minerals, will typically provide a substantial contribution of the foreign exchange required to repay international loans. Much of the capital accruing to rural productivity will be extracted from the rural sector, thus preventing rural growth and capital formation while paying for the irresponsible lending and corruption of past regimes. For example, in the case of Tanzania it is estimated that for every one dollar being spent on education and health, four and nine dollars respectively were being spent on debt repayment. The debt was equivalent to US$267 for every individual in the country although the average per caput income was only US$210.

BOX 2

Characteristics of rural poverty in Cambodia

Since poverty alleviation is a central policy objective of the Kingdom of Cambodia, the characteristics of rural poverty are of utmost importance in ensuring that the institutional framework and response capabilities are commensurate to the task of poverty reduction and post-conflict reconstruction. The Poverty Profile of Cambodia (Royal Government of Cambodia, 1997) outlines a typology of poverty as follows: poverty is highest in rural areas where 43 per cent of the population were considered to be below the poverty line, in contrast to 39 per cent of the population overall (which is 85 per cent rural). In terms of the depth of poverty, 22 per cent of the population have expenditures below the food poverty line or subsistence, thus suggesting absolute poverty. The linkage between poverty and agriculturally based households is particularly significant: 90 per cent of Cambodia's poor live in agricultural households; 46 per cent of farmer-headed households are poor; poverty rates are inversely related to years of schooling, and female-headed households tend to be less represented than male-headed households among the poor.

Two trends in poverty are particularly significant: there was a modest decline in the national incidence of poverty from 39 per cent in 1993–94 to 36 per cent in 1997; however, income distribution worsened in both rural and urban areas with disproportionate gains being made by the rich. For example, the Gini Coefficient indicating levels of inequality of distribution increased in rural areas from 0.27 in 1993–94 to 0.33 in 1997. This increasing income stratification is a cause for concern. However, it may best be addressed by strengthening the productive capacity of smallholders through improved physical and social infrastructure, open market networks including market information, access to inputs, robust rural financial markets and education.

Source: Mullen (1999b)

CHALLENGES AND OPPORTUNITIES IN RURAL POVERTY ERADICATION

The challenge confronting rural poverty eradication include people's own perception of poverty and their ability to address it, problems of local governance lacking in transparency and accountability, rapid population growth, rural–urban migration, poor market infrastructure and the increasing problem of AIDS. These issues are addressed in Table 2.

Besides statistical measures of poverty, the people's own perception of poverty may be captured in participatory poverty assessments (PPAs) which are key instruments of identifying local qualitative characteristics of rural poverty: the problems in micro-markets, weak delivery of basic services and the local culture of deprivation. These perceptions provide major challenges to both rural people and policy-makers. Effective remedies may require radical attitudinal changes to enable people to claim their basic entitlements as citizens, while a responsive and supportive state should articulate the meso and micro policy and planning interventions required to incorporate the PPA conclusions into public expenditure activities.

Poverty itself is global, heterogeneous, multi-causal and geographically configured, and has macro-, meso- and micro-level dimensions. Hence universal prescriptions aimed at reducing poverty have major fault lines. The international community has pledged itself to halve absolute poverty by 2015 (though without graduated 5 yearly benchmarks) which would have a significant effect on rural productivity and incomes. However, one could postulate a number of policy measures or

Table 2 Policies, policy instruments and programmes for rural poverty alleviation

Policy	Policy instruments	Programme/project
Equitable/inclusive development	Redistributive fiscal regimes, parity of urban and rural investment and social provision	• Added-value economic activities in rural areas • Employment generation • Small and micro business promotion, and business incubation – private-sector support
	Infrastructure and public goods provision	• Rural electrification • Water supplies • Schools and a knowledge culture • Information technology • Health; AIDS prevention • Social protection
Good governance	Decentralization	• Devolution to local level • District development programmes targeted on deprivation
	Institution strengthening	• Reinforcing capabilities, training
	Public accountability	• Information flows, public awareness of citizens' rights
	Democracy	• Free and fair elections
	Civil society	• Promotion of human rights and free association
	Gender	• Gender awareness promotion and economic empowerment of women
	Transparency	• Equality in accessing social and economic opportunities; integrity
Stability	Conflict resolution	• Reconciliation • Post-conflict reconstruction • Reduction of military expenditure • Peacebuilding and inter-ethnic collaboration
Enabling economic environment	Liberalization	• Promotion of private-sector initiatives • Venture capital partnership
	Economic diversification	• Marketing infrastructure • Increased competitiveness
	Globalization	• Protection of cultural identity and local economic systems
	Environmental awareness	• Erosion control, regulatory provision • Control of toxic waste and agricultural chemicals • Good arrival husbandry practices • Afforestation • Conservation of flora and fauna
	Sustainability	• Capacity resource availability • Community participation
	Debt management	• Qualification for debt relief • Conditionality fulfilment
Sector-wide approach	Rural development	• Agricultural productivity • Food security • Agribusiness • Sustainable rural livelihoods • Access to financial markets
	International transfers	• Collaborative aid management

mechanisms which could contribute to a significant reduction in rural poverty. These measures include macro, meso and micro policies and policy instruments at sector level, and project/programme interventions. These are outlined in Table 2.

GUIDE TO FURTHER READING

Chambers, R. (1997) *Whose Reality Counts?* London: IT.
Gordon, D. and Spicker, P. (eds) (1999) *The International Glossary on Poverty*, London: CROP/Zed Books.
IFAD (1992) *The State of World Rural Poverty*, London: IT.
IFAD (2001) *Rural Poverty Report 2001*, Oxford: Oxford University Press.
Mullen, J. (1999a) *Rural Poverty, Empowerment and Sustainable Livelihoods*, Aldershot: Ashgate.
World Bank (2000a) *World Development Report 2000/2001: Attacking Poverty*, New York: Oxford University Press.

REFERENCES

Commonwealth Secretariat (1996) *Poverty Reduction Strategies and Programmes*, Regional Workshop, Arusha, Tanzania, London: Commonwealth Secretariat.
Mullen, J. (1999b) 'Local level institutions and poverty reduction: implications for post-conflict village development in Cambodia', Phnom Penh: FAO.
Mullen, J. and Pearce, R. (1993) 'Smallholders and structural adjustment', in L. Demery, M. Ferroni and C. Grootaert (eds) *Understanding the Social Effects of Policy Reform*, Washington, DC: World Bank.
Royal Government of Cambodia (1997) *A Poverty Profile of Cambodia – 1997* (in collaboration with UNDP, World Bank and SIDA), Phnom Penh.
World Bank (1993) *Tanzania: A Poverty Profile*, Washington DC: World Bank.
World Bank (2000b) *Can Africa Claim the 21st Century?* (in collaboration with AFDB, ECA and Africa Economic Research Consortium), Washington DC.

3.2 Rural livelihoods

Colin Murray

Most people who live in the rural areas of poor countries are engaged in an unremitting struggle to secure a livelihood in the face of adverse social, economic and often political circumstances. Two points are central to an understanding of such struggles. The first is that the circumstances of poverty and the reasons for poverty have to be understood through detailed *analysis of social relations* in a particular historical context: between those with land and those without land, for example; between rich and poor households; between men and women; between rural households and the institutions of the market and the state. The second point is that the modes of livelihood that typically prevail both within households and between households are highly *diverse*. Rural households may derive a part-livelihood from farming; a part-livelihood from migrant labour undertaken by absent household members in urban areas or other rural areas; and a part-livelihood from a variety of other activities, more or less informal, such as petty trade or beer-brewing. Variable combinations of activities of this kind, likewise gendered in respect of unequal dispositions of labour and appropriations of income between men and women, are often themselves subject to rapid change over time. For these two reasons, rural livelihoods are not at all easy to study.

Both these points were strongly illustrated in an exemplary text, *Rural Livelihoods: Crises and Responses* (Bernstein *et al.*, 1992). Through exploration of 'agrarian structures and change' in three different regions of the world – Latin America, India and sub-Saharan Africa – and through detailed analysis of 'making a living' and 'survival and change' at the household level, the authors explored the vitally important processes of marginalization, dispossession, accumulation and differentiation that have affected rural communities and go far towards explaining poverty in the late twentieth century.

Two vignettes from the lives of poor people in very different rural areas may be used to illustrate the importance of analysis of social relations and of understanding diversity of modes of livelihood. The first concerns a family of marginalized share-croppers in a Bangladesh village whose circumstances of the mid-1970s were graphically described in Hartmann and Boyce's moving book *A Quiet Violence* (1983). Despite hard work and constant struggle, Sharifa and Abu were forced to sell most of their own fragments of land and even to chop down fruit trees for sale as firewood in order to pay debts and buy a few days' supply of rice.

> We had to borrow money to eat. Sometimes neighbours would lend us money without interest, but we often had to sell our rice before the harvest. Moneylenders would pay us in advance, and take our rice at half the market price. No matter how hard we worked, we never had enough cash. We started selling things – our wooden bed, our cow, our plough. Then we began to sell our land bit by bit. Now we have less than one *dun* left, and most of that is mortgaged to Mahmud Haji.
>
> (quoted in Bernstein *et al.*, 1992: 19)

The second vignette is drawn from Charles van Onselen's massive biography (1996) of an obscure black South African who strove throughout his long life to sustain a tenuous grip on land alienated to white settlers. Kas Maine (1894–1985) was a farmer who did not own land but engaged in many different share-cropping contracts with white landlords in the maize-growing region of the south-western Transvaal. Through the first half of the twentieth century Maine and his family experienced the shifting pressures of the marketplace, the mounting exactions of landlords and the relentless politics of white supremacy. Eventually they were evicted from the land altogether, so that he ended his life in a remote and dusty relocation camp in a former African 'homeland'. Kas Maine met those pressures with hard work, cunning and sometimes desperation. To supplement a livelihood constantly under threat from an arid and volatile climate, and the often arbitrarily tightening screw of the landlords, he engaged in many different activities in the informal economy: shoe- and saddle-repairing, knitting and tailoring, traditional healing. Both stubborn and versatile, he showed single-minded commitment to farming in adverse circumstances and also great enterprise in his pursuit of many other sources of income in a difficult social and political environment. His wives, meanwhile, whose labour in a tough domestic regime was mainly committed to his farming efforts, also strove to secure a small cash income on the side through their own complementary activities: selling cowdung, rearing pigs, brewing beer, occasional 'piece-jobs'.

Closely linked to the observation of diversity of modes of livelihood at any one time is the idea of *diversification* of livelihoods over time. For example, a broad comparative review of a process described as 'de-agrarianization' in sub-Saharan Africa concluded that perhaps 60–80 per cent of rural household income in the late 1990s was derived from non-farming sources, by comparison with an approximate 40 per cent in the 1980s (Bryceson, 1999). There were many different reasons for such changes: structural adjustment programmes, sharply worsening terms of agricultural trade, the collapse of meso-level infrastructures of support for small farmers, devalued currencies, new opportunities and necessities of cross-border smuggling and trade, etc. The literature on diversification, its causes and its implications, is usefully and systematically reviewed by Ellis (1998). It is important to remember that it is not only poor households that are forced to diversify in order to make ends meet as best they can. Richer households also diversify their economic activities – as for example in the case of businessmen who are 'weekend' farmers – and this can be a path to accumulation. It is also important to note that migration for work elsewhere is one typical mode of diversification in the livelihoods of the rural poor that has arguably been inhibited by politicians and undervalued by policy-makers (de Haan, 1999).

Three questions arise out of recent valuable research work undertaken in the mid-1990s and the late 1990s, under the auspices of different projects, for example by the African Studies Centre at Leiden University, the Institute of Development Studies at Sussex and the Overseas Development Institute in London. The first question is how, in view of the complexity of individual household trajectories of change that are illustrated in the two vignettes above, it is possible to derive defensible generalizations about the experience of large numbers of the rural poor over time. The second question is how to achieve a better understanding of the links and the tensions between different levels of analysis: the micro level of the household, the meso level of institutional intervention through local government, development agencies or regional markets, and the macro level of national policy-making. The third question, in the light both of prevalent neo-liberal policy prescriptions and of the reality of diversified rural livelihoods across a number of conventionally discrete economic sectors, is how policies are to be devised in practice that will have an effective impact upon the disparate livelihoods of the rural poor.

It is perhaps helpful to distinguish between the following approaches, separate in principle but closely linked in practice. First, we need to understand diversity at a moment of time (the *circumspective* approach). This may be tackled through a combination of surveys, interviews and various techniques loosely grouped under the heading of participatory rural appraisal. The objective is to open up questions about the proportional importance of and, above all, about significant relationships between different economic activities: for example, that between urban wage earnings and rural consumption or investment in farming. Second, we need to understand change over time (the *retrospective* approach). This requires analysis of the historical context, inference of the broad trends of change, and critical investigation of the institutional framework through which relations between macro, meso and micro levels are worked out over time. It also requires empirical investigation at the household level, which may be undertaken through a combination of methods: longitudinal comparison of household livelihoods, either in a strict sense or in a loose sense, with careful attention to the difficulties that arise out of the fact that a household observed in the mid-1990s cannot be treated as the 'same' household as might have been observed in the mid-1970s, even if partly reliable baseline data of this kind can be identified; and retrospective reconstruction of processes of change through intersecting life histories. The objectives of this approach are to identify 'household' or family trajectories of accumulation and impoverishment and thence particular structural matrices of *vulnerability*. An admirably explicit discussion of the problems that arise in a study of this kind is found in Bagchi *et al.* (1998).

Third, academics are increasingly aware, either by professional inclination or through the pressures of donor funding for their research, of the need to influence policy and action (the *prospective* approach). This should include analysis of the effects of past policies, which are often haphazardly reproduced under different political regimes; a commitment to changing 'mind-sets' amongst government officials, planners, donors, NGOs, etc.; the development of specific rationales for intervention at various levels; and procedures for monitoring and evaluation. The objectives of the prospective approach are better co-ordination of planning and implementation across sectoral boundaries; and building alternative conceptual frameworks for facilitating opportunities for improving livelihoods.

The Sustainable (Rural) Livelihoods framework is one such that has come to dominate recent research, through its official adoption in Britain by the Department for International Development (DfID). It combines, in effect, the circumspective, the retrospective and the prospective approaches outlined above. The term 'Sustainable Livelihoods' may be traced from the work of Robert Chambers and others, through a research programme undertaken by the Institute of Development Studies at Sussex, involving work in Bangladesh, Ethiopia and Mali in particular.

> A livelihood comprises the capabilities, assets (including both material and social resources) and activities required for a means of living. A livelihood is sustainable when it can cope with and recover from stresses and shocks and maintain or enhance its capabilities and assets both now and in the future, while not undermining the natural resource base.
>
> (DfID, 1999: Section 1.1)

Within a particular 'vulnerability context', defined for example by shifting seasonal constraints, short-term economic shocks and longer-term trends of change, people deploy five types of 'livelihood assets' or capital (the 'asset pentagon') in variable combinations, within circumstances influenced by institutional structures and processes, in order to pursue diverse 'livelihood strategies', with more or less measureable 'livelihood outcomes'. Two books, a series of flexible and sensible *Sustainable Livelihoods Guidance Sheets* and a series of more specific working papers elaborate the framework and recent fruitful experience of its practical application (see, for example, Carney, 1998; Scoones, 1998; DfID, 1999, 2000). Further, some practitioners have developed out of their experience of working within the Sustainable Livelihoods paradigm a set of detailed guidelines on the proper conduct of an SL study in practice (for example, Khanya, 2000). The paradigm has a number of strengths and weaknesses, partly reviewed in Murray (2000). One problem is that fundamentally, it may be argued, capital is a social relation, not a 'thing': landlessness, for example, as shown vividly in the example of Sharifa and Abu above, should be understood not simply as a distinctive attribute of the rural poor but as an effect of the working out of unequal social relations over time.

GUIDE TO FURTHER READING

Readers who wish to pursue their understanding of rural livelihoods in detail are referred to Elizabeth Francis's valuable recent book, *Making a Living* (2000), in which she explores the dynamics of struggle over livelihoods through comparative study of change in eastern and southern Africa; and to Frank Ellis's study of livelihood diversification and vulnerability in *Rural Livelihoods and Diversity in Developing Countries* (2000).

REFERENCES

Bagchi, D.K., Blaikie, P., Cameron, J., Chattopadhyay, M., Gyawali, N. and Seddon, D. (1998) 'Conceptual and methodological challenges in the study of livelihood trajectories: case-studies in Eastern India and Western Nepal', *Journal of International Development* 10: 453–68.

Bernstein, H., Crow, B. and Johnson, H. (eds) (1992) *Rural Livelihoods: Crises and Responses*, Oxford: Oxford University Press for the Open University.

Bryceson, D.F. (1999) 'Sub-Saharan Africa betwixt and between: rural livelihood practices and policies', Working Paper 43, Leiden: Afrika-Studiecentrum.

Carney, D. (ed.) (1998) *Sustainable Rural Livelihoods: What Contribution Can We Make?*, London: Department for International Development.

de Haan, A. (1999) 'Livelihoods and poverty: the role of migration – a critical review of the literature', *Journal of Development Studies* 36(2): 1–47.

Department for International Development (DfID) (1999, 2000) *Sustainable Livelihoods Guidance Sheets*.

Ellis, F. (1998) 'Household strategies and rural livelihood diversification', *Journal of Development Studies* 35(1): 1–38.

Ellis, F. (2000) *Rural Livelihoods and Diversity in Developing Countries*, Oxford: Oxford University Press.

Francis, E. (2000) *Making a Living: Changing Livelihoods in Rural Africa*, London: Routledge.

Hartmann, B. and Boyce, J.K. (1983) *A Quiet Violence: View From a Bangladesh Village*, London: Zed Books.

Khanya (2000) 'Guidelines for undertaking a regional/national Sustainable Rural Livelihoods study', see www.khanya-mrc.co.za.

Murray, C. (2000) 'Changing livelihoods: the Free State, 1990s', *African Studies* 59(1): 115–42.

Scoones, I. (1998) 'Sustainable rural livelihoods: a framework for analysis', Working Paper 72, University of Sussex: Institute of Development Studies.

van Onselen, C. (1996) *The Seed is Mine: The Life of Kas Maine, a South African Sharecropper, 1894–1985*, New York: Hill and Wang.

3.3 The Green Revolution

Graham P. Chapman

Thomas Malthus observed two centuries ago that population had the capacity to increase by compounding numbers (i.e. exponentially), while all his experience of 'the qualities of soil' of 'this Island' (Britain) did not allow him to imagine that agricultural produce could increase more than in arithmetic ratio – i.e. in a constant linear manner. His conclusions from these two 'facts' were that, unless preventive measures were taken, such as late marriage and celibacy, human populations would increase until 'positive checks' halted their growth. These checks were those that came to be associated with the eponymous adjective Malthusian – 'all unwholesome occupations, severe labour and exposure to the seasons, extreme poverty, bad nursing of children, great towns, excesses of all kinds, the whole train of common diseases and epidemics, wars, plague and famine' (Flew, 1970: 23).

In the 200 years since Malthus wrote, there have indeed been famines and plagues, but the human population of the planet as a whole has increased exponentially, and on average is better fed and lives longer than ever before – even if there remain far too many people who are malnourished and in dire poverty. This 'success' has proved possible for two reasons: first because more land has been taken under cultivation – in the American prairies for example – as modern transport allows the carriage of bulk commodities like wheat over intercontinental distances; second, because there have been major increases in the productivity of agriculture. Increases in productivity in agriculture often occur in step-like functions as a result of changes in the agricultural system; for example, the change from broadcast rice to transplanted rice, new animal–crop rotations, or the adoption of new fertilizer-responsive varieties. Since both colonization of new land and adoption of new techniques happens incrementally in time, the output of world agriculture seems to increase fairly smoothly and exponentially. However, much of the agricultural experimentation and improvement of the last 200 years has taken place in temperate lands, and that is where in the last century most of the gains in productivity were made.

At a disaggregated level the picture is not always so encouraging. The twentieth century saw several major famines in Asia and Africa, though more often than not it was war or political turmoil that was the cause rather than the result of famine. In the eyes of the industrial world the Malthusian spectre seemed still to threaten. During the Cold War the two ideologies of capitalism and socialism fought for the allegiance of many developing countries, each promising the populace release from poverty and hunger by following their respective political-economic models.

The solutions to these problems were seen differently by the two sides. The socialist camp thought that the problem lay in the relations of production, and that abolition of landlordism and its replacement by collective farming would solve food problems – as enforced in China. Other states believed in the redistribution of land to poor people, though not outright collectivization of land. The developed countries of the West sought to promote growth in agricultural productivity and hence rural incomes by technical means. The Rockefeller Foundation financed the Co-operative Mexican Agricultural Program in Mexico, the forerunner of CIMMYT – Centro Internacional de Mejoramiento de Maiz y Trigo (the International Centre for the Improvement of Maize and Wheat), indelibly linked with the name of Dr Norman Borlaug, who worked there from 1944–60. He was awarded the Nobel Peace Prize in 1970 for his success.

Borlaug was a plant breeder who used hybridization and back-crossing, which over seven or ten generations might produce a new variety with stable and desirable traits. The main strategy adopted was to breed new dwarf varieties that were responsive to artificial fertilizer, particularly nitrogen. The short height of the plants had two advantages: with less leverage from the head acting on the stem, the head could be heavier without causing the stem to bend over and fail ('lodging'), therefore allowing the use of higher doses of fertilizer; and proportionately more of the plant mass would be in grain, and less in unwanted by-products such as the stalk. In breeding selectively for these traits, other unwanted traits emerged. These included a heightened susceptibility to diseases and pests in the early new varieties, so increased use of pesticides and fungicides became part of the revolution. In part the problem resulted from the fact that there were few of the new varieties, and hence rotation of varieties with different disease and pest resistance was difficult. The new monocultural landscapes therefore became good breeding grounds for pests and diseases. Another difference compared with 'traditional' farming systems in which canopy heights are ragged, was that in seeking to help mechanization the canopy height was now kept as constant as possible. This created a different micro-climate, better suited to disease transmission between plant heads which were closer together. A further demand was for water. If inorganic fertilizer is used in dry conditions it competes with the plants for available soil moisture, and can in fact 'burn' the crop. So controlled irrigation became another necessity. In the case of high-yielding varieties (HYV) of rice developed in the Philippines, the economic value did not necessarily increase in line with yield, as the quality of the grain was often inferior, being less savoury and more glutinous, and commanding a lower market price.

In sum the new agriculture required considerable expenditure, and was in a sense not so well adapted to local environments. Thus the more recent name for this agriculture – high external input agriculture – is perhaps more accurate than the evocative label 'the Green Revolution' that was applied to it in the 1960s–90s. The increases in yields obtained pushed production dramatically upwards. Wheat production in Mexico multiplied threefold in the time that Borlaug worked with the Mexican government; and 'dwarf' wheat imported in the mid-1960s was responsible for a massive increase in wheat harvests in Pakistan and India. In 1961 wheat production in India was

11m tonnes, and in 1991 55 m tonnes. From 1967 to 1990 average wheat yields increased by 3.14 per cent compound annually (Bhalla, 1994: 143, 146).

Different aid agencies and foundations started many different agricultural centres to advance the new technologies. In 1971 the CGIAR (Consultative Group for International Agricultural Research) was established as an informal association of 58 public- and private-sector institutions to support a network of 16 international agricultural research centres.[1] CIMMYT and the International Rice Research Institute in the Philippines, which replicated Borlaug's work on wheat by producing in the 1960s (and ever since) new HYVs of rice, came under the CGIAR umbrella, substantially funded now through the World Bank, the Food and Agricultural Organization of the United Nations (FAO), the United Nations Development Programme (UNDP), and the United Nations Environment Programme (UNEP).

In most developing countries the arguments about the desirability of the new technology and the problems with its side-effects got short shrift from hard-pressed governments. In the first two decades after Independence in India population grew at more than 2 per cent per annum, almost the same rate as food production. Food availability per capita hardly changed, and a bad or failed monsoon could easily threaten food security. In India, in 1965 and 1966, famine, supposedly impossible after Independence, again stalked the land. In a country where more than 70 per cent of workers were engaged in agriculture, at the peak of the emergency 10 per cent of available food was imported from the USA on concessional terms. The government response was to embrace the new technology with determination. It particularly pushed irrigation and fertilizer use with the new seeds. It adapted the new seeds on its own agricultural stations, developing new crosses with local improved varieties (LIVs), striving for better adaptation to local conditions. In the short term the success has been outstanding. In many countries in Asia and Latin America for the last quarter of the twentieth century growth in food output exceeded growth in population – the compound rate of the former going up, and the compound rate of the latter falling, for a variety of reasons, one of which may have been increasing food security and wealth. Average rice yields in South and Southeast Asia in 1991–93 were 83 per cent higher than those in 1964–66, the 3 years immediately preceding the introduction of the first modern, high-yielding variety. Total production rose by 120 per cent, ahead of an 85 per cent growth in population. The land planted to rice increased by only 21 per cent. In effect yields have been doubled.

SOCIAL AND ENVIRONMENTAL EFFECTS

Socially the new technology proved divisive, as in the early days the costs of investment meant the new technology was better suited to bigger and richer farms. If the output of large farmers caused prices to fall (but their income terms of trade could still improve because output had grown so much) then poorer small farmers who had not increased their output suffered. Share-croppers and others in limited tenancy were evicted as potential profits grew. But as the wealth of the country-side grew, so did other rural job opportunities, and so did the demand for labour. New seasonal migration streams became established between regions. In the current decade the effects are thought to be more scale neutral, and small farmers have also benefited, particularly with changes in irrigation technology. Environmentally the costs include: the loss of indigenous varieties (particularly of wheat);[2] a purported addiction of some soils to fertilizer, which means that increasing doses have to be applied; persistent pesticides in the environment, which are particularly harmful where rice and fish are cultivated together; a reduced output of straw, which means that animal fodder has to be found from new sources; in some areas rising water tables, which cause salinization of the soil if they reach the surface, and in other areas which are over-pumped a rapid fall in water tables. This again is more likely to impact on poor people, who use traditionally dug open wells, than the rich, who have tube wells drilled in their land. The environmental concerns have given rise to a search for an integration between new and old methods, in particular a quest for a Low External Input Agriculture. This agriculture seeks for more disease-resistant varieties, and integrated pest management, in which natural biological predators are encouraged. It is in some senses moving parallel to the organic farming of the developed countries. It also uses social technologies, to make the sharing and use of water more equitable and more efficient, for example. Other new (or rediscovered) ideas include agroforestry, using trees to draw on nitrogen-rich groundwater, returning leaves of value for fodder and compost. In general, the movement is towards making the new systems sensitive to local environments, rather than independent of them.

A PATCHY RECORD

The Green Revolution provided an increase in agricultural production which undoubtedly has given many governments a breathing space. In comparison with wheat, maize, rice and potatoes, much less has been done for subsistence crops like cassava in Africa or millet in India. Indeed much of African peasant agriculture seems to have been left behind. The number of food-insecure people in sub-Saharan Africa may increase in the next 20 years – the only world region where this is forecast. Equally, the programmes for rain-fed agriculture have lagged behind those for irrigated agriculture, though the situation is changing. For India and China the breathing space has been essential. Rates of population increase continue to fall, but absolute numbers will continue to increase as young populations achieve adulthood and reproduce. By 2050 India and China alone will have added another 800 million people – or an increment equal to three times the current population of the USA. The colonization of new land has essentially ended (apart from the contentious cases of tropical rainforests in Latin America, Indonesia and Africa). And, as with increasing incomes people will seek more dairy products and more meat, the arable output of agriculture will have to increase far faster than population growth. International trade will grow. Russia and East Europe may again emerge as major exporters alongside the USA – a position Russia held before both the First World War and the Revolution.

Technological optimists believe that the age of biotechnology and direct gene manipulation will solve these problems. The slow system of crossing and selecting that Borlaug worked with can be replaced by tailoring new genes to new demands, even transgenically – introducing fish genes into tomatoes to make them withstand freezing, for example. This is one of the big current debates – about Genetically Modified Organisms (GMOs). The big hopes are that plants can be made more disease and pest resistant, so that chemicals need not be used; that the symbiotic bacteria which fixate atmospheric nitrogen on the roots of legumes (enabling beans and peas to create their own fertilizer) can be engineered to grow on the roots of cereal plants; and that plants develop better drought tolerance. Intriguingly, drought tolerance is higher in an atmosphere with heightened CO_2. But even with enhanced drought tolerance, there is no doubt that much of the needed increase in production will come from irrigated areas – and conflict over water will become increasingly tense, particularly as growing urban centres pre-empt more of the supply.

CGIAR still exists and grows, and is still influential. It has added some social science centres to its technical core. But the vanguard of the new technology is no longer with CGIAR. Now it is with the First World big corporations who have invested most in GMOs. The pessimists fear that the rewards will go to the big corporations, and that the small and poor of the third world will be passed by, or forced to pay excessive prices for the new seeds that will undoubtedly be needed. The critics say that big business is interested first in GMOs that increase their profits, and then either not at all, or least and last, in farmers and consumers. They also fear unpredictable consequences as new genes enter the environment. What is clear is that at all stages of human history social revolution has driven changes in agricultural technology, and changes in agricultural technology have driven social changes. As the developing world rapidly urbanizes, new opportunities will arise for new technologies to increase food output. Hopefully these changes will increasingly incorporate Africa; hopefully their impact upon the environment will be increasingly benign. What we do know is that there will be no 'final equilibrium', only a process of constant adaptation and change, leading to a future where, one hopes, all human beings are well fed, and the spectre of Malthus no longer hovers at the table.

NOTES

1. Visit the CGIAR website for more details on centres.
2. In China in 1949, 10,000 wheat varieties were known: by 1970 there were only 1,000 (Shand, 1997).

GUIDE TO FURTHER READING AND REFERENCES

The following text references provide the basis for further reading.

Bhalla, G.S. (ed.) (1994) *Economic Liberalisation and Indian Agriculture*, New Delhi: Institute for Studies in Industrial Development.

Conway, G.R. and Barbier, E.B. (1990) *After the Green Revolution: Sustainable Agriculture for Development*, London: Earthscan.

Conway, G.R. and Pretty, J.N. (1991) *Unwelcome Harvest: Agriculture and Pollution*, London: Earthscan.

Farmer, B.H. (ed.) (1977) *Green Revolution? Technology and Change in Rice-growing Areas of Tamil Nadu and Sri Lanka*, London: Macmillan.

Flew, A. (ed.) (1970) *An Essay on the Principles of Population*, London: Penguin.

Lipton, M. and Longhurst, R. (1989) *New Seeds and Poor People*, London: Unwin Hyman.

Pinstrup-Andersen, P., Pandya-Lorch, R. and Rosegrant, M. (1999) *World Food Prospects: Critical Issues for the Early Twenty-first Century*, Washington, DC: International Food Policy Research Institute.

Shand, H. (1997) *Human Nature: Agricultural Biodiversity and Farm-based Food Security*, Rome: FAO.

Shiva, V. (1993) *Monocultures of the Mind: Perspectives on Biodiversity and Biotechnology*, London: Zed Books.

3.4 Food security

Sudhir Wanmali and Yassir Islam

INTRODUCTION

The concept of food security has been seminal in developing policies to end hunger and malnutrition during the last 25 years. Yet, when planet earth entered the twenty-first century, it did so with more than 800 million hungry people on board. The reason most people are hungry today is not because enough food cannot be produced, but because it does not get distributed fairly and because some people are too poor to buy it. The concept has evolved with full realization that increasing per capita food production alone would not significantly reduce hunger and malnutrition.

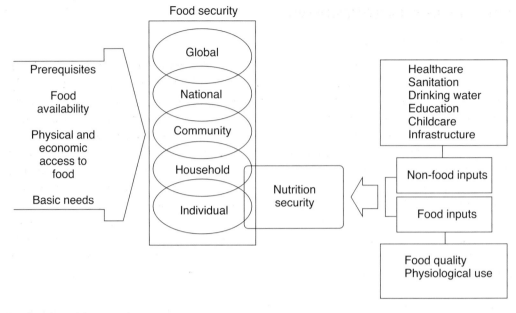

Food and nutrition security

The definition of food security has accommodated various arguments that identify right sequencing, and mix, of policy interventions. Fundamentally, food security means that people have enough food to eat. It can be defined as a goal to be achieved: 'when there is an adequate food supply to which all members of the population have full access' (Christensen, 1991: 1). The operational definition of food security emanated from asking two questions: (i) what does it mean to have 'enough to eat' and (ii) what is the best way of ensuring that all people have full access to food? While the first question has been far less contentious, the second has spawned numerous debates. Tracing the evolution of the concept itself is useful because it reflects changes in approaches to international development, and to policies to end hunger (see figure).

EVOLUTION OF THE CONCEPT

During the World Food Conference of 1974, food security was invoked largely at a national level with an emphasis on maintaining a network of sufficient food reserves to meet the food needs of a country. Many developing countries were quick to identify with this approach but tended to link it to national goals of food self-sufficiency. In this way, they reasoned, they would be less dependent on food imports or food aid from developed countries because the intentions of the latter, with regard to food aid, were often muddied by the objectives of their respective foreign policies. Many countries, however, had an insufficient agricultural resource base to be self-sufficient in food production. The problem, however, was in 'thinking in terms of what *exists*, rather than in terms of who can *command* what' (Sen, 1981: 8). Consequently, food security is understood as having physical and economic access to sufficient food, for an active healthy life, by all people at all times (World Bank, 1986).

POLICIES AND INTERVENTIONS

Household food security

Focusing on aspects of access led to several important, and informed, policy interventions. First, it brought the debate down from national food security to household food security. Subsequently, this led to the rethinking of food security at global, regional, national, local and household levels. While different approaches were advanced, difficulties remained, and continue to remain, in integrating them into a strategy at the level of the individual where it mattered most.

Second, it drew attention to access as a function of household income. Poverty is both a symptom and a cause of food insecurity. Increasing the capacity of poor households to purchase food, in addition to what they might be able to grow, is widely viewed as key to enhancing household food security. This led to investigating *who* the poor are, *why* they are poor, and *where* they are located. Answers to these questions have helped inform policy planning and interventions. The majority of the world's poor people live in rural areas, and many of them on marginal lands, where they face considerable constraints in producing sufficient food. Furthermore, racial, religious, ethnic, class, and caste characteristics of particular groups adversely affect their food security.

Third, it drew attention to intra-household distribution which tends to be biased against women and children, for example in South Asia, which has the largest number of poor and hungry people in the world (UN ACC/SCN, 1992). Gender analysis, therefore, became an important component of research at household level, and policy interventions increasingly attempted to address gender-based inequities in food and income allocation.

Household nutrition security

Looking at differences between individuals within the household reinforced the importance of nutritional security. In one instance, household food insecurity was defined as consumption of fewer than 2,280 kcals per adult equivalent (less than 80 per cent of the adequate daily calorific intake of 2,850 kcals recommended by the World Health Organization) (Reardon and Matlon, 1989: 119). It has been argued that there is too much of a focus on calorific, and too little on protein and micronutrient, consumption in defining food security (Maxwell and Frankenberger, 1992). For example, vitamin A, iron and iodine deficiencies can have serious consequences for the mental and physical health of an individual (UN ACC/SCN, 1992). It is now argued that the quality of the food consumed by an individual, and the differing needs of men, women and children, must be considered in defining food security. It is agreed, however, that without basic food security there can be no nutrition security. Dietary energy supply, however, continues to remain the indicator of choice in assessing food security and when comparing national data (FAO, 1996a).

Transitory and chronic food insecurity

Food insecurity can be transitory and chronic. The first is a temporary phenomenon and the second is more permanent. During seasonal fluctuations in food production, or in times of crisis, impoverished households that are experiencing transitory food insecurity may be pushed into a state of chronic food insecurity. At such times, women and young children especially may be at greater risk than others. Together with lack of access to healthcare, sanitation and other basic needs such as safe drinking water, chronic food insecurity can lead to poor health, lack of energy and further impoverishment. Such concerns have led to an integrated approach in examining how different factors, such as safe drinking water, minimum income, education and small family size interact, and impinge on, people's ability to achieve food security (Swaminathan, 1986).

PREREQUISITES

Achieving food security requires policy interventions at household, community, national and global levels. To identify their nature and scope, conditions that cause food insecurity, and factors that exacerbate it, must be fully understood. What are the prerequisites for achieving food security?

1 *The availability of food*   Global and national grain reserves, and emergency stocks of food can offset shortfalls in production.
2 *The physical and economic access*   Agricultural households need to have sufficient resources to grow food beyond their own requirements, and non-agricultural households have to earn sufficient income to purchase the food they need. Infrastructures are necessary for helping production, distribution, processing and purchasing of food.
3 *The access to basic needs*   Infrastructure of healthcare, sanitation, safe drinking water and education is made available to convert food security into nutrition security.

Unfortunately there are few countries in the world, including even developed countries, where all prerequisites are present. Each becomes a potential constraint leading to food and nutrition insecurity (see figure on p. 160 and, for examples, Table 1).

Table 1 Sources of food and nutrition insecurity

Types of condition or event	Types of population at risk
• Drought • Crop production risks	• Smallholders with limited resources and non-diversified income • Smallholders on marginal lands • Landless farm labourers
• Disruptions in imports/exports • Falling prices of agricultural exports	• Smallholders heavily dependent on export crops • Poor households heavily dependent on imported food
• Unemployment	• Wage-earning households • Informal-sector employees
• Lack of healthcare and sanitation • Poor infrastructure	• Entire communities • Poor households • Vulnerable members (women and children) of households
• Political crisis • Government failure	• Households in areas of civil unrest • Marginalized ethnic groups

Source: Based on von Braun (1999: 50)

ACHIEVING FOOD SECURITY

Demographic factors

The population of the planet earth will increase by more than 70 million people a year through the year 2020. More than 97 per cent of this is expected to be in developing countries, whose share of global population is projected to grow to more than 80 per cent by the year 2020 (Pinstrup-Andersen *et al.*, 1999). Most of this growth will be in already congested urban areas. However, it is also projected that rural populations will outnumber urban populations in the next three to four decades.

These demographic indicators demand innovative approaches to analysing current rural–urban dichotomies in terms of a rural–urban continuum in order to achieve food security through balanced regional economic development.

Agriculture as an engine of growth

Efforts to increase food security will need to be focused on South Asia and sub-Saharan Africa where more than 50 per cent of the world's poor and hungry live, and where more than 75 per cent of the world's malnourished children will live in the year 2020 (Pinstrup-Andersen *et al.*, 1999). Agriculture constitutes about 33 per cent of gross domestic product in these two regions. Very few countries in the world today have experienced significant economic growth without a solid foundation of agriculture. Though many developing countries focused on industrialization, which also accelerated the pace of urbanization through much of the second half of the twentieth century, agriculture is once again seen as the engine of economic growth.

Investments in the agricultural sector, which will lead to increases in food production and household incomes, and to the strengthening of linkages between agricultural and non-agricultural sectors of the rural economy, are seen as an integral component of any future strategy for achieving food security.

Sustainable management of natural resources

In order to feed the population by the year 2020, a 40 per cent increase in grain production is required in the next 20 years (Pinstrup-Andersen *et al.*, 1999). However, more than half of the land area is already used for crop production and pasture; an estimated one billion people already live in households with insufficient land to meet their minimum food needs; and about 500 million people living in abject poverty are already located in areas of high ecological vulnerability. All have contributed to increased deforestation and soil mining, and exhaustive harvesting of water resources.

Sustainable intensification of agricultural production on existing agricultural land through adoption of improved technologies, appropriate agro-ecological farming practices and necessary investments in infrastructure can lead to food security while reducing pressure on fragile lands.

Conflicts and governance

Because agriculture is so important in most developing countries, stagnating agricultural production can lead to social tensions which fuel conflicts. Although causes of conflicts are many, these often have roots in a lack of access to resources and to food. Slow growth of food production per capita has been identified as a major cause of conflict (Nafziger and Auvinen, 1997).

Strategies to increase agricultural production, and to provide economic opportunities, must be equitably implemented to lift people out of poverty and reduce intense competition for limited resources that can lead to conflict.

FOOD SECURITY AS A HUMAN RIGHT

Food and nutrition security, agricultural development, rural development and economic development are parts of ever enlarging and concentric circles. If food and nutrition security is considered as the smallest circle, then constraints in one of the larger circles can have an adverse impact upon it. These constraints need to be understood and addressed before policy options are proposed for achieving food and nutrition security.

Food and freedom from hunger as a fundamental human right was affirmed at the World Food Summit in 1996 (FAO, 1996b). This has led to a 'human welfare and development' approach to food security, where the goal is to empower people and broaden their range of choices (UN/ACC/SCN, 2000). Focusing attention on intra-household allocation of food has further validated this concept. Within the households, improvements in child nutrition in developing countries from 1970 to 1995 were mainly due to higher literacy rates amongst women, better food availability, better health facilities and higher societal status of women than in the past (Pinstrup-Andersen et al., 1999). Empowerment of women is now the cornerstone of all strategies of food security.

This 'human welfare and development approach' is complemented by policies of decentralized administration, finance and rural development that aim to remove bottlenecks in physical and economic access to food at a local level.

If all people are to enjoy food and nutrition security, and lead productive lives, then learning to share the resources of the planet in a more equitable and sustainable manner will be the greatest challenge of the twenty-first century.

GUIDE TO FURTHER READING

El Obeid, A., Johnson, S.R., Jensen, H.H. and Smith, L.C. (1999) *Food Security: New Solutions for the Twenty-first Century*, Iowa: Iowa State University Press. Perspectives on improving food security in the twenty-first century.

Food and Agricultural Organization (FAO) (1999) *The State of Food Insecurity in the World*, Rome: FAO. 'Who, why, and where' of hungry people and food security, and recent statistics.

Kracht, U. and Schulz, M. (1999) *Food Security and Nutrition: The Global Challenge*, New York: St Martin's Press. Strategies for overcoming hunger and malnutrition.

Smith, M., Pointing, J., Maxwell, S. *et al.* (1993) *Household Food Security: Concepts and Definitions: An Annotated Bibliography*, Development Bibliography 8, Brighton: Institute of Development Studies. An annotated bibliography.

REFERENCES

Christensen, G. (1991) *Towards Food Security in the Horn of Africa*, Working Paper No. 4, Oxford: Food Studies Group,

Food and Agricultural Organization (FAO) (1996a) *World Food Summit: Synthesis of the Technical Background Documents*, Rome: FAO.

Food and Agricultural Organization (FAO) (1996b) *World Food Summit: Rome Declaration on World Food Security and World Food Summit Plan of Action*, Rome: FAO.

Maxwell, S. and Frankenberger, T.R. (1992) *Household Food Security: Concepts, Indicators, Measurements*, New York and Rome: UINICEF and IFAD.

Nafziger, E.W. and Auvinen, J. (1997) *War, Hunger, and Displacement: An Econometric Investigation into the Sources of Humanitarian Emergencies*, Working Paper No. 142, World Institute for Development Economics Research, United Nations University.

Pinstrup-Andersen, P., Pandya-Lorch, R. and Rosegrant, M.W. (1999) *World Food Prospects: Critical Issues for the Early Twenty-First Century*, 2020 Vision Food Policy Report, Washington DC: International Food Policy Research Institute.

Reardon, T. and Matlon, P. (1989) 'Seasonal food insecurity and vulnerability in drought-affected regions of Burkina Faso', in D.E. Sahn (ed.) *Seasonal Variation in Third World Agriculture: The Consequences for Food Security*, Baltimore and London: Johns Hopkins University Press.

Sen, A. (1981) *Poverty and Famines*, Oxford: Oxford University Press.

Swaminathan, M.S. (1986) *Sustainable Nutrition Security for Africa: Lessons from India*, San Francisco: The Hunger Project.

UN ACC/SCN (United Nations Administrative Committee on Coordination/Subcommittee on Nutrition) (1992) *Second Report on the World Nutrition Situation: Vol. 1, Global and Regional Results*, Geneva: World Health Organization.

UN ACC/SCN (United Nations Administrative Committee on Coordination/Subcommittee on Nutrition) (2000) *Fourth Report on the World Nutrition Situation: Nutrition Throughout the Life Cycle*, Geneva: World Health Organization.

von Braun, J. (1999) 'Food security: a conceptual basis', in U. Kracht and M. Schulz (eds) *Food Security and Nutrition: The Global Challenge*, New York: St Martin's Press.

World Bank (1986) *Poverty and Hunger: Issues and Options for Food Security in Developing Countries*, World Bank Policy Study, Washington DC: World Bank.

3.5 Rural co-operatives

D.W. Attwood and B.S. Baviskar

Some development goals are best achieved by co-operatives and similar organizations, rather than private corporations or state bureaucracies. This chapter examines the role of co-operatives in rural development, starting with examples from India.

We discuss 'formal' co-operatives (established under official regulatory frameworks), 'informal' co-operation (customary methods of pooling labour, savings, etc.), 'co-operative-like' organizations (e.g., NGOs promoting micro-credit schemes) and institutions managing common-property resources (e.g., irrigation water). What factors cause these varied organizations to succeed or fail, and what benefits accrue to the rural poor if they succeed? Given the huge number and variety of such organizations, our examples are only suggestive.

FORMAL CO-OPERATIVES IN INDIA

Formal co-operatives started under British administration, financed and administered by regional governments. After Independence (1947), more co-operatives were promoted for rural development.

India now has nearly 500,000 rural co-operatives, reaching about 67 per cent of rural households (Agriculture Ministry, 1998).

While impressive in number, these co-operatives suffer many weaknesses. Few become economically viable; many are moribund or defunct. Few operate under democratic control by their members; most are managed by government officials.

Success in sugar and milk processing

Still, there are some genuine, member-controlled co-operatives. Notable examples include sugar factories in Maharashtra state and dairies in Gujarat.

India is the world's largest sugar producer; co-operatives in Maharashtra produce over one-third of the total. Compared with other Indian factories, these co-ops are superior in efficiency, enabling them to pay higher prices for sugarcane (a vital benefit for local farmers). The vast majority of shareholders are small farmers growing sugarcane along with other crops.

Most sugar co-ops in Maharashtra have expanded and diversified into ancillary enterprises. Many have built schools, colleges, clinics and hospitals in their local areas. Their success results from management by members and elected leaders, assisted by hired managers and technicians.

As Maharashtra leads in sugar co-ops, Gujarat leads in dairies. The renowned Kheda District Cooperative Milk Producers' Union has an annual turnover of Rs3 billion (roughly US$100 million). The Gujarat Cooperative Milk Marketing Federation has a distribution network all over India, with an annual turnover of Rs150 billion (Candler and Kumar, 1998). The main benefit for members, as dairy farmers, is access to distant urban markets. Because milk is perishable, access is impossible without industrial processing and transport.

Dairy co-ops in Gujarat are known for their efficiency. They are managed by farmers and elected leaders, assisted by hired managers and technicians. International agencies have promoted similar dairy co-operatives in other countries; 'Operation Flood' (1970–95) sought to replicate these co-ops throughout India.

Understanding patterns of success and failure

Institutional design analysis looks inside organizations for factors promoting efficiency or inefficiency. It helps explain patterns of success and failure among similar organizations in a given region (see Shah, 1996). An example may be taken from our work on sugar factories. Because sugarcane is perishable, the efficiency of a modern sugar factory depends on a steady supply of fresh-cut cane, harvested over several months from an area of several thousand hectares. India's high population density and land scarcity made big sugar plantations unfeasible in most areas. Thus, most private sugar factories had to buy cane from thousands of local farmers. This entailed high transaction costs and irregular cane supply, making private factories inefficient.

After Independence, this problem was overcome in Maharashtra. Thousands of cane growers established a co-operative sugar factory. As co-investors and co-managers (via an elected board of directors), they acquired a stake in the efficient use of heavy industrial equipment and thus needed a centrally managed harvest system. The factory hired and co-ordinated teams of migrant harvest workers to obtain a carefully scheduled supply of fresh cane. Shareholders remained independent farmers; joint ownership meant tying each share to a contract to supply one half-acre of cane to the factory annually.

The first such co-operative factory succeeded, so many others arose in Maharashtra. More efficient than nearby private factories, they drove most out of business. One must wonder, then, why co-operative sugar factories did not flourish in other regions, particularly northern India. This question mirrors a basic one in institutional economics: why does competition not compel all producers to adopt more efficient innovations? Following North's (1990) example, we use a political economy approach to look for answers.

Political economy analysis looks beyond internal design to external context, helping explain patterns of success and failure among regions. For example, 'co-operative' sugar factories in northern India superficially resemble those in Maharashtra yet are highly inefficient. Their main problems stem from state management.

After Independence, India's industrialization policies promoted public-sector enterprises. Five-year plans, modelled on those of the Soviet Union, regulated the economy. In most regions, it seemed logical that 'co-operatives' should also be managed by state officials. However, state-managed 'co-operatives', like state-owned industries, were consistently inefficient.

Managed by state officials, 'co-operative' sugar factories in northern India cannot offer good cane prices. Many farmers look elsewhere to market their crop. The factories cannot obtain a steady supply of cane, so they become even more inefficient, surviving only with heavy subsidies from central government.

CO-OPERATIVES AND THE STATE: OTHER REGIONS

Outside India, similar problems hold. African co-ops resemble India's in several respects. They were first established by colonial rulers and managed by bureaucrats. After Independence, new rulers expected co-operatives to promote development by harnessing customary patterns of informal co-operation to building modern enterprises.

Early hopes soon faded. The much-publicized *ujamaa* programme in Tanzania provides a classic example. National leaders thought state-mandated collectivization would promote equality and productivity. The programme failed due to simplistic assumptions about rural society, coupled with top-down management by state officials (Hyden, 1988). Unlike India, African societies generally lacked established democratic traditions, making it even harder for member-controlled co-operatives to emerge. As in Latin America, many regimes were hostile to organizations not under state control.

Efficient, member-controlled co-operatives are rare in Latin America, but there are exceptions. One Costa Rican co-operative, processing and marketing coffee beans, competes against local private processors and huge sellers on international markets (Sick, 1999). In order to sell to niche markets, the members decided to improve the quality of their product. Among other things, this meant that they, as small growers, had to harvest more carefully. Doing so, they gained higher prices through the co-op.

In Costa Rica, member control is facilitated by democratic traditions. The state supports co-operatives (e.g., via tax concessions) without managing them directly. Unlike northern India, where state-managed 'co-operatives' are propped up by massive subsidies, Cost Rican co-operatives are allowed to fail, and some do. Others succeed because members and elected leaders are committed and innovative. In general, co-operatives perform better with government support, but government control is lethal (see Esman and Uphoff, 1984).

INFORMAL CO-OPERATION AND NGOS

Like corporations, formal co-operatives come under some form of state regulation (not to be confused with state management). Recent research on the 'informal sector' reveals how small, informal enterprises may co-operate in pursuit of common interests. Almost everywhere, rural producers co-operate by pooling or exchanging labour. Informal savings groups seem to be found in villages (and cities) around the world. They pool savings collected in small increments from their members, each member gaining access to the pool by a system of rotation. In some areas of Kenya, for example, women's groups have been quite effective at pooling labour and savings (Thomas-Slayter and Rocheleau, 1995).

NGOs sometimes try to fill the gap between informal savings groups and dysfunctional, state-run 'co-operative' credit systems. In 1976, the Grameen Bank, a new type of NGO, was established in Bangladesh. The bank makes only small loans to poor people, primarily women organized in small groups. As with informal savings groups, group discipline ensures loan repayment. Other NGOs have established similar 'micro-credit' programmes. The system of small-group discipline seems effective in reducing poverty and promoting women's empowerment (Hashemi *et al.*, 1996). Yet cultivation of group discipline entails high administrative costs, often paid by external donors.

In India's Andhra Pradesh state, an experiment in 'Women's Thrift Co-operatives' (WTCs) was launched in 1990 under the auspices of an indigenous NGO. WTCs raise funds solely through small, regular contributions from their members, who earn interest on savings at 1 per cent per month. (For loans they pay 2 per cent.) A village WTC may consist of 200 to 500 women, divided into groups of 10 to 50. Group discipline ensures excellent rates of loan recovery. Loans are used for household expenses, education, healthcare and investments in livestock or small businesses.

In less than a decade, over 33,000 women formed 101 WTCs. On 31 December 1998, their combined savings totalled Rs26 million, with no external grants or loans. The NGO provides advice and support in establishing WTCs, but the latter soon become self-sufficient and self-managing, a source of empowerment for their members. About half the members and leaders come from landless households (Biswas and Mahajan, 1997).

Two points should be added regarding co-operatives and the state. First, India has poured vast sums into formal, state-run credit 'co-operatives', whose assets never consist of members' savings. Their loans mostly go to landowners (mainly men), and many loans are never repaid. Thus, formal 'co-operative' credit is neither self-supporting nor beneficial to the poorest villagers, including women. Second, WTCs were initially not registered as formal co-ops because, as often, state laws governing co-operatives were too restrictive. Persistent lobbying by NGOs in Andhra Pradesh finally led to a new law, under which the WTCs could formally register without jeopardizing their autonomy and internal accountability.

Worldwide, 'micro-credit' programmes appeal to NGOs and donor agencies for various reasons, including their focus on disciplined repayment, their targeting of poor people, and of women in particular. Yet these programmes may have overlooked the potential of 'micro-thrift', which is less dependent on external donors. Micro-thrift more closely resembles age-old patterns of informal co-operation and group discipline.

CO-OPERATIVE MANAGEMENT OF COMMON RESOURCES

Sustainable development and poverty alleviation often depend on common resources. Yet many policies (based on the false assumption that efficiency and sustainability require either privatization or state ownership) have undermined indigenous systems of co-operative resource management. Rangelands have been enclosed in many parts of Africa, with results favourable neither to small livestock herders nor conservation (Webb and Coppock, 1997). In Bali, newly centralized command over old, multi-centric irrigation systems undermined co-ordination, leading to uncontrolled pest damage in the rice fields (Lansing, 1991). In India, colonial and postcolonial governments commandeered forestlands for unsustainable timber extraction, impoverishing small herders and farmers in forested regions.

Prior to such harmful interventions, small producers evolved sustainable systems of common-resource management in many parts of the world (Ostrom, 1990). Fortunately, old systems can sometimes be restored and new ones created. Belated recognition of the crucial role of water temples in co-ordinating Balinese irrigation may avert further pest explosions. An experiment in northern India shows that villagers and the state can co-manage watershed and forest resources, resulting in soil and forest conservation plus higher agricultural output (Chopra and Rao, 1997). Experiments by an indigenous NGO in South India show that community action can restore long-neglected irrigation tanks.

Durable co-operatives are often linked with other co-ops, NGOs or state agencies (in supportive roles). Varied types of co-operatives help people cope with economic, social and environmental problems. To be effective, they must adapt to local conditions, meet the needs of small producers and operate under their control. As creatures of the state, most 'co-operatives' in developing countries embody none of these simple principles.

GUIDE TO FURTHER READING

Attwood, D.W. (1992) *Raising Cane: The Political Economy of Sugar in Western India*, Boulder and London: Westview Press.

Baviskar, B.S. and Attwood, D.W. (1995) *Finding the Middle Path: The Political Economy of Cooperation in Rural India*, Boulder and London: Westview Press.

Shah, Tushaar (1996) *Catalysing Co-operation: Design of Selfgoverning Organizations*, New Delhi: Sage Publications.

Sick, Deborah (1999) *Farmers of the Golden Bean: Costa Rican Households and the Global Coffee Economy*, DeKalb: Northern Illinois University Press.

REFERENCES

Agriculture Ministry (Government of India) (1998) *Cooperative Movement in India: A Statistical Profile*, New Delhi: Government of India.

Biswas, Arun and Mahajan, Vijay (1997) 'Sustainable banking with the poor: a case study on women's thrift co-operative system in Warangal and Karimnagar Districts of Andhra Pradesh', Hyderabad: Co-operative Development Foundation.

Candler, Wilfred and Kumar, Nalini (1998) *India: The Dairy Revolution: The Impact of Dairy Development in India and the World Bank's Contribution*, Washington DC: World Bank.

Chopra, K. and Rao, C.H.H. (1997) 'Institutional and technological perspectives on the links between agricultural sustainability and poverty: illustrations from India', in S.A. Vosti and T. Reardon (eds) *Sustainability, Growth, and Poverty Alleviation: A Policy and Agroecological Perspective*, Baltimore: Johns Hopkins University Press.

Esman, M.J. and Uphoff, N.T. (1984) *Local Organizations: Intermediaries in Rural Development*, Ithaca: Cornell University Press.

Hashemi, S.M., Schuler, S.R. and Riley, A.P. (1996) 'Rural credit programs and women's empowerment in Bangladesh', *World Development* 24(4): 635–53.

Hyden, Goran. (1988) 'Approaches to co-operative development: blueprint versus greenhouse', in D.W. Attwood and B.S. Baviskar (eds) *Who Shares? Cooperatives and Rural Development*, Delhi: Oxford University Press.

Lansing, J.S. (1991) *Priests and Programmers: Technologies of Power in the Engineered Landscape of Bali*, Princeton: Princeton University Press.

North, Douglass (1990) *Institutions, Institutional Change, and Economic Performance*, Cambridge: Cambridge University Press.

Ostrom, Elinor (1990) *Governing the Commons: The Evolution of Institutions for Collective Action*, Cambridge: Cambridge University Press.

Thomas-Slayter, B. and Rocheleau, D. (1995) *Gender, Environment, and Development in Kenya: A Grassroots Perspective*, London: Lynne Rienner.

Webb, P. and Coppock, D.L. (1997) 'Prospects for pastoralism in semi-arid Africa', in S.A. Vosti and T. Reardon (eds) *Sustainability, Growth, and Poverty Alleviation: A Policy and Agroecological Perspective*, Baltimore: Johns Hopkins University Press.

3.6 Regenerating agriculture

Jules Pretty

THE SCALE OF THE CHALLENGE

Despite several decades of remarkable agricultural progress, the world still faces a massive food security challenge. The world population passed 6 billion people in mid-1999, and is predicted to increase to 8.4 billion by 2050, by which time 84 per cent of the world's population will be in those countries that currently make up the 'developing' world. Already, though, there are an estimated 830 million people lacking adequate access to food (Pinstrup-Andersen and Cohen, 1999).

All commentators agree that food production will have to increase, and that this will have to come from existing farmland (cf. IFPRI, 1995; Pretty, 1995, 1998). Many predictions are gloomy, indicating that the gap between demand and production will grow. But solving these problems is not simply a matter of developing new agricultural technologies. Most hungry consumers are poor, and so simply do not have the money to buy the food they need. Equally, poor producers cannot afford expensive technologies. They will have to find solutions largely based on existing resources.

ASSETS-BASED AGRICULTURE

Agricultural and rural systems at all levels, from farms, livelihoods and communities to national economies, rely for their success on the total stock of natural, social, human, physical and financial capital (Costanza *et al.*, 1997; Pretty, 1998; Pretty and Ward, 2001), as follows.

1 *Natural capital* – nature's free goods and services: comprises food (both farmed and from the wild), wood and fibre; water regulation and supply; waste assimilation, decomposition and

treatment; nutrient cycling and fixation; soil formation; biological control of pests; climate regulation; wildlife habitats; storm protection and flood control; carbon sequestration; pollination; and recreation and leisure.

2   *Social capital* – the cohesiveness of people in their societies: comprises relations of trust that lubricate co-operation; the bundles of common rules, norms and sanctions for behaviour; reciprocity and exchanges; connectedness and social institutions.

3   *Human capital* – the status of individuals: comprises the stock of health, nutrition, education, skills and knowledge of individuals; access to services that provide these, such as schools, medical services, adult training; the ways individuals and their knowledges interact with productive technologies; and the leadership quality of individuals.

4   *Physical capital* – local infrastructure: comprises housing and other buildings; roads and bridges; energy supplies; communications; markets; and air, road, water and rail transportation.

5   *Financial capital* – stocks of money: comprises savings; access to affordable credit; pensions; remittances; welfare payments; grants and subsidies.

These five assets are transformed by policies, processes and institutions to give desirable outcomes. Agriculture, though, does more than just produce food. It has a profound impact on many other aspects of local, national and global economies and ecosystems. These impacts can be positive or negative. A fundamental principle of sustainable systems is that they do not deplete capital assets, whilst unsustainable ones do (Goodland, 1998). More sustainable agricultural systems, therefore, tend to have a positive effect on natural, social and human capital whilst also producing food, fibre, oil, etc. A vital feedback loop occurs from outcomes to inputs: agricultural systems impact on the very assets on which they rely for inputs. For example, an agricultural system that depletes organic matter or erodes soil in order to produce food externalizes costs that others must bear; but one that sequesters carbon in soils through organic matter accumulation contributes both to the global good by mediating climate change and to the private good by enhancing soil health.

Agriculture is, therefore, fundamentally multifunctional (FAO, 1999). It delivers many unique non-food functions that cannot be so efficiently produced by other economic sectors. A key policy challenge is to find ways to enhance food production, whilst seeking both to improve the positive functions and to eliminate the negative ones. This will not be easy, as past agricultural development has tended to ignore both the multifunctionality of agriculture and the external costs (Conway and Pretty, 1991; Altieri, 1995; Pretty, 1998; Rosset, 1999: Pretty *et al.*, 2000). Fortunately, there has emerged much evidence to illustrate that it is indeed possible to produce more food whilst accumulating natural, social and human capital.

COMPONENTS OF SUSTAINABLE AGRICULTURE

A wide range of more sustainable forms of agriculture is now emerging and spreading. What, then, are the key components of more sustainable agriculture? And how can transitions in both 'pre-modern' and 'modernized' systems towards greater sustainability be encouraged? Sustainable agriculture is defined as agricultural technologies and practices that maximize the productivity of the land whilst seeking to minimize damage both to valued natural assets (soils, water, air and biodiversity) and to human health (farmers and other rural people, and consumers).

More sustainable agriculture, therefore, seeks to make the best use of nature's goods and services whilst not damaging the environment (Chambers *et al.*, 1989; Altieri, 1995, 1999; Pretty, 1995, 1998). It does this by integrating natural processes such as nutrient cycling, nitrogen fixation, soil regeneration and natural enemies of pests into food production processes. It also seeks to minimize the use of non-renewable inputs (pesticides and fertilizers) that damage the environment or harm the health of farmers and consumers. It makes better use of the knowledge and skills of farmers, so improving their self-reliance. And it seeks to make productive use of social capital – people's capacities to work together to solve common management problems, such as pest, watershed, irrigation, forest and credit management.

Sustainable agriculture is multifunctional within landscapes and economies – it produces food and other goods for farm families and markets, but it also contributes to a range of public goods, such as clean water, wildlife, carbon sequestration in soils, flood protection and landscape quality. It delivers unique non-food functions that cannot be produced by other sectors (for example, on-farm biodiversity, groundwater recharge, urban to rural migration, social cohesion).

MULTIPLE ENTRY POINTS FOR SUSTAINABLE AGRICULTURE TRANSFORMATIONS

A desirable end-point for all agricultural systems is design that enhances both the private benefits for farmers and the public benefits through other multiple functions. Transitions in agriculture are often conceived of as requiring sudden shifts in both practices and values. But not all farmers are able or willing to take such a leap. However, everyone can take small steps, and these added together can bring about big transformations in the end (Pretty, 1998; Pretty and Hine, 2000). The first three improvements involve those that positively affect natural capital in different ways (Types 1–3). The final two focus on improvements to social and human capital (Types 4–5).

Type 1: Better use of available renewable natural capital

A wide variety of technologies and practices are available which farmers and communities can use to make better and more productive use of available natural resources. Water harvesting involves the use of simple technologies to channel and harvest rainfall that was previously being poorly used. Rotational grazing makes better use of potential pasture productivity, and irrigation scheduling ensures water is used efficiently. The options include water harvesting, soil and water conservation; composting, livestock manures; irrigation scheduling and management; restoration of degraded or abandoned land; habitat management for pest-predators; drainage systems and sub-soiling; and raised beds.

A good example is the adoption of water harvesting on 100,000 ha of Burkina Faso and Niger, each now producing some 700–1000 kg of cereal per year, and with the result that households have shifted from being in annual cereal deficit amounting to 644 kg to producing a surplus of 153 kg per year.

Type 2: Intensification of single sub-component of farm system

Another type of improvement to livelihood systems involves the intensification of a single sub-component of a farm, such as through double-dug beds, adding vegetables to rice field borders or digging a fish pond. These technologies can significantly increase total food production for rural livelihoods, particularly of protein and vegetables. The beneficiaries are often children during 'hungry' seasons. Other options include kitchen gardens; micro-environments (for example, gully cropping, silt traps).

A good example is the adoption of bio-intensive gardening in Kenya by some 50,000 households, with the result that food supply continues throughout the dry season.

Type 3: Diversification by adding new productive natural capital and regenerative components

The third type of improvement to natural capital involves the diversification of the whole agro-ecosystem through addition of new regenerative components, such as legumes in cereal rotations, fish in rice, agroforestry and livestock. These technologies can result in synergies – where one component of the system positively contributes to the success of other components. The options include legumes in cropping systems and pastures; integrated livestock (for example, poultry, stall-fed ruminants); fish in rice fields; *Azolla* in rice; trees in cropping systems, including woodlots; natural enemy releases for pest control; and habitat management for pest control and enhancement of beneficials.

A good example is the adoption of integrated pest management in rice in Asia, with farmers now relying on natural predators in wet rice systems to control pests, so allowing them to cut down on pesticide use, and consequently to restock fields with fish. In Jiangsu Province in China, there are some 117,000 ha of rice–fish, rice–crab and rice–shrimp systems. Rice yields have increased by 10–15 per cent, but the greatest dividend is in protein: each hectare can produce 750 kg of fish. Additional benefits come from reduced insecticide use, and measured reductions in malaria incidence owing to fish predation of mosquito larvae. In Bangladesh 150,000 farmers have adopted more sustainable rice production. Rice yields have improved by 5–7 per cent, and 80 per cent of farmers no longer use any pesticides.

Type 4: Social and participatory processes leading to group action for making better use of natural capital

These improvements focus on social and participatory processes that lead to social capital increases, so improving people's capacity to work together on common resource management problems, forming groups for pest, irrigation, watershed, joint forest or credit management. The options include farmers' research and experimentation groups; resource management and users' groups (for example, forest protection, fisheries, irrigation, watersheds); credit groups; and horizontal partnerships between external agencies (for example, government and NGOs; private and public).

A good example is the emergence of 33,000 water users' associations (comprising at least 500,000 farmers) in Sri Lanka. The economic benefits arise mainly from increased water use efficiency, enabling farmers to increase cropping intensity and so raise total production. As farmers took control, so the number of complaints received by the government Irrigation Department about water distribution fell to nearly zero. Since project completion, farmers' organizations have maintained themselves, progressed institutionally and developed their own capacity for dealing with problems.

Type 5: Human capital building through training–learning programmes

These improvements focus on building farmers' knowledge and skills so as to improve analytical skills and capacities to innovate and control their farm systems. A major constraint in the transition towards more sustainable systems is the levels of human knowledge and skills needed for management of more complex systems (it is much easier, for example, to spray a pesticide than it is to farm for beneficial insects). The options include farmer field schools for improving agro-ecological knowledge, leadership training and adult literacy classes.

A good example of new approaches to learning occurs in the farmer field schools in Asia. Vietnam has seen spectacular progress with its implementation of the FFS approach, with some 250,000 farmers trained since the early 1990s. The programme has seen rice yields increase by about 3 per cent, pesticide expenditure fall by 80 per cent, and pesticide application events fall by 79 per cent (from 1.1 to 0.23 per season). In Kenya, the government's catchment approach to soil conservation has helped to build farmers' capacity to learn and experiment, and has resulted in the formation of some 4,500 farmers' groups to institutionalize learning and co-operation.

CONCLUSIONS

Sustainable agriculture can contribute significantly to natural and social capital, as well as make a significant impact on rural people's food security, welfare and livelihoods. But without appropriate policy support at a range of levels, combined with wider social organization and alliances, these improvements will remain at best localized in extent or, at worst, wither away.

The 1990s saw considerable global progress towards the recognition of the need for policies to support sustainable agriculture, and this is beginning to be translated into practice. Most reforms, though, remain piecemeal, with sustainable agriculture still largely at the margins of conventional policy processes and aims. There are additional constraints to overcome. Vested interests in maintaining the status quo will make any reform difficult. Despite the many constraints, it is increasingly clear that sustainable agriculture can bring substantial private and public benefits.

GUIDE TO FURTHER READING

Altieri, M. (1995) *Agroecology: The Science of Sustainable Agriculture*, Boulder, CO: Westview Press.
Pretty, J.N. (1995) *Regenerating Agriculture: Policies and Practice for Sustainability and Self-Reliance*, London: Earthscan Publications; Washington DC: National Academy Press; Bangalore: ActionAid.
Pretty, J.N. (1998) *The Living Land: Agriculture, Food Systems and Community Regeneration in Rural Europe*, London: Earthscan Publications.
Rosset, P. (1999) *The Multiple Functions and Benefits of Small Farm Agriculture*, Food First Policy Brief No 4, Oakland, CA: Food First/Institute for Food and Development Policy.

REFERENCES

Altieri, M.A. (1999) 'Enhancing the productivity of Latin American traditional peasant farming systems through an agro-ecological approach', paper for Conference on *Sustainable Agriculture: New Paradigms and Old Practices?*, Bellagio Conference Centre, Italy, 26–30 April.
Chambers, R., Pacey, A. and Thrupp, L.A. (eds) (1989) *Farmer First: Farmer Innovation and Agricultural Research*, London: IT Publications.
Conway, G.R. and Pretty, J.N. (1991) *Unwelcome Harvest: Agriculture and Pollution*, London: Earthscan Publications.
Costanza, R., d'Arge, R., de Groot R., Farber, S., Grasso, M., Hannon, B., Limburg, K., Naeem, S., O'Neil, R.V., Parvelo, J., Raskin, R.G., Sutton, P. and van den Belt, M. (1997) 'The value of the world's ecosystem services and natural capital', *Nature* 387: 253–60.

FAO (1999) *Cultivating Our Futures: Taking Stock of the Multifunctional Character of Agriculture and Land*. Rome: FAO.

Goodland, R. (1998) 'Environmental sustainability defined for the agricultural sector: leave livestock to the private sector', paper for conference on *Sustainability in Agriculture: Tensions between Ecology, Economics and Social Sciences*, Stuttgart, Germany, 28–30 October.

IFPRI (1995) *A 2020 Vision for Food, Agriculture and the Environment*, Washington, DC: International Food Policy Research Institute.

Pinstrup-Andersen, P. and Cohen, M. (1999) 'World food needs and the challenge to sustainable agriculture', paper for conference on *Sustainable Agriculture: New Paradigms and Old Practices?*, Bellagio Conference Centre, Italy, 26–30 April.

Pretty, J. and Hine, R. (2000) 'The promising spread of sustainable agriculture in Asia', *Natural Resources Forum* 24, 107–26.

Pretty, J. and Ward, H. (2001) 'Social capital and the environment', *World Development* 29(2): 209–27.

Pretty, J., Brett, C., Gee, D., Hine, R., Mason, C.F., Morison, J.I.L., Raven, H., Rayment, M. and van der Bijl, G. (2000) 'An assessment of the total external costs of UK agriculture', *Agricultural Systems* 65(2): 113–36.

3.7 Development and the intermediate classes, with special reference to India

Barbara Harriss-White

However development is defined, it requires the production and distribution of a surplus. Surplus is generated through production in excess of what is required to sustain society from day to day and from generation to generation. This surplus must be consumed, redistributed and reinvested. The productive reinvestment which sustains the system is known as accumulation. Accumulation in turn does not take place in a social and political vacuum but in a mesh of institutions. These social institutions (such as class, ethnicity, religion, gender, locality and the regulations of the state) interact in a complex way to sustain and sometimes to threaten this process. Not only does accumulation take a wide range of forms but also the accumulating class may not be homogeneous. Certainly, all accumulation requires the same logic of surplus appropriation and productive re-investment, but there may be important divergences of interest within the capitalist class. States have an important role to play in the nurture or suppression of divergent forms of accumulation. The legal and coercive framework cradling the market economy, the balance and directions of flows of revenue from taxes to the state, and the productive and distributive backwash from it may sustain one fraction of the accumulating classes over another, one type, one sector, one kind of site, one region over another.

KALECKI'S CONCEPT OF INTERMEDIATE CLASSES

This insight is due to a seminal six-page note by the Polish economist Michal Kalecki written in 1965 (Kalecki, 1972). Considering the then incomplete transition to a mature capitalism of countries such as Indonesia and Egypt, he noted a distinct class force occupying a contradictory location to classes based purely on capital and labour. This distinct force proved as awkward to pin down analytically as peasants and merchants have been, and – now – information workers and the social nature of corporate capital are (see Shanin, 1987, for peasants; Huws, 2000, for teleworkers; and Banaji, 2000, for investor capitalism). But Kalecki thought they could represent a distinctive political interest, a form of politics and a type of development. Kalecki called them 'intermediate classes' (ICs); he called the condition of their dominance or hegemony in a developing country an 'intermediate regime' (IR).

Their common trait is the absence of a contradiction between labour and capital (or labour and management). There are three elements to the IC. First, small-scale or petty commodity producers and traders deploy family labour which is not paid wages. Profit cannot be distinguished from net returns so it cannot be assumed that profit is being maximized as it would be reasonable to do for a capitalist firm. Instead the logic of accumulation may involve a fixed 'target' income or the maximization of production. Second, state officials who corruptly privatize for themselves the sale of public goods and services and/or who, for a private fee, allow tax evasion become self-employed accumulators too. Third, in small family businesses with a combination of family and wage labour, though the exploitation of wage labour may be intense, earnings are not wholly a surplus from labour, nor are they completely a payment to entrepreneurs for their risk taking. There is a component of returns to unpaid family workers and managers. ICs are significant because of their huge numbers and their comprehensive territorial spread. One careful estimate for India in 1980 was over a third of the population (Jha, 1980).

ICs also share in common certain contradictions with other classes. Notably with labour (Kalecki called labour 'paupers'), which has a vital interest in low cost wage goods (particularly food, fuel and basic clothing). ICs have a vital interest in keeping these goods scarce in order to profit from controlling this scarcity. For labour, ICs are the local and immediate manifestation of concentrated capital, the 'masters of the countryside'. But they have contradictory interests with corporate capital for the following reasons. First, while ICs benefit directly from shortages, corporate capital does not. Petty producers, traders and small ('family') capitalist firms can reap immediate rewards from mark-up pricing (pricing not according to the interaction of supply and demand but formed by adding a customary profit component on to costs), and from trade which evades controls ('parallel trade'). They can also benefit from distorted trade resulting from state intervention in domestic markets, where regions in deficit have higher prices and regions in surplus have lower prices than would be the case without state-imposed trade restrictions (Harriss-White, 1996; 2000). By contrast, if big business trades opportunistically in the black and parallel economy, professional managers and minority shareholders cannot reap direct benefits. Those would go to the employees or agents engaged at first hand in such exchanges (Banaji, 2000). Second, economies of scale which give big business competitive advantage (in which production costs are lowered as the volume of production increases) require high levels of capacity utilization (since the higher the capacity at which machinery and plant is used, the lower the fixed cost component in production). High levels of capacity are costly and risky to organize. ICs can undercut corporate capital using family labour, a practice sometimes termed 'superexploitation' because both surplus is produced and wages are not paid. Third, notwithstanding fraud and corruption in corporate capital, highly spatially concentrated corporate capital is easier to regulate and tax. Dispersed ICs with outputs above tax thresholds may escape tax because the cost of revenue raising may exceed the revenue stream. More importantly ICs can, and do, insinuate themselves in a nexus of bribery and evasion to the mutual benefit of the decentralized officials, their political masters, local capitalists and the large shadow state of fixers and intermediaries generated by such arrangements.

A mode of accumulation is thereby created which depends on politics and on the struggle among the various accumulating classes for the control over rent-allocating institutions of the state: banks, tax departments, trading organizations and departments implementing the acts of law through which markets for goods, money and labour are regulated. The struggle is waged through infrastructure and subsidies at the legitimate level and with impacts on electoral politics and also at the illegitimate level through sabotageable policy, clientelist corruption and tax evasion, though the distinctions are often unrecognized by the protagonists.

THE RISE AND FALL OF AN INTERMEDIATE REGIME

Kalecki did not have such a politics in mind when he theorized the preconditions to ICs becoming the ruling class and forming an intermediate regime. There were three such preconditions: land reform to crush feudal agrarian interests; non-alignment in international relations as a defence against imperialist powers supporting national and multinational capital; and a developmental state with an active role in the kind of long duration (infrastructural) investments that private capital will not undertake. Nor did Kalecki bother with the means whereby ICs would take power, or allow for the synergies between two directions of state support: on the one hand to ICs (as certainly happened in the case of the Green Revolution) and on the other to the corporate or public-sector capital necessary for upstream and downstream linkages (iron and steel, vehicles and machinery, fertilizer, pesticides, cement, electrical power, etc.). He also ignored the subsidy-gobbling, concession-snatching political power of big business: he was concerned with the limits to its spatial and social reach. Lastly Kalecki disregarded the functional usefulness of ICs to big business, particularly the reductions in production costs and the real body blows to labour activism which are both made possible with subcontracting and the putting-out of at least parts of the process of production to petty firms, a commonplace process now known as informalization (Sassen, 1997).

Despite such criticism, this set of political and economic arrangements resembles the regulative structure of territorially extensive economies like India's for a good stretch of its post-Independence history. Yet in the last two decades of the twentieth century all Kalecki's predisposing conditions vanished. His own theory can be used to predict the conditions of its irrelevance. A class force, which is more powerful than that of the ICs, has to grow in order to undermine the structure of regulation so beneficial to them. The developmental state degenerates for it is caught in a pincer. On the one hand, poor revenue mobilization is coupled with the delegitimating impact of decades of corrupt politics and indifferent growth. On the other hand, the process of opening-up to global financial markets does little to stop this debilitation, because interest repayments come to form a significant part of state expenditure leaking away to international banks. So public-sector capital investment atrophies for material as well as ideological reasons. Liberalization and globalization are definitely not a project of ICs. The unwinding of the licensing and subsidy policy structure, the imposition of presumptive direct taxation and the lifting of agricultural subsidies are all open attacks on ICs by an apparently increasingly more powerful national capitalist class force.

INTERMEDIATE CLASSES UNDER THREAT FROM GLOBALIZATION

What do ICs look like under threat? The conventional story in India is of an economic crisis caused by the necessity to appease a growing range of interest groups. India's crisis broke in 1991 and was resolved by a drastic reduction in the premium for political power. The state's scope had to be cut back severely under the conditions for structural adjustment loans. At the very period in history when the labouring poor have started to assert themselves in electoral politics, the economic returns from political investments decline. The economy is said to be removed from politics. The state is no longer a means of accumulation.

But the economy can never be removed from politics, if by the latter we understand the practice of power. Indeed a new wave of accumulation has broken upon the shore of Indian capital, powered significantly by entrants from lower castes. Though the era of generalized primary accumulation is long past (the era when the stage is set for productive capitalist investment through the dispossession of labour and the kickstarting of accumulation), each current individual entrant has to develop his/her own starting point for accumulation. Micro-level primitive accumulation pre-exists and co-exists with advanced capital, and spaces for small-scale production are continually being created and reproduced.

Meanwhile, older fractions of the ICs are showing signs of renewed accumulative greed, working through markets as well as states. At the individual competitive level, adulteration, arbitrary deductions, chicanery with weights, measures and prices, counterfeiting with brand labels are propped up by new private protection forces and lubricated by tax evasion. Fraud is currently estimated as being 20 times more important quantitatively than is corruption (Roy, 1996). At the collective level, trade associations are asserting themselves not only in representative roles, but also as regulators of markets. Rules are set. Disputes are resolved. But the most important market for regulation is that of labour. The corporatist regulation of trade has the effect of suppressing the political expression of labour to the advantage of capital and ICs (Basile and Harriss-White, 1999). The current wave of small-scale capital accumulation and corporatist consolidation can be expected to set the parameters for development for decades into the future.

What to make of the fact that ICs remain strong locally? Does their mode of operation affect the current and future prospects of neo-liberal development? Yes it does. The state remains an important means of accumulation. While state regulation in the form of direct participation may be being freed-up (and the process is steeped in procrastination) much regulation has to remain, especially as it pertains to strategic and essential commodities needed everywhere, from the marketing of which ICs benefit. By far the biggest single expenditure item for the eight out of ten of the Indian population who still live in towns and villages below 200,000 remains food (Hazell and Ramasamy, 1991). Staple grains are still in the hands of the powerful and privately lucrative combination of state trading corporations and local traders-cum-moneylenders and small-scale agribusiness. They are still controlled by the state and the ICs. Further, the administration of regulative law cannot be *de*regulated and is of concern to most departments of government. Every aspect is contested in the informal politics of ICs: the definition of tradeable goods, permissible technologies, quality, safety, sites, public health, eligibility criteria for market entry, legitimate contracts, rules of liability, penalties for delinquency, the regulation of information, advertising, the terms and conditions of finance and of work. While India is being reinvented at the levels of images and discourse, there is a great deal of continuity in the real economy at the local level.

Peasants show an unpredicted resilience. ICs show every sign of following suit. A great deal more needs to be known about their regional trajectories of accumulation, grounded in environmental resources, agrarian structures, and the politics of territory and administration. At the turn of the new millennium, if we extrapolate from the cautious estimates of Kumar (1999), half the Indian economy is black. Current estimates from the National Council of Applied Economic Research suggest that 60 per cent of GDP and 93 per cent of employment is in the informal sector and out of the regulative and protective reach of the state (Sinha *et al.*, 2000). Most of this sector corresponds with the political and economic arenas of the ICs. Their developmental achievements are noteworthy, their stamina impressive and their future looks bright.

GUIDE TO FURTHER READING

The following are useful on the intermediate classes.

Harriss-White, B. and White, G. (eds) (1996) *Liberalisation and the New Corruption*, Special Issue, *Bulletin of the Institute of Development Studies* 27(2).

Khan M. and Jomo, K. (2000) *Rents, Rent Seeking and Economic Development*, Cambridge: Cambridge University Press.

Raj, K.N. (1973) 'The politics and economics of intermediate regimes', *Economic and Political Weekly*, 7 July: 119–34.

The following are useful on India's informal economy.

Breman, J. (1996) *Footloose Labour: Working in India's Informal Economy*, Cambridge: Cambridge: University Press.

Cadene, P. and Holmstrom, M. (eds) (1998) *Decentralized Production in India: Industrial Districts, Flexible Specialisation and Employment*, New Delhi: Sage.

Harriss-White, B. and Gooptu, N. (2000) 'Mapping India's world of unorganised labour', in L. Panitch and C. Leys (eds) *The Global Proletariat: Socialist Register 2001*, pp. 89–118.

REFERENCES

Banaji, J. (2000) 'Investor capitalism and the reshaping of business in India', *Working Paper Series*, No. 54, *www.qeh.ox.ac.uk*.

Basile, E. and Harriss-White, B. (1999) 'The politics of accumulation in small town India', Bulletin, *Institute of Development Studies* 30(4): 31–39.

Harriss-White, B. (1996) *A Political Economy of Agricultural Markets in South India: Masters of the Countryside*, New Delhi: Sage.

Harriss-White, B. (2000) 'How India works: the character of the economy', Cambridge Commonwealth Lectures, 1999, drafts at *www.qeh.ox.ac.uk* under 'Working Papers' and (forthcoming), 'What is Indian about the Indian economy?', Cambridge: Cambridge University Press.

Hazell, P. and Ramasamy, C. (1991) *The Green Revolution Reconsidered*, Baltimore: Johns Hopkins University Press.

Huws, U. (2000) 'The making of a cybertariat: virtual work in a real world', in L. Panitch and C. Leys (eds) *The Global Proletariat: Socialist Register 2001*, London: Merlin Press, pp. 1–23.

Jha, P.S. (1980) *The Political Economy of Stagnation*, Delhi: Oxford University Press.

Kalecki, M. (1972) *Essays on the Economic Growth of the Socialist and Mixed Economy*, London: Unwin.

Kumar, A. (1999) *The Black Economy in India*, New Delhi: Penguin Books.

Roy, R. (1996) 'State failure: political-fiscal implications of the black economy' Bulletin, *Institute of Development Studies* 27(2): 22–30.

Sassen, S. (1997) 'Informalization in advanced market economies', *Discussion Paper 20*, Geneva: Development Policy Department, International Labour Office.

Shanin, T. (ed.) (1987) *Peasants and Peasant Societies*, Oxford: Blackwell.

Sinha, A., Sangeeta, N. and Siddiqui, K.S.A. (2000) 'The impact of policies on the Indian economy with special reference to the informal sectors: a multisectoral study', New Delhi: NCAER.

PART 4 | Industrialization and employment

EDITORIAL INTRODUCTION

We are living through an era which many maintain is characterized by globalization. This increasingly global remit seems to apply in the fields of industrialization and employment in particular. The sets of interrelated changes involved have often been referred to under the umbrella title 'global shifts'. On the one hand, there has been a shift whereby some parts of the so-called 'Third World' have become newly industrializing countries (NICs), although it is vital to stress that this is true of a very limited number of nations. On the other hand, there has been another shift which has witnessed the increasing globalization of production via the activities of transnational corporations (TNCs), which are to be found operating in more than one country.

The so-called new international division of labour (NIDL) has to be seen as a vital aspect of globalization, pinpointing shifts in production by world region, and affecting both manufacturing and producer services. At least three NIDLs can be recognized: at the time of European colonization, the industrial development of certain semi-developed areas at the end of the nineteenth century, and the present era, in which foreign direct investment (FDI) has expanded greatly. But ideas concerning globalization have to be qualified. In the sphere of production, for example, the shifts which have occurred have only witnessed the incorporation of a limited number of new locations. Thus, commentators have referred to a process of 'divergence', which is leading to increasing differentation between the places which make up the global economic system. Thus, the thesis of hyper-mobility can be over-stretched, especially in respect of productive capital. In contrast, key aspects of consumption and consumer tastes show signs of becoming ever more uniform at the global scale, and this process of relative homogenization is described as global 'convergence'.

These types of changes need to be seen in a context where perspectives on trade and industrial policy in developing countries have changed greatly over the last 25 years. Recent trends have seen the wholesale promotion of deregulation and liberalization, after an early platform which emphasized protectionism. In this approach, export processing zones (EPZs) and free trade zones (FTZs) are important parts of the so-called new international division of labour, and represent what are seen as relatively easy paths to industrialization. By the end of the twentieth century, over 90 countries had established EPZs as part of their economic strategies.

In the context of all of these market-oriented changes, the informal sector has generally responded by providing more jobs. In effect, the informal sector has compensated for public-sector cut-backs, recession and neo-liberal programmes of economic restructuring. Questions of regulation loom large in this regard, and the high incidence of child labour in Africa, Asia and South America has been a notable point of debate over recent years.

In the context of wide global change, there are many important areas for discussion. In overall terms it has to be recognized that technology is inextricably linked to development, and both are related to knowledge and education. On the other hand, some commentators have argued that at the global level, natural resource endowments are less clearly related to the per capita incomes of nations. Thus, whilst a number of resource-poor nations have grown significantly, a number of resource-abundant ones have performed less well. Energy, often regarded as the fourth basic need, has to be recognized as being vital in the development process. However, the longstanding view that energy use increases progressively with development is in urgent need of revision, and the development of sustainable energy systems has to represent a major goal. In respect of the provision of livelihoods, the net needs to be cast wider than industry alone. Over the last 40 years or so, tourism has been seen as an alternative passport to development, and one with distinctly postmodern overtones. But tourism as a policy of development is beset with sociocultural and environmental problems, and the so-called 'cautionary platform' has increasingly been aired.

4.1 Global shift: industrialization and development

Ray Kiely

The last 30 years have seen a global shift in the international division of labour, in which some parts of the former 'Third World' have become newly industrializing countries (NICs). This is most visible in the case of East Asia, but can also be seen in parts of Latin America, southern Europe and to a lesser extent the Caribbean. The old, colonial-based division of labour in which it was said that the 'advanced' capitalist countries produced the industrial goods and the 'Third World' produced the primary goods was always an over-simplification; now it is simply inaccurate. Thus, according to United Nations Development Programme figures, by the late 1990s almost 50 per cent of manufacturing jobs were located in the developing world and over 60 per cent of developing country exports to the so-called 'First World' were of manufactured goods, a 1,200 per cent increase since 1960 (UNDP, 1998: 17).

One explanation for these changes can be found in the growing globalization of production. Transnational companies (TNCs), which operate in at least one country beyond that of origin, are major agents in this globalization process. They may invest beyond their own country to take advantage of market access, cheap labour, lack of regulation (such as rules concerning the environment) or access to raw materials. Apologists argue that TNCs are therefore developmental, providing host countries with income, employment, technology and so on. Critics argue that TNCs are agents of exploitation, and that they distort the development of nation-states. For instance the use of cheap labour amounts to super-exploitation, and intra-firm trade and capital mobility allows these companies to evade tax payments.

This debate over the character of TNCs is also reflected in disputes over the nature of the changing international division of labour. Apologists such as neo-liberals argue that the rise of some newly industrializing countries is evidence that the global economy is a level playing field in which any nation may develop as long as they follow the correct policies. These are basically the adoption of market-friendly policies of limited government, which will allow a competitive, innovative free market to flourish. Neo-liberals have attempted to explain the rise of East Asia on this basis, though the recession of the late 1990s was somewhat inconsistently put down to too much government. Critics have argued that the changing international division of labour has not changed the basic division of the world – that of core and peripheral countries – and that the newly industrializing countries remain dependent on core countries. This dependence may take the form of reliance on technology, capital or access to Western markets. Critics point to the recession of the last 1990s as evidence that East Asia remains a subordinate, semi-peripheral part of the world economy.

While it is undoubtedly true that there have been enormous changes in the world economy over the last 30 years, many advocates who claim a substantial global shift of industrial production overstate their case. In particular, one sometimes has the impression that *productive* capital is as hypermobile as *financial* capital (which itself is selective in terms of where it locates), and that its movement from one part of the globe to another is a relatively unproblematic task. However, capital continues to concentrate in certain areas. This is because capital faces a number of 'sunk costs' which constitute significant barriers to exit. These may include start-up costs, access to local suppliers, and the acquisition of local trust and acceptance. Once established, growth tends to be cumulative, as earlier developers tend to monopolize technology and skills, established markets and access to nearby suppliers.

Of course these advantages are never absolute, and later developers may leapfrog earlier outmoded production techniques. So, for example, Korean steel and shipbuilding industries developed and ultimately became more competitive than those of Britain in these industrial sectors. This was not however because of a hyper-mobile productive capital that relocated from high-cost Britain to low-cost Korea but was instead a product of a successful alliance between the Korean state and local capital in developing these industries.

Similarly, the partial move away from Fordist mass production to smaller-batch post-Fordist niche production may give some potential to late developers. However the key point is that these changes do not entail the end of capital's tendency to agglomerate in certain parts of the world and thereby marginalize others, thus maintaining uneven development. Indeed, global, 'post-Fordist' flexible accumulation may intensify this tendency as suppliers locate even more closely to final producers as their stock is delivered on a regular just-in-time basis, as opposed to the old irregular just-in-case system.

In some sectors, the barriers to exit are less significant and so industrial capital is more mobile. This is especially the case in labour-intensive industries such as clothing, textiles and semi-conductors. In these and other sectors, fixed costs are lower as technology is not so advanced. This provides former Third World countries with potential comparative advantages over the 'advanced' capitalist countries. But even this advantage is a mixed blessing as employment (often of young women) may involve work for low wages in poor conditions. Employers in these factories are just as likely to be local capitalists as TNCs. Sometimes these employers may be suppliers to Western retailers, who focus their activities on design and marketing. But even in labour-intensive sectors like clothing and footwear, wage costs are not the only factor as manufacturers may have to rely on labour skills, or be close to the final market in an industry where the turnover time for fashion goods can often be very rapid.

Industrial production can therefore be said to be increasingly globalized, but the networks of production processes which lead to a finished commodity remain hierarchically structured. Gereffi (1994: 219) distinguishes two kinds of production process or commodity chain. First, producer commodity chains exist where the site of production is relatively immobile and so production agglomerates in favoured locations. Second, buyer commodity chains exist where there is greater mobility and labour intensity of production. This may give so-called peripheral areas certain advantages in terms of low labour costs, but in these industries barriers to entry exist at the level of brand name merchandising and retail levels. In the first case, marginalization occurs through absence of industrial investment; in the case of the latter, the value added by industrial production tends to be low, at least compared to the marketing and design stages.

The continued concentration of industrial production in selected areas is reflected in the figures on foreign investment. Most direct foreign investment is located in the 'developed' world, and the late 1990s saw a fall in the proportion going to the so-called 'developing countries' (UNCTAD, 1999: 17). This was largely because of the recession in East Asia, which itself shows how concentrated foreign investment is in the developing world. Among those 'developing countries' who received FDI in 1998, the top 5 received 55 per cent of all investment while the 48 least developed countries received less than 1 per cent (UNCTAD, 1999: 17). Foreign investment figures alone do not tell the whole story, as TNCs may raise investment capital from a variety of sources (international money markets, equities and so on), and production may involve cross-border production networks between formally independent firms – the buyer commodity chains discussed above, for example. However, the evidence suggests that in these areas there is also a high rate of concentration, not least in the trade in manufactured goods.

The above outline contrasts sharply with neo-liberal and (some) dependency perspectives outlined earlier. Both neo-liberal and dependency theories assume that productive capital is hyper-mobile but go on to draw very different conclusions. For neo-liberalism, this mobility means that capital will move from areas of abundance to scarcity in order to take advantage of lower costs in the latter. In the long run, so long as there is a global free market unhindered by the operations of interventionist nation-states, this will lead to a system of perfect competition between free and equal producers each exercising their respective comparative advantages. For some versions of dependency theory, this mobility means that capital can move to areas of lower costs in order to increase the rate of exploitation without promoting national development. The result is the continuation of a core–periphery division of the world, as peripheral industrializers suffer from new forms of dependence. Similarly, while neo-liberals regard TNCs as modernizing agents, dependency-oriented writers regard them as agents of underdevelopment.

As already made clear, *both* positions exaggerate the degree of mobility of capital and this weakness leads to other problems. Clearly, given the tendency for capital to concentrate in certain regions and marginalize others, neo-liberal optimism concerning a level playing field in the global economy is seriously misplaced. On the other hand, the tendency of some dependency theorists to regard the newly industrializing countries as being simply peripheral industrializers is also inadequate. To conceptualize the world on the basis of a timeless core–periphery divide is ahistorical, and one is left with the feeling that whatever happens in the 'Third World' (for instance, industrialization or lack of industrialization) occurs because of the will of an all-powerful core, simply pulling the strings of a passive periphery.

Similarly, the debate on the developmental effects of TNCs is too black and white, with one side (neo-liberalism) assuming that the effects are unproblematically favourable while the other (some dependency approaches) assumes that they are all bad. The impact of TNCs will depend on a number of specific factors, such as the particular sector in which the TNC operates, the role of the state in regulating TNC behaviour, and local resistance to the potentially bad effects of a particular transnational company. In a capitalist-dominated world, the question then moves away from a simple one of can or should particular countries open up or do without TNC investment, and instead becomes one of finding the best strategies for dealing with companies which may have different interests from those of the local population. For some socialists, this position may represent a retreat from a pure anti-capitalist position. Given the record of the former so-called socialist countries this may be no bad thing, and anyway socialism is hardly on the agenda in the current period. But perhaps more important, a blanket anti-TNC position can easily become a *nationalist* as opposed to a socialist position. This can have the effect of allowing local capital – equally as likely to be as 'super-exploitative' as TNCs – to behave as it wishes, all in the name of a spurious socialist anti-imperialism.

The global economy therefore continues to be characterized by polarization, with some people and regions at the cutting edge of globalization while others are marginalized. Transnational companies tend to be highly selective in their choice of investment location, concentrating in parts of the former First World or selected parts of the former periphery. There is no longer a clear division of the world between core and periphery (though in fairness this division may never have been as clear as some underdevelopment theorists implied), but at the same time, this does not mean the end of uneven and unequal development. Indeed, the gap between rich and poor is growing; according to Castells (1998: 81), the richest 20 per cent of the world's population has seen their share of world income increase from 70 per cent in 1960 to 85 per cent in 1996, whilst the poorest 20 per cent's share has declined from 2.3 per cent to 1.4 per cent over the same period. The world is divided into many cores and peripheries, which can be located not only between but *within* nation-states.

GUIDE TO FURTHER READING

The following items afford an introduction to global shifts in industrialization.
Castells, M. (1996) *The Rise of the Network Society*, Oxford: Blackwell.
Dicken, P. (1992) *Global Shift*, London: Paul Chapman.
Frobel, F., Heinrichs, J. and Kreye, O. (1980) *The New International Division of Labour*, Cambridge: Cambridge University Press.
Gereffi, G. and Korzeniewicz, M. (eds) (1994) *Commodity Chains and Global Capitalism*, Westport, CT: Greenwood Press.
Held, D., McGrew, A., Goldblatt, D. and Perraton, J. (1999) *Global Transformations*, Cambridge: Polity.
Hirst, P. and Thompson, G. (1996) *Globalization in Question*, Cambridge: Polity.
Hoogvelt, A. (1997) *Globalisation and the Postcolonial World*, London: Macmillan.
Kiely, R. (1998) *Industrialization and Development: A Comparative Analysis*, London: UCL Press.
Ohmae, K. (1991) *The Borderless World*, London: Fontana.

REFERENCES

Castells, M. (1998) *End of Millennium*, Oxford: Blackwell. An important examination of the global economy in the so-called 'information age'.
Gereffi, G. (1994) 'Capitalism, development and global commodity chains', in L. Sklair (ed.) *Capitalism and Development*, London: Routledge, pp. 211–31. A useful summary of the theory of global commodity chains.
UNCTAD (1999) *World Investment Report: Foreign Direct Investment and the Challenge of Development*, New York: United Nations. Annual report on investment flows in the global economy.
UNDP (1998) *Globalization and Liberalization*, New York: United Nations Development Programme. Report on the social effects of development in the global economy.

4.2 The new international division of labour

Alan Gilbert

Both the academic literature and the popular media are currently obsessed with the process of globalization. This process has seemingly generated a new international division of labour (NIDL). Few writing about NIDL and globalization mince their words. According to the World Bank (1995: 1): 'These are revolutionary times in the global economy.' According to the ILO (1995: 68–9): 'Globalization has triumphed.' While it is clear that the world has changed, it is less obvious what has changed. And, if some parts of the world have been fully embraced by the NIDL, others play a rather peripheral role. What few understand, although many claim to, is what effect the NIDL is having on our lives. Perhaps the only certain answer is that it depends on who you are and where you live; some people are doing very well in the NIDL whereas others are most certainly not.

WHAT IS THE NIDL?

Acccording to UNRISD (1995: 24) the NIDL is difficult to define precisely but incorporates six principal forms of change:

- the spread of liberal democracy
- the dominance of market forces
- the integration of the global economy
- the transformation of production systems and labour markets
- the speed of technological change
- the media revolution and consumerism.

The first change is that most areas of the world now constitute part of the global market. Increasingly we all consume the same products and are bombarded with the same kinds of advertising. It is doubtful whether many people around the world would fail to recognize the names Coca-Cola, Nike, Ford, Sony and CNN. The products and images of these companies' products dominate our television screens and our streets.

The second fundamental change is that manufacturing production is no longer confined to a relative handful of industrialized countries. The production of clothes, shoes, bicycles and televisions has become global. Transnational companies produce their goods in an increasing number of countries. Many favour countries where labour is cheap and political conditions are stable, for example, China, Indonesia, Korea, Thailand, Mexico and the Dominican Republic.

Third, NIDL has recently been characterized by the globalization of services and particularly producer services. US investment in Latin America grew by 3.7 times between 1970 and 1996 and much of that investment went into services. Investment in banking, finance and services rose from 32 per cent in 1980 to 54 per cent in 1996.

Finally, the transnational corporations that have managed this transformation have changed their own structure. In the last 40 years or so, they have changed themselves from production companies into the organizers and co-ordinators of production and services (Dicken, 1994: 106). Today, most of these companies operate transnationally and few retain close allegiance to a single country (Reich, 1991). Ford cars are no longer made principally in Detroit, they are made in different places all over the globe. The transnational corporations are the new global brokers, responsible for most of the investment flows flushing around the world system.

THE GEOGRAPHY OF THE NIDL

The dramatic changes that have taken place have not affected every country equally. While Coca-Cola is probably drunk in most parts of the world, per capita consumption is clearly much higher in the United States than it is in India, for example. Most Chinese have only occasional access to a television and perhaps a majority of Africans have never used a telephone. If mass consumption is less than global, production is even less so. Indeed, one of the great concerns about the NIDL is how it has marginalized substantial parts of the world. Some Africans buy global products but very few global products are made there.

IS NIDL NEW?

The technological innovations that have allowed the development of rapid transport links and instant electronic communication are definitely new. But many of the changes have a longer history, what is different is that they are occurring on a larger scale than before. Indeed, in some respects the advocates of fundamental change exaggerate because the massive movement of capital, agricultural products, manufactures, people and ideas has been under way for centuries (Gilbert, 1990). In this sense NIDL is definitely not new. It is merely the latest in a series of major restructurings of the world economy. Walton (1985) has argued that at least two NIDLs have preceded the present one. NIDL mark one was brought about by Europe dividing the world into colonies and reorganizing production and markets in the new colonies. NIDL mark two occurred when previously semi-developed areas of the world began to industrialize from the end of the nineteenth century. The process of import substituting industrialization created major industrial concentrations in countries such as Argentina, Brazil, China, India, Mexico and South Africa. Despite their continuing poverty, these countries contained some of the world's largest industrial economies in 1960.

The current NIDL, which perhaps we ought to call NIDL mark three, is highly significant but so were these earlier shifts. NIDL mark one led to the decimation of aboriginal peoples in Latin America and Australasia, the slave trade across the Atlantic, the incorporation of new food products into the European diet and their production in the colonies, certainly constitute as significant a change to the world as the events of the past 30 years or so. Think of the diet of the average Briton before the potato, the banana, tobacco, sugarcane, tea and coffee reached these shores. NIDL mark two led to the growth of industry and major cities in the periphery of Europe, North and South Africa, India, China and much of Latin America. Again, this represented a major shift in the organization of world production.

WHAT EFFECT HAS NIDL MARK THREE HAD ON THE WORLD AT LARGE?

Some view the impact of NIDL mark three to be wholly positive; others view the process as being totally undesirable. The difference may be due to the fact that NIDL3's effects have been highly variable: whether you gain or lose depends on who you are and where you live.

> Viewed as a whole, . . . the world economy would appear to be creating the basis for rising prosperity and employment growth. The expansion of trade and investment flows against a background of a worldwide shift towards more open economic policies and a greater reliance on market forces should also be contributing to improved resource allocation and efficiency worldwide. Nevertheless, while essentially correct from an overall standpoint, this view of the global economy neglects differences in the position of different countries and of different social groups within these which raise serious adjustment and distributional issues.
>
> (ILO, 1995: 5)

To its critics, and even to some of its advocates, the most worrying outcome of globalization is its impact on poverty and particularly inequality. For, if the world is becoming a richer place, dire poverty remains well entrenched and in many places people are actually becoming poorer. The unleashing of fierce competition between nations has led to Western Europe, North America and parts of the Far East increasing their wealth while most of Africa and parts of Asia and Latin America have been losing out.

In addition, there are major shifts in the distribution of income within countries. 'The owners of capital, along with some managerial and professional groups, have generally gained while the organized working class has lost out' (UNRISD, 1995: 26). If poverty is not actually increasing in most places, there is no doubt that virtually every country in the world is becoming more unequal. Those at the top are reaping huge gains, those at the bottom are gaining little (Londoño and Székely, 1997). As Mittelman (1996: 18) puts it: 'life is marked by a deepening divide between rich and poor'.

One aspect of this divide is the way that NIDL3 has undermined the position of organized labour (Roxborough, 1989). So-called 'post-Fordist' management practices, growing inter-firm competition and less restrictive labour legislation have made employment more precarious (Hayter *et al.*, 1994; Roberts, 1994). Those who are excluded from the global sector and are relegated to informal economic activities seldom thrive.

THE EFFECT ON THE STATE

To some, the most important feature of NIDL3 is the change it has brought in the role of the state (Ould-Mey, 1994; Peck and Tickell, 1994; Cox, 1996; Mittelman, 1996; Panich, 1996). Power has shifted from the nation-state to the transnational corporation.

> The world's 37,000 parent trans-national corporations and their 200,000 affiliates now control 75 per cent of all world trade in commodities, manufactured goods and services. One third of this trade is intrafirm – making it very difficult for governments and international trade organizations to exert any control.
>
> (UNRISD, 1995: 27)

> Globalization has weakened the ability of individual states to manage their economies. At the macroeconomic level, the mobility of finance capital has reduced government control over interest rates and the exchange rate; the flexibility of multinational enterprises has reduced the ability of government to affect the level of investment and its geographical location; and the international mobility of technical and skilled labour has made it more difficult for governments to impose progressive income and wealth taxes and to sustain high levels of public expenditure.
>
> (ILO, 1995: 69)

Today the state is encouraged to spend less on social welfare and more on generating economic growth. Investing in education is deemed to be investment, investing in old people to be unproductive. Pressure is being exerted to cut back on the welfare state, at least in those countries where it developed after the Second World War. Faced with a less paternalistic state, the poor are expected to look after themselves (Leontidou, 1993).

In this sense, the role of the modern state has changed rather than diminished. State power has not declined because transnational corporations cannot run the world alone and rely on national governments to perform a series of important local tasks (Dicken, 1994). The state is now concerned less with protecting its national citizens than with creating the conditions which will attract foreign investment. Sometimes that process makes life more difficult for its own people. According to Mittelman (1994: 431) 'the state no longer serves primarily as a buffer or shield against the world economy. Rather, the state . . . increasingly facilitates globalisation, acting as an agent in the process'.

IS NIDL MARK THREE STABLE?

According to the World Bank (1995: 55) 'Global markets are not only larger than any single domestic market but generally more stable as well – and still have room to accommodate newcomers'. As a result, national economies should be more stable within a globalized economy. On the other hand, Lipietz (1992) argues that the neo-liberal model which sustains NIDL3 is unstable. Social polarization may lead to either disruptive collective action or social breakdown. Swings in the business cycle are exaggerated rather than evened out and the deregulation of international trade leads to forced deflations and states adopting beggar-thy-neighbour policies. Certainly the economic crises that hit Mexico in 1994, the Far East in 1997–98 and Brazil in 1999 demonstrate that in an era of global financial markets, economic disaster always lurks just around the corner.

It is also possible that political discontent will spread under NIDL3. Since one of its key features is the growth of democracy, this could mean that governments are less stable because voters regularly remove them from power. Nowhere is this better seen than in the recent fall from grace of Mexico's PRI, the party that had held power constantly since 1928. But there is a greater danger still to national governments: that their populations will become more radical and hostile. According to this scenario globalization will 'undermine state power and unleash subterranean cultural pluralism' (Mittelman, 1996: 7–8):

> In the face of the declining power of organized labor and revolutionary groups, the powerless must devise alternative strategies of social struggle. . . . New social movements – women's groups, environmentalists, human rights organizations, etc. are themselves global phenomena, a worldwide response to the deleterious effects of economic globalization.

Arguably the 'austerity riots' which greeted national governments' acceptance of IMF structural adjustment agreements are part of the result of a similar process (Walton, 1989, 1998).

THE NEED FOR MULTINATIONAL GOVERNANCE

In order to protect the poor and indeed the majority from the unfavourable side of globalization, there is increasing agreement that it is vital to reform the nature of world government (ODI, 1999; ILO, 1995). To counter the power of the transnational corporations new forms of multinational government must be created. The emergence of huge political alliances and trade blocs like the European Union and NAFTA is possibly a welcome step in this direction. But others would argue that we need world institutions that can control financial flows and tax capital movements. Only in this way will the undesirable face of NIDL be controlled. Without the creation of such a level of government, tax havens, drug flows, international crime, environmental devastation and labour exploitation will get wholly out of control. In this sense, the role of the state with respect to the market has not changed. It is just that in the NIDL, a powerful state is needed at the international level to help the disabled national state look after those who are less able to compete in the new competitive world.

GUIDE TO FURTHER READING AND REFERENCES

The following references provide the basis for further reading.
Cox, R.W. (1996) 'A perspective on globalization', in J. Mittelman (ed.) pp. 21–30.

Dicken, P. (1994) *Global Shift: Transforming the World Economy*, London: Paul Chapman.

Dornbusch, R. and Edwards, S. (eds) (1991) *The Macro-economics of Populism in Latin America*, Chicago: University of Chicago Press.

Edwards, S. (1995) *Crisis and Reform in Latin America*, Oxford: Oxford University Press.

Gereffi, G. (1995) 'Global production systems and third world development', in B. Stallings (ed.) pp. 100–42.

Gilbert, A.G. (1990) 'Urbanisation at the periphery: reflections on the changing dynamics of housing and employment in Latin American cities', in D. Drakakis-Smith (ed.) *Economic Growth and Urbanisation in Developing Areas*, London: Routledge, pp. 73–124.

Hayter, R., Grass, E. and Barnes, T. (1994) 'Labour flexibility: a tale of two mills', *Tijdschrift voor Economische en Sociale Geografie* 85: 25–38.

ILO (International Labour Office) (1995) *World Employment: an ILO Report: 1995*, Geneva: ILO.

Leontidou, L. (1993) 'Informal strategies of unemployment relief in Greek cities: the relevance of family, locality and housing', *European Planning Studies* 1: 43–68.

Lipietz, A. (1992) *Towards a New Economic Order: Post-Fordism, Ecology and Democracy*, Cambridge: Polity Press.

Londoño, J.L. and Székely, M. (1997) 'Persistent poverty and excess inequality: Latin America, 1970–1995', *IADB Working Paper Series* 357.

Mittelman, J.H. (1994) 'The globalisation challenge: surviving at the margins', *Third World Quarterly* 15: 427–43.

Mittelman, J.H. (ed.) (1996) *Globalization: Critical Reflections*, Boulder, CO: Lynne Rienner Publishers.

ODI (1999) 'Global governance: an agenda for the renewal of the United Nations?' *ODI Briefing Paper* July.

Ould-Mey, M. (1994) 'Global adjustment: implications for peripheral states', *Third World Quarterly* 15: 319–36.

Panich, L. (1996) 'Rethinking the role of the state', in J. Mittelman (ed.) pp. 83–113.

Peck, J. and Tickell, A. (1994) 'Jungle law breaks out: neoliberalism and global–local disorder', *Area* 26: 317–26.

Reich, R. (1991) *The Work of Nations: Preparing Ourselves for 21st-century Capitalism*, New York: Simon & Schuster.

Roberts, B. (1994) 'Informal economy and family strategies', *International Journal of Urban and Regional Research* 18: 6–23.

Roxborough, I. (1989) 'Organized labor: a major victim of the debt crisis', in B. Stallings and R. Kaufman (eds) *Debt and Democracy in Latin America*, Boulder, CO: Westview Press, pp. 91–108.

Stallings, B. (ed.) (1995) *Global Change, Regional Response: the New International Context of Development*, Cambridge: Cambridge University Press.

Stoneman, C. (1992) 'The World Bank, income distribution and employment: some lessons for South Africa', in M. Lundah (ed.) *Apartheid in Theory and Practice: An Economic Analysis*, Boulder, CO: Westview Press, pp. 28–39.

UNRISD (1995) *States of Disarray*, Geneva: UNRISD.

Walton, J. (ed.) (1985) *Capital and Labour in an Industrializing World* (Chapter 1), London: Sage.

Walton, J. (1989) 'Debt, protest, and the state in Latin America', in Eckstein, S. (ed.) *Power and Popular Protest: Latin American Social Movements*, Berkeley, CA: University of California Press, pp. 299–328.

Walton, J. (1998) 'Urban conflict and social movements in poor countries: theory and evidence of collective action', *International Journal of Urban and Regional Research* 22: 460–81.

World Bank (1995) *World Development Report 1995*, Oxford: Oxford University Press.

4.3 Global convergence, divergence and development

Robert B. Potter

INTRODUCTION: GLOBALIZATION AND DEVELOPMENT

Globalization is customarily recognized as consisting of three principal strands: the economic, the cultural and the political. In respect of *economic globalization*, distance has become less important to economic activities, so that large corporations sub-contract to branchplants in far distant regions, effectively operating within a 'borderless' world. The stereotype of *cultural globalization* suggests that as Western forms of consumption and lifestyles spread across the globe, there is an increasing convergence of cultural styles on a global norm, with that norm being codified and defined by the global capitalist system. In addition, in the arena of *political globalization*, internationalization is regarded as leading to the erosion of the former role and powers of the nation-state.

One of the most pressing issues, therefore, is what does development mean in a contemporary context which is dominated by processes of globalization and global change? One of the important questions to be addressed is whether globalization is, in fact, a new process in the first place. Does globalization mean the entire world is becoming more uniform? Does it also mean that there is a chance that the world will become progressively more equal over time? If not, is it the case that such a process of accelerated homogenization will come about in the near future? In short, does globalization mean that change and development will trickle down, and that this will occur more speedily than it has in the past?

In respect of homogenization–heterogenization, two generalized views have emerged concerning the relationships between globalization and patterns of development. The first view is the familiar claim that places around the world are fast becoming, if not exactly the same, then certainly increasingly similar. This view dates from the 1960s belief in the process of modernization. Such a perspective tacitly accepts that the world will become progressively more 'Westernized', or more accurately, 'Americanized' (see Roberts, 1978; Massey and Jess, 1995). The approach stresses the likelihood of social and cultural homogenization, with key North American traits of consumption being exemplified by the 'coca-colonization' and the Hollywoodization, or Miamization, of the Third World, replete with McDonald's Golden Arches (see Potter *et al.*, 1999).

The second and far more realistic stance presents almost the reverse view, that rather than uniformity, globalization is resulting in greater difference, flexibility, permeability, openness and hybridity, both between places and between cultures (Massey and Jess, 1995; Potter, 1993). Following on from this perspective, far from leading to a uniform world, globalization is viewed as being closely connected with the process of uneven development and the perpetuation of spatial inequalities.

This view of globalization argues that localities are being renewed afresh. This is particularly so in respect of economic change, where production, ownership and economic processes are highly place- and space-specific. Even in regard to cultural change, it may be argued that although the hallmarks of Western tastes, consumption and lifestyles, such as Coca-Cola, Disney, McDonald's and Hollywood, are available to all, such dominant worldwide cultural icons are reinterpreted locally, and take on different meanings in different places (Cochrane, 1995). This view sees fragmentation and localization as key correlates of globalization.

GLOBAL CONVERGENCE AND DIVERGENCE: CULTURAL AND ECONOMIC GLOBALIZATION

This leads to a major conceptualization of what is happening to the global system in the contemporary world, and what this means for growth and change in present-day developing countries. The basic argument is that the uneven development that has characterized much of the Third World during the mercantile and early capitalist periods has been intensified post-1945, as a result of the operation of what may be referred to as the dual processes of global convergence and global divergence. These terms originate in the work of Armstrong and McGee (1985) (see also Potter, 1990). Together these processes may be seen as characterizing globalization.

Divergence relates to the sphere of production and the observation that the places which make up the world system are becoming increasingly differentiated. Starting from the observation that the 1970s witnessed a number of fundamental shifts in the global economic system – not least the slowdown of the major capitalist economies and rapidly escalating oil prices – Armstrong and McGee (1985) stressed that such changes have had a notable effect on developing nations. Foremost among these changes has been the dispersion of manufacturing industries to low labour-cost locations, and the increasing control of trade and investment by TNCs. It is this trend which has witnessed the establishment of Fordist production-line systems in the newly industrializing countries (NICs), whilst smaller-scale, more specialized and responsive, or so-called flexible systems of both production and accumulation have become more typical of Western industrial nations. Productive capacity is being channelled into a limited number of countries and metropolitan centres. Thus, increasing international division of labour, and the increasing salience of TNCs are leading to enhanced heterogeneity or divergence between nations with respect to their patterns of production, capital accumulation and ownership. Thus, the industrializing export economies of Taiwan, Hong Kong and South Korea can be recognized, along with the larger internally directed industrialized countries such as Mexico, raw material exporting nations like Nigeria, and low-income agricultural exporters such as Bangladesh.

In the contemporary world such changes are highly likely to be non-hierarchic in the sense that they are focusing development on specific localities and settlements. Armstrong and McGee (1985: 41) state that 'Cities are ... the crucial elements in accumulation at all levels, ... and the *locus operandi* for transnationals, local oligopoly capital and the modernising state.' It is these features which gave rise to the title of their book, which characterized cities as 'theatres of accumulation'. Other commentators point to what ostensibly appears to be the reverse trend – that of the increasing similarity which appears to characterize world patterns of change and development. There is at least one major respect in which a predominant pattern of what may be referred to as global convergence is occurring. This is in the sphere of consumer preferences and habits. Of particular importance is the so-called 'demonstration effect', involving the rapid assimilation of North American and European tastes and consumption patterns (McElroy and Albuquerque, 1986).

The influence of the mass media is likely to be especially critical in this respect. The televising of North American soap operas may well lead to a mismatch between extant lifestyles and aspirations (Miller, 1992; Potter and Dann, 1996). Such media systems have become truly global in character in the 1990s. Potter and Dann (1996) show that the ownership of televisions and radio receivers is near universal, even among low-income households in Barbados in the eastern Caribbean. It was also clear that a surprisingly high proportion of households have a video recorder, some 43.24 per cent in 1990. Video ownership was as high as 27.82 per cent for the occupants of all wood traditional houses, and 48.26 per cent for the denizens of combined wood and concrete houses, those which are generally in the process of being upgraded. Other aspects of the wider trend of convergence involve changes in dietary preferences and the rise of the 'industrial palate', whereby an increasing proportion of food is consumed by non-producers (Drakakis-Smith, 1990).

Developing cities may be seen as the prime channels for the introduction of such emulatory and imitative lifestyles, which are sustained by imports from overseas along with the internal activities of transnational corporations and their branch plants. These in turn are frequently related to collective consumption, indebtedness and increasing social inequalities. These changes toward homogenization are ones which are particularly true of very large cities. Such a view sees globalization as a profoundly unsettling process both for cultures and the identity of individuals, and it suggests that established traditions are dislocated by the invasion of foreign influences and images from global cultural industries. The implication is that such influences are pernicious and are extremely difficult to reject or contain (Hall, 1995). Following this line of argument, Hall (1995: 176) has observed that 'global consumerism, though limited by its uneven geography of power (Massey, 1991), spreads the same thin cultural film over everything – Big Macs, Coca-Cola and Nike trainers everywhere'.

However, the impact of standardized merchandising is likely to be highly uneven, especially when viewed in respect of social status. Thus, it is the elite and upper-income urban groups who are most able to adopt and sustain the 'goods' thereby provided – for example, healthcare facilities, mass media and communications technologies, improvements in transport and the like. It may be conjectured that the lower-income groups within society disproportionately receive the 'bads' – for example, formula baby milk and tobacco products. Thus, once again, forces of globalization may be seen to be etching out wider differences on the ground.

A direct and important outcome of this suggestion is a strong argument that the form of contemporary development that is to be found in particular areas of the developing world is the local manifestation and juxtaposition of these two seemingly contradictory processes of convergence and divergence at the global scale. In terms of examples, Armstrong and McGee (1985) look at the ways in which these trends are played out in Ecuador, Hong Kong and Malaysia. Potter (1993, 1995, 2000) has examined how well the framework fits in the examination of the Caribbean, in which context, it is argued, tourism has a direct effect in respect to both trends of convergence and divergence.

CONCLUSIONS

At this point a number of important arguments can be reconciled. The first is that it can be posited that it is the key traits of Western consumption and demand that are potentially being spread in a hierarchical manner within the global system, from the metropolitan centres of the core world cities to the regional primate cities of the peripheries and semi-peripheries, and then subsequently, down and through the global capitalist system. But the actual impact of these will be highly locality-, class- and gender-specific. It is interesting to observe that the innovations that were cited by commentators in the 1960s and 1970s as having spread sequentially from the top to the bottom of the urban system of America were all consumption-oriented ones – for example, the diffusion of television stations and receivers (Potter and Lloyd-Evans, 1998). Thus, it needs to be emphasized that the spread is one of potential, with many real differences evolving between places.

In contrast, aspects of production and ownership are becoming more unevenly spread, and are generally being concentrated into *specific nodes*. This process involves strong cumulative feedback loops. Hence considerable stability is likely to be maintained at selected points within the global system, frequently the largest world cities. Hence, entrepreneurial innovations will be concentrated in space, and are not likely to be spread through the urban system; an argument which has parallels with the view that dependency theory deals with the diffusion of underdevelopment, and not development.

Thus, on the one hand, the culture and values of the West are potentially being diffused on a global scale. By such means, patterns of consumption are spread through time, and there is an evolving tendency for convergence on what may be described as the global norms of consumption. These aspects of global change are primarily expressed hierarchically, and are essentially top-down in nature. In contrast, cities appear to be accumulating and centralizing the ownership of capital, and this process is closely associated with differences in productive capabilities. The tendency toward divergence is expressed in a punctiform, sporadic manner, which stresses activities in area. TNCs and associated industrialization are the most important agents involved in this process. Thus, cities and urban systems have to be studied as important functioning parts of the world economy. In such a role, cities are agents of concentration and spread at one and the same time.

GUIDE TO FURTHER READING

Armstrong, W. and McGee, T. (1985) *Theatres of Accumulation: Studies in Asian and Latin American Urbanization*, London and New York: Methuen. Chapter 3 on 'Cities: theatres of accumulation, centres of diffusion' provides an introduction to the key concepts.

Potter, R.B. (1993) 'Urbanisation in the Caribbean and trends of global convergence–divergence', *Geographical Journal*, 159: 1–21. Considers the appropriateness of the convergence–divergence thesis in the regional context of the Caribbean.

Potter, R.B. (2000) *The Urban Caribbean in an Era of Global Change*, Aldershot, Burlington, Singapore and Sydney: Ashgate. A monograph aiming to bring the Caribbean story of globalization and development up to date.

Roberts, B. (1978) *Cities of Peasants: The Political Economy of Urbanization in the Third World*, London: Edward Arnold. One of the early works pointing to the growing convergence amongst Latin American cities.

REFERENCES

Cochrane, A. (1995) 'Global worlds and global worlds of difference', in J. Anderson, C. Brook and A. Cochrane (eds) *A Global World?* Oxford: Oxford University Press and Open University, pp. 249–90.

Drakakis-Smith, D. (1990) 'Food for thought or thought about food: urban food distribution systems in the Third World', in R.B. Potter and A.T. Salau (eds) *Cities and Development*, London: Mansell, pp. 100–20.

Hall, S. (1995) 'New cultures for old', in D. Massey and P. Jess (eds) *A Place in the World?* Oxford: Oxford University Press, pp. 175–213.

McElroy, J. and Albuquerque, K. (1986) 'The tourism demonstration effect in the Caribbean', *Journal of Travel Research* 25: 31–4.

Massey, D. (1991) 'A global sense of place', *Marxism Today* June: 24–9.

Massey, D. and Jess, P. (1995) *A Place in the World? Places, Cultures and Globalization*, Oxford: Oxford University Press and the Open University.

Miller, D. (1992) 'The young and the restless in Trinidad: a case of the local and the global in mass consumption', in R. Siverstone and E. Hirsch (eds) *Consuming Technology*, London: Routledge, pp. 16–82.

Potter, R.B. (1990) 'Cities, convergence, divergence and Third World development', in R.B. Potter and A. Salau (eds) *Cities and Development in the Third World*, London: Mansell.

Potter, R.B. (1995) 'Urbanisation and development in the Caribbean', *Geography* 80: 334–41.

Potter, R.B. and Dann, G.M.S. (1996) 'Globalisation, postmodernity and development in the Commonwealth Caribbean', in Y.-M. Yeung (ed.) *Global Change and the Commonwealth*, Hong Kong: University of Hong Kong.

Potter, R.B. and Lloyd-Evans, S. (1998) *The City in the Developing World*, Harlow: Longman.

Potter, R.B., Binns, T., Elliott. J.A. and Smith, D. (1999) *Geographies of Development*, Harlow: Prentice Hall.

4.4 Trade and industrial policy in developing countries

David Greenaway and Chris Milner

INTRODUCTION

The last quarter of the twentieth century witnessed a substantial change of attitude in academic and policy circles about the appropriate form of trade and industrial policy for economic development. In this essay we consider the nature, extent and consequences of the resulting liberalization of trade policies in developing countries that this has induced.

RECENT LIBERALIZATION IN DEVELOPING COUNTRIES

Defining liberalization

In a stylized two-sector world defining liberalization is straightforward: removal of a tariff, or indeed any other intervention, which restores the free trade set of relative prices is unambiguously trade liberalization. However, in practice things are more complicated and at least two other concepts are used: changes in policy which reduce anti-export bias and move the relative prices of tradeables towards neutrality; and the substitution of more efficient for less efficient forms of intervention. These are overlapping, but they do not map on to one another on a one-to-one basis. It is possible to engineer a more neutral set of relative prices by introducing an export subsidy with a pre-existing import tariff, or by lowering the tariff, but the resource allocation effects of the two may differ. Although trade theory points to some striking non-equivalences between tariffs and quotas, the theorist might not regard the replacement of the latter with the former as liberalization. Policy analysts do, and this particular reform is a standard ingredient of World Bank liberalization packages.

Rationale for liberalization

There are very powerful economic arguments in favour of free trade (Dornbusch, 1992; Krueger, 1997). It is not too difficult to show that, in the absence of imperfections, free trade is optimal for a small open economy, as most developing countries are. Of course we do not live in a world free of imperfections and there are a great many arguments for second best intervention. However, trade policy is rarely the most efficient form of intervention and even where it is, as the recent analysis of strategic trade policy has shown, the results are not easily generalizable. So the theoretical case for liberal trade policies appears to be a robust one. Why, however, in the early 1980s did it suddenly become so much more persuasive and more acceptable to developing countries to adopt reform measures?

The accumulation of empirical evidence relating to the costs of protection/benefits of liberalization was a factor. Evidence on the former was certainly comprehensive and also fairly convincing. Several influential cross-country studies (Krueger, 1981; Balassa, 1982), together with a multitude of country-specific studies, emphasized the consequences of long-term reliance on import substitution regimes in the form of high and complex patterns of protection, high resource costs, pervasive rent-seeking behaviour, poor macroeconomic performance and stagnating growth (see Greenaway and Milner, 1993).

More controversial was the evidence which appeared to suggest that liberal trade policies were also growth-enhancing; the key piece of data here being the export performance and growth of the so-called 'gang of four': Hong Kong, Taiwan, Korea and Singapore. Although placing great emphasis on the experience of these countries was a little disingenuous, given that only one (Hong Kong) followed a free trade policy, it was nevertheless influential since the others did pursue explicit export promotion policies. Moreover, their growth performance may have had more to do with their ability to react to key macro-economic shocks in the 1970s, rather than their trade policies.

Role of the Bretton Woods agencies

Policy conditionality is routinely applied by the IMF in connection with stabilization loans (SLs). World Bank policy conditionality is a newer phenomenon and dates from the launch of its structural adjustment programme (SAP) in 1980. This involves the disbursement of staged support in the form of structural adjustment loans (SALs) or sector adjustment loans (SECALs), typically on concessional terms, which are conditional upon reforms, often involving trade policy. This arm of the Bank's activities has grown to such an extent that it now accounts for over one-third of its lending portfolio and is its most visible activity.

Ingredients of trade reform programmes

All episodes of trade policy reform typically include measures to reduce anti-export bias, be they import liberalization or export support measures. Tariff reductions, quota elimination, relaxation of import licensing and so on all figure prominently. Note also that measures designed to rationalize and improve the transparency of the protective structure are common: conflating shadow tariffs into actual tariffs; reducing tariff exemptions, substituting tariffs for quotas.

Although the menu of reforms has been fairly standard, the manner of implementation has varied: partly due to genuine professional disagreement over whether a big bang or gradualism is more appropriate; partly due to the fact that the agreement of a package is the outcome of a bargaining process and relative bargaining power differs from one case to another; partly due to a growing recognition that initial conditions and infrastructural support are vital to the prospects for sustainability and these vary from case to case (see Dean, 1995).

EVALUATING EXPERIENCE WITH LIBERALIZATION

It is possible that in the short run liberalization has some undesirable, but inevitable, side-effects. Specifically, in the transition unemployment may rise and/or trade tax revenue may fall. Both are invariably fears on the part of liberalizing governments. A minority of analysts, most notably

Michaely, Papageorgiou and Choksi (1991), claim that such fears are unfounded. In practice however they do occur in many cases: it all depends on initial circumstances and the sequencing of reform.

The evidence

There are some rather important complications associated with conducting an evaluation of a liberalization. First, what is the counter-factual? Should one just assume a continuation of pre-existing policies and performance? Second, how does one disentangle the effects of trade reforms from other effects? Third, supply responses will differ from economy to economy: how long should one wait before conducting an assessment? For a review of these issues and of the evidence on outward orientation and performance see Edwards (1998) and Greenaway (1998).

The evidence suggests that reform programmes tend to be associated with an improvement in the current account of the balance of payments and with an improvement in the growth rate of real exports. Some countries which have undergone adjustment show a subsequent improvement in investment but some experienced a slump. Finally, on balance, the impact on growth may be positive, in the sense that there are more cases of a positive growth impact than a negative growth impact although growth does sometimes deteriorate.

What can one say overall? There have certainly been notable adjustment successes and failures. Some adjustment programmes where trade liberalization has figured prominently, have resulted in rapid adjustment, a rapid supply side response and sustainable growth. In many others, especially in sub-Saharan Africa, stabilization has turned out to be a false dawn as a significant supply response failed to materialize. Are there general lessons?

DESIGN OF TRADE POLICY REFORM

Timing and sequencing issues

Initial timing

A number of arguments have been put forward for conducting any required macroeconomic stabilization in advance of structural adjustment policies. The stabilization programme may, for example, reduce the burdens on the export sector of an overvalued exchange rate. Against these arguments, evidence suggests that the adjustment costs of trade reform are relatively small and likely to go unnoticed alongside stabilization. One might be able to reap efficiency gains from trade reform quickly and before political resistance builds up.

Sequencing

The general view is that liberalization of the capital account should be held back until well into the process of trade reform and that the initial stages of trade reform should see import quota reform before tariff liberalization. The costs of rent-seeking and monopoly associated with quotas, and greater transparency and increased tariff revenue are often cited in the ranking of tariffs over quotas. On export incentives the general consensus appears to be in favour of giving exporters access to inputs at world prices, and against export subsidization.

Speed of liberalization

There are a number of general arguments for rapid reform. First, it gives strong signals to economic agents, demonstrates government commitment and thereby increases the effectiveness and credibility of reforms. Second, it restricts the time and opportunities for resistance from affected lobby groups. There are, however, arguments for gradualism. First, government revenue may decline too rapidly if trade taxes are eliminated in advance of non-trade tax reforms. Second, adjustment costs may justify gradualism on political economy grounds, especially if gradualism slows down the pace of income redistribution. Third, although rapid/radical reform may be viewed as a means of signalling commitment, over-ambitious reforms may also lack credibility if the government already lacks a 'reputation' for good governance or sustaining policies. Finally, given limited foreign exchange reserves and the external credit-worthiness of many developing countries, it is important that liberalizations are compatible with other policy changes. Abrupt liberalization may require abrupt exchange rate depreciation. If this is not politically feasible, then credibility may require gradual trade liberalization (see Falvey and Kim, 1992, for discussion).

Sustainability and credibility issues

The private sector is likely to be sceptical about sustainability and credibility where governments are pressured into trade reform. Commitment is uncertain and external circumstances may change, or internal reaction to reform may undermine resolve. A lack of credibility both blunts the incentives to adjust, for example deterring reallocation of factors to the export sector or deferring investment, and sets in motion forces that undermine sustainability. If consumers expect reforms to be reversed they have an incentive to consume or speculatively accumulate more now of the temporarily cheaper imports. This increases the current account deficit and the probability of policy reversal.

Mitigating strategies can be designed. The need for macroeconomic stability and consistency is obvious. It may also be inadvisable to remove capital controls until trade reforms are fully consolidated. Where lack of credibility is associated with fear of reversion to previous policies once the private sector has reacted to reform – governments need to design strategies to build reputation and demonstrate commitment (see Rodrik, 1989).

Trade policy and macro stability

Direct links between trade policy and macroeconomic stability are limited. Trade policy determines the functional openness of the economy (e.g. trade-to-GDP ratio), but the trade balance is determined by the balance between national income and expenditure. It is exchange rate overvaluation (and fiscal deficit) that is the important link with macroeconomic balances and stability. Although trade reform (if sufficiently radical) can signal government commitment to inflation control, it can also interfere with the prevention of real exchange rate appreciation. Countries liberalizing trade policies often devalue their currency to compensate for the liberalization impact on the balance of payments. The potential inflationary effects of depreciation are likely to constrain the use of nominal exchange rate policy, hence sustained trade liberalization is likely to involve some deterioration in the external balance until there is an export response.

Trade reform and stabilization are linked through trade taxes. Given the high dependence of many developing economies on trade taxes and the slowness of any non-trade tax reforms, fiscal effects must be borne in mind. Replacement of quotas by tariffs, greater simplicity and uniformity in tariff structures which reduce tax evasion through smuggling and under-invoicing are likely to be fiscal-enhancing.

CONCLUSIONS

Economic perspectives on trade and industrial policy in developing countries have changed profoundly over the last quarter century. The current consensus is that deregulation and liberalization can help in growth promotion, but are not in themselves a panacea. The macro-economic environment, the broader infrastructural and social context are all equally important to the design, implementation and eventual outcome of reform.

GUIDE TO FURTHER READING

Greenaway, D. and Milner, C.R. (1993) *Trade and Industrial Policies in Developing Countries*, London: Macmillan. This book explains the analytical toolkit that the economist has to measure and evaluate trade policies and their impacts, illustrating with evidence relating to trade policies and structural adjustment lending (SAL) reforms in the 1980s.

Michaely, M., Papageorgiou, D. and Choksi, A. (eds) (1991) *Liberalising Foreign Trade*, Oxford: Blackwell. This large multi-country study, commissioned by the World Bank, evaluates the impact and success of trade liberalizations during structural adjustment programmes. Though arguably not wholly impartial and using a methodology open to challenge (see Greenaway, 1993), it remains a valuable source of information on the nature and impact of pre- and post-reform trade regimes in many developing countries.

Milner, C.R. (ed.) (1998) *Developing and Newly Industrialising Countries, Vols 1 and 2* Cheltenham: Edward Elgar. This large collection brings together articles by leading writers on trade and openness related issues covering trade liberalization, financial liberalization, regional integration, multinational firms, sectoral issues, multilateral institutions and global policy issues.

Morrissey, W.O. and McGillivray, M. (eds) (2000) *Evaluating Economic Liberalisation*, London: Macmillan. This recent collection of essays on economic liberalization issues from across the developing world includes essays on trade liberalization and on the linkages between wider policy reforms sponsored by the World Bank.

Rodrik, D. (1999) *The New Global Economy and Developing Countries: Making Openness Work*, Washington DC: Overseas Development Council. This essay considers policy responses to globalization and increased openness, the appropriate development strategy and set of domestic policies and institutions required to take advantage of the opportunities created by globalization and to reduce the costs associated with rapid economic and social change.

Also useful are Milner, C.R. (1998) 'Trade regime bias and the response to trade liberalisation in Sub-Saharan Africa', *Kyklos* 51: 219–36 and Rodrik, D. (1998) 'The new global economy and developing countries: globalisation, social conflict and economic growth', *The World Economy* 21: 143–58.

REFERENCES

Balassa, B. (1982) *Development Strategies in Semi-Industrialised Economies*, Baltimore, MD: Johns Hopkins University Press.

Dean, J.M. (1995) 'The trade policy revolution in developing countries', *The World Economy*, Global Trade Policy, Oxford: Blackwell.

Dornbusch, R. (1992) 'The case for trade liberalisation in developing countries', *Journal of Economic Perspectives* 6: 69–85.

Edwards, S. (1998) 'Openness, productivity and growth: what do we really know', *Economic Journal* 108: 383–98.

Falvey, R. and Kim C.D. (1992) 'Timing and sequencing issues in trade liberalisation', *Economic Journal* 102: 908–24.

Greenaway, D. (1993) 'Liberalising foreign trade through rose tinted "glasses"', *Economic Journal* 103: 208–22.

Greenaway, D. (1998) 'Does trade liberalisation promote economic developn
  Economy 45: 491–511.
Krueger, A.O. (1997) 'Trade policy and economic development: how we lea
  87: 1–22.
Krueger, A.O. (ed.) (1981) Trade and Employment in Developing Countries,
  Press.
Rodrik, D. (1989) 'Credibility of trade reform – a policy maker's guide', T

Export processing

202 | Industrializat...
Product and p...
Production...
In EP...
govern...
con...

4.5 Export processing and free trade zones

Robert N. Gwynne

DEFINITIONS

Export processing zones (EPZs) have been defined as labour-intensive manufacturing centres that involve the import of raw materials and the export of factory products (Klak and Myers, 1998: 89). Free trade zones can be classified as zones in which manufacturing does not have to take place in order to gain trading privileges and, hence, such zones have become more characterized by retailing.

Over 90 countries had established EPZs by the end of the twentieth century (Klak and Myers, 1998). The popularity of EPZs in the latter decades of the twentieth century can be attributed to three groups of factors that link the economies of developing countries with those of the world economy in general and the advanced economies in particular:

1   problems of indebtedness and serious foreign exchange shortfalls in developing countries since the 1980s
2   the spread of neo-liberal ideas in the 1990s that encouraged open economies, foreign investment, and non-traditional exports (Gwynne, 1999; Klak and Rulli, 1993)
3   the search by multinational corporations (MNCs) for cost-saving locations, particularly in terms of wage costs, in order to shift manufacturing assembly and component production from locations in the advanced economies.

THEORETICAL CONSIDERATIONS

According to Froebel et al. (1980), the shifting of production by MNCs was part of the *new international division of labour* in which advanced-economy MNCs became actively engaged in shifting productive capacity from locations in advanced economies to those in developing countries. The search for lower costs of production within an increasingly competitive world economy provided the main explanatory factor behind these shifts and led to a progressive disassociation between spaces of production (locations such as EPZs in developing countries) and spaces of consumption (notably in advanced economies, where the purchasing power of consumers remained critical).

The feasibility of MNCs relocating productive capacity to EPZs was also improved by the possibility of decentralizing standardized production processes. The *product life cycle model* (Gwynne, 1990) noted that as production of mature products became more standardized in terms of both

…rocess technology, it proved profitable for MNCs to shift standardized stages of …o low labour cost locations.

… locations, there was normally an added bonus for the MNC, as developing country …ments offered them more favourable investment, trade, tax and labour conditions as …pared with locations in the remainder of the host country. Concessions included:

1 trade – the elimination of customs duties on imports
2 investment – liberalization of capital flows in and out of the EPZs and occasionally access to special financial credits
3 important investments in the provision of local infrastructure by central and/or local government of the host country
4 taxation – reduction or exemption from federal, state and local taxes
5 labour relations – limitations on labour legislation that apply in the rest of the country, such as the presence of trade unions and the adherence to minimum wage and working hours legislation.

EPZs can be spatial enclaves in which export-oriented manufacturing organized largely through MNCs is concentrated. These enclaves are separated from neighbouring areas by the wide range of incentives and exemptions offered to capital within them. Links with surrounding areas are mainly through the attraction of local populations to work in the EPZs. Inputs come from international sources and EPZ production is by definition exported. Within developing countries, EPZs have been established in a wide range of environments – from border areas (as in North Mexico), to relatively undeveloped regions, to locations adjacent to large cities. The most common location has been on the coast, as in the case of China. EPZs have been most concentrated in the Asia Pacific region, where in the 1990s approximately 40 per cent of EPZs were located but where two-thirds of employment in EPZs was generated. Latin America and the Caribbean is the next most significant region for EPZs.

The creation of EPZs has been a popular policy for governments of developing countries because they represent a relatively easy path to begin industrialization in a country. The MNC normally provides technology, capital, inputs and the export markets. Central and local government authorities have relatively few commitments apart from investing in local infrastructure at the site of the EPZ.

Although the establishment of an EPZ could be seen as beneficial in the short term for the developing country, in the long term it offers a major problem as regards economic sustainability. MNCs are normally attracted by trade and tax incentives, low labour costs and labour flexibility to locate a branch plant in an EPZ. These locational attractions do not necessarily last. Governments can gradually withdraw the trade and tax incentives of the EPZs and labour costs can rise if the demand for industrial labour begins to increase rapidly. In these scenarios the type of MNC attracted to an EPZ (interested in reducing costs at a global scale for the manufacture of a labour-intensive product) moves on to a cheaper EPZ location. Thus a reliance on simple export processing would at best perpetuate a reliance on low-skilled, labour-intensive assembly and at worst see the premature end of this type of manufacturing activity within the developing country.

Within East Asia, writers have talked about the *flying geese model* in terms of the dynamic shift of industry from one country (and its EPZ) to another. The model can apply to groups of Japanese firms moving their productive capacity in stages through the countries (and EPZs) of Asia. Thus plants have moved from Japan to first-generation NICs (the newly industrializing countries of South Korea, Taiwan, Hong Kong and Singapore); and then from the NICs to the countries of

ASEAN; then on to China, Vietnam and India (Edgington and Hayter, 2000). Governments of developing countries need to create pathways to more complex forms of industrial growth, including improved supply networks and advances in technological capability. This process has been difficult to achieve. An example from Latin America, that of Mexico, can demonstrate this.

EXPORT PROCESSING ZONES IN MEXICO

One of the largest zones of EPZs in the world is that of the North Mexican border with the United States. In this zone, 13 towns have had EPZ status ever since 1965 and the establishment of the border industrialization programme (BIP) (see figure). Capital goods and parts were imported into Mexico duty free, and then the finished product exported to the USA with Mexico taxing only the value added. The Mexican government set up this programme in an effort to attract the increasing numbers of US businesses which were relocating labour-intensive production plants in Asia. Within these border towns assembly production has predominated in assembly plants known as *maquilas* (Sklair, 1989). The evolution of *maquilas* can best be seen in three stages.

1 The formation of basic EPZs, 1965–1982

Production was typical of the early stage of most EPZs in other parts of the world. The plants were engaged in routine and labour-intensive assembly of mature products and the great majority of workers were unskilled. Most of these (up to 90 per cent) were women, a pattern which created social tensions within the traditional, male-dominated structures of Mexican migrant families. High male unemployment existed side by side with the double workload (assembly plant and home) of women. Virtually all capital and management came from the United States and there was a high dependence on the US market. The Mexican government gave *maquilas* exemptions from some federal labour law requirements. Thus the 13 border towns became set apart from the rest of Mexico in terms of both special trade concessions and conditions for labour.

2 The transformation of the *maquilas*, 1983–1993

Two aspects of changing Mexican political economy became highly relevant to the *maquilas*. First, an outward-oriented approach to economic growth began to be imposed which signified a more competitive exchange rate and less tariff barriers for *maquila* trade with the rest of Mexico. Second, more market-friendly policies were adopted which involved the gradual liberalization of capital and labour markets. The growth in employment and *maquilas* in this period was substantial. Between 1983 and 1993, the number of *maquilas* more than tripled (to 2,050) and employment more than quadrupled to 570,000. Exports grew even faster – by a factor of 12 – to nearly US$24 billion (40 per cent of Mexico's *total* exports). The nature of *maquilas* changed as foreign investors established plants producing high-technology, high value-added components (Gereffi, 1996). Assembly production remained a core activity, with Japanese, European and South Korean corporations now setting up *maquilas* in order to benefit from a location with easy access to the US market and cheap labour costs. US corporations still remained the major investors, particularly in the components industry. The growth of the components industry saw an increase in vertical integration and more complex supply networks in the border towns. The labour markets also began

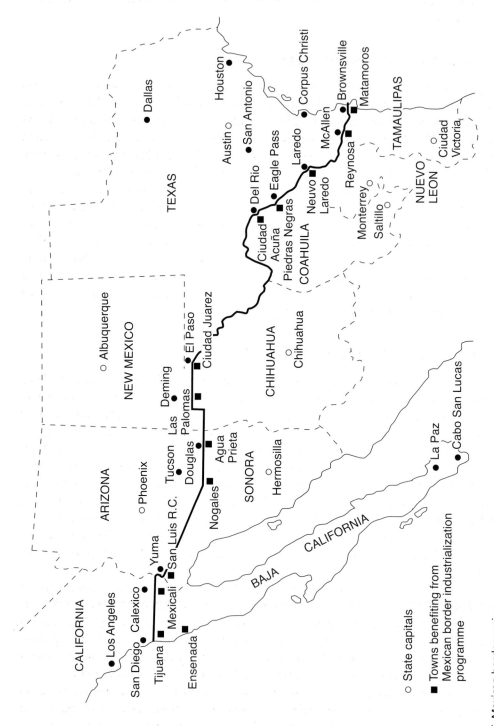

The US–Mexican border region

Source: Gwynne, 1990

to change with a drop in the high proportion of women in the *maquila* labour force. Labour markets in the border towns became older, more skilled and had higher ratios of male workers. Almost all technicians and engineers were Mexican by the late 1980s, along with an increasing number of managers.

3   The maquilization of Mexico? – 1994 onwards

The implementation of the North American Free Trade Area (NAFTA) between the USA, Canada and Mexico in January 1994 brought a distinctive third phase to the EPZs of North Mexico. Their specific advantages for MNC investment within Mexico were reduced in relation to other potential locations away from the border where labour costs were lower. The process of market liberalization intensified after Mexico joined NAFTA. Changes in industrial orientation, technology and labour markets affected industry away from the border towns (Kopinak, 1997) – particularly for those firms that restructured from a domestic (Mexican) orientation to one geared to export markets. Electronics and automotive supply industries have become highly concentrated in the border towns but textile and apparel sectors have a greater presence in the north Mexico interior. The old *maquilas* based on unskilled, low-wage and non-unionized labour are moving from the border region to towns further south in order to benefit from cheaper labour costs. This 'maquilization' of Mexico has significantly reduced the former enclave nature of the border towns. There are more and more complex supply networks with firms in a wide range of north Mexican towns.

EPZS IN MEXICO AND EAST ASIA COMPARED

Gereffi (1996) argued that the Mexican government has plotted a modest pathway from EPZ to a more sustained form of industrial growth. Mexico's 'classic' export-processing stage was characterized by low-skilled, labour-intensive assembly plants specializing in clothing, footwear and basic electronics. The primary economic agents were the MNCs that supplied technology, capital, material inputs and export markets. Mexico's EPZs were able to move to a second stage of component-supply manufacturing in which it was necessary to attract investors in high-technology, high value-added industries and to develop training programmes for workers in these sectors. The production of components was largely organized through subsidiaries of MNCs (such as Ford) rather than by national/local firms producing for MNCs through subcontracts (more the case in East Asian EPZs). The heavy dependence on US MNCs (rather than national firms) in Mexican EPZs makes it difficult for later and more autonomous stages of the industrial pathway to be achieved.

In East Asia, there have been other versions of EPZs (Gwynne, 1990). In certain countries, such as South Korea and Taiwan, EPZs were an important part of the early rapid phase of industrial growth. In these countries, governments were active and successful in promoting EPZs, although their initiatives were associated with a wide range of other inward investment and export promotion incentives. Export destinations of Asian EPZs were more diversified than those of Mexico's northern zones. Whereas the Mexican border has EPZs characterized by a dependent form of industrialization, there is evidence of a more sustainable pathway in East Asia. The key factors in such a comparison are the importance of national firms in export-oriented manufacturing, the technological capability acquired by those firms and the role of government in effectively promoting export-oriented industrialization.

GUIDE TO FURTHER READING

Gwynne, R.N. and Kay, C. (eds) (1999) *Latin America Transformed: Globalization and Modernity*, London: Arnold. Through the analytical lens of political economy, this book examines the shift to neo-liberal and outward-oriented policies in Latin America and thus introduces the wider theoretical and empirical context behind the move to export growth.

Klak, T. (ed.) (1998) *Globalization and Neoliberalism: the Caribbean Context*, Lanham, MD: Rowman & Littlefield. This book assesses the impacts, adjustments and coping strategies found in the small islands of the Caribbean as they experience profound transformations linked to export processing.

Kopinak, K. (1997) *Desert Capitalism: What are the Maquiladoras?*, Montreal: Black Rose Books. A classic study of an export processing zone, namely Nogales in north Mexico.

REFERENCES

Edgington, D.W. and Hayter, R. (2000) 'Foreign direct investment and the flying geese model: Japanese electronic firms in Asia-Pacific', *Environment and Planning A*, 32: 281–304.

Froebel, F., Heinrichs, J. and Kreye, O. (1980) *The New International Division of Labour*, Cambridge: Cambridge University Press.

Gereffi, G. (1996) 'Mexico's "old" and "new" maquiladora industries: contrasting approaches to North American integration', in G. Otero (ed.) *Neo-liberalism Revisited: Economic Restructuring and Mexico's Political Future*, Boulder, CO: Westview Press, pp. 85–106.

Gwynne, R.N. (1990) *New Horizons? Third World Industrialization in an International Framework*, London: Longman.

Gwynne, R.N. (1999) 'Globalization, neo-liberalism and economic change in South America and Mexico', in R.N. Gwynne and C. Kay (eds) *Latin America Transformed: Globalization and Modernity*, London: Arnold, pp. 67–97.

Klak, T. and Myers, G. (1998) 'How states sell their countries and their people', in T. Klak (ed.) *Globalization and Neoliberalism: The Caribbean Context*, Lanham, MD: Rowman & Littlefield, pp. 87–109

Klak, T. and Rulli, J. (1993) 'Regimes of accumulation, the Caribbean initiative and export-processing zones: scales of influence on Caribbean development', in E. Goetz and S. Clarke (eds) *The New Localism*, Beverly Hills: Sage, pp. 117–50.

Kopinak, K. (1997) *Desert Capitalism: What are the Maquiladoras?* Montreal: Black Rose Books.

Sklair, L. (1989) *Assembling for Development: The Maquila Industry in Mexico and the United States*, Boston: Unwin Hyman.

4.6 The informal sector and employment

Sylvia Chant

WHAT IS THE INFORMAL SECTOR?

The 'informal sector' is often equated with precarious, low-productivity, poorly remunerated employment in Third World cities, although in reality the sector is highly heterogeneous (Potter and Lloyd-Evans, 1998). Informal employment usually prevails in commerce and services, but also occurs in manufacturing production (Table 1). Moreover, although many people in the

Table 1 Percentage of production which is informal in different economic sectors for selected developing
countries

	Percentage of production which is informal in:			
	manufacturing	transport	services	total
AFRICA				
Burundi (1990)	35	8	18	25
Congo (1984)	39	10	36	33
Egypt (1986)	21	29	15	18
Gambia (1983)	48	16	57	51
Mali (1990)	45	45	37	40
Zambia (1986)	41	7	48	39
LATIN AMERICA &				
THE CARIBBEAN				
Brazil (1990)	12	23	23	18
Costa Rica (1984)	14	9	16	15
Honduras (1990)	26	17	28	26
Jamaica (1988)	19	23	30	25
Mexico (1992)	9	20	20	16
Uruguay (1985)	16	10	16	16
Venezuela (1992)	16	46	22	23
ASIA & THE PACIFIC				
Indonesia (1985)	38	44	56	49
Iraq (1987)	15	33	7	12
Republic of Korea (1989)	17	34	44	30
Malaysia (1986)	13	20	23	19
Qatar (1986)	1	3	1	1
Syrian Arab Republic (1991)	21	38	22	24
Thailand (1990)	10	40	18	16
Fiji (1986)	14	21	12	13

Source: United Nations, 1995: 135, Table 9

informal sector work on their own account in street-vending, the running of 'frontroom' eater-
ies, stalls or shops, the operation of domestic-based industrial units, and the transport of
passengers and goods (see figure), other informal workers are subcontracted by large firms,
especially in labour-intensive industries such as toys, footwear and clothing (Benería and
Roldan, 1987).

The term 'informal sector' first appeared in the academic and policy literature in the 1970s. It
is usually associated with the work of the anthropologist Keith Hart in Ghana who classified informal employment as that which fell outside the boundaries of formal sector enterprise (factories,
public services, large-scale commerce, for example), and sub-divided the sector into 'legitimate'
and 'illegitimate' activities. The former comprised work which made a contribution to economic
growth, albeit in small ways, such as petty commerce, personal services and home-based production. 'Illegitimate' informal activities, alternatively, described occupations which, if not necessarily
'criminal' in nature, were arguably of dubious worth to national development, such as prostitution,
begging, pickpocketing and scavenging (Hart, 1973).

Hart's work was enthusiastically embraced by the International Labour Organization (ILO),
whose criteria distinguishing the formal and informal sectors comprised relative ease of entry, size,
nature of enterprise ownership, type of production, and levels of skill, capital and technology (ILO,

Pedal power: informal transport in Mexico City

Photo: Sylvia Chant

Table 2 Common characteristics used to define formal and informal employment

Formal sector	Informal sector
Large scale	Small scale
Modern	Traditional
Corporate ownership	Family/individual ownership
Capital-intensive	Labour-intensive
Profit-oriented	Subsistence-oriented
Imported technology/inputs	Indigenous technology/inputs
Protected markets (e.g. tariffs, quotas)	Unregulated/competitive markets
Difficult entry	Ease of entry
Formally acquired skills (e.g. school/college education)	Informally acquired skills (e.g. in home or craft apprenticeship)
Majority of workers protected by labour legislation and covered by social security	Minority of workers protected by labour legislation and covered by social security

Sources: Chant, 1999: 510, Table 38.1; Drakakis-Smith, 1987: 65, Table 5.5; Gilbert and Gugler, 1992: 96

1972; Table 2). The single most important factor which persists in contemporary definitions of the informal sector, however, is regulation (Roberts, 1994: 6).

Regulation and the informal sector

Regulation primarily implies legality, but it is also the case that legality itself is a multi-dimensional concept. Tokman (1991: 143), for example, identifies three types of legality pertinent to the demarcation between formal and informal sector enterprises:

1 legal recognition as a business activity (which involves registration, and possible subjection to health and security inspections)
2 legality concerning payment of taxes
3 legality *vis-à-vis* labour matters such as compliance with official guidelines on working hours, social security contributions and fringe benefits.

Social security tends to be the most costly aspect of legality, so while micro-enterprises may well register themselves as businesses with the relevant authorities, they may avoid paying social security contributions for themselves and their workers. In Latin America, for example, it is estimated that only 2 to 5 per cent of self-employed persons (the largest group of informally employed people in the continent) have access to social security, mainly due to high costs, administrative difficulties, lack of incentives due to the eroding value of pensions, and uncertainty in occupational prospects (Tokman, 1991: 152–3).

RECENT TRENDS IN INFORMAL EMPLOYMENT

Time-series data on informal sector activity need to be treated with extreme caution, not only on account of the irregular and/or clandestine nature of informal work, but because of shifting classificatory schema by different governments and regional organizations (Thomas, 1995). Acknowledging that this also makes international comparisons difficult, the informal sector seems to have grown in most parts of the world in recent decades. In Latin America, for example, informal workers in the urban labour force rose from an overall average of 25.6 per cent to 30 per cent between 1980 and 1990, vastly outstripping growth in the formal sector. For developing regions in general, micro-enterprises have come to employ between 36 and 60 per cent of the labour force (Chickering and Salahdine, 1991: 3).

From the 1980s onwards, most of the growth in informal employment has been forced by recession and neo-liberal economic restructuring. People have been pushed into informal employment through cut-backs in public employment, the closure of private firms and the increased tendency for formal employers to resort to sub-contracting arrangements (Chant and McIlwaine, 1995). Another significant process has been for smaller firms to move wholesale into informality as a result of declining ability to pay registration, tax and labour overheads (Escobar, 1988). As Thomas (1996: 99) summarizes, the 'top-down' informalization promoted by governments and employers has been matched by a 'bottom-up' informalization stemming from the need for retrenched formal sector workers and newcomers to the labour market to create their own sources of earnings and/or to avoid the punitive costs attached to legal status.

The nature of the informal sector during recession and restructuring

In light of the above, it is hardly surprising that the informal sector has become increasingly competitive during the last two decades. Yet although ever more creative strategies to generate income can be found in Third World cities, competition is such that, according to ILO figures for Latin America and the Caribbean, there was a 42 per cent drop in income in the informal sector between 1980 and 1989 (Moghadam, 1995: 122–3). In turn, although the informal sector has continued to expand during the years of crisis and restructuring, it has not been able to absorb all the job losses in the formal sector. In Argentina, for instance, urban unemployment in 1991 was 20.2 per cent, compared with 5.6 per cent in 1986 (Bulmer-Thomas, 1996: 326, Table A9).

Table 3 Percentage of the male and female labour force in the informal sector for selected developing countries

| | Percentage of labour force which is informal in: | | | | | | | |
| | Manufacturing | | Transport | | Services | | Total | |
	Men	Women	Men	Women	Men	Women	Men	Women
AFRICA								
Burundi (1990)	31	60	13	0	17	21	21	32
Congo (1984)	39	43	11	0	21	60	25	67
Egypt (1986)	22	5	31	0	18	3	21	3
Gambia (1983)	38	100	13	0	23	60	25	62
Mali (1990)	63	35	50	0	39	33	45	34
Zambia (1986)	31	81	8	0	31	71	29	72
LATIN AMERICA & THE CARIBBEAN								
Brazil (1990)	14	5	24	2	23	24	19	21
Costa Rica (1984)	14	13	11	0	7	22	8	19
Honduras (1990)	15	52	29	0	26	29	21	34
Jamaica (1988)	21	11	29	0	27	32	25	28
Mexico (1992)	8	11	21	2	30	16	22	15
Uruguay (1985)	15	20	12	0	19	14	17	15
Venezuela (1992)	13	30	50	10	25	20	23	21
ASIA & THE PACIFIC								
Indonesia (1985)	28	57	44	20	47	68	41	65
Iraq (1987)	15	13	34	0	7	4	5	11
Republic of Korea (1989)	24	21	36	40	78	52	48	41
Malaysia (1986)	9	22	22	5	21	26	17	24
Qatar (1986)	0	0	0	0	1	0	1	0
Syrian Arab Republic (1991)	21	18	39	0	91	4	61	7
Thailand (1990)	8	14	43	14	11	30	12	24
Fiji (1986)	15	20	25	0	13	9	15	10

Source: United Nations, 1995: 135, Table 9

Limits to further expansion of the informal sector are threatened by lower purchasing power among the population in general and greater numbers of people entering the workforce (Roberts, 1991: 135). The latter results from high fertility and declining mortality rates throughout most of the developing world during the 1960s and 1970s, and the steadily rising participation of women in the labour force. There are many reasons why more women are joining the labour force, but one of the most significant is economic necessity. In turn, the saturation of the informal sector is often argued to have hit women the hardest because aside from their heavy representation in the sector (Table 3), their limited skills and resources confine them to the lowest tiers of informal activity.

LINKS BETWEEN FORMAL AND INFORMAL SECTORS

The last 20 years of crisis and restructuring have made ever more visible the interconnectedness of the formal and informal sectors, and in particular, the dependence of the latter on the former for contracts, supplies and economic viability. Detailed empirical studies have revealed that the informal sector is linked to the formal sector in many ways (see Table 4), thereby rendering redundant previous notions of labour market dualism.

Table 4 Economic linkages between the formal and informal sectors of the urban economy

---

BACKWARD LINKAGES

a) Informal vendors sell products (e.g. soft drinks, cigarettes) obtained from manufacturers, wholesalers and retailers in the UFS.

b) Informally produced goods such as cooked foodstuffs, home-made clothing and embroidered items are likely to comprise raw materials supplied by the UFS.

FORWARD LINKAGES

a) The UIS may produce intermediate goods destined for final elaboration and distribution through the UFS. This may occur through sub-contracting or purchase on the part of the UFS.

Benefits for UFS of sub-contracting to UIS

    i) Informal employers may avoid paying legal minimum (or above-minimum) wage

    ii) Formal employers avoid obligations to provide social security contributions and fringe benefits to workers in informal enterprises

    iii) Formal employers can respond more flexibly (and at lower cost) to fluctuations in product demand

b) The (cheap) goods and services produced in the UIS, when consumed by UFS workers, arguably subsidise the wages of the UFS.

Source: Thomas, 1996: 56–9
Notes: UFS = urban formal sector; UIS = urban informal sector.

An early attempt to resist the construction of the formal and informal sectors as discrete and autonomous entities was Moser's seminal neo-Marxian exposition on 'petty commodity production'. This theorized urban labour markets as a continuum of productive activities in which large formal sector firms benefited from the existence of micro-entrepreneurs (Moser, 1978). More recently, these ideas have been worked into the thesis of 'stucturalist articulation', which views urban labour markets as 'unified systems encompassing a dense network of relationships between formal and informal enterprises'. Although it is recognized that links between large- and small-scale firms are often exploitative, however, it is also acknowledged that some opportunities may be opened up for informal enterprises by globalization and neo-liberal strategies of export promotion (Portés and Itzigsohn, 1997: 240–1). In many respects, this has encouraged recommendations for more active and sympathetic policy stances towards the informal sector.

THE INFORMAL SECTOR IN URBAN ECONOMIC AND EMPLOYMENT POLICIES

The fact that there was no explicit policy towards the informal sector in most Third World countries until recently was partly due to anticipation that labour surpluses would eventually be absorbed by formal industry and services (Tokman, 1989: 1072). Another factor was the reluctance of economists and civil servants to acknowledge informal activities as anything other than a 'parasitic', 'unproductive' form of 'disguised unemployment' (Bromley, 1997:124). In effect, the informal sector was (and in many circles still *is*) viewed as an employer of 'last resort' or a fragile means of basic subsistence in situations where social welfare provision for those outside the formal labour force is minimal or non-existent (Cubitt, 1995: 163; Gilbert, 1998: 67).

Even where informal entrepreneurs may have wanted to 'become legal', prohibitive costs and convoluted bureaucratic procedures have usually dissuaded them from so doing (Tokman, 1989:

1608). In addition to indirect discrimination resulting from state subsidies to the large-scale capital-intensive sector, informal entrepeneurs have often been subjected to harrassment or victimization (Thomas, 1996: 56–7).

This scenario has tended to change in the last 10–15 years, however, as government authorities, along with planners and social scientists, have come round to the notion that the informal sector is more of a seedbed of economic potential than a 'poverty trap' (Cubitt, 1995: 175). With echoes in Keith Hart's 'popular entrepreneurship' concepts, these more positive constructions have been fuelled by a growing body of empirical research showing that some informal workers earn more than salaried workers, that self-employment can be a source of pride or prestige, that informality permits flexibility and ready adaptation to changing demand and family circumstances, and that people often acquire skills in the formal sector which can subsequently be used to advantage in their own businesses. Theoretical weight has been added to this shift in perspective by the Peruvian economist, Hernando de Soto, whose controversial book *The Other Path* argues that the informal sector is a product of excessive and unjust regulation created by governments in the interests of the society's powerful and dominant groups (Bromley, 1997: 127). Emphasizing the ways in which the existence of the informal sector relieves unemployment, provides a gainful alternative to crime, and harnesses the entrepreneurial talent of the disaffected masses, de Soto asserts that 'illegality' is a perfectly justiable response on the part of the urban poor. Governments should consider tolerating their 'non-conformity' more widely, and give them greater encouragement, protection and freedom (de Soto, 1989).

These ideas have been hotly debated in the literature. One problem with de Soto's eulogization of the informal sector is that it gives a misleading impression of a sector, which is perhaps better understood as '. . . a picture of survival rather than a sector full of entrepreneurial talent to be celebrated for its potential to create an economic miracle' (Thomas, 1995: 130; see also Cubitt, 1995). Another set of problems arises from the potentially perverse implications of proactive informal sector policies. One outcome of advocating decontrol of economic enterprise is that a precedent is set for greater deregulation in the formal sector. This in turn contributes to broader processes promoted by multilaterals such as the IMF and World Bank to liberalize production and markets in developing regions, which have often been harmful to low-income groups.

Nonetheless, accepting that the informal sector is likely to persist for the foreseeable future, measures are arguably needed to help it operate more efficiently and with better conditions for its workers. With reference to the Caribbean, for example, Portés and Itzigsohn (1997: 241–3) suggest that much could be done to diminish the constraints faced by the informal sector. Prominent obstacles at present include lack of working capital through limited access to mainstream financial institutions, concentration in highly competitive low-income markets, the social atomization of informal entrepreneurs due to the irregular and/or chaotic nature of supplies, and the existence of a 'craftsman ethic' which prevents some informal entrepreneurs, particularly in artisanal production, from changing their traditional methods of production (Portés and Itzigsohn, 1997).

While specific policy initiatives in different developing countries are discussed in detail elsewhere, a much-favoured intervention on the institutional/macroeconomic side of the labour market is the repeal of regulations and policies which obstruct entrepreneurship without serving any legitimate public regulatory purpose. There has also been advocacy for governments to consider simpler and diminished requirements and/or allow for progressive implementation (Tokman, 1991: 155).

On the supply side of the labour market, there has been interest in, and/or support for, policies geared to education and training to promote the diversification of the informal sector, to enhance access to credit, to provide assistance in management, marketing and packaging, and to introduce measures to promote greater health and safety. These initiatives are particularly relevant for groups within the informal sector, such as ambulant traders and food vendors, where women are often a large percentage of operatives (Tinker, 1997). There has also been advocacy for decentralized policies to accord with needs and skills in different localities, and the orientation of policies away from individual firms or workers as a means of utilizing the social networks and social capital (reciprocity, trust, social obligations among kin, friends, neighbours and so on) which so frequently fuel the operation of the informal sector (Portés and Itzigsohn, 1997: 244–5).

PROSPECTS FOR THE INFORMAL SECTOR

Regardless of policies which may be implemented by governments and agencies, it is likely that the informal sector will continue to be a significant feature of Third World urban labour markets in the twenty-first century. One important reason for this is demographic pressure. The youthful age structure of most developing nations means that new entrants to the labour force will continue to rise at least until the year 2010. On top of this, the ageing of populations coupled with exiguous state welfare and declining household incomes will probably mean that older people will not be able to exit the labour force. The potential 'crowding-out' of the informal sector is likely to be exacerbated by ongoing increases in the numbers of women in employment.

On the demand side of the labour market, the current climate of deregulation is likely to provoke further contraction in public employment and to foster increasingly 'flexible' labour contracts in the formal sector as firms face ever tougher global competition. In addition, increased capital intensity in the formal sector is likely to push more people into informal occupations over time.

Recognizing that policies to bolster the informal economy will have to address a wide range of concerns simultaneously, one key area is that of extending and enhancing systems of public education and training such that people have greater choice and capabilities in their employment prospects, whether in the formal or informal sector. As such, education which encompasses commercial and managerial skills, alongside instruction in cutting-edge developments such as information technology, could well bring about greater productivity and employment.

Policies geared to supporting people's efforts to sustain their livelihoods should also take due steps to consult the groups concerned. The fact that the informal sector has survived so well through 20 years of severe economic crisis in developing regions testifies to the fact that there are valuable lessons to be learned 'from below', and Third World governments, not to mention multilateral institutions, would be well advised to heed them.

GUIDE TO FURTHER READING

Chickering, A.L. and Salahdine, M. (eds) (1991) *The Silent Revolution: The Informal Sector in Five Asian and Near Eastern Countries*, San Francisco: International Center for Economic Growth. A text primarily concerned with existing and prospective policies for the urban informal sector.

Gugler, J. (ed.) (1997) *Cities in the Developing World: Issues, Theory and Policy*, Oxford: Oxford University Press. Contains various chapters on different aspects of the informal sector, including theory and policy.

Portés, A., Dore-Cabral, C. and Landoff, P. (eds) (1997) *The Urban Caribbean: Transition to a New Global Economy*, Baltimore: Johns Hopkins University Press. A book which combines discussion of contemporary debates on the informal sector, urbanization and globalization, with case studies from the capital cities of Costa Rica, Haiti, Guatemala, Jamaica and the Dominican Republic.

Standing, G. and Tokman, V. (eds) (1991) *Towards Social Adjustment: Labour Market Issues in Structural Adjustment*, Geneva: International Labour Organization (ILO). Examines the impacts of economic restructuring on the growth of the informal sector and the 'informalization' of labour arrangements in large firms in a range of European as well as developing countries.

Thomas, J.J. (1995) *Surviving in the City: The Urban Informal Sector in Latin America*, London: Pluto. A thorough account of the nature and behaviour of the informal sector of employment in Latin America cities.

REFERENCES

Benería, L. and Roldan, M. (1987) *The Crossroads of Class and Gender: Industrial Homework, Subcontracting and Household Dynamics in Mexico City*, Chicago: University of Chicago Press.

Bromley, R. (1997) 'Working in the streets of Cali. Colombia: survival strategy, necessity or unavoidable evil?', in J. Gugler (ed.), *Cities in the Developing World: Issues, Theory and Policy*, Oxford: Oxford University Press, pp. 124–38.

Bulmer-Thomas, V. (1996) 'Conclusions', in V. Bulmer-Thomas (ed.), *The New Economic Model in Latin America and its Impact on Income Distribution and Poverty*, Basingstoke: Macmillan, pp. 296–327.

Chant, S. (1999) 'Informal sector activity in the Third World city', in Michael Pacione (ed.), *Applied Geography: An Introduction to Useful Research in Physical, Environmental and Human Geography*, London: Routledge, pp. 509–27.

Chant, S. and McIlwaine, C. (1995) *Women of a Lesser Cost: Female Labour, Foreign Exchange and Philippine Development*, London: Pluto.

Chickering, A.L. and Salahdine, M. (1991) 'Introduction', in A.L. Chickering and M. Salahdine (eds), *The Silent Revolution: The Informal Sector in Five Asian and Near Eastern Countries*, San Francisco: International Center for Economic Growth, pp. 1–14.

Cubitt, T. (1995) *Latin American Society* (2nd edn), London: Longman.

de Soto, H. (1989) *The Other Path: The Invisible Revolution in the Third World*, New York: Harper & Row.

Drakakis-Smith, D. (1987) *The Third World City*, London: Methuen.

Escobar, L.A. (1988) 'The rise and fall of an urban labour market: economic crisis and the fate of small workshops in Guadalajara, Mexico', *Bulletin of Latin American Research* 7(2): 183–205.

Gilbert, A. (1998) *The Latin American City* (2nd edn), London: Latin America Bureau.

Gilbert, A. and Gugler, J. (1992) *Cities, Poverty and Development: Urbanisation in the Third World*, Oxford: Oxford University Press.

Hart, K. (1973) 'Informal income opportunites and urban employment in Ghana', in R. Jolly, E. de Kadt, H. Singer and F. Wilson (eds) *Third World Employment* Penguin: Harmondsworth, pp. 66–70.

International Labour Organization (ILO) (1972) *Employment, Incomes and Inequality: A Strategy for Increasing Productive Employment in Kenya*, Geneva: International Labour Organization (ILO).

Moghadam, V. (1995) 'Gender aspects of employment and unemployment in global perspective', in M. Simai with V. Moghadam and A. Kuddo (eds), *Global Employment: An International Investigation into the Future of Work*, London: Zed Books, in association with United National University, World Institute for Development Economics Research, pp. 111–39.

Moser, C. (1978) 'Informal sector or petty commodity production? Dualism or dependence in urban development', *World Development* 6: 135–78.

Pineda-Ofreneo, R. (1988) 'Philippine domestic outwork: subcontracting for export-oriented industries', in J.G. Taylor and A. Turton (eds.) *Sociology of Developing Societies: Southeast Asia*, Houndmills, Basingstoke: Macmillan, pp. 158–64.

Portés, A. and Itzigsohn, J. (1997) 'Coping with change: the politics and economics of urban poverty', in A. Portés, C. Dore-Cabral and P. Landoff (eds), *The Urban Caribbean: Transition to a New Global Economy*, Baltimore: Johns Hopkins University Press, pp. 227–48.

Potter, R. and Lloyd-Evans, S. (1998) *The City in the Developing World*, London: Longman.

Roberts, B. (1991) 'The changing nature of informal employment: the case of Mexico', in G. Standing and V. Tokman (eds), *Towards Social Adjustment: Labour Market Issues in Structural Adjustment*, Geneva: International Labour Organization (ILO), pp. 115–40.

Roberts, B. (1994) 'Informal economy and family strategies', *International Journal of Urban and Regional Research* 18(1): 6–23.

Roberts, B. (1995) *The Making of Citizens: Cities of Peasants Revisited*, London: Edward Arnold.

Standing, G. (1989) 'Global feminisation through flexible labour', *World Development* 17(7): 1077–95.

Thomas, J.J. (1995) *Surviving in the City: The Urban Informal Sector in Latin America*, London: Pluto Press.

Thomas, J.J. (1996) 'The new economic model and labour markets in Latin America', in V. Bulmer-Thomas (ed.), *The New Economic Model in Latin America and its Impact on Income Distribution and Poverty*, Basingstoke: Macmillan, in association with the Institute of Latin American Studies, University of London, pp. 79–102.

Tinker, I. (1997) *Street Foods: Urban Food and Employment in Developing Countries*, New York/Oxford: Oxford University Press.

Tokman, V. (1989) 'Policies for a heterogeneous informal sector in Latin America', *World Development* 17(7): 1067–76.

Tokman, V. (1991) 'The informal sector in Latin America: from underground to legality', in G. Standing and V. Tokman (eds), *Towards Social Adjustment: Labour Market Issues in Structural Adjustment*, Geneva: International Labour Office (ILO), pp. 141–57.

United Nations (UN) (1995) *The World's Women 1995: Trends and Statistics*, New York: UN.

4.7 Child labour

Sally Lloyd-Evans

INTRODUCTION: CHILD LABOUR AS A GLOBAL ISSUE

One of the most hotly debated issues in the development agenda over the last decade has been the high incidence of child labour in Asia, Africa and Latin America (Alston, 1994; Roberts, 1998; Bartlett *et al.*, 1999). It is estimated by the International Labour Organization (ILO) (1996), that there are 250 million child labourers between the age of 5 and 15 years of age in the developing world alone. From as young as 3 or 4 years old, children from poor and vulnerable households are seen as potential income earners by their families, whilst numerous others in single-parent families undertake the sole responsibility of financially supporting the household. The heightened concern over the future welfare of millions of the world's poorer children has largely developed from widespread media coverage of child-related issues, such as the murder of Brazilian street children by police death squads, and increased documentation on child work by non-governmental organizations (NGOs) and international institutions such as the United Nations Children's Fund (UNICEF), the World Bank and the ILO.

Child labour is rooted in poverty, history, culture and global inequality (Potter and Lloyd-Evans, 1998). Although the fundamental reason why children work is poverty, there are other important factors which deserve consideration. Whilst global institutions argue that the incidence of child labour will decline as a country's per capita GDP rises, child labour is also seen to be a serious consequence of neo-liberalism and unequal trade resulting from economic globalization. The negative consequences of globalization are centred around the exploitation of workers, including children, in the new international division of labour where developing countries are pressurized to compete in the global export economy. For example, in the 'successful' economies of Southeast

Asia, increases in child prostitution are often linked to macroeconomic policies of governments which have promoted rapid industrialization at the expense of rural development and poverty alleviation.

As a result, the debate over working children is marked by moral indignation and sympathy, which although understandable draws attention away from a more rational interpretation of the processes which draw children into the global labour market (Fyfe, 1994; Robson, 1996). Whilst the horrific stories of Latin America's street children have received the most attention in the media, little consideration is given to the far greater numbers of children who are 'invisibly' employed in the informal sector as agricultural or household workers. Furthermore, prevailing perceptions of children as helpless 'victims' often serve to undervalue the essential contribution they make to household incomes, and denies them the 'right' to help their families in the struggle for a more equitable distribution of resources. As this chapter will highlight, child labour is an extremely complex and multifaceted subject, as 'work' can simultanously be seen as both harmful to a child's development and yet essential for providing for their basic needs.

CHILD LABOUR AND CHILD WORK: CONCEPTUAL ISSUES

What is child labour?

Child labour takes on many forms, from paid work in factories and other forms of waged labour like street selling, which are particularly characteristic in cities, to unwaged labour in the household and predominantly rural areas, to bonded labour and trafficked labour, which are both forms of slavery. Industries, often export-oriented, which employ children have received the most attention and include the production of carpets, glassware, matches, fireworks, gem-polishing and quarrying. 'Dollar Land' in Uttah Pradesh, India, so named due to its profitability, is a region geared to carpet production where 150,000 children over 10 years old work a 10–16-hour day. Similarly, Nepal is famous for its 'kamaiya', bonded child labourers who have been sold into bondage in return for small sums or repayment of rural debts. Trafficked children and bonded labourers are seen to be the most severely exploited and vulnerable child workers, but their invisibility makes policy intervention difficult.

Major geographical differences in the incidence and nature of child labour can be become blurred in the uniform category of 'child labour'. Of the estimated 250 million working children aged between 5 and 15 years in developing countries, the ILO (1996) estimates that 61 per cent are located in Asia, 32 per cent in Africa and 7 per cent in Latin America. World Bank figures on the labour force participation rates of children aged 10–14 differ again, however, with the highest rates believed to occur in Eastern and Western Africa. In Africa, rising poverty and a diminishing adult labour force due to the AIDS epidemic have driven more children into the waged labour force (Robson, 1996). Moreover, UNICEF (1997) has argued that one-third of all children in Africa and Latin America are engaged in some form of economic activity, most commonly in family enterprises. Contrary to popular perception, the ILO estimates that less than 5 per cent of child labourers are employed in export manufacturing, whilst 90 per cent of working children in rural households across the developing world are believed to be engaged in some form of agricultural activity.

Although defintions of child labour vary, they are mainly centred on whether work has a 'detrimental impact' on a child's physical, mental or moral development. Current academic debates centre on whether there is a clear distinction between 'child labour' (usually waged) and 'child work' (unwaged), which is undertaken in the course of everyday life. Action Aid (1992), which has developed programmes to provide children with suitable work and schooling, argue that 'child work', which is often part of normal socialization, becomes 'child labour' when its character changes from 'developmental' to 'economic'. Nieuwenhuys (1994), asks why unpaid household labour is considered to be morally 'neutral' compared to waged work in industry when both are equally detrimental to the development of children. Here, issues of gender are salient, as girls rather than boys are usually expected to undertake a greater proportion of invisible household activities. Whilst there is international condemnation of the employment of children in hazardous industrial activities, there is less agreement over whether household work should constitute 'child labour'. The understanding of children's work has been intertwined by such moral considerations throughout history and, as is highlighted below, it is important to deconstruct child labour in its appropriate social and cultural context.

CHILD LABOUR AND DEVELOPMENT: CONTEMPORARY THINKING

'Western' perceptions of childhood

It has been suggested that the global preoccupation with Third World child workers is further evidence of the enforcement of Western codes of conduct in developing nations, as much of the recent literature on child labour stems from a Western, and predominantly middle-class, construction of 'childhood' (Fyfe, 1994). The idea of 'working children' challenges traditional meanings of childhood, which are predominantly based on Western norms of behaviour. Definitions of childhood have considerable geographical, gendered and cultural implications in relation to whether it is acceptable for children to make decisions about issues that govern their lives (White, 1994).

Socio-spatial dimensions of child labour

There are socio-spatial dimensions to child labour which may explain why some categories of 'child work' are deemed to be more undesirable than others. In particular, many definitions of hazardous 'child labour' are defined by spatial parameters. As Jones (1997) argues, societal and public views on child labour and related issues will depend on the meanings people attach to public 'spaces' and what they see as appropriate places for children. In Latin America, millions of street children are perceived as 'criminal' and a 'threat' to family and social order. Such 'moral imaginations', which are fuelled by the media, led to public tolerance of the murder of street children in Brazilian cities. Across the world, city streets and industrial factories are seen as 'unnatural spaces' for child workers (Marquez, 1999), whilst the household space is deemed to be safe. Such conceptual dilemmas impact upon the development and implementation of global policies which address child labour.

TOWARDS A BETTER FUTURE: CHILD LABOUR AND POLICY INITIATIVES

In light of the above, it is not surprising that issues surrounding child labour have taken centre stage in the development campaigns of agencies and institutions around the world. Global institutions, such as the World Bank and the ILO, have largely adopted a 'paternalistic' approach to child workers which regards them as passive victims of an unfair global system in need of protection (Jones, 1997). Although the existence of child labour is a visible indication of the uneven development and poverty that exists worldwide today, most global institutions believe that hazardous child labour can be eliminated independently of poverty reduction (World Bank, 1997). UNICEF (1997) has

Table 1 The United Nations Convention on the Rights of the Child, 1989

Children have the right to:

- enough food, clean water and healthcare
- an adequate standard of living
- be with their family or those who will care for them best
- protection from all exploitation, physical, mental and sexual abuse
- special protection when exposed to armed conflict
- be protected from all forms of discrimination
- be protected from work that threatens their education, health or development
- special care and training if disabled
- play
- education
- have their own opinions taken into account in decisions which affect their lives
- know what their rights are.

Source: Potter and Lloyd-Evans, 1998: 185

argued that real progress was made in 'realising and protecting' children's rights in the 1990s following the international adoption of the United Nations Convention on the Rights of the Child in 1989. The Convention, documented in Table 1, highlighted the need for child labour to be placed firmly on the international agenda, but the enforcement of child labour standards in many countries has been questioned.

Internationally, the ILO has been identified as the most appropriate 'global' body to deal with child labour issues. Since 1992, it has promoted the International Programme on the Elimination of Child Labour (IPEC) as an effective framework to eliminate child labour and search for alternative solutions to household vulnerability, mainly in the form of providing stable employment for parents and the rehabilitaion, education and training of child workers. Whilst there is reticence by institutions and governments to abolish all forms of child work, the ILO has recently adopted a declaration to place an immediate ban on the 'worst' forms of child labour which include prostitution, work in hazardous industries and bonded labour.

Although a step in the right direction, international solutions to reduce child labour take the decision-making process away from child workers. By contrast, many NGOs and grassroots organizations have attempted to implement small-scale programmes which aim to 'empower' children by supporting their right to work. Ennew (1994) argues for the need to recognize children as rational individuals who can be empowered to take control of their own lives. Grassroots initiatives, such as street drop-in centres, endeavour to give children the opportunity to work in safe environments whilst also providing time for schooling and recreation.

There is still considerable scepticism over whether current policy initiatives will enhance children's quality of life unless there are more fundamental changes to the unequal distribution of global wealth and trade. Although, the ultimate goal of the United Nations remains the worldwide abolition of all child labour, there is now an understanding that progress will be slow, and that change must take into consideration the needs and rights of children and their families.

GUIDE TO FURTHER READING

Bartlett, S., Hart, R., Satterthwaite, D., de la Barra, X. and Missair, A. (1999) *Cities for Children: Children's Rights, Poverty and Urban Management*, London: Earthscan. This book discusses practical measures for meeting the rights of urban children in Africa, Asia and Latin America.

Fyfe, A. (1994) *Child Labour*, Cambridge: Polity. A comprehensive critique of conceptual and development issues relating to child labour, which is supported by case study evidence.

Nieuwenhuys, O. (1994) *Children's Lifeworlds: Gender, Welfare and Labour in the Developing World*, London: Routledge. A detailed study of children's daily work in rural Southern India which examines how gender, class, household structure, education and state ideology combine to structure children's working lives.

UNICEF (1997) *The State of the World's Children, 1997*, New York: UNICEF. Annually produced reports that document the changing geography of children's lives worldwide. The 1997 issue focused on child labour issues.

White, B. (1994) 'Children, work and "child labour": changing responses to the employment of children', *Development and Change* 25(4): 849–78. A thorough critique of changing institutional responses to the child labour debate.

REFERENCES

Action Aid (1992) 'All in a life's work: the labour of children', *Common Cause* 3(12): 1–26.

Alston, P. (ed.) (1994) *The Best Interests of the Child: Reconciling Culture and Human Rights*, UNICEF, Oxford: Clarendon Press.

Bartlett, S., Hart, R., Satterthwaite, D., de la Barra, X. and Missair, A. (1999) *Cities for Children: Children's Rights, Poverty and Urban Management*, London: Earthscan.

Ennew, J. (1994) *Street Children and Working Children: A Guide to Planning*, London: Save the Children.

Fyfe, A. (1994) *Child Labour*, Cambridge: Polity.

International Labour Organization (ILO) (1996) *Child Labour: What is to be Done?*, Geneva: ILO.

Jones, G.A. (1997) 'Junto con los ninos: street children in Mexico', *Development in Practice* 1(1): 39–49.

Marquez, P.C. (1999) *The Street is my Home: Youth and Violence in Caracas*, Stanford: Stanford University Press.

Nieuwenhuys, O. (1994) *Children's Lifeworlds: Gender, Welfare and Labour in the Developing World,* London: Routledge.

Roberts, S.M. (1998) 'Commentary: What about the children?' *Environment and Planning A* 30: 3–11.

Robson, E. (1996) 'Working girls and boys: children's contributions to household survival in West Africa', *Geography* 81: 403–7.

Potter, R.B. and Lloyd-Evans, S. (1998) *The City in the Developing World*, Harlow: Longman.

UNICEF (1997) *The State of the World's Children*, New York: UNICEF.

White, B. (1994) 'Children, work and "child labour": changing responses to the employment of children', *Development and Change* 25(4): 849–78.

World Bank (1997) *Child Labor: Issues and Directions for the World Bank* (accessed 26/04/2000) website: http://www.wbln0018.worldbank.org.

4.8 Technology, knowledge and development

Gordon Wilson

Technology is the purposeful, organized application of knowledge to practical tasks, involving an interaction of tools and people. Technology is inextricably linked to development, because development is ultimately about practical activity. This is the case whether development is thought of as a long, historical process of change, or as deliberate actions in which development agencies of all types engage (Thomas, 2000).

The definition of technology given above is an extension, rather than a negation, of older definitions. When I was at school, I used to think of technology as people working with machines. This is similar to the interaction of tools and people above, although I now contend that tools do not have to be embodied in machines, however simple or complicated these may be. A more formal school-day definition of technology, meanwhile, was the application of science for human purposes. 'Practical tasks' implies something more focused than 'human purposes' perhaps, but science in this definition is no more than shorthand for a particular kind of knowledge. The major differences between the definitions, therefore, lies in what is meant by tools (something broader than machines) and the generalized use of 'knowledge', rather than reducing technology to the application of scientific knowledge.

The main point about tools is that they can be 'hard' (as in machines) or 'soft' as, for example, in a framework for engaging the participation of poor people in development initiatives (where participatory rural appraisal (PRA) would be one such tool). Knowledge too can be classified as 'codified' (i.e. 'hard': written down) or 'tacit', something we feel and which is usually acquired by doing. Thus, we can be told how to use a screwdriver or conduct a PRA (applying codified knowledge), but we become skilled in using these tools with practice – which involves using them in a non-instrumental way, by adapting them, or even discarding them, according to the context and circumstances. This process of becoming skilled through practice is also the process of acquiring tacit knowledge.

Many scholars prefer to think of knowledge, not as a 'thing', but as a 'process of knowing' (Polanyi, 1958). This is because, although the distinction between codified and tacit knowledge is a useful one, the separation in reality is not so easy, nor is the relationship static. Moreover, it invites preferences for one or the other when both are essential. There is thus a literature on the interactions between the two, particularly how such interactions might expand knowledge (Nonaka and Takeuchi, 1995).

Also, there is a related dimension – that knowledge is interpreted through what we already know, through our shared meanings, in other words through our culture (Wilson, 1999) – and in this sense we might wish to speak of not one but many 'knowledges'. This has important implications for technology and development because, given that technology embodies knowledge, it also therefore embodies the culture of those who develop it, which has a bearing on a particular technology's impact, and even acceptance, in different societies.

At an organizational level, there may be attempts formally to 'capture knowledge as knowing' through evaluation of actual practice, and, if it is effective in this regard, it acquires the distinction of becoming a 'learning organization'. This can be represented diagrammatically as a series of three feedback loops, known as single-, double- and triple-loop learning (see figure).

Thus, practical activity becomes a learning process. In single-loop learning, only the practical tasks might be modified in the light of knowledge capture. In double-loop learning the definition of what the practical tasks should be is challenged. In triple-loop learning, the knowledge captured is used to improve the effectiveness of how it might be captured in future, via the evaluation and appraisal processes. This last is often referred to as 'learning how to learn'.

The diagram is, however, only a *model* of how a learning organization *should* work. Just because everyone *knows* how something might be done better, that knowledge is not necessarily translated into practice. Organizations tend to have set, formal and informal, rules and practices, and ways in which people who belong to them behave. Changing these is not easy. Thus, much attention has been directed towards opening the 'black box' of knowledge capture. Within a firm, how can one tap into the knowledge held tacitly on the shop floor via monitoring, evaluation and appraisal?

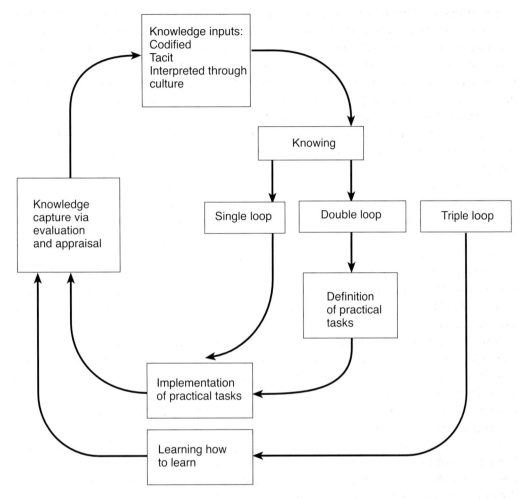

Single-, double- and triple-loop learning for effective knowledge capture

Participatory approaches to social development can similarly be viewed as collective attempts to *construct* a common knowledge out of the different knowledges held by widely different stakeholders. A key question then becomes: 'How can shared, or "social", learning take place?' Answering this has implications for the ways in which evaluations and appraisals of interventions are carried out. It also has implications for the focus of development projects – whether they are ends with measurable objectives, or better conceived as sites of experimentation and learning (Rondinelli, 1993).

It is not my purpose to discuss whether participatory tools, such as PRA, can contribute to empowerment in social development interventions, but they are certainly tools for knowledge capture, used more or less effectively in the hands of more- or less-skilled practitioners. This is interesting, because, if technology is about the application of knowledge, a feature of our times is also to do the opposite – to apply technology to capture knowledge. And, although I have introduced this reversal through the example of PRA, when I normally think of knowledge capture through technology, I think of words like the internet, the World Wide Web, or simply 'information technology' (IT).

By introducing it in an idiosyncratic way, however, IT is put in context. It becomes but one of a list of technologies whose purpose can be described as that of improving the effectiveness of knowledge capture. The development issue for all, however, concerns old questions such as access to the technology, who learns to use it, what do they learn and what do they do with their learning. And, for me, these questions lead to the further question of what more effective knowledge capture does for development. This question has to be examined in terms of both development as deliberate action and development as historical process.

TECHNOLOGY, KNOWLEDGE AND DEVELOPMENT AS DELIBERATE ACTION

Technologies for knowledge capture are here predicated on the assumption that deliberate action for development is a managed process among multiple stakeholders, where no single one has overall control, and where there might be value-based differences between them as to the kinds of intervention needed and how they should be implemented (Thomas, 1996). Within this context, 'soft' technologies tend to focus on enabling shared learning and hence knowledge capture to take place across the stakeholders. PRA, mentioned above, is an example of such a technology. Johnson and Wilson (1999) are also testing 'soft' technologies for institutionalizing shared learning among stakeholders in development interventions, and which attempt to manage the differences in social power between them. This includes managing differences in what the stakeholders know already – for example, the different 'knowing' of professionals and local lay people.

There are also many attempts to use IT in social development. One initiative is the African Virtual University (AVU) launched by the World Bank in 1997, which is: 'bringing knowledge to an undereducated community – via satellite . . . the AVU enables students in 16 African countries to take courses and seminars by professors from universities around the world' (Light, 1999).

Others are more sober in their judgement about IT in relation to social development, taking issue with the focus of its proponents on hardware and knowledge as a commodity to be transferred (Chataway and Wield, 2000). Indeed, estimates suggest that the majority of IT-based initiatives have so far ended in failure of one form or another (Wilson and Heeks, 2000: 418; Heeks and Davies, 1999).

TECHNOLOGY, KNOWLEDGE AND DEVELOPMENT AS HISTORICAL PROCESS

There is a long history of debate accompanying the role of technology in development processes. At one end of the spectrum are the technological determinists who declare that the dominant technologies virtually define the nature of society and its development trajectory; at the other end are the social determinists who contend that the dominant political economy determines the technologies that we develop. This debate is also manifested in analysis of the empirically observed 'long wave' global economic cycles of boom, recession and regeneration that have characterized the past few centuries. Each of these cycles is associated with a 'heartland' technology – the textile industry (late eighteenth century), steel and railroad technologies (mid-nineteenth century), materials-intensive technologies (early twentieth century), and now information and communications technologies (Kaplinsky, 1990: 6).

Running parallel to the above is the current debate of whether the world has entered a 'second great transformation' (Harriss, 2000). If the first 'great transformation' was from craft production to industrial capitalism last century, the second is predicated on information and knowledge. Ideas about the 'second great transformation' have become much associated with the work of Manuel Castells, particularly his trilogy, *The Information Age: Economy, Society and Culture* (Castells, 1996, 1997, 1998).

One of Castells' core theses is that the world is increasingly dominated by networks, which have shared information at their core, and which result in new social and economic relations. Thus networks are a means to shared learning, of knowledge capture, for those included, but, as ever, issues of inclusion or exclusion with respect to networks are crucial when trying to link them to development. Thus we come back to questions of who is included in the network, what do they learn and what do they do with their learning. Networks, of course, do not have to be global, dependent on the internet and World Wide Web. There are examples of 'industrial clusters' – small- (and sometimes large-)scale firms in the same geographical space, who both formally and informally share technological and other knowledge.

The term, 'the great transformation' comes from Karl Polanyi (1957), who used it to describe the original change from craft production to industrial capitalism. But, for Polanyi, there was nothing inevitable about this process. He saw it in terms of a struggle between protectionists on the one hand, and those promoting the commodification of land, labour and productive organization on the other. Today we see a parallel struggle over the commodification of knowledge, epitomized by clashes over intellectual property rights and the patenting of genes between protectionist elements from civil society and corporate interests.

CONCLUSION

Development as deliberate action and development as historical process are linked by knowledge, in that it is essential to know about the latter in order to know what to do in the former. One does not have to be a technological determinist to appreciate that technological development has always been part of the historical process, and currently the predominant generic technology is about knowledge management. Similarly, one does not have to be a proponent of 'technocratic' intervention to understand that knowledge applied to practical tasks is at the core of development intervention.

GUIDE TO FURTHER READING

Castells, M. (1996) *The Rise of the Network Society*, Oxford: Blackwell. This volume of Castells' trilogy, *The Information Age: Economy, Society and Culture*, explores the thesis that the world is increasingly dominated by networks, which have shared information at their core.

Freeman, C., Clark, J. and Soete, L. (1982) *Unemployment and Technical Innovation: A Study of Long Waves and Economic Development*, London: Francis Pinter. This is the classic study of the link between technology and economic long waves, associating each cycle with a 'heartland' technology.

Nonaka, I. and Takeuchi, H. (1995) *The Knowledge-Creating Company*, Oxford: Oxford University Press. This study places the simple notion of knowledge, as a quantity to be created, stored, manipulated and drawn upon, alongside a more complex conceptualization in which tacit and explicit knowledge are different but complementary.

Rondinelli, D. (1993) *Development Projects as Policy Experiments*, London: Routledge. Argues that development projects are more important as experiments than for their immediate impact.

Schmitz, H. and Nadvi, K. (eds) (1999) 'Special Issue on industrial clusters in developing countries', *World Development* 27(9). A wide-ranging analysis of industrial clusters in developing countries.

Wilson, G. and Heeks, R. (2000) 'Technology, poverty and development', in T. Allen and A. Thomas (eds) *Poverty and Development into the Twenty-first Century*, Oxford: Oxford University Press and Milton Keynes: Open University, pp. 403–24. A general introduction to the subject of technology and development linked to poverty reduction.

REFERENCES

Castells, M. (1997) *The Power of Identity*, Oxford: Blackwell.

Castells, M. (1998) *End of Millennium*, Oxford: Blackwell.

Chataway, J. and Wield, D. (2000) Industrialisation, innovation and development: what does knowledge management change?', *Journal of International Development* 12(6): pp. 803–24.

Harriss, J. (2000) 'The second 'great transformation'? Capitalism at the end of the twentieth century', in T. Allen and A. Thomas (eds) *Poverty and Development into the Twenty-first Century*, Oxford: Oxford University Press and Milton Keynes: Open University, pp. 325–42.

Heeks, R. and Davies, A. (1999) 'Different approaches to information age reform', in R. Heeks (ed.) *Reinventing Government in the Information Age*, London: Routledge, pp. 22–48.

Johnson, H. and Wilson, G. (1999) 'Institutional sustainability as learning', *Development in Practice* 9(1): 43–55.

Kaplinsky, R. (1990) *The Economies of Small: Appropriate Technology in a Changing World*, London: IT Publications in association with Appropriate Technology International.

Light, D. (1999) 'Pioneering distance education in Africa', *Harvard Business Review* 77(5): 26.

Polanyi, K. (1957, first published 1944) *The Great Transformation*, Boston: Beacon Press.

Polanyi, M. (1958) *Personal Knowledge*, London: Routledge and Kegan Paul.

Thomas, A. (1996) 'What is development management?', *Journal of International Development* 8(1): 95–110.

Thomas, A. (2000) 'Meanings and views of development', in T. Allen and A. Thomas (eds) *Poverty and Development into the Twenty-first Century*, Oxford: Oxford University Press and Milton Keynes: Open University, pp. 23–48.

Wilson, G. (1999) 'Local knowledges and changing technologies', in T. Skelton and T. Allen (eds) *Culture and Global Change*, London: Routledge, pp. 58–69.

4.9 The 'resource curse' in developing countries[1]

Richard M. Auty

EXPLAINING THE UNDERPERFORMANCE OF RESOURCE-ABUNDANT DEVELOPING COUNTRIES

Since the 1960s the per capita incomes of the resource-poor countries have grown significantly faster than have those of the resource-abundant countries. As Table 1 shows, the worst performers of all in the past 15 years were the mineral-driven resource-rich economies. Yet they have higher growth potential because their capacity to invest and to import is enhanced compared to non-mineral economies by their mineral exports. Explanations for this 'resource curse' fall into two categories, depending on whether they blame external or domestic causes.

Table 1 Natural resources, economic growth, investment efficiency and population, 1960–97

Resource endowment category	Investment (% GDP)	GDP growth (%/year)	ICOR	PC GDP growth (%/year)	Population growth (%/year)
Small non-mineral resource-rich					
1960–73	14.8	4.2	3.5	1.6	2.6
1973–85	20.5	3.4	6.9	0.7	2.7
1985–97	21.9	3.5	6.0	0.9	2.6
Small oil-exporting resource-rich					
1960–73	24.5	6.6	3.7	4.0	2.6
1973–85	31.0	6.5	5.7	2.3	4.2
1985–97	23.9	1.9	12.4	−0.7	2.6
Small ore-exporting resource-rich					
1960–73	17.5	4.9	5.7	2.2	2.7
1973–85	21.8	3.0	7.3	0.1	2.9
1985–97	17.1	2.3	7.5	−0.4	2.7
Large resource-rich					
1960–73	20.3	5.4	4.0	2.7	2.7
1973–85	21.8	3.1	7.1	0.7	2.4
1985–97	20.1	4.0	5.0	1.9	2.1
Small resource-poor					
1960–73	18.8	6.1	3.2	3.5	2.6
1973–85	24.8	4.0	6.2	1.8	2.2
1985–97	23.0	4.4	5.2	2.4	2.0
Large resource-poor					
1960–73	17.7	5.0	4.2	2.4	2.6
1973–85	25.5	5.8	4.4	3.7	2.1
1985–97	26.3	6.0	4.4	4.7	1.3

Source: World Bank, 1999

External causes

Following the Second World War, a controversy arose among development economists with respect to the contribution of primary commodity exports to developing country growth. The structuralists favoured planning and non-market allocation of resources achieved through a variety of controls and government incentives for domestic investment, prices and foreign trade. This approach dominated development theory during the years 1950–80. It advocated reduced dependence on primary commodity exports and favoured heavy investment in manufacturing and infrastructure financed by capital imports. The most influential advocate of this approach was Prebisch (1950) who argued that technological change and policy discrimination by industrial countries were depressing the returns from trade for primary commodities exports in relation to the manufactured goods imported by the developing countries. Prebisch argued that developing countries should accelerate their industrialization by erecting trade barriers to protect infant industry to supply their domestic markets.

This view was opposed by mainstream economists who argued that primary commodity exports are the only way that countries in the early stages of development can generate the foreign exchange necessary to pay for essential imports and to service external debt. Also, an expansion of trade attracts foreign investment and this, in turn, transfers modern technology. In this view, economic growth is maximized by maintaining free domestic and external markets for goods, and by allocating capital in free capital markets. Governments should therefore confine their economic intervention to stabilizing domestic prices and preventing balance of payments disequilibrium.

The basic argument of mainstream economists against Prebisch is that governments misallocate resources and impair domestic and foreign investment. The infant industry policy was invariably captured by the urban pressure groups (workers and owners) that benefited from it so that protection was maintained and the 'infant' industries had little incentive to mature and become efficient (Auty, 1995). This mainstream case gained strong support from studies which showed that the trade policy closure advocated by Prebisch was associated with diminished economic resilience and slower economic growth (Balassa, 1985; Sachs, 1985). Duncan (1993) found that, compared with faster-growing low-income regions like South Asia, sub-Saharan African countries became locked into a dependence of slow-growth commodity exports (the staple trap) instead of promoting diversification into high-growth ones.

A second external factor that might explain the underperformance of resource-abundant countries is the higher volatility of primary commodity prices. Yet several early studies contradicted the hypothesis that instability of export prices of primary commodities constituted a significant obstacle to growth (Coppock, 1962; Michaely, 1962). Rather, variations in the *supply* of exports due to domestic factors appeared to have been more important than fluctuations in overseas demand (Macbean, 1966: 34). However, more recent work shows that regions with the highest primary export shares (Latin America, sub-Saharan Africa, Middle East and North Africa) experienced trade price volatility two to three times that of industrial countries over the 1970–92 period (Westley, 1995). Nevertheless, movements in commodity prices do not cause sharp changes in domestic economic conditions. Governments can therefore adopt policies to reduce or eliminate the effects of changes in the terms of trade on the domestic economy. The evidence therefore points to domestic policy failure as the prime cause of disappointing economic development.

Internal factors: policy failure

Sachs and Warner (1995a and 1995b) examine the effect of policy failure with regard to trade policy. They note that as primary product export dependence increases, trade policy closes as protection of domestic industry is strengthened. Sachs and Warner attribute this to fear of Dutch Disease by the governments of resource-abundant countries. 'Dutch Disease' occurs when a commodity boom strengthens the exchange rate so that imports become more competitive and cause employment-intensive domestic agriculture and manufacturing to contract. Sachs and Warner argue that this fear of unemployment leads the government to strengthen protectionist policies in order to sustain the infant manufacturing sector.

A second 'internal' explanation involves the association between resource abundance and rent-seeking behaviour. Rent-seeking occurs when social groups like unions and businessmen devote energy to lobbying governments for favours (domestic prices set well above world levels, for example) instead of seeking ways to improve their competitiveness. These contests for rents are encouraged by abundant natural resources so that the government in resource-abundant countries is likely to favour politically powerful factions and/or to be predatory. The governments of such states divert revenues, usually from farmers to powerful urban-based groups, into inefficient private or state-owned manufacturing firms that are protected from import competition, or into unnecessary bureaucratic jobs. The revenue to sustain this unproductive activity is provided by the rest of the population so that their welfare suffers.

Rent-seeking behaviour also leads to corruption, which Mauro (1995) and Leite and Weidmann (1999) show is associated with resource abundance and depresses economic growth. Such corruption is most detrimental where the natural resource creates 'point' socioeconomic linkages, as with capital-intensive mining. The revenues from such resources are concentrated upon a few large mining firms, a small mine labour aristocracy and the government officials who set taxes and allocate the tax revenues. Corruption functions as a form of illicit tax that reduces investment and saps its efficiency. Leite and Weidmann (1999) estimate that a one-standard deviation improvement in their corruption index raises the average GDP growth rate by 1.4 per cent. This is equivalent to Venezuela reducing its level of corruption to that of Chile, or of Chile reducing its own corruption level to that of the USA.

It therefore appears that domestic economic policy is more important than natural resources in driving economic growth. The resource-*poor* countries are less prone to policy failure than the resource-abundant countries. Two models show why this is so.

MODELS OF DIVERGENT DEVELOPMENT

The competitive diversification model of resource-poor countries

The intensifying land shortage in resource-poor countries reduces the tolerance of the majority poor for inequitable land distribution. The resulting social tension encourages the political state to align its interests with the majority poor (Auty, 1997). For example, per capita cropland in South Korea and Taiwan was already 0.1 hectares in the 1950s, a level that 'densely settled' Bangladesh and Kenya only reached some 40 years later. Singapore and Hong Kong had even less cropland per capita. The governments of such resource-poor countries tend to appreciate the need to invest efficiently from a very low per capita income and are less likely to pursue policies that divert the economy from its long-term comparative advantage.

The resource-poor countries therefore develop through *competitive* industrialization. Their governments tend to adopt relatively open trade policies at a low per capita income and, since the options for commodity exports are limited in resource-poor countries, labour-intensive manufactured exports expand rapidly. This soon absorbs surplus rural labour and creates pressure for the economy to diversify into *competitive* capital-intensive and skill-intensive manufacturing so that it becomes more resilient to external shocks and rapid growth is sustained. The early elimination of surplus labour also combines with incentives from competitive manufacturing for the poor to acquire skills, to raise wages so that income inequality is curbed. Finally, early industrialization accelerates urbanization in resource-poor countries so that population growth slows sooner and the ratio of dependants to workers falls earlier. This boosts the rates of saving and investment (Table 1).

The staple trap model of resource-abundant countries

An *abundant* natural resource endowment provides greater scope for cumulative policy error. As noted earlier, contests over natural resource surpluses (rents) render resource-abundant countries more likely to engender factional or predatory political states that divert rents to favoured groups at the expense of a coherent economic policy. The economy is therefore increasingly distorted and manufacturing remains protected so that development depends upon a handful of commodities with declining competitiveness.

A longer dependence on primary product exports means that the labour-intensive stage of the competitive industrialization model is leapfrogged. Income inequality therefore remains high and skills also accumulate slowly. Fears of Dutch Disease and unemployment discourage reform to remove trade barriers so that 'infant' manufacturing matures slowly, if at all. In seeking to sustain economic growth, governments either borrow from abroad or squeeze the primary sector still further, instead of reforming. Incentives in farming and mining are thereby depressed, their competitiveness wanes and the economy becomes vulnerable to even mild shocks. This damages social capital (the trust and institutions required to lower transaction costs) and natural capital is wastefully depleted so that growth is not sustainable.

Economic growth collapsed even in oil-rich countries like Saudi Arabia that did not close their economies. This is because the basic policy failure is the use of resource surpluses to relax market discipline so that the efficiency of investment declines, as shown by a high capital/output ratio (ICOR) in Table 1. Recovery from a growth collapse takes decades because it requires not merely a change in policy, but the rebuilding of economic infrastructure and social capital. Table 1 shows that the growth collapse was most acute in the small resource-rich economies (whose diversification options tend to be fewer), and especially where the resource surpluses accrue mainly to the government, as in the mineral economies (and transition economies).

CONCLUSIONS AND POLICY IMPLICATIONS

It is an irony that the growth collapses in resource-abundant countries resulted from the backfiring of the efforts of their governments to reduce their dependence upon primary commodity exports. Domestic policies to promote infant industry (which resource abundance could sustain for longer) weakened their economies through the 1960s and then international policies to reverse the long-run decline in real commodity prices by forming producer cartels such as OPEC triggered severe price volatility and economic shocks in the 1970s.

However, a handful of resource-abundant countries demonstrate that a growth collapse is not inevitable and that policy counts. For example, concern for income inequality led Malaysia's consensual democracy to broker a tacit agreement between the two dominant ethnic groups that economic growth was a prerequisite for poverty alleviation. A conscious effort was therefore made to diversify the economy by avoiding both trade policy closure and repression of economic incentives. As a result, Malaysia first diversified away from rubber and tin production into a widening range of more buoyant commodities like palm oil, timber and oil, before moving strongly into *competitive* manufacturing in the 1980s. Even so, compared with the resource-poor countries of Northeast Asia, industrialization occurred later, economic growth was initially slower and income inequality was higher, but the path of competitive industrialization was eventually reached.

Policy reform in developing market economies and also the transition economies of the former Soviet Union will benefit from recognizing how differences in the political state and natural resource endowment affect economic diversification and social tensions. Reform prospects improve if the political state evolves into a consensual democracy, like those of Malaysia and Botswana, and builds institutions to lower the costs of economic transactions and manage social tension. In addition, the resource-abundant countries need a capital development fund to rationalize the allocation of the revenue surpluses (rents) that their natural resources generate. They also require a commodity revenue stabilization fund to smooth government revenues and make them more transparent so that the opportunity for corruption is curbed. Finally, an evaluation unit to appraise public investment will help to ensure that such investment is efficient.

NOTE

1. This section is based on a research project directed by the author at UNU/WIDER, Helsinki.

GUIDE TO FURTHER READING

Auty, R.M. and Mikesell, R.F. (1998) *Sustainable Development in Mineral Economies*, Oxford: Clarendon Press. Discusses the underperformance of the mineral-rich resource-abundant countries and shows how environmental and natural resource accounting along with social audits can improve the environmental and social sustainability of mineral-driven development.

Gelb, A.H. and associates (1988) *Oil Windfalls: Blessing or Curse?* New York: Oxford University Press. Explains why most oil-rich economies failed to make good use of the additional income from the 1974–78 and 1979–81 oil booms. Presents detailed case studies on Algeria, Ecuador, Indonesia, Nigeria, Trinidad and Tobago, and Venezuela.

Lal, D. and Myint, H. (1996) *The Political Economy of Poverty, Equity and Growth*, Oxford: Clarendon Press. Examines the performance of 21 developing countries, noting the easier development path of the resource-poor countries compared with the resource-abundant countries.

Vincent, J.R. and Ali, M.R. (1997) *Environment and Development in a Resource-Rich Country: Malaysia*, Cambridge MA: Harvard University Press. Applies environmental accounting to examine the successful development of the Malaysian economy.

REFERENCES

Auty, R.M. (1995) 'Industrial policy capture in Taiwan and South Korea', *Development Policy Review* 13: 195–217.

Auty, R.M. (1997) 'Natural resources, the state and development strategy', *Journal of International Development* 9: 651–63.

Balassa, B. (1985) 'Adjusting to external shocks: the newly-industrialising developing countries', *Weltwirtschaftsliches Archiv* 122: 1141–61.

Coppock, J.D. (1962) *International Economic Stability*, New York: McGraw-Hill.

Duncan, R.C. (1993) 'Agricultural export prospects for sub-Saharan Africa', *Development Policy Review* 11: 31–45.

Leite, C. and Weidmann, J. (1999) 'Does Mother Nature corrupt? Natural resources, corruption and economic growth', *IMF Working Paper* 99/85, Washington DC: International Monetary Fund.

Macbean, A.I. (1966) *Export Instability and Economic Development*, Cambridge MA: Harvard University Press.

Mauro, P. (1995) 'Corruption and growth', *The Quarterly Journal of Economics* 90: 681–712.

Michaely, M. (1962) *Concentration in International Trade*, Amsterdam: North-Holland.

Prebisch, R. (1950) *The Economic Development of Latin America and its Principal Problems*, New York: United Nations.

Sachs, J.D. (1985) 'External debt and macroeconomic performance in Latin America and Asia', *Brookings Papers on Economic Activity* 2: 523–75.

Sachs, J.D. and Warner, A.M. (1995a) 'Economic convergence and economic policy', *NBER Working Paper* 2897, Cambridge MA: National Bureau of Economic Research.

Sachs, J.D. and Warner, A.M. (1995b) 'Natural resources and economic growth', Mimeo, Cambridge MA: Harvard Institute for International Development (HIID).

Westley, G. (1995) *Economic Volatility from Natural Resource Endowments*, Washington DC: Inter-American Development Bank.

World Bank (1999) *World Development Indicators*, Washington DC: World Bank.

4.10 Energy and development

B. Sudhakara Reddy

THE NEED FOR ENERGY

Energy is the fourth of the basic needs of people, along with food, clothing and shelter. It is of vital need to human civilization and an intense current concern. The demand for energy depends upon population growth, the rate of economic development, urbanization, changing lifestyles, the availability of resources and the prices of various energy carriers. How are these demands met? People are dynamic and hence are always exploring, experimenting and learning from their surroundings. They are on the lookout for ways of getting energy in a form which is useful to them. They discover raw materials to use, search for them and invent methods of converting them to suitable forms to meet their needs. In other words, the supply of energy depends on the ingenuity and strategy of people's interaction with their environment. The energy issue is primarily a technological problem. An ideal source of energy, to be of some benefit to the society and improve the quality of life, must be economically viable, environmentally sustainable and socially acceptable. Energy, being the need of the day, plays a significant role in the development of society. However, development in energy utilization has been a highly uneven process. While in some countries, per capita energy consumption is increasing exponentially, in others it has even shown a decrease. In India, we see fuelwood stoves alongside nuclear devices; likewise, space vehicles co-exist with bullock carts. The future of energy seems uncertain. At the beginning of the twentieth century, nuclear energy was unheard of. Today, the world abounds with nuclear reactors.

Similarly, contemporary populations cannot imagine life without petroleum products. There is a distinct possibility of the exhaustion of these fuels by the turn of the century. After reckless use of this scarce resource, modern society is now striving hard to avoid this situation.

ENERGY AND DEVELOPMENT: LOOKING BACK

Most thinking in developing countries on energy production and utilization is based on the pattern available in Europe and North America. India adopted virtually an identical path of energy development, following the notion that it is unique, inevitable and unavoidable. However, despite five decades of adherence to this path, it has not met even the basic energy needs of the majority of its people. In such a scenario, a different paradigm of energy development needs to be evolved. This type of energy development goes beyond the traditional supply-side approach, which can contribute to the economically productive activities and improve the quality of life of the people. The main goal of this path is to use energy as a catalytic force to bring about both social and economic development. This type of development embraces the following principles: (i) development orientation; (ii) service-based; (iii) endogenous; (iv) self-reliant; (v) environmentally sound; and (vi) socially acceptable. This section describes the relation between energy and development, looks at past experiences and suggests future directions. Taking an Indian example, the essay provides a summary of the Indian energy scenario, discusses the interactions between energy and development, and argues the need for more effective utilization of energy to make the system more sustainable.

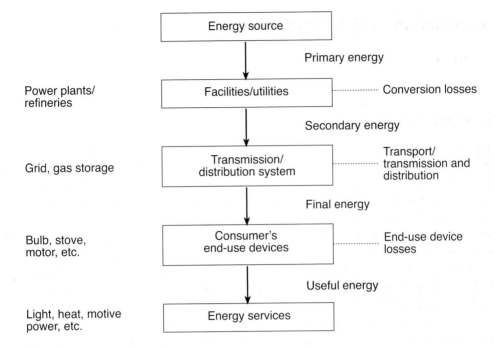

Flow of energy from source to end-use

ENERGY TRANSFORMATIONS: THE BACKDROP

Energy can be broadly classified as commercial and non-commercial. Commercial energy (coal, oil, gas, etc.) is that which can be traded in the market. The non-commercial energy sources, which include fuelwood, dung, agriculture waste, etc., are not traded in the market (even though fuelwood is traded in urban societies). The energy flow from source to end-use is shown in the above figure (Reddy, 1998). At the supply end, the primary energy is in the form found in nature – trees, waterfalls, an oil well, etc. This primary energy is converted into convenient energy carriers designated as secondary energy, for example, firewood logs, charcoal, kerosene, liquified petroleum gas, electricity, etc. Secondary energy, after transportation/transmission and distribution, is delivered as final energy to consumers in the domestic, industrial, agricultural, commercial, transport and other sectors. The final energy delivered to consumers is converted through various end-use devices (stoves, lamps, furnaces, engines, etc.) into useful energy that provides energy services (cooking, illumination, process heating, shaft power, etc.) and satisfies basic needs. There are losses associated with the conversion of one form of energy into the other. These losses are particularly significant in the conversion of final energy into useful energy. In many energy analyses, the efficiencies usually employed pertain only to the end-use of the devices. If we wish to study the energy requirement of a country, it is important to analyse the flow of energy from source to end-use service taking all efficiencies into consideration.

THE INDIAN ENERGY SCENARIO

The study of energy demand and its relation to development is of particular importance in view of its extreme dependence on local energy resources and the way its exploitation affects the economic growth of the country. The process of economic growth is traceable to the substitution of energy for human power in the performance of agriculture, industry and domestic services. Thus, economic development can be accelerated if we learn to use energy in new forms adaptable to a range of needs, which are diversified, based on the social and cultural environments of the society. The two main forces that have an impact on energy demand are population growth and economic development. India has a population of one billion (2000 figures) accounting for 17 per cent of the world's population. India had achieved its highest economic growth rate of 6 per cent per annum during the period 1981–95. With increasing population and economic growth, the need for energy also increases (TEDDY, 1998).

Energy consumption: an overview

Commercial energy consumption

India consumes about 3 per cent of total world commercial energy supplies and the per capita energy consumption is only 5 per cent of that of developed countries (IEA, 1998). In 1998, the total energy demand stood at 1.435 million terajoules (MTJ), of which 64 per cent originated from commercial sources. If sectoral energy consumption is considered, households consume nearly 45 per cent of the total, followed by industry with 40 per cent, transportation 10 per cent and the commercial sector around 3 per cent (Economic Intelligence Service, 2000). The share of the agriculture sector in total, even though small (2 per cent), has increased at a faster rate over the years than any other sector and has been responsible for the major advances made in agricultural productivity, which has made India self-sufficient in food production.

Non-commercial energy consumption

In most developing countries, including India, the utilization of non-commercial energy (not traded in the market) such as fuelwood, dung, agriculture wastes, etc., is significant. For the past few decades, there has been an increase in the consumption of various fuels in absolute terms, but their growth rates are declining significantly. Since non-renewable sources of energy like petroleum are limited, and hence expensive, the vast potential of renewable energy sources merits serious and immediate consideration.

Environmental implications

In recent years, there has been growing concern about global warming due to the increased concentration of greenhouse gases (GHGs) and the resulting socioeconomic impact. These emissions are derived from a number of human activities, namely energy production and utilization, deforestation, agricultural practices, etc. Of these, energy (production and use) contributes to nearly 50 per cent of GHG emissions (TEDDY, 1998). In India, carbon emissions reached 238 mt, of which 85 per cent came from the burning of fossil fuels (emission coefficients (tC/toe): coal – 1.08; oil – 0.86 and gas – 0.62). Technological developments in energy demand and changes in fuel mix are therefore of greatest significance from an environmental perspective. Table 1 provides an overview of economic development, energy consumption and environmental implications for India.

Rural and urban household energy consumption

Households account for nearly 50 per cent of total energy consumption and hence it is important to look at the pattern of utilization. The quantity and type of energy carriers used by households

Table 1 An overview of India's energy and economic development, 1998

Economic overview	Units	
Population	(million)	981
Urbanization	(%)	32
Per capita gross domestic product	(Rs in 1980–81 prices)	3177
Energy overview		
Reserves		
Coal	(billion tonnes)	82.3
Oil	(billion barrels)	4
Natural gas (Tcf)		19
Consumption		
Coal	(million tonnes)	342
Oil products	(million tonnes)	1.8
Natural gas	(Tcf)	0.7
Electricity	(TWh)	475
Fuelwood	(million tonnes)	280
Energy intensity	(Btu/US$)	31000
Environment overview		
Energy-related carbon emissions	(million tonnes)	238

Source: Economic Intelligence Service, 1999

Table 2 Utilization of various energy carriers in rural and urban households

	Per cent of households		
Energy carrier	Rural	Urban	Total
Cowdung	19.6	2.5	15.4
Fuelwood	75.7	30.2	60.5
Coal/charcoal	1.63	8.5	8.2
Biogas	0.43	0.5	0.5
Kerosene	1.34	23.6	7.2
LPG	1.1	26.6	7.9
Electricity	0.2	8.1	0.3
Total	100	100	100

Source: based on the estimates by Ramani *et al.*, 1995

depends on the price, and on the household income. Another important consideration is the availability of commercial carriers, which is high in urban areas. The process of urbanization is traceable to the substitution of commercial energy for non-commercial energy in the industrial, commercial and domestic sectors (the share of consumption of commercial fuels by urban areas is about 80 per cent, whereas that of the urban population is only 31 per cent) (Reddy, 1998). In the case of rural energy consumption, the main fuels are fuelwood, dung and agricultural wastes, which are used mainly for cooking/heating purposes, while kerosene and electricity are used for lighting (Table 2).

Energy thresholds and the development path

After assessing the total energy consumption, it is important to find out whether the present pattern of consumption meets the minimum requirements of its people and whether enough energy will be available for increasing the pace of development. The per capita minimum energy

Table 3 Minimum energy requirements for rural and urban households

Energy requirements for a household per day (Kwh)

Service	Rural	Urban	Average
Cooking	1	2	1.3
Water heating	0.6	1	0.72
Lighting	0.6	1.2	0.78
Other services	0.3	1.8	0.75
Total	2.5	6	3.55
For total population (GWh)	350	660	1010

requirement is the one which supports daily life at a bare minimum and is necessary for human survival (Parikh, 1980). After crossing this threshold, the country enters into the phase of development. How can one arrive at these norms for services like cooking, lighting and transport? When can the country cross this threshold and enter into the path of development? The minimum energy requirements for urban and rural India are shown in Table 3.

ENERGY TECHNOLOGY AND ECONOMIC DEVELOPMENT

The relation between energy technology and economic development is crucial for developing countries, since the process of substitution of energy for human power in the performance of industry, agriculture and households is taking place slowly. Here the role of technology diffusion is crucial. To increase productivity and develop economically, the energy inputs have to be increased significantly (between 1950 and 1990 energy consumption has increased fourfold, from 86 to 350 mtoe). But this requires the raising of resources (the costs of power plants, over the past few decades, have gone up from Rs10,000 to Rs50,000 per kW). Also, increasing energy consumption results in the consumption of precious non-renewable energy resources like coal and petroleum products and, more importantly, degrades the environment. The scale of the problems created by this pattern of development, suggests that a change in direction, without a compromise to growth, is essential. Efficient technologies and various demand-side management options (efficient lighting, motor drives, fans and pumps, co-generation systems, etc.) induce consumers to use energy more effectively, so as to reduce the demand without compromising the services (Johanson et al., 1993). However, there exist many economic, environmental and social barriers for their effective penetration (Parikh et al., 1994). For this, one has to study the relationship between the type of energy production with the natural resource system and the capital before adopting a particular technology. Table 4 provides data on various efficient technologies and the marginal cost of savings.

SUSTAINABLE ENERGY SYSTEMS

There is an urgent need to strive for a sustainable energy system. The modern world faces a choice: either to return to the austerity level of the pre-industrial period, or opt for a development-oriented approach (using renewable energy sources, energy efficient technologies, etc.), instead of a growth-oriented approach. The latter path is possible only if politicians, planners, equipment manufacturers, financial institutions and researchers begin, without delay, to re-channel available human, technical and financial resources into the mass production and marketing of efficient/renewable

Table 4 Efficient technologies and the marginal cost of savings

Option/service	Standard technology	Efficient technology	Marginal cost of savings (Rs/kWh)
Power generation		Combined cycle power plants	0.76
		Sugar co-generation	1.19
		Integrated gasifier combined cycle	1.15
Technologies	Standard motors	Efficient motors	0.66
	No variable-speed drive	Variable-speed drive	0.44
	Standard pumps/fans	Efficient pumps/fans	0.47
	Incandescent lamps	Compact fluorescent lamps	0.18
	Mercury lamps	High-power sodium vapour lamps	0.5
	Magnetic ballasts	Electronic ballasts	1.04
	Standard arc furnace	Efficient electric arc furnace	0.31
Process	No vapour absorption refrigeration systems	Vapour absorption refrigeration systems	0.36
Residential cooking	Traditional wood stoves (10% efficiency)	Efficient stoves	−0.17
	Traditional wood stoves (10% efficiency)	Kerosene stove	−0.10
	Traditional wood stoves (10% efficiency)	LPG stove	0.10
Water heating	Traditional wood stoves (10% efficiency)	Solar water heater	0.48
	Electric water heater	Solar water heater	0.94
Commercial lighting	Incandescent lamp	Compact fluorescent lamp	0.56

Sources: for power generation, transmission technologies: ALCGAS, 1999; for industrial, commercial and residential technologies: Parikh *et al.*, 1994

Notes: All costs are in 1995 prices; the negative costs mean that the gains from these measures completely compensate the additional costs incurred; in addition they provide substantial returns to the investors.

energy technologies. This path also has the potential to provide employment opportunities, as they are more labour intensive than the resource-intensive fossil fuel systems. The implementation of such a system requires the reorientation of energy planning and of the priorities of governments/utilities; multiplying research efforts for clean, renewable energy systems; and changing the mind-set of the consumers. Efficiency measures are, on average, less capital intensive per kilowatt than the supply-side options. Future energy projections should not be examined simply according to supply calculations and planning should not be confined to energy experts. It is important that the consumers who are affected by the policy decisions should be consulted. The evolution of the needs of the people and the services that require energy (lighting, cooking, transport, motive power, etc.) have to be analysed along with demographic and social trends. Finally, for a sustainable energy strategy, policy and planning should be thought out as part of a global policy involving land use, infrastructure, urbanization and lifestyles, and not simply confined to a particular state or country.

GUIDE TO FURTHER READING AND REFERENCES

The following items provide a guide to further reading in connection with the issues dealt with above.

Asia Least Cost Greenhouse Gas Abatement Strategy (ALGAS) (1999) *Report of the Phase I of GEF Project*, New Delhi: TERI.

CMIE (2000) Economic Intelligence Service – Energy, Centre for Monitoring Indian Economy, Mumbai.

Economic Intelligence Service (1999 and 2000) *Energy*, Mumbai: Centre for Monitoring Indian Economy.

International Energy Agency (IEA) (1998) *World Energy Outlook*, Paris: (IEA).

Johanson, T.B., Kelly, H., Reddy, A.K.N. and Williams, R.H. (1993) *Renewable Energy: Sources for Fuels and Electricity*, Washington: Island Press.

Parikh, J.K. (1980) *Energy Systems and Development*, New Delhi: Oxford University Press.

Parikh, J.K, Reddy, B.S. and Banerjee, R. (1994) *Planning for Demand Side Management in the Electricity Sector*, New Delhi: Tata McGraw-Hill Publishing House.

Ramani, K.V., Islam, M.N. and Reddy A.K.N (eds) (1995) *Rural Energy System in Asia-Pacific Region: A Survey of the Status, Planning and Management*, Kuala Lumpur: Asia-Pacific Development.

Reddy, B.S. (1998) *Urban Energy Systems*, New Delhi: Concept Publishers.

TEDDY (1998) Tata Energy Directory Year Book, New Delhi: Tata Energy Research Institute.

4.11 Tourism and development

Graham M.S. Dann

In the 1960s, and with the advent of jet aircraft, mass tourism soon entered a phase when it became rapidly established in the 'costas' of the Centre and, before long, it stretched to the pleasure peripheries of the Third World. In those heady hedonistic days it was largely and uncritically accepted by economists and such international organizations as the World Bank and United Nations that tourism's financial benefits, in terms of balance of payments surpluses, foreign exchange earnings, job creation and infrastructural development well outweighed the potential costs, so much so that tourism came to be unilaterally regarded as a 'passport to development' (de Kadt, 1979), if not something of a cargo cult. The adoption of this favourable position has been described as the 'advocacy platform' (Jafari, 1989).

However, the antithesis was not long in coming. Beginning with popular criticism, it quickly took root in scholarly circles. Here the combined message was that the negative sociocultural consequences of tourism far outstripped any positive economic considerations – an approach which came to be known as the 'cautionary platform' (Jafari, 1989).

By way of dialectical synthesis, another group began to clamour for what it variously called 'alternative tourism', 'soft tourism', 'green tourism', etc., a form of tourism which, it maintained, was consonant with the aims of 'alternative development'. Small-scale, ecologically viable projects, such as that found in the high-profile Lower Casamance region of Senegal (with its discovery tours in locally made boats and stays in native village huts), were paraded as examples of best practice, and they, together with their underpinning beliefs, were said to constitute the 'adaptancy platform' (Jafari, 1989).

So far, the debate had been high on rhetoric and low on theoretical awareness and methodological sophistication, a situation that paved the way for a 'knowledge based platform' (Jafari, 1989), one that attempted to blend theory with empirical investigation. In its initial stages, the principal advances were in the realm of paradigms that had been derived from the disciplines of sociology and anthropology (Dann, 1996: 6–33). Three major perspectives dominated the intellectual scene – those of 'authenticity/sacred quest', 'strangerhood' and 'play'. These approaches were respectively based on the insights of Durkheim and Goffman, Schutz and Simmel, and postmodernism. Although theoretically disparate, they had a shared concern with understanding the tourist and how (s)he was attracted by difference, the latter being provided by the destination and the 'Other'. Subsequently, a fourth perspective, grounded in 'conflict' and the insights of constructivism attempted to give voice to contested alterity. Still later, a fifth paradigm, that of tourism as 'language' (Dann, 1996), sought to explore the ways that places and their peoples were promoted to the tourist, a discourse of hyperbole that, not only paradoxically proclaimed the infinite delights of a finite set of locations, but was itself a rhetoric that was quite unsustainable.

However, still missing from the discussion, though coterminous with it, was another strand of debate which had been initiated mainly by geographers, one that focused more directly on problems of tourism development. In this vein, Doxey (1976) argued that tourism passed through various stages. While its introduction was characterized by euphoria on the part of a given host population, as the industry consolidated from small catering and accommodation establishments to large multinational hotel chains, so too was initial joy transformed to grudging acceptance, apathy and even outright hostility. Indeed, Doxey, basing himself on case studies of Niagara and Barbados, relatedly designed an 'irritation index' which sought to capture these transitions of indigenous sentiment, while Plog (1973) made the complementary point that sociocultural impacts were predicated on the differential motivation of tourists.

A few years later, Butler (1980), in a much-cited paper, attempted to spell out Doxey's insights with greater accuracy and detail in his well-known model of the tourism resort cycle. Although Butler's was a development model that similarly outlined various unilinear stages, where it differed from Doxey's, however, was in allowing for the possibility of rejuvenation or decline in the penultimate phase of a destination's evolution. Subsequently, Butler's model was tested, re-tested and given greater precision by others, especially as regards different types of resort and the varied conditions under which they were operating. At the theoretical level, perhaps the most sophisticated variant was that supplied by Doğan (1989), whose overview of the sociocultural impacts of tourism had benefited from an important intervening contribution by Mathieson and Wall (1982). And so it was that towards the end of the 1980s consensus was reached that sociocultural change could not be attributed solely to tourism. Other co-present factors, such as industrialization, urbanization and the mass media, had to be taken into joint consideration and assessed for partial explanation.

However, it was not until the Brundtland Report and the filtering through of those insights to research, that tourism scholars began adopting or challenging them. Texts, such as those of Pearce (1989) and Gartner (1996), were generally neutral, while analyses by Butler (1992), de Kadt (1992), Mowforth and Munt (1998), Wall (1997) and Wheeller (1994), for example, were decidedly more critical. Additionally, there were several influential edited works (e.g., Bramwell *et al.*, 1996; Pearce and Butler, 1999; Smith and Eadington, 1992; Wahab and Pigram, 1997) which supplied an eclectic pot-pourri of approaches. Furthermore, for the last few years there has been a publication – *The Journal of Sustainable Tourism* – which has provided a forum for academic debate on the topic.

By way of appraisal of these various offerings, Wall (1997) points out that the term 'development' can be understood as a philosophy, process, plan or product. It is a slippery value-laden word containing moral ideas, a number of dimensions (e.g., economic, social, environmental) at various levels (e.g., individual, regional, national, international), while using several indicators (e.g., poverty, unemployment, inequality, self-reliance). The expression 'sustainable development' which, he argues, is something of an oxymoron (cf. Butler, 1992), is similarly ideological in nature since it is predicated on differential access to power and such related considerations as gender, age, class and race. As for 'sustainable tourism', Wall observes that it is a highly problematic concept, given the difficulty and undesirability of maintaining an activity for an indefinite time without degrading the environment and while excluding other activities and processes. It is therefore necessary to ask whether tourism should be sustained or allowed to decline, which trade-offs are required for the common good and, when identified, who decides whether the needs of present and future generations will be met, whether ecotourism is more sustainable than mass tourism and whether the clean green image of the former is not just another marketing gimmick. Wall believes that currently there is insufficient empirical evidence to answer these fundamental questions. He also feels that the present state of development theory (e.g., modernization, dependency, neo-classical, alternative development) is conceptually inadequate to act as a basis for interpreting sustainable tourism.

De Kadt (1992), as a specialist both in tourism and the sociology of development has, by way of anticipation, been able to offer a further critique of neo-classical, Marxist and structuralist theories for their state-centredness. He has also been critical of the evangelical fervour sometimes displayed by proponents of alternative tourism, along with their wholesale indignant rejection of mass tourism, transnational capitalism and rampant consumerism (cf. Butler, 1992). Instead, de Kadt suggests, it might be better to re-examine dispassionately those elements comprising alternative development from which alternative tourism borrows (ecological soundness, scaling down the operations of production and government, recognition of needs other than those of material consumption, equal consideration of the needs of all (including future generations), and political involvement from below). Thus, instead of alternative development and alternative tourism registering common outrage over violated nature (tourism's exploitation of the Third World as comprising the last unspoilt areas), materialism (modernity, consumerism, elitism) and culture (lack of concern over what people want out of development and why), it might be more useful and practical to centralize ecological considerations within cost/benefit frameworks, to treat the environment as an internality and to extend economic analyses beyond mere patterns of growth in order to include the dynamics of nature and survival. By the same token, it will additionally be necessary to examine the role of state intervention in counteracting the exceeding of capacity limits and including tourism in its development plans (via taxes, incentives and foreign exchange rates), to tackle the problem of local decision-taking (lack of expertise, dependency on elites and developers), to encourage the monitoring by internal NGOs and to acknowledge the need for flexible specialization.

It is worthwhile noting that today many of the recommendations of Wall and de Kadt have been accepted and adopted. In particular, environmental impact assessments are now quite standard in tourism research. There are several studies, for instance, which employ impact attitude scales in order to evaluate the acceptance or otherwise of tourism expansion by competing interest groups in well-patronized destinations. Further refinement has been added in those investigations which seek to measure trade-offs for tourists and different types of residents. Additionally, there are inquiries in Third World countries where development extends beyond the environment to the domains of economic growth and social welfare, which seek to discover what improvements, if any, are reflected in local quality of life as many of the inhabitants move from residential areas to those of greater tourist concentration.

Even so, and in spite of these advances, there are more and more problems that need to be tackled satisfactorily and on a continual basis. Butler (1999), for instance, poses further questions about integrated development (cf. Innskeep, 1991) in which all elements of tourism need to mix with those existing and traditional elements of the destination community according to the criteria of acceptability, efficiency and harmony. Relatedly, there is renewed concern about community involvement in decision-taking, policy formulation and planning (Murphy, 1985).

Then there is the huge matter of globalization which, in the hands of tourism scholars, critically explores the impact of increasing internationalization and its erosion of boundaries and identities, that is to say, the removal of indigenous involvement and its replacement by the interests of multi-national corporations. The McDonaldization and Disneyfication of society are both germane to tourism, and both are replete with ideology and ethnocentrism. Now also might be as good a time as any to re-examine the developmental implications of promoting pre-modern authentic differences of Third World host cultures for a postmodern clientele of generating countries nurtured on an ethos of de-differentiation. Currently, too, tourism academics have been highlighting a number of sidelined ethical dilemmas and have suggested replacing 'sustainable tourism' with the idea of 'responsible tourism'. Although the latter expression is difficult to conceptualize, let alone operationalize, at least the notion of responsibility sensitizes researchers to the many moral dimensions associated with tourism development. Indeed, while all the forecasts consistently continue to predict dramatic and uninterrupted growth for tourism well into the new millennium and beyond, developmental issues surrounding the world's largest industry will similarly multiply and require careful examination.

GUIDE TO FURTHER READING

Butler, R. (1992) 'Alternative tourism: the thin edge of the wedge', in V. Smith and W. Eadington (eds) *Tourism Alternatives: Potentials and Problems in the Development of Tourism*, Philadelphia: University of Pennsylvania Press, pp. 31–46.

de Kadt, E. (1992) 'Making the alternative sustainable: lessons from development for tourism', in V. Smith and W. Eadington (eds) *Tourism Alternatives: Potentials and Problems in the Development of Tourism*, Philadelphia: University of Pennsylvania Press, pp. 47–75.

Wall, G. (1997) 'Sustainable tourism – unsustainable development', in S. Wahab and J. Pigram (eds) *Tourism Development and Growth: The Challenge of Sustainability*, London: Routledge, pp. 33–49.

REFERENCES

Bramwell, W., Henry, I., Jackson, J., Prat, A., Richards, G. and Straaten, J. (eds) (1996) *Sustainable Tourism Development: Principles and Practice*, Tilburg: Tilburg University Press.

Butler, R. (1980) 'The concept of a tourist area cycle of evolution: implications for management of resources', *Canadian Geographer* 24(1): 5–12.

Butler, R. (1992) 'Alternative tourism: the thin edge of the wedge', in V. Smith and W. Eadington (eds) *Tourism Alternatives: Potentials and Problems in the Development of Tourism*, Philadelphia: University of Pennsylvania Press, pp. 31–46.

Butler, R. (1999) 'Problems and issues of integrating tourism development', in D. Pearce and R. Butler (eds) *Contemporary Issues in Tourism Development*, London: Routledge, pp. 65–80.

Dann, G. (1996) *The Language of Tourism: A Sociolinguistic Perspective*, Wallingford: CAB International.

de Kadt, E. (ed.) (1979) *Tourism: Passport to Development?* New York: Oxford University Press.

de Kadt, E. (1992) 'Making the alternative sustainable: lessons from development for tourism', in V. Smith and W. Eadington (eds) *Tourism Alternatives: Potentials and Problems in the Development of Tourism*, Philadelphia: University of Pennsylvania Press, pp. 47–75.

Doğan, H. (1989) 'Forms of adjustment: sociocultural impacts of tourism', *Annals of Tourism Research* 16: 216–36.

Doxey, G. (1976) 'A causation theory of visitor–resident irritants: methodology and research inferences', in *The Impacts of Tourism, Proceedings of the 6th Annual Conference of the Travel and Research Association*, Salt Lake City: Travel and Research Association, pp. 195–98.

Gartner, W. (1996) *Tourism Development: Principles, Processes and Policies*, New York: Van Nostrand Reinhold.

Innskeep, E. (1991) *Tourism Planning: An Integrated and Sustainable Development Approach*, New York: Van Nostrand Reinhold.

Jafari, J. (1989) 'Sociocultural dimensions of tourism: an English language literature review', in J. Bystrzanowski (ed.) *Tourism as a Factor for Change: A Sociocultural Study*, Vienna: Centre for Research and Documentation in the Social Sciences, pp. 17–60.

Mathieson, A. and Wall, G. (1982) *Tourism: Economic, Physical and Social Impacts*, London: Longman.

Mowforth, M. and Munt, I. (1998) *Tourism and Sustainability: New Tourism in the Third World*, London: Routledge.

Murphy, P. (1985) *Tourism: A Community Approach*, New York: Methuen.

Pearce, D. (1989) *Tourist Development*, Harlow: Longman.

Pearce, D. and Butler, R. (eds) (1999) *Contemporary Issues in Tourism Development*, London: Routledge.

Plog, S. (1973) 'Why destination areas rise and fall in popularity', *Cornell Hotel and Restaurant Association Quarterly*, November: 13–16.

Smith, V. and Eadington, W. (eds) (1992) *Tourism Alternatives: Potentials and Problems in the Development of Tourism*, Philadelphia: University of Pennsylvania Press.

Wahab, S. and Pigram, J. (eds) (1997) *Tourism Development and Growth: The Challenge of Sustainability*, London: Routledge.

Wall, G. (1997) 'Sustainable tourism – unsustainable development', in S. Wahab and J. Pigram (eds) *Tourism Development and Growth: The Challenge of Sustainability*, London: Routledge, pp. 33–49.

Wheeller, B. (1994) 'Egotourism, sustainable tourism and the environment: a symbiotic, symbolic or shambolic relationship?' in A. Seaton, C. Jenkins, R. Wood, P. Dieke, M. Bennett, R. MacLellan and R. Smith (eds) *Tourism: The State of the Art*, Chichester: Wiley, pp. 647–54.

PART 5

Urbanization

EDITORIAL INTRODUCTION

The Second United Nations Conference on Human Settlements, customarily referred to as 'Habitat II', held in Istanbul, Turkey, in 1996, attested to the continuing importance of the urbanization process in developing societies. In the period since 1950, rapid urbanization has become one of the principal hallmarks of developing nations. It is the magnitude of the changes that are occurring which underscores the salience of urban processes, for it is generally accepted that, on average, the conditions to be found in the rural areas of developing countries are much poorer than those that are to be encountered in the towns and cities.

It is now well established that in the contemporary world, for every urban dweller living in the affluent developed world, two exist in the poorer cities and towns of the developing world. In fact, by the end of the first quarter of the twenty-first century, this ratio will have risen to three to one in favour of urban residents in the developing world. This rapid rise in both urbanization (the proportion of the population living in urban places), and urban growth (the physical expansion of cities on the ground), is exemplified in a number of different ways. Globally, these include increases in the number of large cities, as well as increases in the size of the largest cities themselves. It is also associated with the ever-larger number of cities which have reached the million population mark. By 1990, the average population of the world's 100 largest cities was in excess of 5 million. In 1800, the equivalent statistic had stood at fewer than 200,000 inhabitants. Further, by 1990, there were 12 'mega cities' with over 10 million inhabitants; and, most notably, seven were to be found in Asia, three in Latin America and two in the United States of America.

Over the last 10 years, the concept of the 'world' or 'global city' has come to prominence. This approach stresses that cities have to be seen as key points in the articulation of the global economic system, and are dominated by transnational corporations (TNCs) and transnational capital. However, recent research has pointed to the fact that in many regions – for example, in South America – it is medium-sized cities that are now showing the fastest overall rates of growth. In short, over the Third World as a whole, big and small cities are growing and exhibiting great dynamism.

Within these fast-growing urban settlements, poor housing is perhaps the most conspicuous manifestation of generalized poverty. Possibly the second most overt sign of the stresses and strains of rapid urban change are witnessed in the urgent need for sound and effective environmental management. Whilst more urban residents die due to preventable diseases than as the result of disasters, it is earthquakes, storms and floods that receive far greater media coverage on a day-to-day basis. Housing and environmental conditions are major areas calling for good governance in Third World cities, and perhaps more than anything else, the political will to improve matters on a broad social and economic front is pressingly required. This is a vital area when one considers that the very existence of urban areas is predicated on economies of scale, which should therefore allow environmental and health hazards to be tackled more effectively than in rural areas.

A closely related issue is the need to provide food for growing city populations, and urban food security has emerged as an increasingly important topic over the last few years. So-called 'urban' and 'peri-urban' agricultures are seen as potentially very significant in supplying growing urban populations with affordable and relatively secure food supplies. This is a key area which has been identified by policy-makers for further investigation, not least in relation to the disadvantages and limits pertaining to such agriculture, as well as the obvious advantages.

5.1 Urbanization in developing countries

David Satterthwaite

URBAN TRENDS

More than two-thirds of the world's urban population is now in Africa, Asia, Latin America and the Caribbean. Between 1950 and 1995, the urban population of these regions grew more than fivefold – from 346 million to 1.8 billion (Table 1). Although Asia and Africa still have more rural than urban dwellers, they both have very large urban populations. Asia alone has close to half the world's urban population – with more than half of its urban population within just two countries, China and India. Africa now has a larger urban population than Northern America; so too does Latin America and the Caribbean – which also has close to three-quarters of its population living in urban centres.

GROWTH OF LARGE CITIES

Two aspects of this rapid growth in urban population have been the increase in the number of large cities and the historically unprecedented size of the largest cities (see Table 2). Just two centuries ago, there were only two 'million-cities' worldwide (i.e. cities with one million or more inhabitants): London and Beijing (Peking). By 1990 there were 293 and most were in developing

Table 1 Trends and projections in urban populations by region, 1950–2010

Region	1950	1965	1980	1995	2010*
Urban population (millions of inhabitants)					
Africa	33	66	130	251	458
Asia	244	426	706	1192	1816
Latin America and the Caribbean	69	133	233	350	463
Rest of the world**	404	559	685	781	849
Percentage of population living in urban areas					
Africa	14.6	20.7	27.3	34.9	43.6
Asia	17.4	22.4	26.7	34.7	43.6
Latin America and the Caribbean	41.4	53.4	64.9	73.4	78.6
Rest of the world**	55.3	64.1	70.5	74.2	78.0
Proportion of the world's urban population living in					
Africa	4.4	5.6	7.4	9.8	12.8
Asia	32.5	36.0	40.3	46.3	50.6
Latin America and the Caribbean	9.2	11.2	13.3	13.6	12.9
Rest of the world**	53.9	47.2	39.0	30.4	23.7

Source: Hardoy *et al.*, 2001, drawing on United Nations, 1998
Notes: *Projected. The most recent population data for most countries are from censuses held around 1990 and it will take until 2002 or later before there is new census data from enough countries to have an accurate idea of the scale of urban change during the 1990s. There is also a group of countries (mostly in Africa) for which there has been no census data since the 1970s or early 1980s so all figures for their urban (and rural) populations are based on estimates and projections. **Rest of the world includes all countries in Europe, Northern America and Oceania.

Table 2 The distribution of large cities by region, 1950–1990*

Region	1800	1900	1950	1990
Number of 'million-cities'				
Africa	0	0	2	27
Asia	1	4	26	126
Latin America and the Caribbean	0	0**	7	38
Rest of the world	1	13	45	102
Number of the world's 100 largest cities				
Africa	4	2	3	6
Asia	64	22	32	44
Latin America and the Caribbean	3	5	8	16
Rest of the world	29	71	57	34

	Average size of the world's 100 largest cities for different years			
	1800	1900	1950	1990
Number of inhabitants	187,000	724,000	2.1 million	5.3 million

Sources: Hardoy *et al.*, 2001; data for 1950 and 1990 from United Nations (1998); data from 1800 and 1900 from the authors' analysis of some 250 censuses, and from Chandler and Fox, 1974.
Notes: *1990 is still the latest year for which there are statistics based on census data for most of the world's large cities. **Some estimates suggest that Rio de Janeiro had reached one million inhabitants by 1900 while other sources suggest that it had just under one million.

countries. Many have populations that grew more than tenfold between 1950 and 1990 – including Abidjan, Amman, Bhopal, Curitiba, Dar es Salaam, Dhaka, Harare, Khartoum, Kinshasa, Lagos, Nairobi, Lusaka, Maputo and Seoul.

Table 2 also highlights how the size of the world's largest cities has grown dramatically over the last 200 years: in 1800, the average size of the world's 100 largest cities was less than 200,000 inhabitants, but by 1990 it was over five million. By 1990, there were 34 urban agglomerations within the world which had more than five million inhabitants, including 18 in Asia, 6 in Latin America and 2 in Africa. By this date, there were also 12 'mega-cities' with 10 million or more inhabitants: 7 in Asia, 3 in Latin America and 2 in the United States.

KEY CHARACTERISTICS OF URBAN CHANGE

These statistics give the impression of very rapid urbanization that is focused on large cities. But some care is needed when making generalizations, because there is such diversity in the scale and nature of urban change between nations and, within nations, over time. Also, for the larger and more populous nations, such diversity in urban trends occurs between different regions. In addition, certain general points need to be highlighted.

More than half the world's population does not live in cities   Although it is often stated that more than half the world's population live in cities, this is not the case. According to the most recent UN statistics (United Nations, 2000), the world's urban population will only come to exceed its rural population around 2007. The proportion of people living in cities is also considerably below the proportion living in urban centres as a significant proportion of the urban population lives in urban centres too small to be called cities (because they lack the size and the economic, administrative or political status that being a city implies).

Less urbanized populations, smaller cities　In all regions of the world, most of the urban population live in urban areas with less than one million inhabitants. 'Mega-cities' with 10 million or more inhabitants had less than 3 per cent of the world's population in 1990. Even in Latin America with its unusually high concentration of population in mega-cities, more than four times as many people live in urban areas with fewer than one million inhabitants than in 'mega-cities'.

Most of the world's mega-cities had slower population growth rates during the 1980s (the last decade for which census data are available). In addition, the more decentralized patterns of urban development evident in many nations suggest that the proportion of the world's population living in mega-cities will not increase much. Mega-cities can only develop in countries with large non-agricultural economies and large national populations; most nations have too small a population and too weak an urban-based economy to support a mega-city.

Although the size of the world's largest cities is historically unprecedented, most of the largest cities are significantly smaller than had been expected. For instance, Mexico City is likely to have around 18 million people in 2000 – not the 31 million people predicted 20 years ago (United Nations, 1980). Calcutta is likely to have had fewer than 13 million inhabitants in 2000, not the 40–50 million people that had been predicted during the 1970s (Brown, 1974). Most very large cities experienced slow-downs in their population growth rate in the last inter-census period for which there are data, with many having more people moving out than moving in (including Calcutta, Buenos Aires, Sao Paulo, Mexico City and Rio de Janeiro).

A range of factors helps explain this. For most large developing-country cities, one reason was slow economic growth (or economic decline), so fewer people moved there; this helps explain slower population growth rates for many cities in Africa and Latin America during the 1980s. A second factor was the capacity of cities outside the very large metropolitan centres to attract a significant proportion of new investment. In various nations that have had effective decentralization, urban authorities in smaller cities have more resources and capacity to compete for new investment. Trade liberalization and a greater emphasis on exports during the 1980s also increased the comparative advantage of many smaller cities. Meanwhile, advances in transport and communications lessened the advantages for businesses of concentrating in the largest cities. A third factor, evident in many cities, was lower rates of natural increase, as fertility rates came down.

However, there are also large cities whose population growth rates remained high during the 1980s – for instance, Dhaka (Bangladesh) and many cities in India and China, and strong economic performance by such cities is the most important factor in explaining this. In other regions, especially in sub-Saharan Africa, there are various cities whose population growth was much boosted by the movement there of people displaced by wars, civil strife or drought, but in many instances this is largely a temporary movement, not a permanent one.

The concentration of large cities in large economies　There is an economic logic to the location of large cities. In 1990, the world's five largest economies (United States of America, China, Japan, Germany and the Russian Federation) had half of the world's mega-cities (with 10 million plus inhabitants) and more than a third of its 'million-cities' Within developing countries, the largest cities were concentrated in the largest economies (which also tend to be among the most populous countries): Brazil and Mexico in Latin America; China, India, Indonesia and the Republic of Korea in Asia. These nations had all but one of the 'mega-cities' in these regions and nearly half of all the 'million-cities'. When data from censuses held in 2000 or 2001 become available, they are likely to show that this concentration of large cities in the largest economies has increased.

There is a strong association between a nation's per capita income and its level of urbanization. Most of the nations with the most rapid increase in their level of urbanization between 1960 and 1990 were also the nations with the most rapid economic growth (UNCHS, 1996).

Beyond a rural–urban division   Perhaps too much emphasis is given to the fact that the world is soon to become predominantly urban, because of the imprecision in defining 'urban' and 'rural' populations, and the large differences between countries in the criteria used to define urban centres. These differences limit the validity of inter-country comparisons. For instance, it is not comparing like with like if we compare the 'level of urbanization' (the percentage of population in urban centres) of a nation that defines urban centres as all settlements with 20,000 or more inhabitants with another that defines urban centres as all settlements with more than 1,000 inhabitants. The comparison is particularly inaccurate if a large section of the population lives in settlements of between 1,000 and 19,999 inhabitants (which is the case in most nations). The proportion of the world's population living in urban areas could be increased or decreased by several percentage points simply by China, India or a few of the other most populous nations changing their definition of what is an urban centre. Thus, the proportion of the world's population currently living in urban centres is best considered not as a precise percentage (i.e. 47.0 per cent in 2000) but as being between 40 and 55 per cent, depending on the criteria used to define what is an 'urban centre'.

There is a tendency in the discussions of urban change to concentrate too much on changes in levels of urbanization, and too little on the economic and political transformations that have underpinned urbanization – at a global scale, the very large increase in the size of the world's economy and the changes in the relative importance of different sectors and of international trade – and how this has changed the spatial distribution of economic activities, and the social and spatial distribution of incomes. The distinction between 'rural' and 'urban' populations has some utility in highlighting differences in economic structure, population concentration and political status (as virtually all local governments are located in urban centres) but it is not a precise distinction.

First of all, large sections of the 'rural' population work in non-agricultural activities or derive some of their income from such activities, or commute to urban areas. Distinctions between rural and urban areas are also becoming almost obsolete around many major cities as economic activity spreads outwards – for instance around Jakarta (McGee, 1987), around Bangkok and within Thailand's Eastern Seaboard, around Mumbai (and the corridor linking it to Pune), in the Pearl River Delta in China and in the Red River Delta in Vietnam (World Bank, 1999).

Conversely, large sections of the 'urban' population work in agriculture or in urban enterprises that serve rural demand. In addition, discussing 'rural' and 'urban' areas separately can ignore the multiple flows between them in terms of migration movements and the flow of goods, income, capital and information (Tacoli, 1998). Many low-income households draw goods or income from urban and rural sources.

An uncertain urban future   Most publications discussing urban change assume that the world will continue to urbanize far into the future. Such assumptions should be viewed with caution. Given the historic association between economic growth and urbanization, a steady increase in the level of urbanization in low-income nations is only likely to take place if they also have steadily growing economies. While stronger and more buoyant economies for the world's lower-income nations should be a key development goal, the current prospects for most such nations are hardly encouraging, within the current world economic system. Many of the lowest-income nations have serious problems with political instability or civil war, and most have no obvious 'comparative advantage' on which to build an economy that prospers and thus urbanizes.

There are also grounds for doubting whether a large proportion of the world's urban population will come to live in very large cities. As noted above, many of the largest cities have slow population growth rates and much new investment is going to particular medium-sized cities well located in relation to the largest cities and to transport and communications systems. In addition, in prosperous regions with advanced transport and communications systems, rural inhabitants and enterprises can enjoy standards of infrastructure and services, and access to information, that historically have only been available in urban areas. Thus, both low-income and high-income nations may have smaller than expected increases in their urban populations, although for very different reasons.

GUIDE TO FURTHER READING

This chapter draws on a longer description of urban change in Hardoy, Jorge E., Mitlin, Diana and Satterthwaite, David (2001) *Environmental Problems in an Urbanizing World*, London: Earthscan Publications.

For more details of urban change within each of the world's regions, see UNCHS (*Habitat*) (1996) *An Urbanizing World: Global Report on Human Settlements, 1996*, Oxford and New York: Oxford University Press.

For statistics on the scale and nature of urban change, see the biennial publication of *World Urbanization Prospects* by the United Nations Population Division. This summary drew on United Nations (1998) *World Urbanization Prospects: The 1996 Revision*, Population Division, Department of Economic and Social Affairs, United Nations ST/ESA/SER.A/170, 190pp and United Nations (2000) *World Urbanization Prospects: The 1999 Revision*, Population Division, Department of Economic and Social Affairs, ESA/P/WP.161, 128pp.

For a discussion of urban change and world cities, see Sassen, Saskia (1994) *Cities in a World Economy*, London and New Delhi: Pine Forge Press, Thousand Oaks, 157pp.

REFERENCES

Brown, L. (1974) *In the Human Interest*, New York: W.W. Norton and Co.

Chandler, T. and Fox, G. (1974) *3000 Years of Urban Growth*, New York and London: Academic Press.

McGee, T.G. (1987) 'Urbanization or Kotadesasi: the emergence of new regions of economic interaction in Asia', Working paper, Honolulu: East West Center, June.

Tacoli, C. (1998), *Bridging the Divide: Rural–Urban Interactions and Livelihood Strategies*, Gatekeeper Series No. 77, London: IIED Sustainable Agriculture and Rural Livelihoods Programme, 17pp.

United Nations (1980) *Urban, Rural and City Population, 1950–2000, as assessed in 1978*, ESA/P/WP.66, June, New York, 38pp.

World Bank (1999), *Entering the 21st Century: World Development Report 1999/2000*, Oxford and New York: Oxford University Press.

5.2 World cities and development

Robert B. Potter

INTRODUCTION

The dominant role that leading cities play in the current process of global development has recently been given explicit expression in the concept of the 'world city'. Although nebulous in size-definitional terms, the idea is that certain cities dominate world economic affairs and trans-actions. At one level, this is a very straightforward and obvious proposition, and indeed, Peter Hall drew attention to the significance of what he specifically referred to as world cities in the devel-oped world in the mid-1960s (see Hall, 1966). However, the contemporary relevance of world cities has been elaborated by the American social scientist and academic planning and development analyst, John Friedmann (see Friedmann and Wolff, 1982; Friedmann, 1986; see also Friedmann, 1995). In the 15 years since Friedmann's original work served to make the term popular, a number of other writers have contributed to what Friedmann (1995) now refers to as the 'world city para-digm' (see King, 1990; Sassen, 1991, 1996; Knox and Taylor, 1995). However, both King and Sassen have written under the modified title the 'global city'.

THE BASIC IDEAS

However, as originally formulated, even Friedmann (1995) noted that there was an element of ambiguity attached to what at that juncture he referred to as 'the world city hypothesis'. Was it heuristic, providing a way of asking pertinent questions about cities in general, or was it a state-ment about a particular group or class of cities which displayed distinctive characteristics? In the paper Friedmann published in 1996 explaining 'the world city hypothesis', he started by noting that it was only in recent years that the study of cities had come to be directly connected with the dispo-sition of the world economy (Friedmann, 1986). It was emphasized that certain cities had become the 'basing points' for international capitalism, and that the world city hypothesis was essentially about the spatial arrangements involved in the new international division of labour. In other words, world cities served to articulate regional, national and international economies into a global economic system. Of course, the argument is far from new and represents a central proposition of classical dependency theory according to Frank (1966).

In his early formulation, seven interrelated theses were put forward by Friedmann (1986) concerning what he saw as the nature of world cities.

1 The form and extent of a city's integration with the world economy and its role in the new international division of labour, will be decisive for any structural changes within it.
2 Key cities throughout the world are used by global capital as 'basing points' in the spatial orga-nization and articulation of production and markets. Thus, the resulting linkages make it possible to arrange world cities into a complex hierarchy.
3 The global control functions of world cities are directly reflected in the structure and dynam-ics of their production sectors and employment.
4 World cities are major sites for the concentration and accumulation of international capital.

5 World cities are points of destination for large numbers of both domestic and/or international migrants.

6 World city formation brings into focus the major contradictions of industrial capitalism, among them spatial and class polarization (giving rise to cores and peripheries and semi-peripheries at the global scale, and developed and less-developed regions at the national scale).

7 World city growth generates social costs at rates that tend to exceed the fiscal capacity of the state (for example, those that arise from the rapid influx of poor workers into world cities and the massive needs for housing, education and health that this generates).

THE PATTERN OF WORLD CITIES IDENTIFIED BY FRIEDMANN

When Friedmann proceeded to actually identify what he regarded to be the system of world cities at the global scale, he distinguished between primary and secondary world cities in terms of their overall impact and influence. These two classes were not rigorously defined. He also distinguished between those occurring in what he referred to as 'core' and 'semi-peripheral' countries. Whilst most of the primary world cities, such as London, Paris, Rotterdam, Frankfurt, Zurich, New York, Chicago, Los Angeles and Tokyo were to be found located in the 'core' countries of the developed world, Singapore and Sao Paulo were recognized as primary world cities in the semi-periphery. In addition, Hong Kong, Bangkok, Taipei, Manila, Seoul, Mexico City, Caracas, Rio de Janeiro, Buenos Aires and Johannesburg were recognized as part of an emerging network of secondary world cities in the less developed world (Friedmann, 1995). In short, world cities may be seen as points of articulation in a TNC-dominated capitalist global system. Thus, Africa is the least developed continent, and it had the smallest number of world cities: just the one in the form of Johannesburg. African cities show relatively low numbers of international business and other headquarters (see Simon, 1993).

POLICY IMPLICATIONS

As a descriptive statement, the world city hypothesis or paradigm seems little more that a statement of the obvious. In stressing that the salience of cities derives much more from their roles within the global capitalist system, rather than their size, the approach performs a more valuable function in a fast-globalizing world order. If one links the idea of world cities to the joint processes of global convergence and divergence, then clear policy implications start to emerge and the framework becomes a valuable tool for the analysis of development patterns and processes (see Potter and Lloyd-Evans, 1998, in relation to this specific point).

There is the implication, for example, that uneven development is particularly likely to be associated with developing countries, and that their paths to development in the late twentieth century will be infinitely more difficult than those that faced developed countries in former times. This argument has been reviewed in the case of poor countries by Lasuen (1973). He started from the premise that in the modern world, large cities are the principal adopters of innovations, so that natural growth poles become evermore associated with the upper levels of the urban system. Lasuen also observed that the spatial spread of innovations is generally likely to be slower in developing countries, due to the frequent existence of single plant industries, the generally poorer levels of infrastructural provision and, in some instances, the lack of political will.

Thus, developing countries facing spatial inequalities have two policy alternatives. The first is to allow the major urban centres to adopt innovations before the previous ones have spread through the national settlement system. The second option is to attempt to hold and delay the adoption of further innovations at the top of the urban system, until the filtering down of previous growth-inducing changes has occurred. This may sound theoretical, but these options represent the two major strategies which can be followed by developing nations. The former policy will result in increasing economic dualism, but also, some would argue, the chance of a higher overall rate of economic growth. On the other hand, the latter option will lead to increasing regional equity, but potentially lower rates of national growth. Most developing countries have adopted policies close to the former alternative of unrestrained innovation adoption, seeking to maximize growth rather than equity. This all intimates the problems which are inherent in circular or cumulative growth in particular global urban places.

It is just this sort of patterning of entrained growth that was identified by Pred (1973, 1977) in his examination of the historical growth and development of the urban system of the United States. Pred noted that the growth of the mercantile city was based on circular or cumulative causation, linked to multiplier effects. Further, Pred argued that the growth of large cities was based on their interdependence, so that large city stability has been characteristic. However, Pred maintained that key innovation adoption sequences were not always hierarchic, frequently flowing from a medium-sized city up the urban hierarchy, or from one large city to another. Pred (1977) looked at the headquarters of TNCs in post-war America, and stressed the close correspondence with the uppermost levels of the urban system. Thus, growth within the contemporary urban system is increasingly linked to the locational decisions of multinational firms and government organizations. The recognition of global cities suggests that such patterns of uneven and non-hierarchical development are highly applicable at the international and global scales.

A modern expression of the value of the concept of the world city is provided by airline transport and the formation of airport hubs. The idea that transport is a key dimension in the development of world cities in the contemporary context is an interesting one which is relatively easy to exemplify, together with its developmental implications. The idea that globalized improvements in transport and communications are leading to the intensification of the functional importance of certain places or nodes is confirmed if we look at the evolution of airline networks in the 1990s. This has been considered by Keeling (1999), who produced a map showing the international air connections between the major cities. The map opposite shows the number of outward and return non-stop flights per week from various nodes. The outcome illustrates all too clearly the predominance of three global cities, namely London, New York and Tokyo, and the role these cities play as dominant global hubs. Together, these three cities receive 36.5 per cent of global non-stop flights to the world airline network's 20 dominant cities. Beyond these three cities, Paris, Cairo, Singapore, Los Angeles and Miami appear as secondary global hubs, and Johannesburg, Moscow, Bombay, Bangkok, Hong Kong, Sydney, Sao Paulo, Rio de Janeiro and Buenos Aires as secondary hubs. The flows mapped out in the figure show just how marked is the concentration. The essential similarity between this map of airline flows and a figure simply depicting world cities is highly apparent. This is a practical affirmation that increasing globalization is leading to strong local concentration within continents and that it can be seen as increasing the differences which exist between urban nodes. Thus, Johannesburg is the single airline hub in Africa south of the Sahara, and only Cairo stands out as a hub in the north of the continent.

But, of course, such patterns are most certainly not fixed for all time. The pattern changes. Thus, Friedmann (1995) suggests that both Rio de Janeiro and Buenos Aires have both lost significant potential as world cities over the last 10 to 15 years, and that they should no longer be listed among

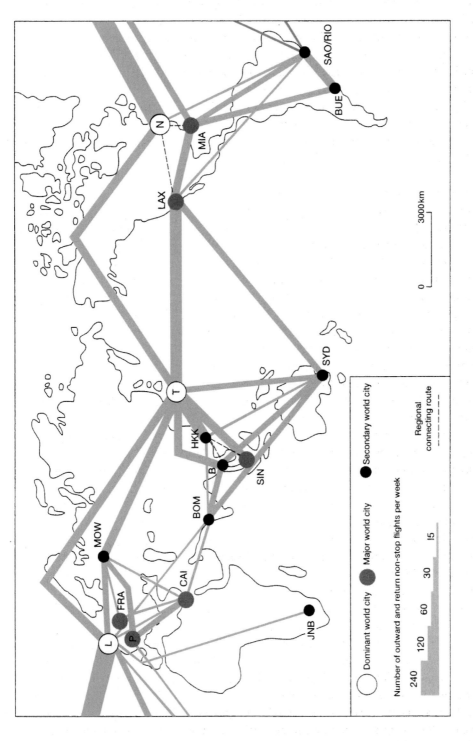

Dominant flows on the world airline network in the mid-1990s

Source: Potter *et al*., 1999, Figure 4.3

even the third rank of world cities. As with all aspects of modern capitalist development in a neo-liberal world order, generally gradual and incremental changes are in-built to what otherwise appears to be a system based on inertia and stability. Interestingly in this context, Friedmann (1995) relates how he was co-opted by the Government of Singapore, in an effort to find ways of enhancing the city state's standing as a world city.

GUIDE TO FURTHER READING

Friedmann, J. (1986) 'The world city hypothesis', *Development and Change* 17: 69–83. The article in which Friedmann promulgated, and made popular, the idea of the world city, arguing that only recently had the study of cities become directly linked to the examination of the world economy.

Friedmann, J. (1995) 'Where we stand: a decade of world city research', Chapter 2 in P. Knox and P. Taylor (eds), *World Cities in a World-System*, Cambridge: Cambridge University Press, pp. 21–47. An eclectic essay exploring the genesis and contemporary development of the global city hypothesis.

Keeling, D.J. (1995) 'Transport and the world city paradigm', in P. Knox and P. Taylor (eds) *World Cities in a World-System*, Cambridge: Cambridge University Press, pp. 155–31. Argues that the role of transport linkages in the shaping of the world city system has been underexplored and, using contemporary data, looks at the current hierarchy of world airline network nodes.

Potter, R.B. and Lloyd-Evans, S. (1998) *The City in the Developing World*, Harlow: Prentice Hall. A basic introduction to urban dynamics and urban structuring in developing countries. The book embraces an overview of the nature of urban systems in the Third World and as such, the world city concept is overviewed.

REFERENCES

Frank, A.G. (1966) *Capitalism and Underdevelopment in Latin America*, New York: Monthly Review Press.

Friedmann, J. (1986) 'The world city hypothesis', *Development and Change* 17: 69–83.

Friedmann, J. (1995) 'Where we stand: a decade of world city research', Chapter 2 in P. Knox and P. Taylor (eds) *World Cities in a World-System*, Cambridge: Cambridge University Press, pp. 21–47.

Friedmann, J. and Wolff, G. (1982) 'World city formation: an agenda for research and action', *International Journal of Urban and Regional Research* 6: 309–43.

Hall, P. (1966) *The World Cities*, London: Weidenfeld and Nicolson.

Keeling, D.J. (1999) 'Transport and the world city paradigm', in P. Knox and P. Taylor (eds) *World Cities in a World-System*, Cambridge: Cambridge University Press, pp. 115–31.

King, A.D. (1990) *Global Cities: Post-Imperialism and Internationalization of London*, London: Routledge and Kegan Paul.

Knox, P. and Taylor, P. (eds) (1995) *World Cities in a World-System*, Cambridge: Cambridge University Press.

Lasuen, J.R. (1973) 'Urbanisation and development: the temporal interaction between geographical and sectoral clusters', *Urban Studies* 10: 163–88.

Potter, R.B. and Lloyd-Evans, S. (1998) *The City in the Developing World*, Harlow: Prentice Hall.

Pred, A. (1973) 'The growth and development of systems of cities in advanced economies', in A. Pred and G. Tornqvist (eds) *Systems of Cities and Information Flows: Two Essays*, Lund Studies in Geography, Series B 38: 9–82.

Pred, A. (1977) *City-Systems in Advanced Economies*, London: Hutchinson.

Sassen, S. (1991) *The Global City*, Princeton NJ: Princeton University Press.

Sassen, S. (1996) 'The global city', in S. Fanstein and S. Campbell (eds) *Readings in Urban Theory*, Oxford: Blackwell, pp. 61–71.

Simon, D. (1993) *Cities, Capital and Development: African Cities in the World Economy*, London: Belhaven.

5.3 Prosperity or poverty? Wealth, inequality and deprivation in urban areas

Carole Rakodi

Cities and towns hold out great promise, but also can be unforgiving environments; opportunities abound, but the risks are great; the successful live well, but life for those who do not succeed is a struggle, marked by poverty, ill-health and insecurity.

PROSPERITY OR POVERTY?

The correlation between urbanization and economic development, statistics which show the disproportionate share of GDP generated in urban areas, and the modern buildings and ostentatious wealth of central business districts, industrial estates, shopping malls and high-income residential areas combine to reinforce a view of cities as 'engines of economic growth' and sites for wealth generation. Many do not regard urban poverty as a serious problem. In earlier models, the path to development was expected to be industrialization and urbanization. For a time, progress appeared to be promising. Protected industrialization and the expansion of public-sector activities resulted in increased formal-sector wage employment, mostly in urban areas.

Not all entrants to the urban labour force could obtain full-time employment or earn wages sufficient to support a family. However, the good prospects that were thought to encourage high rates of rural–urban migration despite rising unemployment led to a perception of urban areas as favoured environments. By the 1970s, it was clear that the basic needs of many, especially in Africa and South Asia, were not being met: trickle down was not working as expected, especially for those living in rural areas. An influential explanation was Michael Lipton's 'urban bias' thesis. Lipton (1977) asserted that the major mistake in development policy was the 'urban bias' in expenditure and pricing policies. Failure to recognize the necessity of increased productivity in peasant agriculture for both sustained economic growth and increased prosperity for the majority of the population had, he suggested, led to a disproportionate emphasis on industrialization and thus concentration of investment in urban infrastructure. The political importance of concentrated urban populations reinforced this pattern and helped to explain the widespread adoption of cheap food policies. Subsidized food was paid for by low producer prices, which constrained the production and marketing of food crops and maintained small farmers in poverty, further fuelling out-migration.

The extent to which urban bias was a valid and sufficient explanation of development failure (especially persistent rural poverty) was questioned from the outset. It was noted that not all countries had an anti-rural policy bias; that other identities and political interests (ethnic, religious, class) cut across the rural–urban divide; and that rural/urban boundaries are arbitrary (Varshney, 1993). Thus, although there was much truth in Lipton's analysis, which average income/expenditure figures for urban and rural areas appeared to bear out, the 'urban bias' thesis and the use of averages also served to conceal a more complex reality.

WEALTH, INEQUALITY AND POVERTY

While some urban residents were able to secure employment, housing and access to services, many were not. Increasingly, since the 1960s, wage employment, the formal housing development process and public provision of infrastructure have failed to keep up with population growth. An increasing proportion of workers was forced, in the absence of social security systems, to seek economic opportunities in the so-called informal sector. Residents unable to rent or buy in the formal housing sectors were forced to become house owners or tenants in informal settlements, with a variety of insecure tenure arrangements. Although physical infrastructure and social facilities were available, many poor households could not access them and had to rely on self-provision (wells, pit latrines), the purchase of relatively costly private-sector services (water from vendors) or illegal tapping of publicly provided services (electricity, water).

The urban bias thesis, which labelled urban areas as 'wealthy' and rural areas as 'poor', failed to recognize high degrees of urban inequality and the exclusion of a large proportion of residents from the wealth, opportunities and good living conditions supposedly typical of urban areas. Nevertheless, it was widely accepted, and the economic reforms of the 1980s had, as a result, a strong 'rural bias'. The need to address trade and budget deficits led, in countries subject to structural adjustment policies, to trade and financial liberalization, the abolition of price controls and subsidies, and the commercialization of physical and social services. The effect, deliberately, was to remove 'urban bias' and other economic 'distortions' in order to encourage agricultural production and exports of all kinds. The results, in urban areas, included falling real incomes and job losses from all formal employment sectors. Thus much of the brunt of typical structural adjustment policies has been borne by the urban poor and the gap between average rural and urban incomes has, more or less, been eliminated, undermining the continued validity of the 'urban bias' explanation for underdevelopment (Varshney, 1993).

Before examining some evidence on the extent of inequality and poverty, and trends in the 1980s and 1990s, a few methodological difficulties must be mentioned. The most common measure of poverty is household consumption or expenditure. An absolute poverty line represents the cost of a basket of necessities, including food (the food poverty line) and other needs. However, money-metric measures of poverty have limitations, many of which adversely affect comparisons of the incidence of poverty in urban and rural areas. In particular, prices and patterns of consumption vary between regions. However, many poverty assessments do not allow for differences in prices between urban and rural areas, and even more fail to allow for differences in consumption bundles, especially the need for the urban poor to pay for housing and services which may not be monetized in rural areas, as well as the higher costs of transportation (especially for journeys to work). Further, the poorest urban residents often live in temporary accommodation or on the streets and may not be captured in sample surveys. Lastly, changes in, and the arbitrary nature of, urban boundaries affect estimates of poverty incidence in urban and rural areas, either excluding large numbers of residents in informal settlements beyond urban boundaries or including rural households living within them (Rakodi, 1995; UNCHS, 1996).

Inequality is generally greater in urban than rural areas. For example, in Sri Lanka the Gini coefficient for urban areas in 1985/6 was 0.62 compared to 0.55 for rural areas (Gunatilleke and Perera, 1994). The incidence of poverty varies, but was at least a third higher in rural than in urban areas in most countries in the 1980s and 1990s (UNCHS, 1996: 113). Trends often show urban poverty shadowing rural poverty. In countries where overall levels of poverty have decreased, such as India, the incidence of urban poverty has also decreased (Haddad et al., 1999). Economic growth in the industrializing countries of Asia was associated with declines in both urban and rural poverty, but the economic crisis of the late 1990s precipitated a dramatic increase, especially in urban poverty, as formal-sector jobs were lost. In Indonesia, for example, where there had been a steady decline in urban poverty from 39 per cent in 1976 to 10 per cent in 1996, the level tripled to 30 per cent by mid-1998 (Firman, 1999: 76). In Zambia, during the long economic decline of the 1970s and 1980s, urban poverty increased more rapidly than rural poverty.

The contribution of urban poverty to total poverty depends on both the incidence of poverty in urban and rural areas and the extent of urbanization. It thus varies from 8 per cent in Uganda (where only 11 per cent of the population is urban) to 57 per cent in Brazil (where 75 per cent of the population is urban). Although still small in many countries, the contribution of urban to overall poverty generally grew in the 1980s and early 1990s (Haddad *et al.*, 1999). Average consumption figures and estimates of poverty incidence thus appear to show a lesser problem of poverty in urban than in rural areas, but high inequality and trends showing a shift in the locus of poverty demonstrate that these indicators conceal much of the reality.

DEPRIVATION, VULNERABILITY AND INSECURITY

All headcount measures of poverty have been challenged on the basis that, even if refined, they do not recognize the life-cycle trajectories of households and therefore do not distinguish between permanent and transient poverty. Moreover, a consumption-based conceptualization of poverty may not coincide with the perceptions of the poor themselves, who define poverty to encompass not merely low incomes, but also deprivation and insecurity.

In high-density urban environments, housing and utilities of adequate standard are critical to health (Satterthwaite, 1997). Their availability is an outcome of the interaction between private provision and public policy. In the monetized economies of towns and cities, access to housing, utilities and social services is determined not just by availability, however, but also by household financial resources. To the poor, good-quality accommodation, education and healthcare are unaffordable. Their access to secure tenure, services and social facilities may, moreover, be constrained by social and political discrimination, affecting groups differentially by gender, ethnicity, caste, religion and so on.

Some basic health indicators, such as childhood mortality, are generally lower in urban areas. However, in some countries the reverse is true for other indicators, such as morbidity rates from infectious diseases (Haddad *et al.*, 1999). Higher population densities, combined with absent or inadequate piped water, drains, sanitation and refuse collection, mean that urban populations are more at risk from faecal contamination and other environmental hazards (Satterthwaite, 1997). The high incidence of infectious diseases is associated with acute malnutrition, the absolute and relative incidence of which increased faster in urban than rural areas in many countries between the late 1980s and mid-1990s. Thus although the incidence of both poverty and under-nutrition remains lower in towns and cities, their locus is changing from rural to urban areas (Haddad *et al.*, 1999).

Moreover, there is greater variation in rates of mortality and morbidity and nutritional status *amongst* urban than rural populations, consonant with the greater inequality referred to above. Although overall levels of morbidity and mortality due to disease or injuries and accidents vary between cities, all are greater in poor areas: studies suggest that death and disease rates for infants and children are between 2 and 10 times higher in deprived than non-deprived areas of cities (Stephens, 1996).

Insecurity is related to vulnerability: the sensitivity of well-being to a changing environment and households' ability to respond to negative changes. Households have assets that may be drawn down in times of need and built up in better times to provide defences against shocks and stresses and to improve well-being. Assets of particular importance to urban households may be physical (housing, equipment for economic activities), human (labour power, skills, good health), financial (savings, credit), social (membership of formal or informal social organizations, which provide information, contacts and support) or political (channels of representation and influence) (Moser, 1998; Rakodi, 1999). Households which lack assets that they can mobilize in the face of hardship are more vulnerable to impoverishment. The assets available to households are determined in part by their characteristics and strategies. However, the potential for accessing and building up assets is also influenced by wider circumstances, including the operation of labour, land and housing markets; levels of crime and violence; arrangements for infrastructure and service provision; and the regulatory regimes governing urban activities, which may discriminate against self-help housing construction or informal-sector economic activities.

Access to labour market opportunities is a key element in the livelihood strategies of urban households. Wider economic circumstances, trade and industrial policies, availability of land and infrastructure, and the characteristics of the local labour market influence the opportunities available. Access to them depends on the resources available to and constraints on particular households: education and skills, dependency ratios, health status, relative location of affordable residential areas and employment centres, and access to public transport. Poor households with adults in work tend to depend on informal-sector activities, especially services, or on casual employment. They are, however, characterized by high unemployment rates amongst adults and also include households with limited labour resources: young households with children, especially single mothers; and those containing disabled, sick or elderly adults.

Much of the discussion so far has referred to households as though consumption is equally distributed amongst all their members, but there is extensive evidence to show that this is not the case: some individuals within households are disadvantaged in terms of access to resources, including the economically inactive (some elderly people, women and children) and unpaid family workers (especially domestic servants).

In times of wider economic difficulties or in the face of household-level shocks, such as bereavement, illness or retrenchment, some households are better equipped than others to defend themselves against impoverishment. The key strategy seems to be diversification, so that households with multiple adults of working age, more than one source of income, an asset such as a house which can generate income, urban or rural land for food production, and urban or rural social networks that can be called upon for support, cope better with economic crisis (Rakodi, 1995). For some, impoverishment may be temporary, and improved well-being may follow national economic recovery or the development of alternative income sources. Others, however, may be forced to sell physical assets, move into inferior accommodation, send children out to work, reduce the quality and quantity of food consumed, postpone medical treatment, and/or withdraw from reciprocity arrangements, such as rotating savings and credit associations. The chronic poor are unable to take advantage of the opportunities offered in cities and become trapped in a vicious circle of poverty and deprivation.

CONCLUSION: POLICY RESPONSES

The most powerful policies with a direct or indirect impact on urban poverty are national economic and social policies. Their effects are mediated through markets and through the activities of local government, which has varying capacity to adopt pro-poor policies. The urban poor depend heavily on their assets of labour and human capital, tying them strongly into the money economy and labour markets. Access to housing and capital assets for informal economic activities is also important to their livelihoods. The role of social networks and the ways in which local political processes determine access by the poor to resources and assets are less well understood. However, increased understanding of poverty and vulnerability, and identification of constraints on the ability of individuals, households and communities to access key assets and services provide pointers to appropriate policy interventions.

GUIDE TO FURTHER READING

There are several special issues of journals on the topic of urban poverty: *Habitat International* 19(4) (1995); *IDS Bulletin* 28(3) (1997); *Environment and Urbanisation* 7(1/2), (1995); and *Asian Development Review* 12(1) (1994). See also Jones, S. and Nelson, N. (eds) (1999) *Urban Poverty in Africa: From Understanding to Action*, London: IT Publications.

REFERENCES

Firman, T. (1999) 'Indonesian cities under the "Krismon"', *Cities* 16(2): 69–82.

Gunatilleke, G. and Perera, M. (1994) 'Urban poverty in Sri Lanka: critical issues and policy measures', *Asian Development Review* 12(1): 153–203.

Haddad, L., Ruel, M.T. and Garrett, J. (1999) 'Are urban poverty and undernutrition growing? Some newly assembled evidence', *World Development* 27(11): 1891–904.

Lipton, M. (1977) *Why Poor People Stay Poor: Urban Bias in World Development*, London: Temple Smith.

Moser, C.O.N. (1998) 'The asset vulnerability framework: reassessing urban poverty reduction strategies', *World Development* (26)1: 1–19.

Rakodi, C. (1995) 'Poverty lines or household strategies? A review of conceptual issues in the study of urban poverty', *Habitat International* 19(4): 407–26.

Rakodi, C. (1999) 'A capital assets framework for analysing household livelihood strategies', *Development Policy Review* 17(3): 315–42.

Satterthwaite, D. (1997) 'Urban poverty: reconsidering its scale and nature', *IDS Bulletin* 28(2): 7–23.

Stephens, C. (1996) 'Healthy cities or unhealthy islands? The health and social implications of urban inequality', *Environment and Urbanisation* 8(2): 9–30.

United Nations Centre for Human Settlements (UNCHS) (1996) *An Urbanizing World: Global Report on Human Settlements, 1996*, New York: Oxford University Press.

Varshney, A. (1993) 'Introduction: urban bias in perspective', in Varshney, A. (ed.) *Beyond Urban Bias*, London: Frank Cass, pp. 1–22.

5.4 Housing the urban poor

Alan Gilbert

Millions of families in the cities of the so-called Third World live in adequate accommodation and some even live in luxury. Unfortunately, the majority of households do not. Most of the poor tend to live in homes without adequate sanitation, with an irregular electricity supply, built of flimsy materials and without adequate security. Millions of others live in more solid and serviced accommodation but in overcrowded conditions. Apart from the households living in shacks or overcrowded tenements and those lacking adequate services, millions more would claim to have a housing problem. They live in houses that do not match their hopes and needs: they have difficulty paying their rent or mortgage, they have a long journey to work, their home is too small, they wish to own a house rather than rent. The Third World housing problem, therefore, is vast (UNCHS, 1996; Potter and Lloyd-Evans, 1998; Gilbert, 1998; Gilbert and Gugler, 1992).

If there can be little doubt about the severity of the problem to be tackled, it is important to recognize that there is no simple way of defining precisely what the housing problem is. While the plight of some is indisputable, any precise definition of the extent of the housing problem is complicated by the fact that it cannot be computed accurately. In any society, the housing problem is defined socially and culturally. The kind of house that may be tolerated in one society may be damned in another; what may be regarded as desirable in one city may be anathema in another.

What constitutes poor housing is not just about physical standards. As John Turner (1968) long ago demonstrated there is little point providing a poor family with a fully serviced, three-bedroom house if the family cannot afford the rent or mortgage payment. The most suitable shelter for such a family may be something rather flimsy. Adequate accommodation is that which fits the circumstances of the family rather than being determined on purely physical grounds. In the short term, at least, a poor family can survive in inadequate shelter; it cannot survive without food or water.

As such, the housing problem is not something that can be solved by architects and planners. It is a multi-faceted problem that can only be helped through raising living standards, improving employment opportunities and applying sensible urban regulations. Unfortunately, the nature of the housing problem in Third World countries is often diagnosed in excessively simple ways. Politicians are often forced to recommend simplistic solutions; newspapers publish exposés of deplorable housing conditions and the public demand action. Unfortunately, as the housing problem is multi-faceted, any simple solution is unlikely to help. Complex problems require complex responses.

The rest of this chapter considers some of the ideas that are held generally about Third World housing and shows how frequently reality diverges from our assumptions.

Homelessness

In general, homelessness is a major problem in relatively few Third World cities. According to the World Bank (1992: 14), only 0.8 per cent of Africans, 0.4 per cent of East Asians and 0.6 per cent of Latin Americans 'sleep outside dwelling units or in temporary shelter in charitable institutions'. It is only in South Asia where homelessness seems to be a significant issue, with 7.8 per cent of the population living on the streets. Beyond the Indian sub-continent, most people in Third World cities have homes. Indeed, the homelessness rate is lower than in industrialized countries (0.9 per cent). The problem in most Third World cities is not the lack of shelter, but the overcrowded, poorly serviced and flimsy accommodation that often constitutes a home (Devas and Rakodi, 1993; Desai, 1995; Potter, 1995; Gilbert, 1998).

Variations in the nature of the housing problem

The housing problem differs considerably between countries both in form and severity. In general, the poorer the country, the worse the urban housing situation: African and Indian shelter standards are far below those of Latin America (UNCHS, 1996). There are also major differences between housing conditions in different cities within the same country. The quality of housing between cities varies according to the nature of the land market, the state of the economy, the ability of governments to provide services, and local climate and topography. The principal housing problems facing one city may be of little significance in another. One city may have poor infrastructure and services although its houses may provide families with plenty of space. In another city, families may suffer from severe overcrowding but have plenty of services.

Urban housing is worse than rural housing

Public concern is often expressed about the state of housing in urban areas, particularly that in the largest cities. It is a reaction both to the huge self-help areas that have developed and to fears about the likely political repercussions. In practice, urban housing conditions are generally far better than those in rural areas. In Colombia, for example, crowding in rural homes is far worse than in the urban areas; every room in the countryside contains an average of 2.3 persons compared to 1.6 persons in urban homes. The differential is still worse when measured in terms of services; only 35 per cent of rural households in Colombia have electricity, compared with 97 per cent of urban homes.

Concern about illegality

Most urban governments are concerned about illegality. When land has been stolen, when green areas have been invaded, or when basic building standards are ignored, illegality can be a vital issue. In many cities, however, the problems of illegality are frequently exaggerated. In many places, housing is illegal only in the sense that it offends the planning regulations (Gilbert and Ward, 1985; Ward, 1982; Baken and van der Linden, 1992). The illegality consists of a lack of services, something that can easily be resolved by the provision of infrastructure. Elsewhere, perfectly decent and well-serviced homes simply lack properly registered title deeds; they are illegal only in a technical sense.

Even where illegality relates to more serious issues such as the ownership of land, the real problem often lies elsewhere. More often than not, land has been invaded with the connivance of the authorities (Gilbert, 1998). Some major cities of Latin America have a large proportion of the population living in illegal settlements, but the quality of that accommodation is actually superior to the housing found in other cities where there is little or no 'illegality' (Gilbert, 1998). The illegality of land and housing tenure, therefore, is only sometimes a problem. In general, most forms of illegality can be removed through the provision of title deeds, the supply of services or the modification of planning regulations.

Concern about tenure

Many Third World governments consider that a key ingredient in housing improvement is to make ownership available to all. They do so because they think that this will win them votes, and they are not entirely wrong in this belief. Certainly, most families aspire to home ownership. They do so because they believe it is a good investment, that the house is something they can leave to their children, that it offers security in times of hardship and that it boosts their self-esteem (Gilbert, 1999). Television and advertising has turned the desire for ownership across the globe into a cultural norm; it is where everyone expects to end up. In addition, home ownership also provides

Table 1 Tenants as a proportion of total households by city, c.1990

City	% tenants	Year
Mexico City	22	1990
Guadalajara	24	1990
Bogotá	42	1993
Lima	17	1991
Santiago	20	1992
Caracas	26	1991
Buenos Aires	13	1991
Delhi	30	1991
Accra	71	1991
Ibadan	54	1987
La Paz	36	1992
Quito	49	1990
Seoul	57	1990
Istanbul	39	1985

Sources: official census figures plus Tipple *et al.*, 1997: 113; Arimah, 1997: 108; Schteingart and Solís, 1996; UNCHS, 1996: 473–6

a series of alternative ways of generating incomes. Rooms can be let and small businesses operated from the premises (Gilbert, 1987).

Even if much of this is true, it does not mean that governments should strive to create universal home ownership. Indeed, there are good reasons why they should not. In particular, they should remember that there will always be some kinds of people who require rental accommodation, even when they have the resources to be home owners. Among these are those planning short stays in the city, those who like living close to the city centre, those without family responsibilities and those who do not want the complications that home ownership brings. Table 1 shows how important renting is in many Third World cities, particularly in West Africa and parts of Asia.

There is also evidence that, although it is not an unproblematic tenure, renting has had a bad press. Conventional wisdom holds that tenants detest paying rent, that tenants are constantly being evicted, that they live in deplorable conditions and that landlords are grasping and vindictive (Mohamed, 1997). However, survey results frequently provide another picture. Landlords and tenants do not always see eye to eye but strife is relatively infrequent (Gilbert and Varley, 1991; Gilbert *et al.*, 1993; Rakodi, 1995; Kumar, 1996). If rental accommodation is often inadequate, tenants generally have better services than most families living in self-help settlements. Most landlords are neither exploitative nor grasping; indeed, rents in many cities are low relative to incomes (Tipple, 1988). Nor is renting always an insecure tenure, for many tenants stay years in the same home, and the danger of eviction has been greatly exaggerated in most cities (Gilbert, *et al.*, 1993; UNCHS, 1989).

Rental housing in many Third World cities does not only accommodate the poor. In Egypt and India, many affluent families also rent accommodation. And if tenant families generally have lower incomes than owner families, they are not poorer, because their families are much smaller.

Government policy

Third World governments would not be able to solve their housing problems even if they were to try. The best that they could be expected to do in an environment of general poverty is to improve living conditions They should try to reduce numbers of people living at densities of more than 1.5 persons in each room; increase access to electricity and potable water; improve sanitary facilities; prevent families moving into areas that are physically unsafe; and encourage households to improve the quality of their accommodation.

A sensible approach is to destroy slums as seldom as possible, on the grounds that every displaced family needs to be rehoused and removing families is often disastrous. Governments should also avoid building formal housing for the very poor, because this housing tends to be expensive and the poor cannot afford to pay for the accommodation. Sensible governments will attempt to upgrade inadequate accommodation by providing it with infrastructure and services of an appropriate standard (Skinner et al., 1987). Where land prices permit, sites-and-services programmes should be developed which will provide space for low-income families and pre-empt the temptation to invade land. How far this kind of action will improve conditions, however, depends on other variables like the efficiency of the servicing companies and the employment situation. It also depends on governments only intervening in areas where they can genuinely help (World Bank, 1993).

There are no easy solutions to Third World housing problems because poor housing is merely one manifestation of generalized poverty. Decent shelter can never be provided while there is widespread poverty. Nor is the housing problem something that can be considered apart from the rest of the society, the type of economy and the nature of the state (Gilbert and Gugler, 1992; Potter and Lloyd-Evans, 1998). At the same time, sensible policies can help mitigate shelter problems. We now know enough about the housing situation to be able to design sensible policies. Unfortunately, it has rarely been the lack of knowledge that has stopped us improving living standards. More often it has been the inability of governments to introduce the necessary policies that has constituted the critical barrier. Their inability and sometimes reluctance to adopt new legislation or to modify inappropriate policies have been determined by political realities (Matthey, 1992; Gilbert and Gugler, 1992). At root, therefore, the Third World housing problem is about politics and economics. Without appropriate political reforms and sustained economic growth, housing conditions will not get much better. Appropriate action will not cure the housing problem but it could help a substantial minority of Third World citizens to improve their shelter situation.

GUIDE TO FURTHER READING AND REFERENCES

The following text references provide the basis for further reading.

Arimah, B.C. (1997) 'The determinants of housing tenure choice in Ibadan, Nigeria', Urban Studies 34: 105–24.

Baken, R-J. and van der Linden, J. (1992) Land Delivery for Low Income Groups in Third World Cities, Aldershot: Avebury.

Desai, V. (1995) Community Participation and Slum Housing: A Study of Bombay, London: Sage.

Devas, N and Rakodi, C. (eds) (1993) Managing Fast Growing Cities: New Approaches to Urban Planning and Management in the Developing World, Harlow: Longman.

Gilbert, A.G. (1987) 'Latin America's urban poor: shanty dwellers or renters of rooms?' Cities 4: 43–51.

Gilbert, A.G. (1998) The Latin American City, London: Latin America Bureau and New York: Monthly Review Press.

Gilbert, A.G. (1999) 'A home is for ever? Residential mobility and home ownership in self-help settlements', Environment and Planning A 31: 1073–91.

Gilbert, A.G. and Gugler, J. (1992) Cities, Poverty and Development: Urbanization in the Third World (2nd edn), Oxford: Oxford University Press.

Gilbert, A.G. and Varley, A. (1991) *Landlord and Tenant: Housing the Poor in Urban Mexico*, London: Routledge.

Gilbert, A.G. and Ward, P.M. (1985) *Housing, the State and the Poor: Policy and Practice in Latin American Cities*, Cambridge: Cambridge University Press.

Gilbert, A.G., Camacho, O.O., Coulomb, R. and Necochea, A. (1993) *In Search of a Home*, London: University College London Press.

Gilbert, A.G., Mabin, A., McCarthy, M. and Watson, V. (1997) 'Low-income rental housing: are South African cities different?', *Environment and Urbanization* 9: 133–48.

Kumar, S. (1996) 'Landlordism in Third World urban low-income settlements: a case for further research', *Urban Studies* 33: 735–82.

Matthey, K. (ed.) (1992) *Beyond Self-help Housing*, London: Mansell; Munich: Profil Verlag.

Mohamed, S-I. (1997) 'Tenants and tenure in Durban', *Environment and Urbanization* 9: 101–17.

Potter, R. (1989) 'Urban housing in Barbados, West Indies', *The Geographical Journal* 55: 91–93.

Potter, R.B. (1995) *Housing and the State in the Eastern Caribbean*, The University of the West Indies Press.

Potter, R.B. and Lloyd-Evans, S. (1998) *The City in the Developing World*, Harlow: Longman.

Rakodi, C. (1995) 'Rental tenure in the cities of developing countries', *Urban Studies* 32: 791–811.

Schteingart, M. and Solís, M. (1996) *Vivienda y familia en México: un enfoque socio-espacial*, Aguascalientes: INEGI, and Mexico City: Colegio de Mexico and UNAM.

Skinner, R.J., Taylor, J.L. and Wegelin, E.A. (eds) (1987) *Shelter Upgrading for the Urban Poor: Evaluation of Third World Experience*, Nairobi: UNCHS and Rotterdam: Institute of Housing Studies.

Tipple, A.G. (1988) *The Development of Housing Policy in Kumasi, Ghana, 1901 to 1981*, Newcastle: University of Newcastle-upon-Tyne, Centre for Architectural Research and Development.

Tipple, A.G., Korboe, D. and Garrod, G. (1997) 'Income and wealth in house ownership studies in urban Ghana', *Housing Studies* 12: 111–26.

Turner, J.F.C. (1968) 'The squatter settlement: an architecure that works', *Architectural Design* 38: 357–60.

United Nations Centre for Human Settlements (UNCHS) (*Habitat*) (1989) *Strategies for Low-income Shelter and Services Development: the Rental-housing Option*, Nairobi: UNCHS.

United Nations Centre for Human Settlements (1996) *An Urbanizing World: Global Report on Human Settlements, 1996*, New York: Oxford University Press.

Ward, P.M. (ed.) (1982) *Self-help Housing: a Critique*, London: Mansell.

World Bank (1992) *The Housing Indicators Program: Volume II, Indicator Tables*, Washington, DC: World Bank.

World Bank (1993) *Housing: Enabling Markets to Work*, a World Bank Policy Paper, Washingon, DC: World Bank.

5.5 Urbanization and environment in the Third World

David Satterthwaite

INTRODUCTION

Most of the world's urban population and most of its large cities are now in the Third World. The quality of environmental management in these urban centres (and of the governance structures within which they occur) has very significant implications for development. Despite great diversity in the size and economic base of urban centres, they all share certain characteristics. All combine concentrations of human populations and a range of economic activities. Their environment is much influenced by the scale and nature of these economic activities – both directly in the resources they use and the pollution they generate, and indirectly in the environmental impacts of their workforce and dependants and the other enterprises on which they draw. Urban environments are also much influenced by the quality and extent of provision for supplying fresh water and for collecting and disposing of solid and liquid wastes.

In most countries in Africa, Asia and Latin America, the expansion in the urban population has occurred without the needed expansion in the services and facilities essential to a healthy urban environment, especially provision for water, sanitation, drainage and solid waste management. It has usually occurred with little or no effective pollution control.

URBAN OPPORTUNITIES AND DISADVANTAGES

The fact that large urban centres have high concentrations of people, enterprises and motor vehicles – and their wastes – can make them very hazardous places in which to live and work. With inadequate or no environmental management, environmental hazards become the main cause of ill-health, injury and premature death. Average life expectancies can be below 40 years and one child in four may die before the age of 5. The urban poor face the greatest risks as their homes and neighbourhoods generally have the least adequate provision for water supplies, sanitation, drainage, garbage collection and healthcare.

But urban centres also provide many environmental opportunities. High densities and large population concentrations usually lower the costs per household and per enterprise for the provision of infrastructure and services. The concentration of industries reduces the unit cost of making regular checks on plant and equipment safety, as well as on occupational health and safety, pollution control and the management of hazardous wastes. There are also economies of scale or proximity for reducing risks from most disasters. There is generally a greater capacity among city dwellers to help pay for such measures, if they are made aware of the risks and all efforts are made to keep down costs. With good environmental management, cities can achieve life expectancies that compare favourably with those in Europe and North America.

Cities also have many potential advantages for reducing resource use and waste. For instance, the close proximity of so many water consumers gives greater scope for recycling or directly re-using waste waters. In regard to transport, cities have great potential for limiting the use of motor vehicles (and thus also the fossil fuels, air pollution and greenhouse gases that their use implies). This might sound contradictory, since most large cities have problems with congestion and motor-vehicle-generated air pollution. But also, in cities many more trips can be made through walking or bicycling. Cities make a greater use of public transport and a high-quality service more feasible.

Good environmental management can also limit the tendency for cities to transfer environmental costs to rural areas, for example, through:

- enforcing pollution control to protect water quality in nearby water bodies, safeguarding those who draw water from them, and also fisheries
- an emphasis on 'waste reduction, re-use, recycle' to reduce the volume of wastes that are disposed of in the area around cities
- comprehensive storm and surface drains, and garbage collection systems which reduce non-point sources of water pollution.

More resource-conserving, waste-minimizing cities can also contribute much to addressing global environmental problems, including de-linking a good quality of life from increased resource use, waste generation and greenhouse gas emissions. However, realizing these potential advantages of urban concentrations requires competent city governments that are accountable to their populations.

THE IMPORTANCE OF GOVERNANCE

All urban areas require some form of government to ensure adequate quality 'environments' for their inhabitants. Governments must also act to protect key resources and ecosystems in and around the city – for instance, to regulate land use, to protect watersheds, to control pollution and the disposal of wastes, and to ensure adequate provision of environmental infrastructure and services. Ensuring good-quality environments becomes increasingly complex, the larger the population (and the scale and range of their daily movements) and the more industrial the production base.

In all cities, environmental management is an intensely political task, as different interests compete for the most advantageous locations, for the ownership or use of resources and waste sinks, and for publicly provided infrastructure and services. The most serious environmental problems in urban areas are largely the result of inadequate governance and inadequate investment. Two concerns are particularly pressing:

- reducing environmental hazards, and
- reducing the loss of natural resources and the damage or disruption of ecosystems.

The emphasis on 'governance' rather than 'government' is because good environmental management needs city authorities and politicians to be accountable to their citizens and to work with them. The term governance is understood to include not only the political and administrative institutions of government, but also the relationships between government and civil society (McCarney, 1996).

THE SCALE AND RANGE OF ENVIRONMENTAL PROBLEMS

Infectious and parasitic diseases

Many of the most serious diseases in cities are 'environmental' because they are transmitted through disease-causing agents (pathogens) in the air, water, soil or food, or through insect or animal disease vectors. Many diseases and disease vectors (for instance, the mosquitoes that transmit dengue fever or yellow fever) thrive when provision for water, sanitation, drainage, garbage collection and healthcare is inadequate. Around half the Third World's urban population is suffering from one or more of the diseases associated with inadequate provision for water and sanitation.

Official statistics often over-state the proportion of urban dwellers adequately served. Many governments assume that all urban dwellers within 100 metres of standpipes or latrines are 'adequately served', despite the difficulties of access. They remain classified as 'adequately served' even when water supply is irregular and of poor quality. Tens of millions of urban dwellers have no toilet they can use so they either defecate in the open or in plastic bags. Improved provision for water and sanitation can bring great benefits in terms of improved health, reduced expenditures (on water vendors and on treatment from diseases) and much reduced physical effort (especially for those who collect and carry water from standpipes or other sources far from their shelters).

Airborne infections are among the world's leading causes of death. For many, their transmission is aided by the overcrowding and inadequate ventilation that is common in the tenements, boarding houses or small shacks in which most low-income urban dwellers live. While improving housing and other environmental conditions can reduce their incidence (and by reducing other diseases also strengthen people's defences against these) medical interventions such as immunization or rapid treatment are more important for reducing their health impact.

Chemical and physical hazards

The scale and severity of many chemical and physical hazards increases rapidly with urbanization and industrialization. While controlling infectious diseases centres on provision of infrastructure and services (whether through public, private, NGO or community provision), reducing chemical and physical hazards is largely achieved by regulating the activities of enterprises and households.

A great range of chemical pollutants affect human health. Controlling exposure to chemicals in the workplace ('occupational exposure') is particularly important, with action needed from large factories down to small 'backstreet' workshops. In most cities, there is an urgent need for measures to promote healthy and safe working practices and to penalize employers who contravene them. In many urban areas, domestic indoor air pollution from open fires or poorly vented stoves that use coal or biomass fuels has serious health impacts. Lower-income households are affected most as people tend to move to cleaner, safer fuels when incomes rise.

There is also a growing need for more effective control of outdoor (ambient) air pollution from industries and motor vehicles. Worldwide, more than 1.5 billion urban dwellers are exposed to levels of ambient air pollution that are above the recommended maximum levels. Urban air pollution problems are particularly pressing in many Indian and Chinese cities.

Accidents in the home are often among the most serious causes of injury and premature death, especially where much of the population live in overcrowded accommodation made from temporary materials and use open fires or unsafe stoves and candles or kerosene lights.

Traffic management which protects pedestrians and minimizes the risk of motor vehicle accidents is also important. Motor vehicle accidents have become an increasingly significant contributor to premature deaths and injuries in many cities. The number of fatalities and serious injuries per road vehicle is often much higher than in high-income countries.

Achieving a high-quality city environment

Attention should be given not only to reducing environmental hazards but also to ensuring provision or protection of those facilities that make urban environments more pleasant, safe and valued by their inhabitants, including parks, public squares/plazas and provision for children's play and for sport/recreation. This should be integrated with a concern to protect each city's natural landscapes with important ecological and aesthetic value, for instance wetland areas, river banks or coasts.

Managing wastes

Municipal agencies are generally responsible for providing or contracting out waste collection services. Most lack the technical knowledge, institutional competence and funding base to meet these responsibilities. In many urban centres, more than a third of the solid wastes generated are not collected and it is usually the low-income districts that have the least adequate collection service. This means that wastes accumulate on open spaces and streets, clogging drains and attracting disease vectors and pests (rats, mosquitoes, flies).

Many industrial and institutional wastes are categorized as 'hazardous' because of the special care needed to ensure they are isolated from contact with humans and the natural environment. In most urban centres, governments do little to monitor their production, collection, treatment and disposal. Businesses generally have large incentives to avoid meeting official standards and little risk in doing so.

Reducing the impact of disasters

Disasters are considered to be exceptional events which suddenly result in large numbers of people being killed or injured, or large economic losses. As such, they are distinguished from the environmental hazards discussed above. This distinction has its limitations, since far more urban dwellers die of easily prevented illnesses arising from environmental hazards in their food, water or air than from 'disasters', yet the death toll from disasters gets more media attention.

Cyclones/high winds/storms have probably caused more deaths in urban areas than other 'natural' disasters in recent decades. Earthquakes have caused many of the biggest urban disasters. Flood disasters affect many more people than cyclones and earthquakes, but generally kill fewer people. Landslides, fires, epidemics and industrial accidents are among the other urban disasters that need attention.

Global warming will increase the frequency and severity of disasters in many urban areas. For instance, the rise in sea level will increase the risk of flooding for many port cities. It will also disrupt sewers and drains and may bring seawater intrusion into freshwater aquifers. Changes in rainfall regimes may reduce the availability of freshwater resources or bring increased risk of floods.

Increasingly, urban authorities recognize the need to integrate 'disaster prevention' within 'environmental hazard prevention'. Even where disasters have natural triggers that cannot be prevented, their impact can generally be greatly reduced by understanding who within the city population is vulnerable and acting to reduce this vulnerability before the disaster occurs. There are also important overlaps between 'the culture of prevention' for everyday hazards and for disasters.

DEVELOPING MORE SUSTAINABLE INTERACTIONS WITH NATURE

Cities transform natural landscapes both within and around them.

- The expansion of cities reshapes land surfaces and water flows. In the absence of effective land-use management, urbanization can have serious ecological impacts such as soil erosion, deforestation, and the loss of agricultural land and of sites with valuable ecological functions.
- The 'export' of solid, liquid and airborne pollutants and wastes often brings serious environmental impacts to regions around cities, including damage to fisheries by untreated liquid wastes, land and groundwater pollution from inadequately designed and managed solid waste dumps and, for many of the larger and more industrial cities, acid rain.

- Freshwater resources are being depleted. Many cities have outgrown the capacity of their locality to provide fresh water or have over-used or mismanaged local sources so these are no longer usable. Increasingly distant and costly water sources have to be used, often to the detriment of the regions from which these are drawn.

A focus only on such regional damages can obscure the fact that city consumers and enterprises provide the main market for rural produce while rural inhabitants and enterprises draw on urban enterprises for goods and services. Urban markets can provide not only rural incomes but also the basis for rural investments in better environmental management. Many low-income rural households also depend on urban markets or urban employment for a significant part of their livelihood.

Global impacts

The demands that larger and wealthier cities concentrate for food, fuel and raw materials are increasingly met by imports from distant ecosystems. This makes it easier to maintain high environmental standards around such cities, including preserving natural landscapes, but this may simply be transferring costs to people and ecosystems in other regions or countries. Other cost transfers are projected into the future. For instance, air pollution may have been cut in some wealthy cities but emissions of carbon dioxide (the main greenhouse gas) remain high and may continue to rise. This is transferring costs to the future through the human and ecological costs that atmospheric warming will bring.

All cities have to develop a more sustainable interaction with the ecocycles on whose continued functioning we all depend. But to promote a sustainable development-oriented urban policy needs a coherent and supportive national policy. It is difficult for city governments to reduce cost transfers to their region or the future because they are accountable to the populations living within their boundaries, not to those living in distant ecosystems on whose productivity the city producers or consumers may draw. It is also difficult for city authorities to take account of the needs and rights of future generations and of other species without a supportive national sustainable development framework.

GUIDE TO FURTHER READING AND REFERENCES

This article draws on Hardoy, Jorge E., Mitlin, Diana and Satterthwaite, David (2001) *Environmental Problems in an Urbanizing World*, London: Earthscan Publications.

For more detail on the transfer of cities' environmental costs, see McGranahan, G., Jacobi, P., Songsore, J., Surjadi, C. and Kjellén, M. (2001) *Citizens at Risk: From Urban Sanitation to Sustainable Cities*, London: Earthscan Publications.

For a review of approaches to addressing urban environmental problems, see Leitmann, Josef (1999) *Sustaining Cities: Environmental Planning and Management in Urban Design*, New York: McGraw-Hill, 412pp.

For air pollution and cities, see Elsom, Derek (1996) *Smog Alert: Managing Urban Air Quality*, London: Earthscan, 226pp.

For a discussion of sustainable development and cities, see Hardoy and others (2001), McGranahan and others (2001) and Haughton, Graham and Hunter, Colin (1994) *Sustainable Cities*, Regional Policy and Development series, London: Jessica Kingsley, 357pp.

For a discussion of governance, see McCarney, Patricia L. (ed.) (1996) *Cities and Governance: New Directions in Latin America, Asia and Africa*, Toronto: Centre for Urban and Community Studies, University of Toronto, 206pp.

5.6 Urban agriculture

Kenneth Lynch

INTRODUCTION

The phrase 'urban agriculture' initially sounds like a contradiction in terms; however, the phenomenon has grown in significance in the cities of the South over the last 20 years. A number of key events have contributed to this growth. These include the United Nations University's Food Energy Nexus Programme, the International Development Research Centre's *Cities Feeding People* programme and the preparation of a report on urban agriculture by the Urban Agriculture Network (1996) for the Second United Nations Conference on Human Settlements (*Habitat II*) held in Istanbul in 1996. A number of annual reports by international organizations have contributed to this by devoting their themed sections to cities (World Commission on Environment and Development (WCED), 1987; United Nations Population Fund, 1996; World Resources Institute, 1996). The issue of provisioning the rapidly growing cities of the world's poorest countries is included as a major challenge for the future in these reports.

One of the main reasons for the growing concern about provisioning fast-growing cities is the sheer speed at which they are growing. For example Potter and Lloyd-Evans (1998) report that towns and cities of the world's poorest countries are receiving 45 million new inhabitants each year. The total urban population of Africa is estimated to increase from 250 million in 1995 to 804 million by the year 2025 (World Resources Institute, 1996). The nature of urban development in many ex-colonial countries means that much of this growth is concentrated in one primate city. Already, research shows that many cities in the developing world are making great demands of their countries, either through the transportation of food and fuel over considerable distances, or through the process of selective migration of rural young people to the cities in search of better prospects (United Nations Population Fund, 1996). One of the greatest challenges for the city planning authorities in rapidly growing cities, therefore, will be to provide for the needs of these expanding urban populations without depleting the natural resource base (WCED, 1987).

One key focus for concern is that of urban food security, as these cities grow very quickly. The concern was brought to wider attention through the report to the *Habitat II* conference in 1996 (Urban Agriculture Network, 1996). In this report the Urban Agriculture Network reported on a range of aspects of urban agriculture, including a number of successes. Such successes have encouraged urban agriculture proponents that urban and peri-urban agriculture is an important strategy in supplying growing urban populations with affordable food (Smit and Nasr, 1992). Evidence suggests that in some cities urban agriculture may already occupy up to 35 per cent of the land area, may employ up to 36 per cent of the population, and may supply up to 50 per cent of urban fresh vegetable needs.

There is recent evidence from large urban centres across Africa which reveals that urban and peri-urban cultivation has steadily increased since the late 1980s (Binns and Lynch, 1998; Drakakis-Smith, 1994). One explanation for the growth in prominence is that it is a response to the economic downturn during the 1980s that affected city dwellers in particular. However, Rakodi (1995) also reports that in Harare, despite its illegal status, urban agriculture has increased since the severe drought of 1991–92. Field research in cities in northern Nigeria has found that urban cultivation

Urban farmers in Kano, Nigeria

has intensified considerably in the last decade. Oral evidence collected in Kano suggests that before then such cultivation was largely restricted to dry-season production under the small-holder irrigation system. Further Kano research has also revealed that the amount of horticultural production among resource-poor farmers (such as those in the above figure) has increased significantly, motivated by the impact of government policies and increasing urban poverty (Binns and Lynch, 1998).

Urban and peri-urban agriculture is therefore one possible response to the demand created by rapidly growing city populations and accentuated by particular difficulties associated with specific cities.

PROMOTING URBAN AGRICULTURE

Food produced locally in urban areas may have several added benefits (see Table 1). First, it employs a proportion of the city's population. For example, Binns and Lynch (1998) reported that 24 per cent of the residents of Dar es Salaam were farming within the city and a further 30 per cent were involved in cultivation outside the city. Second, it can reduce the cost of food because it is not transported over increasingly long distances. For example Egziabher *et al.* (1994) estimated that in Addis Ababa urban dwellers can save between 10 and 20 per cent of their income through urban cultivation. Third, it diversifies the sources of food, resulting in a more secure supply. This is particularly important during periods of disruption – for example, a severe rainy season may result in some roads being closed in tropical countries, a drought may lead to failing crops, or – more drastic – during periods of political or military disruption, supply lines from rural supply areas may be cut. During the siege of Sarajevo in the 1990s, the city's people were forced to produce their own food to supplement the meagre supplies shipped in. In Uganda reports suggest that the prevalence of urban agriculture in the city of Kampala may have resulted in much lower than expected child malnutrition problems during the conflicts of the late 1970s and early 1980s.

Table 1 Summary of the findings of urban agriculture research

Advantages	Concerns
• Vital or useful supplement to food procurement strategies • Various environmental benefits • Employment creation for the jobless • Providing a survival strategy for low-income urban residents • Urban agriculture making use of urban wastes	• Conflict over water supply, particularly in arid or semi-arid areas • Health concerns, particularly from use of contaminated wastes • Conflicting urban land issues • Focus on urban cultivation activities rather than in relation to broader urban management issues • Urban agriculture can benefit only the wealthier city dwellers in some cases

Proponents of urban agriculture point out that farming is not incompatible with urban systems if planned and managed carefully. There is much archaeological evidence to suggest that most pre-colonial cities across Africa, the Americas and South and East Asia had forms of food production as an integral part of their morphology. European cities had a lot of agricultural activities up until the Victorian era (Egziabher *et al.*, 1994). There is some evidence that urban dwellers continued to be involved on a small scale in cultivation during the colonial period (Egziabher *et al.*, 1994). Indeed, many modern European and North American cities are experiencing a resurgence of allotment gardens or a growth of high-value commercial horticultural activities.

A key principle of the promotion of urban agriculture in both developed and developing societies is that of environmental improvement. This, it is argued, can be brought about through a number of aspects of this activity. First, most promoters of urban agriculture point to the energy and emission savings of *in situ* production over transporting foods long distances.

Second, many urban wastes, both commercial and domestic, can form valuable inputs to urban agricultural systems, thus closing resource loops and reducing the waste management problems of many advanced and developing cities. Urban agriculture has also been identified as fulfilling a temporary holding function, making productive use of vacant land in Manila, Lusaka and Mexico City. Third World city authorities could set aside areas in spontaneous settlements for temporary urban agriculture. For example, as the settlements mature these sites could be used to provide vital infrastructure, such as schools, health centres, or if the urban agriculture sites formed corridors, for the construction of roads and other infrastructure, such as water, electricity and waste disposal.

POTENTIAL PROBLEMS

There are, however, a number of concerns that also arise in the literature on urban food supply in developing countries (see Table 1). These relate to key strategic and planning issues which are going to become of crucial importance in the relatively near future. The first relates to the issue of water. In some Third World cities the water authorities are already struggling to provide sufficient water supplies to the current population – a particularly acute problem in North Africa and the Middle East. This situation could be exacerbated if the development of urban agriculture is allowed to develop in cities where water supply is already a major problem. This conflict is most acute where urban agriculturists tap into water supplies illegally. The question which needs to be asked here is whether the food supply for the city is better produced in the city or in rural areas where the demand for water is considerably less and unlikely to increase relative to the cities.

The second major issue relates to land. Urban agriculture often takes place on land over which the producers have little or no claim. This is not a problem where the land is vacant and unused, which is often the case. However, conflict arises where the demand for land is high and the land is needed by the owners to meet pressures from other urban sectors, such as housing or industry. This is likely to become particularly acute where growing city populations find that access to land around the city is restricted. These restrictions can be the result of peri-urban physical barriers (such as mountains, common in cities in Latin America, or swamps or rivers, common in Africa and Southeast Asia) or institutional barriers (such as military bases or other large-scale institutional land uses).

The third issue relates to known and perceived health problems associated with urban agriculture (Egziabher *et al.*, 1994). For example, tuberculosis is often linked to cattle keeping, while the cholera outbreak in Santiago, Chile, in 1992 was partly traced to vegetables grown in the city that had been contaminated by polluted irrigation water (Urban Agriculture Network, 1996). In addition to this, there are justifiable health concerns relating to the lack of monitoring of inputs, such as chemical pesticides, used to grow foods, and of the food-processing and preparation practices in uncontrolled informal markets. The authors of the UNDP report (Urban Agriculture Network, 1996) are more positive. Doubt is expressed about many of the perceived concerns, pointing out that some are based on accepted wisdom and have not been scientifically addressed. They suggest that many of these problems can be overcome with good management and the promotion of best practice.

Finally, Ellis and Sumberg (1998) point out that a classical locational analysis of farming suggests that high-value and highly perishable crops are likely to be produced close to the urban market. However, in reality this is not necessarily the situation and they argue that an understanding of local circumstances may provide information about the functioning of land markets and transactions supporting urban cultivation. The particular circumstances that make urban agriculture viable frequently involve a complex set of arrangements relating to household needs, household food procurement strategies, employment opportunities, and the issue of land regulation and market factors. This can result in urban cultivation activities being temporary, risky and non-replicable. They therefore argue that more research should be undertaken to seek a clearer understanding of particular situations, before shrinking development budgets are committed to promoting urban agriculture.

For example, there is conflicting evidence that households which engage in urban agriculture as a survival strategy are not always recent migrants to the city, nor are they necessarily the most resource-poor urban dwellers (see, for example, Egziabher *et al.*, 1994). Some writers have suggested that such cultivation may only benefit households that are themselves directly involved and which are not necessarily 'resource poor' (Drakakis-Smith, 1994). The argument here relates to the issue of whether urban agriculture provides the elites with an additional opportunity for making income or whether it underpins the survival strategies of the lowest-income urban residents.

CONCLUSION

The most appropriate way forward is likely to be different for each city according to its geographic, economic and social circumstances. However, clearly some form of strategic planning is required to examine the appropriateness of the various options for food supply. The issues raised in this chapter demonstrate the potential advantages and disadvantages of promoting urban-based production as opposed to rural-based production. The promotion of urban agriculture should be considered as part of a broader comprehensive strategy taking into account the environmental and social, as well as the economic consequences of promoting one aspect of the food system over others.

It is ironic that at a time when attention is being focused on urban problems in developing countries more analytical work has not been undertaken to ensure that the promotion of urban agriculture does not cause more harm than good. For example, some researchers have cautioned that little research has been done on the changing relations between urban and rural areas, particularly under structural adjustment policies, despite a considerable amount of research on related topics.

GUIDE TO FURTHER READING AND REFERENCES

The following text references provide the basis for further reading.

Binns, J.A. and Lynch, K. (1998) 'Sustainable food production in sub-Saharan Africa: the significance of urban and peri-urban agriculture', *Journal for International Development* 10(6): 777–93.

Drakakis-Smith, D. (1994) 'Food systems and the poor in Harare under conditions of structural adjustment', *Geografiska Annaler* 76 B(1): 3–20.

Egziabher, A.G., Lee-Smith, D., Maxwell, D.G., Memon, P.A., Mougeot, L. and Sawio, C. (1994) *Cities Feeding People: An Examination of Urban Agriculture in East Africa*, Ottawa: International Development Research Centre.

Ellis, F. and Sumberg, J. (1998) 'Food production, urban areas and policy responses', *World Development* 26(2): 213–25.

Potter, R. and Lloyd-Evans, S. (1998) *The City in the Developing World*, Harlow: Longman.

Rakodi, C. (1995) *Harare – Inheriting a Settler-colonial City: Change or Continuity?* World City Series, Chichester: John Wiley.

Smit, J. and Nasr, J. (1992) 'Urban agriculture for sustainable cities: using wastes and idle land and water bodies as resources', *Environment and Urbanization* 4(2): 141–52.

Smith, D.W. (1998) 'Urban food systems and the poor in developing countries', *Transaction of the Institute of British Geographers* 23(2): 207–20.

United Nations Population Fund (1996) *The State of World Population 1996; Changing Places: Population, Development and the Urban Future*, New York: United Nations. Also published at http://www.unfpa.org/publications/swp.htm.

Urban Agriculture Network (1996) *Urban Agriculture: Food, Jobs and Sustainable Cities*, publication series for *Habitat II*, Vol. 1, New York: United Nations Development Programme.

World Commission on Environment and Development (1987) *Our Common Future*, Oxford: Oxford University Press.

World Resources Institute (1996) *World Resources 1996–97: The Urban Environment*, Oxford: Oxford University Press with the United Nations Environment Programme and the World Bank. Also published at http://www.wri.org/wri/wr-96–97/index.html.

Environment

EDITORIAL INTRODUCTION

Over the last 15 years or so, the environment has become a major dimension of development thinking. In the future, it needs to become a major component of development practice. In the past, undoubtedly, too much attention has been paid to economics, and far too little emphasis has been placed on the environment–development interface. However, since the Brundtland Commission in 1987, attention has increasingly focused on the concept of sustainable development. Although there are many discourses on sustainability, reflecting the interests of many different groups, most adopt the Commission's working definition of sustainability as meeting the needs of the present, without compromising the ability of future generations to do the same. But it has to be recognized that the concept of sustainable development is complex and contradictory. For example, it is generally harder for the poor to operationalize, as it is tempting for them to 'discount' the future, in order to provide for the pressing needs of the present.

A major threat to the environment is posed by global climatic change, and it is now generally accepted that climate is changing, due at least in part to human activity. Once again, the concomitants of global warming, such as land degradation, desertification and flooding, appear to threaten to impact on the poor disproportionately, rather than the rich. Such environmental circumstances are also expressed in terms of problems of food security. In this connection, urban environmental circumstances are also salient, not least as witnessed in waste dumping in watersheds, which causes major pollution problems downstream, where such waters may then be employed for irrigation and domestic purposes, thereby leading to a variety of health risks.

The United Nations Conference on Environment and Development (UNCED) held in Rio de Janeiro in 1992, and generally referred to as the 'Rio Earth Summit', was designed as a major effort to catalyse a more sustainable approach to development. However, some commentators have argued that the needs of national governments and business lobbies were too dominant in the various discussions which took place as part of the conference. Another major issue was that during the proceedings, the nations broadly making up the North and the South seemed to adopt and stress different objectives. The nations of the North seemed intent to argue that environmental problems can be cured by the application of technology. In contrast, the governments of the South emphasized the need for real structural reforms in order to change the international economy, so as to impact directly on the effects of debt, structural adjustment programmes and the like.

Agenda 21 was, in many eyes, one of the most important outcomes of the Rio Earth Summit, and was signed by all 176 participating nations. Local Agenda 21, which was presented as Chapter 28 of Agenda 21, encourages local governments to facilitate increased community involvement in all forms of environmental decision-making. However, it is frequently maintained that not enough emphasis is being placed on Brown Agenda issues. These environmental problems, which are primarily encountered in urban environments, serve to put many millions of lives at risk. They are also expressed in the emergence of so-called 'pollution havens' in developing countries, where the pollutants of the North are effectively dumped in the South. Another major area of enquiry has re-examined the nature of disasters and vulnerability. Here views have been changing quite dramatically, in so far as there has been a move to recognize that even natural events need not turn into disasters, and that steps may be taken to avoid the harmful consequences of such events. The vulnerability and entitlement explanatory models are of particular salience in this connection. Another major focus has been on the developmental issues faced within particular environments, notably within tropical and sub-tropical savannas and tropical moist forest ecosystems.

6.1 Sustainable development

Michael Redclift

DISCOURSES OF 'SUSTAINABLE DEVELOPMENT'

The expression 'sustainable development' has been used in a variety of ways, particularly within the context of development studies. Today we are confronted with several different discourses of 'sustainable development', some of which are mutually exclusive. For example, campaigners for greater global equality between nations, huge international corporations and local housing associations have all had recourse to the term 'sustainable development' to justify, or embellish, their actions.

We might begin our analysis of these different discourses by returning to essentials. Each scientific problem which is resolved by human intervention, using fossil fuels and manufactured materials, is usually viewed as a triumph of management and a contribution to economic good, when it might also represent a future threat to sustainability. In the 1970s there was a fear that our major environmental problems would be associated with resource scarcities (Meadows *et al.*, 1972). At the beginning of the twenty-first century we are faced by another challenge: that the means we have used to overcome resource scarcity, including substitution of some natural resources, and 'cleaner' environmental products and services, may have contributed to the next generation of environmental problems. This realization provides an enormous challenge to conventional social science thinking, encapsulated in the term 'sustainable development', which has served as a concept, a policy prescription and a moral imperative.

Sustainable development was defined by the Brundtland Commission in the following way: 'development that meets the needs of the present without compromising the ability of future generations to meet their own needs' (Brundtland Commission, 1987). This definition has been brought into service in the absence of agreement about a process which almost everybody thinks is desirable. However, the simplicity of this approach is deceptive, and obscures underlying complexities and contradictions. It is worth pausing to examine the apparent consensus that reigns over sustainable development.

First, following the Brundtland definition, it is clear that 'needs' themselves change, so it is unlikely (as the definition implies), that those of future generations will be the same as those of the present generation. The question then is, where does 'development' come into the picture? Obviously development itself contributes to 'needs', helping to define them differently for each generation and for different cultures.

This raises the second question, not covered by the definition, of how needs are defined in different cultures. Most of the 'consensus' surrounding sustainable development has involved a syllogism: sustainable development is necessary for all of us, but it may be defined differently in terms of each and every culture. This is superficially convenient, until we begin to ask how these different definitions match up. If in one society it is agreed that fresh air and open spaces are necessary before development can be sustainable, it will be increasingly difficult to marry this definition of 'needs' with those of other societies seeking more material wealth, even at the cost of increased pollution. It is precisely this kind of trade-off which is apparent in developing countries today.

Furthermore, how do we establish which course of action is *more* sustainable? Recourse to the view that societies must decide for themselves is not very helpful. (Who decides? On what basis are the decisions made?) At the same time there are problems in ignoring culturally specific definitions of what is sustainable in the interest of a more inclusive system of knowledge. There is also considerable confusion surrounding *what* is to be sustained. One of the reasons why there are so many contradictory approaches to sustainable development (although not the only reason) is that different people identify the objects of sustainability differently.

WHAT IS TO BE SUSTAINED?

For those whose primary interest is in ecological systems and the conservation of natural resources, it is the natural resource base which needs to be sustained. The key question usually posed is the following: how can development activities be designed which help to maintain ecological processes, such as soil fertility, the assimilation of wastes, and water and nutrient recycling? Another, related, issue is the conservation of genetic materials, both in themselves and (perhaps more importantly) as part of complex and vulnerable systems of biodiversity. The natural resource base needs to be conserved because of its intrinsic value.

There are other approaches, however. Some environmental economists argue that the natural stock of resources, or 'critical natural capital', needs to be given priority over the flows of income which depend upon it (Pearce, 1991). They make the point that human-made capital cannot be an effective substitute for natural capital. If our objective is the sustainable yield of renewable resources, then sustainable development implies the management of these resources in the interest of the natural capital stock. This raises a number of issues which are both political and distributive: who owns and controls genetic materials, and who manages the environment? At what point does the conservation of natural capital unnecessarily inhibit the sustainable flows of resources?

Second, according to what principles are the social institutions governing the use of resources organized? What systems of tenure dictate the ownership and management of the natural resource base? What institutions do we bequeath, together with the environment, to future generations? Far from taking us away from issues of distributive politics, and political economy, a concern with sustainable development inevitably raises such issues more forcefully than ever (Redclift, 1987; Redclift and Sage, 1999).

The question 'what is to be sustained?' can also be answered in another way. Some writers argue that it is present (or future) levels of production (or consumption) that need to be sustained. The argument is that the growth of global population will lead to increased demands on the environment, and our definition of sustainable development should incorporate this fact. At the same time, the consumption practices of individuals will change too. Given the choice, most people in India or China might want a television or an automobile of their own, like households in the industrialized North. What prevents them from acquiring one is their poverty, their inability to consume, and the relatively 'undeveloped' infrastructure of poor countries.

Is there anything inherently unsustainable in broadening the market for TV sets or cars? The different discourses of 'sustainable development' have different answers to this question. Many of those who favour the sustainable development of goods and services that we receive through the market, and businesses, would argue that we should broaden the basis of consumption. Others would argue that the production of most of these goods and services today is inherently unsustainable – that we need to 'downsize', or shift our patterns of consumption. In both developed and, increasingly, developing countries, it is frequently suggested that it is impossible to function effectively without computerized information or access to private transport.

The different ways in which 'sustainability' is approached, then, reflects quite different under-lying 'social commitments', that is the patterns of everyday behaviour that are seldom questioned. People define their 'needs' in ways which effectively exclude others from meeting theirs and, in the process, can increase the long-term risks for the sustainability of other people's livelihoods. Most important, however, the process through which we enlarge our choices, and reduce those of others, is largely invisible to people in their daily lives.

Unless these processes are made more visible, 'sustainable development' discourses beg the question of whether, or how, environmental costs are passed on from one group of people to another, both within societies and between them. The North dumps much of its toxic waste and 'dirty' technology on poorer countries, and sources many of its 'needs', for energy, food and miner-als, from the South. At the same time, the elevated lifestyles of many rich and middle-class people in developing countries are dependent on the way in which natural resources are dedicated to meeting their needs. Finally, of course, the inequalities are also intergenerational, as well as intra-generational: we despoil the present at great cost to the future. Discounting the future (as econo-mists call it), valuing the present above the future, is much easier to do in materially poor societies, where survival itself may be at stake for many people.

There are other forms of inheritance from the past. Economics developed, historically, around the idea of scarcity. The role of technology was principally that of raising output from scarce resources. Among other benefits of economic growth was the political legitimacy it conferred, within a dynamic economy, on those who could successfully overcome the obstacles to more spending, and wealth was usually regarded as a good thing in itself. This assumption of scarce resources and technological benefits sits uneasily with sustainability in the industrial North today, and underlines the difficulty in reconciling 'development' with 'sustainability'. It strikes at the legit-imization of only one form of 'value', albeit the principal one, within capitalist, industrial societies. The German sociologist Habermas expressed his criticism of this view forcefully, in the following way:

> Can civilisation afford to surrender itself entirely to the . . . driving force of just one of its subsystems – namely, the pull of a dynamic . . . recursively closed, economic system which can only function and remain stable by taking all relevant information, translating it into, and processing it in, the language of economic value.
>
> (Habermas, 1991: 33)

HUMAN RIGHTS, DEMOCRACY AND SUSTAINABLE DEVELOPMENT

Finally, since the various discourses of sustainable development began to flourish, it has become evident that another dimension to the problem of diminished sustainability needs to be consid-ered. This is the extent to which, at the beginning of the twenty-first century, we need to refer to processes of democracy and governance in the context of sustainable development. The Brundtland Report took a highly normative view of both the environment and development, as did the Earth Summit deliberations in 1992. With the second Earth Summit in 2002 in mind, it may be useful to pause to consider whether we can ever achieve 'sustainable development' without increased democratization at all levels of society. Today questions of sustainability are linked, intel-lectually and politically, to other issues, such as human rights and 'identity', with which they are connected. But notions of 'rights' and 'identity' are themselves changing. In the era of genetic engi-neering, the genetic modification of humans, as well as plants and animals, is shaping new senses of 'identity'. As individuals change, so do the groups to which they belong. In the era of globalization it is sometimes argued that 'sustainable development' may be more difficult to achieve, as economies converge towards shared economic objectives. At the same time it may prove impossible to achieve 'sustainable development' (if it *is* achievable) without acknowledging quite distinctive accounts of human rights in nature, and even the rights *of* nature, which were hitherto ignored. The concept of 'sustainable development', as understood by different people, is both contradictory, obscure and illuminating at the same time.

REFERENCES AND GUIDE TO FURTHER READING

Brundtland Commission (World Commission on Environment and Development) (1987) *Our Common Future*, Oxford: Oxford University Press. This report led directly to the term 'sustainable development' passing into common use. It was also the first overview of the globe which considered the environmental aspects of development from an economic, social and political perspective; cf. *Man and the Biosphere* (*MAB*) almost a decade earlier. Among the principal omissions was detailed consideration of non-human species, and their 'rights'. The 'Brundtland Report' (named after its Chairperson, the Norwegian Prime Minister at the time) also opened the way for non-governmental organizations (NGOs) to be considered a serious element in environment and development issues.

Habermas, J. (1991) 'What does socialism mean today?' in R. Blackburn (ed.) *After the Fall*, London: Verso.

Meadows, D.H., Meadows, D.L., Randers, J. and Behrens, W. (1972) *The Limits to Growth*, London: Pan Books. This book was a milestone in thinking about the environment in the 1970s. It identified the main problem for development as the shortage of natural resources – these were the 'limits' to growth. This view changed in the 1970s and 1980s, largely because the price of oil rose very quickly and alternative substitutes for many natural resources were exploited in their place. In addition, of course, the 'Green Revolution' in staple cereal crops, which was largely undertaken in the 1970s and 1980s, appeared to show that the same land base could produce very much more food . . .

Pearce, D. (1991) *Blueprint 2: Greening the World Economy*, London: Earthscan. Following on from Blueprint One, David Pearce illustrated the applications of economic analysis to environmental problems, in a way that particularly interested policy-makers.

Redclift, M.R (1987) *Sustainable Development: Exploring the Contradictions*, London: Routledge. This was the first, and probably the best, treatment of 'sustainable development'. The case studies and ethnographic illustrations, combined with the accessible intellectual discussion, make this a 'classic'.

Redclift, M.R. and Sage, C.L. (1999) 'Resources, environmental degradation and inequality', in Andrew Hurrell and Ngaire Woods (eds) *Inequality, Globalisation and World Politics*, Oxford: Oxford University Press. A good general overview of the relevance for development of inequality in resource endowments.

6.2 Climate, environment and development

Duncan McGregor

INTRODUCTION

Climate and environment are inextricably interlinked. Whilst climate is relatively easy to define and to classify, and has in the past been considered to be an independent arbiter of human activity, 'environment' has had numerous definitions over the years. Though 'environment' has traditionally been used to describe the surroundings in which we live, increasingly people modify their environmental conditions to the extent that the environment in turn moulds human activity (Gupta and Asher, 1998: 3). This is perhaps most critical in the development context in terms of agriculture and of human living conditions both rural and urban. That global climates are changing, due at least in part to human activity, is generally accepted by the scientific community, and the implications of this are potentially most important for the poorer of the World's societies.

The developing countries are principally located within the tropics and the sub-tropics, and in areas ranging in climate from humid to arid, but predominantly hot except at altitude. Whilst natural vegetation is balanced with its environment, and the land has a balanced natural 'carrying capacity' of flora and fauna, interference through human activity almost invariably gives rise to problems. In the humid tropics, the combination of high temperatures and copious rainfall encourages high rates of chemical weathering and the production of leached clay soils of low inherent fertility. Towards the drier zones, sandy soils support low biomass and are in general highly susceptible to erosion. In both cases, where population or development pressures (or both) have led to the breakdown of traditional, adaptive forms of agriculture such as shifting cultivation, deepening land degradation is a frequent consequence.

THE CLIMATIC ENVIRONMENT AND AGRICULTURAL DEVELOPMENT

Climate imposes direct constraints on agriculture, most critically in determining whether or not there is a sufficient growing season for a particular crop. Critical to this is the balance between precipitation and potential evapotranspiration, which largely defines the availability of water for plant growth. The combination of water availability and adequate temperature defines the plant growing period, as, for example, in the Food and Agricultural Organization's (FAO) Agro-ecological Zones project (FAO, 1978). Here, the growing period is taken as the continuous period from the time when precipitation reaches a value of half of the potential evapotranspiration, through the period of rainfall above full evapotranspiration, plus the number of days required to evaporate an assumed soil moisture storage equivalent to 100 mm of precipitation (FAO, 1978). This applies to rain-fed agriculture, still the predominant form of agriculture in developing areas.

This moisture requirement for crop growth may be over-ridden by use of some form of irrigation, but at a cost. The major problems associated with irrigation are waterlogging, aquifer depletion and salinization. Salinization, in particular, is a major problem in arid and semi-arid lands, where net evaporative environments predominate (with potential evapotranspiration greater than precipitation for the major part of the year). To take one example, in India, it is estimated that 4.5 million hectares have been affected by salinization (Agnew and Anderson, 1992: 159), while in semi-arid Haryana, more than 60 per cent of the soil area within the state has been classified as marginal to saline.

Changing rainfall patterns lead to changing crop patterns. Short-term climatic fluctuations have occurred throughout history, and many farming societies have evolved a range of strategies to cope with this. In semi-arid lands, for example, vegetation is in a constant state of flux, responding to minor variations in local or regional climate. What may be perceived by the outsider as 'land degradation' may in fact be part of a normal, longer-term variability (Warren, 1995; Sullivan, 1996). Risk-spreading strategies have been evolved, including diversification of food production involving livestock, the use of varieties of seeds with a shorter growing season, a flexible, more opportunistic, approach to sowing with the use of more drought-resistant seeds such as millet and sorghum, and grain storage.

Longer-term drought, sometimes classed as dessication, is more difficult to deal with, as has been seen in the case of the Sahel area of sub-Saharan Africa. Here, a number of years of above-average rainfall in the 1950s and 1960s, which encouraged intensification of agriculture and the northward displacement of nomadic pastoralism, were followed by an intense period of drought through the 1970s and into the 1980s, which led to widespread famine in the region and the deaths of millions of animals and an estimated 50,000 to 250,000 people. The term 'desertification', originally coined in the late 1940s, has been used to describe the particular form of land degradation in arid and semi-arid lands due to human activities such as over-grazing, over-cultivation, mismanagement of irrigation systems, and deforestation, exacerbated by the onset of drought conditions. The term was institutionalized by the United Nations Conference on Desertification, held in Nairobi in 1977. As Thomas and Middleton (1994) demonstrate, the institutionalized 'myth' of desertification, and the uncertainties surrounding it, can only be resolved through more sophisticated monitoring of climate and its effects on vegetation, through analysis of population trends, and through a better understanding of the social dynamics involved at the interface between climatic fluctuation, vegetational response to it, and traditional and introduced land use systems. The natural resilience of Sahelian ecosystems to short-term climatic fluctuations has been overprinted in a detrimental way by human activity.

Climate fluctuation and change, therefore, have significant implications for food security, both in terms of the sustainability of particular crops in particular climatic circumstances, the changing susceptibility of crops to pests and diseases, and the heightened susceptibility of intensely used land to degradation. At the heart of the problem in many developing areas is the uneven distribution of population and the mismatch with the availability of good-quality agricultural land (Greenland et al., 1998). Much of the presently cultivated land in developing areas is classed as marginal, either in climatic or pedological terms, and the pool of potentially cultivable land is unevenly distributed. Food security is therefore tenuous in many developing areas, though a change in climate may be a positive benefit to some as well as a disbenefit to others.

THE CLIMATIC ENVIRONMENT AND HUMAN SETTLEMENT

A critical factor in the placement of human settlements has always been access to a supply of water, whether for domestic, agricultural or industrial consumption. Progressive increases in water use inevitably lead to resource marginality in many areas of the globe, particularly in cases where there is an increasing concentration of population. For example, although the evidence is equivocal, many authorities link deepening environmental degradation to rural–urban migration and rapid urbanization in marginal lands such as the Sahel. The limiting factor here is rainfall.

Elsewhere, larger urban areas produce their own microclimate. Rapid and ongoing urbanization is a reality in many developing areas, and this is reflected in a range of climatically linked environmental changes (Gupta and Asher, 1998: Ch. 10), Particularly in the humid tropics, intense tropical downpours lead to increased flooding and surface run-off, to accelerated slope failure where building has encroached on to steeply sloping terrain, and to increased sediment production. Urban 'heat island' effects include increased temperatures, reduced humidity and increased precipitation in and around the urban area. As urbanization proceeds, air quality deteriorates, helped by reductions in wind speed within the urban area, and water quality is invariably reduced due to the discharge of wastes into the hydrological system.

Many inland cities in the tropics have developed on higher ground, often for reasons of defence, and this leads to significant off-site environmental degradation. For example, in Kumasi, Ghana, situated across the meeting of two watersheds, inadequate waste collection and poorly enforced regulation relating to the dumping of waste have led to large-scale dumping of domestic and industrial wastes into the river systems, in turn polluting river water and contaminating ground-water. Major problems occur downstream, where the floodplain farmers use river water for irriga-tion and, in the dry season, for domestic use (McGregor *et al.*, 2000). Amongst these problems, particularly affecting younger children, are reported increases in skin and respiratory complaints.

CLIMATE CHANGE AND DEVELOPMENT

As noted earlier, there is general agreement amongst scientists that global warming is in progress. There is still much debate as to how much of this is due to underlying climatic trends and how much to human activity. Principal amongst the human contributions to contemporary climate change are the burning of fossil fuels and deforestation by burning, both of which lead to increases in the prin-cipal 'greenhouse gas', carbon dioxide. The nature and likely causes of contemporary climate change are reviewed elsewhere (see, for example, Houghton, 1997), but two-way linkages between defor-estation and regional-scale climate change seem increasingly likely. For example, in South America, Amazonian deforestation, estimated at rates of around 5 million ha per annum through the 1980s (Grainger, 1993: 131), appears to have led to sub-regional decreases in precipitation, increases in run-off, erosion and sediment delivery to rivers, and increased risk of flooding downstream.

Although it must be said that conclusive studies have yet to emerge, there is an increasing sense that we are dealing with an environment which is becoming progressively more 'risky'. Though this must be set against a longer-term historical context where extreme events have been reported with varying frequency in the past, the present-day ocean–atmosphere interaction appears to be one of progressive change. Among the effects cited are increased levels of El Niño/Southern Oscillation (ENSO) activity, increased hurricane activity and rising sea levels.

El Niño events in the Pacific region appear to have become more frequent and stronger in the last two decades. In the 'normal' situation (shown in Figure A) cold water upwelling off the west coast of South America, bringing nutrient-rich water to the sea surface, is associated with an east to west sea ocean surface current and coincides with the low-level airflow. At the onset of an El Niño event, the easterly winds and sea surface current weaken and are replaced by west to east flows (Figure B). The deep sea current weakens and then reverses (Moore *et al.*, 1996: 94–8). As well as causing a catastrophic decline in fish populations off the Peruvian coast and unusually heavy rains inland in Peru and Ecuador, ENSO events have been associated in recent years with extreme weather events such as drought in parts of Indonesia and Australia. Conversely, unusually heavy rains in areas as far apart as the Sahel, northern Kenya and eastern Australia, have been asso-ciated with the non-appearance of El Niño. Clear causal connections have not been established as yet, but Reading *et al.* (1995: 48) suggest that the occurrence of sea surface temperature anomalies seems to coincide with disrupted atmospheric patterns worldwide.

Linked to global warming, rising sea surface temperatures have led to increased probabilities of the formation of hurricanes. As Wigley and Santer (1993) have pointed out in the case of the Caribbean, such a rise in sea surface temperatures could lead not only to an increased likelihood of hurricane storms, but changes in their patterns. In the last five years, the Caribbean has experienced an increased incidence of hurricane storms, its worst hurricane seasons since the 1930s (1995 and 1999), and the first hurricane in more than 100 years to track from west to east across the Caribbean

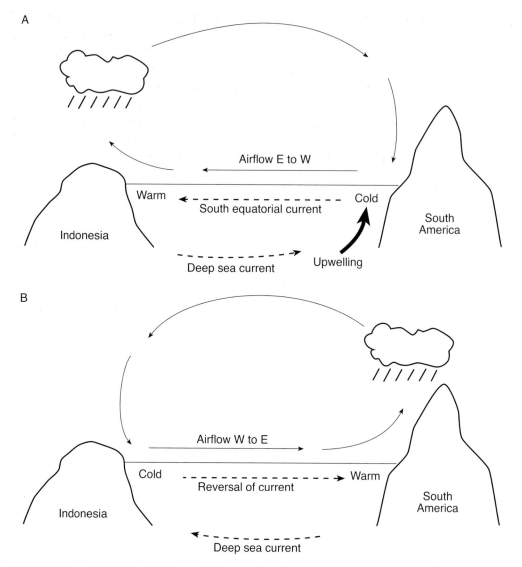

A

B

El Niño/Southern Oscillation: (A) 'normal' situation; (B) El Niño reversal

(Hurricane Lenny in 1999). When allied to a situation where precipitation levels appear to be falling in parts of the Caribbean Basin (Walsh, 1998), a condition of increased storminess allied to generally drier conditions indicates more frequent drought conditions and more intense land degradation through accelerated soil erosion on agricultural land at the start of the rainy season.

Many primate cities in developing areas are situated in the coastal zone. In small islands such as the coral islands of the Indian and Pacific Oceans, the entire land surface is within a few metres of sea level. In these conditions, suburban growth is frequently concentrated on reclaimed coastal lands at significant risk from rising sea levels and storm surge conditions. From current projections, it seems likely that sea levels will rise by between 5 and 40 cm by 2050. In island groups such as the Maldives, a risein sea level of 40 cm would inundate coastal land and tourism infrastructure, would flood valuable agricultural land, and would prejudice the limited groundwater aquifer through saline incursion. Coastal deltaic areas, such as the southern part of Bangladesh, present particular risk, since these are potentially at risk of flooding from both land and sea. The densely populated delta lands of Bangladesh present a critical problem for the nation and for the world's aid agencies.

In conclusion, it may be argued that, in the past, development has focused more on economics than on the environment. However, driving the response of the environment, the nature and scale of contemporary climatic change presents developing areas with a particular challenge. In many developing areas, there is a critical lack of data on basic physical processes and on the likely effects of ongoing climate change which will impact on agriculture and living conditions. Proactive strategies are required to focus on food security in particular, and living conditions in general, and such strategies must be underpinned by sound data on environmental behaviour.

GUIDE TO FURTHER READING

Gupta and Asher (1998) provide an all-round introduction to the interactions of physical and human environments in developing areas.

Middleton (1999), although not focusing specifically on developing areas, covers a wide range of relevant material.

For more information on physical processes in the humid tropics, and for an introduction to the problems of land management in that zone, see Reading *et al.* (1995).

A most readable introduction to the causes and consequences of global warming is given by Houghton (1997).

People – environment relationships in developing areas are explored in Morse and Stocking (1995), while Greenland *et al.* (1998) contains an up-to-date review of land and water resources.

REFERENCES

Agnew, C. and Anderson, E. (1992) *Water Resources in the Arid Realm*, London: Routledge.

FAO (1978) *Report of the Agro-ecological Zones Project: Volume 1. Methodology and Results for Africa.* World Soils Resources Report 48, Rome: FAO.

Grainger, A. (1993) *Controlling Tropical Deforestation*, London: Earthscan.

Greenland, D.J., Gregory, P.J. and Nye, P.H. (eds) (1998) *Land Resources: on the Edge of the Malthusian Precipice?*, Wallingford: CAB International and London: Royal Society.

Gupta, A. and Asher, M.G. (1998) *Environment and the Developing World: Principles, Policies and Management*, Chichester: Wiley.

Houghton, J. (1997) *Global Warming: the Complete Briefing* (2nd edn), Cambridge: Cambridge University Press.

McGregor, D.F.M., Simon, D. and Thompson, D.A. (2000) 'Peri-urban natural resources management at the watershed level: Kumasi, Ghana, at http://www.gg.rhul.ac.uk/kumasi/

Middleton, N. (1999) *The Global Casino: an Introduction to Environmental Issues* (2nd edn), London: Arnold.

Moore, P.D., Chaloner, W. and Stott, P. (1996) *Global Environmental Change*, Oxford: Blackwell.

Morse, S. and Stocking, M. (eds) (1995) *People and Environment*, London: UCL Press.

Reading, A.J., Thompson, R.D. and Millington, A.C. (1995) *Humid Tropical Environments*, Oxford: Blackwell.

Sullivan, S. (1996) 'Towards a non-equilibrium ecology: perspectives from an arid land', *Journal of Biogeography* 23: 1–5.

Thomas, D.S.G. and Middleton, N.J. (1994) *Desertification: Exploding the Myth*, Chichester: Wiley.

Walsh, R.P.D. (1998) 'Climatic changes in the Eastern Caribbean over the past 150 years and some implications in planning sustainable development', in D.F.M. McGregor, D. Barker and S. Lloyd-Evans (eds) *Resource Sustainability and Caribbean Development*, Kingston, Jamaica: The Press, University of the West Indies, pp. 26–48.

Warren, A. (1995) 'Changing understandings of African pastoralism and nature of environmental paradigms', *Transactions of the Institute of British Geographers* NS20: 193–203.

Wigley, T.M.L. and Santer, B.D. (1993) 'Future climate of the Gulf/Caribbean Basin from the global circulation models', in G.A. Maul, (ed.) *Climatic Change in the Intra-Americas Sea*, London: Edward Arnold, pp. 31–54.

6.3 The Rio Earth Summit

Mark Pelling

INTRODUCTION

The United Nations Conference on Environment and Development (UNCED) was held in 1992 in Rio de Janeiro, from which its more popular title the 'Rio Earth Summit' was derived. The conference's aim was to formulate a number of voluntary frameworks and legally binding conventions for nation-states to catalyse a more sustainable global development. Most commentators agree that UNCED fell far short of this goal. The individual interests of national governments and business lobbies dominated negotiations. Les Gibbard's cartoon from the *Guardian* newspaper (below) sums up the frustration that the lack of internationalism caused. This present chapter reviews the

'There's an awful lot of coughin' in Brazil'

Source: Original cartoon reproduced by permission of Les Gibbard, first published in the *Guardian*, 3 June 1992, p. 5

process of decision-making as well as the outputs from Rio, and critically assesses their contribution to sustainable development discourse and policy.

THE RUN-UP TO RIO

In 1989, the Canadian diplomat Maurice Strong was appointed Secretary-General of UNCED and over the following months, four preparatory committees, or PrepComs, were convened, where the agenda for UNCED was set. At this stage, it became clear that two very different approaches to sustainable development were being promoted. The Northern, industrialized nations held that environmental degradation was only a short-term problem which could be tackled through the application of technological solutions (an approach called ecological modernization). In opposition to this, countries of the South argued that technological solutions could deal only with the symptoms and not the causes of the crisis, and that the real targets for action should be the international economy, debt, structural adjustment programmes and the role of transnational corporations (TNCs) (Connelly and Smith, 1999).

UNCED

Delegations from 176 nations participated in the main conference, with over 30,000 NGOs participating in the Global Forum. At the end of the conference, five agreements had been signed:

- the Rio Declaration
- the Biodiversity Convention
- the Framework Convention on Climate Change
- the Agreement of Forest Principles
- Agenda 21.

The Biodiversity Convention and the Framework Convention on Climate Change were both signed at Rio, although they had been negotiated beforehand outside the PrepCom system. Steps were also taken towards a Convention on Desertification.

The Rio Declaration

This is a statement of principles for sustainable development which framed the entire conference. It is a much watered down version of an originally proposed 'Earth Charter'. It is a product of a compromise between Maurice Strong, who envisioned it as a pro-environment document, and the developmental priorities of the G77 (Group of 77, then representing 128 nations from the South). The influence of dominant neo-liberal developmental philosophy underlies the declaration, which advances industrialization as the preferred path to development, and nation-states as the principal actors. Green and Alternative Development agendas are conspicuous by their absence. The Declaration has no binding authority, but presents 27 principles to guide national and international environmental behaviour in which the basic inseparability of the environment and development is recognized. In what is perhaps the most important statement of principle, the North acknowledges its special responsibility for the environmental crisis.

The Biodiversity Convention

This convention was initially conceived as a response to concerns for the ecological integrity of tropical rainforests, as voiced by Northern conservationist NGOs. In the latter stage of negotiations, the wider issue of biotechnology was introduced by G77 who feared the loss of rights over forest resources. The issue of biotechnology became contentious, with the USA finally refusing to sign, under pressure from the business lobby that wanted open access to the genetic resources of tropical forests. Despite this setback, 156 counties did sign the Biodiversity Convention. Part of the reason for the Convention's success (and for subsequent criticism) was its simultaneous provision for the environmental and business concerns of governments from both the North and South. In the process of negotiation, biodiversity was transformed into biotechnology, with no ownership rights for 'source' countries or communities. Moreover, the issue of ecological degradation through forest destruction – the original basis for the convention – was sidelined by the negotiation of biotechnology rights.

The Framework on Climate Change

The origins of this non-binding Framework Convention lie in the Intergovernmental Panel for Climate Change (IPCC) which stated in 1990 that growing rates of greenhouse gas emissions, principally from industry and transport, were linked to global climate change and sea-level rise, with consequences for 'natural' and human systems worldwide. Carbon dioxide was identified as a key agent in anthropocentric global warming and the IPCC recommended that global emissions be cut by at least 60 per cent. The industrialized nations of the North were the prime culprits in the production of carbon dioxide: the USA alone accounted for 23 per cent of global emissions (IPCC, 1990). Negotiations in the run-up to Rio were blighted by the mutually incompatible positions of the industrialized and oil-producing states on the one hand, and the developing nations on the other (Elliott, 1994).

During UNCED, talks were brought to a deadlock by the USA, which refused to set a target for stabilizing carbon dioxide emissions. The refusal to restrict emissions was first argued on the premise that the US economy would be hard hit by such a reduction, but later it became apparent that the US believed that it could mitigate or adapt to the possible consequences of climate change and that this would give the country a strategic international advantage (Chatterjee and Finger, 1994). Without the USA any formal convention on climate change would be meaningless and eventually the programme was scaled down to a Framework Convention without any legal commitments for industrialized countries to stabilize their carbon dioxide emissions. Debates about climate change go to the heart of the environment/development dilemma. There is a clear link between the products of fossil fuel-based industrialization, and environmental change and risk to future development options. The Framework Convention offers in response, a preference for facing the uncertainties of human and ecological adaptation to climate change, rather than stimulating any more fundamental movement away from fossil fuel-based industrial production as an engine for economic growth.

The Agreement on Forest Principles

This is a non-binding statement of principles for the management, conservation and sustainable development of forests. It is all that remains of a potential convention on forests. Conflict between the North and South (especially Malaysia and Indonesia, both major logging nations) was, again, the reason for this failure. Southern states claimed that moves by the North to promote the preservation of tropical forests threatened national sovereignty by removing the right to exploit their own forest resources. Most Northern nations had already benefited from the exploitation of their forests and it seemed unfair that these same Northern states should put pressure on the South, which would limit opportunities for macroeconomic development. The Agreement on Forest Principles is perhaps the greatest lost opportunity of the Rio Earth Summit. No limits were placed on deforestation, or regard for the need to preserve the biodiversity of forests (which in any case had been transformed into industrial resources of biotechnology in the Convention on Biodiversity).

Agenda 21

The most far-reaching and influential outcome of the Rio Earth Summit has been Agenda 21 – a guide towards a more sustainable future in the twenty-first century. The document is a non-binding framework for action. It was signed by all 176 nations participating in UNCED and incorporates the results of lobbying from NGOs and business interests. Given the breadth of participation, it is not surprising that the need to reach consensus has led to contradictions within the text. Critical areas of contention were population control (opposed by the Vatican), reduction in fossil-fuel use (opposed by the oil-producing states) and the renegotiation and cancellation of debt. The final document has 40 chapters, all dealing with substantive issues concerned with different sectors of, and actors involved in, development and the environment. The present review tackles the document by looking at its six main themes, as discerned by Chatterjee and Finger (1994): quality of life on earth, efficient use of the earth's natural resources, sustainable economic growth, protection of our global commons, management of human settlements and chemicals and the management of waste.

The opening chapters of Agenda 21 contain a number of grand objectives that frame the goals of the subsequent chapters. These objectives, which outline a vision for quality of life on earth, have long been at the heart of UN policy and include the eradication of poverty, full employment, promoting good health and controlling population growth. The second theme for Agenda 21 is to promote the efficient use of the earth's natural resources, through the extension of economic valuation and decision-making frameworks. There are a number of philosophical and methodological problems with such an approach – such as whether it is appropriate or possible to put economic values on natural assets – which are not tackled. The emphasis on maintaining economic growth, which runs throughout the Earth Summit documents is reiterated in the third theme on sustainable economic growth. The environmental crisis is seen as a problem to which ongoing economic activities must adapt, rather than any suggestion of a more radical departure.

The fourth theme, on oceans and the atmosphere, deals with common ownership resources. There is a preference for exploitation over conservation and preservation, with a number of recommendations for regulation through international agreements. The theme of human settlements is dealt with in several chapters that seek to promote energy and resource efficiency. Given the deterioration of the urban environment, particularly in the world's mega-cities, it is unfortunate that UNCED did not place greater emphasis on critical Brown Agenda issues, such as polluted air, filthy water and inadequate sanitation, which affect a growing proportion of the world's population. The dangers and costs of waste and the management of hazardous chemicals are examined in the final thematic group of chapters, but there is no mention of the benefits of recycling, of reducing the production of waste or of the need to improve waste disposal techniques.

UNSAID AT UNCED: A CONCLUDING ASSESSMENT OF THE EARTH SUMMIT

Many argue that a great deal was left unsaid at Rio. The limits to the Rio agenda were constrained from the outset by its ecological-modernist perspective, which put emphasis on the need for continued economic growth, coupled with environmental regulation, rather than altering the basic relationship between development and the environment, for which many NGOs lobbied. There were no binding agreements on debt, structural adjustment programmes, population control, North–South technological and financial transfer, the role of TNCs and global militarism (Connelly and Smith, 1999). This reflects the strong influence of international industrial and business interests and the Vatican, which were effective in lobbying at the national level during the PrepComs and within the UNCED process. The intransigence of the USA was a serious limiting factor. The USA was 'prepared to veto any initiative that could be viewed as redistributing economic power at the global level, that would create new institutions, or that would require additional budgetary resources, technology transfers, or changes in domestic US policies' (Porter and Brown, 1996: 117–18). These problems raise two general issues of deeper concern for sustainable development: first, the tension between national sovereignty and international obligations; second, the erosion of government accountability to the electorate, and its replacement with interest politics – most clearly shown in the funding of presidential candidates in the USA.

Despite these profound weaknesses in the UNCED process, some positive movement was achieved. Public awareness of environmental issues was raised. The need to renew democracy through an increased stress on participation ran throughout the conference, and especially in Agenda 21. Governments and NGOs were forced to find ways to talk to each other, and a great many relationships were forged which have strengthened the network of contacts and alliances that have contributed to more recent debates on sustainable development. Finally, but most tangibly, two Conventions were signed and Agenda 21, with all its flaws, has emerged as an important catalyst for further action towards a sustainable future (Grubb, 1993).

GUIDE TO FURTHER READING

For a concise and balanced critique of the UNCED process and its outputs see International Institute for the Environment and Development (1994) *Earth Summit '92*, Wickford: Regency Press.

A spirited critique of Rio, from two environmentalists who witnessed the conference at first hand, is provided by Chatterjee, P. and Finger, M. (1994) *The Earth Brokers: Power, Politics and World Development*, London: Routledge.

For a view which contextualizes the Rio Earth Summit in the international political-economy of the time see Thomas, C. (ed.) (1994) *Rio: Unravelling the Consequences*, Newbury: Frank Cass.

REFERENCES

Chatterjee, P. and Finger, M. (1994) *The Earth Brokers: Power, Politics and World Development*, London: Routledge.

Connelly, J. and Smith, G. (1999) *Politics and the Environment: From Theory to Practice*, London: Routledge.

Elliott, J.A. (1994) *An Introduction to Sustainable Development*, London: Routledge.

Gibbard, L. (1992) 'Gibbard's view cartoon', the *Guardian*, 3 June, p. 5.

Grubb, M. (1993) *The 'Earth Summit' Agreements: A Guide and Assessment*, London: Earthscan.

Intergovernmental Panel on Climate Change (IPCC) (1990) *The IPCC Scientific Assessment*, Cambridge: Cambridge University Press.

Porter, G. and Brown, J. (1996) *Global Environmental Politics*, Boulder CO: Westview Press.

6.4 Local Agenda 21 and the Third World

Jonathan Pugh

SUSTAINABLE DEVELOPMENT AND INCREASING CONCERN WITH 'THE LOCAL'

Sustainable development became a key global concern during the last part of the old millennium and is likely to remain so well into this millennium. This suggests an apparent paradigm shift, or change in world-view of the way in which countries should develop, from a concentration upon pure economic growth to a wider concern with environmental, social and economic sustainability. Whilst much of the focus of this new agenda has been upon national government and the way in which it can control pollution emissions, there is also increasing concern with local-level environmental management. This is because it is increasingly acknowledged that local communities may in some cases be in a better position to understand and manage the local environment than government at the national level (Warburton, 1998).

This theme is developed here by first discussing the relationship between local participation in environmental management and sustainable development before introducing the concept of institutional capacity. This concept suggests that the capacity of local institutions to manage the local environment will be enhanced by bringing together the wide range of different interest groups from within the area and forming a consensus as to the way in which development should take place (Healey, 1997). The discussion then identifies the support which has been given to this approach by Local Agenda 21 which was adopted internationally at the Rio Earth Summit in 1992 (see Chapter 6.3). By means of two case studies from the Caribbean, the second half of this discussion focuses on the issues associated with the reaching of a consensus for environmental management at the local level and the enhancement of local institutional capacity.

INSTITUTIONAL CAPACITY – LINKING PUBLIC PARTICIPATION TO SUSTAINABLE DEVELOPMENT

The linkages between increased local participation in decision-making and sustainable development can be understood by considering the interrelated issues of *inequity*, *empowerment* and *consensus*. Inequitable access to resources confines many people to poverty. This means that whilst a few people can use resources wastefully, the majority of the world's population is forced to degrade the environment.

Inequity and poverty are a reflection of a few interest groups having greater power over decision-making processes which effect the use of resources. As an example, the development of a hotel complex, supported by a limited number of powerful businesspeople and politicians, can lead to the relocation of a local community from the littoral zone of a tropical island. This may mean that the local community moves inland and cuts down rainforests to grow crops, resulting in reduced soil fertility and productivity of land. At the same time the hotel development may allow a few tourists to use electricity, water and so on in an unsustainable manner.

Thus, the dominance of a few interest groups in decision-making processes may lead to unsustainable development. The empowerment of a local community so that it can have a greater input into decision-making processes will increase the community's capacity to consider and propose new and alternative strategies for development. One concept which has been developed as a means of increasing the involvement of more people, and reducing the dominance of a few interest groups in decision-making, is the notion of institutional capacity.

The capacity of local institutions to implement more sustainable development will be enhanced when they address the range of needs of the different groups in society – governmental and non-governmental, gender, religious, kinship, social and so on. A concern with institutional capacity thus involves a concern with the 'web of relations' embedded in societies (Healey, 1997). It involves the identification and forging of relationships between different interest groups, with the aim of reaching a consensus between these groups as to the way in which an area should be developed. A high level of interaction between different interest groups, a wide range of civic associations, coalitions between interest groups and consensus for the way in which a locality is to be developed are thus central to the development of local institutional capacity and more sustainable development (Amin and Thrift, 1995). This approach was given support at the international level by the set of principles put forward at the Rio Earth Summit of 1992 for the achievement of participatory environmental management.

PUTTING INSTITUTIONAL CAPACITY ON THE AGENDA

Agenda 21 is one of the most significant documents to have encouraged debate on the implementation of sustainable development in recent history. It is a product of the United Nations Commission on Environment and Development (UNCED), or the Rio Earth Summit. Chapter 28 of Agenda 21, entitled Local Agenda 21, encourages local governments to facilitate the involvement of community groups and the wider public in decision- and policy-making processes.

Local Agenda 21 was initially formulated by the International Council for Local Environmental Initiatives in 1991 'as a framework for local governments world-wide to engage in implementing the outcomes of the United Nations Conference on Environment and Development' (www.iclei.org). However, as will be seen shortly, the principles of Local Agenda 21 have implications for many local-level institutions, not just local government. These principles suggest that there should be:

1 multi-sectoral engagement in the planning process through a local stakeholder group that serves as the co-ordination and policy body for preparing a long-term sustainable development action plan
2 consultation with community groups, NGOs, businesses, churches, government agencies, professional groups and unions in order to create a shared vision and to identify proposals and priorities for action
3 participatory assessment of local social, economic and environmental conditions and needs
4 participatory target-setting through negotiations among key stakeholders in order to achieve the vision and goals set forth in the action plan, and
5 monitoring and reporting procedures, including local indicators, to track progress and to allow participants to hold each other accountable to the action plan.

(www.iclei.org)

THE IMPLEMENTATION OF LOCAL AGENDA 21

In 1997, the International Council for Local Environmental Initiatives reported the findings of a worldwide study into the implementation of the five principles of Local Agenda 21 outlined above (www.iclei.org). Local Agenda 21 initiatives are most notable in Australia, Bolivia, China, Denmark, Finland, Japan, The Netherlands, Norway, Republic of Korea, Sweden and the United Kingdom. A total of 1,487 local governments in these countries are implementing Local Agenda 21 processes, representing 82 per cent of Local Agenda 21 activities worldwide. Thus, by far the major-ity of Local Agenda 21 initiatives are found in the 'developed world'. This may be because many of the processes are already in place in local government institutions of the 'First World' or those in place may more readily be adapted to fit the principles of Local Agenda 21. 'First World' Local Agenda 21 initiatives tend to concentrate on environmental issues, whereas 'Third World' initia-tives most often focus on social and economic issues. This is arguably a reflection of the issues of poverty and lack of social infrastructure facing many of the world's poorest countries (www.iclei.org).

However, all Local Agenda 21 processes have included consultation with local communities and just over half have involved the establishment of local groups to oversee the implementation of Local Agenda 21. Approximately two-thirds of Local Agenda 21 initiatives have resulted in the production of a local environmental action plan for the area, with over one-quarter establishing monitoring procedures for this plan. The fact that monitoring is more prevalent in the developed world can be seen as a reflection of the resources which these countries have to devote to contin-uous environmental improvement. As indicated in Table 1, in many cases, a wide range of differ-ent interest groups is involved in Local Agenda 21 initiatives. Table 1 indicates that business interests are most likely to be represented when a Local Agenda 21 initiative is established, with indigenous and ethnic minorities being least likely to be involved (www.iclei.org).

This account now turns to two case studies and concentrates on the interactions which take place between different interest groups during participatory processes for environmental manage-ment. The discussion highlights the issues associated with enhancing institutional capacity and establishing Local Agenda 21 initiatives. The case studies are taken from the Caribbean – one from Barbados and the other from St Lucia.

Table 1 The participation of different interest groups in Local Agenda 21 initiatives

Interest group	Percentage of Local Agenda 21 initiatives which include interest group
Business sector	83
Community organizations	82
Non-governmental organizations	79
Educational sector	70
Scientific institutions (universities)	58
Government other than municipal	53
Youth	53
Women	53
Trade unions	51
Ethnic minorities	22
Indigenous people	22

Source: adapted from www.iclei.org

BRINGING TOGETHER DIFFERENT INTEREST GROUPS: THE ISSUE OF CONSENSUS

The town of Soufriere, on the west coast of St Lucia, is one of the most scenic areas in the world. The area is largely covered in thick rainforest and has some of the most diverse coral reefs in the Caribbean. The Soufriere Marine Management Area (SMMA) is a local institution which has been established by the national government of St Lucia, in order to address the conflicts between tourist and fishing sectors in the area which have negatively impacted upon the marine environment. These conflicts are a reflection of the increase in tourism and the competition between fisherpeople and yacht and dive operators over access to the marine environment, plus the decrease in the numbers of fish due to over-fishing. This exercise in the devolution of power formally started in 1995 with the production of the SMMA Plan – the environmental action plan for Soufriere. Before this final agreement for the management of resources was produced, there had been at least three years of intensive consultations between all the different interest groups from the area, from local businesspeople to fisherpeople and hoteliers. It was this level of consultation which led to the SMMA being recognized as a Local Agenda 21 initiative.

The conflicts between the fishing and tourism sectors have also been the impetus for the establishment of the Folkestone Marine Park and Reserve on the west coast of Barbados. The Folkestone area is one of the most intensively developed coastal zones of the Caribbean, and in recent years has witnessed over-fishing and hotel construction. As in the case of Soufriere, the response has been to establish a consultative process for environmental management. An attempt is presently being made in Folkestone to involve a wide range of fisherpeople, hotel owners, local businesspeople and others who conduct activities on the west coast of Barbados, in order to produce an environmental action plan for Folkestone. A local institution – the Folkestone Roundtable – has been established comprising these different interest groups, with the aim of mirroring the success of the SMMA. Although the Folkestone process has adopted many of the principles of Local Agenda 21, it has not been recognized as such, arguably due to the process only beginning in 1999.

Thus, attempts are being made in the case of both Barbados and St Lucia to establish local institutions which involve a diverse range of interest groups in order to develop local plans for the environmental management of local areas. Both countries are attempting to enhance local institutional capacity for sustainable development and are adapting many of the principles of Local Agenda 21. However, the following discussion illustrates that, in both cases, there are a number of issues which are influencing the creation of a consensus for environmental management at the local level (Potter and Pugh, 2000).

First, fisherpeople arguably do not have as much of an influence over the processes as the other interest groups, even though all interest groups are supposed to have an equal input. In Soufriere, the meetings of the local institution are largely conducted in English. However, the main language of fisherpeople is patois, a form of French. Many fisherpeople have suggested that this enables other interest groups to concentrate on steering the meetings to the issue of over-fishing, with less emphasis being placed on the impact of hotels upon the marine environment. Second, fishing has traditionally been viewed as a 'second class' occupation in both Barbados and St Lucia, and fisherpeople have tended to be seen as resource consumers, with the impact of the tourism industry on the environment only recently being acknowledged. This and the fact that tourism brings more money into the islands, gives greater credibility to the voices of the tourist representatives. Third, those in the tourist industry have stronger political connections than fisherpeople. These factors enable those in the tourist sector to have a significant impact over the development of the coastlines of Soufriere and Folkestone. However, many hotels continue to pump raw sewerage into the sea which has a negative impact on coral reefs; and the continued expansion of hotel developments on the littoral zone has significantly reduced access to beaches for local communities.

This brief discussion illustrates that dominant interest groups can have a severe impact upon the enhancement of local institutional capacity and the achievement of a new local environmental agenda. Whilst in both Barbados and St Lucia many different interest groups are being involved, some interest groups have a greater 'say' concerning the use of resources. As a result, these groups are allowed to continue to pollute and have a greater chance of their vision of development being realized, whilst other groups and cultures are effectively being suppressed. Even though local institutions have been established, the connections between inequity, empowerment and consensus have not been addressed.

CONCLUSION

This chapter has discussed and given examples of the increasing number of attempts to involve different interest groups and to develop local institutions for decision-making, with the aim of achieving more sustainable development. However, the development of local institutional capacity for environmental management and the development of a Local Agenda 21 initiative require much more than just bringing these groups together. They involve the forging of new relationships between different interest groups and the breaking down of old and entrenched barriers in order to implement a new local agenda in which all interest groups feel that they have a stake. They involve a greater concern with a new political disposition of power. The argument is therefore that whilst it is important to continue to focus upon 'the local' and bring different local interest groups together to manage the environment, we should also look closely at the relationships between these different groups if the new local environmental agenda is to be successful.

GUIDE TO FURTHER READING

For two differing approaches to the study of local planning, compare Flyvbjerg, B. (1998) *Rationality and Power: Democracy in Practice*, Chicago: University of Chicago Press, with Healey, P. (1997) *Collaborative Planning: Shaping places in Fragmented Societies*, London: Macmillan. The former concentrates on an account of how planning processes are rationalized by those in power. The latter is a justification of the need for collaborative planning.

For further studies on Caribbean planning refer to Potter, R.B. and Pugh, J. (2000) 'Caribbean urban futures', in R.B. Potter (ed.) *The Urban Caribbean in an Era of Global Change*, Aldershot, Brookfield USA, Singapore, Sydney: Ashgate, pp. 173–88.

The International Council for Local Environmental Initiatives website at www.iclei.org contains information on the Local Agenda 21 initiative.

REFERENCES

Amin, A. and Thrift, N. (1995) 'Globalisation, "institutional thickness" and the local economy' in P. Healey, S.J. Cameron, S. Davoudi, S. Graham and A. Madani Pour (eds) *Managing Cities: the New Urban Context*, London: John Wiley, pp. 91–108.

Warburton, D. (1998) *Community and Sustainable Development: Participation in the Future*, London: Earthscan.

6.5 The Brown Environmental Agenda

Tim Forsyth

The 'Brown' Environmental Agenda refers to environmental problems associated with urban or industrial locations, such as pollution, poor sanitation and waste disposal. The term is used in contrast to the 'Green' Agenda, which describes environmental problems associated with vegetation and wildlife, such as biodiversity and deforestation. In contrast to the Green Agenda, almost all 'Brown' environmental problems are relevant in some way to environmental health, although environmental health is an important topic in its own right.

The importance of the Brown Agenda in comparison to the Green Agenda is controversial. Taken together, Brown environmental problems are immense throughout the world and increasing. According to the United Nations, at the beginning of this century, only 14 per cent of people lived in cities, yet by 2000 the proportion had risen to more than 50 per cent; 90 per cent of global population growth occurs in cities. By 2025 the urban population will be 5.2 billion, of whom 77 per cent will live in developing countries. Cities such as Lagos, Mexico City, Shanghai and Cairo are set to contain tens of millions of people by 2010 (United Nations, 1998).

Yet despite this importance, there has been generally little attention to Brown environmental issues in global environmental debate. More people are currently at risk from Brown environmental problems such as contaminated drinking water than commonly thought. Indeed, in 1994, at least 220 million people still lacked a source of potable water near their homes. Diarrhoeal diseases alone killed more than 3 million children in 1993 and caused some 1.8 billion episodes of illness annually (World Resources Institute *et al.*, 1996; World Health Organization, 1999). But at the Earth Summit in 1992, for example, most discussion concerned biodiversity, deforestation and climate change (Grubb *et al.*, 1993).

Some theorists have argued that the lack of attention to Brown environmental issues reflects the fact that most environmentalism in developed countries has emerged contemporaneously with a middle-class urban elite, who have focused mainly on 'Green' concerns such as threats to wilderness and wildlife (Nash, 1982). Moreover, environmental policy in developing countries tends to be formulated by international organizations in conjunction with local elites who may share this concern for wilderness. Local elites may also be the main owners of industry, and therefore are likely to resist environmental regulations that may risk profits. The people most affected by Brown environmental problems tend to be among the poorest inhabitants of developing countries, such as shantytown dwellers or migrant workers, and therefore have little direct influence on the direction of environmental policy. This is not to suggest that problems relating to natural resources are unimportant, but that the importance of the Brown Agenda is often underestimated (Guha and Martinéz-Alier, 1997).

The nature of environmental problems in cities is commonly seen to pass through two main stages over time (Satterthwaite, 1997, 1999). In the first stage, during the early stages of development of the city, hazards include pathogens from human waste or bacteria- and insect-borne infections such as dysentery and cholera, caused by poor sanitation, over-crowding and inadequate water management. The second stage includes hazards resulting from industrialization and technological advancement, such as traffic fumes, heavy metal poisoning (such as from lead and cadmium), or threats inside factories such as solvent poisoning (solvents are highly toxic fluids used for cleaning, and if inhaled in sufficient quantity can kill within seconds). The World Health Organization (WHO and UNEP, 1992) has estimated that in Mexico City, suspended particulate matter from vehicles and others sources contributes to 6,400 deaths each year, and 29 per cent of all children have unhealthy blood lead levels. The World Bank estimates that if particulate levels alone were reduced to WHO guidelines, between 300,000 and 700,000 premature deaths per year could be avoided globally (WHO and UNEP, 1992).

Yet although the nature of hazards produced in cities undergoes a transition over time, the underlying vulnerability of people to environmental problems is also influenced by institutional factors such as effective education or the existence of emergency healthcare. For example, one of the largest causes of deaths among young children in developing countries today is scalding from hot water (Bartlett et al., 1996). Better healthcare and access to medicine by citizens would radically decrease this number. Furthermore, many factories in developing countries are staffed mainly by women, and so they are at greater risk from certain industrial hazards. Another often unrecorded cause of death is indoor air pollution resulting from dirty fuel sources such as animal dung and charcoal. Indoor pollution is often more serious in terms of risk than many outdoor and industrial pollutants, yet it is often overlooked by environmental legislation, and is difficult to monitor. Moreover, implementing safeguards requires communicating to millions of people at the household level.

The incidence of Brown environmental problems also changes over space as cities grow and become more developed. As pollution grows, many authorities are tempted to transport waste elsewhere by physically moving it in containers, waste pipelines, or by using high stack chimneys that can spread pollution in the atmosphere. Acid rain in Germany or New England, for example, has been blamed in part on industrial emissions in Britain or the United States Midwest. Waste dumps are often again based in land inhabited by poor and politically powerless people. Local authorities often lack the infrastructure, training or funding to collect all urban and industrial waste created under rapid urbanization, leading to such inadequate and dangerous dumping. Indeed in 1993, the World Bank estimated that of India's 3,119 towns and cities, only 8 had full waste-water collection and treatment facilities, and 209 partial treatment facilities. The rest simply pumped untreated waste water and sewage into lakes, rivers and coastal areas (Brandon and Ramankutty, 1993).

A related spatial implication of Brown environmental problems is the emergence of so-called 'pollution havens', or locations in developing countries that attract the most polluting industries because of comparatively less stringent environmental regulations or other costs, compared to surrounding locations. South Korea, for example, became the location for much shipbuilding from Japan, and many high-technology companies relocated from California in the 1980s to Southeast Asia because of cheaper labour costs. Three-quarters of all Thai factories dealing with hazardous chemicals are located within Bangkok's metropolitan area and the neighbouring provinces. This includes five of Thailand's seven lead smelting plants and more than 90 per cent of its chemical, dry-cell battery, paint, pharmaceutical and textile manufacturing plants (Linden, 1993). Similarly, some countries have also unwittingly imported toxic waste from industrialized countries because of lax legislation or the wishes of local authorities to receive payment for accepting such waste without knowing how to treat it effectively. In 1987, for example, two Italian firms sent almost 4,000 tonnes of PCB-contaminated waste to Koko, Nigeria, under the label of substances 'relating to the building trade', where they were stored in a farmer's backyard for a small fee. The waste eventually leaked, causing injury to local inhabitants and cleanup workers (Krueger, 1999).

In response to such problems, international efforts to address the Brown Agenda are gradually increasing. The Basel Convention of 1989 provided the first international restrictions on the transport of toxic waste. Furthermore, the United Nations created a Sustainable Cities programme in 1990, and the United Nations Second Conference on Human Settlements (*Habitat II*) in 1996 highlighted environmental problems. The latest series of industrial standards proposed by the International Standards Organization (ISO 14,000) include a variety of environmental guidelines, which are gradually being implemented around the world.

Some analysts are also optimistic that economic globalization – or increasing investment in developing countries by international companies – will also decrease environmental problems. Transnational companies have often proved stricter than local manufacturers in implementing international standards. Furthermore, international investors may also introduce new and environmentally better forms of industry to developing countries such as photovoltaics (technology that converts sunlight to electricity), or industrial waste treatment plants (Forsyth, 1999). Indeed, some initial research represented by the so-called environmental 'Kuznets Curve' has indicated that environmental pollution increases during the early stages of industrialization, but then decreases as industry finds more money to invest in cleaner technologies, and new legislation is passed (Auty, 1997).

However, the enforcement or measurement of environmental standards established on an international basis may not always indicate the totality of incidence of hazards experienced locally. Measurement of greenhouse gas emissions from factories may enable factories to adhere to some international standards, but it may not benefit local populations if the factories also emit waterborne waste that is not measured, or if shantytowns develop around factories with poor sanitation or healthcare. Some theorists have therefore criticized the Kuznets Curve for overlooking the political distribution of hazards resulting from industrialization, and instead only focusing on a limited number of risks, excluding the problems most relevant to local inhabitants (Satterthwaite, 1997). Furthermore, the increasing dependency of many developing countries on international investment opens their economies to the risk of industry relocating to new countries if costs rise. Few governments wish to increase these costs by insisting on enforcing new environmental standards. Host countries therefore have to consider how far foreign investment may enhance industrialization and improve environmental standards; or how far it may lead to pollution havens, and consequent damage to the competitiveness of domestic companies. In some cases, governments have chosen to concentrate foreign investment in specially selected export-processing zones or industrial estates that can often be hotspots for industrial pollution or environmental health problems (Eskeland and Harrison, 1997).

The environmental impact of foreign investment is also related to the inclusivity of economic development, and the ability for authorities to implement regulation. In Central and Eastern Europe, it is almost uniformly agreed that the environmental standards under communism were poor, and that the influx of investment from Europe and North America may increase environmental quality. Yet, in common with all countries undergoing rapid industrialization, the distribution of environmental benefits depends partly on the ability of the new economic growth to include all sectors of society, and for environmental standards and laws to be enforced. Unfortunately, the lack of progress in both of these factors so far has indicated that industrialization has to be accompanied by the evolution of political infrastructure that can undertake the formulation and implementation of equitable environmental policy. Furthermore, a large proportion of new investment in Eastern Europe and developing countries will be in commodities, such as cars, that add to environmental problem. In 1990, the global vehicle fleet (excluding two- and three-wheel vehicles) totalled some 580 million, but this will grow to more than 810 million by 2010 (Faiz and Gautam, 1994).

The Brown Environmental Agenda, then, refers to some of the most pressing and widespread environmental problems in development, which often affect the poorest and least powerful people. The production of environmental hazards also reflects the influence of powerful groups such as local elites and international investors. Consequently, Brown environmental problems are intricately linked to political and social change, and the ability to change the direction of policy towards the needs of groups that are politically unrepresented.

But achieving such change is difficult as it involves challenging many deep-seated interests and assumptions common in global environmental policy. Under the Kyoto Protocol of 1997, for example, a new investment fund called the *Clean Development Mechanism* was established in order to encourage investment in developing countries by countries who had to reduce greenhouse gas emissions. The Mechanism was created partly in order to satisfy the long-term demands of many developing countries for more effective environmental technology. However, since 1997, most discussion of how to use the Mechanism has concentrated on investing in the Green Agenda topics such as reforestation for carbon sequestration rather than methods to reduce industrial emissions at source (Grubb *et al.*, 1999). Some analysts have explained this redirection of funds from Brown to Green Agenda as a result of greater support in industrialized nations for projects that can allegedly combine carbon sequestration with biodiversity conservation. Moreover, some industrialized countries fear that upgrading industrial technology in developing countries will incur greater costs and threaten the industrial competitiveness of investors (Forsyth, 1999). Meanwhile, industrialization and urbanization in developing countries continue rapidly, with many of their hazards going unchecked.

The future management of Brown environmental problems seems dependent on achieving change both locally and globally. At the local level, new political institutions are needed to enable local citizens to gain access to the environmental policy process in order to ensure that their needs are being met and that environmental education about new industrial hazards can be communicated effectively. At the global scale, a new attitude is required to understand that millions of lives are at risk from Brown environmental problems, and that global environmental agreements need to prioritize new forms of investment and political action to address them fully.

GUIDE TO FURTHER READING

For readers seeking case studies and policy updates from the developing world, the most informative journal is *Environment and Urbanization*, which is published in the United Kingdom by the International Institute for Environment and Development, see http://www.iied.org/eandu/index.html.

New, and informative, publications are also made available from the websites of international organizations such as the World Bank, http://www.worldbank.org/, World Health Organization, http://www.who.int/ and United Nations, http://www.un.org/, and specialist research institutes such as the Royal Institute of International Affairs, http://www.riia.org/, and the World Resources Institute, http://www.wri.org/. These organizations publish annual reports of environmental problems that provide up-to-date statistics and news.

For readers seeking a general introduction to the Brown Agenda, there are two important textbooks: Hardoy, J., Mitlin, D. and Satterthwaite, D. (1992) *Environmental Problems in Third World Cities*, London: Earthscan; and Satterthwaite, D. (ed.) (1999) *The Earthscan Reader in Sustainable Cities*, London: Earthscan.

REFERENCES

Auty, R. (1997) 'Patterns of pollution during the industrial transition', *The Geographical Journal* 163(2): 206–15.

Bartlett, S., Hart, R., Satterthwaite, D., de la Barra, X. and Missair, A. (1996) *Cities for Children: Children's Rights, Poverty and Urban Management*, London: Earthscan and UNICEF.

Brandon, C. and Ramankutty, R. (1993) *Toward an Environmental Strategy for Asia*, World Bank Discussion Paper No. 224, Washington DC: World Bank.

Eskeland, G. and Harrison, A. (1997) 'Moving to greener pastures?: multinationals and the pollution haven hypothesis', World Bank, Policy Research Dept, Public Economics Division, Washington DC: World Bank.

Faiz, A. and Gautam, S. (1994) *Motorization, Urbanization, and Air Pollution, Discussion Paper*, Washington DC: World Bank.

Forsyth, T. (1999) *International Investment and Climate Change: Energy Technologies for Developing Countries*, London: Earthscan and the Royal Institute of International Affairs.

Grubb, M., Koch, M., Munson, A., Sullivan, F. and Thomson, K. (1993) *The Earth Summit Agreements: a Guide and Assessment*, London: Earthscan and the Royal Institute of International Affairs.

Grubb, M. with Brack, D. and Vrolijk, C. (1999) *The Kyoto Protocol: a Guide and Assessment*, London: Earthscan and the Royal Institute of International Affairs.

Guha, R. and Martinéz-Alier, J. (1997) *Varities of Environmentalism*, London: Earthscan.

Krueger, J. (1999) *International Trade and the Basel Convention*, London: Earthscan and the Royal Institute of International Affairs.

Linden, E. (1993) 'Megacities', *Time* 141(2), 11 January.

Nash, R.F. (1982) *Wilderness and the American mind* (3rd edn), revised, New Haven: Yale University Press.

Satterthwaite, D. (1997) 'Environmental transformations in cities as they get larger, wealthier and better managed', *The Geographical Journal* 163(2): 216–24.

Satterthwaite, D. (ed.) (1999) *The Earthscan Reader in Sustainable Cities*, London: Earthscan.

United Nations (1998) *World Urbanization Prospects, the 1996 Revision: Estimates and Projections of Urban and Rural Populations and of Urban Agglomerations*, Department of Economic and Social Affairs, Population Division, New York: United Nations.

World Health Organization (1999) *The World Health Report 1999: Making a Difference*, Geneva: World Health Organization.

World Health Organization and United Nations Environment Programme (1992) *Urban Air Pollution in Megacities of the World*, Oxford: Blackwell.

World Resources Institute, United Nations Environment Programme, United Nations Development Programme and the World Bank (1996) *World Resources 1996–97: A Guide to the Global Environment*, Washington DC: World Resources Institute.

6.6 Vulnerability and disasters

Piers Blaikie

DEFINITION

A disaster is a great, sudden and unexpected misfortune. Its consequent disruption may involve mortality, morbidity, severe mental and physical privation as well as the destruction of or damage to property. It can also disturb existing social structures and processes including systems of production; the division of labour, norms and social roles, the course of national and international politics, as well people's expectations, outlook and motivations. A disaster typically involves a discrete and natural event such as storm-force wind, flood, drought, pest attack, earthquake, landslide or avalanche, as well as events caused wholly by human action, such as industrial accidents and acts of war. The term 'disaster' has also been stretched to include longer-term events such as the AIDS pandemic in the worst affected regions of the world (Barnett and Blaikie, 1994), and to complex human emergencies, in which a number of these events and their repercussions play themselves out over a considerable period of time.

EXPLANATIONS OF DISASTERS

It is likely that the number and scale of disasters has steadily risen over the past 40 years and this has contributed to the rising significance of the field of disaster studies. These focus upon improving understanding of why and how disasters happen; predicting and monitoring the type and degree of damage and loss; and evolving practical methods of forecasting, prevention, mitigation and assisting recovery. Unfortunately, it is true to say that the gap between the intellectual/academic analysis and the practice of disaster mitigation remains wide.

The dominant and technocratic view

Disaster studies have focused on the search for causes and understanding processes by which a disaster is initiated and subsequently unfolds. One of the earliest authoritative attempts was made in the Indian Famine Codes from 1880, which still remain central to Indian government policy today. Usually, explanations for disasters do not identify a single direct cause, but rather a coming together of both direct and indirect causes. Until the mid-1980s, natural causes of disasters were given prominence, and the direction of explanation tended to run from the physical environment to its social impacts. Thus, famine was seen to be caused by drought and consequent crop failure, leading to an insufficient supply of food. Loss of life through drowning and damage to property in a coastal area were seen to be caused by storm-force winds and exceptional high tides concurring at low-lying coastal locations. Deaths from the collapse of buildings following an earthquake were seen to be caused by the severity of the earthquake itself, and so on. This seemed a common-sense approach, but as we shall see, common sense, while having an alluring appeal, sometimes proves unreliable. This type of explanation, which focuses on the natural rather than the social, underlines the 'exceptional', 'unprecedented', 'unexpected', 'unmanaged' and 'unforeseen' nature of the event for which people were 'unprepared' and 'unaware' (Hewitt, 1983: 10). It led to policy measures which favoured physical protection, forecasting and monitoring geophysical processes, physical protection from physical hazards, and emergency measures.

The political economy view

Increasingly over the last 15 years, explanations have shifted from the 'dominant' approach described above to a political economy approach. The latter, while not excluding the role of nature, emphasizes the social reasons of why people are susceptible to these natural events. Natural events such as storms, earthquakes and floods do occur, the explanation goes, but they need not become a disaster. Adequate warning, protection, knowledge, skills and access to both material resources and to knowledge, networks and sources of support can greatly mitigate the impact of a natural event and increase the ability of people to recover from its effects. Attention is thus directed to the structural processes which create and distribute material resources, wealth, influence and power in a society, that is to say the preconditions for a disaster – which is indeed the focus of political economy. Specifically, attention is turned to normal, day-to-day life in which people with different human and material resources earn a livelihood. When a natural event occurs, which could potentially have disastrous impacts, the pre-existing distribution of these resources shapes in a direct way the distribution of access and capability to avoid, cope with successfully and recover from the natural event in a given population.

There are clear political and moral advantages from this more recent approach to disasters. First, it implies that disasters are preventable – that natural events need not turn into disasters at all, which points to the accountability of people, processes and institutions which may have either increased the susceptibility to the natural event or have some responsibility for preventing or mitigating its impacts. Second, people are seen not as hapless and helpless victims of a disaster, but as actors who are capable in varying degrees of coping in the wake of a natural event, or avoiding it altogether. Therefore, instead of blaming nature and people for an unprecedented event for which they had been inadequately prepared, people's own resources become central to their recovery. Third, issues of justice are highlighted. The rich seldom suffer from the impact of a disaster as much as the poor. Most frequently, it is women (rather than men), the very old and very young, those of low social status, those of ethnic and religious minorities who are discriminated against by the majority, those with poor access to appropriate resources and reserves and those who cannot draw upon a supply of social capital (that is, trust and support networks) who fare worst and fail to recover.

VULNERABILITY

The concept of vulnerability attempts to operationalize this degree and type of susceptibility to different natural events. Unfortunately the term has been used in many different ways and it has generated almost as much confusion as insight. Here is one definition, among many others, which may be identified as mainstream:

> the characteristics of a person or group in terms of their capacity to anticipate, cope with, resist, and recover from the impact of a natural hazard. It involves a combination of factors which determine the degree to which someone's life and livelihood is put at risk by a discrete and identifiable event in nature or society.
>
> (Blaikie, *et al.*, 1994: 9)

Therefore the term 'vulnerability' refers to people rather than to areas, buildings or agricultural systems, and is a statistical condition which applies to people during 'normal' (pre-disaster) life, but which is not realized and tested until it is triggered by a natural event (see the alternative but similar definitions by Cannon, 1994; Deyle *et al.*, 1998 and Maskrey, 1989). Much of the explanatory power of vulnerability derives from its basis in how people earn a livelihood. Figure 1 describes in graphic terms the iterative process of earning a livelihood from a sample number of individuals (men, women, young, old etc.) in different households with different demographic characteristics and with different access to the range of necessary resources to gain a livelihood.

People make regular decisions to plant crops, sell produce, invest in economic activity or sell cattle, and normal life continues. For some, this may well involve privation, oppression and hardship, but for others, the opposite. It is not until the natural event intervenes – very suddenly as in the case of an earthquake or *tsunami* (tidal wave) or over a period of months or even years as in the case of a famine (as illustrated in Figure 1) – that the pre-existing patterns of vulnerability are called into effect.

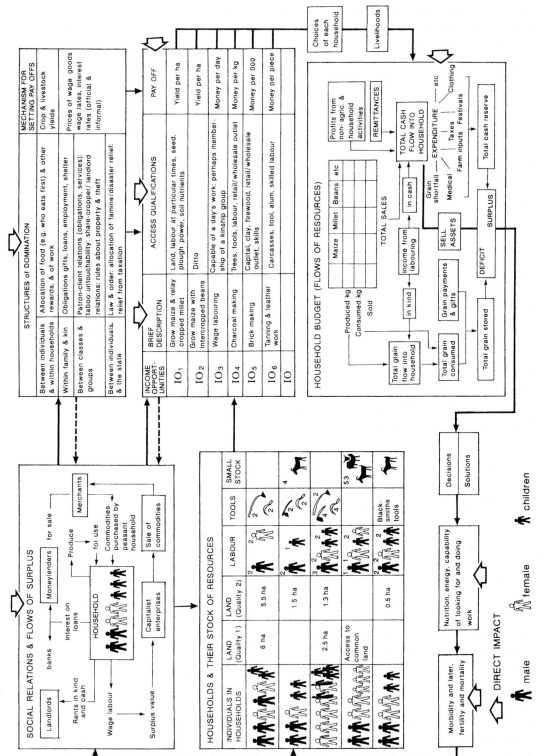

Figure 1 Impact of natural events upon livelihoods

The natural event is coped with in different ways by those with very different capabilities. Those with a low vulnerability have a high resilience to this natural shock; have better access to early warning systems; can take preventative action (e.g. stockpiling food or vacating a hazardous area by private transport); and can generally buy their way out of trouble. Access to sources of official assistance is superior for these people as they are usually literate, have friends and relatives in the local administration, and know how to handle and benefit from networks of distribution. Those with a high vulnerability show the converse characteristics.

This explanatory scheme of vulnerability is then 'cycled through' iteratively following the natural event. Sometimes instantaneously, there are both direct and indirect impacts. For example, some members of the household may have died or been injured as a direct result of the impact of the natural event. Others will have been traumatized and will have to divert their energies and resources to looking after the injured or burying their dead. Many of their material resources may become unusable. The range of practicable choice of income opportunities may thus be drastically curtailed, and simply no longer available to them. Also, the access qualifications for some income opportunities may rise beyond the capabilities of the more vulnerable. Others may be able to sell surpluses at greatly inflated prices. The outcomes of these differentiated coping strategies may be reflected in reduced consumption for some, but great wealth for others. For example, inequality in the distribution of valuable assets, particularly land, was greatly increased as a result of the floods and famine in Bangladesh in 1987. This model can be cycled a number of times following the natural event as values in the livelihood system may radically change over a matter of days.

Entitlements

A parallel and similar explanatory model deriving from approximately the same date is the 'entitlement' approach developed by Sen (1981). Both the access and entitlement approaches are explained, not because they are substantially different, but because the reader in disaster studies is bound to encounter both.

People obtain food through a number of different types of 'entitlement relationships' in private ownership market economies. Instead of the notion of access, structures of domination and the market which determine access qualifications and pay-offs as in the explanatory scheme above, a range of 'entitlements' are identified. These can be production-based entitlements which are the right to own food that one produces with one's own or hired resources; trade-based entitlements associated with ownership when they are transferred through commodity exchange; own labour entitlement when one sells one's own labour power; inheritance and transfer entitlement; and extended entitlements based upon legitimacy and expectations regarding access to resources. This formulation has, in the case of famine to which it was originally applied, allowed innovative and important insights which, at first might seem contrary to common sense. People starve, entitlements theory claims, because their entitlements to food fail and not necessarily because there are insufficient aggregate food supplies to feed everyone. Thus, there have been famines where the total food availability has not declined at all, but instead there has been a failure of effective demand (not need!) for food through the failure of their entitlements. People simply became too poor to afford food which is physically available. A number of protracted debates about the operation of the two competing causes of famine (Food Availability Decline versus Food Entitlement Decline) have complicated the issue, and it is clear that they are not as mutually exclusive in many cases as the protagonists of each position claim. In many famines, it is clear that both an initial food availability decline occurred on either a national or regional scale

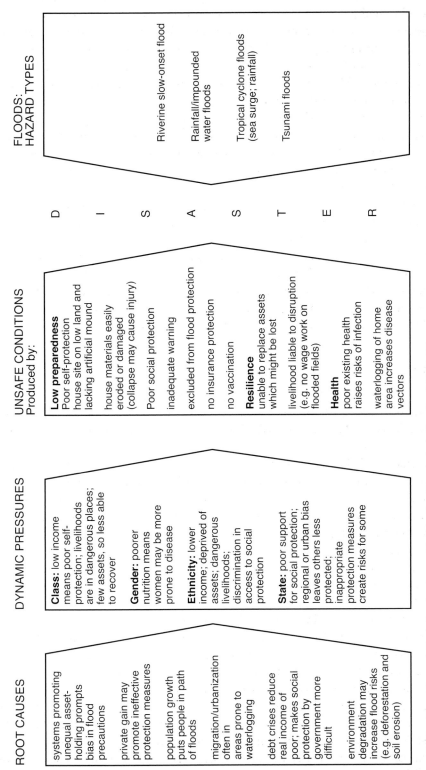

Figure 2 The 'Crunch model' of disasters as applied to the Bangladesh floods of 1987–88

Source: Blaikie et al., 1994, Figure 6.1, p. 134

(for example, brought about by extended civil war or drought), as well as entitlement failure for certain vulnerable groups.

WIDER CONTEXTS OF DISASTERS

While the notion of vulnerability – either employing the access or entitlement model – throws light upon the local and regional context of the impact of disasters, it is still necessary to put patterns of vulnerability in a wider social context. One attempt to do this has been called 'pressure' or, perhaps less elegantly, the 'crunch' model. This identifies what it calls a hierarchy of factors, from the international to the local, which are labelled 'root causes', 'dynamic pressures', 'unsafe conditions'. These bear down upon people differentially as preconditions of long standing from the one side of Figure 2 and the hazard event from the other. When the hazard event occurs, people are 'squeezed' differentially by what is termed 'a disaster'. Figure 2 indicates an example of the Bangladesh floods in 1987–88.

IMPLICATIONS FOR POLICY

Turning finally to the implications for policy of these developments in disaster studies, the most important generalization is that in practice the dominant, technocratic view prevails, in spite of the new insights of political economic approaches. It is easier for national governments and the international disaster relief agencies to respond to an emergency than to track and tackle the structural (and politically sensitive) preconditions of vulnerability. There is much more political mileage to be made for governments from physical protection (bunds, flood shelters, sea defences) and conspicuous handouts of food and medical supplies than from the supposed benefits in the reduction of vulnerability through such measures as redistributive land reform, easily accessible micro-credit or the provision of do-it-yourself earthquake-resistant housing. Furthermore, disaster relief when it does arrive, is frequently inappropriate and is not targeted to the most vulnerable. Most importantly, 'outsiders', while vital in providing resources to mitigate disasters and for implementing policies to decrease vulnerability and injustice, also have the greatest capacity to undermine the most effective resource of all – local community self-help, local organizations and local networks. Also, once the emergency is over, institutional memories are short. The window of opportunity for structural reform to reduce vulnerability, and to integrate disaster relief into longer-term development policy is usually all too limited.

GUIDE TO FURTHER READING

Interested readers can consult the following three texts.

Blaikie. P.M., Cannon, T., Davis, I. and Wisner, B. (1994) *At Risk: Natural Hazards, People's Vulnerability and Disasters*, London: Routledge.

Hewitt, K. (1997) *Regions of Risk: A Geographical Introduction to Disasters*, London: Longman.

Oliver-Smith, A. and Hoffman, S. (eds) (1999) *The Angry Earth: Disaster in Anthropological Perspective*, New York: Routledge.

REFERENCES

Barnett, A. and Blaikie, P.M. (1994) 'AIDS as a long wave disaster', in A. Varley (ed.) *Disasters, Development and Enviroment*, Chichester: Wiley, Ch. 10.

Cannon, T. (1994) 'Vulnerability analysis and the explanation of "natural disasters"', in A. Varley (ed.) *Disasters, Development and Environment*, Chichester: Wiley, Ch. 2.

Deyle, R., French, S., Olshansky, R. and Paterson, R. (1998) 'Hazard assessment: the factual basis for planning and mitigation', in R. Burby (ed.) *Cooperating with Nature*, Washington DC: National Academy Press.

Hewitt, K. (ed.) (1983) *Interpretations of Calamity*, Boston: Allen and Unwin.

Maskrey, A. (1989) *Disaster Mitigation: A Community Based Approach, Development Guidelines*, Development Guidelines, No. 3, Oxford: Oxfam.

Sen, A. (1981) *Famines and Poverty*, Oxford: Oxford University Press.

6.7 Savannas and development

Jayalaxshmi Mistry

INTRODUCTION

Savannas are tropical and sub-tropical ecosystems with a continuous and important grass/herbaceous stratum, a discontinuous layer of trees and shrubs of variable height and density, and where growth patterns are closely associated with alternating wet and dry seasons (Bourlière and Hadley, 1983). The key ecological determinants of savannas are plant available moisture (PAM), plant available nutrients (PANs), fire and herbivory (Stott, 1991). Savannas cover over a third of the tropics in South America, Asia, Australia and large tracts of Africa, and are home to over a fifth of the world's population. Many of these human communities rely on subsistence agriculture or pastoralism for survival, and are therefore governed by the seasonal and sometimes unpredictable nature of PAM, as well as by the typically nutrient-poor PAN status of many soils.

There are many developmental issues in savannas. These include the rising population increasing the demand for both agricultural and urban land, advances in agricultural technology and its commoditization, inequalities in land distribution, insecure tenure and the commercialization of natural products. Although these issues affect savannas around the world, a large amount of work has been focused on Africa, especially in the more semi-arid regions. In particular, emphasis has been on land degradation problems and the role of pastoralists in this process. However, a common element of much development work in savannas has been a general lack of understanding of savanna ecology, as well as traditional ways of life and culture. The three environmental issues I would like to focus on in this essay illustrate this point well. They are land degradation in savannas, wildlife management through community-based projects, and traditional and indigenous resource use and management.

EQUILIBRIUM/NON-EQUILIBRIUM PARADIGMS IN SAVANNAS: THE CAUSES OF LAND DEGRADATION

There has been widespread belief that as a result of over-use of natural resources, many semi-arid lands, including savannas, are threatened by wide-scale and irreversible land degradation. Dramatic statements about the rate of desertification and bush encroachment have been made by academics and development professionals alike, exacerbated by media coverage, particularly in sub-Saharan Africa. Local pastoralists have invariably been regarded as the culprits, and development efforts have been aimed at changing their management strategies, and ultimately their way of life. Yet what is incredible is that many claims of land degradation have no supporting scientific evidence. Prince *et al.* (1998), for example, used remotely sensed data to show that sub-continental desertification in the Sahelian savanna zone of West Africa is not taking place. Then where do these ideas of impending doom in pastoral lands come from?

Traditional ideas on land degradation on pastoral lands in savannas can be traced to ecosystem concepts of fragility and equilibrium (Sullivan, 1996). These views see ecosystems as isolated, closed biotic systems, gradually equilibrating to stable, external conditions until a 'climax' equilibrium state is reached. Stability in the biotic closed system is maintained through intra- and interspecific interactions among species, and any disturbance to this system is perceived as being external to the dynamic functioning of the ecosystem. In regards to pastoral lands, these assumptions about ecosystem dynamics have had a fundamental impact on development policies and interventions. They have been the framework of maintaining livestock and harvesting at 'sustainable' (i.e. constant) levels through time, and of assuming that there is an inherent 'carrying capacity' for land, which if exceeded, will cause degradation. They have also been the basis of claims of irreversible land degradation when successive dry years have resulted in tracts of bare ground, and that local resource management strategies designed to capitalize on good years in order to survive drought, are destructive.

However, there is one fundamental characteristic of semi-arid savannas that the development community has chosen to ignore: the variable and unpredictable nature of rainfall and, therefore, PAM. Sullivan (1996: 1) gives the example of Namibia, where an area of her research was described in 1995 as being 'on the brink of collapse' and one year later, as a result of above-average rainfall, an 'uninterrupted ocean of waving grassland'. The recognition by some workers that indeed rainfall may not be 'external', but a critical biotic-interacting component of the ecosystem, has led to a paradigm shift to a non-equilibrium ecology (Warren, 1995). In this model, the biotic component, reflecting factors such as biological productivity, are primarily PAM-limited and driven by aperiodic and idiosyncratic rainfall events. Therefore, in many cases, so-called 'land degradation' may in fact be a temporary transition stage governed by the variable PAM, as well as other 'disturbances', including fire.

An illustration of this is given by studies in the eastern Kalahari, which have characterized bush encroachment as major land degradation, associated with the intensification of cattle grazing over the last 30 years. Dougill *et al.* (1999) investigated this hypothesis by comparing the impact of boreholes of various ages on bush encroachment. They found that bush encroachment was not directly related to the age of a given borehole, and there were no changes in soil characteristics between boreholes. This supports the idea that frequent disturbance such as fires, frosts, and wood harvesting, but particularly droughts, provide savannas with some degree of ecological resilience to permanent change. Dougill *et al.* (1999) conclude that the bush encroachment presently seen in the eastern Kalahari is not permanent, but a stage in a dynamic system that may either lead to quasi-permanent ecological change or be reversed, depending on environmental conditions and management strategies (see figure).

That is not to argue that degradation is not occurring. It is, but in more localized patches, and can be attributed to development policies encouraging the settlement of pastoralists and their livestock by providing boreholes in areas without permanent water. Ringrose *et al.* (1996), using satellite data in south-eastern Botswana, found that most natural vegetation had been removed within walking distance of villages and adjacent to boreholes. Similar results were found by Perkins and Thomas (1993).

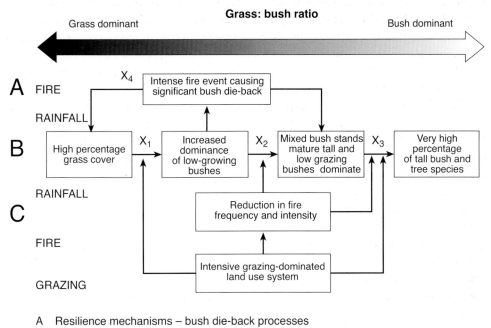

A   Resilience mechanisms – bush die-back processes
B   Vegetation state
C   Degradation processes – bush encroachment processes
Note: all trasitions are regulated by the inherent variability in rainfall regimes

State and transition model of ecological change on Kalahari rangelands
Source: after Dougill *et al.*, 1999

Sullivan (1996) stresses the need for development policies to switch their focus from trying to maintain pastoral lands in a state of 'equilibrium', to the idea of 'persistence' (i.e. the adaptability of plants, animals and humans to changing conditions). More emphasis needs to be placed on studying and promoting local resource management strategies, as has already been done for some pastoral groups (e.g. Behnke *et al.*, 1993). However, as Sullivan (1996: 4) points out 'dominant thinking about arid and semi-arid systems remains largely focussed on exactly the opposite'.

WILDLIFE MANAGEMENT

In African savannas, wildlife and humans have been in conflict for decades. It was after the peak of big-game hunting during colonial times that European colonists realized that animal populations had been severely reduced. A conservation strategy, the 'fences and fines' approach (based on the American National Park model), was adopted, resulting in the displacement of many local communities, as well as a restriction on utilizing natural resources that they had had access to for hundreds of years.

By the 1970s, it became obvious that this form of conservation was not working. Shrinking habitats and economies of local communities was one problem; the other was the high levels of 'illegal' hunting. Media coverage mainly highlighted the huge numbers of elephants being hunted for their ivory, but many other animals were also affected, and still are. A study by Hofer *et al.*

(1996) estimated that in the Serengeti National Park, the total annual off-take between 1992 and 1993 was 159,811 wildlife, including 44,958 resident and 111,691 migratory mammalian herbivores. These were mainly wildebeest, zebra and impala. However, what government and development agencies failed to recognize was that wildlife had always been a vital resource for local communities, and so-called 'poaching' is a means of sustaining livelihoods.

In the early 1980s, conservationists began a search for alternative ways to protect wildlife and involve local communities in the process. A new approach, 'community-based wildlife management' (CWM), was introduced, with the underlying idea that local communities should have the right to manage and benefit from local resources and, as a result, they would protect and conserve wildlife because it would be in their economic interest to do so. Various programmes were established, the most well-known being CAMPFIRE (Communal Area Management Programme for Indigenous Resources) in the savannas (*miombo*) of Zimbabwe (Campbell, 1996). Although in principle the idea is good, and some positive outcomes occurred, recent research indicates that there are still many fundamental problems with CWM (Songorwa, 1999). These are principally the failure to adopt the bottom-up, participatory approach which CWM advocates, and the inability to address basic community needs, and distribute benefits equally. These studies indicate that local elites were gaining the most from such projects.

INDIGENOUS RESOURCE MANAGEMENT

Development in the area of resource management in savannas has made an interesting U-turn, and there have been concerted efforts to learn more about indigenous and traditional techniques of resource management. Reij *et al.* (1996) describe various soil conservation techniques used by local communities in African savannas. Researchers are also looking more closely at traditional grazing management strategies by pastoralists, as already mentioned.

Fire has been an age-old management tool in savannas, mainly for agricultural and pastoral purposes. However, the arrival of European colonists in many savanna regions both altered the fire regime to one of late dry season burning, and imposed restrictions on burning per se. In many savanna regions, the latter has been upheld until today, with policy-makers opting for fire suppression rather than any proper management strategy involving the use of fire. The consequences have been large-scale illegal burning, and the occurrence of catastrophic burns resulting in ecological and economic damage to land and property.

Recent research has, therefore, turned back to traditional and indigenous methods of fire management. For example, Mistry (1998), interviewing traditional small farmers in the Brazilian savannas, found that indicators such as the lunar cycle were important in determining the use of fire. The farmers claimed that burning during certain phases of the moon has beneficial effects on post-fire plant growth, although as yet there is no scientific evidence to support this. The influence of the moon is also significant in that it suggests that some traditional burning is being carried out at various times throughout the dry season, not only during the late dry season. The use of indigenous fire management, however, is most evident in the Australian savannas. Research there has been ongoing since Haynes (1985) first described the fire strategies of a group of Aborigines in north-central Arnhem Land. This, and more recent research, indicates that Aboriginal fire management involves burning at different times of the year and of different vegetation types within the savanna region. A practical implication of adopting the traditional fire management model is that considerable effort must be given to breaking up grassy fuels in the early to mid dry season, in effect to create a mosaic of burnt and unburnt patches across the landscape (Russell-Smith, 1995). This is in contrast to the European model of fire management whereby a few large areas of savanna are burned within a limited period of the year.

With the recognition of Aboriginal land rights, and traditional resource management, fire management policies in the Australian savannas are now aimed at incorporating Aboriginal techniques. At Kakadu National Park, for example, policies for fire management are based on Aboriginal regimes. These prescribed fires are applied by park staff, but around Aboriginal settlements and areas used for hunting, burning is carried out by Aborigines. The nature and practice of Aboriginal burning has relevance for contemporary and future land management. Aboriginal burning has both ecological and social significance, the latter illustrated by the 'cleaning' burns that are set in the early to mid dry season (Russell-Smith *et al.*, 1997). The mosaic of early, late and unburnt patches also has implications for conservation, with studies showing that a range of fire regimes is required to adequately conserve certain faunal groups, as well as biodiversity in general.

CONCLUSION

Development in savannas is constrained by many factors, particularly the physical environment limited by PAM and PAN. However, as the examples above demonstrate, development in savannas is also affected by perceptions of ecosystem dynamics, as in the case of land degradation, and the influence of European values, as in the cases of wildlife management and indigenous resource use. This is juxtaposed with many social and economic injustices, especially problems of land tenure. The unequal distribution of land and any wealth generated from it is a major barrier to development. Although there are movements in some savanna regions, such as the Aboriginal movement in the Australian savannas and 'Sem Terra' (People Without Land) in the Brazilian savannas, addressing inequality in land ownership is still a major hurdle. However, hopefully, the fact that people are increasingly questioning past methods and values of management in savannas will mean recognition for change and a better future for all savanna lands.

GUIDE TO FURTHER READING

Behnke, R.H., Scoones, I. and Kerven, C. (eds) (1993) *Range Ecology at Disequilibrium: New Models of Natural Variability and Pastoral Adaptation in African Savannas*, London: ODI and IIED. A good description of the ideas of equilibrium and disequilibrium, and their application to traditional pastoralism in Africa.

Campbell, B. (ed.) (1996) *The Miombo in Transition: Woodlands and Welfare in Africa*, Bogor, Indonesia: Center for International Forestry Research (CIFOR). A useful guide to wildlife and traditional resource management in the central African savannas.

Mistry, J. (2000) *World Savannas: Ecology and Human Use*, Harlow: Pearson Education. A comprehensive account of various development issues in savannas around the world.

REFERENCES

Bourlière, F. and Hadley, M. (1983) 'Present-day savannas: an overview', in F. Bourlière (ed.) *Tropical Savannas: Ecosystems of the World 13*, Amsterdam: Elsevier Scientific Publishing Company, pp. 1–17.

Dougill, A.J., Thomas, D.S.G. and Heathwaite, A.L. (1999) 'Environmental change in the Kalahari: integrated land degradation studies for nonequilibrium dryland environments', *Annals of the Association of American Geographers*, 89(3): 420–42.

Haynes, C.D. (1985) 'The pattern and ecology of munwag: traditional Aboriginal fire regimes in north-central Arnhemland', *Proceedings of the Ecological Society of Australia* 13: 203–14.

Hofer, H., Campbell, K.L.I., East, M.L. and Huish, S.A. (1996) 'The impact of game meat hunting on target and non-target species in the Serengeti', in V.J. Taylor and N. Dunstone (eds) *The Exploitation of Mammal Populations*, London: Chapman and Hall, pp. 117–46.

Mistry, J. (1998) 'Decision-making for fire use among farmers in the savannas of central Brazil', *Journal of Environmental Management* 54: 321–34.

Perkins, J.S. and Thomas, D.S.G. (1993) 'Spreading deserts or spatially confined environmental impacts? Land degradation and cattle ranching in the Kalahari desert of Botswana', *Land Degradation and Rehabilitation* 4: 179–94.

Prince, S.D., Brown de Colstoun, E. and Kravitz, L.L. (1998) 'Evidence from rain-use efficiencies does not indicate extensive Sahelian desertification', *Global Change Biology* 4: 359–74.

Reij, C., Scoones, I. and Toulmin, C. (eds) (1996) '*Sustaining the Soil: Indigenous Soil and Water Conservation in Africa*, London: Earthscan.

Ringrose, S., Vanderpost, C. and Matheson, W. (1996) 'The use of integrated remotely sensed and GIS data to determine causes of vegetation cover change in southern Botswana', *Applied Geography* 16(3): 225–42.

Russell-Smith, J. (1995) 'Fire management', in T. Press, D. Lea, A. Webb and A. Graham (eds) *Kakadu: Natural and Cultural Heritage and Management*. Darwin: Australian Nature Conservation Agency, North Australia Research Unit, Australian National University, pp. 217–37.

Russell-Smith, J., Lucas, D., Gapindi, M., Gunbunuka, B., Kapirigi, N., Namingum, G., Lucas, K., Giuliani, P. and Chaloupka, G. (1997) 'Aboriginal resource utilisation and fire management practice in western Arnhem Land, monsoonal northern Australia: notes for prehistory, lessons for the future', *Human Ecology* 25(2): 159–95.

Songorwa, A.N. (1999) 'Community-based wildlife management (CWM) in Tanzania: are the communities interested?', *World Development* 27(12): 2061–79.

Stott, P. (1991) 'Recent trends in the ecology and management of the world's savanna formations', *Progress in Physical Geography*, 15(1): 18–28.

Sullivan, S. (1996) 'Towards a non-equilibrium ecology: perspectives from an arid land', *Journal of Biogeography* 23: 1–5.

Warren, A. (1995) 'Changing understandings of African pastoralism and the nature of environmental paradigms', *Transactions of the Institute of British Geographers* 20: 193–203.

6.8 Tropical moist forests and development

Alan Grainger

INTRODUCTION

The deforestation of tropical moist forests is a major global environmental problem, threatening the survival of half of all species of plants and animals, and contributing to global climate change via the greenhouse effect. According to some projections, all tropical moist forests could be lost in 100 years if present deforestation rates continue (Myers, 1985). Yet from the point of view of tropical countries, these forests cover land that could be put to more productive uses, and there is no reason why such countries should not clear their forests for agriculture just as temperate countries have done in the past.

This is a classic sustainable development dilemma: should forest be cleared to improve social and economic conditions, or be protected to safeguard environmental welfare? The problem is made more acute by the international dimension: the loss of these particular forests would diminish the environmental welfare of the whole world. But who should pay for their protection: the developing countries through the costs of lost development, or the developed countries who will gain disproportionate benefits? Is this merely yet another instance of the North exploiting the South?

This chapter interprets tropical deforestation within frameworks of national and international development. It argues that deforestation is best viewed as a residual of land use change, and that the future of tropical moist forests depends heavily on the success of developing countries in reducing their traditional dependency on developed countries and avoiding environmental coercion.

TROPICAL FOREST RESOURCES

Types of Forest

Tropical forest can be divided into closed forest, which has a closed canopy and is more prevalent in the humid tropics near the Equator, and open forest, which is more common in the drier and more seasonal tropics and has an open canopy because its trees are scattered. Tropical moist forest refers to all types of closed forest in the humid tropics (Sommer, 1976), and has two main types: tropical rainforest and tropical moist deciduous forest (or 'monsoon forest') (Schimper, 1898).

Human impacts on forests

There are two main human impacts on tropical moist forests: deforestation and degradation. Deforestation can be defined as 'the temporary or permanent clearance of forest for agriculture or other purposes'. The key word here is clearance: if forest is not cleared, then deforestation does not take place according to this definition. Lesser impacts, which involve a temporary or permanent reduction in the density or structure of forest cover, or its species composition, are referred to as degradation. The dominant forestry practice in the humid tropics is not clearfelling, as in many temperate forests, but selective logging. As this usually only removes 2–10 trees per hectare (ha) out of a total of about 300 good-sized trees, it does not clear forest, and so does not cause deforestation as defined here (Grainger, 1993). But it does degrade forest and can be an indirect cause of deforestation if farmers use logging roads to gain access to forest after logging ends.

Extent and rate of change

Estimates of tropical forest areas and deforestation rates are still quite inaccurate, as might be expected from the traditional spatial bias in natural resource exploration and exploitation. In 1980 all tropical closed forest (i.e. both humid and dry) covered 1,202 million ha, according to the United Nations Food and Agriculture Organization (FAO), and was being deforested at 7.3 million ha per annum between 1976 and 1980 (Table 1) (Lanly, 1981). The corresponding figures for tropical moist forest only were estimated at 1,081 million ha and 6.1 million ha per annum (Grainger, 1984). A further 4 million ha per annum were logged from 1976 to 1980, some of which was subsequently deforested for farming. A follow-up survey by FAO for 1990 did not produce an estimate comparable with the 1980 figures, owing to the use of a different forest classification system, a flawed map of forest zones, and the use of outdated national surveys and modelling adjustments, which meant that the area of tropical moist forest could not be calculated reliably (Grainger, 1996).

Table 1 Estimates of tropical forest area, 1980 (million ha) and deforestation rates, 1976–80 (million ha per annum)

	All closed tropical forest[a] (Lanly, 1981)		Tropical moist forest[b] (Grainger, 1983)	
	Area	Deforestation rate	Area	Deforestation rate
Africa	217	1.3	205	1.2
Asia-Pacific	306	1.8	264	1.6
Latin America	679	4.1	613	3.3
Total[c]	1201	7.3	1081	6.1

Notes: [a] refers to 76 countries; [b]refers to 63 countries; [c]totals may not always equal the sum of regional figures due to rounding

Table 2 The immediate causes of deforestation

A Shifting agriculture
  Traditional shifting cultivation
  Short-rotation shifting cultivation
  Encroaching cultivation

B Permanent agriculture
  Permanent field crop cultivation
  Government-sponsored resettlement schemes
  Commercial ranches
  Cash-crop plantations

C Other land uses
  Mining
  Hydroelectric power schemes
  Narcotic plant cultivation

Source: Grainger, 1993

CAUSES OF DEFORESTATION

The immediate causes of deforestation need to be distinguished from the underlying causes. The immediate causes are the wide range of land uses that replace forest, including various types of shifting and permanent agriculture, as well as non-agricultural land uses (Table 2).

The underlying causes are the socioeconomic factors and government policies that lead to demand for a change in land use (Table 3). Two major underlying causes are population growth and economic growth. When population rises, more farmland is needed to feed the extra people, and deforestation rates are statistically correlated with population growth rates in international cross-sectional regression studies. Links with economic growth rates are more difficult to model, since economic growth not only leads to higher food consumption per capita and so to higher deforestation rates, but also allows investment in farming that will increase yields per ha and reduce deforestation rates (Lambin, 1994, 1997; Brown and Pearce, 1994; Grainger, 1998).

Other underlying causes are poverty and landlessness, as poor people flee from cities or other overpopulated areas to clear forest to feed themselves. Governments influence deforestation rates directly, by specifically planning or promoting forest clearance, and indirectly through their social and economic policies. These key driving forces of deforestation are mediated by environmental factors (for example, soil fertility, topography), ease of access (for example, proximity to rivers and

Table 3 The underlying causes of deforestation

A   Socioeconomic factors
    Population growth
    Economic growth
    Poverty and inequality

B   Facilitating factors
    Proximity of rivers and roads
    Fragmentation of forests
    Topography
    Soil fertility

C   State intervention
    Agriculture policies
    Forestry policies
    Other policies

D   External factors
    Demand for exports
    Financing conditions

roads), and land use sustainability (unsustainable farming can lead to declining yields and hence more deforestation is needed to maintain overall food production).

DEFORESTATION AND NATIONAL DEVELOPMENT

Deforestation is an entirely predictable consequence of development in forested countries, not an aberration. The people of the United Kingdom, for example, do not seem to find it abnormal to live in a country with only 10 per cent forest cover – and even this has doubled since the end of the nineteenth century. The key challenge is to try to understand the mechanisms driving deforestation and how these are likely to change in the future as development proceeds.

Statistical links between contemporary rates of deforestation, population growth and other underlying causes do not provide much insight into likely long-term trends in forest area. But if population density is taken as a proxy for development status, then international cross-sectional analysis suggests that percentage national forest cover should decline as a country develops and population density rises, but then approach a lower limit (Palo *et al.*, 1987).

This has provided the basis for useful conceptual models of long-term land use change. For example, all forested countries are expected to undergo a period of significant reduction in forest cover, called their national land use transition (see figure) (Grainger, 1995). The point where forest cover starts to increase again, as forest regenerates on abandoned low-productivity farmland, or intensive plantations are established, has been called the forest transition (Mather, 1992). However, national land use transition curves are actually the inverse of agricultural expansion curves, as the pattern of change in farmland area in response to rising population greatly depends on the availability of fertile land in each country. In the absence of any intervention to conserve natural ecosystems, this will have a major influence on long-term trends in forest cover.

A CORE–PERIPHERY PERSPECTIVE

Development involves much more than the expansion of human population and economic activity, and the role of forests in development should also be seen in its wider political context. From

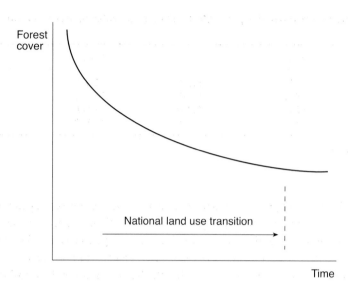

The national land use transition

the perspective of core–periphery theories of development, tropical countries are generally found in the global periphery, relative to the core represented by the industrialized nations. Remaining forests in most tropical countries are also concentrated in peripheral areas, e.g. outlying islands, swampy areas or mountainous regions remote from the urban core.

Within each country, events inside tropical forests go largely unnoticed by politicians in capital cities. The ability of state institutions to monitor deforestation and the sustainability of forest management, and to protect forests against deforestation, is severely limited by physical distance, the inefficiencies of hierarchical institutions linking core to periphery through multiple organizational layers, and an over-concentration of personnel in headquarters offices. Indigenous peoples, shifting cultivators and other smallholder farmers in forested areas have limited political influence over national governments, and so receive little technical assistance in making their land uses more productive and sustainable, which again exacerbates deforestation. Forested areas are often regarded as convenient 'sinks' for landless people, and help to obscure the failures of development policies.

Peripheral areas can become important to national governments for two main reasons. First, to redistribute population from other over-crowded areas of the country: the Indonesian Transmigration Programme and various resettlement schemes in Brazilian Amazonia provide good examples of this. Second, the state may regard settlement and forest clearance as essential to ensure the security of national borders, and this was a major motivation for the many initiatives of the Brazilian government in Amazonia from the 1960s onwards (Eden, 1990).

At the international level, tropical forests seem to conform with the predictions of the economist David Ricardo in becoming important peripheral sources of timber in the period after the Second World War, when temperate forests were increasingly unable to meet demand for timber in the industrialized countries. Before the war, tropical hardwoods like teak and mahogany were mainly used as luxury cabinet timbers, but afterwards they were exploited in large volumes as lower-value utility timbers for both furniture and construction. Tropical hardwood exports grew by a factor of 14 between 1950 and 1980 (Table 4), the main importers being Japan, the European Union and East Asian countries (such as South Korea, Taiwan and Singapore) which processed them into plywood for re-export.

Table 4 Trends in tropical hardwood exports, 1950–1980 (million cubic metres roundwood equivalent volume)

	1950	1960	1970	1980
Africa	1.107	5.518	8.645	8.290
Asia-Pacific	2.448	9.527	38.779	50.751
Latin America	0.809	0.714	1.408	2.185
Total	4.364	15.759	48.832	61.226

Source: Grainger, 1998

Of the various theories that portray links between developed and developing countries using a core–periphery model, dual economy theory predicts the gradual, but heterogeneous, diffusion of economic growth, resource extraction and processing into the periphery (Hicks, 1969). On the other hand, dependency theory and world systems theory predict that the global core will continue to exploit the periphery's economic surplus, keeping the latter in a dependent position so that it underdevelops, rather than develops (Frank, 1969; Wallerstein, 1974). Although this latter view is rather static and deterministic, it does explain many features of international development. Thus many developing countries continue to rely on the export of a few primary commodities, but most of the value added to these accrues to the developed countries that process them. Until 1980, two-thirds of all tropical hardwood was exported as logs, and processed either in the industrialized countries or in the newly industrializing countries of East Asia, such as Taiwan, Singapore and South Korea. As with other primary commodities, access to developed country markets for processed products is limited by higher tariffs (Bourke, 1988). This share fell to a half during the 1980s when Indonesia vastly expanded its plywood production capacity, but this may be explained by several unique features of this country, and tends to support the growth pole variant of dual economy theory.

Plantations are still prominent features of the dependency relationship between developed and developing countries, just as in colonial times. In most tropical countries, the state has promoted the expansion of oil palm, rubber, cocoa, coffee and coconut plantations since becoming independent, clearing large areas of tropical forests in the process. Pulpwood exports will also rise substantially in the future, following the massive expansion of low-cost pulpwood plantations in Brazil.

TROPICAL FORESTS AND ECO-IMPERIALISM

The informal imperialism that has dominated relationships between North and South since the Second World War has been subtly refined in recent decades to include a new 'eco-imperialism', as both states and non-governmental organizations in developed countries have exerted pressures to protect tropical forests 'for the good of all humanity'. Tropical deforestation has been portrayed as 'bad', and the role of forests in development completely neglected. Co-operative mechanisms to improve tropical forest management (for example, through the First International Tropical Timber Agreement) have been increasingly replaced by more overt coercive pressures, e.g. setting a timetable for sustainable forest management in the Second International Tropical Timber Agreement, attempting to introduce both individual bans on the import of tropical hardwood not deemed to have come from sustainably managed forests, and more generalized environmental trade barriers through the World Trade Organization.

Tropical forests are likely to be a key battleground between developed and developing countries in the coming decades as the former continue to press their demands for protecting the global environment, while the latter seek to reverse their age-old inferiority in world trade and the global economy generally. Developing countries managed to fight off a proposed Forest Convention at the UN Conference on Environment and Development in Rio de Janeiro in 1992, which would have formalized overseas intervention in the management of sovereign resources, and only a weak, non-binding Statement of Forest Principles was produced.

CONCLUSIONS

From a developmental perspective, 'saving the tropical moist forests' seems to be a hollow and naïve slogan, and leads to the question: 'saving them for whom?' The future of the tropical moist forests will be determined by the development strategies of the countries in which they are found but, as this essay has shown, these strategies cannot be divorced from the dependency relationships that are at the heart of international development, and that have gradually taken on an environmental dimension in recent decades. If tropical countries do adopt more sustainable development paths than temperate countries have followed in the past, then the omens are good; but this is more likely to occur as a result of internal pressures rather than overseas coercion, which only creates antagonism. So it will all depend on how fast democracy and pluralism can grow, so that the people of the tropics can express their own preferences for safeguarding their environmental heritage while also improving the social and economic dimensions of their quality of life.

FURTHER READING

For extended overviews consult Brown and Pearce (1994); Eden (1990); Grainger (1993, 1998); and Myers (1985).

REFERENCES

Bourke, I.J. (1988) 'Do forest products trade barriers disadvantage the developing countries?', *Resources Policy* 14: 47.
Brown, K. and Pearce, D.W. (1994) *The Causes of Tropical Deforestation*, London: UCL Press.
Eden, M. (1990) *Ecology and Land Management in Amazonia*, London: Bellhaven Press.
FAO (1993) *Forest Resources Assessment 1990: Tropical Countries*, FAO Forestry Paper No. 112, Rome: UN Food and Agriculture Organization.
Frank A.G. (1969) 'Latin America: underdevelopment or revolution', *Monthly Review*, New York.
Grainger A. (1983) 'Improving the monitoring of deforestation in the humid tropics', in S.L. Sutton, T.C. Whitmore and A.C. Chadwick (eds) *Tropical Rain Forest: Ecology and Management*, Oxford: Blackwell Scientific Publications, pp. 387–95.
Grainger, A. (1993) *Controlling Tropical Deforestation*, London: Earthscan Publications.
Grainger, A. (1995) 'National land use morphology: patterns and possibilities', *Geography* 20: 235–45.
Grainger, A. (1996) 'An evaluation of FAO's Tropical Forest Resource Assessment 1990', *Geographical Journal* 162: 73–9.
Grainger, A. (1998) 'Modelling tropical land use change and deforestation', in F.B. Goldsmith (ed.) *Tropical Rain Forest: A Wider Perspective* London: Chapman and Hall. pp. 303–44.
Hicks, J. (1969) *A Theory of Economic History*, Oxford: Oxford University Press.

Lambin, E.F. (1994) *Modelling Deforestation Processes. A Review*. TREES Series B, Research Report No.1, Ispra, Italy: Institute for Remote Sensing Applications, European Commission Joint Research Centre.

Lambin, E.F. (1997) 'Modelling and monitoring land-cover change processes in tropical regions', *Progress in Physical Geography* 21: 375–93.

Lanly, J.P (ed.) (1981) *Tropical Forest Resources Assessment Project (GEMS): Tropical Africa, Tropical Asia, Tropical America*, 4 vols, Rome: UN Food and Agriculture Organization/UN Environment Programme.

Mather, A.S. (1992) 'The forest transition', *Area* 24: 367–79.

Myers, N. (1985) *The Primary Source*, New York: W.W. Norton.

Palo, M., Mery, G. and Salmi, J. (1987) 'Deforestation in the tropics: pilot scenarios based on quantitative analyses', in M. Palo and G. Mery (eds) *Deforestation or Development in the Third World? Vol. III*, Bulletin No. 349, Helsinki: Finnish Forest Research Institute, pp. 53–106.

Schimper, A.F.W. (1898) *Plant Geography Upon a Physiological Basis*, English translation by W.R. Fisher, G. Groom and I.B. Balfour (1903), Oxford: Oxford University Press.

Sommer, A. (1976) 'Attempt at an assessment of the world's tropical forests', *Unasylva* 28(112–13): 5–25.

Wallerstein E. (1974) *The Modern World System*, New York: Academic Press.

Gender, population and development

EDITORIAL INTRODUCTION

It is widely accepted in the present times that development must be informed by gender analysis and that particular attention must be paid to the needs of the poor. The last four decades have seen four World United Nations Conferences on Women. Far-reaching blueprints have been produced for eliminating discrimination against women. The major development agencies include a mandatory framework for all activities to check that gender is considered, even in neutral projects. The World Bank has recently accepted a women's monitoring committee to keep 'Women's Eyes on the Bank'.

Some might even argue that the way gender is integrated into development thinking and practice indicates a high degree of co-option or neutralization of feminist objectives, rather than their success in transforming the development agenda. Increasingly, the political participation of women has become crucial to access the male-dominated world of policy-making. Empowerment involves challenging existing power relations and gaining greater control over sources of power.

This section argues that gender remains central to development and offers a lens through which to deconstruct gender-related processes and issues. It enhances understanding of women's lives and the gendered nature of economic, social and political processes. It traces the dominant approaches to gender and development, charting the changes from *women* in development (WID) to a broader use of gender analysis: *gender* and development (GAD), as a reflection of the changing paradigms of feminist orthodoxy and development analysis.

UNICEF has identified women, or rather mothers and young children, as the groups most vulnerable to economic adjustment programmes. Although there has been a very rapid growth of women's employment, the availability of women is constrained by family responsibilities. Women's willingness to work is partly determined by the extent to which they have control over income generated in the household. This relates to gender bias in the household, and the gendered nature of negotiation and exchange within households. In addition, there is extensive evidence that women's income is almost exclusively used to meet household needs, whereas men tend to retain a considerable portion of their income for personal spending. Women gain self-worth from increased economic participation and visible contribution to household income.

More egalitarian gender relations in, and outside, the household impact positively on women's development. Women with access to better education and employment opportunities rely less on their children for economic security and social recognition.

Technological change raises gender issues. Where machinery was introduced into traditional women's activities, men either completely replaced women or the activity became subdivided and men took over skilled technological tasks while women were relegated to less skilled, menial tasks. Technological development, since it can disrupt cultural norms, need not however be detrimental.

Disagreement exists over whether there is a population problem and what this problem is. Are there too many people in the world or not? The traditional Malthusian view sees population growth as a source of problems that will sooner or later run up against the limits of the Earth's resources. This has long been the message from the major Western aid donors, at least until the 1994 International Conference on Population and Development in Cairo. This has contributed to the excesses of some family planning programmes, notoriously negligent of human rights, such as China's one child programme. Another view sees no problem other than in relation to distribution/redistribution.

Human rights, human development, women's empowerment, and reproductive and sexual health are themes requiring an approach to population based on a solid ethical foundation, aimed at sustainable human development and centred on the role of women.

7.1 WID, GAD and WAD

Kate Young

WID (Women in Development), GAD (Gender and Development) and WAD (Women and Development) are the acronyms for different approaches to development work involving women. By the end of the twentieth century all the approaches have been amalgamated into what is usually called the GAD approach, but this bears little resemblance to its former configuration; as a consequence many feminists prefer not to use it. The term gender has been very widely adopted but usually stripped of its original meaning; often it is merely a synonym for woman/women.

WID

WID first appeared in the 1970s when women in aid agencies argued that development programmes ignored and excluded women. A key text for the incipient WID movement was Ester Boserup's *Women's Role in Economic Development*, which argued that modernization was not benefiting women, denying them access to land, training, education and technology; she condemned the tendency of planners to see women as secondary earners and to concentrate on their roles as housewives (Boserup, 1970). A major early WID theme was that programme designers and planners held false but unstated assumptions/stereotypes and prejudices about women's roles, consigning them merely to household and family, and assuming that resources channelled to the household would automatically benefit them (Rogers, 1980).

With a growing and vocal women's movement in the USA and Europe, aid agencies were pressured into taking a more complex view of women's activities, not just their familial roles but also their economic contributions (potential or actual). Many responded by adding on a women's component to pre-existing development programmes/projects, often focusing on handicraft production, small-scale income generating or home economics. The United Nations responded to similar pressure by organizing the first Women's Conference in 1975 – Equality, Development and Peace – the three topics covering the concerns of the Western world, the Developing World and the Eastern European countries. The following year it announced the Decade for Women.

WID practitioners – largely working within the UN or state aid agencies – were initially primarily concerned with giving women access to work within development agencies, to resources distributed through such agencies, and later on to getting women's perspectives on development objectives included in policy-making. They argued that resources should be targeted to women – for example, appropriate technologies to lessen much of the drudgery involved in domestic work – and to improve the productivity of women's economic activities. Credit programmes, agricultural extension and other training were needed to provide access to modern knowledge and the market economy. They pushed for equity strategies – getting women into the public sphere and paid employment – as well as the appointment of more women to higher positions in the government and in development agencies. The need for more women-friendly policies required that planners learn what women really do, and this required the systematic collection of sex-disaggregated data. To monitor policy and to ensure inclusion of women's needs by policy-makers required that women's units be set up within donor agencies and governments.

WID advocates faced a great deal of resistance to their demands from planners and aid bureaucrats alike (Staudt and Jaquette, 1988). To overcome this they found it expedient to under-play equality arguments and stress anti-poverty ones. They focused on women's crucial role in developing countries in alleviating family poverty, and their role in the provision of basic needs. Later, and more instrumentally still, they stressed the positive relationship between women's increased educational levels, access to paid employment, raised age of marriage and lowered birth rates.

WID advocates saw themselves as pragmatic, non-ideological development practitioners (Tinker, 1982), but in fact most accepted the basic postulates of neo-classical economic theory and were influenced by the liberal feminist arguments for women's equality (Jagger, 1983). As liberal feminists tended to gloss over biological differences between men and women – stress-ing their similar mental capacities and capacity for rationality – WID tended to ignore moth-ering and caring rather than arguing that they should be equally valued as income earning and producing. Nor did WID proponents criticize the model of development being promoted – modernization or the promotion of the market economy – but rather the way that 'malestream' planning ignored women. Worse still, the economic changes being introduced were leading to women losing some of the resources they had previously had; their status was being lowered, rather than raised, by development. To ensure that all project interventions would be sensitive to the sexual division of labour, WID scholars designed the Harvard 'gender roles' model to help planners direct appropriate project benefits to women as well as men (Overholt *et al.*, 1984).

By the 1980s with the increasing concern with waste and failure of development efforts, WID advocates shifted from exposing the negative effects of development planning and programmes on women to arguing how much the development effort was losing by ignoring women's actual or potential contributions. Research showed that programmes/projects which denied women resources actually undermined project performance; that projects were failing to reach targets due to women's unwillingness to provide unpaid 'family' labour to projects from which only men would benefit (Buvinic *et al.*, 1983). Rather than the piecemeal approach of women-only projects, women's concerns should be set squarely within the project mainstream.

These efficiency arguments resonated with development planners concerned to allocate resources more effectively; they now accepted that women were rational economic agents respon-sive to incentives (World Bank, 1984). Furthermore as research showed that women used what little they had to good effect and invested more of their income in their children, development efforts to increase their productivity and range of economic activities were doubly beneficial. More resources were targeted at enhancing women's economic activities. However, ignoring women's dual areas of activity and their need to balance their productive and reproductive activities led to the dilemma of the intensification of women's work burden. And this at a time when structural adjustment programmes were leading to major cuts in public expenditure, with the implicit assumption that services hitherto provided by the state could now be provided by 'the family' – in other words: women.

GAD

In the mid-1970s a critique of WID was emerging from the analytical work of feminist scholars at the Institute of Development Studies. Their point of departure was that unequal power relations between men and women prevent women from benefiting from greater access. Furthermore that women's inequality is not solely a problem of developing countries; women in the so-called developed countries also face a gendered labour market with women's jobs (and pay levels) at the lower end of the job hierarchy; women are also absent from the corridors of power (whether in politics, religion or finance). Women's reproductive work is not given social value. As such, they avoided the division that the WID approach appeared to make between First and Third World women (Young *et al.*, 1984).

Using the concept of gender (the socially acquired notions of masculinity and femininity) and gender relations (the socially constructed form of relations between men and women) they analysed how development strategies reshape these power relations. They noted how economic and social change, whether planned or unplanned, often gives greater opportunities to one gender and showed how, in many societies, the development of the market economy had shifted the balance sharply in men's favour (Young, 1989). In so doing they questioned the conventional liberal belief that the market economy would help spread egalitarian values and undermine authoritarian and male-biased traditional attitudes. GAD activists also highlighted an aspect of unequal relations – violence against women – which in many areas inhibited women from taking up opportunities targeted to them, whether literacy classes, credit, agricultural extension, etc.

The early GAD theorists were mainly socialist feminists and were thus highly critical of the economic growth model of development. They did not censure planners for their ignorance and prejudice, but in their critique of economic theory they argued for the need to give economic value to women's bearing and caring roles. Women's double day (paid employment and unpaid domestic work) benefited both capital – domestic labour subsidizing the cost of male labour – and male workers. They also contested the claim that women were not integrated into development, arguing rather that they are central to it in providing unpaid family labour as a 'natural' aspect of being women. Lastly they questioned the WID approach of treating women as a homogeneous category, and emphasized the differences between them based on class, age, marital status, ethnicity or race, and religion, which could constitute their specific aims as being antagonistic (Young, 1979).

WAD

Differences between women was also the finding of an influential early study prepared for the Government of India's presentation to the 1975 UN Women's Conference. Scholars who collected the data for the study were shocked to find how large segments of the female population had been pushed into ever-greater poverty, while middle-class and educated women had benefited.

Many WAD activists from the Third World argued that the development model being promoted not only did not include women's perspective, it lacked the perspective of developing countries as well. Dependency theorists made similar arguments, privileging the oppression of class relations to gender. The DAWN Network of largely Third World researchers argued that gender inequality was of little interest to the majority of women in developing countries, who were concerned about lack of food, housing, drinkable water, and employment rather than equality (Sen and Grown, 1987).

CONVERGENCE

By the late 1980s there was a degree of convergence between the three approaches. Women's empowerment became the critical demand. WID/GAD/WAD advocates attacked the assumption that women could be used to carry out policies designed without their active participation, and argued that women should be integrated into all aspects of development assistance and involved centrally in planning and implementing development policies, programmes and projects. But they also argued that women would not accept a model of development which was premised on individual self-interest and privileged profit-making over meeting the needs of the majority. Many of their arguments were taken up by development scholars working with UNDP which began to call for a focus on human development rather than economic development alone, and whose elaboration of the approach is published in the annual Human Development Report (UNDP, from 1990).

By the 1990s one of the major concerns of women activists was why 30 years of activism has at one level apparently been successful – UN agencies and most national governments all pay lip service to the importance of gender equality – yet closer analysis shows that from the family through to the highest institutional levels women are still not men's equals.

Throughout the preparatory work leading to the 1995 UN Women's Conference in Beijing women activists tried to create a Platform for Action which would bind governments to a series of strategic actions favouring women's equality and empowerment, and urged the thousands of women's non-governmental organizations to oversee implementation. After much debate and considerable resistance the Platform was adopted by member governments, but it remains to be seen how many will in fact implement it.

In trying to understand the persistence of inequality at the family level an influential economist who was part of the Human Development team characterized intra-household relations as ones of co-operative conflict (Sen, 1987, 1990). Men and women, each following their own livelihood strategies, have to make choices between co-operating (not always to the equal benefit of both parties) or not co-operating (conflict). Choices are influenced by the parties' relative bargaining strength; the latter being a product of differences in how each member's contribution to household well-being is perceived, the degree to which members identify their own self-interest as being equivalent to other members' well-being, the ability/willingness to threaten or wreak violence on others, and each member's fall-back position, i.e. the options available to each one should co-operation collapse. Not surprisingly he found that, inter-generationally, women's position was weaker than that of men.

While the family is seen as the basic institution which sets the tone for gender relations within a society, it is now becoming clear that other institutions are equally gendered and reproduce women's inequality in varying degrees (Agarwal, 1997). Despite all the efforts to persuade policy-makers and planners of the importance of gender issues, and to get women into positions of power within development agencies, discriminatory incentives and procedures as much as active resistance effectively block women's advancement or serious consideration of women's alternative vision of development. As a consequence, activists' and scholars' attention is now turning to the analysis of institutions and how to get a level playing field for women by changing institutional rules and practices (Goetz, 1997).

GUIDE TO FURTHER READING

Rathgeber, E.M. (1990) 'WID, WAD, GAD: trends in research and practice', *The Journal of Developing Areas* 24(4): 489–502.

Razavi, S. and Miller, C. (1995) 'From WID to GAD: conceptual shifts in the women and development discourse', UNRISD Occasional Paper No. 1, Geneva: UNRISD.

Young, K. (1993) *Planning Development With Women: Making a World of Difference*, London: Macmillan.

REFERENCES

Agarwal, B. (1997) 'Bargaining and gender relations within and beyond the household', *Feminist Economics* 3(1): 1–51.

Boserup, E. (1970) *Woman's Role in Economic Development*, London: Allen and Unwin.

Buvinic, M., Lycette, M. and McGreevey, W. (1983) *Women and Poverty in the Third World*, Baltimore: Johns Hopkins University Press; especially 'Women's issues in Third World poverty: a policy analysis', pp. 14–33.

Goetz, A.M. (1997) *Getting Institutions Right for Women in Development*, London: Zed Books.

Jagger, A. (1983) *Feminist Politics and Human Nature*, Brighton: Harvester Press.

Overholt, C., Anderson, M., Cloud, K. and Austin, J. (1984) *Gender Roles in Development*, West Hartford, Connecticut: Kumarian Press.

Rogers, B. (1980) *The Domestication of Women: Discrimination in Developing Societies*, London: Kogan Page.

Sen, A. (1987) *Gender and Co-operative Conflicts*, WIDER Working Papers 18, Helsinki; also in I. Tinker (ed.) (1990) *Persistent Inequalities*, Oxford: Oxford University Press, pp. 123–49.

Sen, G. and Grown, C. (1987) *Development, Crises and Alternative Visions*, New York: Monthly Review Press.

Staudt, K. and Jaquette, J. (1988) 'Bureaucratic resistance to women's programs: the case of women in development', in C. Boneparth and E. Stoper (eds) *Women Power and Policy*, New York: Pergamon Press, pp. 263–81.

Tinker, I. (1982) *Gender Equity in Development: a Policy Perspective*, Washington DC: Equity Policy Center.

UNDP (1990 *et seq.*) *Human Development Report*, New York: Oxford University Press.

World Bank (1984) *World Development Report, 1984*, Washington DC: World Bank.

Young, K. (1979) 'Editorial and conference resolution, recommendations and research guidelines', *IDS Bulletin* 10(3).

Young, K. (ed.) (1989) *Serving Two Masters*, New Delhi: Allied Publishers.

Young, K., Wokowitz, C. and McCullagh, R. (eds) (1984) *Of Marriage and the Market: Women's Subordination in International Perspective*, London: Routledge and Kegan Paul.

7.2 Women and the state

Kathleen Staudt

Until the last two decades, the state has been relatively neglected in political studies. Analysts had long referred to the 'nation-state', but were much more taken with the nation: the growth of nationalism, national and cultural values, political participation, popular attitudes toward government and society. The state, defined in its Weberian sense as the exercise of sovereign authority within territorial boundaries, was the empty box that structural-functional theorists drew in their political systems graphics, seemingly relegating that box to the sometimes-tedious studies of public administration.

Even women and gender analysts succumbed to these tendencies. They studied 'inputs' to the box with research on social movements, revolutions, public opinion and political participation. They studied 'outputs' from the box in their analyses of public politics and laws that 'developed' women and men differently in different class, cultural and geographic contexts. In this 1970s era, the fields of Women in Development and Gender and Development were born.

STATE ANALYSIS WINDS UP

With the publication of *Bringing the State Back In* (Evans *et al.*, 1985) comparative political theorists put the state on the analytic agenda. With historical and comparative perspectives, they ended the pretence (so common in studies of the United States) of an irrelevant or minimalist state, as in the classic liberal ideal. This focus led people to examine government institutions more carefully for the way they opened or closed doors to people and policy debates.

The study of institutions experienced some revival, with analysts attentive to the grand institutions and rules that enveloped the political scheme of legislative bodies, administrative agencies and electoral systems. As far back as 1955, Maurice Duverger compared the single-member and proportional representation electoral systems for their impacts on geographical or ideological politics and two- or multi-party systems. Soon analysts of female under-representation in high-level political decision-making positions would embrace these grand-level approaches. Would proportional representation systems seat more elected women? What about parliamentary systems? And, most importantly, what difference would that make in the gendered decisions and outcomes of the political process? Policy analysts searched for ways to understand the connections between policies, institutions and decision-makers for their resistance to gender justice and the persistence of deep inequalities.

These connections began to be made with attention to the state. Statist critique and analysis became attached to grand explanatory narratives, from pluralism to Marxism, but with attention to women and gender. States were conceptualized as historical and institutional shells that protected and advanced male interests. Theorists challenged existing conceptions of the state as neutral umpire between competing interests (the pluralist view ingrained in US politics), or as the instrument of the dominant economic class (the Marxist view). The institutionalization of male interests reached beyond capitalist profiteering rationales. Moreover, although socialist models were few and flawed, gender inequality persisted in seemingly intractable ways.

During the 1980s, the wind-up period on women and the state analyses, the state and its ideology were tied to development policies (before the word 'development' was critically challenged). Several debates emerged which would lead to a wind-down period on women and the state analyses. Debates existed among 'feminists' (another word yet to be critically challenged (Staudt, 1998)): should feminists work with the state or against the state? To draw on Audre Lorde's eloquence (1984), the state was the Master's House from which development policies operated. Few states had a positive track record on women and gender justice, and analysts judged many states as doomed to perpetuate gender subordination. Power and authority emanated from the state, and states were subject to little analytic differentiation. In this conception, the Master had agency, or the ability to act; the inhabitants had no agency.

Several collections emerged on the state–development–women connections in the 1980s. Charlton *et al.* (1989) reviewed literature on statism, calling for analysts to examine state officials and their gender ideologies, state policies and institutions, and state definitions of the parameters of politics. The area-studies chapters in their collection made theoretical use of the public–private divide that emerged in Western theory, separating male and female domains and agency to gender-differentiated spheres. Deere and León (1987) set their collection in terms that linked agricultural and land policies in Latin America to national economic policies and the global debt problem. Afshar's collection (1987) did not address theory, but instead focused on nation-state case studies of policies in Asia and Africa. In their edited collection, Parpart and Staudt (1989) drew on critical theoretical perspectives of dependency and mode of production analysis to examine the origins of the state in Africa, women's access to the state, and state management of resources. These collections traced state origins to Europe in centuries past, with the transnational spread of state structures and ideologies through world capitalism, colonization and imperialism. Yet even before the rise of the modern state, it appeared that men dominated women, drawing in part on public, institutional authority.

In another debate, analysts wondered about the extent to which one could generalize about states. Despite the framing discourse on 'the state' in book titles and theoretical introductions, many contributors to these collections used the nation-state as a unit of analysis. And these nation-states were not all alike. It was refreshing and long overdue that country case studies emerged, for comparative politics had rarely integrated women and gender into analyses. Yet this flurry of country cases made it clear that analysts could not generalize about states in the nearly 200 countries worldwide.

STATE ANALYSIS WINDS DOWN

Analysis on women and the state quickly went into a wind-down period for a variety of reasons. Related analyses re-emerged with new conceptual language such as democracy, governance, political representation and accountability. Why the wind-down? Some of the debates led to answers, pointing toward new analytic trends.

First, states began to be differentiated, not only in their strength and weakness as agents of control, authority and power, but also in the degrees to which they opened space to women's claims to be active and heard, for space within the state, and for justice in policy and legal terms. States were never all alike, and some of the most overdrawn feminist analyses treated them as monolithic, with men and women as monolithic inhabitants within them. All but the most simplistic research acknowledges the diversity among women and men by class, nationality, culture and geographic space, among other factors (Mohanty et al., 1991). Further, international financial institutions began structural adjustment programmes in the 1980s that aimed to reduce the size of states, make them more efficient and expose more economic resources to market forces. It was an analytic mistake to assume that states were static, not dynamic, or as dynamic as the societies which they try to envelop (or which envelop them).

Second, weak states and even some strong states never had nor have full power, authority and agency to envelop the societies they claim (Midgal, 1988). Important theorizing on power recognized that another part of power was the ability of inhabitants to resist, sabotage and ignore state machinery. In parallel fashion, women exercise power in resistance to men and to the state. It was an analytic mistake to accept theoretical or state claims of omnipotence.

Third, states are not monolithic, but rather bundles of contradictions that do not work in perfect harmony. Some of the most overdrawn statist analysis emerged from the US with over-generalized, almost biological notions of women as victims and men as sexual aggressors (MacKinnon, 1989). The welfare state began to emerge as a category worth analysis and engagement. Canada and the Scandinavian states emerged as models for ways that rights and justice agendas might be consolidated within (Vickers et al., 1993; Gelb, 1989; Hernes, 1987).

STATES REVISITED: DEMOCRACY, GOVERNANCE AND POLITICS

With democratic space and process, along with healthy judicial systems, people make use of contradictions within the state to achieve gains. In the 1990s, with the so-called transitions to democracy beginning to emerge, a new context led to greater analytic attention to the kinds of institutions and democracies which permit democratic openings to women and to gender justice agendas. A mammoth collection with 43 country case studies allowed focus on political institutions (Nelson and Chowdhury, 1994). Collections on women engaging state and international bureaucracy institutions offered insights into openings for women and gender justice agendas (Staudt, 1997). Goetz (1997) aptly titled a collection *Getting Institutions Right for Women in Development*.

With globalization increasing in full force, in a context lacking accountable global governance, it is increasingly becoming clear that claims for gender rights and justice are operable primarily in existing nation-state governance and transnational organizations. Thus, analysts have put institutional rules and processes on the agenda to examine which kinds of system open space to women and new policy agendas (Rule and Zimmerman, 1994; Goetz, 1997). Even United Nations agencies put women's political participation on the agenda, with the Division for the Advancement of Women regularly collecting data on women in high-level political decision-making positions, such as cabinets, parliaments and chief executive roles. The United Nations Development Programme's *Human Development Report, 1995*, prepared for the World Conference on Women in Beijing, 1995, contains a chapter on women (see also Staudt, 1996).

At Beijing, participants resolved to follow up its elaborate Platform for Action. Accountability is now a key concept for organization and for research. Currently, debates are less likely to be anti-state or pro-state, but rather: how do people engage the state and public affairs for accountability, not only on traditional women's policy issues but also on mainstream policy issues (Staudt, 1998)?

CONCLUSIONS

The rise and fall of women and the state analysis parallels the contemporary challenge to meta-analysis and grand narratives. The state as all-powerful agent of male control is one of those grand, but wobbly scaffolds that, with a critical eye, falls with its own flaws. Women and the state analysts now pursue various paths that examine national and global governance with a wide variety of institutional rules and policies.

Debates on women and the state moved analysts beyond the pro- or anti-state stance, useful in applications to women's activism. Analysts also moved beyond the notions of states as static and the same. What emerged after statist analyses was a comparative approach that examined institutions and accountability strategies. Yet a common thread of male control lingers in the institutions, policies and laws in countries worldwide, part of a growing global economy. Hopefully, comparative studies of women in politics will not regress to a pluralist approach, worldwide, for the analysis convincingly demonstrated that few, if any, states have operated as neutral umpires in gender terms.

GUIDE TO FURTHER READING

Readers should start with the collections of Evans *et al.* and Charlton *et al.* for conceptual analyses of the state. They should continue with the institutional and accountability collections of Nelson and Chowdhury, and of Goetz. See references for full citation information.

REFERENCES

Afshar, Haleh (ed.) (1987) *Women, State and Ideology: Studies from Africa and Asia*, Albany: SUNY/Albany Press.

Charlton, Sue Ellen M., Everett, Jana and Staudt, Kathleen (eds) (1989) *Women, the State, and Development*, Albany: SUNY/Albany Press.

Deere, Carmen Diana and León, Magdalena (eds) (1987) *Rural Women and State Policy: Feminist Perspectives on Latin American Agricultural Development*, Boulder: Westview.

Duverger, Maurice (1955) *The Political Role of Women*, Paris: UNESCO.

Evans, Peter B., Rueschemeyer, Dietrich and Skocpol, Theda (eds) (1985) *Bringing the State Back In*, Cambridge: Cambridge University Press.

Gelb, Joyce (1989) *Feminism and Politics: A Comparative Perspective*, Berkeley and Los Angeles: University of California Press.

Goetz, Anne Marie (ed.) (1997) *Getting Institutions Right for Women in Development*, London: Zed Books.

Hernes, Helga Maria (1987) *Welfare State and Woman Power*, Oslo: Norwegian University Press.

Lorde, Audre (1984) 'The Master's tools will never dismantle the Master's house', in *Sister Outsider*, Freedom, CA: Crossing Press.

MacKinnon, Catharine (1989) *Toward a Feminist Theory of the State*, Cambridge, MA: Harvard University Press.

Migdal, Joel S. (1988) *Strong Societies and Weak States: State-Society Relations and State Capabilities in the Third World*, Princeton: Princeton University Press.

Mohanty, Chandra Talpade, Russo, Ann and Torres, Lourdes (eds) (1991) *Third World Women and the Politics of Feminism*, Bloomington, IN: Indiana University Press.

Nelson, Barbara and Chowdhury, Najma (eds) (1994) *Women and Politics Worldwide*, New Haven, CT: Yale University Press.

Parpart, Jane and Staudt, Kathleen (eds) (1989) *Women and the State in Africa*, Boulder: Lynne Rienner Press.

Rule, Wilma and Zimmerman, Joseph F. (eds) (1994) *Electoral Systems in Comparative Perspective: Their Impact on Women and Minorities*, Westport, CT: Greenwood.

Staudt, Kathleen (1996) 'Political representation: engendering politics', in *Background Papers: Human Development Report, 1995*, New York: United Nations Development Programme.

Staudt, Kathleen (ed.) (1997) *Women, International Development and Politics: The Bureaucratic Mire* (2nd edn), Philadelphia: Temple University Press.

Staudt, Kathleen (1998) *Policy, Politics & Gender: Women Gaining Ground*, West Hartford, CT: Kumarian Press.

United Nations Development Programme (UNDP) (1995) *Human Development Report, 1995*, New York: Oxford University Press.

Vickers, Jill, Rankin, Pauline and Appelle, Christine (1993) *Politics as if Women Mattered: A Political Analysis of the National Action Committee on the Status of Women*, Toronto: University of Toronto Press.

7.3 Gender, families and households

Ann Varley

FAMILY AND HOUSEHOLD AS CULTURAL CONSTRUCTS

The distinction between 'The Family' and 'families' is a key faultline in contemporary social and political thought. Preference for the term 'families' signifies rejection of the nuclear family household as universal norm. Insistence on the definite article signals either support for the nuclear family as ideal family form or repudiation of 'Western' influences allegedly undermining local traditions. 'Family' is often used as a touchstone by which nations or ethnic groups differentiate themselves from each other or gauge how they have changed over time. Changes in family life may therefore come to symbolize the effects of development or modernization processes, for better or for worse.

Debates about the family are often, in reality, debates about women's behaviour. The figure of the young woman leaving the family home to find work in the city, where her sexuality can less easily be monitored, has served as a symbol of modernity displacing tradition in many different societies. Women may be blamed for a range of social ills, whilst men's behaviour too often remains unquestioned. For example, to explain an observed rise in teenage pregnancies in Africa, the most important question may be why young *men* are refusing to marry (Moore, 1994). There is a similar danger in isolating families and households as a subject for discussion. Families may be blamed for the consequences of structural forces because it is convenient to the state to individualize responsibility for poverty.

Families are clearly an emotive subject. The term 'household' is often seen as more neutral. Households are usually defined in functional terms as 'task-oriented residence units', whereas families are kinship units that 'need not be localized' (Netting *et al.*, 1984: xx). Confusion arises because household membership is also generally based on kinship. Although households may consist of single individuals, friends or homosexual partners, members are usually recruited through heterosexual partnerships, childbearing or the incorporation of other kin (such as elderly parents). Many discussions about 'the family' thus refer to the family *household*.

Household functions include co-residence, economic co-operation, reproductive activities such as food preparation and consumption, and socialization of children. It is mistaken, however, to regard 'household' as unproblematically descriptive by comparison with the value-laden 'family'. Households are also cultural constructs (Yanagisako, 1984). We should not assume that our own society's understanding of 'household' is shared by others. For example, the functions mentioned above are often assumed to take place within the same household unit, with different functions neatly overlapping. That is not the case in parts of sub-Saharan Africa, where these functions may take place across several residential units (Guyer and Peters, 1987).

Functional accounts of the household unit run the risk of portraying it as isolated from the rest of society. In practice, members' survival and well-being is also influenced by their connections with other households – kin, friends or neighbours. The importance of social networks in this context was demonstrated by Larissa Lomnitz's classic (1977) work in a Mexican 'shantytown'.

An emphasis on households as bounded units can also lead us to 'misconstrue them as social actors endowed with human consciousness' (Yanagisako, 1984: 331). The difficulty with treating a group of people like an individual is that it is tempting to identify the group with one actual human actor. The 'head of household' concept has been much criticized, particularly where the head is automatically assumed to be male. For one person to represent the household implies that there are no systematic conflicts of interest between members and that the head will act altruistically and equitably. A major contribution of feminist scholarship has been to challenge this assumption that family life is based on consensus and co-operation. Economic co-operation, for example, cannot be taken for granted (Dwyer and Bruce, 1988). Family households are, rather, characterized by inequality structured around the axes of gender, age and generation.

GENDER, HOUSEHOLD HEADSHIP AND HOUSEHOLD RELATIONS

The theme of gender and households is often narrowly interpreted as meaning 'woman-headed households'. Many people believe that the proportion of households headed by a woman is increasing dramatically. The statistical evidence available is not however that clear cut. A modest upward trend has been recorded for some parts of the world, but a few countries have even reported declining figures (Chant, 1997; United Nations, 2000). Some discussions of the subject are, moreover, seriously flawed, statistically and conceptually.

Statistically, problems of definition and data quality are daunting. There are good arguments for preferring an economic definition of headship, but this is not practical for census purposes. Many census agencies allow respondents to define who heads their household or explicitly exclude the possibility of a woman being counted as head unless there is no male above a certain age in the household. They therefore 'considerably understate women's household responsibilities' (United Nations, 2000: 42).

Many authors nonetheless confidently assert that one-third of the world's households are headed by a woman. This figure comes from an 'educated guess' made by participants in the 1975 International Women's Year conference (Tinker, personal communication, 1995). It has no basis in census data (Varley, 1996). We do not know how national data should be adjusted to counter male bias in enumeration or the apparently growing trend for married women to take responsibility for household maintenance. As such, the best available information, however flawed, is as summarized in Table 1. Excluding the developed countries, the figure is just under one in six households headed by a woman, and one in five overall.

Table 1 Percentage of household heads who are women, by region (1985–1997)

Region	Percentage		No. of countries for which data available
Africa	18.3		26
Northern Africa		12.1	3
Southern Africa		43.4	2
Rest of sub-Saharan Africa		21.0	21
Latin America and the Caribbean	20.2		20
Caribbean		34.3	5
Central America		18.3	6
South America		20.4	9
Asia	11.6		17
Eastern Asia		17.9	3
Southeastern Asia		16.5	4
Southern Asia		9.1	4
Central Asia		23.0	2
Western Asia		10.2	4
Oceania	15.2		7
Developed regions	29.5		24
Eastern Europe		26.9	8
Western Europe		28.7	11
Other developed regions		30.4	5
All	19.6		94
Excluding developed regions		14.1	70

Source: author's calculations, from United Nations (1999); source of Wistat data is varied: principally United Nations Demographic Statistics database as at December 1998, national census or survey data.
Note: no data available for China (other than Hong Kong and Macau), Pakistan, Russian Federation or Nigeria, as well as many smaller populations.
Where household numbers are not available (Wistat, Topic 4.7), the 1990 census round figure for total households (Topic 4.8) has been used with the percentage female headship for each country (Topic 4.7) in order to calculate weighted regional totals. The regional headings used are as in United Nations (2000), Chart 2.24, which also uses Wistat data, but the figures presented differ, because those in the United Nations publication are unweighted averages. For a few countries only households where the head is aged 10/12/15+ are considered.

Why do people nonetheless keep repeating that one-third of the world's households are headed by a woman? It is not difficult to find even more dramatic pronouncements about the extent of female headship in urban areas or amongst the world's poorest households. The reason for this is suggested by Cecile Jackson (1996: 492): 'the poverty of . . . women-headed households has been obscured by the inclination . . . to "talk up" the numbers of women-headed households, and their poverty, to justify GAD [Gender and Development] in numerical terms'. 'One in three' grabs the attention.

There are however a number of dangers in prioritizing impact over accuracy. First, however useful global statistics may prove for advocacy purposes, such claims 'have the potential to back-fire and discredit feminist research' (Baden and Goetz, 1998: 23). Second, the evidence linking poverty and female headship is far from clear-cut (Jackson, 1996; Chant, 1997). Intra-household poverty – in particular, the denial to women and children of full access to men's income – has been described as a more important concern. There is 'overwhelming evidence that resources under the control of women are more likely to be devoted to children than are resources in the hands of men' (Moore, 1994: 8).

The evidence about the poverty of woman-headed households is inconclusive. This is partly because of compensating mechanisms such as household extension (bringing in more income-earners) or remittances from kin (Varley, 1996; Chant, 1997; Lloyd and Gage-Brandon, 1993). Ultimately, however, the problem with the 'feminization of poverty' discourse surrounding woman-headed households is 'that gender justice is not a poverty issue . . . [in spite of] the tendency in development organisations to collapse all forms of disadvantage into poverty' (Jackson, 1996: 501).

The focus on woman-headed households also has other dangers. First, some authors conflate households headed by women and those headed by men with, respectively, 'women' and 'men'. This renders women who are *not* heads of household invisible. Second, there is a tendency to over- or under-play the agency of female household heads. Arguing, for example, that 'one out of every three women is opting out of patriarchal families to head her own household' (Tinker, 1990: 11) is not only statistically questionable but also overlooks the significance of widowhood in relation to female headship. Table 2 shows that, in developing regions, the highest proportion of

Table 2 Percentage of household heads who are women, by region and age, and percentage of household heads aged 60+, by region and sex of head (1985–1996)

Region	Where head is 24 or less	Where head is 25–44	Where head is 45–59	Where head is 60 or over	% of women heads aged 60+	% of men heads aged 60+	No. of countries
Africa	26	28	32	37	21	15	9
Latin American and Caribbean	15	14	22	32	31	15	10
Asia and Oceania	9	9	15	26	33	15	9
Europe	39	19	21	43	47	24	19
Other developed regions	43	27	25	40	30	20	5
All	28	20	23	38	34	19	52

Source: author's calculations, from United Nations (1999), see Table 1.
Note: In addition to countries for which no headship data are available (see Table 1), the data for India, Indonesia and Bangladesh are not disaggregated by age.
The regional figures allow for different numbers of households in each country included (cf. United Nations, 2000, Chart 2.25, which presents unweighted averages).
There is some variation in age categories (for example, in a few cases the national figures cited in the age category 15–24 in practice include ages 15–29).

woman-headed households occurs where the householder is aged 60 or over. The difference between the percentages of male and female household heads in this age group underlines the importance of widowhood in contributing to female headship.

Underplaying women's agency makes those heading their households the victims of male desertion. Desertion is certainly a major issue (Chant, 1997). However women are not always innocent, or men guilty. Recent interest in masculinities and development is helping to counteract the 'straw man' problem. There is also an existing literature examining conflict between women in extended households, particularly in rural south and east Asia and Latin America. Ultimately, such conflict stems from patriarchal norms denying women access to influence except via their relationships with men (Caplan and Bujra, 1978).

Conflict between women household members has implications for the welfare of elderly women. Older women have been marginalized by the literature's emphasis on 'lone mother' households with young/dependent children (Varley, 1996). In societies where brides have traditionally moved in with their husband's parents, there has long been a problem of mothers-in-law teaching the new family members to 'know their place' in a sometimes brutal fashion. Where greater prosperity and female employment has made young couples less dependent on their parents, the unhappiness created by shared living arrangements has encouraged household nucleation (Jackson, 1996).

Down the line, what this means must be considered in the light of the observation that developing countries are currently ageing much faster than developed countries (Wilson, 2000). Fertility decline means that older people will in future have fewer children to care for them. In addition, 'the growing number of young married couples who live on their own away from the husband's parents means that care by a daughter-in-law is no longer automatic' (Wilson, 2000: 120). Older women can find themselves in a vulnerable position – in extreme cases, as victims of abuse – even when they do live with relatives. Research in urban Mexico and south India suggests that the balance of power in the mother-in-law/daughter-in-law relationship is shifting towards the younger woman (Varley and Blasco, 2000; Vera-Sanso, 1999).

The significance of gender in relation to families and households is, in short, far broader than the persistent emphasis on woman-headed households would suggest.

GUIDE TO FURTHER READING

Chant, Sylvia (1997) *Women-Headed Households: Diversity and Dynamics in the Developing World*, Basingstoke: Macmillan. A comprehensive review of the literature plus the author's case studies of lone mother households in Costa Rica, Mexico and the Philippines.

Dwyer, Daisy and Bruce, Judith (eds) (1988) *A Home Divided: Women and Income in the Third World*, Stanford: Stanford University Press, pp. 1–19. A ground-breaking collection of articles from around the world investigating inequality and negotiation within the household over income and expenditure.

Moore, Henrietta (1994) *Is There a Crisis in the Family?*, Occasional Paper No. 3, Geneva: World Summit for Social Development. A concise, balanced and justifiably much-cited overview of family changes in different parts of the world. Available on the internet at http://www.unrisd.org/engindex/publ/cat/publdni.htm.

Varley, Ann (1996) 'Women heading households: some more equal than others?', *World Development* 24(3): 506–20. Explores the validity of global headship statistics and argues that the literature on woman-headed households marginalizes older women and those who live alone.

Wilson, Gail (2000) *Understanding Old Age: Critical and Global Persectives*, London: Sage, Chapter 9, 'Family and community in later life', pp. 115–30. A good, concise, introduction to families' role in caring for older people worldwide.

REFERENCES

Baden, S. and Goetz, A.M. (1998) 'Who needs [sex] when you can have [gender]? Conflicting discourses on gender at Beijing', in C. Jackson and R. Pearson (eds) *Feminist Visions of Development: Gender Analysis and Policy*, London: Routledge, pp. 19–38.

Caplan, P. and Bujra, J.M. (eds) (1978) *Women United, Women Divided: Cross-Cultural Perspectives on Female Solidarity*, London: Tavistock.

Guyer, J.I. and Peters, P.E. (1987) 'Introduction – conceptualising the household: issues of theory and practice in Africa', *Development and Change* 18(2): 197–214.

Jackson, C. (1996) 'Rescuing gender from the poverty trap', *World Development* 24(3): 489–504.

Lloyd, C. and Gage-Brandon, A. (1993) 'Women's role in maintaining households: family welfare and sexual inequality in Ghana', *Population Studies* 47: 115–31.

Lomnitz, L. (1977) *Networks and Marginality: Life in a Mexican Shanty Town*, London: Academic Press.

Netting, R.McC., Wilk, R.R. and Arnould, E.J. (1984) 'Introduction', in R.McC. Netting, R.R. Wilk and E.J. Arnould (eds) *Households: Comparative and Historical Studies of the Domestic Group*, Berkeley: University of California Press, pp. xiii–xxxviii.

Tinker, I. (1990) 'A context for the field and for the book', in I. Tinker (ed.) *Persistent Inequalities: Women and World Development*, New York: Oxford University Press, pp. 3–13.

United Nations (1999) *Women's Indicators and Statistics Database (Wistat)*, Version 4 CD-Rom, New York: UN.

United Nations (2000) *The World's Women 2000: Trends and Statistics*, New York: UN.

Varley, A. and Blasco, M. (2000) 'Intact or in tatters? Family care of older women and men in urban Mexico', *Gender and Development* 8(2): 47–55.

Vera-Sanso, P. (1999) 'Dominant daughters-in-law and submissive mothers-in-law? Cooperation and conflict in South India', *Journal of the Royal Anthropological Institute* 5: 577–93.

Yanagisako, S.J. (1984) 'Explicating residence: a cultural analysis of changing households among Japanese-Americans', in R.McC. Netting, R.R. Wilk and E.J. Arnould (eds) *Households: Comparative and Historical Studies of the Domestic Group*, Berkeley: University of California Press, pp. 330–52.

7.4 Feminism and feminist issues in the South

Linda Peake and D. Alissa Trotz

INTRODUCTION

In discussing this chapter we asked ourselves whether it is possible to speak of 'feminist issues in the South' without reductions to stereotype or gate-keeping concepts.[1] Certainly a number of issues spring immediately to mind: women's human rights and legal autonomy; poverty, access to equitably paid work and continuing non-recognition of unwaged work; violence against women; reproductive health and rights; access to services such as education and housing as well as land and other assets; environmental issues; heterosexism; nationalism; war; religion; HIV/AIDS; and economic citizenship, structural adjustment policies and debt. However, this chapter is not a consideration of a 'list' of feminist issues (a list, any list, risks omissions and generalizations) but rather of some of the epistemological and methodological risks that are raised by the terms 'feminist' and 'South'. Not least, for example, we write this as a woman of colour from the South and a white woman from the North, both now living in Canada, both working in Guyana. Who then represents 'feminist issues in the South'? Who decides which issues matter at any one particular time and place? What might they be by the time this Companion is published? While not wishing to deny or demean the very real and pressing issues and problems faced by millions of women in the South, the ways in which feminists approach their study is very much bound up in questions of representation and the degree of importance attached to making connections between women's activities on the ground and theorizing.

FEMINISM AND THE SOUTH?

One consequence of 'development' thus far has been the (not uncontested) marginalization and misrepresentation of women in the South. What Alexander and Mohanty (1997) refer to as 'historical and newly emergent forms of colonisation' continue to play their role in keeping women of the 'South' in their place as the other, while simultaneously stabilizing gendered, racialized and classed identities in the 'North'. Indeed, gendered ideologies and relations in the South cannot be fully comprehended outside of this global matrix.

The spatial dimensions of this arrangement rely upon discrete categorizations – for example, of nations, of 'developed' and 'un(der)developed' countries, of 'First' and 'Third' World – providing important discursive resources for the continual (re)production of essentialized identities of the 'Third World woman', denying and obliterating their historic and geographic variability. Third World women are too often depicted monolithically as passive and as victims, a worldview that not only ignores their agency but also the vast differences among Southern women across regions and countries as well as within them. Women of the South may have had (to paraphrase Corbridge, 1995: x–xi), 'a past in common, if not a common past' i.e., an engagement foisted upon them with colonialism and postcolonialism, but their futures cannot be contained within a single script. When we refer to the South as a contingent community, then, it is with the understanding that historic and contemporary patterns of global inequality have produced resonances across places that are in so many other ways dissimilar.

Meanwhile, the lack of consideration of the tensions between structural imperatives, such as class, and subjectivities has largely disconnected Western feminist theorizing from a consideration of the material effects of power and inequalities that are the hallmark of neo-liberalism and the new global order. For example, in analyses of the body Western feminists appear to be restricting their attention either to theorizing the body or to focusing on bodily constructions of desire and pleasure. Indeed, the Western female body is increasingly being articulated as sexuality. Relatively little reference has been made to the issue of violence as a bodily regulator or to the ways in which the inscription of bodies occurs in openly aggressive and other coercive ways, either in relation to female or male bodies. Hence the increasing levels of violence permeating the everyday relations of women in the South, symbolic of the lack of democracy and of fundamental human rights that characterize existence for so many, have hardly entered into Western feminist projects on the body.

Issues over the representation of 'Third World' women are also being raised by academic feminist (and postcolonial and poststructuralist) questionings around the 'death of the subject'. While these impel us to take seriously questions around the constitution of subjectivities, they most importantly require a shift in visioning that does not continually reinvoke notions of the 'Third World woman' as passive, victim and other. Moreover, women of the 'North' and 'South' are not separate; gendered ideologies and practices are produced, sustained and challenged through inequalities across, as well as within, both 'places'. It is from such a positioning that we define feminism as the art of crafting inclusive and democratic practices that work towards increasing the self-determination of women as part of the global project of rethinking and transforming hierarchies. It requires a critical analysis based on local feminist praxis which connects to broader, i.e. global, relations of domination and subordination that are inclusive of social divisions such as 'race', class and sexuality as well as gender.

WOMEN AND EMPLOYMENT

To emphasize the necessity of careful contextualization, we turn now to an example of a 'feminist issue in the South'. The international division of labour, structural adjustment programmes and increasingly the general devaluation of work to resemble conditions that previously existed largely for women, paint a depressing picture of employment prospects for women in the South. But against the backdrop of the consolidation of capitalist relations through globalization and the neo-liberal economic agenda, researchers have traced both promise and threat in the spaces between structural imperatives and the ongoing constitution of subjectivities. One locus that has created contradictory spaces for women is export-oriented industries. Early research in this field appeared to paint a single portrait of the female factory worker as young, single, female and exploited, but these findings obscured the uneven geographies of these industries being largely based on some (by no means all) experiences, largely in Southeast Asia. We now understand that there are differences not just across countries and regions, but also within them. Localized studies indicate how global capitalism intersects with specific gendered regimes to produce different types of demands and struggles for power (see, for example, Freeman, 1998; Hsiung, 1996; Pearson, 1998; Wolf, 1992). They also allow us to understand how women create 'opportunities' and change, ranging from strikes and other forms of resistance through reworking of gender relations in the household, to renegotiation of personal and social identities.

Our focus on export-oriented industries and formal-sector work is not meant to be exclusionary. While important, it represents only a small share of women's income-earning activities with informal-sector activities forming the bulk of women's work. Neither is this only a scenario of the South. Work is becoming increasingly globalized, not just in terms of capital but also in terms of labour, but the same promises and conditions that enable capital to enjoy unfettered mobility do not exist for labour. Examples include sex workers who travel abroad and who are criminalized and vulnerable, and women who cross borders to perform cheap unregulated labour in North America, such as domestic workers, but who enjoy little or no protection under the law.

TENSIONS AND RESOLUTIONS: ORGANIZING FOR CHANGE?

Tensions around the representation of 'feminist issues in the South' became clear in the first conferences following the Declaration of the United Nations Decade for Women in 1975. Constituencies from the South challenged the hegemonic vision of Western feminism, raising questions over the universality of female sisterhood as well as the issue of who is defining a feminist agenda and from where. While questioning of the liberalist growth models of development of the 1950s–1960s that had created a space through which issues of women and development could be inserted – albeit in Women in Development (WID) ways – into mainstream development discourse, Southern-based groups, such as Development Alternatives with Women for a New Era (DAWN), argued that the question was not whether women were left out of development, but the skewed manner in which they were incorporated (Sen and Grown, 1987).

Nonetheless, we are not arguing here for any simplistic attempt to differentiate between 'bad' North and 'good' South brands of feminism. Indeed, Andaiye, a prominent Caribbean feminist/woman's activist, suggests that since 1975 there has arisen a loose grouping of feminists of the North and South. She claims that while women of the South give priority to issues of economic injustice, 'often the economic injustice focused on is North/South, not that inside the South and between women of the South. . . . These same women, who are global in their activism, also have a more active and stronger relation to feminists of the North than to the struggles of poor women in the South, where they (partly) live.' She concludes that perhaps the real issue for 'feminism' in the South is its frequent disconnection from women's struggles on the ground. It is to these that we now turn.

What has been significant about women's responses in the present conjuncture is that the traditional spaces in which women are located and which tend to be designated their main arenas of responsibility – the neighbourhood, the household – have become politicized and transformed into sites of struggle. In Latin America, for example, it is virtually impossible to ignore the critical and ongoing contributions made by countless women to the transitions to democracy. And in the Caribbean there is a long history of women's organizations – social, religious and political – engaged in struggles to improve women's lives, although it was not until the 1970s and 1980s that feminist-oriented groups started to emerge. Women in these organizations are working to address such issues as the persistent and increasing burden of poverty on women; inequality in healthcare; violence against women; and inequality between men and women in the sharing of power. They are also seeking ways to work together, across generational, 'race', ethnic, religious, class and other divides including national and global concerns (Peake and Trotz, 1999). We need to acknowledge the very real constraints under which these efforts to mobilize are operating, including – perhaps not least – a hostile international environment.

In many instances it is women in the South who are at the forefront of working to change the conditions within which they work and live, a situation that is increasingly leading to migration across national borders. Indeed, the figure of the migrant female worker is emblematic not only of the inequalities between North and South but also of resonances that are occurring globally, such as women's visibility in an increasingly casualized and flexible workforce in both the North and South. What does this tell us about the choices women are prepared to and have to make, in a society in which caring work does not come with a similar or equal set of obligations for everyone? The DAWN platform for Beijing argues that:

> women stand at the crossroads between production and reproduction, between economic activity and the care of human beings, and therefore between economic growth and human development. They are the workers in both spheres – the most responsible, and therefore with most at stake, those whom suffer the most when the two work at cross-purposes, and most sensitive to the need for better integration between the two.

(DAWN, 1995: 21)

Women can lead the challenge to globalization in the 1990s and 2000s as we did in challenging the policies of structural adjustment in the 1980s and 1990s. If globalization has increased the political, economic and social marginalization of women it has also enabled the mobilization of women across disparate spaces and borders. The challenge surely now lies in creating transnational feminist critiques while not losing sight of the specific sites through which struggles for social justice are waged.

NOTE

1. We are deeply indebted to Andaiye and Ruth Pearson for their comments on an earlier draft. The usual disclaimers apply.

GUIDE TO FURTHER READING

A historically important text on feminism and development from a Southern perspective is Sen and Grown (1987). Two of the most recent texts on feminists theorizing development are Pearson and Jackson (1998), which revisits earlier debates on feminism and development, and Alexander and Mohanty (1997) which offers a variety of case studies. For case-studies of women's organizing across the South see Basu with McGrory (1995). Porter and Judd (1999) meanwhile provide practical examples of the strengths and pitfalls of feminist interventions in development processes. See also Peake and Trotz (1999) for a text that has arisen directly from the authors' engagement with women in the South in the Red Thread Women's Development Programme in Guyana.

REFERENCES

Alexander, J. and Mohanty, C.T. (eds) (1997) *Feminist Genealogies, Colonial Legacies, Democratic Futures,* Andaiye (2000), personal communication, 19 July London: Routledge.

Basu, A. with McGrory, C.E. (eds) (1995) *The Challenge of Local Feminisms: Women's Movements in Global Perspective,* Boulder, CO: Westview Press.

Corbridge, S. (ed.) (1995) *Development Studies: A Reader,* Edward Arnold: London.

DAWN (1995) *Markers on the Way: the Dawn Debates on Alternative Development,* Dawn's Platform for the Fourth World Conference on Women, Beijing.

Freeman, C. (1998) 'Island-hopping body shopping in Barbados: localising the gendering of transnational workers', in C. Barrow (ed.) *Caribbean Portraits: Essays on Gender Ideologies and Identities,* Kingston, Jamaica: Ian Randle Publishers, pp. 14–27.

Hsiung, P. (1996) *Living Rooms as Factories: Class, Gender and the Factory Satellite System in Taiwan,* PA: Temple University Press.

Peake, L. and Trotz, A. (1999) *Gender, Ethnicity and Place: Women and Identities in Guyana,* London: Routledge.

Pearson, R. (1998) 'Nimble fingers revisited: reflections on women and Third World industrialization in the late twentieth century', in R. Pearson and C. Jackson (eds) *Feminist Visions of Development,* London: Routledge.

Porter, M. and Judd, E. (eds) (1999) *Feminists Doing Development: A Practical Critique,* London: Zed Books.

Sen, G. and Grown, C. (1987) *Development Crises and Alternative Visions: Third World Women's Perspectives,* New York: Monthly Review Press.

Wolf, D. (1992) *Factory Daughters: Gender, Household Dynamics and Rural Industrialization in Java,* Berkeley: University of California Press.

7.5 Gender and empowerment: new thoughts, new approaches

Jane L. Parpart

Empowerment has become a popular, largely unquestioned 'goal' of such diverse and contradictory development institutions as the World Bank, Oxfam and many more radical non-governmental organizations (NGOs). Initially associated primarily with alternative approaches to development, by the 1980s empowerment was being advocated as a necessary ingredient for challenging and transforming unequal political, economic and social structures. It was regarded as a weapon for the weak – best wielded through participatory, grassroots community-based activities. However, empowerment has many meanings and by the mid-1990s, some mainstream development agencies had begun to adopt the term. While not abandoning their belief in liberal economic policies, the language of consultation, participation and partnership with Southern clients has increasingly infiltrated mainstream development discourse (World Bank, 1995). These discursive similarities obscure differences in interpretation and practice. Mainstream institutions and their practitioners for the most part envision empowerment as a means for enhancing efficiency and productivity within the status quo rather than as a mechanism for social transformation.

These debates and perspectives have influenced (and been influenced by) development theorists and practitioners concerned with women, gender and development as well. An initial focus on integrating women into development in the 1970s, shifted to a concern with gender and gender relations in the late 1980s (Moser, 1993; Parpart *et al.*, 2000). However, some activists and theorists from the South, and a few from the North, began to recognize the limitations of even this advance. They began to argue that women would never develop unless they are empowered to challenge patriarchy and global inequality. Gita Sen and Caren Grown introduced the term in their landmark book, *Development, Crises, and Alternative Visions* (1987). They offered a vision of empowerment rooted in a commitment to collective action growing out of the lived experiences of women (and men) in the South, as well as a concern for political and economic inequality. While rather utopian in tone, the book calls for a collective vision, a set of strategies and new methods for mobilizing political will, empowering women (and poor men) and transforming society. The authors put considerable faith in the transformative potential of 'political mobilization, legal changes, consciousness raising, and popular education' (p. 87).

Writings on empowerment and gender as an approach to development have continued to emerge in the alternative development literature, especially from the South. In 1994, for example, Srilatha Batliwala warned that 'empowerment', which had virtually replaced terms such as poverty alleviation, welfare and community participation, was in danger of losing its transformative edge. She called for a more precise understanding of power and empowerment, one that sees power 'as control over material assets, intellectual resources, and ideology' (1994: 129). For Batliwala, empowerment is 'the process of challenging existing power relations, and of gaining greater control over the sources of power' (1994: 130). It requires political action and collective assault on cultural as well as national and community power structures that oppress women and some men. Thus, while acknowledging the need to improve the lives of grassroots women, Batliwala insists that women's empowerment requires transformative political action as well.

Naila Kabeer (1994) also insists on the centrality of empowerment for the struggle to achieve gender equality. Drawing on the work of Lukes (1974), she criticizes the liberal and Marxist emphasis on *power over* resources, institutions and decision-making, and adds Lukes' focus on power as the ability to control discussions/discourses and agendas. She argues, however, for a more feminist analysis of power, one that emphasizes the transformative potential of *power within*. This power is rooted in self-understanding that can inspire women (and some men) to recognize and challenge gender inequality in the home and the community (1994: 224–9). Like Batliwala, she emphasizes collective, grassroots participatory action – the *power to* work *with* others 'to control resources, determine agendas and to make decisions' (1994: 229). More concerned with action than theory, she continues to explore practical, measureable ways to empower women (Kabeer, 1999).

Jo Rowlands (1997) brings a broader analytical perspective to the discussion of gender and empowerment. She argues that 'empowerment is more than participation in decision-making; it must also include the processes that lead people to perceive themselves as able and entitled to make decisions' (1997: 14). It is personal, relational and collective. She recognizes that empowerment is not just a gender issue, but a development issue affecting women and men. While acknowledging the complexity and difficulties of empowerment as a concept and a practice, she remains convinced that the key to empowerment lies in mobilizing marginalized people, especially women. She cautions, however, that empowerment is a process rather than an end product, neither easily defined nor measured. At the same time, she believes that:

there is a core to the empowerment process . . . which consists of increases in self-confidence and self-esteem, a sense of agency and of 'self' in a wider context, and a sense of *dignidad* (being worthy of having a right to respect from others).

(1997: 129–30)

Initially, mainstream development agencies concerned with women ignored the language of empowerment, but as top-down development policies failed to alleviate poverty in the 1990s, especially among women, the discourse began to change. Empowerment entered the lexicon of mainstream women and development discourse. For example, the Beijing Platform states unequivocally that women's empowerment is 'fundamental for the achievement of equality, development and peace' (United Nations, 1995: para. 13). The Canadian International Development Agency's (CIDA) 'Policy on Gender Equality' includes women's empowerment as one of the eight guiding principles for its policy goals (1999). Of course, mainstream development agencies generally focus on empowerment as a means for improving women's productivity and efficiency within neo-liberal economic systems and 'solutions' (World Bank, 1995). At the level of discourse, however, development practitioners and policy-makers from all perspectives increasingly seem to agree that empowerment is a necessary ingredient for women's development.

This seeming congruence of policy and approach obscures the difficulties faced by those trying to understand, implement and measure women's empowerment. While the instability of the term has its advantages – for empowerment varies by context and condition – that same fluidity impedes our understanding of the ways one might enhance both the process and outcomes of empowerment projects. Some practitioners and scholars focus on personal empowerment, arguing that, without it, collective empowerment is impossible. Indeed, Caroline Moser places self-reliance and internal strength at the centre of empowerment, which she defines as the ability 'to determine choices in life and to influence the direction of change, through the ability to gain control over crucial material and non-material resources' (1993: 74–5). Others emphasize collective empowerment, noting the fragility of individual efforts (Kabeer, 1994). Always concerned with transforming ideals into practice, Moser remains sceptical about the willingness of mainstream development agencies to embrace the grassroots, participatory small-scale methods championed by the empowerment approach (1993: 77–79). Moreover, as Naila Kabeer points out, attempts to measure (and direct) empowerment are often based on the assumption that 'we can somehow predict the nature and direction that change is going to assume. In actual fact, human agency is indeterminate and hence unpredictable in a way that is antithetical to requirements of measurement' (1999: 462).

Despite different emphases and perspectives, discussions of empowerment have for the most part remained rooted in the local, in the needs of the 'poorest of the poor'. This is particularly true of attempts to empower women. While acknowledging the importance of the local, and of grassroots knowledge and activism, this focus on the local and the uncritical use of the term em(power)ment constrains the transformative ability of the empowerment approach. *Rethinking Empowerment* (Parpart *et al.*, 2002) argues that empowerment will only become an effective tool for challenging gender inequality when it moves beyond the local to address the following issues.

Discussions of empowerment must move beyond the assumption that power is defined only as *power over* others, that the powerless need to be brought into the charmed circle of the powerful. This approach ignores the internal inhibitions facing marginalized groups, the need for *power within*. It ignores the difficulties of organizing together to carry out effective action. Empowerment requires a nuanced, holistic approach to power, one that draws on thinkers such as Michel Foucault (1991) and feminist writings on power (see articles in Hekman, 1996) as well as the scholar/activists discussed above. It requires attention to the role of language and meanings, identities and cultural practices as well as the forces that enhance *power to* act *with* others to construct and carry out effective change, often in hostile and difficult environments.

Second, while empowerment is often a local affair, the local is embedded in the global and the national, and vice versa. We need to understand the interconnectedness of the three levels that frame our debates about struggles for empowerment. Global competitiveness affects job opportunities in even the smallest communities, drawing women and men into transnational migration networks and creating diasporas which can both help and hinder local and national development. Global economic policies often define the limits of government policy and action at the national and regional level; witness the impact of structural adjustment policies on many Third World economies. Cyberspace both enables people to move beyond their locale and yet ties them to the limits of their technical skills and access. Improved representations of women in government are influenced by local as well as national/regional cultural practices towards women, as well as international discourses and practices regarding women and politics.

Third, the empowerment literature has focused on consciousness raising, and individual and group activity/agency without perhaps paying enough attention to the ways in which institutional structures and politics frame, constrain and enable these activities. The institutional, material and discursive framework within which individual and group agency can develop must be taken seriously. This does not mean that the process of implementing 'empowerment' policies and projects, and the agency involved, is less important. It does, however, point to the need to situate individual and group action/agency within the material, political and discursive structures in which it operates. This requires careful, historically situated analyses of women's struggles to gain power in a world rarely of their own choosing.

Finally, we see empowerment as both a process and an outcome. At times the two are indistinguishable, at others outcome becomes part of the process itself, and at still others the process is the outcome. While recognizing that specific outcomes should (and often can) be measured, empowerment is often difficult to measure. Many subtle and often unexpected strategies have the potential, but not the certainty, of empowerment (Kabeer, 1999). Others, such as international covenants and gender-sensitive laws, seem to guarantee empowerment but fail due to patriarchal cultural practices and structures. Thus, while conceptual clarity demands some distinction between process and outcome, the process of empowerment is often just as important as the outcome. While attempts to measure outcomes are important for keeping development practitioners and policymakers honest, and comparing intent with performance, an obsession with outcomes and measurement can endanger the very processes most apt to nurture women's empowerment, even if not apparent at the time.

These four themes offer a way to make both the concept and the practice of empowerment strategies for women more rigorous, effective and perhaps complex. Women's groups, movements and feminist scholars would then be able to reflect upon the interconnectedness that empowerment requires if it is to be more than a 'motherhood' term. This approach pushes the existing boundaries of analysis about women's empowerment to make it more effective, nuanced and grounded. It is intended as a means for strengthening empowerment, both as a concept and as a practice for enhancing women's equality and gender equity in an increasingly complex, global/local world.

GUIDE TO FURTHER READING AND REFERENCES

Batliwala, S. (1994) 'The Meaning of Women's Empowerment: new concepts from action', in G. Sen, A. Germain and L.C. Chen (eds) *Population Policies Reconsidered: Health, Empowerment and Rights*, Boston: Harvard University Press.

Canadian International Development Agency (CIDA) (1999) *Policy on Gender Equality*, Ottawa: CIDA.

Foucault, M. (1991) *The Foucault Reader: An Introduction to Foucault's Thought*, P. Rabinow (ed.) Harmondsworth, UK: Penguin.

Hekman, S. (1996) *Feminist Interpretations of Michel Foucault*, University Park, PA.: Pennsylvania State University Press.

Kabeer, N. (1994) *Reversed Realities: Gender Hierarchies in Development Thought*, London: Verso.

Kabeer, N. (1999) 'Resources, agency, achievements: reflections on the measurement of women's empowerment', *Development and Change* 30(3): 435–64.

Lukes, S. (1974) *Power: a Radical View*, London: Macmillan.

Moser, C. (1993) *Gender Planning and Development: Theory, Practice and Training*, London: Routledge.

Parpart, J., Connelly, P. and Barriteau, E.V. (eds) (2000) *Theoretical Perspectives on Gender and Development*, Ottawa: International Development Research Centre.

Parpart, J., Rai, S. and Staudt, K. (eds) (2002) *Rethinking Empowerment: Gender and Development in a Global/Local World*, London: Routledge.

Organization for Economic Co-operation and Development (OECD) (1998) *Report on Gender Equality*, Paris: OECD.

Rowlands, J. (1997) *Questioning Empowerment: Working with Women in Honduras*, Oxford: Oxfam Publications.

Sen, G. and C. Grown. (1987) *Development, Crises, and Alternative Visions: Third World Women's Perspectives*, New York: Monthly Review Press.

United Nations (1995) *Beijing Platform for Action*, New York: United Nations.

World Bank (1995) *World Bank Participation Source Book*, Washington, DC: World Bank Environment Department Papers.

7.6 Women in the global economy

Bama Athreya

INTRODUCTION

Women participate in formal and informal economies worldwide in a number of ways. In the past few decades one of the most noteworthy aspects of women's participation in the so-called 'global economy' has been the dramatic rise in participation of women workers in light manufacturing industries. The figure of the female factory worker has caught the imagination of many feminist scholars, in particular, and it is no wonder. In many newly industrializing countries, young women from rural agricultural families are entering the manufacturing workforce in large numbers. The peasant girl-turned-factory daughter provides a dramatic symbol of the woman caught in the crossfire between traditional and modern roles and norms. Furthermore, the barely post-adolescent girl, controlled by an older, male factory manager, is often seen as a victim not only of traditional patriarchies but also of new ones created by the expanding influence of multinational corporations. Are women victims, or agents of change in the global economy?

VICTIMS OF THE GLOBAL ECONOMY

The literature on women workers can be divided roughly into two categories, the first of which sees the factory experience as adding to women's oppression, and the second of which sees it as in some ways liberating. Maria Mies' 1986 work, *Patriarchy and Accumulation on a World Scale*, provides an explanation of women's oppression as intensified by the spread of global capital. Mies posits that corporations based in developed countries have spread their arms overseas primarily in search of the cheapest possible labour. Because of the relative worthlessness assigned to women and women's work in societies throughout the world, women are always the cheapest source of labour. Mies asserts that women are also more easily controllable than men, because as housewives they have been 'atomized', or cut off from social support structures (Mies, 1986: 116). She then gives examples of common stereotypes which illustrate that Third World women are perceived as the perfect workers because they are nimble and docile. The sexual dimension to Asian women's passivity, in particular, adds to their desirability as workers, she asserts, citing advertisements from Malaysia recommending the talents of 'the oriental girl'.

Many factory managers themselves will admit they prefer young women workers. In Southeast Asia, factory managers have repeatedly and openly stated that women workers are more adept than men at detail work, and also that they are less likely to organize or strike. In other developing countries, garment factory managers have stated frankly that they prefer to hire young women because they have no experience and are therefore easier to control. Industrialists throughout Asia prefer to hire children where possible for similar reasons. To whatever extent possible, in the developed as well as the developing world, businesses are interested in hiring the workers who will be least likely to complain about poor wages or working conditions.

Aihwa Ong's research on Malaysian factory women provides one of the most thorough and interesting examples of the woman worker-as-victim genre (Ong, 1987). Ong suggests that the modern workplace adds to women's oppression, and that women react by invoking symbols of a traditional past in which, presumably, they were treated more equitably. Her work presumes that the women themselves are 'mystified' by state rhetoric into thinking they prefer modern industrial employment to agrarian village life, but their sublimated true desires manifest themselves through episodes of spirit possession.

A prominent theme throughout Ong's work is that of the extension of control into all aspects of the factory girls' lives. Not only, says Ong, are they subjected to rigorous discipline within the factory itself, but the patterns of their external lives are changed and controlled as well. For example, she notes, some firms organize local activities and contribute to village activities and funds, for good public relations. A 'parents' night' at one factory is described as having been particularly successful. Ong sees such activities as an ill-intended extension of control into all realms of these girls' lives. Furthermore, she implies, they are a way of 'co-opting' peasant families into valuing factory work for their daughters by insidiously integrating such work with traditional village patterns of life. The factories' message seems to be that they will not corrupt these good village girls, but instead teach them to respect the old ways and mores.

Yet, Ong notes that these very factory girls are feared to be succumbing to a 'capitalist . . . individualist and materialist culture'. She notes, 'Indeed, many factory women, especially those working in urban-based free trade zones, acquired eye-catching outfits and spent their off-hours shopping and going to the movies.' She notes that local bureaucrats, feeling threatened by the new autonomy of such women, reacted by vilifying their morality (Ong, 1987: 181).

The actions and comments of the women themselves are relevant in this regard. Their newfound sexual autonomy is evident in several examples and Ong concurs that control over earnings has translated into control over reproductive destiny. She writes, 'young women and men exhibited a striking sense of self in their matrimonial choices and negotiations. . . . Family conflict, broken betrothals, divorces and the unwedded condition are the loose ends and ragged edges of the kampung society in transition' (Ong, 1987: 116).

These writings, typifying the woman factory worker as a victim both of traditional culture and of the state, are typical of the new industrial division of labour (NIDL) school of scholarship which emerged in the early 1980s, and examples of which may still be found. The failure of the NIDL school was thus that it overlooked early signs of grounds for resistance and empowerment in women's proletarianization. The significant role played by women in the labour movements and democracy movements of South Korea, the Philippines and Bangladesh, for example, has been largely invisible in this body of literature, despite numerous writings on gender and industrialization in Asia.

Interestingly, Ong revisited the subject of working women's consciousness in a 1991 article, 'The gender and labor politics of postmodernity', which summarized the state of the NIDL studies. The essay concludes by noting exactly what such studies have missed: the development of militant labour movements featuring women. Ong notes in particular the development of women's unions in South Korea, in which 'female workers learned to be sovereign subjects, acting as self-determining agents of social change' (Ong, 1991: 305). These observations led her to reconsider her own data on Malaysian factory women and to suggest the possibility that they, too, are in a process of transformation.

Although the NIDL writings correctly identified ways in which mass production might serve to intensify existing forms of oppression, these writings failed to note the cultural transformations that economic change would inevitably cause. Mies and others correctly noted that peasant women were, by and large, atomized. However, once they have entered the industrial realm, such women can no longer either think or act in an atomized fashion; a sense of shared experience, not only with other workers but with other women, must begin to emerge. This transformation will be explored in the following section.

WOMEN TRANSFORMED

There is another point of view regarding the neophyte woman factory worker. This alternate school suggests that women may actually be empowered by their experience as formal wage earners. This argument is not unique to Asia; it has been argued that the movement for women's liberation in the United States and Britain was in part an outgrowth of women's transition to wage work (Thompson, 1963: 414–18). Gillian Foo and Linda Lim note that Singaporean and Malay factory women, particularly those that work in multinational corporations, are economically better off than their rural counterparts. Furthermore, they show that in addition to economic motivations, women are socially motivated to take on industrial wage employment.

> Young single women say they welcome the opportunity that factory work provides to delay marriage and childbearing, to enjoy the companionship of their peers and lead independent lives, and to 'broaden their horizons' through new experiences. Married women say they feel bored staying at home and miss the companionship of colleagues. Among both single and married women are many who say they would choose to work even in the absence of economic need.
>
> (Foo and Lim, 1989: 215)

Diane Wolf's work provides additional evidence for the argument that young women may seek wage employment because of desire for increased economic and social autonomy. Her 1992 study of young women workers in Indonesia is largely devoted to showing that far from being major contributors to the household income, young single factory women tend to spend their earnings on their own personal needs, entertainment and luxury goods. Their new economic power is accompanied by changing social roles: 'There was considerable social experimentation in their behaviour; many factory daughters frequently negotiated their position as they tested the limits of parental boundaries' (Wolf, 1992: 258). Wolf notes that similar changes were not apparent among village girls who did not work in the factories.

Increased social autonomy may also enhance the political awareness of the young female factory worker. Foo and Lim cite a striking example of a young Malaysian woman's realization of her political potential:

> Before I started working, I was very timid, whatever I did, I was scared. I was scared of the supervisor, of my work, and so on. Now, I'm brave enough to speak up, to explain and to clarify my mistakes, to speak my objections and to lead the society that I'm a member of. . . . After working in a factory, I've met a lot of friends and got to know a lot of people so I'm not scared of asking questions and making my points to others. I'm not shy about doing whatever I think is right. I'm brave enough to be a party leader in politics too.
>
> (Foo and Lim, 1989: 221)

In short, there is some evidence that young girls, making their way from rural areas to urban industrial employment, may be emboldened by their new surroundings and occupations. In a subsequent article, Lim noted that in comparison with other forms of employment, industrial-sector employment has provided women throughout Asia with the opportunity to organize and thereby to enhance their social and political power (Lim, 1990: 5). Jane Hutchison, writing about the Philippines, has also found that the incorporation of women into the formal labour force actually enabled women to organize toward goals that advanced not only their status as workers but as women (Hutchinson, 1992: 441).

CONCLUSION

These few pages have examined the sociological/anthropological perspectives on women's engagement in light manufacturing industries worldwide, and particularly in Asia, where women have entered the industrial workforce in striking numbers in recent years. It has not examined the economic realities for such women workers. To be sure, jobs in light manufacturing in developing countries tend to be poorly paid, in most instances offering workers minimum wages, with little hope of advancement or increased incomes in future. Women may thus become secondary contributors to household income, but in most cases developing-country households cannot be supported on a single earner's factory wages. Moreover, this chapter has not explored numerous other facets of women's engagement in global manufacturing enterprises, let alone in the global economy more generally. In many countries women produce for manufacturing enterprises not as formal workers in a defined workplace, but as home-based workers, unprotected by labour legislation, paid on piece rates that fall far below established minimum wages and unable to organize for better protections as their factory-based sisters might.

Nevertheless, women's engagement in the global economy has not been a simple story of unmitigated exploitation. In some countries, even as secondary wage earners women have found that factory employment has played into overall changes in societal options regarding marriage and childbearing. In other settings, injustices imposed by the workplace have served as a catalyst to new forms of political action by women. These are the unintended consequences of globalization and, more broadly, of economic development.

GUIDE TO FURTHER READING

Afshar, Haleh and Agarwal, Bina (eds) (1989) *Women, Poverty and Ideology in Asia*, London: Macmillan.

Beneria, Lourdes and Roldan, Martha (1987) *The Crossroads of Class and Gender: Industrial Homework, Subcontracting, and Household Dynamics in Mexico City*, Chicago: University of Chicago Press.

Deyo, Frederic C. (1989) *Beneath the Miracle: Labor Subordination in the New Asian Industrialism*, Berkeley: University of California Press.

Kung, Lydia (1978) *Factory Women in Taiwan*, New York: Columbia University Press.

Mies, Maria (1982) *The Lace Makers of Narsapur: Indian Housewives Produce for the World Market*, London: Zed Books.

Mies, Maria (1986) *Patriarchy and Accumulation on a World Scale*, London: Zed Books.

Nash, June and Fernandez-Kelly, Maria Patricia (eds) (1983) *Women, Men and the International Division of Labor*, Albany: State University of New York Press.

Ong, Aihwa (1987) *Spirits of Resistance and Capitalist Discipline: Factory Women in Malaysia*, Albany: State University of New York Press.

Safa, Helen I. (1995) *The Myth of the Male Breadwinner: Women and Industrialization in the Caribbean*, Boulder, CO: Westview Press.

REFERENCES

Foo, Gillian H.C. and Lim, Linda Y.C. (1989) 'Poverty, ideology and women export factory workers in Southeast Asia', in Haleh Afshar and Bina Agarwal (eds) *Women, Poverty and Ideology in Asia*, London: Macmillan.

Hutchinson, Jane (1992) 'Women in the Philippines garments exports industry', *Journal of Contemporary Asia* 22(4).

Lim, Linda (1990) 'Labor organization among women: workers in multinational export factories in Asia', *Journal of Southeast Asia Business* 6(4).

Ong, Aihwa (1991) 'The gender and labor politics of postmodernity', *Annual Review of Anthropology* 20.

Thompson, E.P. (1963) *The Making of the English Working Class*, New York: Vintage Books.

Wolf, Diane (1992) *Factory Daughters: Gender, Household Dynamics, and Rural Industrialization in Java*, Berkeley: University of California Press.

7.7 Gender and structural adjustment

Lynne Brydon

INTRODUCTION

From the early 1980s the IMF and World Bank granted loans to the majority of states in the 'South' for the 'stabilization' and 'adjustment' of their economies. These loans were to be used to fund policies devised in accordance with the WB/IMF's dominant ideologies, broadly neo-liberal, encouraging the shrinking of the state, removal of subsidies and the growth of competition. Adjusting countries had to agree to implement measures calculated to restore their balances of payments and create entrepreneurially driven economies. There were incentives to produce 'tradable' goods (goods that could be traded for hard currency). The medium-term aim of adjustment was 'recovery with growth', the idea that Third World states could develop into middle-income countries by 2020.

IDEAL OUTCOMES OF STRUCTURAL ADJUSTMENT POLICIES

So structural adjustment policies and programmes (SAPs), derived as they were from neo-liberal economic theory, were supposed to create employment in new enterprises competing (from a baseline presumed to ape a 'level playing field') in growing national, regional and global markets. 'Recovery with growth' is a laudable aim, and the SAP policy-makers assumed that efficient growth would involve the whole of a state's labour force, irrespective of gender (women's as well as men's labour would be included in the *efficient* workings of a state's economy), particularly those who were educated and liable to be flexible in their approaches to work. But early empirical studies of the effects of SAPs indicated a range of hardships, apparently affecting women more than men: for example, declines in maternal and child health status (Cornia et al., 1987), cash shortages because of devaluation, removal of subsidies and increased competition in the informal sector (Afshar and Dennis, 1992). Initial responses from the Bank regarded the problems as temporary blips but they did agree to monitor the situation. In the later 1980s the Bank set up both Living Standards Measurement Surveys,[1] to monitor the grassroots effects of adjustment, and packages of short-term alleviatory policies[2] designed to target the worst-hit ('vulnerable') sectors of populations.

GENDER AWARENESS?

Some, at least, of the problems in achieving 'recovery with growth' can be blamed on gender-blindness. Informed by the neo-liberal ideologies of the World Bank, SAPs provide a prime example of the gender-blindness and 'male bias' (Elson, 1995a) of supposedly gender-neutral theory. In addition, the LSM surveys were also based on economic theories, assuming specific household forms and power relations also incorporating a 'male bias'. Only after early gendered criticisms, both of SAPs and LSM surveys, were serious attempts made to take gender into account, both in the design and analysis of policies and surveys, and in the analysis of stratification within local labour markets. In short, economic theory and classical survey design do not provide 'level playing fields' with respect to gender: they are not gender neutral.

There were thus attempts at 'adding on' gender (Brydon and Legge, 1996) to SAPs. Ghana's PAMSCAD, for example, targeted some policies specifically at women, but at women as 'reproducers' (nutrition and feeding programmes). Policies focused on income generation (loans for business or agricultural ventures) tended to favour men. Where women were the focus of loan policies, their prospective enterprises were confined within the range of conventionally recognized 'women's work', for example, trading or food processing. Cultural assumptions of 'women's work' were not challenged. Any attempt to disaggregate ostensibly gender-neutral survey data by gender ran into difficulty as gender was not an integral analytical axis in the LSM surveys.

EMPIRICAL CRITIQUES

Early critiques showed in what ways women's lives were made more difficult as a result of the workings of SAPs (Dennis, 1991; Afshar and Dennis, 1992; Elson, 1995a): increasing health problems for mothers (the implications being that mothers sacrifice their own nutrition and health for the sake of their children); women's household manager roles are made more difficult because of price rises (through devaluation and subsidy cuts); opportunities for women's earning in formal and informal sectors decline. Cash shortages might mean switching to cheaper foods, either less nutritious (health risks) or, where pulses are introduced as protein, taking longer to prepare and cook (taking more of both, women's time and fuel).

Inefficient formal enterprises are 'rationalized' with the introduction of SAPs, resulting in mass unemployment. Even though fewer women than men tended to be employed in these enterprises, disproportionately high numbers of women were laid off when enterprises were 'rationalized'. Whether this is because women were in low-level and unskilled positions (either through lack of education or connections/networks,[3] or because of the gender division of labour within the market), or even because of blatant discrimination against women in downsizing the labour force, is a moot point: these points merit discussion in their own right. The point here is that women are more likely to have been 'downsized' than men.

But men have also been made redundant and they, too, have to make a living, to survive and 'cope'. The informal sector has been the most obvious destination for the newly unemployed, so much so that it has become overcrowded. The practicalities of living are more difficult: there are only so many seamstresses, hairdressers, bakers and traders (women), and carpenters, electricians, plumbers and barbers (men) that a neighbourhood can support. The pool of SAP-created available labour is supposed to have been mopped up by new businesses attracted by the availability of skilled labour and attractive conditions of production. Although a few new locally owned companies have been founded, international capital has been shy of investing in adjusting countries, apart from under the favourable conditions of an export processing zone (EPZ) or free trade area. But even where there are such zones, inward investment in many cases, and particularly in sub-Saharan Africa, has been minimal.

In EPZs most locally hired workers are women. The usually quoted rationale for this is their docility, because of women's 'natural' (sic) subordination to men (whether bosses or male relatives) and dexterity (because of the gendered training of women from childhood in 'nimble-fingered' tasks (Elson and Pearson, 1981) of women workers). This means that women become family breadwinners, the power derived from their earnings at odds with 'traditional' household responsibilities[4] where formerly they either had no or minimal control of cash (crudely summarizing, Asia, Latin America and the Middle East) or responsibility for specified areas of household expenditure (sub-Saharan Africa). Elson (1995a) has suggested that these changes lead to tension in domestic gender relations, and depression in the cases of husbands (resulting in stress for wives), as has happened with economic restructuring in the 'North'.

These are direct effects of SAPs on women, but there are also gendered indirect consequences of SAPs. Although the World Bank has denied that SAPs must necessarily mean cut-backs in social-sector spending, particularly health and education, in practice most adjusting countries have focused their revenues on the economy and balance of payments. While sectors like health and education have not been ignored under the dispensations of adjustment, neither have they been recipients of significantly increased central funding, and their overall share of GDP often declines, leaving women to pick up the burdens of providing education for children and healthcare for all family members at home. UNICEF reports: 'The region (*Sub-Saharan Africa*) includes over 30 heavily indebted countries, and governments spend as much on debt repayment as on health and basic education combined – $12 billion in 1996, and per capita education spending is less than half that of 1980' (1999: 10). In addition, neo-liberal thinking has been introduced into both health and education sectors in various ways.

EDUCATION

Although primary education remains nominally free in many adjusting states, 'cost recovery' principles have been introduced: costs such as uniform, books, pens and paper and, in some cases, classroom furniture, are borne by parents. Because there is still a bias towards educating sons rather than daughters, girls lose out where poor families have to pay. If fewer of today's girls have no or little education, there is less chance that their children will be educated and healthier (a mother's education level is positively associated with nutrition and her children's, especially daughters', education). In addition, overall economic growth of the country may be adversely affected: women's educational levels have been shown to be positively correlated with smaller family sizes.

HEALTH

In the health sector the cost-recovery measures have been a strong feature, particularly with respect to drugs budgets. Prescribed drugs must now be paid for (at market rates) while costs of record-keeping, consultation and hospital care may also be borne by patients. Where sick people are too poor to pay for consultations or drugs, the costs of caring for the sick fall on women who must both nurse and spend time looking for either cheaper patent, or local herbal medicines. Elson (1995a) cites the case of a woman who had to sacrifice an entire season's crops because she had to cook for a hospitalized relative throughout the planting season, hospital catering being an aspect of care that has been 'rationalized' with the introduction of SAPs.

In short, the empirical effects of adjustment for women have been increases in their 'work' loads as the state sloughs off responsibility for a wide range of services. The burden of these services has shifted from the public to the private sectors, from the 'production'/visible account to the 'reproduction'/invisible account, and has fallen largely to the lot of women.

GENDER, ADJUSTMENT AND ECONOMICS

These are some of the empirical consequences of adjustment policies for women and they come about because, although the theories might be assumed to be gender neutral, the policies (again ostensibly 'gender neutral') they inform are put into practice in social environments which are emphatically not 'gender neutral'. More recent work on gender and structural adjustment has moved away from the empirical and has focused on the underlying assumptions of economic theories, particularly those of gender neutrality. Diane Elson (1993, 1995b, for example) has been at the forefront of this work and has painstakingly deconstructed the assumptions underlying both neo-liberal and structural theories. The 'problems' with different varieties of economic theory stem mainly from two sources:

1 a failure to take into account (largely) women's unpaid 'work': social and biological reproduction

2 a failure to recognize gender as an axis for stratification in societies. The potential for gender disaggregation is not incorporated into models: there are women farmers and men farmers, women workers and men workers, and the parameters needed to describe their opportunities and constraints are different.

But beyond this, aggregation *per se* is gendered. We have to question 'how priorities are established, and who gives way when agents' decisions do not add up to a coherent whole' (Elson, 1995b: 1852), thus taking on board issues of power and entitlements in domestic contexts. Only by deconstructing economic theories in this way might distortions from the expected outcomes of SAPs (changes in divisions of labour, ambiguous gender relations within households, and more work for women through transferring tasks from public to private sectors), resulting in failure to achieve expected 'efficient' economic performance, be overcome.

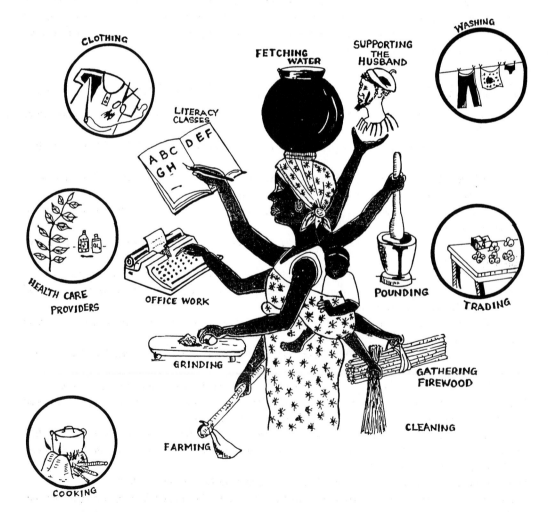

A woman's daily activities – workload on women in Ghana

NOTES

1. Large-scale statistical surveys done on a yearly basis, designed to monitor not only income and spending, but also health indicators.
2. For example, Ghana's PAMSCAD, the Programme of Actions to Mitigate the Social Costs of Adjustment (Brydon and Legge, 1996).
3. Generally the outcome of gender stereotyping rather than any choice on the part of women themselves.
4. Unless they are female household heads.

GUIDE TO FURTHER READING

Diane Elson's excellent edited collection *Male Bias in the Development Process* is a good introduction (1995a): Elson's own chapters for theoretical overviews and empirical material by Dennis (Nigeria), MacEwen Scott (informal sector) and Pearson (Mexico). Haleh Afshar and Carolyne Dennis's edited *Women and Adjustment Policies in the Third World* has an excellent introductory section and case studies from Latin America and Africa. Other books of case studies include Sparr (1994) and Emeagwali (1995). More detail on the theoretical underpinnings of economic theories can be found in Elson (1993 and 1995b). Recent work on 'gender-and-structural-adjustment' has tried to incorporate donors' current focus on 'poverty' as an all-embracing issue. For this, see for example, Curtin and Nelson, 1999; Dewan, 1999; Kanji, 1995 and Sen, 1999. A follow-up special issue (Grown *et al.*, 2000) of *World Development* (28(7)) to Cagatay *et al.*, (1995) brings advances in gender awareness in economics up to date.

REFERENCES

Afshar, Haleh and Dennis, Carolyne (1992) *Women and Adjustment Policies in the Third World*, Basingstoke: Macmillan.

Brydon, Lynne and Legge, Karen (1996) *Adjusting Society: The World Bank, the IMF and Ghana*, London: I.B. Tauris.

Cagatay, Nilufer, Elson, Diane and Grown, Caren (1995) 'Introduction', *World Development* (Special Issue on *Gender, Adjustment and Macroeconomics*), 23(11): 1827–36.

Cornia, Andrea, Jolly, Richard and Stewart, Frances (eds) (1987) *Adjustment With a Human Face* (2 vols), Oxford: Clarendon Press.

Curtin, T.R.C. and Nelson, E.A.S (1999) 'Economic and health efficiency of education funding policy', in *Social Science and Medicine* 48(11): 1599–611.

Dennis, Carolyne (1991) 'Constructing a "career" under conditions of economic crisis and structural adjustment: the survival strategies of Nigerian women', in Haleh Afshar (eds), *Women, Development and Survival in the Third World*, Harlow: Longman, pp. 88–106.

Dewan, R. (1999) 'Gender implications of the "new" economic policy: a conceptual overview', *Women's Studies International Forum* 22(4): 425–29.

Elson, Diane (1993) 'Gender aware analysis and development economics', *Journal of International Development* 5(2): 237–47.

Elson, Diane (ed.) (1995a) *Male Bias in the Development Process*, Manchester: Manchester University Press.

Elson, Diane (1995b) 'Gender awareness in modeling structural adjustment', *World Development* (Special Issue on *Gender, Adjustment and Macroeconomics*), 23(11): 1851–68.

Elson, Diane and Pearson, Ruth (1981) 'Nimble fingers make cheap workers . . .', *Feminist Review* 7: 87–107.

Emeagwali, Gloria T. (ed.) (1995) *Women Pay the Price: Structural Adjustment in Africa and the Caribbean*, Trenton, New Jersey: Africa World Press.

Grown, Caren, Elson, Diane and Cagatay, Nilufer (eds) (2000) *World Development* 28(7).

Kanji, Nazneen (1995) 'Gender, poverty and economic adjustment in Harare, Zimbabwe', in *Environment and Urbanization* 7(1): 37–55.

Sen, G. (1999) 'Engendering poverty alleviation: challenges and opportunities', *Development and Change* 30(3): 685–92.

Sparr, Pamela (ed.) (1994) *Mortgaging Women's Lives*, London: Zed Books.

UNICEF (1999) *The State of the World's Children, 1999*, New York: UNICEF.

7.8 Gender, technology and livelihoods

Andrew Scott and Margaret Foster

INTRODUCTION

Most of the world's poor are women. Of the 1.3 billion people living on less than US$1 a day, 70 per cent are women (UNDP, 1995). Women are at the forefront in meeting the basic needs of their families as well as being responsible for subsistence food production and income generation. At least 80 per cent of all food crops in sub-Saharan Africa, 70–80 per cent in South Asia, and 50 per cent in Latin America and the Caribbean are produced by women (UNDP, 1995). The majority of micro- and small-scale enterprise operators are women, and there are more women than men employed in the informal sector (Sethuraman, 1998). Women more than men assume responsibility for the care of children, the sick, the incapacitated and elderly, as well as nurturing their community and ensuring the sustainability of their family's livelihood.

In this chapter, we describe the gendered nature of poor people's livelihoods, the holistic context of their lives and their technology, and we consider the factors that influence and are influenced by these gender differences. The chapter also describes ways that practitioners can take account of and address these differences in order to target very poor people.

POVERTY

When targeting poverty the emphasis has to be on women's development needs and on building women's assets, reducing women's vulnerabilities and tackling those problems which women themselves identify. It must be possible

> to convince decision makers in governments and multi- and bilateral donors of the fact that many of the poorest people in the world depend for their survival on the innovatory technical skills of women, and that women's scientific and technical knowledge is too valuable to ignore.
>
> (Appleton, 1995; 304)

Such knowledge is undervalued by society and even by women 'technologists' themselves.

It is extremely difficult for prosperous 'outsiders' to understand the complex nature of poverty and to appreciate that 'the poor' are not a homogenous group. With disaggregation it becomes clear that the effects of wealth or poverty, age, physical and mental abilities, ethnic group and religion, etc., are all reinforced by the effects of gender. To understand the social context of development we must therefore take a gendered and disaggregated perspective of poor people's production.

GENDER

Women and men absorb the norms and values of the society around them. They learn the roles and responsibilities, behaviour and expectations which relate to each sex and define for each their position in society. The skills and technology that they use, and the technical knowledge to which they have access are conditioned by this process as are the options open to them to extend existing knowledge and skills and thus to increase their livelihood options.

In their daily activities women use their technical skills and knowledge, and they continually innovate and adapt technologies in response to the changing context of their lives. Although the popular notion of an inventor or an artisan is male, it is frequently women who adapt and refine tools to fit their varying circumstances. Women, however, often claim that they only 'help out' while in fact supporting family businesses in essential ways, book-keeping, marketing or even in light engineering (Foster, 1999).

Women and men, living in the same place, may experience differently their economic, social, cultural, political and geographical environment. Women do not have the same access as men to the services, resources and opportunities within their communities. Exploiting available assets requires access to support mechanisms, to credit, raw materials, transport, market information, etc., yet all of these are more difficult for women to secure. If they do manage to do it, they often then lose control over their initiative to the men who made the services available to them.

Women's work can be perceived differently by development workers. They are often ignorant of women's contribution and depend on men to describe or 'translate' women's production processes to them. One study revealed that male extension workers in Africa think that women do not make significant contributions to agriculture, that women are tied down with household chores and children, are shy and difficult to reach, and that they are 'unprogressive' when considering innovations (Gill, 1987).

Women lack the self confidence and the social status to participate directly in community organizations, in training courses or in representing their interests to decision-makers. They are often invisible, literally in some societies where women avoid social interaction, and because of lack of representation they are voiceless. Their crucial role is frequently overlooked by outsiders, who may themselves be men. Few women are involved in extension work, research or technology development, with the result that information available about these women 'technologists' is scarce.

WOMEN AND LIVELIHOODS

As a result of their wide-ranging responsibilities, domestic, productive and community duties, women are generally involved in a broader range of tasks than men, and they will therefore frequently have a wider range of technical skills on which to draw for livelihood strategies.

Considering the livelihoods of very poor women helps us to appreciate the differential value and availability of their time. Women have more responsibilities during the day and less available time to learn about new techniques, attend meetings or training. Many poor women in poor countries spend the majority of their productive lives either pregnant or lactating, usually with very small children to care for. As a result they are frequently severely anaemic and always extremely tired. They cannot afford any risky investment of time or energy, which may or may not lead to an improvement of life in the future.

The pattern of women's daily activities is quite different from men's. Characteristically women spend less time on any one activity and frequently carry out two or more tasks at the same time (e.g. cooking and child minding). Men are more likely to be able to commit larger blocks of unin-terrupted time to working with a particular technology or process. They are more likely to be avail-able to participate in project interventions, and as a result tools are frequently designed for use by men rather than for women.

TECHNOLOGY

'Technology' is the human skills, knowledge and organization, as well as the tools or 'hardware' involved in production. This definition highlights the separate and specific value of women's tech-nology. Inherited knowledge, unique to location and culture, is often passed from mother to daughter, and symbolized in many countries in Africa and South America by the traditional wedding present from mothers to daughters of trays of seeds or tubers. These enshrine the community's own biodiversity and the special responsibility women have to protect food crops for the future, and illustrate how technical information passes by word of mouth between women.

Technical information and skills are communicated to women and between women using different channels (Appleton, 1995). Women have different social networks and different access to education. Though women are more likely than men to be illiterate, uneducated or to speak only a minority language, they are not ignorant and if information is appropriate to their needs they will welcome it.

Technical change is influenced by access to resources, which can be allocated according to the perceptions and priorities of outsiders. Firewood is an example of such biased priorities. Biomass, the most common cooking fuel, accounts for 90 per cent of all the energy used in poor countries (World Bank, 1996). It is a woman's task to ensure cooked food is available, and to collect the fuel. It has been estimated that poor people spend up to a third of their income and their time on accessing this energy (Gamser et al., 1990).

Such a huge demand affects other decisions, expenditure on heating and shelter, on food choice, security and nutrition, and the effects of these on health and productivity imply that energy choice fundamentally affects other aspects of development. It is possible to trace energy scarcity to high fertility, low literacy rates, a lack of participation and decision-making ability at local level, and a lack of empowerment.

Developing appropriate energy technologies is therefore central to the conservation of women's time and health, and the effective development of women's production. However, cooking fuel is used by women and is not linked in an obvious way to the generation of family income. This may account for the lack of technological innovation in cooking fuel technology which could not only save time and effort but increase food security and possibly have a positive effect on other devel-opment indicators (Gamser et al., 1990).

The distinction between 'reproductive' and 'productive' tasks is often meaningless when the producer is very poor. Activities involving the same tasks with the same technologies (e.g. process-ing food) are often used for both subsistence and income generation. Consequently the technical innovations that women make are based on their own priorities and their understanding of the risks involved across the full range of their responsibilities (Appleton, 1995: 10). Female micro-entrepreneurs, for example, often do not aim for growth of their enterprise to the same degree as male entrepreneurs. Women's micro-enterprises are generally more security-oriented than growth-oriented (Everts, 1998: 25).

Lack of recognition of women's technical knowledge and their contribution to family liveli-hoods has led to the neglect of important subsistence crops, usually grown by women, on which families and communities survive (Mpande and Mpofu, 1995). Poor women's access to land where such crops can be produced has been restricted by developments favouring cash-cropping and involving irrigation, 'improved' seeds and chemical fertilizers.

The introduction of new technology to men in sectors previously controlled by women has brought about a loss of women's authority over activities from which they once gained an income. The evidence suggests that in 'the invention and development of technology, women's technical expertise has been displaced with particular efficacy' (Crewe and Harrison, 1998: 34).

PARTICIPATION AND CHANGE

External support for improving technology for poor people should not be restricted to an 'outsider's' understanding of the situation. Successful intervention requires recognition of who the 'experts' are, who is doing what, and what their needs and priorities are. This should be the result of a rigorous gender analysis of the existing situation, and an analysis of interest groups that includes all stakeholders and does not allow one group to speak on behalf of another. 'Participation' will not by itself lead to technologies that serve the interests of all users (Appleton and Scott, 1994), and some participative approaches have in fact marginalized women and benefits have gone to local elites (Mosse, 1994). It depends on who participates, where, when and how.

The only effective way to work within such constraints is to involve poor women at every stage, to go at their pace and in their direction, working in their place and in their language. Involvement of poor women in this way, the sharing of means as well as ends, the sensitive appreciation of the uniqueness of place and time, helps not only to design more appropriate hardware and processes, but also builds on existing indigenous technical capacity, without threatening culture or traditional values.

Behaviour, social processes and concepts underlie the use of technical knowledge by women, and these deserve respect. New technological ideas will be accepted by poor women only if they are an obvious improvement, if they do not impose an extra burden and if they are culturally acceptable. A technique is required that will enable the invisible and silent 'technologists' to find their voice and to improve their ability to inform outsiders about their needs as well as to improve their access to useful information.

CONCLUSION

For men and women, different life experiences impact differently on their livelihood capabilities and priorities with respect to the use and development of technology. The implicit undervaluing of their skills, knowledge and organization of technology use has had serious implications for the status of women as technology producers and users, and for their involvement in the development process.

Gender analysis is important in the assessment of the impact on poverty of technology-focused development projects. Employing gendered frameworks of technology use and capability allows disaggregation of areas of existing and potential technical expertise. Gender analysis also enables recognition of the gendered nature of livelihood activities within households and communities. Understanding of how such activities shape, and are shaped by, this gendered technological context, enables a picture of the technological capabilities of women and men to be formed.

GUIDE TO FURTHER READING

Appleton, H. (ed.) (1995) *Do It Herself: Women and Technical Innovation*, London: IT Publications.

Everts, S. (1998) *Gender and Technology: Empowering Women, Engendering Development*, London: Zed Books.

Gender, Science and Technology Gateway: http://gstgateway.wigsat.org/gw.html.

Gender, Technology and Development (journal), Sage Publications.

ITDG (in press) *Discovering Technologists: Women's and Men's Work at Village Level*, London and ITDG South Asia, Colombo: ITDG Publishing.

Sweetman, C. (ed.) (1995) Editorial in 'Gender and technology' issue of *Gender and Development* 7(2): 2–7.

REFERENCES

Appleton, H. (ed.) (1995) *Do It Herself: Women and Technical Innovation*, London: IT Publications.

Appleton, H. and Scott, A. (1994) 'Gender issues in agricultural technology development', paper presented at agricultural engineers' conference, FAO.

Crewe, E. and Harrison, E. (1998) *Whose Development? An Ethnography of Aid*, London: Zed Books.

Everts, S. (1998) *Gender and Technology: Empowering Women, Engendering Development*, London: Zed Books.

Gamser, M., Appleton, H. and Carter, N. (eds) (1990) *Tinker, Tiller, Technical Change*, London: IT Publications.

Gill, D.S. (1987) 'Effectiveness of rural extension services in reaching rural women: a synthesis of studies from five African countries', paper presented at FAO Workshop on Improving the Effectiveness of Agricultural Extension Services in Reaching Rural Women, Harare, Zimbabwe.

Foster, M. (1999) 'Supporting the invisible technologists: the Intermediate Technology Development Group, *Gender and Development* 7(2): 17–24.

Mosse, D. (1994) 'Authority, gender and knowledge: theoretical reflections on the practice of participatory rural appraisal', *Development and Change* 25(3): 497–525.

Mpande, R. and Mpofu, N. (1995) 'Survival skills of Tonga women in Zimbabwe', in H. Appleton (ed.) *Do It Herself: Women and Technical Innovation*, pp. 188–93.

Sethuraman, S.V. (1998) *Gender, Informality and Poverty: A Global Review*, WIEGO.

UNDP (1995) *Human Development Report, 1995*, New York: UNDP.

World Bank (1996) *Rural Energy and Development: Improving Energy Supplies for Two Billion People*, Development in Practice Series, Washington: World Bank.

7.9 Women and political representation

Shirin M. Rai

Why is representation an important issue for development? Development policies are highly politically charged trade-offs between diverse interests and value choices. 'The political nature of these policies is frequently made behind the closed door of bureaucracy or among tiny groups of men in a non-transparent political structure' (Staudt, 1991: 65). The question then arises, how are women to access this world of policy-making so dominated by men? The answers that have been explored within women's movements have been diverse – political mobilization of women, lobbying political parties, moving the courts and legal establishments, constitutional reform, mobilization and participation in social movements such as the environmental movement, and civil liberties campaigns at local/global levels.

Representation has been the focus of reformist, inclusionary strategies in public policy in many political systems. Of itself, the concept is not such that it can bear the burden of close scrutiny – there are too many caveats that have to be taken on board for it to work. It is attractive largely in contrast to other political arrangements. Lack of representation is perceived as a problem, and citizens largely accept democratic institutions as important to the expansion of possibilities of political participation. Further, exclusion generates political resentment adversely affecting not only the political system but also social relations within a polity; no individual or group likes being regarded as part of an excluded, and therefore disempowered, group.

Representation as a concept makes certain assumptions that are problematic. These affect the policy-making and functioning of political institutions. The first set of assumptions are related to representation of interests – that there are identifiable (women's) interests, that (women) can represent. For women this raises issues about what are women's interests when they are being constantly disturbed by categories of race, ethnicity and class, and whether women can be homogenized in terms of their sex/gender without regard to their race, ethnic and class positionings. Martha Nussbaum has emphasized the importance of equality and human rights as the irreducible minimum rights for women in the development of their capabilities (Nussbaum and Glover, 1995). Iris M. Young has addressed these issues through her exploration of the idea of group interests (1990). She suggests that group interests can be formulated by groups meeting as groups supported by public resources; that the interests thus formulated would be more reflective of group concerns, securing greater legitimacy within the group. As such these interests should be made part of policy, and policy-makers asked to justify their exclusion from processes of policy-making. As a final protection of interests, Young suggests that these more cohesive groups should have power of veto over policy affecting them. This analysis would presumably take account of class-based groups such as trade unions, though most research which has taken on board Young's framework has focused on issues of race, ethnicity, sexuality and gender.

A second set of assumptions regarding representation is about appropriate forms of representative politics, and the levels of government and policy-making. Despite an enduring interest in direct participatory politics, representative government operates largely through a party political system. Political parties thus form an important constraint for individual representatives, especially if the representative seeks to support certain group interests. Group interests have often been regarded as too particularistic; 'general interests' or more often 'national interests' take precedence in party political rhetoric. Political parties also perform 'gate-keeping' functions – interests are given recognition through the agenda-setting of political parties. My study of Indian women parliamentarians suggests that institutional constraints, and systems of organizational incentives and disincentives are important explanations of the limited role that women can play in advancing the agenda of gender justice through party-based political work (Rai, 1996).

Representation is a key concept in liberal understandings of governance – it focuses on institutions, organization and practices. Representation is also central to the concept of citizenship – in both its normative sense, participation in politics as a prerequisite for the subjective public self, and in the practical, the inclusion within state boundaries where particular development agendas take shape. The framework of citizenship has recently been used by corporate-sector engagements with the policy world, and civil society organizations – 'corporate citizenship' is an emergent field of enquiry in development studies as well as business studies. Representation is also important in terms of accountability – of both public and private organizations. Increasingly we see a critique of not only state-based institutions, but also of INGOs and NGOs in terms of an accountability deficit and how this might influence interest articulations and formulations and implementation of policy. As it signifies consent, representation is also an essential element of good and therefore legitimate government which is increasingly becoming the focus of the delivery network institutions of development (World Bank, 1992: 6; 2000). Representation is, however, used as a universal and an undifferentiated concept which does not take into account particular positionings, needs and claims of groups constituting a particular civil and political society.

WOMEN IN POLITICAL INSTITUTIONS

A headcount of the officers of the state in all sectors – legislature, executive and the judiciary – in most countries of the world reveals an overwhelming male bias despite many mobilizations furthering women's presence at both national and global levels. An Inter-Parliamentary Union Study found that the number of sovereign states with a parliament increased sevenfold between 1945–95, while the percentage of women MPs worldwide increased fourfold (Pintat in Karam, 1998: 163). The UN *Atlas of Women in Politics: 2000* shows that women form 13.4 per cent of members of parliament as a whole. The Nordic states lead with women constituting 38.8 per cent of members of both houses of parliament, while the Arab States had only 3.5 per cent (UN, 1999). Furthermore, data shows that there is no easy positive corelation between economic indicators and the presence of women in public bodies. While in Europe (without the Nordic countries) women were 13.4 per cent of the total number of MPs, the figure in sub-Saharan Africa was 11.7 per cent. In recognition of the slow improvement in women's representation in national parliaments, enhancing women's presence within state bodies is now being pursued as a goal both by women's movements as well as international institutions. This suggests that an engagement with state structures is now considered an appropriate means of bringing about shifts in public policy.

FEMINIST DEBATES ON REPRESENTATION

Why are debates on women's representation important? First, women have recognized that interests need to be articulated through participation and then represented in the arena of politics. Within the women's movements there has been a significant shift in the 1980s towards engaging positively with state feminism as a strategy that could be effective in furthering the cause(s) of women. The argument about women's presence in representative politics, as Anna Jonasdottir (1988) has pointed out, concerns both the *form* of politics and its *content*. The question of form includes the demand to be among the decision-makers, the demand for participation and a share in control over public affairs. In terms of content, it includes being able to articulate the needs, wishes and demands of various groups of women. The interest in citizenship has also been prompted by the shift in women's movements, in the 1980s, from the earlier insistence upon direct participation to a recognition of the importance of representative politics and the consequences of women's exclusion from it (Lovenduski and Norris; McBride Stetson and Mazur, 1995; and Rai, 2000). It is here that politics – public and private, practical and strategic – begins to formalize within the contours of the state.

Gender and representation is also an important issue in the international sphere. Good governance has become important to the political discourses of world aid agencies and financial institutions. After having concentrated attention on the processes and practices of structural adjustment programmes (SAPs) in the Third World countries during the 1970s and 1980s, the World Bank and other aid agencies are faced with decelerating growth in many countries accompanied by a rise in social tensions, in many cases the consequence of SAPs. Issues of governance have therefore become important and the focus has shifted to supporting processes of institution-building that would help manage the social and political fallout of economic policies supported by international aid agencies and Western governments (World Bank, 2000). The UN has also played an important role in placing the issue of women's exclusion from political processes on the international agenda. The Platform for Action agreed upon in Beijing in September 1995 emphasized both the need to increase the levels of women's participation in politics, and also the need for the development of national machineries for the advancement of women (Rai, 2000).

While we cannot assume that more women in public offices would mean a better deal for women in general, there are important reasons for demanding greater representation of women in political life. First, is the intuitive one – the greater the number of women in public office, articulating interests, and seen to be wielding power, the more disrupted the gender hierarchy in public life could become. Without a sufficiently visible, if not proportionate, presence in the political system – 'threshold representation' (Kymlicka, 1995) – a group's ability to influence either policy-making or, indeed, the political culture framing the representative system is limited. Further, the fact that these women are largely elite women might mean that the impact that they have on public consciousness might be disproportionately bigger than their numbers would suggest.

Second, and more important, we could explore the strategies that women employ to access the public sphere in the context of a patriarchal sociopolitical system. These women have been successful in subverting the boundaries of gender, and in operating in a very aggressive male-dominated sphere. Could other women learn from this cohort? The problem here is, of course, precisely that these women are an elite. The class from which most of these women come is perhaps the most important factor in their successful inclusion into the political system. We can, however, examine whether sociopolitical movements provide opportunities for women to use certain strategies that might be able to subvert the gender hierarchy in politics. Finally, we can explore the dynamic between institutional and grassroots politics. The 'politicization of gender' in the Indian political system, for example, is due largely to the success of the women's movement. Women representatives have thus benefited from this success of the women's movement. There has, however, been limited interaction between women representatives and the women's movement. This, perhaps, is the issue that the women's movement needs to address as part of its expanding agenda for the 1990s.

STRATEGIES FOR INCREASING WOMEN'S REPRESENTATION

Many strategies have been discussed for increasing women's representation in politics – party lists in South Africa and the UK, and quotas at the local governance levels in India are two important experiments. There has also been discussion of parity representation for women and men, especially in the Nordic states (Karam, 1998). All three are contested strategies, as the following discussion of quotas demonstrates. The arguments for quotas for women in representative institutions are fairly well rehearsed. Women's groups are now arguing that quotas for women are needed to compensate for the social barriers that have prevented women from participating in politics and thus making their voices heard: that in order for women to be more than 'tokens' in political institutions, a level of presence that cannot be overlooked by political parties is required, hence the demand for a 33 per cent quota: that the quota system acknowledges that it is the recruitment process, organized through political parties and supported by a framework of patriarchal values, that needs to carry the burden of change, rather than individual women. The alternative, then, is that there should be an acknowledgement of the historical social exclusion of women from politics, a compensatory regime (quotas) established, and 'institutionalized ... for the explicit recognition and representation of oppressed groups' (Young, 1990: 183–91). However, there is some unease felt by many women's groups with elite politics and elite women, and the role that quotas might play in consolidating rather than shifting power relationships.

CONCLUSIONS

In this chapter I have argued that while political representation is crucial to women's empowerment, there are also some critical issues that we need to reflect upon. State institutions cannot be the major focus of women's political struggles. Both spaces – the informal and formalized networks of power – need to be negotiated by the women's movements in order to best serve women's interests (Rai, 1996). This would include the work of civil society associations, increased representation of women in state and political bodies that allows for a wide-ranging set of interests to be represented by women, and also a discursive shift in the way in which politics is thought about to enable women to function effectively in politics. Women's participation in representative institutions can be effective only in the context of such continuing negotiations and struggles.

GUIDE TO FURTHER READING AND REFERENCES

The following text references provide the basis for further reading.

Goetz, A.M. (ed.) (1997) *Getting Institutions Right for Women in Development*, London: Zed Books.

Karam, A. (ed.) (1998) *Beyond Numbers: Women in Parliaments*, Stockholm: IDEA.

Jonasdottir, A.G. (1998) *The Political Interests of Gender: Developing Theory and Research with a Feminist Face*, London: Sage.

Lovenduski, J. and Norriss, P. (1993) *Gender and Party Politics*, London: Sage.

Kymlicka, W. (1995) *Multicultural Citizenship*, Oxford: Oxford University Press.

McBride Stetson, D. and Mazur A. (1995) *Comparative State Feminism*, London: Sage.

Nussbaum, M. (1995) 'Human capabilities, female human beings', in Nussbaum, M. and Glover, J., *Women, Culture and Development*, Oxford: Clarendon Press.

Rai, S.M. (ed.) (1996) 'Women and the state: some issues for debate', in S.M. Rai and G. Lievesley (eds) *Women and the State: International Perspectives*, London: Taylor and Francis.

Rai, S.M. (ed.) (1997) 'Women in the Indian Parliament', in A.M. Goetz (ed.) *Getting Institutions Right for Women in Development*, London: Zed Books.

Rai, S.M. (ed.) (2000) *International Perspectives on Gender and Democratisation*, Basingstoke: Macmillan.

Rai, S.M. (ed.) (2001) *Mainstreaming Gender, Democratizing the State? National Machineries for the Advancement of Women*, Manchester: Manchester University Press.

Staudt, K. (1991) *Managing Development*, London: Sage.

World Bank (1992) *Good Governance*, Washington: World Bank.

World Bank (2000) *World Development Report: Attacking Poverty*, Washington: World Bank.

Young, I.M. (1990) *Justice and the Politcs of Difference*, Princeton, NJ: Princeton University Press.

7.10 Population trends in developing countries

Ernestina Coast

At the beginning of the twenty-first century, the global population had exceeded 6 billion; it took just 12 years for the population to increase from 5 to 6 billion. Developing countries[1] currently account

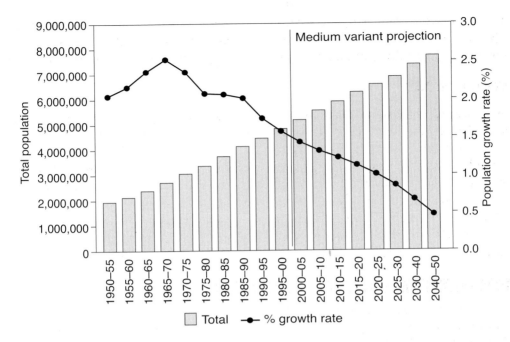

Population trends, less developed regions, 1950–2050

for 80 per cent of the world's population and 61 per cent of the global total is accounted for by Asia alone, driven by the population giants China and India. The global annual rate of population increase peaked at 2.04 per cent per year in the late 1960s, and had declined to 1.33 per cent per year by 1999. Developing region population is currently growing at a rate of 1.59 per cent per year (see figure), and growth rates in Africa still exceed 2.3 per cent per year, the highest growth rate of any major area.

The absolute annual increase in global population peaked at 86 million people per year in the late 1980s, and is currently 78 million people per year; 97 per cent of this population increase takes place in the less developed regions. Behind these 'statements of account' of global population lies a multitude of regional and individual country population trends. In the following discussion, the approach will be descriptive, focusing on the three demographic variables of fertility, mortality and migration.

DATA SOURCES

A consideration of detailed population trends in developing countries must take into account the data available for analysis. There are three main sources of demographic data: censuses, vital registration (e.g. birth and death registration) and surveys (e.g. World Fertility Survey (WFS), Demographic and Health Surveys (DHSs)). Cleland states that pre-1945 'studies of the demography of less developed countries hardly existed' (1996: 433). Over the last five decades, considerable advances have been made in the collection of demographic data in developing countries, although vital registration continues to be very deficient (both in terms of coverage and quality). For some countries, particularly those with recent or ongoing conflicts, estimates of population data continue to be little more than educated guesswork. Publications such as the *United Nations World Population Prospects and Demographic Yearbook* provide country-level comparable data sets with which to work, although there are still concerns about data validity and reliability for some countries.[2]

AGE AND SEX STRUCTURE

Many developing countries are experiencing very rapid changes in the relative numbers of children, working-age population and older persons. Less developed countries have tended to be characterized by relatively youthful age structures. For example, children under the age of 15 currently account for one-third of less developed regions' populations, and 42 per cent of least developed[3] populations. Mainly as a result of declining fertility these proportions have declined significantly since the mid-1960s (Table 1). By 2050 it is estimated that children will account for only 20 per cent of less developed regions' populations.[4]

As the proportions accounted for by children decline, there has been an accompanying increase in the proportions of elderly (aged 60 years and above) (Table 2). People aged 60 and over currently account for less than 8 per cent of the population in less developed regions. In reality this means 33 million oldest-old people (aged 80 years and older) are currently estimated to be living in less developed countries (Mirkin and Weinberger, 2000).

The proportions of elderly are predicted to continue to increase, and by 2050 it is estimated that 3 per cent of the population in less developed regions will be aged 80 years or older. The speed of the ageing of the populations in these areas is more rapid than has occurred in developed regions, mainly due to the rapidity of the fertility decline. Improvements in post-childhood mortality have also added to the process of population ageing in less developed countries.

There are profound implications for the care and support of the elderly, particularly in contexts where resources and civil institutions are already limited. Because women tend to live longer than men, issues of long-term care and support are especially acute for women. Demographic dependency ratios[5] provide a crude measure of the relative sizes of the economically active and inactive populations. With increasing ageing in developing regions, the elderly dependency ratio is projected to increase by almost three times between 2000 and 2050. However, this trend must be set against a background of declining child dependency ratios. The overall effect is therefore one of declining net dependency ratios over the next five decades in developing regions.

Table 1 Percentage of population aged under 15 years, 1950–2000

	Major region			Geographical region		
Year	World	Less developed	Least developed	Africa	Asia	Latin America and Caribbean
1950	34.3	37.8	41.3	42.5	36.6	40.0
1955	35.6	39.3	41.8	42.8	38.1	41.0
1960	36.9	40.7	42.7	43.5	39.4	42.2
1965	37.7	41.8	43.4	44.2	40.4	42.8
1970	37.4	41.8	44.3	44.7	40.3	42.4
1975	36.9	41.3	44.9	45.0	39.9	41.3
1980	35.2	39.3	44.9	44.8	37.7	39.6
1985	33.5	37.1	45.0	44.6	34.9	37.9
1990	32.4	35.6	44.5	44.3	33.2	36.0
1995	31.2	34.3	43.4	43.6	31.8	33.7
2000	29.7	32.5	42.1	42.5	29.9	31.6

Table 2 Percentage of population aged 60 years and older, 1950–2000

| Year | World | Major region | | Geographical region | | |
		Less developed	Least developed	Africa	Asia	Latin America and Caribbean
1950	8.1	6.4	5.4	5.1	6.7	5.9
1955	8.1	6.3	5.2	5.0	6.7	6.1
1960	8.1	6.2	5.1	4.9	6.5	6.2
1965	8.2	6.1	5.0	4.9	6.4	6.3
1970	8.4	6.1	5.1	5.0	6.5	6.4
1975	8.5	6.1	5.0	4.9	6.6	6.5
1980	8.6	6.3	5.0	5.0	6.8	6.6
1985	8.8	6.6	4.9	4.9	7.2	6.8
1990	9.2	6.9	4.9	4.9	7.6	7.1
1995	9.6	7.3	4.8	4.9	8.2	7.4
2000	10.0	7.7	4.9	5.0	8.8	7.9

MORTALITY   rate of people death.

Life expectancy at birth is one of the 'benchmark' indicators of development,[6] and in developing countries it increased from 40.9 years in 1950 to 63.3 years by 2000, a remarkable and rapid achievement. The difference in longevity between the more and the less developed regions also decreased over this period, from 25.7 years to 11.6 years. There are still major regional disparities in life expectancy at birth, from 48.4 years in Sub-Saharan Africa to 70.4 years in Latin America and the Caribbean. Sierra Leone, following nearly two decades of conflict, has the dubious honour of being the country with the lowest life expectancy, at 37.2 years.

Livi-Bacci states that 'Reduced mortality and establishment of the chronological age-linked succession of death are prerequisites to development' (1992: 152). Improvements in mortality generally occur first at younger ages, particularly the first 12 months of life. The infant mortality rate (IMR)[7] in less developed regions is seven times higher than that recorded for more developed regions, at 63/1,000 and 9/1,000, respectively. Improvements in early-age mortality have been achieved throughout the developing world (Table 3) during the second half of the twentieth

Table 3 Trends in infant mortality rates, 1950–2000 (expressed per 1,000 live births)

| Year | World | Major region | | Geographical region | | |
		Less developed	Least developed	Africa	Asia	Latin America and Caribbean
1950–1955	155	178	194	179	180	126
1955–1960	139	160	179	166	162	113
1960–1965	117	134	166	153	131	101
1965–1970	102	115	154	143	110	91
1970–1975	93	104	146	131	98	81
1975–1980	87	98	138	120	94	69
1980–1985	78	87	128	110	83	57
1985–1990	69	76	116	99	72	48
1990–1995	62	68	108	94	63	40
1995–2000	57	63	99	87	57	36

century due to a combination of health interventions (including disease control, immunization, oral rehydration therapy) and broader socioeconomic development (including nutrition and parental education). Sub-Saharan Africa still continues to lag behind other major world regions, with an IMR of 93/1,000. The impact of improvements in early age mortality extends far beyond a contribution to an increase in life expectancy; it has profound implications for fertility through a range of mechanisms[8] (Preston, 1978).

Maternal mortality[9] continues to be a major issue for adolescent and adult women in developing countries, despite initiatives such as Safe Motherhood (1987) and the ICPD[10] 'Programme of Action' (1994). It is estimated that, globally, a woman dies of maternal causes every minute, with an estimated 585,000 maternal deaths annually. Of these deaths 99 per cent are in developing countries (Ganges and Long, 1998), with concomitant negative implications for the survival of any existing children.

Mention must be made of the HIV/AIDS epidemic, with an estimated 33.6 million infected individuals at the end of 1999; 95 per cent of infected people live in developing countries, and it is likely that this proportion will continue to rise. The region most severely affected by HIV/AIDS is sub-Saharan Africa, which accounts for approximately 70 per cent of global HIV/AIDS cases. The demographic impacts of the HIV/AIDS epidemic are many and complex. Twentieth-century increases in life expectancy are predicted to reverse as a direct result of HIV/AIDS. For example, life expectancy at birth in Botswana rose from 42.5 years in 1950 to 60.4 years in 1990, but is predicted to have declined to 47.4 years by 2000. HIV/AIDS will also have an indirect effect on morbidity and mortality through the spread of 'opportunistic' diseases such as tuberculosis (UNAIDS, 1997).

Future trends in adult mortality will depend upon changes in health technology and expenditure, lifestyle, disease patterns and economic development (and reversal). For example, the recent rapid rise[11] of tobacco smoking in many developing countries will have an impact upon adult mortality patterns. Garenne's (1996) study of mortality trends in Africa includes changing diets (leading to obesity and diabetes), chemical-resistant disease development, migration (and its role in communicable disease spread), road traffic accidents, HIV/AIDS (and associated opportunistic diseases such as TB), conflict and urbanization (though its effect on disease ecology) as important future influences on developing-country mortality levels.

FERTILITY

Pre-1960, there was little evidence of any fertility decline in developing countries, and the total fertility rate (TFR)[12] was estimated at 6.16 children per woman for all developing regions (1950–55). Countries such as Argentina and Uruguay, which had TFRs of less than 3.5 children per woman by 1950, were the exception rather than the rule. The TFR for all developing regions was estimated at 3.00 at the end of the twentieth century, representing a decline of more than 50 per cent since the 1950s (Table 4). It must be remembered, however, that much of the decline in fertility in the developing world can be accounted for by the dramatic decline in fertility in China alone.

Extreme heterogeneity in fertility levels and trends, between and within regions and countries, cannot be ignored. Sub-Saharan Africa is the world region with the highest overall levels of fertility, with little evidence of sustained fertility declines beyond Kenya, Botswana and Zimbabwe. In some countries, substantial fertility decline has not yet been recorded. For example, TFRs in Yemen remained virtually unchanged at 7.6 children per woman from the 1950s to the mid-1990s.[13] In

Table 4 Trends in total fertility rates, 1950–2000

		Major region		Geographical region		
Year	World	Less developed	Least developed	Africa	Asia	Latin America and Caribbean
1950–1955	4.99	6.16	6.54	6.58	5.91	5.89
1955–1960	4.92	5.99	6.54	6.68	5.63	5.94
1960–1965	4.95	6.01	6.59	6.78	5.62	5.97
1965–1970	4.91	6.01	6.67	6.75	5.69	5.55
1970–1975	4.48	5.43	6.71	6.60	5.09	5.03
1975–1980	3.92	4.65	6.60	6.52	4.22	4.49
1980–1985	3.58	4.15	6.50	6.37	3.70	3.86
1985–1990	3.34	3.79	6.03	5.97	3.39	3.35
1990–1995	2.93	3.27	5.37	5.47	2.85	2.97
1995–2000	2.71	3.00	5.05	5.06	2.60	2.70

contrast, rapid and marked fertility declines have occurred elsewhere, particularly in Asia. For example, between 1970 and 1995 the TFR in Bangladesh fell from 7.02 to 3.40 children per woman.

Explanations for the decline in fertility in developing countries cannot rely on single variable explanations. In terms of the proximate determinants of fertility (Bongaarts and Potter, 1984), increased contraceptive prevalence is generally agreed to be the main cause of the fertility decline. The proportion of couples using modern contraception has increased dramatically, from approximately 1 in every 10 couples in the 1960s to 1 in 2 couples by 1999 (Black, 1999). Other contributory proximate determinants include rising age at marriage for women and increased rates of induced abortion. Broader socioeconomic changes such as rising levels of female education and employment, and increased urbanization have contributed to the fertility decline in developing countries.

MIGRATION

Migration[14] is very important in determining population (size and composition) at the local level. The speed and scale with which population movements can take place means that net migration can far outweigh fertility and mortality changes in sub-national areas. Much of the rapid urbanization of many developing-country populations may be accounted for by rural–urban migration. Migration flow data (both international and national) are notoriously difficult to obtain (International Migration Review, 1987). Globally, it is estimated that developing countries contribute just over half (54.7 per cent) of the international migrant population (Zlotnik, 1998). Internal population movements (both voluntary and involuntary) have profound implications for populations. For example, refugees and internally displaced persons tend to have little or no access to healthcare provision, and the result can be increased morbidity and mortality (Gardner and Blackburn, 1996). Conflict-related population migration continues to be a major contributor to national population levels in many developing countries.[15]

CONCLUSION

The twentieth century witnessed unprecedented change in population dynamics and the implications for future generations are uncertain. Demographers can make population projections from current population figures, plus assumptions about mortality and fertility. These projections serve as a useful planning tool, but they do not tell the whole story. Rapid fluctuations in population movements will be caused by unpredictable internal instability, natural disasters and conflict. Migration within countries has already changed the composition of many developing countries, driving rapid urbanization. The future ability of developing countries to cope with increasingly aged populations also remains to be seen, especially in combination with increasingly unpredictable economic futures.

NOTES

1. Africa, Latin America and the Caribbean, Asia (excluding Japan) and Melanesia, Micronesia and Polynesia.
2. This overview of population trends will use the most recent United Nations World Population Prospects (1998 revision), a source which is readily available in most reference libraries.
3. The grouping 'least developed' uses the framework as defined by the United Nations General Assembly, as of 1998, and includes 48 countries, of which 33 are in Africa, 9 in Asia, 1 in Latin America and the Caribbean, and 5 in Oceania. They are included in the less developed regions.
4. UN medium variant projections.
5. Net dependency ratio = number of children aged below 15 years and adults aged 65 years or older per 100 people of working age; child dependency ratio = number of children aged below 15 years per 100 people of working age; elderly dependency ratio = number of people aged 65 years or older per 100 people of working age
6. The calculation of life expectancy at birth is heavily biased by levels of infant mortality. In populations with high levels of infant mortality, life expectancy at birth provides a very poor representation of the age at which people are likely to die.
7. The number of deaths before their first birthday, of live-born infants during a year, divided by the number of live births in the year, and usually expressed per 1,000.
8. Including the 'insurance' effect (the hypothetical result of parents choosing to have more births than their desired number of children due to a fear that some children will die), interruption of lactation, the 'replacement' effect (the replacement of dead children by subsequent births) and societal supports for fertility.
9. A maternal death is defined as a death during pregnancy, childbirth, or six weeks *postpartum*. It therefore also includes deaths attributable to induced abortion.
10. International Conference on Population and Development, Cairo.
11. Cigarette consumption per adult increased by 60 per cent between 1970–72 and 1990–92 in all developing countries (UNDP, 1999).
12. Total Fertility Rates (TFRs) are the most commonly used indicator of fertility. TFRs will therefore be used throughout this discussion, and represent the number of children a woman would have during her lifetime if she were to experience the fertility rates of the period at each age.
13. A recent decline in fertility has been recorded in the 1997 Yemen Demographic and Health Survey, with a TFR of 6.5.
14. Migration refers here to population movements involving a permanent or semi-permanent change of usual residence. Mobility refers to 'all phenomena involving the displacement of individuals' (Pressat, 1985: 148).
15. See www.unhcr.ch for up-to-date information.

GUIDE TO FURTHER READING

Demeny, P. and McNicoll, G. (1998) *The Earthscan Reader in Population and Development*, London: Earthscan.

Livi-Bacci, M. (1992) *A Concise History of World Population*, Oxford: Blackwell.

Livi-Bacci, M. (1997) *A Concise History of World Population* (2nd edn), Cambridge, MA: Blackwell.

Lutz, W. (1996) *The Future Population of the World: What Can we Assume Today?*, London: Earthscan.

Population Division, Department of Economic and Social Affairs of the United Nations Secretariat (1998) *World Population Prospects: The 1998 Revision*, New York: United Nations.

REFERENCES

Black, T. (1999) 'Impediments to effective fertility reduction', *British Medical Journal* 319: 932–3.

Bongaarts, J. and Potter, R.G. (1984) *Fertility, Biology, and Behaviour: An Analysis of the Proximate Determinants*, New York: Academic Press.

Cleland, J. (1996) 'Demographic data collection in less developed countries 1946–1996', *Population Studies* 50(3): 433–50.

Ganges, F. and Long, P. (1998) 'Safe motherhood: successes and challenges', *Outlook* 16 (Special Issue).

Gardner, R. and Blackburn, R. (1996) 'People who move: new reproductive health focus', *Population Reports* Series J, No. 45.

Garenne, M. (1996) 'Mortality in Sub-Saharan Africa: trends and prospects', in W. Lutz (ed.) *The Future Population of the World: What Can we Assume Today?*, London: Earthscan.

International Migration Review (1987) 'Measuring international migration: theory and practice', Special Issue 21(4).

Mirkin, B. and Weinberger, M.B. (2000) *The Demography of Population Ageing*, paper presented at the *Technical Meeting on Population Ageing and Living Arrangements of Older Persons: Critical Issues and Policy Responses*, Population Division, United Nations, New York, 8–10 February 2000.

Pressat, R. (1985) *The Dictionary of Demography*, Oxford: Basil Blackwell.

Preston, S.H. (1978) *The Effects of Infant and Child Mortality on Fertility*, New York: Academic Press.

UNAIDS (1997) *Tuberculosis and AIDS: UNAIDS Point of View*, Geneva: UNAIDS.

UNDP (1999) *Human Development Report, 1999.* Oxford: Oxford University Press.

Zlotnik, H. (1998) 'International migration 1965–96: an overview', *Population and Development Review* 24(3): 429–68.

7.11 Sexual and reproductive rights

Sonia Corrêa

HISTORICAL THREADS

- Throughout history, nomadic and agricultural societies have exercised varied forms of fertility regulation. Roman, Greek and medieval societies investigated biological reproduction. Across cultures abortion has been subject to legal, religious and medical regulation.
- In the West, from the seventeenth century on, human reproduction and sexuality – while remaining determined by moral and religious norms – was increasingly subject to scientific inquiry, statistical quantification and state intervention. From late eighteenth century, utopian socialists, Marxist parties, Malthusian and neo-Malthusian eugenic groups, and feminist organizations developed ideas and proposals for transforming these two domains.

- In the second half of the nineteenth century, mass-produced condoms became available and were promoted by neo-Malthusians and activists, sometimes on eugenic convictions. Feminists claimed women's citizenship by struggling for voting rights. They considered fertility control unnatural, but supported women's rights to refuse sex and control their own bodies. Socialist streams articulated women's reproductive freedom, and ideas for broader and deeper social and economic transformation. The scientific study of sexuality was inaugurated.
- By the early twentieth century Margaret Sanger coined the term 'birth control' and from there on the diffusion of related ideas spread unevenly beyond Europe and North America. By the 1930s, progressive voices lost ground to medical, health and eugenic approaches to fertility control. Sanger-associated networks developed links to ideologies of class, caste, ethnic and racial domination that played a major role in the second wave of global efforts aimed at controlling fertility in the second half of the century.
- In the 1950s and 1960s, population control became a 'grand ideology'. The United Nations, global financial institutions, bilateral donors and private foundations developed arguments to demonstrate that rapid demographic growth *would* curtail economic development in the South. In reaction, at the UN World Population Conference of Bucharest in 1974, developing countries advocated 'development the best contraceptive'. But soon afterwards few of these countries, particularly in Asia, adopted population control policies.

CONTEMPORARY FACTS

- 1993: the International Conference on Human Rights, Vienna, acknowledges that human rights are universal, indivisible and interrelated, and that women's human rights must be respected both in the public and in the private sphere.
- 1994: the Programme of Action of the International Conference of Population and Development (ICPD, Cairo, 1994) defines reproductive rights as:

  [Embracing] certain human rights that are already recognized in national laws, international human rights documents and other consensus documents. These rights rest on the recognition of the basic right of all couples and individuals to decide freely and responsibly the number, spacing and timing of their children and to have the information and means to do so, and the right to attain the highest standard of sexual and reproductive health. It also includes their right to make decisions concerning reproduction free of discrimination, coercion and violence.

  (paragraph 7.3)

- 1995: Platform of Action of the IV World Women Conference, Beijing, reaffirms ICPD principles and spells out the substantive contents of women's sexual rights as:

  The human rights of women include their right to have control over and decide freely and responsibly on matters related to their sexuality, including sexual and reproductive health, free of coercion, discrimination and violence. Equal relationships between women and men in matters of sexual relations and reproduction, including full respect for the integrity of the person, require mutual respect, consent and shared responsibility for sexual behavior and its consequences.

- 1997: the Treaty of Amsterdam that amends the Treaty of the European Union considers sexual orientation an unjustifiable ground for discrimination.
- 2000: the Council of Europe requests the inclusion of sexual orientation in the list of unjustified grounds for discrimination in the European Convention on Human Rights.

CONTEMPORARY SOCIAL MOVEMENTS

While nineteenth-century feminist pioneers perceived sexuality as a male-dominated domain in which women were de-moralized, contemporary feminism streams – having surged concurrently with the 1960's 'sexual revolution' – openly advocate women's rights to both reproductive self-determination and sexual pleasure. They argue in favour of free contraception and abortion to emancipate women's personal and sexual potentialities. By the early 1970s, when the pill and IUDs were made available worldwide, feminist analysis had also started documenting how states, religious doctrines and political movements throughout history and across cultures had manipulated women's sexuality and fertility.

By then in Northern socities, progress was being achieved in women's civil and political rights and labour participation. But this had not been accompanied by legal reforms in family law and regulations concerning sexuality, contraception and abortion. Consequently, campaigns calling for sexual and reproductive self-determination blossomed in Europe and in the United States. In developing nations, women's organizations initially supported the position of their governments in resisting population control. But gradually Southern feminists perceived that neither developmentalist approaches nor population control programmes responded to women's needs and aspirations.

In 1984, in Amsterdam, the first International Reproductive Rights Conference legitimized reproductive rights as a global feminist concept. Concurrently, gay and lesbian issues were becoming globalized. From the mid-1980s, the upsurge of the HIV/AIDS pandemic also spurred the spread of ideas about rights in relation to sexuality. These various strands would create, North and South of the Equator, the political and policy environment favouring the conceptualization of sexual and reproductive rights.

INSTITUTIONAL INITIATIVES

This political and conceptual evolution occurred predominantly in civil societies. But it was preceded and surrounded by relevant institutional processes. As early as 1974, in Bucharest, a United Nations agreement had already been reached with respect to the right of couples and individuals to decide the number of their children. Similar rights language was adopted in the final document of the 1975 Women's Conference in Mexico City and, most importantly, in the Convention for the Elimination of Discrimination against Women (CEDAW) adopted in 1979. In both cases gender equality principles were added to general principle of individuals' and couples' reproductive choice.

This climate would, nevertheless, change during the 1980s. In 1984, at the International Population Conference of Mexico City, broader acceptance of family planning programmes was expressed by developing countries, and women's right to contraception was reiterated. But an alliance between the United States' Reagan Administration and the Holy See made abortion a major controversy. From then until 1993, the United States cut funding for international family planning activities on the grounds that they would facilitate access to pregnancy terminations.

Consequently, at the 1985 UN Women's Conference in Nairobi, abortion was excluded from the governmental debates, although it was openly and widely debated in the NGO Forum. By the end of the decade, despite prevailing conservatism, the World Health Organization formally adopted the definitions of sexual and reproductive health. This institutional move provided a strategic platform to further advance sexual and reproductive rights in global policy areas.

CONCEPTUAL CONTROVERSIES

Although letigimized in international documents, sexual and reproductive rights remain a contested political terrain, a clear illustration of this being the harsh political controversies surrounding abortion. Both in the North and in the South, religious norms and dogmatic legal or ethical frames stigmatize and criminalize abortion, while feminists advocate access to legal and safe abortion as a non-negotiable dimension of sexual equality. But tensions occur in other domains, as in the case of development debates. While scholars and planners take the economy and demography as their basic point of departure, feminists focus on women's rights and gender inequality, maintaining that women should be the subjects, not the objects, of any related policy. Similarly, gay and lesbian scholars and activists question biomedical and legal discourses that impose heterosexuality as a norm.

Inside the feminist field itself the foundations of sexual and reproductive rights are subject to constant inquiries. The struggle for legal abortion was to a large extent at the core of early struggles for reproductive rights. But, during the 1980s, it was questioned whether abortion should be addressed as a single issue in Southern countries as it had been in the United States. This controversy was overcome when consensus was reached that abortion is both a health and rights issue, an approach allowing for integrating the claim for abortion rights within a broader reproductive rights and women's health framework.

A deeper controversy developed – and still revolves – around the Western imprint of the two concepts. The argument in this case is that ideas about an individual's ownership of her body and women's autonomy are inappropriate for many Southern women. This perspective converges with the broader critique of human rights that is framed on the grounds of cultural relativism. A related point of view concerns the disjunction between the individual and social dimensions of sexual and reproductive rights. It claims that autonomy or choice in matters relating to reproduction and sexuality may be meaningless where livelihood is endangered, public health and education systems are inadequate, and cultural diversity is not respected.

During the 1990s these critiques were responded to with an ethical frame based on four principles: equality, diversity, personhood and bodily integrity. Feminist research shows that while few women use the terms sexual and reproductive rights, they understand them as being able to make decisions about procreation, to be free from harassment by men, and to protect themselves against domestic violence and preventable illness. Southern feminists also advocate that the language of sexual and reproductive rights must be firmly placed within a larger frame that also includes adequate nutrition, housing, a job and social assistance (i.e., education, daycare, healthcare and contraception).

The sexual and reproductive rights framework implies both positive rights, such as reproductive healthcare and employment, and negative rights, such as protection against rape and discrimination, regardless of sexual orientation or marital status. Nevertheless, unresolved tensions and problems persist, particularly in the realm of sexuality. There is currently plenty of political space to develop and sharpen the notion of sexual rights, but developing 'universal' ideas of sexuality is an exceedingly complex task.

POLICY AND POLITICAL CHALLENGES

A human rights approach to sexual and reproductive politics is confronted with major technical and political difficulties, including non-binding provisions in United Nations documents. Even if these new principles are made legally binding, effective enforcement requires a rigid and continuing distinction between public/private in international human rights law and national legal systems. This is particularly important for women, whose lives in many cultures are still locked within the domestic domain in which most abuses such as sexual coercion, marital rape, female genital mutilation and virginity codes occur.

There are even greater challenges in the contradictory picture that is found at the nexus between economic dynamics and the transformation of gender relations. In reaction to the negative effects of poorly understood and unregulated globalization, there is a strengthening of political, national, religion-based, ethnic and other identities that are reviving traditional gender systems and controls over sexuality. Racism, nationalism and ethnic hatreds also pose immense threats to gender equality, and reproductive and sexual self-determination.

Often, those who promote a globalized and unregulated economy often support the breaking down of traditional gender systems and lessening of sexual constraints. But they are largely unconcerned with the negative effects of current economic trends that, in most circumstances, underlie the expansion of fundamentalism, patriarchal revivals and ethnic conflict. These forces have been systematically at play in global arenas during the last decade of the twentieth century, most particularly at the United Nations. The experience of these debates suggests that the fulfilment of gender equality as well as of sexual and reproductive freedom will be curtailed unless these complex and contradictory trends are not better understood, challenged and eventually tamed.

GUIDE TO FURTHER READING AND REFERENCES

Cook, Rebecca (1995) *Human Rights and Reproductive Self-Determination*, The American University Law Review, Vol. 44–4, Washington DC.

Corrêa, Sonia with Reichmann, Rebecca (1994) *Population and Reproductive Rights: Feminist Perspectives from the South*, London: Zed Books.

Corrêa, S. and Petchesky, R. (1994) 'Reproductive rights: a feminist perspective', in *Population Policies Reconsidered: Health, Empowerment and Rights*, G. Sen, A. Germain and L.C. Chen (eds) Boston: Harvard School of Public Health.

International Planned Parenthood Federation (IPPF) (1995) *IPPF Charter on Sexual and Reproductive Rights* London: IPPF.

Kerr, J. (1993) *Ours by Right: Women's Rights as Human Rights*, London: Zed Books.

Petchesky, Rosalind P. and Judd, Karen (eds) (1998) *Negotiating Reproductive Rights: Women's Perspectives Across Countries and Cultures*, London and New York: Zed Books.

Sen, G., Germain, A. and Chen, L.C. (1994) *Population Policies Reconsidered: Heath, Empowerment and Rights*, Cambridge, MA: Harvard School of Public Health.

United Nations (1994) *Programme of Action of the International Conference on Population and Development*, New York: UN.

United Nations (1994) *Report of the International Conference on Population and Development, Cairo, 5–13 September*, Sales E.95.XIII.18. New York.

United Nations (1995) *Report of the Fourth World Conference on Women Beijing, 6–15 September*, A/CONF.177/20, 7. New York.

United Nations (1996) *Beijing Declaration and Platform for Action*, adopted by the Fourth World Conference on Women, New York: UN.

7.12 Indigenous fertility control

Tulsi Patel

INTRODUCTION

Demographic studies have generally seen the world as divided into two broad parts: one afflicted by high growth of population and the other better balanced by low growth of population. The less developed societies (because of their proclivity for high fertility) are seen to be under the spell of religious superstition and tradition, while the developed world is seen as capable of rational choice. Anthropological (Handwerker, 1990; Patel, 1994; Greenhalgh, 1995) and historical (Harris and Ross, 1987; Hufton, 1995) studies situate population and fertility amidst cultural and political-economic considerations. It is evident that though barrenness was regarded as a curse, an over-abundance of living children was seen as something less than a blessing.

This chapter focuses on indigenous fertility control in two ways: mortality control on the one hand, and fertility on the other. Though many of the indigenous practices and techniques may not be of proven effectivity, they are not totally ineffective.

SOCIAL MECHANISMS AND POPULATION REGULATION

The prevalence of indigenous population control (fertility) is reported in many societies. Heer (1964) reports for Indian-speaking communities in parts of Andean countries, Freebeme (1964) for traditional China, Smith (1977: 142–3) for Japan, Bledsoe (1997) for Gambia, Harris and Ross (1987) for societies ranging from Paleolithic times to the present, Patel (1994 and 1998) for rural North Indian peasant and tribal society, and Ram and Jolly (1998) for Asia and the Pacific during the colonial times.

Limiting fertility within marriage

Matters related to marriage and fertility are intimate, gendered and elicit intense interest from surrounding kin, community and state (cf. MacCormack, 1982; Patel, 1994). The German ethnologist, Felix Speiser (1990) attributes low birth rates to the pre-colonial sexual economy – the way in which older, less virile men monopolized women, and sterility in women ensuing from being 'used' for sexual purposes at a very early age.

Celibacy

Prayer to have self-control is known besides the New Testament praising virgins as Christ's brides or jewels. Hindu *sadhus* and *sadhvis*, and some wrestlers in India remain celibate for life. A strict and elaborate regimen is prescribed for wrestlers to control semen loss (Alter, 1992: 133).

Unwelcome babies

Infanticide, especially female infanticide, has for centuries depressed the number of surviving children, with fewer girls to replace their mothers as reproducers. Vishwanath (2000) provides figures for the reduced population of Patidars during 1820s and 1890s in Gujarat. In twentieth-century India and China, millions of girls were not allowed to survive. Douglas (1966) describes the customary beliefs and practices of eliminating babies among a few primitive communities. The neglect of female children is customary in south Asia and son preference is characteristic.

Colonial discourses have denounced as pathological infanticide other indigenous practices, such as abortion, neglect, widow strangulation and denial of remarriage, protracted periods of sexual abstinence, etc., and decrease of population (see Ram and Jolly, 1998). Though it is impossible to quantify them, accounts of female infanticide are available from autobiographical accounts (Dureau, 1998).

Eugenics politics

Many colonizers encouraged breeding among the middle and upper classes. The colonies however, did not always respond to the desires of the colonial masters or missionaries (see Ram and Jolly, 1998). Speiser (1990: 50) evokes this clearly from a mother, 'Why should we go on having children? Since the white man came they all die' (cf. Rivers, 1922: 104).

Scheper-Hughes (1984) in her study of northeast Brazil talks of ethno-eugenics. Mothers expressed a belief in a child's innate constitution relating to 'readiness or fitness for life' as opposed to traits displayed by a child 'who wanted to die'. The life-boat ethics explains the absence of grief over such deaths, and is also excused by the widespread folk belief in Latin America that such infants are not affected by original sin and rise immediately to heaven to become little angels (Hutchinson, 1957: 145, cited in Harris and Ross, 1987). Fijian mothers were under strict surveillance to increase the population of Fiji, and were often accused of procuring abortions and liable to inquests.

Abortion

In the early stages of pregnancy abortion was widely tolerated all over the world for centuries as one of the only dependable methods of fertility control. Even the Catholic Church took the conveniently loose view that the foetus became animated by the rational soul, and abortion therefore became a serious crime at 40 days after conception for a boy and 80 days for a girl.

Among the Javanese (Alexander, 1986) there are occasional reports of the occurrence of abortion. Treating delayed menstruation with herbs and massage is evidently common (see also the theme issue of *Social Science and Medicine*, 1996). Herbs purchased at fairs and/or prepared from garden plants to bring on 'women's courses' before the pregnancy was far advanced are also reported for fifteenth- to seventeenth-century European society, and their knowledge passed on from one generation of women to another. Midwives were thought to be well versed in preparing these concoctions, as were whores. Dureau (1998: 248) reports the use of abortifacients by women in the Solomon Islands during the colonial period (cf. Fortes, 1949: 167; Patel, 1994). Some of the herbal preparations are also used as a contraception (cf. Patel, 1994).

MECHANISMS OF FERTILITY REGULATION

Some of the practices of fertility control are related directly to the belief and value structures of a given society, while others might be related to the political and economic structures.

Abstinence

Abstinence within marriage has been effectively used for centuries in most cultures. Handwerker (1986: 103) refers to an old Liberian farmwoman stating that the foolproof method of contraception was to avoid your husband. A Rajasthani woman in her 80s had confided that she had borne only two children because she had sternly kept her husband at an arm's distance. Besides institutional practices prescribing avoidance, women have used their ingenuity as well. They are known to introduce a barrier to reduce or prevent a congenial possibility of sex. A demographer from the Philippines corroborated Patel's (1997) observation of the enticing of children to sleep in one's bed with the specific aim of deterring any sexual advances.

> Madame de Sevigne, in seventeenth-century France, urged upon her daughter after three pregnancies in quick succession, the desirability of having her maid sleep in the same room to depress the sexual urges of the Comte de Grigan. Lower down the social scale, keeping children in the marital bed may have been used by women to lessen the prospects of pregnancy.
>
> (Hufton, 1995: 178)

An Indian village elder eulogized the much-reduced possibility of undesirable self-indulgence and sin when surrounded by people in a joint family (Wadley, 1994).

Sleeping arrangements

The architecture of housing provides for only one, or at the most two proper rooms. The rest of the large house space is either open or consists of half-covered structures that allow a rather generous ventilation and disallow privacy (see Patel, 1994: 173, 188–9; Wadley, 1994: 13). Except for very young couples, closed rooms are not used for sleeping. The middle aged and elderly sleep in common open spaces like the courtyard. Streets are lined with cots at night and men talk themselves to sleep. Sex relations of the elderly do not remain a secret for long and become a subject for gossip (cf. Dureau, 1998: 244).

Even among the younger couples who are expected to be sexually active, mothers, mothers-in-law and grandmothers often intervene to restrict sexual intercourse. Sleeping close to the daughter-in-law restrains her man from making sexual advances. The Kusasi of Savanna in Ghana (Cleveland, 1986) would report the matter to a mother or a father and reprimand the man if he were observed not abstaining from sex or making advances without his wife's desire (cf. Patel, 1994).

Social onomastics

The pattern of nomenclature signals the uncalled-for births after parents have had the socially optimum number of children of both sexes. The names indicating the parents' unwelcome attitude to their later children are Madi (one who has barged in), Aichuki (enough of coming), Santi (peace/quiet), Santos (satisfaction/complacency) and Dhapuri (satisfied/full/complete).

Pregnant grandmother syndrome

In Mogra (the village of Patel's 1994 study), a grandmother ceases to bear children. The norms prescribe the time when a couple should opt out of having a baby once their children are married. If elderly (parents of married children) display undue concern over sensual enjoyment they risk criticism and ridicule (cf. Vatuk 1990: 75 for Uttar Pradesh and Caldwell, 1982 for the Yoruba of Nigeria).

Lactation practices

Prolonged breast-feeding is widely reported. Among the Asia-Pacific communities (Ram and Jolly, 1998) children were ideally suckled for about four years. Studies from Java in Indonesia and Africa (Handwerker, 1986) report at least two years of *postpartum* breast-feeding sans coitus.

There exists ethnographic evidence of the association between lactation and anovulation. In Mogra, mothers breast-feed their infants on demand and consider mother's milk as the only vital nutrient for the infant. It is believed that mother's milk is the only feed that leads neither to diarrhoea nor to malodorous stools (cf. Hufton, 1995). MacCormack reports for Sierra Leone, 'Sande women, with their secret knowledge, public laws, legitimate sanctions and hierarchical organization, bring women's biology under the most careful cultural control' (1977: 94). Also, in rural Rajasthan if an infant were to die, the older sibling is put to the breast with the clear purpose of avoiding an early conception.

Political and ritual considerations

Some African and Pacific tribes prolong breast-feeding and abstinence with the explicit purpose of having only one or two children per woman. The Bhils in Rajasthan (Patel, 1998) practise abstinence for a month during the Gavari worship festivities, and once or twice a week when either spouse is fasting. A good fraction of men wear the ritually processed copper ring (called a *gole*) as part of a ritual which expects them to abstain on still more occasions.

Besides, the popular practice of *pomanchar*, literally guesting, involves frequent reciprocal visits of kin, relatives and even caste members. Sleeping is especially gender-segregated. During guesting, except for very young couples, sexual activity is inhibited.

Contraception

Coitus interruptus or withdrawal, has been practised and passed on from generation to generation. Though the semiology varies from culture to culture, the seed and soil (*beej–kshetra*) for sperm and womb respectively is the most common metaphor in many parts of the world (Cleveland, 1986; Dube, 1986; Delaney, 1991; Patel, 1994). The preference for the right kind of field/soil for a seed is a widespread concern in most societies. Hufton records a case, 'When Isabella de Moerloose of the region of Ghent married a pastor in 1689, he tried by coitus interruptus and oral sex to avoid making Isabella pregnant' (1995: 174), as he did not want children from Isabella (who came from lower social stock) to claim his descent and inherit his property.

CONCLUSION

Conflicts between the reproductive desires of a society's fecund women and other individuals, groups and political elite are present. Differential access to power determines how conflicts over reproduction are conducted and resolved (or if they are resolved). State/colonial power exercises surveillance and intervenes for eugenic change in stock of populations or for labour supply.

The use of intentionality in power dynamics relates with real-life situations where fertility decisions like sexual intercourse, conception, positions to retain or expel the seed, abort, kill, throw away, etc. are taken. All household members are rarely likely to have a total consensus. Nor are macro-level results merely aggregates of the micro-level fertility decisions.

GUIDE TO FURTHER READING

Greenhalgh's edited collection develops the cultural and political approaches to human reproduction. Handwerker's edited volumes cover both ethnographic and theoretical issues of fertility processes and politics and explore the link between the macro and micro phenomena through which population processes and politics work. He highlights cultural and biological constraints within which people make fertility decisions.

Patel's work explores the household and community processes and their politics as they are unravelled over the life cycle of women in rural north India. Interesting social and folk practices of indigenous fertility regulation are exposed. Ram and Jolly's edited volume is an analysis of the politics of colonial and postcolonial surveillance and interventions to increase the population of colonies in Asia and the Pacific. It also deals with the discourses on the politics and cultural differences between the colonialists and the colonies. Additionally, Delaney's book (Delaney, 1991) is a graphic account of the suffering and anguish infertility can cause to men and especially to women in the patriarchal society of Turkey. Derived from Islamic monotheistic cosmology, the seed gains supremacy over the soil (see also Dube, 1986).

REFERENCES

Alexander, P. (1986) 'Labour expropriation and fertility: population growth in nineteenth century Java', in W.P. Handwerker (ed.) *Culture and Reproduction*, Boulder: Westview Press.

Alter, J. (1992) *The Wrestler's Body*, Berkeley: University of California Press.

Bledsoe, C. (1997) 'Reproduction and aging in rural Gambia: African empirical challenges for the culture of Western science', unpublished manuscript.

Caldwell, J.C. (1982) *Theory of Fertility Decline*, London: Academic Press.

Cleveland, D.A. (1986) 'The political economy of fertility regulation: the Kusasi of Savanna West Africa (Ghana)', in W.P. Handwerker (ed.) pp. 263–93.

Delaney, D. (1991) *The Seed and The Soil: Gender and Cosmology in Turkish Village Society*, Berkeley: University of California Press.

Douglas, M. (1966) *Purity and Danger: An Analysis of the Concepts of Pollution and Taboo*, London: Routledge and Kegan Paul.

Dube, L. (1986) 'Seed and earth: the symbolism of biological reproduction and sexual relations in reproduction', in L. Dube, E. Leacock and S. Ardener (eds), *Visibility and Power*, Delhi: Oxford University Press.

Dureau, C. (1998) 'From sisters to wives: changing contexts of maternity on Simbo, Western Solomon Islands', in K. Ram and M. Jolly (eds) *Maternities and Modernities: Colonial and Postcolonial Experiences in Asia and the Pacific*, Cambridge: Cambridge University Press.

Fortes, M. (1949) *The Web of Kinship Among the Tallensi*, London: Oxford University Press.

Freebeme, M. (1964) 'Birth control in China', *Population Studies* 18(1): 5–16.

Greenhalgh, S. (ed.) (1995) *Situating Fertility: Anthropology and Demographic Inquiry*, Cambridge: Cambridge University Press.

Handwerker, W.P. (ed.) (1986) *Births and Power: Social Change and Politics of Reproduction*, Boulder: Westview Press, pp. 1–33.

Handwerker, W.P. (1990) *Culture and Reproduction*, Boulder: Westview Press.

Harris, M. and Ross, E. (1987) *Death, Sex, and Fertility: Population Regulation in Preindustrial and Developing Societies*, New York: Columbia University Press.

Heer, D.M. (1964) 'Fertility differentials between Indian and Spanish speaking parts in Andean countries', *Population Studies* 18(1): 71–84.

Hufton, O. (1995) *The Prospect Before Her, Vol. 1: 1500–1800*, London: HarperCollins.

MacCormack, C.P. (1977) 'Biological events and cultural control', *Signs* 3(1): 93–100.

MacCormack, C.P. (ed.) (1982) *Ethnography of Fertility and Birth*, New York: Academic.

Patel, Tulsi, (1994) *Fertility Behaviour: Population and Society in a Rajasthan Village*, Delhi: Oxford University Press.

Patel, Tulsi, (1997) 'The fit between sterilization and traditional fertility in rural India', paper presented at the East–West Center Alumni Association International Conference, New Delhi, 23–26 November 1997.

Patel, Tulsi, (1998) 'Reproduction and tribal society: a study in Southern Rajasthan', Project Report submitted to the ICSSR, Delhi.

Ram, K. and Jolly, M. (eds) (1998) *Maternities and Modernities: Colonial and Postcolonial Experiences in Asia and the Pacific*, Cambridge: Cambridge University Press.

Rivers, W.H.R. (ed.) (1922) *Essays on the Depopulation of Melanesia*, Cambridge: Cambridge University Press.

Scheper-Hughes, N. (1984) 'Infant mortality and infant care: cultural and economic constraints in nursing in Northeast Brazil', *Social Science and Medicine* 19: 535–456.

Smith, T.C. (1977) *Nakahara: Family Planning and Population in a Japanese Village, 1717– 1830*, Stanford: Stanford University Press.

Social Science and Medicine (1996) 42(4) (for several articles in the special issue on abortion).

Speiser, F. (1990 [1923]) *The Ethnology of Vanuatu: An Early Twentieth Century Study*, Bathurst: Crawford House.

Vatuk, S. (1990) ' "To be a burden on others": dependency anxiety among the elderly in India', in O.M. Lynch (ed.) *Divine Passions: The Social Construction of Emotion in India*, Berkeley: University of California Press.

Vishwanath, L.S. (2000) *Female Infanticide and Social Structure*, Delhi: Hindustan.

Wadley, S. (1994) *Struggling with Destiny in Karimpur, 1925–1984*, Delhi: Vistar.

7.13 China's single child family policy

Delia Davin

INTRODUCTION

At the end of 1970s, the Chinese government called on all Chinese couples to limit their families to a single child. Other governments have, of course, tried to persuade couples to have fewer children in the interests of reducing population growth, but none has adopted a policy as strict as China's. This chapter will lay out the background to the policy, and discuss its implementation and its impact.

THE DEMOGRAPHIC BACKGROUND

The establishment of civil order and of a comparatively effective health system in the 1950s in China produced a steep decline in the death rate. The birth rate remained high and the population grew from 583 million in the 1953 census to just one thousand million by 1982 (Banister, 1987). There were many debates about the need for birth control in the 1950s and 1960s in China. Policy-makers were early concerned about China's huge population, worrying about the difficulty of feeding it. Mao Zedong rebuked the experts for seeing people as 'mouths not hands'. He argued that China's population could be an asset if everyone was made productive. By the early 1960s, however, the government had begun to advocate family planning, and in the 1970s it presented the 'two-child family' as the ideal. The slogan 'late, spaced, few' was used to sum up the new demands: couples should delay the birth of their first child, they should leave a long gap before the second and they should stop at two (White, 1994).

Mao's death in 1976 was followed by a reassessment of China's economic record since the establishment of the People's Republic in 1949. There was concern that economic growth had been too slow, especially in agriculture. Worthwhile gains had been cancelled out by population growth, with the result that by the late 1970s the per capita output of grain was not much greater than it had been in 1957. A shortage of cultivable land imposed severe limitations on the potential for further growth. China was already feeding almost a quarter of the world's population on only 7 per cent of its cultivated land. The age structure of China's population was another cause for concern. Demographers warned that China's population of close to one billion would double within less than half a century if each woman had just three children. Figures from the 1982 census confirmed this potential for growth. It was found that 45 per cent of the population were under 20 and nearly two-thirds were under 30. The policy response was the one child family rule, first announced in the late 1970s and implemented with increasing severity in the early 1980s (Croll *et al.*, 1985).

ONE CHILD REGULATIONS

Although the one-child limit is national policy, no national law has been agreed to underpin it. Instead, the provinces and many of the big cities have all produced their own regulations. These vary in the detail but it is nonetheless possible to give a general summary. All couples are asked to have only one child unless they fall into certain exempt categories. These include ethnic minorities, returned Overseas Chinese, those whose first child is handicapped and will not be able to work, and parents who themselves were both only children. The most important exception, which has become general in regulations for rural areas since 1986, is that peasant couples whose first child is a girl may have a second child (Davin, 1990a).

There are incentives to conform to the policy and penalties for ignoring it. Parents who promise to have only one child receive a small monthly allowance and privileged access to housing, healthcare and schooling. Those who have a second or third child without permission are penalized for out-of-plan births. They may be fined or may have 10 per cent or more of their salaries withheld for 14 to 16 years to represent the supposed costs to the state of the additional child. The medical fees for the birth and subsequent health and educational costs fall wholly upon the parents. The state has produced extensive materials to justify the policy arguing that rapid population growth threatens living standards and makes rapid economic growth unattainable.

IMPLEMENTATION AND IMPACT

The one child policy has been unpopular and difficult to implement, especially in the countryside where children are still seen as a source of prosperity and security. Sons are traditionally preferred to daughters in China because they remain members of their natal families when they marry. They are thus available to support their parents in old age and their sons carry on the family name. Daughters marry out of their natal families. A daughter cares for her husband's parents in old age and her sons carry on her husband's family name. When a couple also have a son, a daughter can be loved and welcomed, but her birth may be felt as a disaster if the one child rule is strictly enforced and it means that her parents lose the chance to produce a son. According to Chinese statistics, boys increasingly outnumber girls among Chinese children. Several factors are responsible. First, there is clear evidence that there has been some female infanticide although this is hard to quantify. Some parents simply fail to register female births in order not to be barred from having further children. Another factor is the preferential treatment accorded to boys that may improve their survival chances. It is probable, however, that there really are fewer female births than male ones in China. Sex-selective abortion, although illegal, is widely practised. The distorted sex ratio and the abandonment of girl babies has given rise to considerable government concern, and has forced modifications of the one child policy in the countryside (Greenhalgh, 1994).

Acceptance of the one child policy has been easier in China's cities (Milwertz, 1997). In the established urban areas, accommodation, childcare and education are becoming increasingly expensive, dual-career families are the norm and consumerism is transforming people's aspirations. Few couples now have more than one child. Much time, attention and money is lavished on these single children as parents invest in the future through them. This consequence of reduced fertility fits in well with the state advocacy of 'reducing the quantity and enhancing the quality' of the population. On the other hand there is concern about the likely character of a generation without brothers and sisters. It is often claimed that these children will be spoilt, selfish and lacking in social skills. Another worry is that the enormous pressure on children to succeed academically may have some negative consequences (Davin, 1990b).

The main resistance to the single child family policy has been in the countryside where the economic need for sons is greatest and where peasants see children as a source of prosperity and old-age security. Conflict has been reduced by the concession that allows rural couples a second child if their first is a girl, but many other aspects of population policy still clash with rural traditions and aspirations. The minimum ages for marriage are set very high, at 22 for a man and 20 for a woman. Couples whose circumstances qualify them to have a second child are still required to seek permission to do so and to leave a four-year gap between births. Women who have an unauthorized pregnancy come under heavy pressure to abort. Those who have had a second child are supposed to undergo a sterilization or employ an approved method of contraception. Many families defy such regulations. Rural officials, who are frequently related to the people they are supposed to police, sometimes ignore infringements of these regulations. On the other hand there have been many reports of coercive behaviour on the part of local officials who may themselves be fined or demoted if they fail to meet targets set for their area concerning the number of single child families, births and contraceptive use.

In the past three decades the state in China has relaxed its control over many areas of the economy, cultural life and even politics. Yet as a result of the single child family policy, it now intrudes into what are normally the most private areas of life to an extraordinary degree. Improvements in contraception have not brought reproductive freedom for Chinese women. They are subject to conflicting pressures from the state and from their husbands' families over the number of children they will have. Their menstrual cycles are officially monitored and they bear the main burden of contraception and sterilization. If they give birth to a girl when a boy is desired their husbands and their in-laws may blame them. On the other hand women have also benefited in some ways from population policy. Even in the poorest and most remote parts of the Chinese countryside women have access to the contraceptive knowledge and supplies that are still denied to women in much of the developing and even the developed world (Davin, 1990a).

Internationally, there has been widespread controversy over the one child policy. It has been condemned, especially in the United States, by campaigners against abortion and also by those who regard reproductive freedom as a basic human right (Aird, 1990). Others argue that there can be no absolute right to reproductive freedom where it threatens the nation's development goals. They applaud the Chinese success in lowering fertility and raising living standards (Brown, 1995).

The total fertility rate in China declined from 6.66 in 1968 to 3.19 in 1979 and 2.32 in 1987, an extraordinary achievement in what was still overwhelmingly a poor agricultural country[1] (Feeney and Wang, 1993). Urban rates were 3.2 in 1970 and 1.3 in 1987 (Feeney et al., 1989). Chinese birth rates increasingly resemble those of a developed country. The factors that contributed to this decline certainly include those that have been associated with demographic transition all over the world: increased urbanization, rising living standards, improved literacy rates, especially among women, and higher female labour participation rates. Birth rates had begun to fall in the 1970s when the state was already advocating birth planning but before the introduction of the draconian one child policy. It is difficult to know just how much of the fertility decline can be attributed to this policy. It is clear, however, that the state's promotion of small-family goals, its constant pressure on the population to accept these goals and its huge investment in making contraception available everywhere, have contributed to China's extraordinarily rapid fertility reduction. Most families still have more than one child, but the vast majority now practise contraception and, even in the countryside, families with more than three or four children are very rare. It is a mark of the achievement of China's population policy that the state is now concerned with the problems that will arise with the greying of the population over the next few decades as the proportion of the elderly rises.

NOTE

1. Total fertility rate or TFR is a measure that indicates the number of children a woman who completed her fertile period would have across a lifetime given the birth rate prevailing in a particular year.

GUIDE TO FURTHER READING

The most recent and most up-to-date study of China's population policy is Thomas Scharping (2001) *Birth Control in China, 1949 to 1999*, Richmond, Surrey: Curzon Press. The first detailed discussion of the one child policy to be published in English was Croll, E., Davin, D. and Kane, P. (eds) (1985) *China's One Child Family Policy*, London: Macmillan. It contains much that is still relevant. Milwertz, C. (1997) *Accepting Population Control: Urban Women and the One-child Family Policy*, Richmond, Surrey: Curzon Press, discusses the way urban women and their families feel about the pressure to restrict their families. Coverage of other aspects of the policy will be found in articles on China's population policy regularly published in the journal *Population and Development Review*.

REFERENCES

Aird, John (1990) *Slaughter of the Innocents*, Washington: AEI Press.

Banister, Judith (1987) *China's Changing Population*, Stanford: Stanford University Press.

Brown, Lester (1995) *Who will Feed China: Wake-up Call for a Small Planet*, London: Earthscan.

Croll, E., Davin, D. and Kane, P. (eds) (1985) *China's One Child Family Policy*, London: Macmillan.

Davin, D. (1987) 'Gender and population in the People's Republic of China', in Haleh Afshar (ed.) *Women, State and Ideology: Studies from Africa and Asia*, London: Macmillan, pp. 111–29.

Davin, D. (1990a) 'Never mind if it's a girl, you can have another try: the modification of the one-child family policy and its implications for gender relations in rural areas', in Jorgen Delman, Clemens Stubbe Ostergaard and Flemming Christiansen (eds) *Remaking Peasant China: Problems of Rural Development and Institutions at the start of the 1990s*, Aarhus: Aarhus University Press, pp. 81–91.

Davin, D. (1990b) 'The early childhood education of the only child generation in urban areas of mainland China', *Issues and Studies* 26 (4 April): 83–109.

Feeney, Griffith, Feng Wang, Mingkun Zhou and Baoyu Xiao (1989) 'Recent fertility dynamics in China', *Population and Development Review* 15(2 June): 297–322.

Feeney, Griffith and Wang Feng (1993) 'Parity progression and birth intervals in China: the influence of policy in hastening fertility decline', *Population and Development Review* 19(1): 61–100.

Greenhalgh, S. (1994) 'Controlling births and bodies in village China', *American Ethnologist* 21(1): 3–30.

Milwertz, C. (1997) *Accepting Population Control: Urban Women and the One-child Family Policy*, Richmond, Surrey: Curzon Press.

White, T. (1994) 'The origins of China's birth planning policy', in C.K. Gilmartin, G. Hershalter, L. Rofel and T. White (eds) *Engendering China: Women, Culture and the State*, Cambridge: Harvard UP, pp. 250–78.

Health and education

EDITORIAL INTRODUCTION

Should poor countries be concerned about the implications for human welfare when they cannot afford to provide health and educational needs and when their economic resources are heavily constrained? There are three reasons for concern. First, the basic health, nutritional and educational needs of the most vulnerable groups – the under-5s, pregnant women and nursing mothers – are urgent and compelling. If these are neglected, they can set back the health and welfare of the whole future generation of a country, in addition to adding to present human and economic miseries. Second, there is considerable evidence that there are positive economic returns to interventions supporting basic nutrition, health and education; and third, human welfare and progress is the ultimate end of all development policy.

Infectious diseases, many of which are relatively easy to cure, remain the major killers in low-income countries. Poverty is clearly connected with vulnerability to these infections, and under-nutrition is often a major contributing factor. Over the last two decades there has been great concern about the transmission of HIV/AIDS. It also raises serious problems with the prevalent approaches to primary healthcare. There are 880 million people worldwide who do not have access to health services.

The poor and the very young in low-income countries seem particularly vulnerable to disease and there is evidence to suggest that, in many countries, the position of women in society relative to that of men makes them more prone to disease. High fertility may indeed be advantageous to some women (despite the possible health risks) as a route to higher status, economic security or access to financial and other resources. Many of those concerned with women's reproductive health argue that family planning services should be available not for population control but for birth control, and only as part of comprehensive health and welfare provisions.

Adult literacy is a huge problem for human resource development; 880 million adults (aged 15 or over) worldwide are illiterate. Education greatly strengthens women's ability to perform their vital role in creating healthy households. Much emphasis has been placed on the role of female education in promoting good health. It increases their ability to benefit from health information and to make good use of health services; it increases their access to income and enables them to live healthier lives. Similarly, children out of school and in work should be targeted to secure long-term development goals. There are something like 100 million primary school-age children who are out of school.

8.1 Malnutrition and nutrition policies in developing countries

Prakash Shetty

INTRODUCTION

A critical examination of the global causes of mortality and morbidity indicates that malnutrition (and infectious diseases) continue to be significant contributors to the health burden in the developing world as we enter the new millennium. Despite reductions in the prevalence (per cent) of malnutrition, the numbers of individuals affected remain much the same or have even increased, largely the result of increases in the population in these countries. What is striking, however, is that the health burden due to non-communicable diseases such as heart disease and cancer is dramatically increasing in some of these developing countries with modest per capita GNPs, particularly those that appear to be in some stage of rapid developmental transition. It would appear that even the modest increases in prosperity that accompany economic development seem to be associated with marked increases in the mortality and morbidity attributable to these non-communicable diseases. These dramatic changes in the disease burden of the population are probably mediated by changes in the dietary patterns and lifestyles which typify the acquisition of an urbanized and affluent lifestyle. Countries in rapid developmental transition, like China, India and Brazil, seem to bear a 'double burden' of poverty and undernutrition coupled with problems acquired due to urbanization and affluence.

WHAT IS MALNUTRITION?

The term malnutrition refers to all deviations from adequate nutrition, including under- and over-nutrition, and encompass both inadequacy of food or excess of food relative to need. Undernutrition is defined as being the result of insufficient food caused primarily by an inadequate intake of dietary energy, whether or not any specific nutrient is an additional limiting factor. This emphasis on dietary energy as a general measure of food adequacy seems justified since an increase in food energy, if derived from normal staple foods, brings with it most other nutrients. Thus, in most situations, increased dietary energy is a necessary condition for nutritional improvement, even if it is not always sufficient in itself.

Malnutrition also encompasses specific deficiencies of essential nutrients such as vitamins and minerals. Thus malnutrition arises also from deficiencies of specific nutrients, or from diets based on wrong kinds or proportions of foods. Goitre, scurvy, anaemia and xerophthalmia are forms of malnutrition, caused by inadequate intake of iodine, vitamin C, iron and vitamin A respectively. Conditions such as obesity, though not the result of inadequacy of food, also constitute malnutrition. The terms 'malnutrition' and 'undernutrition' are often used loosely and interchangeably although a distinction exists and may need to be made.

Malnutrition refers to nutritional situations characteristic of relatively poorer socioeconomic populations of 'low-income' developing countries. Although it is possible to arrive at the prevalence (per cent) and the numbers of individuals within a population manifesting signs of specific nutrient deficiency, for instance anaemia as a result of iron deficiency, they are almost always associated with marginal or low food energy intakes. Thus the term 'malnutrition' is often used in the broader sense, referring to any physical condition implying ill-health or the inability to maintain adequate growth, appropriate body weight and to sustain acceptable levels of economically necessary and socially desirable physical activities brought about by an inadequacy in food – both quantity and quality.

THE CAUSES OF MALNUTRITION

To develop policies related to food and nutrition that affect the health of populations in developing countries, it is helpful to review the factors that determine malnutrition. The causes of malnutrition are multidimensional and its determinants include both food and non-food related factors, which often interact to form a complex web of biological, socioeconomic, cultural and environmental deprivations. Although establishing a relationship between these variables, and the indicators of malnutrition do not necessarily imply causality, they do demonstrate that in addition to food availability many social, cultural, health and environmental factors influence the prevalence of malnutrition. Although, in general, people suffering from inadequacy of food are poor, not all the poor are undernourished. Even in households that are food secure, some members may be undernourished. Income fluctuations, seasonal disparities in food availability and demand for high levels of physical activity, and proximity and access to marketing facilities may singly or in combination influence the nutritional status of an individual or a household. For example, the transition from subsistence farming to commercial agriculture and cash crops may help improve nutrition in the long run, however, they may result in negative impacts over the short term unless accompanied by improvements in access to health services, environmental sanitation and other social investments. Rapid urbanization and rural to urban migration may lead to nutritional deprivation of segments of society. Cultural attitudes reflected in food preferences and food preparation practices, and women's time constraints including that available for child-rearing practices, influence the nutrition of the most vulnerable in societies. Inadequate housing and over-crowding, poor sanitation and lack of access to a protected water supply, through their links with infectious diseases and infestations, are potent environmental factors that influence biological food utilization and nutrition. Inadequate access to food, limited access to healthcare and a clean environment and insufficient access to educational opportunities are in turn determined by the economic and institutional structures as well as the political and ideological superstructures within society.

Poor nutritional status of populations affects physical growth, intelligence, behaviour and learning abilities of children and adolescents. It impacts on their physical and work performance and has been linked to impaired economic work productivity during adulthood. Inadequate nutrition predisposes them to infections and contributes to the negative downward spiral of malnutrition and infection. Good nutritional status, on the other hand, promotes optimal growth and development of children and adolescents. It contributes to better physiological work performance, enhances adult economic productivity, increases levels of socially desirable activities and promotes better maternal birth outcomes. Good nutrition of a population manifested in the nutritional status of the individual in the community contributes to an upward positive spiral and reflects the improvement in the resources and human capital of society.

Economic growth and prosperity can also contribute to the problem of malnutrition in a population by creating conditions that are conducive to the development of chronic diseases of adulthood which include heart disease, diabetes and cancer. Urbanization, which characterizes economic development of developing societies, alters several environmental factors including the pattern of diet and changes in lifestyles of individuals. It is well recognized that economic prosperity helps attain adequacy of food in quantitative terms for much of the population. This improvement, however, is accompanied by a qualitative change in the diet with increased dietary energy being provided by fat in the daily diet replacing the carbohydrates from staples or cereals. There is an increase in the consumption of food from animal sources which has other ecological consequences. Consumption of salt and sugars also increases. Lifestyle changes, particularly with relation to the level of occupational and leisure time activities, also occurs, predisposing populations to an increasingly sedentary lifestyle which consequently leads to the occurrence of obesity. These developmental changes in largely rural societies break down social support systems and networks, favour inequalities in societies and increase stress levels of individuals. In addition the deterioration of the physical environment, particularly the increase in levels of environmental pollution, contributes to increase the health burden of societies in transition.

POLICIES AND PROGRAMMES TO PROMOTE GOOD NUTRITION IN DEVELOPING COUNTRIES

A recognition and proper understanding of the range, complexity and interplay of the factors that sustain the problem of malnutrition in developing societies is essential to help develop policies and programmes that meet the nutritional needs of the populations and to reduce the burden of malnutrition in these countries.

Improving household food security is one of the stated objectives of all democratic societies and constitutes an important element of the human rights to adequate food now endorsed by the international community. *Food security* is defined as the access by all people at all times to the food they need for an active and healthy life. The inclusion of the term household ensures that the dietary needs of all the members of the household are met throughout the year. The achievement of household food security requires an adequate supply of food to all members of the household, ensuring stability of supply all year round, and the access, both physical and economic, which underlines the importance of the entitlement to produce and procure food.

The pre-eminent determinant of household food insecurity is poverty in societies. Several policy measures undertaken by governments in developing countries are aimed at ensuring food supply and household food security. These include the following.

- Macroeconomic policies and economic development strategies that ensure both public-sector and private-sector investment in agriculture and food production.
- Appropriate policies to promote expansion and diversification of food availability and agricultural production in a stable and sustainable manner, and to regulate the import or export of foods and agricultural products to ensure food security.
- Policies that help create adequate employment opportunities for the rural poor and improving market efficiencies and opportunities.
- Policies that improve distribution and access to land, and to other resources such as credit, as well as other agricultural inputs.
- Legislating for policies that deter discrimination and ensure equal status for women, and ensuring their effective implementation.
- Identification of good and culturally appropriate caring practices and policies that protect, support and promote good care and nutrition practices for children.
- Policies that enable public health measures to reduce the burden of infectious diseases and to ensure access to primary healthcare.

Several programmes have been initiated in developing countries to improve the current situation with regard to nutrition of their population. These programmes have been aimed at the immediate or short-term amelioration of the nutritional situation. Strategies used include the following:

1 *Supplementation* of food or specific nutrients to meet the immediate deficits. Examples include food supplementation during acute food shortages such as famines or disasters and the mandatory provision of iron and folate supplements to all pregnant mothers attending ante-natal clinics in primary healthcare centres.

2 *Fortification* of food items in the daily diet is another successful strategy that has been adopted to deal with specific nutritional problems or nutrient deficiencies. A good example is the fortification of common salt with iodine (iodised salt) to tackle the problem of iodine deficiency and goitres; one of the most successful strategies that has helped reduce the burden of iodine deficiency disorders globally.

3 *Food-based approaches* include attempts to improve the nutrition of households by promoting kitchen gardens to enable families to produce and consume a diversified diet rich in vitamins. This has been promoted as a programme to reduce vitamin A deficiency in developing countries.

Preventing malnutrition is just as important as solving the problem, and both goals require the need to assess the severity of the problem as well as the ability to predict its occurrence to make prevention a realistic goal. *Nutritional surveillance* plays an important role in assembling information to assist the development of policy and programme decisions. Nutritional surveillance involves the regular and timely collection of nutrition-relevant data, as well as its analysis and dissemination. There are obvious advantages in the collection of nutrition-relevant information since the nutrition of a population is the outcome of social, economic and other factors, and is hence a good indicator of the overall development, and often a better indicator of the equitable development, of the society. Nutritional surveillance systems may vary depending on the immediate objective for which they have been set up and some developing countries have more than one system in place. National governments of developing countries are also involved in *improving food quality* and *ensuring food safety*. Most countries have legislation to help ensure safety and quality of foods from production to retail sale. They also have established institutions or ministries to oversee food safety and quality.

Economic growth and development should reduce the burden of undernutrition even if the reduction is slow and many people continue to suffer needlessly. There is thus a need for well-conceived policies for sustainable economic growth and social development that will benefit the poor and the undernourished. The deleterious consequences of rapid growth and development need to be guarded against and policies need to be in place to prevent one problem of malnutrition replacing another in these societies. Given the complexity of factors that determine malnutrition of all forms, it is important that appropriate food and agricultural policies are developed to ensure household food security and that nutritional objectives are incorporated into development policies and programmes at national and local levels in developing countries.

GUIDE TO FURTHER READING

ACC/SCN (2000) *Nutrition Through the Life Cycle*, Fourth Report on World Nutrition Situation, Geneva: UN Sub-Committee on Nutrition.

Berg, A. (1987) *Malnutrition: What Can be Done?*, Baltimore: Johns Hopkins University Press.

Brun, T.A. and Latham, M.C. (1990) *Maldevelopment and Malnutrition*, World Food Issues 2. Ithica: Cornell University.

FAO (1993) *Developing National Plan of Actions for Nutrition*, Rome: Food and Agriculture Organization.

Gopalan, C. (1992) *Nutrition in Developmental Transition in South-East Asia*, New Delhi: World Health Organization, SEARO.

Gopalan, C. and Kaur, H. (1993) *Towards Better Nutrition: Problems and Policies*, New Delhi: Nutrition Foundation of India.

Latham, M.C. (1997) *Human Nutrition in the Developing World*, Rome: Food and Agriculture Organization.

World Bank (1994) *Enriching Lives: Overcoming Vitamin and Mineral Malnutrition in Developing Countries*, Washington DC: World Bank.

8.2 Quality of maternal healthcare and development

Maya Unnithan-Kumar

Most developing countries in South Asia and sub-Saharan Africa are typical of high-mortality settings which in particular are related to maternal and infant deaths.[1] While maternal mortality is perhaps the most visible manifestation of the ill-health of women, it is maternal morbidity (the reproductive ailments which can translate into life-threatening conditions) which is a better indicator of the widespread and deep-rooted nature of the risks associated with motherhood. Poverty and the poor quality of the public health services are some of the main factors contributing to maternal morbidity in developing countries. An obvious means of enhancing the quality of services is to focus on the building up of the infrastructure (equipment, personnel) of the health delivery system. Such an approach has been limited especially where it has been guided by the demographically driven objectives of population planning.

The recent 'quality of care' approach has arisen from the need to approach the issue of health service delivery through the experiences and life circumstances of the users rather than in terms of the objectives of the population planners. In the area of maternal health the quality of care has been defined as 'the degree to which maternal health services for individuals and populations increase the likelihood of timely and appropriate treatment for the purpose of achieving desired outcomes that are both consistent with current professional knowledge and uphold basic reproductive rights' (Hulton *et al.*, 1999: 4).[2] When applied to maternal health services, the quality approach takes as its starting point the idea that all pregnant women, not just those who experience problems during pregnancy (the focus of previous healthcare programmes), are at risk of obstetric complications as, in reality, there are few indicators or predictors of the actual risks involved in childbirthing.

WHEN MOTHERHOOD IS UNSAFE

Six months previous to writing this article, Munga lived in a village on the outskirts of Jaipur, the capital city of Rajasthan in N.W. India. She was 20 years old and expecting her third child. She already had a daughter and a son. When her labour pains started, she called for Samina (her father's younger brother's wife) and Munaan, an elderly relative, both known in the local area for their expertise in birthing babies. A boy was born at 6 p.m. that day. Samina and Munaan left shortly after this. Munga continued to bleed profusely and twice vomited the milk she was given to drink. Some six hours later she was dead.

Why did Munga die? It could have been for any one, or all, of the following reasons. Munga's parents were poor, she had little nutrition as a child and later suffered from tuberculosis. When she married, her husband earned enough but never gave her any money. As a result, she could not afford to pay for doctors or medicines, or for transport to the government centres which were far away and, in any case, it was uncertain that the doctors would be there. She relied on the local midwives. The midwives, competent in delivering normal babies, were anxious as Munga was weak and could not push hard enough during her contractions. They exerted abdominal pressure during the last stages of her labour contractions (a risky procedure because of the danger of rupture to the uterus). Munga also received an injection by a local doctor to speed up her labour (the unassessed provision of intramuscular oxytocin also greatly enhances the risk of rupture to the uterus).

Munga, like a number of other young women in her village was at risk in becoming a mother. With their negligible resort to contraception, motherhood for most of these women is simultaneous with their entry into the reproductive span of their life. This means that, for most of their child-bearing life, from menarche to the menopause, Munga and women like her are in continuous cycles of bearing, birthing and breastfeeding their children. Given the poverty-related nutritional deficiencies, scarcity of water for washing, and sheer physical work that frame the contexts of their continuous biological reproduction, it is not surprising that motherhood is a physically debilitating and unsafe period for rural and urban poor women.

High and closely spaced fertility along with poor nutrition and poor healthcare are the primary reasons for the high mortality and morbidity figures for women and children in India (Jejeebhoy and Rama Rao, 1998). The risks associated with closely spaced deliveries and an early initiation into child-bearing are also among the factors identified in East Africa where mothers with inter-pregnancy intervals of less than a year, or aged either below 15 years (at the birth of their first child) or above 35 years (in their seventh or eighth pregnancy) were regarded as at high risk (McDonagh, 1996). As a result, some of the important effective interventions which address the risks associated with motherhood are considered to be the distribution of contraceptives to space out pregnancies and the provision of iron, folate and malarial prophylaxes to strengthen women. However, empirical observations of health-seeking behaviour show that the provision of contraceptive devices and nutritional supplements will not in themselves ensure a reduction in maternal morbidity. There are both cultural reasons for this (gender ideologies make it difficult to discuss sexual matters across the sexes; the cultural expectations and value placed on women's reproduction make child-bearing a social imperative; women's subservience to men in decisions relating to child-bearing) as well as physiological reasons (the low-cost contraceptive technologies available are not sustainable by weak, anaemic and nutritionally deficient women). Moreover, the supply of contraceptives is misplaced as it ignores the local demand for reducing high levels of reproductive tract infections and the resulting secondary infertility. This disjunction between the nature of the supply and the kinds of demand for maternal healthcare is reflected in the local perceptions of the health services as being of poor quality.

ENHANCING THE QUALITY OF MATERNAL HEALTH SERVICES

The provision of a high quality of maternal healthcare is related to an understanding of what constitutes good quality of care, on the one hand, and a commitment on the part of the state to invest resources towards this end. In their framework for assessing the delivery of institutional maternal care, Hulton *et al.* (1999) suggest two basic levels which must be addressed: first, the elements of the provision of care (such as the use and quality of the personnel employed and the infrastructure available to provide the essential obstetric care as laid down by WHO regulations, an efficient referral system, universal emergency provisioning and the use of appropriate technologies, and an awareness of internationally recognized good practice). And, second, the elements of the experience of care (dealing with the patients' cognition of the services, the respect received and emotional support during care).

In her review of the effectiveness of antenatal services in reducing maternal morbidity and mortality, McDonagh (1996) suggests there is more rather than less evidence to cast doubt on the positive effects of antenatal care where it exists. She finds the greatest impact made by antenatal care in places like Gambia, Lesotho and Tanzania, where a domiciliary midwifery service is supported by local efficient obstetric services. Such findings support my observations on antenatal care in rural India as well.

It is the trained auxilliary nurse midwife (ANM) who acts as the first point of professional contact for women with the public health sector in developing countries. The training in midwifery is critical in a situation such as that in rural India, where most births take place at home rather than in institutional settings. Yet, it is common to find that the ANM who is trained in delivering children is very rarely called upon to do so. When her assistance is sought, it is in emergency situations which she has neither the qualifications nor the authority to handle on her own. As most women and families only seek institutional assistance in crisis conditions and there is no culture of antenatal check-ups, the inability of ANMs to deal with emergencies immediately curtails their importance as health providers in local perceptions.

As the ANMs are not trained or equipped to deal with obstetric complications, it becomes vital for the routes of referral through the system to the appropriate institution to be efficient and failsafe to ensure the quality of health service provisioning. Referral services are of particular importance in child delivery complications as these are usually emergency cases with late presentation. Little cognisance has been taken of the vital significance of providing good referral services in health planning circles, mainly because there has been a focus on increasing the infrastructural facilities available as compared to the other elements of the quality of care approach, and because little attention has been paid to the functioning of the maternal health services as a whole. In the absence of good and timely referral services, as I have argued elsewhere (Unnithan-Kumar, 2001), it may be more appropriate to provide gynaecological expertise for women at their first point of institutional contact in health matters, either by upgrading the skills and qualifications of the ANMs or providing them with the necessary technical expertise to consult in emergencies near at hand. This would allow for obstetric and gynaecological professional care to be provided at the level of the sub-centre itself, where emergency care is most needed. The recent experiences of the few NGOs providing healthcare services, such as SEARCH in Maharashtra, who train local midwives and also provide local gynaecological expertise, has proved to be very effective (Mavlankar *et al.*, 1999).

The quality of public health service provision is significantly linked to the state financial allocations for the health sector. The economic reforms brought in by structural adjustment programmes have often led to a constriction in public spending on health. In India, it is noted, there has been a deceleration in the real per capita revenue and capital expenditure on health since the mid-1980s (Seeta Prabhu, 1999),[3] which is a trend in accordance with the World Bank's recommendations to confine the role of the public sector to providing preventive rather than curative health services. Given the recent constraints in public spending on health, it is unlikely that there will be any change in the quality of maternal services provided in countries like India. This is unfortunate as I believe the problem of the unsafe initiation of poor women into motherhood in Rajasthan is not because they desire domestic rather than institutional antenatal care;[4] rather they are caught in a bind, between the poor quality of public health service delivery on the one hand, and the lack of indigenous expertise to cope with obstetric complications on the other. The most effective solution seems to lie in the provision of locally trained midwives working alongside gynaecological experts. In the absence of appropriate antenatal expertise at the local level of the health service structure, and where there exist exacting cultural expectations which devalue the health risks of motherhood, the reproductive phase will continue to be a period in which poor women in developing countries face high health risks.

NOTES

1. Maternal mortality is generally estimated as 500,000 maternal deaths each year, of which 99 per cent occur in developing countries (Royston and Armstrong in Jejeebhoy and Rama Rao, 1998).
2. In the area of maternal health, the quality of care approach is influenced by the concept of reproductive health, which, following the International Conference on Population and Development in Cairo in 1994, emphasizes the provision of safe and consumer-driven services.
3. From 1989 to 1995, the Union government's revenue expenditure on the social sector, which includes expenditure on medical, public health and family welfare, fell from 3.04 per cent of the total revenue expenditure to 3.01 per cent of the same (Seeta Prabhu, 1999: 121).
4. The preference for home deliveries is an often cited argument which traces the problem of the poor access to health services to 'traditional' patterns of health-seeking behaviour rather than to the poor quality of services. On the contrary, I argue that a traditional resort to home births is more a result of an unequal access to health services as well as the poor nature of the services.

GUIDE TO FURTHER READING

Government of India (1995) *National Family Health Survey (NFHS), India: 1992–93*, Bombay: International Institute for Population Sciences.

McDonagh, M. (1996) 'Is antenatal care effective in reducing maternal morbidity and mortality?', *Health, Policy and Planning* 11(1): 1–15, Oxford: Oxford University Press.

Patel, T. (1994) *Fertility Behaviour: Population and Society in Rajasthan*. Delhi: Oxford University Press.

Rao, M. (ed.) (1999) *Disinvesting in Health: The World Bank's Prescriptions for Health*, New Delhi: Sage.

Thaddeus, S. and Maine, D. (1994) 'Too far to walk: maternal mortality in context', in *Social Science and Medicine* 38(8): 1091–110.

Unnithan-Kumar, M. (1999) 'Households, kinship and access to reproductive healthcare among rural Muslim women in Jaipur', in, *Economic and Political Weekly*, Vol xxxiv, Nos 10, 11 (March 6–13), pp. 621–30.

Unnithan-Kumar, M. (2000) 'On the empowerment of midwives in Rajasthan: implications for healthcare policy', *Economic and Political Weekly*, Bombay: Hitkari house (in press).

REFERENCES

Hulton, L., Matthews, Z. and Stones, R. (1999) *A Framework for the Evaluation of the Quality of Care in Maternity Services*. University of Southampton: Department of Social Statistics.

Jejeebhoy, S. and Rama Rao, S. (1998) 'Unsafe motherhood: a review of reproductive health', in M. Dasgupta, L. Chen and T.N. Krishnan (eds) *Women's Health in India: Risk and Vulnerability*, Oxford: Oxford University Press.

Mavlankar, D., Bang, A. and Bang, R. (1999) 'Quality reproductive health services in rural india: the SEARCH experience', in *Services on Upscaling Innovations in Reproductive Health in Asia* 2, India: Selangor; Malaysia: International Council on the Management of Population Programmes.

Seeta Prabhu, K. (1999) 'Structural adjustment and the health sector in India', in Mohan Rao (ed.), *Disinvesting in Health,* New Delhi: Sage, pp. 120–9.

Unnithan-Kumar, M. (2001) *Traditional Healers and Reproductive Health Services in NW India* (under review), Reproductive Health Matters, London: Blackwell.

8.3 The social and economic impact of HIV/AIDS on development

Tony Barnett

HIV AND AIDS

HIV (Human Immunodeficiency Virus) causes a breakdown of the human body's ability to defend itself against infections and other diseases. The process of immune system failure can take several years. When the immune system no longer functions effectively, a person's health fails with a characteristic range of opportunistic infections finally overwhelming the system. This is called AIDS (Acquired Immunodeficiency Syndrome). Infection with HIV may occur through human body fluids – blood, semen, vaginal secretions and breast milk. Most people who catch HIV do so through sexual intercourse. When people's health is poor to begin with, the chances of infection increase. This is often the case with poor people who do not have access to medical care, who are likely to live in unhealthy conditions and/or do dangerous or unhealthy work. Where people's poor health status includes untreated or partially treated sexually transmitted infections, such as genital warts, genital herpes or any of a range of common sexually transmitted infections, the chance of contracting HIV from an infected partner increase dramatically.

Without expensive drug treatments (Anti-Retroviral Therapy (ART) or Highly Active Anti-Retroviral Therapy (HAART)) which are available to many people with HIV infection and AIDS in richer communities, the end result of HIV infection is death from AIDS. In poor communities a typical period from initial infection to death is between six and eight years. Initial infection results in a mild flu-like illness and the person soon recovers. During the intervening period – which may last several years, they may lead a normal life and be completely unaware of their status. They are infectious during this period and so each person may infect each of his/her sexual partners.

Because this disease is mainly sexually transmitted, it has very important social and economic implications for development. It affects the structure of populations and therefore the supply and quality of labour.

HIV/AIDS – THE GLOBAL SITUATION

Table 1 summarizes the global HIV/AIDS situation as at the end of 1999. In 1999, there were about 15,000 new HIV infections per day. Of these more than 95 per cent are in developing

Table 1 Global HIV/AIDS estimates at the end of 1999: children and adults

People living with HIV/AIDS	34.3 million
New HIV infections in 1999	5.4 million
Deaths due to HIV/AIDS in 1999	2.8 million
Cumulative number of deaths due to HIV/AIDS	18.8 million

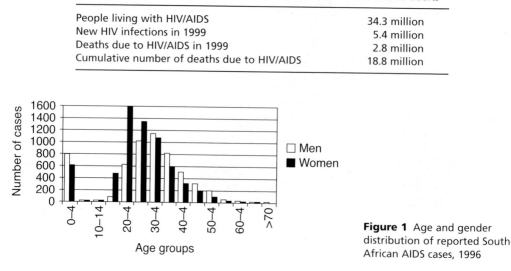

Figure 1 Age and gender distribution of reported South African AIDS cases, 1996

countries. It is also noteworthy that 1,700 are in children under 15 years of age – some of these infections are sexually transmitted while others are transmitted from mother to child during birth or through breast milk. However, of the 15,000 new infections each day, about 13,000 are in persons aged 15 to 49 years, of whom almost 50 per cent are women and about 50 per cent are 15–24 year olds. Figure 1 shows the typical distribution of HIV infection by age and gender in South Africa in the mid-1990s. This distribution can now be seen in many other countries in Africa and elsewhere.

HIV/AIDS AND POPULATION

The most seriously affected areas of the world are in Africa. It is quite possible that some countries and regions in South Asia, Southeast Asia and China will follow this pattern in the next decade. The source for this section and much that follows is UNAIDS (2000).

In the hardest-hit countries, AIDS is altering population structures in ways not seen before. Because it is mainly sexually transmitted, HIV/AIDS picks off society's young adults.

- Since the epidemic began, over 18 million lives have been claimed globally by AIDS. The majority, about 15 million, have been in sub-Saharan Africa. These numbers can be expected to double over the next decade because it is estimated that 34 million people are now living with HIV or AIDS, and that about 5 million new infections can be expected to occur annually.
- AIDS deaths are *premature deaths*. In developing countries where HIV spreads mainly through unsafe sex between men and women, the majority of infected people acquire HIV by the time they are in their 20s and 30s. On average they can be expected to die of AIDS within 10 years of initial infection.
- In sub-Saharan African countries, where such large proportions of the population have HIV or have already died of AIDS, these premature deaths are radically altering the structure of the population.
- HIV will kill at least a third of the young men and women of countries where it has its firmest hold and in some places up to two-thirds.

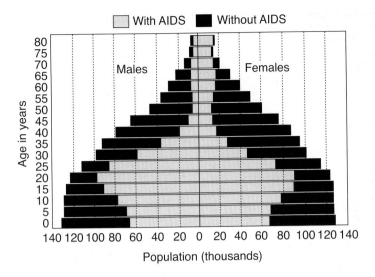

Figure 2 Projected population structure with and without the AIDS epidemic, Botswana, 2020

Source: US Census Bureau, *World Population Profile, 2000*

THE POPULATION CHIMNEY

It has been traditional to describe the population structure of 'developing countries' as approximating a pyramid. Because life expectancy has tended to be low and birth rates high, the youngest age groups of the population – babies, children and healthy young people up to 19 – form the broad base of the pyramid, which then tapers up gradually through the older age groups, which have begun shrinking through illness and death.

The US Census Bureau has suggested that there is now a completely new shape – the 'population chimney'. This was seen in early studies of impact (see Barnett and Blaikie, 1992: 36) and is now confirmed by national projections of, for example, Botswana in 2020. Compared with the population structure that Botswana would have in the absence of an AIDS epidemic, the base is less broad. Many HIV-infected women die or become infertile long before the end of their childbearing years, so fewer babies will be born. Up to a third of the infants born to HIV-positive women become infected themselves before or during birth, or through breast milk. Hence, fewer babies survive to childhood and adolescence.

The most dramatic change in the pyramid occurs at the ages when young adults infected early in their sex lives begin to die of AIDS. In sub-Saharan Africa, young women are typically two or three times more likely to have become infected by age 24 than young men. Thus, starting with women in their mid-20s and men in their mid-30s, the adult population shrinks radically. Only those adults who escape HIV infection can survive to middle and old age. In 2020, Botswana is expected to have more women in their 60s and 70s than women in their 40s and 50s.

The chimney (Figure 2) shows the predicted dramatic impact of AIDS on the structure of the population of Botswana, where over a third of the 775,000 adults are currently estimated to be infected with HIV.

AIDS AND DEVELOPMENT

The implications of the preceding sections is that, in the absence of effective and available vaccines or economically feasible and effective treatments, AIDS may be expected to wipe out half a century of development gains as measured by life expectancy at birth. From 44 years in the early 1950s, life expectancy rose to 59 in the early 1990s. Now, a child born between 2005 and 2010 can once again expect to die before his or her 45th birthday. Analysts have looked at the prospective risk of dying of AIDS that today's 15-year-olds will face throughout their lifetime (see data from Baba, 2000: 36). The analyses are based on the assumption that, in each country studied, AIDS prevention programmes will be successful enough to cut in half the risk of becoming HIV-infected over the next 15 years. They do not take into account possible improvements in treatment or the availability of an HIV vaccine. According to these conservative analyses, in countries where 15 per cent of adults are currently infected, around a third of today's 15-year-olds will die of AIDS. Where adult prevalence rates exceed 15 per cent, the lifetime risk of dying of AIDS is much greater. Hence, in countries such as South Africa and Zimbabwe, where a fifth or a quarter of the adult population is infected, AIDS is set to claim the lives of around half of all 15-year-olds. In Botswana, where about one in three adults is already HIV-infected – the highest prevalence rate in the world – it is estimated that two-thirds of today's 15-year-old boys will die prematurely of AIDS.

Life expectancy and child mortality rates have been widely used as markers for development. In Botswana, life expectancy at birth is now estimated to be 39 years instead of 71 without AIDS. In Latin America and the Caribbean, the impact on life expectancy is not as great as in sub-Saharan Africa because of lower HIV prevalence levels. However, they are still lower than they would have been without AIDS. In the Bahamas, life expectancy at birth is now 71 years instead of 80. In Haiti, life expectancy is now 49 instead of 57. Asia, Thailand, Cambodia and Myanmar have lost three years of life expectancy.

The impact on child mortality is highest in countries which had significantly reduced child mortality due to other causes and where HIV prevalence is now high. Many HIV-infected children survive their first birthdays, only to die before the age of 5. In Zimbabwe, 70 per cent of all deaths among children under 5 are due to AIDS. In South Africa that percentage is 45. In the Bahamas, 60 per cent of deaths among children under 5 are due to AIDS. In Myanmar, Cambodia and Thailand, 1 per cent of deaths among children are due to AIDS. Due to these substantial increases in child mortality, only 5 out of 51 countries in sub-Saharan Africa will reach the International Conference on Population and Development (ICPD) goals for decreased child mortality.

WIDER DEVELOPMENT IMPACTS

The premature death of half of the adult population, typically at ages when they have already started to form their own families and have become economically productive, can be expected to have a radical effect on virtually every aspect of social and economic life. While it is difficult to measure the precise impact of HIV at a national level in most hard-hit countries, a great deal of information exists about how the epidemic is affecting everything from households to the public and private sector of the economy. The impacts on households, education, agriculture, health and the conducts of business will be severe.

CONCLUSION

HIV/AIDS presents a wide range of development challenges. There is no area of development policy which can omit to take HIV/AIDS into account. It will affect industrial production, agriculture, mining and, above all, households in poor countries. Inasmuch as households are essential to social and cultural reproduction but their contributions are not measured in official statistics, it is inevitable that the full social and economic impact of HIV/AIDS will go unnoticed until the effects are already very large.

GUIDE TO FURTHER READING

For those who want information about HIV/AIDS and health and welfare matters, there are few better points of departure than Alcorn, K. (ed.) (1999) *AIDS Reference Manual*, available from NAM Publications, 16a Clapham Common Southside, London SW4 7AB. This is published annually in an updated form.

An excellent general survey of the global situation in relation to many aspects of HIV/AIDS, from bio-medical through clinical to public health, social, and economic and legal aspects, is contained in Mann, J. and Tarantola, D. (eds) (1996) *AIDS in the World II: Global Dimensions, Social Roots and Responses*, New York and Oxford: Oxford University Press.

The World Bank has been concerned about the social and economic implications of HIV/AIDS for many years and has now published a wide-ranging review of the health economic, health system and public policy issues in World Bank (1997 and 1998) *Confronting AIDS: Public Priorities in a Global Epidemic*, New York and Oxford: Oxford University Press for the World Bank.

A useful source of up-to-date information about the state of the epidemic globally and in particular regions and countries is the internet site of UNAIDS. The URL is: http://www.unaids.org/. In addition, the United States Census Bureau is also a source of information on rates of infection and illness in countries other than the US. The address of its internet site is: http://www.census.gov/.

Early but still useful discussion of the macroeconomic impact of HIV/AIDS is to be found in Over, M. (1992) *The Macroeconomic Impact of AIDS in Sub-Saharan Africa*, Technical Working Paper No. 3 (June), Washington: World Bank, Population, Health and Nutrition Division, Africa Technical Department.

An early case study of the impact of HIV/AIDS on communities in Africa is to be found in Barnett, T. and Blaikie, P. (1992 and 1994) *AIDS in Africa: Its Present and Future Impact*, London: Belhaven Press.

On the implications of HIV/AIDS for South Africa, see Whiteside, A. and Sunter, C. (2000) *AIDS: The Challenge for South Africa*, Capetown, South Africa: Human and Rousseau Tafelberg.

REFERENCES

Baba, Z. (2000) *Report on the Global HIV/AIDS Epidemic*, Geneva: UNAIDS.

Barnett, T. and Blaikie, P. (1992) *AIDS in Africa: Its Present and Future Impact*, London: Belhaven Press.

The Status and Trends of the HIV/AIDS Epidemics in the World, Provisional Report, 5–7 July 2000 – this report is available through the following websites: Family Health International http://www.fhi.org, Francois-Xavier Bagnoud Center for Health and Human Rights http://www.hri.ca.partners/fxbcenter.

UNAIDS (2000) *Report on the Global HIV/AIDS Epidemic*, June 2000, Geneva: UNAIDS. This is available from the UNAIDS website http://www.unaids.org.

US Census Bureau http://www.census.gov/ipc. In addition, these sites are excellent sources of information about HIV/AIDS and development in general. An additional source is the website of the World Bank http://www.worldbank.org and, on that site, the section featuring the International AIDS and Economics Network.

8.4 **Managing health and disease in developing countries**

Stephen J. Connor

Despite calls for 'Health for All by the Year 2000' (WHO, 1978) the new millennium sees many of the world's poorer communities suffering health status decline. The reasons for this are many-faceted and contextually diverse. To understand this situation it is useful to begin with a few basic questions. What is health? How is it measured? What are the major health problems? Who is responsible for healthcare provision? Why isn't it provided adequately? Here differing definitions of health, some aspects of ill-health and development, and a focus on one particular health problem are used to explore some of the issues surrounding the management of disease in developing countries.

DEFINING HEALTH

While health is an integral component of development (Sen, 1999) it is a condition which is beguilingly difficult to define (Phillips and Verhasselt, 1994). The 'medical model' views health as 'the absence of disease'. Attempts to include a more human-ecological approach are apparent in disease ecology (Learmonth, 1988) and public health (Turshen, 1989). Recognition of health as a broad social construct is reflected in WHO's definition: 'a state of complete physical, mental and social well-being and not merely the absence of disease or infirmity' (WHO, 1992). Health-care studies among rural communities support this broad perspective. Respondents in a study in Zaire included parents living, cultivated land and windows in their house within their definition of healthy. They included crime among health problems and social reconciliation as an intervention. These broad global and community definitions confirm health as an integral aspect of development, and demonstrate the significance of development as a major public health issue.

HEALTH PROBLEMS IN DEVELOPING COUNTRIES

Clearly one would expect health problems facing rural communities in Africa to be different from those facing urban populations in Europe. One aid to understanding these differences is the 'epidemiological transition' which links changing disease patterns over time with changes in the social, economic, demographic and ecological conditions prevailing. For example: first phase – subsistence agriculture, high fertility, high infant death rate, low life expectancy, infectious disease and periodic famine are the main causes of death; second phase – gradual improvements in agriculture, nutrition and sanitation reduce crude death rate; third phase – intensive agriculture/industrialization, lower fertility, longer life expectancy, non-communicable degenerative diseases become the main cause of death. This theoretical 'one-way' process has clear parallels with the modernization theories of development and the demographic transition. The model is based on historical assessment of 200 years in Europe and the USA (Omran, 1971). Japan, Taiwan and the Eastern European countries underwent the transition more quickly, while the latter (Eastern Europe) challenges the one-way nature of the process.

Diseases affecting the elderly may be less of a constraint to development prospects than those of the young and middle years. However, beyond such a generalization we ought not to lose sight of the fact that health problems are not homogenous in any country, at any time, regardless of its stage of development, and disparities occur with social class, gender and region; with the poorest at greatest risk (Phillips and Verhasselt, 1994).

RESPONSIBILITY FOR HEALTHCARE

That each individual has a basic responsibility to value their own health may be unequivocal. Beyond that, responsibilities for health become more complex and may include employers, family, health workers, hospitals, insurers, local or national government, international legislative/advisory bodies, etc. Likewise, there is the equally complex issue of cost of healthcare provision. Is an individual's health something they alone benefit from, and should pay for, or is there a wider community benefit? Where are the community boundaries? Communicable, or infectious, diseases clearly pose a threat to others. Malaria, one example of a communicable disease, may serve as a focus to explore these issues further.

MALARIA AS A 'GLOBAL' HEALTH PROBLEM

Malaria is considered a 'tropical disease', i.e. geographically determined. This is not strictly accurate; malaria has occurred close to the Arctic Circle, and poverty and social conditions play an important role in the distribution and persistence of the disease. Currently it is in the countries of Africa that malaria poses the greatest public health problem, accounting for 80 per cent of the world's malaria and 90 per cent of its estimated 1.7–3.4 million deaths annually (WHO, 1993).

Malaria results from a complex interaction between parasite, the mosquito vector, its human host, and the broader environment (social and ecological). Control may focus on any, or all, of these components. In 1948 the World Health Organization was established and malaria quickly became its highest priority.

1   The global malaria control strategy, 1946–1954

The world had seen the mobilization of huge forces during the Second World War and it was felt that concerted efforts could now be made, as a major international humanitarian initiative, against one of the world's major public health problems. Intervention relied primarily on spraying the interior walls of dwellings with DDT to kill resting mosquito vectors, any malaria cases were treated with Chloroquine to reduce the parasite pool. In the USA, Europe, North Africa and the Middle East malaria control campaigns were so successful that global eradication was seen as a realistic possibility.

2   The global malaria eradication campaign, 1955–1969

Fears over growing resistance to these cheap and effective control tools and the costs of maintaining recurrent control measures spurred the drive for eradication. While eradication in the developed nations of Europe and the USA was expected, India and Ceylon looked as if they, too, might succeed (Kondrachine and Trigg, 1997). In India prevalence levels of 70 million per year declined by 1967 to about 100,000 cases (Learmonth, 1988).

Eradication efforts did not include most sub-Saharan African (SSA) countries. There were two basic schools of thought on control in SSA. The interventionists with their strong commitment to eradication were convinced of the need to vanquish malaria from every continent (Macdonald,

1951). The conservationists argued that the equilibrium reached between humans and parasites under intense malaria transmission offered a high degree of adult protection and should not be interfered with (Wilson *et al.*, 1950). Ultimately vector control campaigns were not considered feasible in SSA, due to the technical difficulties of intense malaria transmission, requiring extensive control efforts in countries which had very limited health infrastructure (Bradley, 1992). However, Ethiopia, South Africa and the former Rhodesia did carry out effective malaria control campaigns. Major research experiments which included vector control in Kenya, Tanzania, and Nigeria also produced significant reductions in infant and child mortality.

During the later part of this phase the considerable gains made began to lose ground. Donors saw that eradication was going to be a long process. While prepared to invest significant funding for limited-term intervention, they were reluctant to maintain recurrent vector control operations. They argued that further improvement in the malaria situation could only be achieved through greater national commitment and improved public health infrastructure. In recognition of this, the devastating epidemics in Sri Lanka during 1968 and the widescale re-emergence of malaria in Asia, the 1969 World Health Assembly radically re-examined the malaria eradication strategy. This was followed by an immediate reduction in bilateral and international financial support to anti-malarial campaigns.

3   Malaria control with the ultimate goal of eradication, 1969–1978

During this period the capability of many endemic countries to continue anti-malarial operations, especially those involving vector control, were further reduced and many countries, including India, experienced a dramatic resurgence of malaria. While anti-malarial programmes were in decline the efforts to establish basic healthcare services in the more peripheral areas of endemic countries met with little success. Extensive resurgence of malaria in South Asia and Latin America led to calls to develop malaria control programmes appropriate to the infrastructure existing in endemic countries.

4   Malaria control as part of primary healthcare (after 1978)

This approach was formulated at Alma-Ata in Russia in September 1978. It centred on an actively participating community working closely with health services. Its aims were to ensure that malaria control activities would be integrated into the priority setting of the general health services, to reflect the prevailing infrastructure and level of service delivery possible, and to be able to maintain the gains achieved. It was argued that the fundamental element of the new approach reflected recognition of the variability of epidemiological situations, the feasibility of their modification and the availability of resources.

A decade after Alma-Ata, progress towards 'Health for All by the Year 2000' remained slow and disappointing. Only China had made significant inroads against malaria, elsewhere the situation was stagnant or deteriorating, especially in sub-Saharan Africa (Kondrachine and Trigg, 1997). Financial resources available to healthcare in developing countries continued to decline. To support primary healthcare provision UNICEF launched the 'Bamako Initiative' in 1987 to encourage financing through cost recovery. In many countries malaria control had been carried out as a public health measure; people were now expected to meet the cost of treatment themselves. By the end of the 1980s the global malaria control strategy was in crisis.

THE PHOENIX RISING

In view of the increasing prominence of malaria as a major public health problem, the Executive Board of WHO and the World Health Assembly adopted resolutions in 1989 asserting that control of malaria must again become a global priority. Malaria was seen as an excessive drain on limited health resources, a major constraint on child survival programmes, and maintained poverty through low productivity and impaired economic growth. International meetings in Brazzaville, New Delhi and Brasilia during 1991 and 1992, followed by consultation with experts at national and regional levels, led to the formulation of a new strategy which was adopted by the Ministerial Conference on Malaria in October 1992. The *New* Global Malaria Control Strategy recognizes that malaria has no single formula for its control, but is a disease of differing epidemiological types determined by a diversity of social, ecological and economic settings.

Strong political support for concerted action against malaria, especially in Africa, grew throughout the 1990s. In 1996 an Accelerated Strategy for Malaria Control in the Africa Region was approved by WHO and in 1997 the Meeting of Heads of State of the Organization of African Unity made its declaration on malaria control. Further international support came in 1997 with the Multilateral Initiative on Malaria and in 1998 with the 'Roll Back Malaria' Global Partnership, which includes the United Nations Development Programme and the World Bank. Roll Back Malaria aims to identify stakeholders, consolidate research and deliver concerted support to malaria control through strengthened health systems development. It aims to draw more commitment from the private sector in a drive for new control tools through its Medicines for Malaria Venture, and the Malaria Vaccine Fund which is supported by the Bill and Melinda Gates Foundation.

THE CHALLENGE FOR THE FUTURE

The malaria parasite respects few boundaries, and with increased international mobility comes an increased threat to all. The new momentum for tackling malaria comes at a time when the old control tools have lost much of their acceptability and effectiveness. There is pressure for a worldwide ban on DDT, and Chloroquine resistance is now so widespread as to make the drug virtually useless. Hopes for an effective vaccine remain just that. However, there are promising new treatments and preventative measures in the Chinese herbal derivative Artemether and the insecticide-treated 'bednet'. The latter is seen as an appropriate tool for many rural African situations and widespread trials have shown it to be very effective in reducing malaria mortality (Lengeler and Snow, 1996).

Recent macroeconomic analysis of the burden of malaria suggests a loss of GDP to sub-Saharan African countries of between US$3–12 billion per year due to malaria and argues that the required financial inputs into malaria control would pay for themselves many times over. Through Roll Back Malaria calls have been made for commitments of at least US$1 billion per year (at the time of writing pledges received total US$750 million) and commitments have been made to ensure that within 5 years every African child should sleep under the protection of a treated bednet.

Though this brief discourse we have seen perspectives of the malaria problem and responsibilities for its control shift from that of a global problem, to a national health problem, a community problem, an individual's problem and finally a regionalized health issue, involving multiple stakeholders recognizing common interests and requiring concerted action at all levels. The political will to tackle malaria is more promising than it has been at any time since the mid-1960s. Malaria is curable and preventable, and an estimated one-third of the world's population, living in previously malarious regions, are now free from the disease. The challenge to health and development agencies remains to extend this achievement to the poorer countries of the world.

GUIDE TO FURTHER READING

Phillips, D. and Verhasselt, Y. (1994) *Health and Development*, London: Routledge.
WHO (1992) *Our Planet, Our Health: Report of the WHO Commission on Health and Environment*, Geneva: World Health Organization.
Learmonth, A. (1988) *Disease Ecology*, Oxford: Basil Blackwell.
Turshen, M. (1989) *The Politics of Public Health*, London: Zed Books.
Desowitz, R.S. (1991) *The Malaria Capers*, London: W.W. Norton.

REFERENCES

Bradley, D.J. (1992) 'Malaria: old infections, changing epidemiology', *Health Transition Review* 2: 137–53.
Kondrachine, A. and Trigg, P.I. (1997) 'Control of malaria in the world', *Indian Journal of Malariology* 34: 92–110.
Lengeler, C. and Snow, R.W. (1996) 'From efficacy to effectiveness: insecticide-treated bednets in Africa', *Bulletin of the World Health Organization* 74: 325–32.
Macdonald, G. (1951) 'Community aspects of immunity to malaria', *British Medical Bulletin* 8: 33–6.
Omran, A.R. (1971) 'The epidemiologic transition: a theory of the epidemiology of population change', *Milbank Memorial Fund Quarterly* 4: 509–38.
Sen, A. (1999) 'Health in development', *Bulletin of the World Health Organization* 77: 619–23.
WHO (1978) *Alma-Ata 1978: Primary Health Care*, Report of the International Conference on Primary Health Care (Alma-Ata, USSR, 6–12 September), Geneva: WHO.
WHO (1993) *A Global Strategy for Malaria Control*, Geneva: WHO.
Wilson, D.B., Granham, P.C.C. and Swellengrebel, N.H. (1950) 'A review of hyperendemic malaria', *Tropical Diseases Bulletin* 47: 677–98.

8.5 Children's work and schooling: a review of the debates

Ramya Subrahmanian

INTRODUCTION

The elimination of child labour is an intrinsic component of discussions on both globalization and international trade, and on the challenges of universalizing elementary education. With large numbers of children out of school, the spotlight is being placed increasingly on the wide range of activities that children undertake, paid or unpaid, compelled or chosen. While children out of school and in work are the target group for effective policy intervention, there is much ethical and economic wrangling over the extent and nature of child labour, the quality of schooling in developing countries, and the economic factors that continue to encourage child labour rather than curb it. This chapter will sketch the debates, disputes and complexity of the child rights agenda,[1] with a view to encapsulating the multiple policy agendas to which these give rise.

Data reveal the complexities of defining children's work, and the political and ethical nuances of the approaches advocated to address the problem. Policy debates centre around the desirability of imposing bans on child labour, and the adequacy of such interventions where a relatively small proportion of working children are employed in trades and services where such bans can be enforced. International responses are deemed increasingly important in the fight for defending child rights universally across economically and culturally diverse societies, and particularly in the context of globalization where economic actions undertaken in one place have repercussions elsewhere. However, there is also caution expressed in different quarters in relation to the danger of universalizing a standardized conception of 'childhood'. Especially emphasized is the concern that in the search for a morally just solution to problems of endemic poverty and inequality, children's own agency and interpretations of household needs and their obligations may be lost, ultimately affecting possibilities for child-centered approaches to the achievement of their rights.

DEFINING THE POLICY TARGET GROUP

Estimating the number of children in work, and out of school yields the number of children who are deemed to be in need of policy intervention, although this is a task as complex as the moral dimensions of the debate. ILO data from 1998 point to a regionally diverse picture of child labour, with an estimated quarter of a billion children aged between 5–14 at work worldwide, half of whom are estimated to work full-time. Africa, South Asia and Latin America/Caribbean account for the largest number of children out of school (collectively 60 per cent), with Africa having the largest proportion (40 per cent), and South Asia having the largest absolute numbers (54 million) of working children (cited in Grote *et al.*, 1998). Estimates vary depending on the definition of child labour that is used, and on the measurability of different forms of work. The definitional spectrum includes those that recognize as child labour either only children working in hazardous industries,[2] or those undertaking activities that are considered to jeopardize their safety, health or morals, and not all forms of work (ILO), to those who define the 'working' child as any one out of school on the basis that children's activities are fluid across different types of work, and hence cannot be isolated merely in terms of the 'hazardous' (Sinha, 2000).

The latter definition is demanded by those who find the distinctions drawn between different types of work ambiguous, and the focus on children employed in industries an underestimation of the number of children engaged in economic activity. Focusing on the small number of children who work in industries is implicitly gender-biased, as it obscures from consideration the amount of work carried out by girls as part of household labour, which has an equally deleterious impact on their ability to attend school. Many commentators point to the problem of 'missing children', or those children who appear to be out of school but are not necessarily captured in data on child labour.

Statistical estimates reveal little of the complexities of the seasonal patterns of children's work, the regularity of school attendance, and the quality of educational outcomes to which school attendance gives rise. The definitional disagreements and consequent measurement problems in ascertaining the scale of the issue form one part of the difficulty of devising a child rights agenda that will get them out of employment and into school. Thus a suggested approach is to define the population of children in need of attention as those out of school, rather than in work, a percentage that would be easier to calculate. This would then net a total global population of 130 million or 21 per cent of all children who are out of school (UNICEF, 1999).

CURRENT POLICY APPROACHES

Policy responses are focused broadly on two types of approach. The first type includes conventions and agreements, aimed at defining minimum labour standards. These operate at the multilateral level, and include ILO conventions (for example, on minimum age), and regionally operational charters such as the EU's Social Charter and the North American Free Trade Agreement (NAFTA) ancillary agreement on labour standards. Debate still rages on the labour standards to be incorporated in the WTO. The ILO's International Programme on the Elimination of Child Labour (IPEC) launched in 1991–92 is a more intensive programmed aimed at supporting partner countries' efforts to eliminate child labour at national and sub-national levels. The second type are conventions and agreements that emphasize the importance of education for all children, especially the all-encompassing Convention on the Rights of the Child (CRC), and agreements reached at international conferences such as the Jomtien Education for All conference (1990). Compulsory education policies and the legal elimination of child labour are also emphasized to compel governments to work towards children's rights. NGOs offer a wide variety of approaches at community level, providing interventions that in the interim seek to create enabling conditions to move children out of work and into school (Marcus and Harper, 1997).

While conventions and international agreements may create an enabling environment for progressive change in the conditions that deny children their rights, the efficiency and desirability of coercive tools, particularly bans on goods that are produced using the labour of children, form the basis of disputes about the best means for achieving desired ends.[3] Much of the debate on desirability, however, rests on the underpinning analysis of why it is that children are in work and out of school in the first place, and the recognition of the diverse conditions that give rise to children's economic engagement.

INTERLOCKING DEBATES ON CHILDREN'S WORK AND EDUCATION

Why do children work?

Debates on children's work centre around the rationale for households to send children to work, the value of their economic contributions to household income and the need to differentiate between different forms of work performed by children. Poverty, and the 'limited options' (Marcus and Harper, 1997: 8) open to children who belong to families at the edge of survival, are most commonly cited factors explaining why households may 'choose to send a child to work rather than invest in human-capital accumulation in the form of schooling' (Grote et al., 1998: 9). Gupta and Voll (1999) note that without income from children's employment in factories, over half the households surveyed in the match and fireworks industries in South India would lose a substantial portion of their income. Grote et al. (1998) note that the economic contributions of children who work as wage labourers, self-employed or in family enterprises, often help tide adult household members over difficult economic patches where livelihoods are insecure or employment casual. This is indicated by data which shows that approximately 70 per cent of all children are engaged in the rural sector, in activities relating to agriculture, hunting, fishing or forestry (Grote et al., 1998). It is also argued that children are sent to work at young ages to develop their skills in preparation for adult employment (Gupta and Voll, 1999), or to form social networks with future employers where there is a high degree of competition for employment. Other evidence suggests, however, that child labour exists in those areas where there is high adult unemployment, reinforcing the point that children's wages are not supplementary, but often substitute adult labour, thus undermining household economic welfare (Gupta and Voll, 1999). However, a counter-argument points to the role that children often play in sustaining family enterprises, thus enhancing adult employment. A further set of explanatory factors rests in the mortality and fertility determinants of family size, and the impact that this may have on household economic decision-making (Grote *et al.*, 1998; Kabeer, 2000b).

Data on the nature of economic contributions is also disputed. It is argued that children's contributions are often over-emphasized, and contribute little to overall household income (Swaminathan, 1998). These arguments support the view that economic activity for children is a 'default activity' (Bhatty, 1998), arising from the inadequacy or even non-availability of schools, leaving children little option but to help in the home and at work. The increase in schooling availability in recent years may clarify this picture, although issues of quality are invariably invoked to explain why children drop out of school.

Why don't children go to school?

A major factor explaining the poor educational outcomes in many developing countries is underinvestment in education by governments. Poor quality of schools gives rise to poor performance of children in examinations, with attendant consequences for the interest of children who are enrolled to stay in school. In some situations, truancy exists despite parents' best efforts (Subrahmanian, 2000). In others, the introduction of policies to elicit fees for attending even primary school has led to significant equity impacts, particularly for girls.

Curriculum reform is a major requirement in countries where deep-rooted biases reinforce the exclusion of poor, female and ethnically marginalized groups, and where the curriculums of schools privilege the world of the male, urban, affluent actor engaged in intellectual labour – a far cry from the world of the poor, and particularly female, child from a labouring household. In addition, the lack of accountability of teachers to the communities they serve, gives rise to malpractice in the functioning of schools (Dreze and Sen, 1995).

The intersections between work and schooling

Child labour and education are not polarized choices for poor households and, in the decisions to either educate or send a child to work, not mutually exclusive. Children often work *in order* to attend school (Nieuwenhuys, 1994) and to free up household resources from investment in their education. The ability to contribute towards household livelihoods also contributes to their self-esteem (Subrahmanian, 2000). Further, the combination of school and work can also be seen as a strategic choice for parents who wish to balance the benefits of minimum education with the discipline of economic activity in contexts where employment opportunities are scarce, or demand prior investments of social or financial capital.

However, recognizing that children may be engaged both in schooling and work does not resolve the debate on how to address their well-being. While seasonally adjusted school calendars, and flexible schooling are ways to address the immediate constraints facing children who would otherwise be deprived of schooling, the physical costs for children who do both are high.

THE AGENDA AHEAD

A central position in this highly contested, morally and ethically challenging debate, is that any form of child work is exploitative if it denies children their right to education and a childhood that is free from adult responsibility (Burra, 1995). However, the recognition that poverty and economic uncertainty constrain the options available to households who send their children to work 'out of need, not greed' (Grote *et al.*, 1998) is not a justification for continued policy neglect of the rights of children, but a recognition that the responses need to be far more comprehensive than legislating either a ban on child work or enforcing compulsory education.

The polarization of the worlds of work and schooling in policy approaches is problematic because it does not reflect the intersections between the two for poor households. Navigating complexities of household short-, medium- and long-term planning fundamentally involves the provision of an array of choices that enable them to select the most rational one, and the provision of incentives for investment in children's long-term well-being. Such an approach automatically widens the range of policy interventions necessary, including improving adult wages, regulating labour markets to address equity concerns, enhancing the bargaining power of the poor, and strengthening the accountability of public services to the needs of the poorest households. The need for a gender-aware approach must not be underemphasized, given that rationales for not investing in girls' education rest in socially embedded norms that cannot be easily addressed through economic interventions.

NOTES

1. While the chapter will draw largely on material from India, many of the issues raised have a more global resonance.
2. For example, the proposed Convention on the Immediate Abolition of the Worst Forms of Child Labour, 1999.
3. See Kabeer (2000a) on the impact of the Harkin Bill on children employed in Bangladesh's garment industry.

GUIDE TO FURTHER READING

Journal of International Development (1996) Special Issue on 'New approaches to children and development', 8(6).

Kabeer, N., Nambissan, G. and Subrahmanian, R. (eds) (forthcoming) *Needs Versus Rights: Child Labour and the Right to Education in South Asia*, New Delhi: Sage Publications.

Weiner, M. (1991) *The Child and the State in India*, New Delhi: Oxford University Press.

REFERENCES

Bhatty, K. (1998) 'Educational deprivation in India: a survey of field investigations', *Economic and Political Weekly*, 4 and 18 July, Bombay.

Burra, N. (1995) *Born to Work: Child Labour in India*, New Delhi: Oxford University Press.

Dreze, J. and Sen, A. (1995) *India: Economic Development and Social Opportunity*, New Delhi: Oxford University Press.

Grote, U., Basu, A. and Weinhold, D. (1998) 'Child labour and the international policy debate: the education/child labour trade-off and the consequences of trade sanctions', *ZEF Discussion Papers on Development Policy*, Bonn.

Gupta, M. and Voll, K. (1999) 'Child labour in India: an exemplary case study', in Voll (1999).

Kabeer, N. (2000a) *The Power to Choose: Bangladeshi Women in Dhaka and London*, London: Verso.

Kabeer, N. (2000b) 'Inter-generational contracts, demographic transitions and the "quantity–quality" trade-off: parents, children and investing in the future', *Journal of International Development* 12: 463–82.

Marcus, R. and Harper, C. (1997) 'Small hands: children in the working world', *Working Paper No. 16*, London: Save the Children Fund.

Nieuwenhuys, O. (1994) *Children's Lifeworlds: Gender, Welfare and Labour in the Developing World*, London and New York: Routledge.

Sinha, S. (2000) 'Child labour and education' in R. Wazir (ed.) *The Gender Gap in Basic Education: NGOs as Change Agents*, New Delhi: Sage.

Subrahmanian, R. (2000) 'Coproducing universal primary education in a context of social exclusion: households, community organisations and state administration in a district of Karnataka, India', unpublished PhD thesis, Open University, Milton Keynes, UK.

Swaminathan, M. (1998) 'Economic growth and the persistence of child labor: evidence from an Indian city', *World Development* 26(8): 1513–28.

UNICEF (1999) *The State of the World's Children 1999: Education*, New York: UNICEF.

Voll, K. (ed.) (1999) *Against Child Labour: Indian and International Dimensions and Strategies*, New Delhi: Mosaic Books and Third Millenium Transparency.

8.6 Young people, education and development

Rob Bowden

At the turn of the millennium there remain some 130 million children out of school, most of them living in developing areas and 56 per cent of whom are girls (UNICEF, 1999). This shortfall not only deprives those children of their fundamental right to education, as enshrined in the 1948 universal declaration of human rights and numerous international agreements since, but is widely recognized as *the* major hindrance to development.

EDUCATION FOR DEVELOPMENT

Education, and particularly the education of girls, is known to have a dramatic impact on development. UNICEF (1999), for example, reports an anticipated decrease in infant mortality levels of 4.1 deaths per 1000 if girls' primary school enrolment were to increase by 10 per cent, and a further reduction of 5.6 deaths per 1000 for a similar increase in secondary enrolment. Education has also been closely correlated to fertility rates such that in Brazil secondary-educated women have an average of 2.5 children, compared to 6.5 children for illiterate women (UNICEF, 1999). Beyond social indicators, a recent Oxfam report, 'Education Now', suggested that four years of primary schooling in Uganda raises farmer output by 7 per cent, whilst a secondary education in Bangladesh is said to treble the participation rate of women in political meetings (UNESCO, 1999a). Perhaps the best example of the benefits of education can be seen in Kerala (India), which with universal literacy has the lowest infant mortality rate in the developing world and the lowest fertility rates in India (UNICEF, 1999). Kerala is also among the poorest states, suggesting that commitment is perhaps more important than finance in achieving education for all. However it also suggests that education does not necessarily lead to economic growth and therefore should not be relied upon as a panacea for development.

Many countries have adopted policies to provide education for all, such as Malawi which in 1994 declared universal free primary education and saw enrolment rates increase from 1.9 million children to over 3.2 million (UNICEF, 1999). In 1996 the Ugandan government announced a universal primary education (UPE) programme to fund the first four children in every family and saw enrolment levels double virtually overnight to over 5.3 million children (UNDP, 1998).

QUALITY OF EDUCATION

Such progress is (perhaps justifiably) applauded by the international donor community, but critics point out that education is about more than boosting statistics and that what really matters is the quality of education received. High levels of enrolment can mask erratic attendance, irrelevant curricula, poorly trained teachers, gender insensitivity and a lack of facilities that often combine to result in low completion levels. For example, in Nepal just under half of primary school entrants fail to reach grade 5, whilst in Malawi and Angola almost two-thirds will have dropped out by this stage (UNICEF, 2000). In addition, and often as a precursor to high drop-out rates, millions of pupils repeat school years several times such that in Latin America and the Caribbean 13 per cent of primary pupils in 1995 were repeaters, 30 per cent of them repeating grade 1 (UNESCO, 1998).

Together the problem of repeaters and high drop-outs has become known as 'school wastage', an issue that is considered central to achieving education for all, owing to its absorption of scarce resources and its disproportionate impact on the most vulnerable groups in society (UNESCO, 1998). As social budgets are constrained by stringent structural adjustment programmes (SAPs) the need for a child to repeat, or their failure to complete a year, represents a significant financial undertaking for both the state and families, that might have been otherwise invested. According to UNESCO figures this amounts to US$49 per repeating pupil in sub-Saharan Africa, or more tellingly 32.8 per cent of the region's education expenditure being spent on wastage up to grade 5 (UNESCO, 1998: 25). In addition to the financial burden, school wastage may inadvertently enhance social differentiation and economic inequalities by affecting most severely those who are least able to afford the costs of repetition (UNESCO, 1998: 5).

In my own research in rural Uganda school wastage appears also to reduce the self-esteem of pupils and certainly erodes the confidence of parents and children alike in the education system.

Table 1 Repeaters and wastage in primary education by region

Region	Primary repeaters as % of total enrolment (1995)	First-grade repeaters as % of total repeaters (1995)	Estimated cost per pupil in US$ (1995)	Education (public current expenditure) – % spent on wastage before grade 5 (1995)
Less developed regions	8	30	n/a	15.8
Sub-Saharan Africa	17	31	49	32.8
Arab states	10	17	n/a	12.6
Latin America/Caribbean	14	30	312	26.6
Eastern Asia/Oceania	7	44	89	10.2
Southern Asia	12	25	121	n/a
Least developed countries	16	35	19	37.8

Source: UNESCO, 1998

But it is not just the unpredictability of completion that concerns them, it is also the value of the education that they emerge with and the opportunities (or lack of) that it affords them. As one boy of 14 stated 'What is the point in going to school if you end up digging sweet potatoes?' In many parts of the developing world school curricula are founded on Western urban principles with scant regard to local needs in terms of the skills they impart.

Programmes to create more appropriate curricula are now under way in many countries, such as the 'village schools' programme in Mali that encourages instruction relating to local village life, health, work and knowledge, and the BEND (basic education for national development) programme in Uganda that is developing a vocational curriculum suited to learners' needs. Vocational and practical skills are also being emphasized in Tanzania; the core curriculum being reduced from 13 to 7 subjects to accommodate more locally appropriate learning (Ouane, 1996).

In the past, curricula have been particularly irrelevant for many rural areas, the problem being exacerbated by school calendars competing with the demand for children's assistance as agricultural labourers. In the lake-shore economy of Uganda, for example, children return to school just as the planting season starts and sit their year-end exams during the peak harvest period. This means that many return to school several weeks late and find it difficult to catch up, whilst others are withdrawn from school in the period leading up to their exams, resulting in poor pass rates and high levels of repetition or drop-out.

Some countries have begun to accommodate this difference, such as in the Philippines where the assimilation of the school and agricultural calendars has led to increased attendance and reduced wastage (UNESCO, 1998). Among the earliest and best-known examples of a more flexible education system are the schools run by the Bangladesh Rural Advancement Committee (BRAC). Established in 1985, the BRAC schools work in close co-operation with parents to determine not only the school calendar, but also the hours of the school day that are most suited to local needs. The sensitivity behind BRAC schools has reduced drop-out rates from around 60 per cent in state schools to just 3 per cent (Mahmud, 1993) and a measure of their success can be seen in their expansion from the initial 22 schools in 1985 to some 34,000 by 1998 (UNICEF, 1999).

EXPECTATIONS AND REALITY

The focus on basic (primary) education since 1990 has detracted attention from secondary education in many developing countries resulting in a system unable to meet the expectations of burgeoning primary leavers looking to continue their education. This shortfall is more than a logistical dilemma, though, because the secondary-age cohort are of that critical age where they begin to make choices regarding their futures and hence determine the future of society as a whole (UNESCO, 1999b).

When expectations are not realized, young people can become despondent with their position. In my research, young people spoke of being trapped with one foot in the modern, literate future and another in their illiterate village past. Some spoke of feeling socially marginalized, of losing their identity as a consequence of a partial education. Adults treat them with suspicion, ignoring or dismissing their 'educated' insights, leading to frustration and, increasingly, to intergenerational conflict. For example, one youth of 15 who had learnt about composting and natural fertilizers met with outright rejection when attempting to inform his parents about the potential benefits. In what might be perceived as defiance of his parents, he proceeded to implement the techniques in his own garden (children are given a small 'garden' to grow crops as part of their upbringing in Uganda), but when his crops visibly yielded better than his parents', his father destroyed them and the compost store. Similar stories of conflict and resistance were common and frequently associated with the role education plays in altering child/adult relationships. In contrast, peers who did not attend school, but were educated through traditional socialization or as apprentices were becoming respected members of the community, offering valued services and knowledge. And, those fortunate enough to continue in education become rapidly distanced both socially and geographically, owing to the low density of secondary and tertiary institutes.

Besides the personal implications (self-esteem, etc.) of such situations, there are broader ramifications for education and development as a whole. Parents may become sceptical as to the value of education if they see it providing inappropriate skills and knowledge at the same time as children who did not attend school succeed in the local community. Children themselves may make similar judgements based on what one head teacher referred to as 'success motivation' – witnessing the relative success or failure of older siblings and peers. Both of these factors could affect education enrolment and/or the willingness of parents/carers to fund it.

Neither should it be considered that a guarantee of secondary education will resolve these problems. In fact it may exacerbate them, in that by this time they are even further removed from the realities of their community and yet in many instances lack employment opportunities appropriate to their education and/or expectations, thus being forced to return to their homes.

EDUCATION AND THE 'MISSING LINK'

In the quest for education for all, it is possible that the full potential of education for development is being overlooked in favour of a 'quick fix' statistical achievement. This may not only lead to a waste of valuable resources, but could inadvertently erode future confidence and investment in education for development. For education to be successful in achieving its development intentions it must be contextually located and not treated as an isolated variable. Synchronizing curricula to local needs and school timetables to seasonal calendars have proven the benefits of such approaches, but there is another dimension that is perhaps even more significant. An investment in education is an investment in human capital, but this is of limited utility in the absence of a supportive environment. Such environments are increasingly the focus of a literature on 'social capital' that considers networks and affiliations as a foundation for development (Johnston *et al.*, 2000). The examples from Uganda suggest that education may in fact erode social capital by creating social divides and marginalization. Education has been removed from the community as part of a process that Kilbride and Kilbride (1990) refer to as 'delocalization' – a significant proportion of a young person's socialization now taking place under state auspices.

For education to realize its full potential for development, this missing link is in need of greater attention. Parents and communities should be encouraged to appreciate education as an investment shared by the community as a whole and not an individual asset. Such an environment would allow young people to better utilize their education within the local community, simultaneously raising the profile of education and the self-belief of individuals. Young people are rightly considered by many to be an invaluable and largely untapped resource for development, but at present the link is rarely made. For it to become a reality there is a need to address children's rights to participate, to demonstrate the value of children as social actors and to empower them to utilize their knowledge effectively. It is for these reasons that education should not be treated as an isolated variable that, if improved, will miraculously lead to development – such views are naïve. Consideration of young people, education and development must instead be appreciated as a complex set of social relations that extend beyond the classroom, effecting the transformation of relations of production and reproduction of society as a whole. Until this is given its due importance, education for all, it is suggested, will remain a recurring ambition.

GUIDE TO FURTHER READING

UNICEF's annual report *The State of the World's Children* for 1999 is dedicated to education and provides detailed background material, case studies and statistical analysis to help explain general patterns and key issues.

UNESCO produces a quarterly bulletin called *EFA 2000* for the International Consultative Forum on Education for All that contains regular features, news updates and references to new publications. Located at http://www.education.unesco.org/efa, it can be accessed or downloaded free of charge.

REFERENCES

Johnston, R.J., Gregory, D., Pratt, G. and Watts, M. (eds) (2000): *The Dictionary of Human Geography* (4th edn), London: Arnold.

Kilbride, P.L. and Kilbride, J.P. (1990) *Changing Family Life in East Africa*, London: Pennsylvania State University Press.

Mahmud, A. (1993) 'Rural schools win back the children', *Guardian*, 1 October, p. 12.

Ouane, A. (1996) 'Mid-decade review of progress towards education for all', policy review seminars in Africa, February 1996, Issues Paper for discussion by the International Consultative Forum on Education for All, Paris: UNESCO. Located at http://www.unesco.org/efa/07E3afri.htm.

UNDP (1998) *Uganda Human Development Report, 1998*, Kampala: UNDP.

UNESCO (1998) 'Wasted opportunities: when schools fail', Paris: UNESCO for the International Consultative Forum on Education for All.

UNESCO (1999a) 'Poverty hampers progress in basic education', in *EFA 2000* 36, July–September, available at http://www.education.unesco.org/efa.

UNESCO (1999b) 'Reforming secondary education', located at: http://www.unesco.org/efa/newsoctober1999/unesco.thm.

UNICEF (1999) *The State of the World's Children, 1999*, Oxford: Oxford University Press for UNICEF.

UNICEF (2000) *The State of the World's Children, 2000*, Oxford: Oxford University Press for UNICEF.

8.7 Adult literacy and development

Raff Carmen

LITERACY FOR ALL BY THE YEAR 2000

As recently as ten years ago there was still enough confidence in the promise of education in general and the positive links between literacy and development for the United Nations to announce the decade of 'Education for All by the Year 2000', inaugurated by UNESCO's events-packed 'ILY90' (International Literacy Year, 1990) and the International Conference 'Education for All' in Jomtien, Thailand, in the same year. This was despite the fact that, during the 1980s, known as the 'lost decade of development', the looming debt repayment crisis and a severe regime of SAPs (structural adjustment policies) imposed by the World Bank and IMF, combined with wholesale privatizations and the demise of the state as universal provider, signalled a reversal in the advances made in the area of social development in the previous decades. Fundamental entitlements, such as the human right to health and education, previously provided for free, were now to be paid for, which meant that millions simply could not afford those services.

Among the education targets set in the 1990 Jomtien Declaration was UPE (universal primary education) by the year 2000. UPE is important because if education ever became truly universal the festering problem of adult illiteracy which has stood adamantly at about one billion, 750 million of them women (Chlebowska, 1990: 17), would have been eliminated long ago.

Depending on what literacy 'means' in an ever-changing globalizing world with ever-changing and sophisticated channels of communication, the very criteria on which such statistics are based are at best elusive, as is, indeed, the problem of poverty itself with which it to a large extent overlaps. 'Literacy' has been variously defined, starting from the most literal and narrow sense of 'the ability to read and write a short statement' (Hutton, 1992: 10), passing through Street's litera*cies* or 'shorthand for the social practices and conceptions of reading and writing' (1990: 32), to the even broader meaning of oral, camcorder, drama, TV, computer and internet literacy, embracing both traditional oral as well as novel electronic forms of human communication.

In this chapter I will even go further and call the cross-cultural transition from the world of simple, seamless production of the *artisan*/small producer to the complex world of organization for production of the '*worker*', also, a form of literacy, or '*entrepreneurial*' literacy.

Promises about the global UPE started as early as the 1960s, when Ministers of Education at conferences held on all three continents predicted UPE 'by 1980'. Some 20 years on, there (still) is no school to go to for many of the world's children. Where there is a school, classes are likely to be severely overcrowded, with a besieged untrained teacher in charge. For one in three African children, 'schools' have not even a blackboard, and a 'classroom' may be anywhere, under a tree, with not a pencil or book in sight. In rural Tanzania, once-proud home of 'Education for Self-Reliance' and, among many others, state-funded nationwide Radio Learning Programmes-cum-Adult Literacy Campaigns (for example, the *Mtu ni Afya* health campaign in the 1970s), one schoolbook has now to be shared among 30 pupils. As for 'adult basic education' programmes (ABE includes the 3Rs but is not confined to them, see Hutton, 1992), these are invariably the first to be axed in times of crisis and budget cuts.

Mwalimu Nyerere, the teacher-turned-president, whose lifetime ambition it had been to triple school attendance and at the same time wipe out illiteracy in Tanzania, had to depart this world (14 October 1999) with one-third of his countrymen and two-thirds of Tanzanian women still illiterate. Virtually all African, and many Asian and Latin American countries, continue to labour under an unbearable debt-repayment burden which means that in many cases twice as much may have to be spent on repaying debt to the already rich than for providing education and health to their own citizens. Mali, Zambia, Burkina Faso and Chad have seen their educational budgets dwindle from as high as 25 per cent (in the case of Zambia) to less than 1 per cent of an already pathetically meagre GDP (McGreal, 2000).

This notwithstanding, the World Education Forum, the Jomtien follow-up held in Dakar in April 2000, set the year 2015 as the (new) target for UPE worldwide and opted for a 'substantial reduction' (by at least 50 per cent) – not elimination – of the number of adult illiterates by 2015.

ADULT LITERACY AND DEVELOPMENT

Myths

That illiteracy will be 'eradicated' any time soon is, indeed, according to the National Center on Adult Literacy (NCAL, Philadelphia), one of the more abiding myths spun around the relationship between literacy and development (Wagner, 1999). Equally to be relegated to the realm of myths is the notion that the acquisition of literacy would bring immediate developmental benefits in terms of generic changes in the human psyche and in the way people think. Since the 1940s, literacy and modernity have been taken to be interchangeable with a scientific turn of mind. For modernity and, hence, 'development' to properly take root, the 'traditional' (in actual fact, people's cultural identity) had, so the theory went, to 'pass away' (Lerner, 1964; Rogers, 1969) while the 'savage' mind had to be 'domesticated' (Goody, 1984). Educational economists and planners held a 40 per cent literacy rate as a threshold for development 'take-off' (Atkinson, 1983: 60).

The belief in the quasi-automatic benefits of literacy, and the interventionist strategies which go with it, have been dubbed the '*autonomous*' model, as compared to the '*ideological*' model which starts from the understanding that 'literacy' is first and foremost a social practice or rather, a whole range of culturally embedded social practices, which means that there is not just one, set-piece, monolithic literacy but a multitude of litera*cies* (Street, 1984). Literacy and orality are 'embedded in an oral context'. Unless the cultural complexity of 'literacy-in-practice' is taken into account 'UNESCO and other international aid agencies will continue to register high dropout rates' (Street, 1990: 33).

In an age where the monopoly of the printed word and reverence for the book are increasingly being eroded by the onslaught of omnipresent digital, electronic and virtual communications, it is salutory to remember that literacy is another 'media' skill among many. Given humankind's common oral roots (not forgetting their 'oral' or 'street' numeracy – for example, Nuñez, 1993), the 'autonomous' model of literacy has always been, at best, an ill-advised aberration. Visual literacy (e.g. Linney, 1995), video, camcorder, TV, computer and internet literacy, drama literacy (in which passive spectators become *spectactors* – Boal, 1992), puppetry and popular expression in general, all belong, as we have indicated above, quite appropriately to the wider realm of literacy as a 'media' discipline. Moreover 'was not literacy invented by illiterates?' (Enzensberger, 1987).

Approaches and methods

Laubach's (1960) phonically-based 'Each One Teach One' (EOTO) method – (also known as the 'missionary' approach because of its close links to proselytizing Bible-reading – Hutton, 1992: 30) – clearly is part of the 'narrow' pedagogical (vs andragogical) transmission-of-skills approaches to literacy teaching and training. This does in no way take away from the Laubach school's claim to have made 100 million people literate.

UNESCO's 'functional' approach of the 1970s, tried out under its experimental world literacy programme (EWLP), starts from the belief that 'literacy as an essential element in overall development, must be linked to economic and social priorities and to present and future manpower needs' (UNESCO, 1988, in Hutton, 1992: 32). As will be pointed out below, in view of the vastness of the problem, modern workplaces in which that 'future manpower' can 'function' are, invariably, few and far between where they are most needed: *another* literacy is necessary, too.

'Liberating' literacy became an integral part of the 'popular education' movement of the 1970s and 1980s and is closely linked to the famous Brazilian adult educationist Paulo Freire (1972). His starting point was 'conscientizing' literacy (from the Portuguese word *conscientização*) by which poor peasants and slum-dwellers denied voting rights because of their inability to read and write could, autonomously, gain 'critical consciousness', in the process itself of learning how to read and write, not just the alphabet (the 'Word') but also the 'World' (Freire and Macedo, 1985). Freire always insisted that his extremely effective (Brown, 1975) andragogical educational approach was not intended as a 'method' in the first place. He was equally opposed to the use of 'Janet and John' literacy primers, as learners themselves are quite capable of generating their own 'codifications'. Cutting the umbilical cord with the primer, however, in actual practice in the field, always proved more easily said than done.

The 'stranglehold' of the primer was finally broken thanks to REFLECT (regenerated Freirean literacy through empowering community techniques). REFLECT takes on board Freire's sound andragogical principles and complements them with learner-driven, 'bottom-up' rapid/participatory rural appraisal research methods borrowed from agronomy and social anthropology (Chambers, 1997) which were adapted to literacy work (Archer and Cottingham, 1996).

'WHERE THERE IS NO WORKPLACE': THE *OTHER* LITERACY

The above approaches, for all their rich methodological diversity, nevertheless share the alphabet as their common learning focus and starting point. However personally and socially enriching the alphabet undoubtedly is, when it comes to 'Literacy and Power' issues, as they are known nowadays (Archer and Costello, 1990; Street, 1990), in other words, issues of ownership and control of 'the economic factor' (sustainable development), the alphabet on its own is obviously 'not enough': even in Europe, where illiteracy is not an immediately obvious problem, 50 million people are unemployed. This has to be set against the backdrop of one billion unemployed and under-employed worldwide (ILO, 1998).

Western understandings of enterprise, of organization development (known as OD) and of *training* or the *verbal* transmission of knowledge and skills which traditionally have also dominated the development co-operation scene, start from the taken-for-granted assumption that there always are or will be workplaces to go to. The Brazilian sociologist Clodomir Santos de Morais, is on record as having both a theory and a *capacitating*[1] methodology in place which allows the illiterate and the socially excluded to *create,* for themselves and by themselves, workplaces and income in the process itself of learning to become 'entrepreneurially literate'.

If, indeed, by alphabetic literacy is meant the cross-cultural transition from one culture of communicating (three-dimensional *orality*) to another (i.e. the two-dimensional world of the *alphabet*), then the cross-cultural transition from the world of simple, seamless production of the *artisan*/small producer to the complex world of organization for production of the '*worker*', then the process of becoming 'entrepreneurially' literate is a genuine '*other*' form of literacy, too, and a very important one.

CONCLUSION

In the course of the moraisean Organization Workshop (Carmen and Sobrado, 2000) the '*need*' – for literacy, no doubt, but for a host of other skills needed in the complex world of work – 'learns to know its object, it becomes a motive' (Leont'ev, 1978).

While there ought not to be the slightest doubt about the social impact of literacy and its benefits for the person and society at large, starting with its role in women's emancipation (Bown,

1990), literacy, at best, can only be an instrument, not one of the primary means by which economic development is brought about.

The 50 years of literacy programmes and mass campaigns have been a tale of enormous heroism, sacrifices, and individual and collective achievements of which the initiators can be justly proud. With the number of illiterates, the unemployed and underemployed remaining stubbornly stuck at the 1 billion mark, and mounting, it may be time, first, for the existence of the 'other' literacy to be realized and recognized by the 'big players' in the field and, second, that its implications for poverty alleviation and development promotion, in view of the massive nature of the job which remains to be done, are taken seriously.

NOTE

1. Just as 'conscientization', 'capacitation' ('objective activity' – from the Portuguese '*capacitação*') represents a generically different adult educational concept and practice: in objective activity it is not the trainer or teacher, but the 'object' which 'teaches'. 'Capacitation' includes 'training' but is neither defined nor confined by it (see Carmen and Sobrado, 2000: xvii).

GUIDE TO FURTHER READING

For general reading see Hutton, B. (1992), Wagner, D. (1999), and for literacy-related bibiliography see http://literacyonline.org/products/ili/webdocs/wagner.html. For practitioners see Archer, D. and Cottingham, S. (1996) and Fordham, P. *et al.*, (1995) *Adult Literacy, A Handbook for Development Workers*, Oxford: Oxfam.

REFERENCES

Archer, D. and Costello, P. (1990) *Literacy and Power*, London: Earthscan.

Archer, D. and Cottingham, S. (1996) *The REFLECT Mother Manual*, London: Action Aid.

Atkinson, G.B. (1983) *The Economics of Education*, London: Hodder & Stoughton.

Boal, A. (1992) *Games for Actors and Non-Actors*, London: Routledge.

Bown, L. (1990) *Women, Literacy and Development*, London: Action Aid.

Brown, C. (1975) *Literacy in 30 Hours*, London: Readers and Writers Co-op.

Carmen, R. and Sobrado, M. (2000) *A Future for the Excluded: Job Creation and Income Generation by the Poor. Clodomir Santos de Morais and the Organization Workshop*, London: Zed Books.

Chambers, R. (1997) *Whose Reality Counts?*, London: IT Publications.

Chlebowska, K. (1990) *Literacy for Rural Women in the TW*, UNESCO.

Correia, J. (2000) 'From Paulo Freire to Clodomir Santos de Morais', in R. Carmen and M. Sobrado, p. 39.

Enzensberger, H.M. (1987) 'In praise of the illiterate', in *Adult Education and Development* 28: 96, Bonn.

Freire, P. (1972) *Cultural Action for Freedom*, Harmondsworth: Penguin.

Freire, P. and Macedo, A. (1985) *Reading the Word and the World*, London: Routledge.

Fordham, P., Holland, D., and Millicam, J. (1995) *Adult Literacy: A Handbook for Development Workers*, Oxford: Oxfam/VSO.

Goody, J. (1984) *The Domestication of the Savage Mind*, Cambridge: Cambridge University Press.

Hutton, B. (ed.) (1992) *Adult Basic Education in South Africa*, Oxford: Oxford University Press.

ICAE (1991) *Popular Theatre Workshop – Rehoboth, Namibia*, Toronto, Canada: ICAE.

ILO (1998) 'Grim and getting grimmer', *ILO Magazine* 27, December, Geneva.

Laubach, F. (1960) *Toward World Literacy*, Syracuse: Syracuse University Press.

Leont'ev, A.N. (1978) *Activity, Consciousness and Personality*, New York: Prentice Hall.

Lerner, D. (1964) *The Passing of Traditional Society. Modernizing the Middle East*, New York: Free Press.

Linney, B. (1995) *Pictures, People and Power*, London: Macmillan.

McGreal, C. (2000) 'Nigerians denied the power of words', *Guardian*, 8 August, London, p. 19.

Nuñez, T. (1993) *Street Mathematics*, Cambridge: Cambridge University Press.

Rogers, E. (1969) *Modernization among Peasants*, New York: Holt.

Rostow, W. (1960) *The Stages of Growth*, Oxford: Oxford University Press.

Street, B. (1984) *Literacy in Theory and Practice*, Cambridge: Cambridge University Press.

Street, B. (1990) 'Which literacies?', in B. Street (ed.) *Literacy in Development: People, Language and Power*, London: Commonwealth Institute.

Wagner, D. (1999) *Literacy and Development. Rationales, Myths and Future Directions*, literacyonline.org.

8.8 How pedagogical changes can contribute to the quality of education in low-income countries

John Shotton

INTRODUCTION

During the 1960s and 1970s the educational systems of the newly independent and mostly low-income countries of the South underwent rapid quantitative and qualitative change. This was most often under the influence of the international donor and lending agencies (IDLAs), but in certain cases also as a result of independent initiatives from individual national governments. The bulk of financial input, whether aid or not, as King (1991) has outlined, went to system maintenance and expansion, but slowly the South became a greenhouse for educational programme experimentation instigated by both Northern and Southern agencies and governments.

The overall failures of these development initiatives were being articulated during the 1970s and 1980s by a range of researchers (International Development Research Committee, 1972; Vulliamy *et al.*, 1990). The Education for All (EFA) Conference at Jomtien in Thailand in 1990 provided a forum where these inadequacies and failings were aired, and where the IDLAs and Southern national governments were openly challenged by Southern NGOs in particular, to contribute towards the development of a new approach, hopefully learning lessons from the mistakes of the era which began with the post-independence education projects.

Those lessons were both general and specific. Generally a consensus on the part of delegates emerged at Jomtien and later in New Delhi in 1993, that levels of both actual multilateral and bilateral educational aid and national government funding were appallingly low and had certainly not been targeted at basic education. More importantly the project mode had failed to consider issues of sustainability and the problems of proceeding to scale in low-income countries which were facing severe problems of debt and increased impoverishment. There was also agreement that it was no longer appropriate to send large numbers of teachers from the North to staff primary schools, to pilot enclave curriculum development and teacher training projects which operated out-of-context and were too expensive. Sending cohorts of administrators to the North for expensive training in higher education institutions did little to build local capacity in the long term. Technical support from highly paid Northern consultants was often inappropriate; national experimentation was often not strategic; and reaching the poor with centrally directed programmes was too paternalistic to work (Menon, 1993: 15). Most important of all there was a recognition that more serious attention had to be paid to specific pedagogical issues with a focus on critiquing existing practice and seeking reform, particularly at the primary school level, to enhance and contribute to quality improvement in the lives of the poorest and weakest children in society.

I try to raise here what the key issues are in developing a critique of pedagogy in the primary school classrooms in low-income countries in the South, and consider what might underpin an alternative approach.

EDUCATIONAL BANKING FOR THE POOR

Critiquing existing practice is complex. The nature of pedagogy in a typical primary school class-room in a low-income country in the South is that they are often the victims of the imposition of an imperial educational system. This conforms closely to the model that Freire has labelled the pedagogy of the oppressed where teachers and students are trapped within a debilitating milieu that resembles a banking system of education (1974). The characteristics of the model are first its definition of knowledge. Knowledge is a thing 'out there', a 'cognizable object' in Freire's terms. A person acquires it by an act of cognition and it then becomes their private property. It can be passed on but it retains, as it were, its objective status, so that the learner receives it as a thing from outside, a gift. The concept is essentially static and encourages submission to certain modes.

Second, there is the model view of the learner. The scope of action allowed to the learner is restricted to receiving, filing and storing deposits. The learner's role is essentially passive and submissive. Thinking is to be shaped, behaviour modified. Banking education thus begins with an understanding of people as objects. Implicit in the notion is the assumption of a dichotomy between people and the world. People are spectators not creators.

Third, the model views the teaching process as merely the transfer of information where the teacher has only to make a deposit in the mind of the learner.

Fourth, the model disregards the continuum of experience. The banking approach will never propose to learners that they consider reality critically. It will deal instead with such vital questions as whether Gopal gave green grass to the goats. Through its censorship of knowledge it confirms people in their status as objects to be manipulated by others.

My observations of the typical primary school classroom in low-income countries in the South led me to conclude that pedagogically a banking model exists where, especially for the poor and weakest sections of society,

- the teacher teaches and the students are taught
- the teacher knows everything and the students know nothing
- the teacher thinks and the students are thought about
- the teacher talks and the students listen
- the teacher disciplines and the students are disciplined
- the teacher chooses and enforces a choice, and the students comply
- the teacher acts and the students have the illusion of acting through the action of the teacher
- the teacher chooses the programme content and the students, who were not consulted, adapt to it.
- the teacher confuses the authority of knowledge with her/his own professional authority, which is set in opposition of the freedom of the students.

The teacher is the subject of the learning process, while the students are objects, it is a pedagogy of the oppressed in action.

NO MASTER HIGH OR LOW: DEVELOPING AN ALTERNATIVE

In order to counteract this it is important that we consider and develop an alternative way of thinking which will contribute to the enhancement of the teaching and learning experience for those who are most oppressed by schooling in low-income countries in the South. Challenging the pedagogy of the oppressed is no easy task but one that I would argue is crucial in the pursuit of greater teaching and learning effectiveness. Let me first define what I mean by teaching and learning effectiveness as I use it hereafter.

The debate about teaching and learning effectiveness has become rooted in performance indicators and attainment targets, supposedly quantifiable measures. These are merely one measure of effective teaching and learning, and one rooted in an essentially positivist framework. I want to posit an alternative view of an effective teaching and learning paradigm built on the principle of a learning partnership between teacher, child and community that has at its heart high aspirations for children. The crucial indicator is respect and here I draw on the inspiration of Lawrence Stenhouse who suggested that effective teaching and learning can be identified, almost singularly by the degree of respect it affords to its learners (1971). Rudduck suggests that Stenhouse felt that respect can be signalled in different ways (Rudduck, 1995). It is communicated when teachers listen to children and are prepared to take their ideas seriously. It is demonstrated in the care teachers take to ensure that curriculum content links in an important way with children's own lives and developing perspectives. And it is reflected in the extent to which teachers make accessible to children the logic behind the structures and procedures that shape, but often remain implicit in, classroom practice. In some ways, his thinking echoes that of Dewey who wrote: 'There is no defect in traditional education greater than its failure to secure the active co-operation of the pupil in the construction of the purpose involved in his studying' (1938: 67).

The concern not to underestimate children was a major theme in Stenhouse's work. He was wary of simplifying things, for simplification can communicate low expectations of children and it can trivialize content. He wanted teachers to help children struggle with difficulty, to enjoy the challenge of things that are tough, and to feel that if they struggle with meaning then they are gaining. Failure is about avoiding struggle. He was in sympathy with Sarason who asked why we are not deeply upset 'that so many students come to view the life of the mind, the world of ideas . . . as derogated arenas of experience' (1991: 163).

Changes in the structure of schooling do not seem to have kept pace with the earlier maturity of young people. The new curriculum frameworks that are emerging in low-income countries have perhaps not given sufficient thought to ways of learning that stretch children's minds and to ways of connecting school knowledge with the child's world outside school. What Sarason says of reform in the US is true of reform anywhere:

> The educational reform movement has not come to grips with these overarching aims. One can alter curricula, change power relationships, raise standards . . . but if these efforts are not powered by altered conceptions of what makes children tick and keeps them intellectually alive, willingly pursuing knowledge and growth, their results will be inconsequential.
>
> (Sarason, 1991)

Going back to Stenhouse, he was writing in the 1960s about standards and how they could be used to help children develop a stronger sense of control over their own learning. The values that informed his discussion were somewhat different from the values that structure the debate about standards and achievement in most low-income countries today. By standards he meant the criteria adopted in the criticism of classrooms, and not the attainment in classwork. He wrote: 'Whenever classroom work is judged, standards are implied, and within the classroom there are at least two different standards operative, that of the teacher and that of the class' (1967: 49). Stenhouse urged teachers to discuss criteria for judgement with children so that the children themselves might begin to understand how judgements of excellence are constructed and how they might more confidently use the criteria for judgement in relation to their own work.

The question now is, what might an effective school look like that accorded to the kind of definition that I, standing on the shoulders of Stenhouse and Rudduck, have tried to give? The answer is that I do not know, but a step in the right direction might be one where the teachers do not regard themselves as the 'masters' of knowledge at any level, 'high ' or 'low', to quote from William Morris who believed that nothing could be taught as opposed to much that can be learned.

In practice what this might mean is that schools should be places where children are accorded a set of rights similar to those suggested by Stenhouse himself (1983: 153–4) that by their very nature challenge the pedagogy of the oppressed; namely, the right to:

- demand that the school shall treat them impartially and with respect as persons
- demand that the school's aims and purposes shall be communicated to them openly, and discussed with them as the need arises
- demand that the problems and organizational arrangements of the school should be capable of rational justification and that the grounds of them should be available to them
- expect that the school will offer them impartial counsel on academic matters, and, if they desire it, with respect to personal problems
- expect special consideration and compassion from the school should they live in home or environmental circumstances which make it difficult for them to meet the demands which the school places on them
- expect that the school will make unabated efforts to provide them with the basic skills necessary to live in modern society
- expect that the school will provide them with a general education which will equip them to enter upon a livelihood and which will provide the basis for further specialized education and training
- expect that the school will do its best to make available to them the major public traditions in knowledge, arts, crafts and sports
- expect that the school will enable them to achieve some understanding of society as it stands and that it will equip them to criticize social policy and contribute to the collective development of society.

In the final analysis actual progress is probably dependent on transforming the role of the teacher in the primary school by involving him or her in decision-making processes in the school. By placing all teachers at the heart of the development of a child-centred pedagogical and curricula development, and according them greater professionalism and involvement in active research.

In conclusion I want to focus on the issue of research, for in many ways it ties the strategies together. Returning to Stenhouse just for a moment, it is not insignificant that teachers with whom he had worked contributed a plaque to his memory after he died, on which they inscribed his own words: 'It is the teachers who in the end will change the world of the school by understanding it' (1975: 208).

This is the essence of a theory of teacher professionalism, autonomy and development. I believe that it is indeed the teacher, purposive and free, informed by knowledge and understanding, with clearly articulated values and a repertoire of practical skills, that can be the central agent of change in the primary school classroom in low-income countries. Research is crucial to this.

It is my contention that teachers can be researchers in that, with encouragement, they can try to get better at teaching by consciously identifying some significant aspect of practice that they need to understand better and to work on. They can learn by careful enquiry into their own practice and, where possible, by bringing to bear on their practice ideas from research and from some kinds of educational theory. The idea of teachers as researchers implies professionalism and suggests that the quality of teachers' work should not be static but rather continually advanced by teachers themselves.

To summarize, perhaps what is needed is progress in the art of teaching as a public tradition and a personal achievement.

GUIDE TO FURTHER READING

Berhanu Dibaba (1997) *Contextualising Teaching and Learning in Rural Primary Schools: Using Agricultural Experience,* London: Department for International Development.

Bloom, J.W. (1992) *The Development of Scientific Knowledge in Elementary School Children: A Context of Meaning Perspective, Science Education* 76(4): 399–413.

Gulliford, R. and Widlake, P. (1997) *Teaching Materials for Disadvantaged Children. Schools Council Curriculum Bulletin* 5, London: Evans/Methuen Educational.

Shotton, J. (1996) 'Learning from the South', *Development Education Journal* 1(7): 19–24, London: DEA.

Shotton, J. (1997) *Learning and Freedom: Policy, Pedagogy and Paradigms in Indian Education,* New Delhi: Sage.

UNESCO (1996) *Education for All – Achieving the Goal,* Paris: UNESCO.

REFERENCES

Dewey, J. (1938) *Experience and Education,* New York: Macmillan.

Freire, P. (1974) *Pedagogy of the Oppressed,* London: Penguin.

International Development Research Committee (1972) *Education, Research and Aid,* Paris: IDRC.

King, K. (1991) *Aid and Education in the Developing World,* London: Longman.

Menon, S. (1993) 'How much Education for All?', *Economic Times,* New Delhi, India, 9 December, pp. 14–15.

Rudduck, J. (ed.) (1995) *An Education that Empowers,* London: Bera.

Sarason, B. (1991) *The Predictable Failure of Educational Reform,* New York: Josey Bass.

Stenhouse, L.A. (1971 [1967]) *Culture and Education,* London: Nelson.

Stenhouse, L.A. (1975) *An Introduction to Curriculum Research and Development,* London: Nelson.

Stenhouse, L.A. (1983) *Authority, Education and Emancipation,* London: Heinemann.

Vulliamy, G., Lewis, K. and Stephens, D. (1990) *Doing Educational Research in Developing Countries,* London: Falmer.

8.9 Management challenges in achieving education for all: South Asian perspectives

Caroline Dyer

ACHIEVING EDUCATION FOR ALL: THE CHALLENGES

Education and development

Education is positively associated with human development, reflected in economic growth, a productive labour force, improved health and controlled fertility; and its status as a basic human right was recognized by the United Nations in 1948. Many developing countries, once liberated from colonial rule, made a Constitutional pledge to provide universal primary education. Commitments to providing basic education for all (EFA) were made at the World Conference on Education For All in Jomtien, 1990, and re-affirmed in Dakar, 2000. Basic education comprises life skills which include reading and writing. The main vehicle for gaining these skills is the formal primary school, on which we focus here.

National literacy rates in South Asia provide some indication of progress made, and the challenges ahead (Table 1). Over the years, policies have gained sophistication and clarity about the multi-stranded approaches required to make good-quality education available to all. Initially lack of access to a school was seen as a key barrier to universal primary education: the response was to expand the network of schools and numbers of teachers. This focus on quantity overshadowed the issue of quality. Quality is notoriously difficult to define: traditional, key indicators of the quality of systems providing basic education have included rates of school enrolment, retention, achievement of learning outcomes, and national literacy (e.g. UNESCO, 1998) (see Table 2). Quantitative measures such as these have prompted concerns over the rates of return to investment, and highlighted a lack of internal efficiency, e.g. relatively low levels of participation in primary schooling, early drop-out, and low levels of student achievement.

Schools: sustaining or breaking down social inequality?

Read differently, these indicators reflect how schools are contextually situated within unequal socioeconomic power relations. Non- or low participation, wastage and achievements are more

Table 1 National literacy rates, South Asia, 1995

	Total (%)	Male (%)	Female (%)
India	62.0	65.5	37.7
Pakistan	37.8	50.0	24.4
Bangladesh	38.1	49.4	26.1
Nepal	27.5	40.9	14.0
Sri Lanka	90.2	93.4	87.2

Source: UNESCO, 1998

Table 2 Indicators of internal efficiency in primary education, South Asia, 1985–1995

	Gross enrolment ratio				Net enrolment ratio				Percentage of repeaters				Percentage of cohort reaching			
	1985	1995	1985	1995	1985	1995	1985	1995	1985	1995	1985	1995	Grade 2		Grade 5	
	Male		Female		Male		Female		Male		Female		Male	Female	Male	Female
India	111	110	80	90	–	–	–	–	4	–	4	–	81	81	65	59
Pakistan	56	101	30	45	–	–	–	–	–	–	–	–	–	–	–	–
Bangladesh	72	–	53	–	65	–	48	–	–	–	–	–	–	–	–	–
Nepal	108	129	50	89	–	–	–	–	–	28	–	24	68	62	52	52
Sri Lanka	104	114	102	112	100	–	100	–	8	–	9	–	100	100	98	99

Source: UNESCO, 1998

pronounced among minority/low-caste/economically weaker/special needs groups, and among women. Existing educational provision may reinforce longstanding social stratification rather than promote social equity.

Historically, educational systems of former colonies have been centralized, with formal decision-making powers concentrated in the hands of a small elite at the top, and orders passed from the top down to teachers at the bottom (Dyer, 2000). Bureaucrats adhere to rigid and undemocratic operating principles embedded into the bureaucracy during colonial times; teachers' autonomy or creativity is not encouraged; and in the process, public participation in the management of education is largely excluded. Government provides the school building, the teacher, the package of knowledge encapsulated in the textbooks, the inspector, and so on. Wide discrepancies between the knowledge that children gain from school, and its relevance or usefulness in their daily lives, are part of this pattern of schooling (e.g. PROBE, 1999). The nature of curricular content and limited school success in attracting and retaining children (particularly girls) from minority groups are reflections of the need to search out ways of making education more equitable and inclusive. Focusing reform efforts on making this happen is a key challenge for managers of educational systems.

MANAGEMENT CHALLENGES AT THE PRIMARY SCHOOL LEVEL

Promoting cultures of learning

Equity concerns over the lower-school success of disadvantaged groups strongly implies the need to bring about radical shifts in the culture of teaching and learning. Centrally devised curricula and textbooks have tended to assume that all children are homogenous. The focus has been on what is to be taught, rather than on children's learning, assuming that if the teacher teaches, children will learn. But if schools are to promote greater social equity, they need to operate in more democratic, participatory ways, with greater emphasis on learning, so that children's own knowledge and experiences are valued and validated.

A crucial shift is to encourage the one-way traffic of 'teacher as expert', transmitting a predetermined body of knowledge to give way to two-way interactions, with a teacher as the facilitator of children's discovery. This entails valuing and encouraging individual difference, and giving all children opportunities to progress comfortably at their own speeds. Endorsement of these principles has led to the introduction of competency-based education. The competencies all children should gain are identified nationally and the teacher is expected to facilitate the gaining of those competencies. This role demands a different approach to teaching, classroom management and to ideas about knowledge itself, and teachers may experience the demands of the new approach as a loss of control, subversion of their power in the classroom, and a challenge to their traditional standing as the gatekeeper of knowledge. Reforming teacher education to promote improved teacher quality is another priority area for educational managers.

Ultimately, if classrooms are to become more democratic, substantial changes need to be made to the way teachers are managed, as well as trained. Teachers are still seen as implementers of ideas generated by 'experts' elsewhere. McNiff (1991: xiv) explains:

> Instead of being encouraged to build up the wisdom to judge their own practice in terms of its educational competence, teachers are expected to implement identified criteria of excellence . . . to 'come up to standard', but the standards are external to, and often have little bearing on, the reality of their immediate everyday practice. This view of teachers in classrooms denies them a self-image of reflective educators, and turns them into . . . technicians.

Releasing the creative potential of teachers is a challenge for educational managers: and unless progress is made in this respect, policy aspirations towards better-quality education may remain unrealized. Current reform efforts need to have a core concern with shifting the balance of teacher accountability to the children in their care, and to ensuring learning outcomes, rather than accountability to an impersonal bureaucracy.

This places an onus on management too, to improve their commitments to ensuring sound operating conditions, including appropriate and good-quality teaching/learning materials so that all teachers, and all children, are assured the best possible chances of success.

Community participation and non-governmental organizations

In recognition of the distance (often physical as well as in terms of status) between educational management, in the form of government officials, and primary school teachers, a thrust of recent policy initiatives has been to try and boost more locally accountable structures. The state, in so doing, is trying to redress the imbalances created by its own past interventionist activities, which excluded local communities from any say in school management. Greater community participation has been promoted by the formation of bodies such as village education committees to oversee the regular attendance of a teacher, or upkeep of school buildings. Although relatively recent initiatives, there are encouraging signs that such committees are having a positive impact in improving relationships between teachers and the communities in which schools are embedded.

Non-governmental organizations (NGOs) are significant educational actors, often pioneering innovative approaches or reaching communities which are omitted from other educational provision. Relations between government and NGOs are intrinsically complex: NGOs can be more flexible, more rapidly responsive and innovative, but their sphere of operation is limited unless they can work in partnership with government. Such partnership can be highly productive: the curricular innovations of Eklaviya in Madhya Pradesh State, central India, were adopted across the state; in Bangladesh the Bangladesh Rural Advancement Committee (BRAC) operates some 30,000 non-formal primary schools in areas where there is insufficient or no government provision; the Aga Khan Foundation has undertaken a significant School Improvement Programme in Pakistan.

DECENTRALIZATION AS A DEMOCRATIC RESPONSE

This overview has illustrated some key challenges facing educational managers within the formal system in enhancing the quality of schools. Globally, the reform of management in the educational sector is increasingly seen as an essential component of enhancing relevance and of promoting social justice. Decentralization is advocated as a means of improving public participation in decision-making, redistributing political power, and enhancing the efficiency, quality and stability of educational systems.

Decentralization is 'a willingness to broaden or change the distribution of educational power ... a transfer of decision-making power from the nation-state to some socially organic local community' (Davies, 1990: 11). Its advocates argue that efficiency improves because local units of government can make more locally sensitive decisions about how and where to allocate resources. The financial burden on central government is reduced but quality is enhanced because nationally devised curricula or learning outcomes can be adapted to accommodate local cultural variations. Greater institutional and political stability should result because more is known about local or regional conditions, and there will be better support for national development policies if they are better understood, and local support for them is mobilized. But since power and finances are central issues, decentralisation may create more opportunities for political agendas of elected officials or powerful bureaucrats to undermine measures designed to improve the efficiency of the education system. It may also increase power tussles, and provide more opportunities for corruption. Defining a local community is difficult, and disparate groups may not combine appropriately to represent 'community' interests.

Decentralization may take one of several forms. Under *deconcentration*, a limited amount of decision-making authority is passed on to local agencies of central administrative units – this may result in greater central control. Under *delegation*, decision-making responsibility is assigned to the elected officials of local agencies – but this power can be withdrawn again. Under *devolution*, local bodies with legal status are created. Prawda (1993) identifies from work in Latin America a series of preconditions for successful decentralization: full political commitment from leaders at all levels; a model setting out appropriate roles and responsibilities, and resulting levels of accountability, of all participants; a timetabled and clear implementation strategy; clear operational procedures; continuous skill training for all participants; relevant performance indicators which are monitored through a management information system; adequate financial, human and physical resources to sustain the process. He also argues that decentralization stands a much better chance of success if there is a realistic gestation period and stability among senior personnel.

Davies (1990: 12) adds a fourth form: *privatization*, where market forces determine the operation of educational institutions. In South Asia, one response to unsatisfactory public-sector school is a rapid, under-regulated mushrooming of private schools. These also cater to the high demand for English language education, which is connected with access to better-paid jobs locally, and entry into the international sector. Advocates of marketization argue that it not only promotes efficiency and accountability, but also advances the democratic principles of free choice. The poorest, however, cannot afford private education of any variety, so marketization does not enhance choices for those who still depend on state facilities – indeed, private-sector expansion has failed to generate healthy competition and has labelled state education even more clearly as the preserve of those without choice. Furthermore, because education is widely seen as a public good, marketization does not lead to the retreat of the state. The state still has a duty to provide education, and to invest in education for the collective social good.

The democratic impulse behind decentralization – the notion that all are equal, and equally entitled to success, is a powerful ideology. It implies that there is no rationing of social and economic goods, and that everyone is entitled to an equal share. Yet, historically, schools have played a major role in apportioning privilege. Through examinations, for instance, schools regulate who becomes 'successful'. In terms of social equity, appropriate financial measures, proactive policies and innovative structures must underpin management reform, but they are not in themselves enough. Educational systems also need managers whose horizons stretch beyond technicist concerns with efficiency to question the role of schooling in upholding or breaking down unjust social structures, and who engage with the wider discourse of privilege and structural inequalities in which schools are situated.

GUIDE TO FURTHER READING AND REFERENCES

Colclough, C. with Lewin K. (1993) *Educating All the Children: Strategies for Primary Schooling in the South*, Oxford: Clarendon.

Davies, Lynn (1990) *Equity and Efficiency? School Management in an International Context*, Lewes: Falmer Press.

Dyer, Caroline (2000) *Operation Blackboard: Policy Implementation in India's Federal Polity*, Wallingford: Symposium Books.

Fullan, Michael with Stiegelbauer, S. (1991) *The New Meaning of Educational Change*, London: Cassell.

Graham-Brown, Sarah (1991) *Education in the Developing World: Conflict and Crisis* London: Longman.

Harber, Clive and Davies, Lynn (1997) *School Management and Effectiveness in Developing Countries*, London: Cassell.

Hawes, H. and Stephens, D. (1990) *Questions of Quality: Primary Education and Development*, London: Longman.

Kwong, Julia (2000) 'Introduction: marketisation and privatisation in education', Special Issue on Marketisation and Privatisation in Education, *International Journal of Educational Development* 20(2): 87–92.

Lockheed, Marlaine and Verspoor, Adriaan (1992) *Improving Primary Education in Developing Countries*, Oxford: Oxford University Press/World Bank.

McNiff, Jean (1991) *Action Research: Principles and Practice*, London: Routledge.

Prawda, Juan (1993) 'Educational decentralisation in Latin America: lessons learned', *International Journal of Educational Development* 13(3): 253–64.

PROBE (1999) *Public Report on Basic Education in India*, the PROBE team, New Delhi: Oxford University Press.

UNESCO (1998) *World Education Report: Teachers and Teaching in a Changing World*, Paris: UNESCO.

Political economy of violence and insecurity

EDITORIAL INTRODUCTION

For many people concerned about development, the most disturbing aspect of the 1990s was the apparent spread of war, particularly civil war, as illustrated by images of distraught and destitute fleeing people. Human rights violations resulting from current conflicts and rising violence are unprecedented. The costs are to be measured in deaths, broken lives, destroyed livelihoods, lost homes and increased vulnerability.

The first Article of the United Nations Charter committed governments to maintain international peace and security, to take effective collective measures to prevent and remove threats to peace, and to suppress acts of aggression. Yet international response to conflict appears ever more inadequate. The United Nations operations have proved very costly, in terms both of the funding required and of political credibility.

International NGOs have gained considerable experience of providing relief aid to traumatized populations. Interventions not intended to be sustainable have created aid dependency (for example, in Mozambique). The possibilities of providing for human security do not seem to have been enhanced. Embarrassing failures have resulted, the effectiveness of humanitarian aid has been questioned and funding has sharply declined.

The *Human Development Report* of 1994 reported 52 major conflicts in 42 countries and another 37 countries affected by political violence. Of these 79 countries, 65 were in the developing world. Recent 'inter-ethnic strife' was noted in about half of the world's states. Most major armed conflicts in the 1990s took place in Africa and Asia. Relatively few wars happened in eastern Asia or South America, both severely affected during the Cold War. This suggests a shift in the concentration of major war towards the world's most impoverished places, many now in a state of 'complex emergency', characterized by protracted crisis and the collapse of state structures.

Many commentators have suggested that the end of the Cold War allowed scores of ethnic groups to compete ferociously for power and influence, encouraging demands for greater autonomy for populations within states and the restricting of central government controls. The international arms trade increased the availability of modern military equipment, strongly affecting the way in which civil wars break out and escalate. It is well known that industrialized countries compete with each other to secure lucrative export contracts for military hardware and know-how. The end of the Cold War has also led to falling demand for newly manufactured products, as former superpowers withdraw support for client regimes' defence budgets.

Increased access to highly effective military equipment has been a major catalyst. Small arms have become profitable for powerful organizations and commercial companies prepared to engage in illegal trade. The availability of these modern weapons has indubitably facilitated escalating violence.

Similarly, violence against women and children increasingly concerns development agencies as women challenge structures and practices of subordination – such as violence against women and/or discriminatory political structures and regulations.

Total numbers of official refugees are difficult to measure, with official data on refugee flows never consistently collated and some very large displaced groups never formally registered as refugees. Many governments are increasingly unwilling to recognize and take responsibility for displaced populations. Rich countries attempt concertedly to restrict the arrival of asylum seekers on their territory and their exit from war zones.

In civil wars civilians tend to be the object of fighting and bear most consequences. Material resources and social networks, which made daily life possible, are destroyed. Longstanding arrangements of exchange between groups are often forcibly broken down. Levels of violence are less regulated in civil wars. It is important to recognize that contemporary internal conflicts have beneficiaries as well as victims. They include young men whose livelihoods become bound up with ongoing violence, and 'war lords' powerful because no authority can impose the rule of law. In some places, such as parts of Afghanistan and Sudan, civil wars are so prolonged that they have become the norm. Much of the population has had no experience of peace.

Economic deprivation is both cause and consequence of war. Social stratification linked to highly inequitable distributions of income is not new, and has often caused violent conflict. Recently, however, the exclusion of populations from benefits of economic growth has assumed a more overtly structured and regional dimension.

Approximately 10 million people per year are estimated to have been displaced through infrastructural programmes in developing countries. Most recent literature is dominated by reservoir-caused displacement. Displacement operations have not only grown considerably but have also been handled disastrously, generating unprecedented resistance and high international visibility, e.g. the Narmada dam in India. Population densities keep increasing, and every new major infrastructural programme requires 'space' that is often inhabited or already otherwise used. 'Displacement' is not just an economic transaction, substituting property with monetary compensation; it also involves 'resettlement' and requires true 'rehabilitation'.

9.1 Women, children and violence

Cathy McIlwaine

Violence has recently become an important development issue. This is due to a number of factors including worldwide increases in everyday violence, the globalization of crime and violence, and the recognition that violence undermines economic growth and sustainable development (McIlwaine, 1999). Implicit in these debates is violence against or involving women and children. However, the international community has generally been slow in recognizing gender-based violence. Only in 1989 was the United Nations Convention on the Rights of the Child ratified, identifying the rights of children to protection from various forms of violence. Similarly, not until 1993 was a United Nations declaration on the elimination of violence against women instituted, with global action only called for during the UN Fourth World Conference on Women in Beijing, 1995 (Spindel *et al.*, 2000).

IDENTIFYING GENDER-BASED VIOLENCE

Violence refers simply to the use of physical force that causes hurt to others in order to impose one's wishes (Keane, 1996: 66). Within a huge diversity of categorizations, one of the most useful distinctions is between political, economic and social violence. These are identified in terms of the primary motivating factor, either conscious or unconscious, for gaining or maintaining political, economic or social power through force or violence. These three types of violence are not mutually exclusive and overlap in varying degrees. Gender and age cross-cut all types of violence, although violence against women and children is usually classified as social (Moser and McIlwaine, 2000).

Violence against women is widespread regardless of country, class, race, education or age. According to the 1993 UN declaration, it includes 'any act of gender-based violence that results in, or is likely to result in, physical, sexual or psychological harm or suffering to women, including threats of such acts, coercion or arbitrary deprivations of liberty, whether occurring in public or private life' (Heise *et al.*, 1994: 3). It is essential to reiterate that violence against women occurs in two key arenas – the private sphere of the home, as well as the public sphere of the community and workplace. Too often, it is assumed that gender-based violence is confined to the home, and it is therefore ignored and deemed immune from intervention. The most common types of gender-based violence within the private sphere include sexual, verbal or physical violence between conjugal partners, or by fathers against daughters. These can also occur in the public arena, along with rape, sexual attack or harassment among strangers. Some occupations are also more likely to be associated with violence against women than others, such as prostitution and domestic service. In some cultures there are specific forms of violence against women. These may include acid-throwing in Bangladesh, involving men throwing acid on women's faces as a form of attack, or the dowry deaths common in South Asia where women are killed when their families do not provide sufficient material goods (Zaman, 1999). Often, gender-based violence is institutionalized and condoned by state legislation, and some cultures even tacitly condone female murder by male intimates (Rude, 1999).

It is important to stress that women tend to be the victims of violence perpetrated by men. However, women also perpetrate violence, especially against children, and have considerable agency to resist gender-based violence (El-Bushra, 2000). They may also commit or collude with violence against other women. Despite its association with social violence, gender-based violence may also form part of economic or political violence. For instance, gender-based violence is common during political conflict and war (Cockburn, 1998). With an upsurge in the victimization of civilians during wars, women and children have suffered the most, comprising around 90 per cent of all those affected (UNICEF, 2000). Indeed, the use of male rape and torture of women as political tools of war have been reported throughout the world. Further violence against women is incorporated in militarization around the world in terms of the functioning of the sex trade around military zones. While women tend to be the main victims of political violence, they have also been perpetrators, especially as soldiers and combatants.

TRENDS IN GENDER-BASED VIOLENCE

Under-reporting of violence against women is widespread. This is mainly due to the taboo and shame attached to it in many cultures, as well as male impunity from prosecution. Therefore there are few statistics on the extent of violence against women, with most studies based on anecdotes, newspaper reports or small-scale studies (Davies, 1994). Yet there have been some attempts to measure violence against women at national and international levels. For example, the UNDP now lists rape in its annual *Human Development Report*. UNICEF has also produced some figures for violence against women by intimate male partners which highlight the sheer extent of violence against women (see Table 1).

Despite problems with measurement, there is a general consensus that violence against women has been increasing in the last few decades. Often this is linked with transition to peace in countries previously beset by political conflicts. In South Africa, the transition to democracy has been accompanied by a spiralling of violence against women, with the highest rate of rape in the world (Baden *et al.*, 1998). Elsewhere, gender-based violence has increased due to changing male–female relationships during socioeconomic change, often linked with structural adjustment policies (Chant, 1997).

Table 1 Prevalence of violence against women by an intimate male partner

Country	Percentage of adult women who have been physically assaulted (not including sexual abuse or rape)
Bangladesh	47
Canada	29
Colombia	19.3
Egypt	34.4
Ethiopia	45
Mexico	27
Nigeria	31.4
Papua New Guinea	56.1
Paraguay	9.5
Philippines	5.1
Uganda	57.9

Source: WHO database on violence against women (1984–98) cited in UNICEF, 2000
Note: country studies are not necessarily comparable

CAUSES OF GENDER-BASED VIOLENCE

There are multiple and complex causes of gender-based violence. In general, though, it is rooted in ideological differences between women and men, usually related to the concentration of power in men's hands and a belief that women are men's possessions to be treated as they wish. As such, gender-based violence is closely associated with the construction of gender identities, and especially masculinities (Greig, 2000). Furthermore, it is often thought that development strategies in the South may also exacerbate violence against women by challenging the status quo.

There are two main ways of viewing violence against women. The first is to accept male violence as 'natural' and rooted in biological differences; this view makes it difficult to try and change male behaviour. The second, shaped by feminist scholarship and action, relates male violence to the social constructions of patriarchal forces and, in theory, it may be prevented (O'Toole and Schiffman, 1997). A study of a fishing village in South India illustrates the pervasiveness of the former viewpoint. The women interviewed saw wife-beating as an inevitable part of conjugal life. They felt that nothing could be done about men wanting to beat their wives in the first place, but thought they could reduce it by restricting alcohol consumption (Busby, 1999).

IDENTIFYING VIOLENCE INVOLVING CHILDREN

Many of these causes also relate to violence involving children. While all children encounter gender-based violence, girls in particular may experience the most severe forms of abuse. It should be highlighted that there is even less information on violence specifically involving children than on gender-based violence. In a rare attempt at quantification that excludes infant and child mortality rates, UNICEF suggests that since the introduction of the Convention on the Rights of the Child, more than 2 million children have been killed and more than 6 million disabled by armed conflicts, mainly due to landmines (UNICEF, 2000).

Most work on the issue of children and violence deals with the public sphere in terms of street children, child soldiers and gang activity. In terms of the former, many debates have focused on street children and their perpetration of economic violence. Street children are associated with petty theft such as stealing food from shops and markets, pick-pocketing, mugging and robbery. This is reflected in some of the slang words used for street children such as 'the plague' (Colombia), 'vermin' (Ethiopia) and 'mosquitoes' (Cameroon). From a gender perspective, street children tend to be mainly male. For example, studies in Colombia and Ethiopia found that the street child population was 75 per cent male (Lalor, 1999).

Street children are also victims of violence. Because of their association with crime, they are often targeted by authorities and private individuals, and killed or harmed. For example, in Guatemala City, street children have been targets of 'social cleansing' (killing) because of their assumed involvement in petty crime, prostitution and begging. Furthermore, the National Police and private police forces have been identified as the main perpetrators. In Brazil, thousands of street children and youth have been killed by 'death squads', with 5,000 children and youth murdered between 1988 and 1990 (Scheper-Hughes, 1996). The reasons for children turning to the streets usually focus on poverty and the need to generate income. Recently, however, it has been shown that sexual and physical abuse have also played a crucial role (Jones, 1997).

The second area deals with child soldiers. While some work has revolved around the psychosocial effects of children as witnesses of war, much has considered the role of child soldiers. Indeed, an estimated 300,000 children are serving in 36 wars around the world. A study from Mozambique shows how boys as young as 9 were forcibly recruited as soldiers to Renamo (Mozambique National Resistance) and then required to kill, rape and beat people that in some cases were their parents. Girls, on the other hand, were recruited as 'slave wives' and allocated to male soldiers to provide all reproductive and sexual needs. Recruitment of children was considered desirable, first, because children had high energy levels, second, they were more obedient and easier to manipulate than adults, third, they were less likely to escape and, finally, they did not demand pay (Thompson, 1999).

The final area relates to gang activity. Although this usually involves youth, children are also members. These are largely an urban phenomenon in the cities of the South. There is a huge diversity of different types of gangs, although most are male-dominated. As a phenomenon, they have different generic names, such as *maras* in El Salvador and Guatemala, as well as specific names such as the Area Boys of Lagos, Nigeria. Gang membership reflects an attempt by young men to assert their social identity in the context of dysfunctional families, as well as in response to high rates of unemployment and recruitment by political organizations (Moser and McIlwaine, 2000).

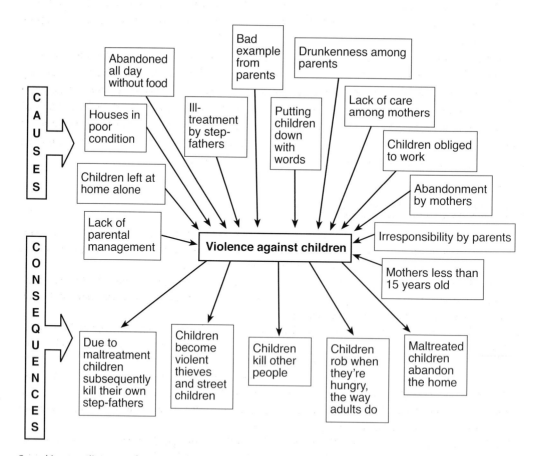

Causal impact diagram of causes and effects of violence against children in Aguazul, Colombia, identified by a mixed-sex group of adults

Source: Moser and McIlwaine, 2000

INTERRELATIONSHIPS BETWEEN VIOLENCE INVOLVING WOMEN AND CHILDREN

While the specific reasons for children living on streets, or being involved in gangs or as soldiers have already been mentioned, it is also important to mention that power relations underlie why children may be victims or perpetrators of violence. Children of both genders are embedded in gendered systems of power through their position as the property of fathers (O'Toole and Schiffman, 1997). Their unequal position in the home and wider society makes them vulnerable targets for those stronger than themselves; these may be fathers or elder siblings who take advantage of those younger and less powerful, regardless of their gender. Power relations are also central to why children perpetrate violence too; besides those forced into it, children will often commit acts of violence as a way of empowering themselves in difficult situations.

There is often a continuum of causality that runs over generations, which is critical in understanding why people end up committing or being victims of violence. It is significant that violence against children in the home as victims may also lead them to be perpetrators in later life. For instance, children who turn to perpetrating violence will often come from families where they have suffered from or witnessed violence themselves. Another example is shown in the figure opposite, drawn by a focus group in Colombia using participatory appraisal techniques. It illustrates how violence against children will often lead them to kill their step-fathers or become violent thieves or street children.

In terms of looking ahead to the future and trying to deal with violence against and involving women and children, it is therefore important to recognize different types of violence as causally interlinked (Moser and McIlwaine, 2000). The widespread nature of violence against women and children also needs to be recognized, especially in countries that implicitly condone it. The task of eliminating these types of violence must therefore be at the forefront of sustainable development strategies. Indeed, UNIFEM's recent 'Trust Fund to Eliminate Violence against Women' launched in 1996 (Spindel *et al.*, 2000) is an important step in the right direction.

GUIDE TO FURTHER READING

Davies, M. (ed.) (1994) *Women and Violence: Realities and Responses Worldwide*, London: Zed Books. This book includes chapters from scholars and activists about the universal nature of violence against women. It adopts a global perspective and covers examples from 30 countries.

Gender and Development (1998) Special Issue on 'Violence Against Women', 6(3). This collection considers gender-based violence as a development problem. It includes case studies on India, Indonesia and South Africa, as well as some theoretical and policy papers.

Jacobs, S., Jacobson, R. and Marchbank, J. (eds) (2000) *States of Conflict: Gender Violence and Resistance*, London: Zed Books. This edited collection concentrates on gender and political violence. It includes some general papers, as well as case studies from China, Brazil and South Africa.

O'Toole, L.L. and Schiffman J.R. (eds) (1997) *Gender Violence: Interdisciplinary Perspectives*, New York and London: New York University Press. This text adopts an interdisciplinary approach to gender-based violence. Comprising 35 chapters, it examines the causes and consequences of different types of violence with specific sections on children and gender violence.

Spindel, C., Levy, E. and Connor, M. (2000) *With an End in Sight: Strategies from the UNIFEM Trust Fund to Eliminate Violence Against Women*, New York: UNIFEM. This text describes a series of practical initiatives to eliminate violence against women, developed by a network of women's organizations throughout the world.

REFERENCES

Baden, S., Hasim, S. and Meintjes, S. (1998) *Country Gender Profile: South Africa*, Bridge Report no. 45, University of Sussex, Brighton: IDS.

Busby, C. (1999) 'Agency, power and personhood: discourses of gender and violence in a fishing community in South India', *Critique of Anthropology* 19(3): 227–48.

Chant, S. (1997) 'Women's roles in recession and economic restructuring', *Geoforum* 27(3): 297–327.

Cockburn, C. (ed.) (1998) *The Space Between Us: Negotiating Gender and National Identities in Conflict*, London: Zed Books.

Davies, M. (ed.) (1994) *Women and Violence: Realities and Responses Worldwide*, London: Zed Books.

El-Bushra, J. (2000) 'Transforming conflict: some thoughts on a gendered understanding of conflict processes', in S. Jacobs, R. Jacobson and J. Marchbank (eds) *States of Conflict: Gender Violence and Resistance*, London: Zed Books, pp. 66–86.

Greig, A. (2000) 'The spectacle of men fighting', *IDS Bulletin* 31(2): 7–17.

Heise, L., Pitanguy, J. and Germain, A. (1994) *Violence Against Women: The Hidden Health Burden*, Washington DC: World Bank.

Jones, G.A. (1997) 'Junto con los Niños: street children in Mexico', *Development in Practice* 7(1): 39–49.

Keane, J. (1996) *Reflections on Violence*, Verso: London.

Lalor, K.J. (1999) 'Street children: a comparative perspective', *Child Abuse and Neglect* 23(8): 759–70.

McIlwaine, C. (1999) 'Geography and development: violence and crime as development issues', *Progress in Human Geography* 23(3): 453–63.

Moser, C. and McIlwaine, C. (2000) *Urban Poor Perceptions of Violence and Exclusion in Colombia*, Washington DC: World Bank.

O'Toole, L.L. and Schiffman J.R. (eds) (1997) *Gender Violence: Interdisciplinary Perspectives*, New York and London: New York University Press.

Rude, Darlene (1999) 'Reasonable men and provocative women: an analysis of gendered domestic homicide in Zambia', *Journal of Southern African Studies* 25(1): 7–27.

Scheper-Hughes, N. (1996) 'Small wars and invisible genocides', *Social Science and Medicine* 43(5): 889–99.

Spindel, C., Levy, E. and Connor, M. (2000) *With an End in Sight: Strategies from the UNIFEM Trust Fund to Eliminate Violence Against Women*, New York: UNIFEM.

Thompson, C.B. (1999) 'Beyond civil society: child soldiers as citizens in Mozambique', *Review of African Political Economy* 80: 191–206.

UNICEF (2000) *State of the World's Children 2000*, www.unicef.org/sowcoo/.

Zaman, H. (1999) 'Violence against women in Bangladesh: issues and responses', *Women's Studies International Forum* 22(1): 37–48.

9.2 War and famine

Jean Drèze

War is one of the last bastions of famine in the contemporary world. Almost every famine in the last 30 years or so has been connected with armed conflict of one sort or another. The connection is particularly evident in sub-Saharan Africa, where conflict-related famines have struck country after country – Angola, Ethiopia, Kenya, Mozambique, Nigeria, Somalia, Sudan, Uganda, to name a few. The two main food crises of the 1990s outside Africa, in Iraq and North Korea, were also related to military hostilities, if not (in the latter case) active combat.

One reason why famine is strongly associated with armed conflict is that most countries are now able to prevent famine in peacetime. This is a relatively recent development. During the twentieth century, major famines have occurred in India, China, Russia, Brazil, Bangladesh and many other countries even in the absence of armed conflict. This happened at a time when large numbers of people lived in conditions of extreme poverty and vulnerability, and when public assistance systems (national as well international) were also poorly developed. In both respects, the situation has considerably improved in many countries, making them much less vulnerable to peacetime famine. The political compulsions to respond to an impending famine are also much stronger than they used to be, especially in relatively democratic societies. In most countries today, it would take a major economic and political crisis for a famine to occur in the absence of war.

In wartime, however, it is easy for the normal economic and political safeguards against famine to break down, even in relatively affluent countries. In economic terms, armed conflicts may contribute to 'entitlement failures' (i.e. a breakdown of the ability of households to acquire the commodities they need to survive) in at least five distinct ways.[1] First, there is often a 'recession effect': aggregate output and income decline as the physical, legal and administrative basis of productive activity is destroyed or disrupted. Second, even when there is no recession effect (war economies sometimes do quite well in terms of aggregate output), entitlements are often threatened by a 'composition effect': the composition of output shifts towards the production of military supplies, leading to severe shortages of civilian goods and sharp increases in the prices of essential commodities. Third, there is a 'distribution effect': the burden of wartime deprivation tends to fall heavily on underprivileged families, as the latter have to cope with forgone earning opportunities, rising prices, reduced public services, and sometimes also the direct destruction or appropriation of their possessions. Fourth, the vulnerability of underprivileged households is further enhanced by a 'risk effect', associated with the breakdown of ordinary insurance arrangements (e.g. reciprocal credit, patronage relations, labour migration and various forms of state support). Fifth comes what might be called an 'environmental effect': the epidemiological and health environment deteriorates due to population displacement, water pollution, the collapse of health services and related processes. Broadly speaking, it is typically through some combination of these different effects that vulnerable households are driven to destitution or even starvation in situations of armed conflict.

Turning to the political factors, one major issue is that armed conflicts foster authoritarian regimes that are not accountable to the population. This makes it easier for a famine to develop, as there is no guarantee that remedial action will be taken in the event of a food crisis.[2] In some conflict situations, unaccountable leaders may even stand to gain from the emergence of famine conditions in specific areas.

It would be inaccurate to say that the political leadership is always indifferent to the plight of the civilian population in times of armed conflict. In fact, there have been interesting instances where the role of the state in protecting and promoting the well-being of the citizens *expanded* in wartime. Here a useful distinction can be made between inter-state conflicts and civil wars. Inter-state conflicts, particularly 'patriotic wars', often involve an increase in social cohesion and an expansion of the role of the state (indeed, the historical emergence of 'nation-states' has been closely connected with this process). In some cases, this process also includes an expansion of social provisions, and possibly even an improvement in the living conditions of disadvantaged sections of the population. In relatively democratic societies, in particular, the expansion of social provisions in wartime sometimes plays an essential role in sustaining popular support for the war effort. This is one reading, for instance, of Britain's experience during the First World War.[3]

The situation is radically different in situations of internal conflict ('civil war'), which typically involve disintegration rather than consolidation of the social role of the state. The catastrophic breakdown of health and education services, for instance, is a well-documented feature of many civil wars in the contemporary world. In many cases, this breakdown has been intensified by direct military attacks on schools, health centres and the civilian infrastructure in general. The food economy, too, is a common target, damaged through means such as destruction of crops, disruption of transport networks and looting of relief supplies.

Thus, the political antecedents of famine vulnerability in wartime include not only the possible abdication of state responsibility for the prevention of famine, but also the active use of food (or famine) as a weapon. In many countries, for instance, the disruption of food supplies by the ruling government has been used to cut the lifelines of rebel forces or their supporters.[4] Inter-state conflicts, too, have frequently involved the deliberate undermining of food entitlements. One recent example is the creation of quasi-famine conditions in Iraq in 1990–91, when the combination of intensive bombings and draconian economic sanctions (even involving food imports) caused widespread hunger and a dramatic increase in mortality rates.[5] Restrictions on food imports were relaxed in mid-1991, but widespread hunger persists to this day as general economic sanctions continue to paralyse the Iraqi economy and undermine food entitlements. A recent UNICEF study estimates that economic sanctions on Iraq have caused up to half a million excess deaths among children alone in the 1990s (UNICEF, 1999). This is one of the worst cases of the use of food as a weapon in the gruesome history of conflict-related famines in the twentieth century.

Helping to force the opponent into submission is only one example of the possible 'uses' of famine in a context of violent conflict. There are also other ways in which particular classes or groups (e.g. traders, speculators, warlords, political leaders) may derive economic or political benefits from conflict-related famine. While sectional advantages of this type exist in most famines, war situations often provide exceptional opportunities for particular groups to take advantage of famine conditions, e.g. by seizing the property of displaced persons. In some cases, these 'benefits of famine' can even be seen to play a crucial role in the causation of famine itself. This is, for instance, a plausible interpretation of the politics of famine in Southwestern Sudan in 1985–89 (Keen, 1994).

Famine relief operations initiated by third parties in situations of armed conflict, particularly civil wars, tend to generate serious moral and strategic dilemmas. The basic issue is that there is no 'neutral' space in which to conduct such operations. Famine relief may even end up fuelling the conflict in question, as when humanitarian aid becomes a military resource or an object of contention for the parties involved. Some authors even view the 'disaster relief industry' as a major cause of continued war and famine in Africa (de Waal, 1997). While this sensational interpretation may not do justice to the genuine dilemmas faced by humanitarian agencies in conflict situations, it is a useful reminder of the potential dangers of ill-considered intervention. It also points to the need for integrating humanitarian concerns with political analysis and pressure.[6]

Recent research on war and famine has done a great deal to clarify the issues, and also to bring armed conflicts closer to the focus of attention in development studies. Let us hope that this will help to prevent war-related famines in the future. However, given the intrinsic economic as well as political fragility of food entitlements in situations of armed conflict, war-related famines are likely to continue as long as wars themselves persist. Ultimately, the safest way of eradicating the former is to abolish the latter. This may sound utopian, but it is even more utopian to think that the human race can survive much longer without achieving on a worldwide basis the 'pacification' that has already occurred to a large extent within specific countries.[7] Human beings are a long way behind most other species in this field: one has to look rather far down the biological scale (e.g. among some species of ants) to find anything resembling the institution of war in the animal world (Andreski, 1992). There is no reason to think that we cannot catch up with monkeys, dogs and rats in this respect. If we don't, our days are numbered.

NOTES

1. The 'entitlement approach' to famine analysis was pioneered by Amartya Sen (1981). On the debates surrounding this approach, see Osmani (1995).
2. On this issue, see particularly Sen (1992); also Drèze and Sen (1989).
3. See Winter (1986), Bourne (1989) and Marwick (1991); for a related analysis with reference to the Second World War, see Titmuss (1950).
4. See e.g. Sanders (1982) and Macrae and Zwi (1994).
5. On this, see Drèze and Gazdar (1992).
6. On this point, see particularly Keen (1994) and Keen and Wilson (1994). For a candid account of the moral dilemmas involved in humanitarian emergencies, see Vaux (2001).
7. For an illuminating discussion of the prospects of eliminating war as an institution, see Anatol Rapoport (1992).

GUIDE TO FURTHER READING

de Waal, Alex (1997) *Famine Crimes: Politics and the Disaster Relief Industry in Africa*, Oxford: James Currey. A thought-provoking analysis of the politics of famine relief in Africa.

Drèze, Jean and Sen, Amartya (1989) *Hunger and Public Action*, Oxford: Clarendon. Part 2 discusses famines and famine prevention, building on the entitlement approach developed earlier by Amartya Sen. It is short on war, but the general framework may be of interest.

Keen, David (1998) *The Economic Functions of Violence in Civil Wars*, Adelphi Papers 320, Oxford: Oxford University Press for the International Institute for Strategic Studies. An insightful essay on the political economy of civil wars.

Macrae, J. and Zwi, A. (eds) (1994) *War and Hunger: Rethinking International Responses to Complex Emergencies*, London: Zed Books. A useful collection of papers on the dilemmas of humanitarian intervention in conflict situations.

Rapoport, Anatol (1992) *Peace: An Idea Whose Time has Come*, Ann Arbor: University of Michigan Press. The scientific case for revolutionary pacifism. Essential reading for anyone concerned about the future of the planet.

REFERENCES

Andreski, Stanislav (1992) *Wars, Revolutions, Dictatorships*, London: Frank Cass.

Bourne, John M. (1989) *Britain and the Great War 1914–1918*, London: Edward Arnold.

de Waal, Alex (1997) *Famine Crimes: Politics and the Disaster Relief Industry in Africa*, Oxford: James Currey.

Drèze, Jean and Gazdar, Haris (1992) 'Hunger and poverty in Iraq, 1991', *World Development* 20: 921–45.

Drèze, Jean and Sen, Amartya (1989) *Hunger and Public Action*, Oxford: Clarendon.

Keen, David (1994) 'The functions of famine in Southwestern Sudan: implications for relief', in Macrae and Zwi, pp. 111–24.

Keen, D. and Wilson, K. (1994) 'Engaging with violence: a reassessment of relief in wartime', in Macrae and Zwi, pp. 209–21.

Macrae, J. and Zwi, A. (eds) (1994) *War and Hunger: Rethinking International Responses to Complex Emergencies*, London: Zed Books.

Marwick, Arthur (1991) *The Deluge: British Society and the First World War* (2nd edn), London: Macmillan.

Osmani, Siddiq (1995) 'The entitlement approach to famine: an assessment', in K. Basu, P. Pattanaik and K. Suzumura (eds) (1995) *Choice, Welfare, and Development: Essays in Honour of Amartya Sen*, Oxford: Clarendon Press; reprinted in Drèze, J.P. (ed.) (1999) *The Economics of Famine*, International Library of Critical Writings in Economics, Cheltenham, UK: Edward Elgar, pp. 182–241.

Rapoport, Anatol (1992) *Peace: An Idea Whose Time has Come*, Ann Arbor: University of Michigan Press.

Sanders, D. (1982) 'Nutrition and the use of food as a weapon in Zimbabwe and Southern Africa', *International Journal of Health Services* 12: 201–13.

Sen, Amartya (1981) *Poverty and Famines*, Oxford: Clarendon.

Sen, Amartya (1992) 'Wars and famines: on divisions and incentives', in W. Isard and C.H. Anderson (eds) (1992) *Economics of Arms Reduction and the Peace Process*, Amsterdam: North-Holland.

Titmuss, R.M. (1950) *History of the Second World War: Problems of Social Policy*, London: HMSO.

UNICEF (1999) *Child and Maternal Mortality Survey 1999: Preliminary Report*, New York: UNICEF.

Vaux, Tony (2001) *The Selfish Altruist*, London: Earthscan.

Winter, Jay M. (1986) *The Great War and the British People*, Cambridge, MA: Harvard University Press.

9.3 Refugees

Richard Black

INTRODUCTION

The relevance of a chapter on refugees in a compendium on development may not be immediately obvious. The plight of refugees might be seen at best as irrelevant to the goals of international development agencies. Instead, specialized international institutions are concerned with refugees, notably the United Nations High Commission for Refugees (UNHCR). At worst, the production of refugees might be seen as the *opposite* of development, especially as development has come to be defined more in terms of human rights, democracy and the rule of law.

Yet refugees are more than simply symptoms of the absence of development. Analysis of refugee flows both within the developing world and from 'South' to 'North', throws up discourses, policies and socioeconomic processes that directly parallel wider development issues. In this context, interesting opportunities exist for enhanced learning and understanding in both directions between 'refugee studies' and 'development studies'.

DEFINING REFUGEES

Refugees exist in both 'North' and 'South'. In the North, they are commonly defined (by states) according to the 1951 Geneva Convention on refugees, as those who have a well-founded fear of being persecuted for reasons of race, religion, nationality, membership in a particular social group, or political opinion. In contrast, in many Southern countries a wider definition is often employed, as in Africa where 'victims of war or external aggression' are included, and accordingly much greater numbers proportionally are held to fall within the purview of 'refugee policy'. Based mainly on government figures, which involve a mixture of these two definitions, the UNHCR estimated that at the end of 1999, there were some 11.7 million refugees worldwide. Of these, 30 per cent were in Africa and 41 per cent in Asia. There were also a further 1.2 million 'asylum-seekers', mostly in Europe and North America – those who had claimed refugee status but whose claims were not yet recognized (UNHCR, 2000).

Such geographical variations in the definition of who is a refugee stand as an initial warning of the lack of robustness of the category, and the potential for confusion. Indeed, recent years have seen attempts both to narrow and to widen the definition of refugees. States in both the North, and increasingly also the South, have sought to justify more restrictive immigration policies, by cracking down on those they label as 'bogus' asylum-seekers. The result has been a progressive narrowing of practical applications of the refugee definition, with greater insistence on the need for asylum-seekers to prove *individual persecution* to gain the status of 'refugee'. Refugees are emphatically not seen as those left behind by 'development' even if ongoing wars have prevented the return of some who fail to meet the narrow interpretation of the refugee definition employed by Northern states.

At the same time, though, moves have come from both academic and policy quarters to widen the refugee definition – or at least to focus on the broader issue of 'forced migration' rather than a narrow definition of 'refugees'. As a result, terms such as 'internally displaced person' (IDP), 'environmental refugee', 'relocatee' and even 'economic refugee' have entered the literature. For example, nearly five million IDPs were recently 'of concern' to the UNHCR – in effect treated as if they were refugees – whilst up to 25 million further IDPs were estimated to lie beyond the organization's reach (Cohen and Deng, 1998). Estimates of the number of 'environmental refugees' range from 10 to 25 million, though such estimates – and indeed the concept itself – have been widely criticized. Although far from unproblematic in themselves, these additional categories of forced migration testify to the overlapping causes and consequences of migration. These range from situations of forced displacement across international borders as a result of essentially political events, to instances where state borders are not crossed, or environmental degradation, large-scale development schemes, or economic crisis play a significant role in producing migration.

A major part of this difficulty in defining refugees is the dual context in which the term is used. In the policy world, the term 'refugee' is first and foremost a legal category. It confers rights to protection, but also to assistance, and possibly the right to stay in a country that offers far better conditions in terms of its economic opportunities or human rights record (Shacknove, 1985). Yet the transplanting of the term to social science as a term with any explanatory power or analytical worth requires at the very least a consistent application of the term by policy-makers, and preferably a conceptual basis that lies independent of its policy implementation. It is far from clear that either exists. Even a simple division of migration into 'forced' (refugees) and 'voluntary' (not refugees) is problematic, as people who are displaced have varying degrees of choice over when, where and how to move even in conditions of extreme crisis.

EXPLAINING FORCED MIGRATION

If the term 'refugee' itself is not self-explanatory, the next step is to explore different explanations of forced migration, to see whether any more consistency can be found. One view is that increasing numbers of refugees and forced migrants are the result of a breakdown of order in a post-Cold War world. During the Cold War, there was a perception in the West that refugees were mainly those fleeing persecution under communist regimes, even if some observers recognized that proxy wars being fought between the US and the Soviet bloc had also produced mass flows of refugees in Africa and Asia. In contrast, in the post-Cold War world, the 'security' of superpower rivalry is argued to have given way to a much more localized and bloody series of wars and internal conflicts. In these new wars, 'tribal' or 'ethnic' hatreds are seen as driving an ever-expanding number of refugees out of their homes. This is linked to environmental degradation caused by poverty, conflicts over increasingly scarce natural resources and a declining commitment to development aid amongst the world's leading donor nations.

Such a perspective at the very least suggests that moves to draw up typologies of refugees and forced migrants, and to identify the distinguishing features of different categories, may be misplaced. From this standpoint, the wars that cause displacement increasingly mix political, economic, social and environmental factors. The result is a new 'vicious circle' of poverty, violence and displacement that makes a rigid categorization of refugees as 'political', 'economic' or 'environmental' highly problematic. Meanwhile, as poverty, violence and displacement are interlinked, the promotion of development – especially a pro-poor, pro-human rights and pro-good governance version of development – might be seen as a potential solution to the world's 'refugee crisis'. Yet much as it is compelling, such a perspective arguably misses both the main causes of forced migration, and also the importance of the links between refugees and development.

A first clue is provided by the one form of forced migration that does not fit neatly into the 'downward spiral' hypothesis of poverty, violence and displacement – namely so-called 'development-induced displacement'. Those who have been displaced by dams and other major public works bear many of the hallmarks of the refugee – they are forced to leave their homes and land, often at short notice and with little or no compensation. Yet by definition their flight is caused not by a lack of development, but by 'development' itself, albeit a particular vision of what development should be.

A number of major wars that have produced refugees in the last decade can be seen not as conflicts of poverty, but as wars driven by political elites seeking power over resources, territory or the state (or all three). In Bosnia, the war was between nationalist leaders, fighting for control of territory and access to lucrative business opportunities in the post-communist era. In Rwanda, the genocide can be seen as rooted in colonial oppression and state-sponsored violence. In both cases, ethnic rivalries were deliberately inflamed by leaders intent on gaining and/or maintaining power. Where environmental factors are relevant, it is often an abundance, rather than a lack of natural resources that leads to conflict. Thus in the Congo, Angola, Sierra Leone and Liberia, access to major deposits of diamonds, oil and other minerals has both caused and sustained long-running conflicts that have displaced millions of people. Meanwhile, external intervention has often been neither absent nor benign, as Western companies (and even in some cases aid agencies and 'peace-keeping' forces) have played a partisan role in bolstering the position of one or more of the warring factions.

REFUGEES AND THE DISCOURSE OF DEVELOPMENT

The above discussion suggests that there are links between development and the production of forced migration, even if the latter is not the simple consequence of the former, or its absence or failure. Meanwhile, such links do not stop at the causes of refugee flight. In their responses to the humanitarian crises created by massive refugee flows, international aid agencies and donor governments have mirrored the policy shifts that have occurred in the development field. They have also used similar representations of the 'other' as they try to promote what Silk has described as 'caring at a distance' (Silk, 1997). This leads us to probe further the connections between refugee and development discourse.

In the 1980s, discussion of the need to promote a 'relief to development continuum' was laudable in principle. Yet it led to grandiose projects for refugee resettlement based on development ideas that were already well out of date. In a review of over 100 such schemes in Africa since 1962, Kibreab (1989) found that just nine had reached the point of self-sufficiency by 1982. More recently, in refugee assistance, attention has shifted to the basic needs of refugees – food, water, shelter and healthcare – before moving on to a growing concern with environmental awareness and ensuring the sustainability of emergency interventions (Black, 1998). Yet at each stage, external interventions have been dogged by bureaucratic, technical and political problems, linked in grand part to a failure to heed the warnings derived from development experience.

Yet another, and arguably more important, element of these problems of refugee (and development) assistance has been the characterization of both the intended recipients of aid (passive, powerless, poor) and the problem itself (technical, unicausal, easily defined). Although development and refugee agencies have grappled with how to promote participation of 'beneficiaries' in assistance programmes, it has proven difficult to break a pattern that Harrell-Bond (1986) describes as simply 'imposing aid'. Indeed, international humanitarian agencies have their own political and bureacratic motives for involvement in refugee assistance, which may be far from benign or disinterested.

In this sense, refugee situations provide us with similar dilemmas and challenges to the broader development scene – how to deal with complex situations, in which poverty and need are not simply technical issues, but also political ones. Humanitarian aid may be driven as much by supply (excess food stocks, defence of strategic interests, guilt), as by demand (i.e. hunger or poverty). Increasing amounts of aid are provided by non-governmental organizations (NGOs), whose numbers have mushroomed. Around 250 NGOs are estimated to have operated in Albania and FYR Macedonia at the time of the Kosovo crisis, causing immense co-ordination problems. The proliferation of agencies is encouraged by donor policies that favour the channelling of funds through NGOs.

It is important to hold up to scrutiny the role and motivations of these aid givers, as much as those who receive assistance. For example, whilst there has been some progress towards the definition of minimum standards for humanitarian assistance agencies, there is little to prevent NGOs from moving into refugee emergencies, whatever their objectives or capabilities. The results can be disastrous, as was seen in the 1994–96 emergency in eastern Zaire, when uncontrolled international agency activity may well have contributed to suffering, rather than relieving it. At the same time, whether we are concerned with emergencies or not, the task of engaging with recipients of aid requires us to understand peoples' own strategies and constraints, and resist the temptation to categorize and stereotype.

GUIDE TO FURTHER READING

Ager, A. (ed.) (1999) *Refugees: Perspectives on the Experience of Forced Migration*, London: Cassell Academic. This edited collection contains papers from a range of anthropological, sociological and psychosocial perspectives.

Black, R. (1998) *Refugees, Environment and Development*, London: Longman. Provides a critical analysis both of the growing literature on environmental causes of migration and also on attempts to make refugee assistance more linked to sustainable development priorities.

Harrell-Bond, B.H. (1986) *Imposing Aid: Emergency Assistance to Refugees*, Oxford: Oxford University Press. A classic study with a major impact across the field of refugee studies. It provides a detailed anthropological account of the situation of Ugandan refugees in southern Sudan in the mid-1980s.

UNHCR (2000) *The State of the World's Refugees – Fifty Years of Humanitarian Agenda*, Oxford: Oxford University Press. Sets out basic facts and figures about refugees worldwide, and looks back on the organization's history.

Zolberg, A., Suhrke, A. and Aguayo, S. (1989) *Escape from Violence: Conflict and the Refugee Crisis in the Developing World*, Oxford: Oxford University Press. Another classic study on the causes of forced migration, which tries to identify key features of forced migration that set it apart as a field of study.

REFERENCES

Black, R. (1998) *Refugees, Environment and Development*, Harlow: Longman.

Cohen, R. and Deng, F. (1998) *Masses in Flight: The Global Crisis of Internal Displacement*, Washington DC: Brookings Institution Press.

Harrell-Bond, B.H. (1986) *Imposing Aid: Emergency Assistance to Refugees*, Oxford: Oxford University Press.

Kibreab, G. (1989) 'Local settlements in Africa: a misconceived option?', *Journal of Refugee Studies* 2(4): 468–90.

Shacknove, A. (1985) 'Who is a refugee?', *Ethics* 95(2): 274–84.

Silk, J. (1997) *The Roles of Place, Interaction and Community in Caring for Distant Others*, Geographical Papers No. 121, University of Reading, Department of Geography.

UNHCR (2000) 'Refugees and others of concern to UNHCR: 1999 Statistical Overview', Geneva: UNHCR.

9.4 War and development

Tim Unwin

Earlier this year I was part of the West African peacekeeping force (ECOMOG) that was sent to Sierra Leone. Our orders were to disarm and if necessary kill anyone suspected of being from the rebellion. In practice, this means killing anyone in the line of fire who poses a threat to you or your fellow soldiers. I killed many people during our operation. I remember killing two young guys, not older than 13 or 14, who fired on me at close range. I don't think they even knew how to use their weapons properly. I was very lucky not to be killed, as they came at me from behind and caught me by surprise. Luckily I had an automatic weapon.

After I shot them, I saw one of them was only wounded and I had to shoot him again. I still remember the look on his face as he was dying – anger rather than anything else. I think about him most days, and I prayed for him once. Whole families were wiped out if they were suspected of supporting the rebels. During one particularly bad day of fighting the killing was quite random. Old people, the handicapped and babies were killed. We violated women, stole and hit people just for fun, just because we had the power. I am not proud of what I did – we were brothers, but we were killing each other and destroying everything. We were supposed to be the peacekeepers, but we became killers and robbers. I resigned from the army because of Sierra Leone. There was very little difference between the rebels, the mercenaries and us.

(Johnson, 1999)

The central argument of this contribution is that we need to understand the horrors of war if we are truly to grapple with the complexity of 'development'. For millions of people across the world, war and violence are as much parts of daily life as are going to school, shopping in the supermarket, or surfing the net for people in Western Europe or North America (Unwin, 1994). Yet war is largely ignored by those who write about development, and it features only very rarely in theoretical texts addressing development issues. This chapter therefore seeks not only to provide an outline of the extent and character of global warfare, but also to account for this failure of Western academics sufficiently to incorporate war into their interpretations of development. In so doing it argues that we need to make warfare central to such interpretations.

War is a notoriously difficult notion to define. At its most basic, the idea of war implies conflict. But conflict of what kind? Does it have to be armed conflict? Do certain numbers of people have to be involved? Do people have to be killed? Furthermore, even when more precise definitions of warfare are adopted, it is difficult to reach general agreement on what any one particular kind of conflict actually is. A peacekeeping operation in one person's mind might be a repressive act of warfare to somebody else. Moreover, as emphasized in the quotation with which this chapter begins, what might have started in someone's mind as a peacekeeping operation can rapidly turn into a frenzy of violence and death.

One of the most widely accepted classifications of armed conflicts is nevertheless that adopted by the Stockholm International Peace Research Institute (SIPRI). As Williams (1994) has emphasized, SIPRI has sub-divided the majority of post-1945 conflicts other than those associated with de-colonization into three categories. First, there are *inter-state conflicts*, which have generally been relatively rare phenomena, but which have, for example, in the last decade included the Gulf War (1990–91) between the US-led coalition and Iraq following the latter's invasion of Kuwait, and the conflict between Pakistan and India in 1998. Second, there are *internal conflicts*. These have been the most frequent category of conflict in the post-1945 period, and involve disputes over control of government by an armed opposition, often with the intervention of external powers. Third, there are *state formation conflicts*, involving non-government forces seeking to secede or change the constitutional status of territory, with recent examples including the violence that came to a peak in East Timor in 1999, as well as the conflicts continuing in Chechnya during the late 1990s and the beginning of 2000.

Not all authors, though, are happy with this definition. As Craft (1999) for example emphasizes, the idea of warfare needs to be separated from that of the state. In his words:

> War is actually . . . much closer to other definitions that encompass a more fundamental aspect of human relations prior to the state – as a deadly struggle for power, and all that comes with it, within society. As such, and because war predates the state, to confine its definition to 'a violent conflict between states' . . . is a distortion of what war actually is in preference to what many would have it be
>
> (Craft, 1999: 5)

Following such an argument, it is useful therefore to distinguish between fundamental struggles for power between different social groups, and the institutionalization of such struggles within the contemporary global political system.

Another recent attempt to grapple with the complexity of warfare and political instability in the contemporary world, has been the introduction of the term 'complex political emergencies' or CPEs. These have been described as a shorthand expression of conflicts which combine some or all of the following: conflict within and across state boundaries, political origins, protracted duration, social cleavages and predatory social formations (Goodhand and Hulme, 1999; see also Cliffe and Luckham, 1999). As Goodhand and Hulme (1999: 23) emphasize, 'Contemporary conflicts are not events with clear beginnings and ends, but are an element of a broader process of social change which is turbulent, discontinuous and the result of combinations of contingent factors'. As such, their resolutions can never be easy, and must lie largely within the societies within which they occur.

However we choose to define warfare, it is evident that it is something that is endemic to human society. The naïve optimism with which some world leaders acclaimed the end of the Cold War during the late-1980s, was short-lived. Far from there being a 'peace dividend', the 1990s and early 2000s have witnessed increasing political instability and fragmentation across many areas of the world, with little sign of their abatement. Despite tendencies towards an increasingly global economy and a new world order (for contrasting views of this see Fukuyama, 1992; Huntington, 1996), violence, death and all of the horrors associated with war continue to dominate the lives of tens of millions of people across the globe. SIPRI (1999) thus reported that there were 25 major internal armed conflicts across the world in 1998, and it has been estimated that in 1999 alone, some 48 million people suffered or died in conflicts around the globe (*The Times*, 5 January 2000). Such conflicts are no respecters of persons, and at least six million children were killed or maimed in armed conflicts during the 1990s. Moreover, as recent conflicts across Africa have shown, many children are directly involved in the warfare themselves, carrying guns from a young age and being forced to fight in the conflicts that have swept the continent (for a wider discussion of child soldiers see Goodwin-Gill and Cohn, 1994; for the linkages between war and hunger see Macrae and Zwi, 1994).

Despite the significance of armed conflict for the lives of so many of the world's people, theorists of 'development' have remained remarkably unwilling to incorporate any consideration of warfare into their analytical frameworks. This is well illustrated by the following examples drawn from some recent popular texts on development. One of the best short introductions to 'development' for sociologists is McMichael's (1996) succinct analysis of development and social change in a global context. This provides a compelling account of the replacement of the 'development project' by 'globalism', and the interconnectivists between international markets and commodity chains. However, neither 'war' nor 'armed conflict' receive an entry in his index, and there are only negligible mentions of the many internal conflicts or civil wars that have beset the poorer countries of the world in recent years. Likewise, major texts in geography, such as Dickenson *et al.*'s (1996) account of the *Geography of the Third World*, and Potter *et al.*'s (1999) *Geographies of Development*, fail to incorporate any detailed analysis of warfare, including it only in passing in contexts such as its role in generating refugee movements, or though its linkage with the arms trade. Equally, Hoff *et al.*'s (1993) comprehensive text on the economic theory, practice and policy of rural organization entirely ignores the possible effects of warfare or armed conflict on the credit markets, land markets, taxation systems and technological changes examined.

At least three main causes can be suggested in seeking explanations for this dearth of attention to warfare in the 'development literature' drawn from different disciplines. First, the idea of 'development', however defined, almost always implies some kind of progress. Warfare, by its very character, is in contrast usually seen as the antithesis of such progress, and cannot therefore readily be incorporated into a development-oriented theoretical scheme. Second, very few academics have practical empirical experience of the horror of modern warfare, the smell of burning flesh, the sounds of screaming men, women and children as their houses disintegrate under the incessant rainfall of bombs, or the terror as women are raped over and over again at gunpoint by rampaging soldiers. In our alienated academic writing we therefore sanitize the experiences of countless people for whom these experiences are all too frequent, and all too real. Third, warfare raises profound and difficult ethical questions, which are far from easy to resolve. Debates over whether or not there can ever be 'just wars' continue, as do those over the linkage between arms sales and the propagation of such warfare (Keegan, 1993; Snow, 1997).

Recognizing and accepting these and the many other reasons why we have failed sufficiently to incorporate warfare into our understanding of 'development' will of itself enable us to develop more sensitive interpretations of the complex changes that are affecting the lives of the poor, exploited and underprivileged across the globe. However, we need to go beyond this, if we are to help such people gain access to the relative peace that so many of us take for granted. Global military expenditure does indeed seem to have declined since its peak in 1987 (SIPRI, 1999), but there is little evidence that any of this reduced expenditure is being used directly to benefit the poorest of the world's people. Moreover, 1997 once again saw a slight increase in expenditure, and precise figures for much of the world remain unclear. Furthermore, arms production figures, although falling in the early 1990s, levelled off in 1995, and have since then remained on an approximately level trend (SIPRI, 1999). It is likely that violence and war will always be with us, but rather than fuelling these conflicts, there is a powerful moral argument that arms-producing countries should make much greater efforts than they may already be doing to limit their production of weapons of all kinds, and likewise to restrict their distribution.

Finally, rather than being seen as something extraordinary, we need to incorporate an understanding of warfare and violence as being commonplace to the changes taking place in the world today. Rather than ignoring war, we need to confront it. Only then will we be able to devise mechanisms which can effectively reduce the levels of deprivation, misery and psychological anguish that are caused by its practice.

GUIDE TO FURTHER READING

The following texts and source books provide useful material for exploring further the issues highlighted in this chapter.

Cliffe, L. (ed.) (1999) *Complex Political Emergencies*, Special Issue of *Third World Quarterly* 20(1). This Special Issue of *Third World Quarterly* provides very useful case study material of recent conflicts in Central America, Sri Lanka, the Horn of Africa, Sierra Leone, Liberia and Mozambique, as well as theoretical accounts of complex political emergencies.

Craft, C. (1999) *Weapons for Peace, Weapons for War: The Effect of Arms Transfers on War Outbreak, Involvement, and Outcomes*, New York: Routledge. This provides a useful account of the various trade-offs between weapons sales and the probability of conflict.

SIPRI (Stockholm International Peace Research Institute) *SIPRI Yearbook*, Oxford: Oxford University Press (annual; summaries available at http.//www.editors.sipri.se). These annual yearbooks provide a wealth of useful data on armaments, disarmament and international society, as well as comprehensive essays on key issues relating to conflict and arms control.

REFERENCES

Craft, C. (1999) *Weapons for Peace, Weapons for War: The Effect of Arms Transfers on War Outbreak, Involvement, and Outcomes*, New York: Routledge.

Cliffe, L. and Luckham, R. (1999) 'Complex political emergencies and the state: failure and the fate of the state', *Third World Quarterly* 20(1): 27–50.

Dickenson, J., Gould, B., Clarke, C., Mather, S., Prothero, M., Siddle, D., Smith, C. and Thomas-Hope, E. (1996) *A Geography of the Third World*, London: Routledge.

Fukuyama, F. (1992) *The End of History and the Last Man*, New York: Free Press.

Goodhand, J. and Hulme, D. (1999) 'From wars to complex political emergencies: understanding conflict and peace building in the new world disorder', *Third World Quarterly* 20(1): 13–26.

Goodwin-Gill, G. and Cohn, I. (1994) *Child Soldiers: The Role of Children in Armed Conflicts*, Oxford: Clarendon Press.

Hoff, K., Braverman, A. and Stiglitz, J.E. (eds) (1993) *The Economics of Rural Organization: Theory, Practice and Policy*, Oxford: Oxford University Press for the World Bank.

Huntington, S. (1996) *The Clash of Civilizations and the Remaking of World Order*, New York: Simon and Schuster.

Johnson, M.O. (1999) 'Eyewitness, Sierre Leone, 1999', *The Times* MM, The World at the Millennium Week 5, Death (http://www.the-times.co.uk/MM/week5/portfolio5.html, 24 February 2000).

Keegan, J. (1993) *A History of Warfare*, New York: Vintage Books.

Macrae, J. and Zwi, A. (eds) (1994) *War and Hunger: Rethinking International Responses to Complex Emergencies*, London: Zed Books.

McMichael, P. (1996) *Development and Social Change*, Thousand Oaks: Pine Forge.

Potter, R.B., Binns, T., Elliott, J.A. and Smith, D. (1999) *Geographies of Development*, Harlow: Longman.

SIPRI (Stockholm International Peace Research Institute) (1999) *SIPRI Yearbook 1999: Armaments, Disarmament and International Security*, Oxford: Oxford University Press.

Snow, D. (1997) *Distant Thunder: Patterns of Conflict in the Developing World* (2nd edn), Armonk, NY: M.E. Sharpe.

The Times (2000) 'Last year's wars claimed 48 million victims', *The Times*, 5 January, p. 24.

Unwin, T. (1994) 'States, wars and elections: the political structure of development', in T. Unwin (ed.) *Atlas of World Development*, Chichester: Wiley, pp. 239–40.

Williams, S.W. (1994) 'Warfare', in T. Unwin (ed.) *Atlas of World Development*, Chichester: Wiley, pp. 252–3.

9.5 Complex emergencies and development

Barry Munslow

NEW GROWTH INDUSTRY

Complex emergencies is a relatively new concept in the lexicon of development studies. Yet it is now a major growth industry within the international aid community, as more and more countries experience internal civil strife with a breakdown of political, economic and social order and stability accompanied by the attendant humanitarian crises. The concept first emerged at the end of the 1980s as a 'neutral metaphor for civil war' (Duffield, 1994: 4). Political sensitivities concerning national sovereignty made the governments of Sudan and Mozambique unwilling to accept the designation of 'civil war' to characterize the ongoing conflicts within their borders. Yet an internal war was most certainly taking place. In both cases, drought combined with internal conflict to create the need for considerable international assistance to meet the humanitarian need. Not only were there massive numbers of refugees congregating in neighbouring countries, there were as large, or even greater numbers of internally displaced people inside those countries affected, in equal need of humanitarian assistance.

The international community already possessed a great deal of knowledge and experience of dealing with traditional emergency situations where drought, floods, mud-slides, volcanoes or other such trigger events were concerned. When combined with the increasing vulnerability of large sections of the population of developing countries these trigger events created the need for emergency assistance. What was making the new emergencies 'complex' was that either internal wars alone were creating a somewhat similar set of circumstances of humanitarian need, or these 'traditional emergencies' were occurring within an added complexity of internal war. Wars within states were replacing wars between states with some chilling repercussions. According to the *New York Times* (5 July 1997), 'Worldwide, 90 per cent of war casualties now are civilians.' Both the people on the ground directly affected and in desperate need, and those who proposed to help them, had to confront and deal with these new complex emergencies. At the end of the twentieth and the beginning of the twenty-first century, the African continent alone faced a torrent of complex emergencies. The states involved included Guinea Bissau, Sierra Leone, Liberia, Sudan, Ethiopia, Eritrea, Somalia, Congo, Democratic Republic of the Congo, Rwanda, Burundi and Angola.

'Humanitarian interventions' was another term employed to capture the problem of international action being taken under such circumstances. For Bhikhu Parekh (1997: 5):

> humanitarian intervention means external interference with the internal affairs of a country with a view to ending or at least reducing the suffering caused by such events as civil war, genocide and starvation. . . . It respects the integrity of the state and is committed to preserving its territorial boundaries; but it also insists on our common humanity and the concomitant duty under certain circumstances to disregard the state's autonomy and intervene in its internal affairs.

Herein lies the rub. The whole system of international relations and diplomacy has been built around the concept of national sovereignty. When the Berlin wall crumbled in 1989 the era of complex emergencies was released upon the world. Whilst the Cold War was in place, a nation's sovereignty was protected by whichever camp, capitalist or socialist, that the sovereign nation lay within. Those who opted to stay non-aligned, could play off the superpower rivalry and try thereby to maintain national sovereignty. The post-Cold War world saw a questioning of national sovereignty and a rash of internal conflicts bursting forth, most notably in the Balkans and in Africa. War has become decentralized. Asia was not excluded, in particular the plight of the people of East Timor, which was finally resolved following international intervention and secession from Indonesia. Increasing concern with international humanitarian issues, including ethnic cleansing and genocide, has led to a critical questioning of the supremacy of the concept of national sovereignty. The mass genocide in Rwanda in 1994 served as a warning to the international community of the horrors that could happen if effective and timely international intervention does not occur. This opened a Pandora's box for the international community. In essence, was it justified and/or expedient to launch a war in order to prevent worse human suffering if the status quo was left in place? One need look no further than the United Nations' use of armed force from the 1990s onwards in Bosnia, Kosovo, northern Iraq, Somalia and Sierra Leone for evidence of this. In the words of Adam Roberts (1993: 1): ' "Humanitarian War" is an oxymoron which may yet become a reality.'

There were two major difficulties for the international community in tackling the problems of complex emergencies. One was *which* institutions should be dealing with this issue and the second involved *how* to deal with them, in essence the question of policy. The institutional challenge was far from easy.

INSTITUTIONAL COMPLEXITIES

The former superpowers no longer had the same interest in military or political intervention in far-off conflicts following the collapse of communism. Concerning institutions, therefore, the United Nations is generally regarded as having primary responsibility. Marrack Goulding (1993: 464) a former UN Under-Secretary-General for peacekeeping operations has captured well the essential conditions which need to be in place to ensure some chance of successful UN intervention:

> The mandate or task must be clear, practicable and accepted by the parties; the parties must pledge themselves to co-operate with the peacekeepers and their pledges must be credible; and the member states of the United Nations must be ready to provide the human and material resources needed to do the job.

Angola provides a worst-case scenario of what can happen when the conditions laid out by Goulding, concerning how to deal with the complex emergency, are breached on not just one, but on two occasions to date. The Bicesse peace agreement signed in 1991 between the ruling MPLA government and the UNITA armed opposition culminated in elections in September 1992, with UNITA returning to war immediately thereafter because it lost the UN-supervised elections. Margaret Anstee, the UN Special Representative to Angola at that time, has argued that the UN had neither a viable mandate nor the resources, and one at least of the two warring parties (UNITA) did not make a credible pledge to ensure peace (Anstee, 1996).

A new peace initiative, the 'Lusaka Accords' was signed in November 1994. Again the UN oversaw the peacekeeping operation and four years later war broke out once again. Worst of all was that the failures of the first initiative were repeated. UNITA opposition troops were not demobilized and disarmed. Their leader, Jonas Savimbi, never left the 'bush' to join formal political life within the established institutions in the capital city of Luanda. Above all, as in the case of Sierra Leone's armed opposition, UNITA control of the diamond fields was allowed to continue, hence the financial resources for the rebels to fund arms purchases and renew the conflict as and when it suited them remained in place. The Sierra Leone complex emergency in 2000 demonstrated yet again the dangers of not providing a credible UN operation. A considerable number of UN troops were captured by the rebels and some were killed.

In general, the UN military capability has not been sufficiently effective. For this reason, NATO troops were brought in both in Bosnia and in Kosovo. NATO has provided a credible military force, the UN has to develop such a capacity.

In practice, a good deal of the complexity in complex emergencies emerges from the institutional problems of those institutions which have assumed the task of humanitarian intervention. A number of difficulties exist. The initial model for interventions was based upon that of 'natural' disasters with a linear continuum envisaged for interventions progressing in stages from relief to rehabilitation to development. Critiques of this approach grew throughout the 1990s. Duffield (1994) argued that this continuum assumed development was the norm, interrupted by an emergency, whereas it was precisely the failure of the development process itself which had contributed to the emergency. Beyond this, there exists a fundamental divide between the emergency institutions and the development institutions, they have different mandates and funding, which frequently precludes or impedes any effective bridging mechanism from humanitarian relief to sustainable development being established by the various institutions involved. This divide is further exacerbated by institutional rivalries and the struggle for institutional funding at a time when development assistance budgets have universally been squeezed (Munslow and Brown, 1997).

The criticism of the fallacies of the development continuum approach eventually found some acknowledgement in the institutional structures. The European Commission (1996) proposed linking relief, rehabilitation and development. In essence, all three initiatives need to be pursued in parallel and be combined together to maximize the overall impact. Stating this as a goal is a step forward, but achieving it in practice has yet to be proven in the successful resolution of numerous ongoing complex emergencies.

An overly long institutional chain of command adds to the complexity. The OECD governments of the advanced industrialized countries fund multilateral agencies such as the World Food Programme or the United Nations High Commission for Refugees, which in turn work in parallel with bilateral government funding organizations, and they finance international non-governmental organizations (NGOs), which in turn contract local NGOs, who work with community organizations and people on the ground. Along this complex chain there is ample scope for delay, confusion, duplication, crossed or inappropriate mandates and institutional self-interest in an era of restricted aid budgets, clouding the issue of effective delivery. All too often in the past, the outside agencies have taken responsibility themselves for delivery of humanitarian assistance. Too often, interventions have weakened rather than strengthened indigenous structures. Building up local capacity to manage the situation is another vital component in creating bridges to move from complex emergency to sustainable development.

Greater co-operation and flexibility is required if there is to be a successful transition from a complex emergency to a more sustainable development future. There have been success stories, albeit not without setbacks along the way, such as Mozambique (Ferraz and Munslow, 1999). There were also repeated failures, as in Angola (Munslow, 1999).

HELP OR HARM?

In policy terms, there are a number of contentious issues. Critics have argued that disaster relief efforts, initially in the Horn of Africa, contributed to the transfer of assets from the weak to the strong rather than the reverse (Duffield, 1993). Such critiques have mounted and grown more sophisticated. The African Rights group (1997) has argued that whilst huge amounts of humanitarian assistance have been given to Sudan since the early 1980s, overall, relief resources have become part of the machinery of oppression and of inflicting the opposite of what was intended, namely destitution and famine for the citizens of Sudan.

In situations of civil conflict, sources of aid become an additional object of contention between the warring parties. Hence conflicts between Ethiopia and Eritrea and between the government and the southern opposition in Sudan seriously affected the relief efforts precipitated by drought, for many peoples in the Horn of Africa in 2000. Humanitarian interventions have sometimes been undermined in their effectiveness by local asset transfer. In essence the groups which are strongest ensure that they receive the lion's share of assistance. This is precisely the reason why Ethiopia did not wish to use the ports of Eritrea for the international humanitarian relief effort in 2000. Opposing sides try to co-opt the injection of resources for their own political, and often in addition, private economic benefit. Yet this does not have to be the case. The counter-argument is that the international community has a duty to help those in need and the aid just needs to be better targeted.

A further contentious policy issue concerns international law, weighing the balance between national sovereignty and human rights abuses involving 'ethnic cleansing' and even genocide. A major rethink in international legislation is required to temper the current inviability of national sovereignty. Making policy in the context of a legal vacuum is never easy. Policy considerations depend upon political will and in the age of the global village, the news media play an important role. One school of thought argues for the 'CNN effect' whereby the media drives the policy agenda, whereas the 'manufacturing consent' school argues that the news media is manipulated into supporting government policy (Robinson, 1999).

GUIDE TO FURTHER READING

The following texts provide further reading on complex emergencies.

Harris, J. (ed.) (1995) *The Politics of Humanitarian Intervention*, London and New York: Pinter.

Kumar, K. (ed.) (1997) *Rebuilding Societies after Civil War: Critical Roles for International Assistance*, Boulder and London: Lynne Rienner.

Macrae, J. and Zwi, A. (eds) (1994) *War and Hunger: Rethinking International Responses to Complex Emergencies*, London: Zed Books.

Munslow, B. and Brown, C. (1997) Complex emergencies and institutional complexes', *Contemporary Politics* 3(4): 307–20

REFERENCES

African Rights (1997) *Food and Power in Sudan. A Critique of Humanitarianism,* London: African Rights.

Anstee, M. (1996) *Orphan of the Cold War. The Inside Story of the Collapse of the Angolan Peace Process 1992–3,* London: Macmillan.

Commission of the European Communities (1996) *Communication from the Commission to the Council and the European Parliament on Linking Relief, Rehabilitation and Development*, Brussels, 30 April.

Duffield, M. (1993) 'NGOs, disaster relief and asset transfer in the Horn: political survival in a permanent emergency', *Development and Change* 24(1): 131–57.

Duffield, M. (1994) *Complex Political Emergencies – an Exploratory Report for UNICEF*, University of Birmingham: School of Public Policy.

Ferraz, B. and Munslow, B. (eds) (1999) *Sustainable Development in Mozambique*, Oxford: James Currey.

Goulding, M. (1993) 'The evolution of United Nations peacekeeping', *International Affairs* 69(3): 451–64.

Munslow, B. (1999) 'Angola: the politics of unsustainable development', *Third World Quarterly* 20(3): 551–68.

Munslow, B. and Brown, C. (1997) 'Complex emergencies: the institutional impasse', *Third World Quarterly* 20(3): 551–68.

Parekh, B. (1997) 'The dilemmas of humanitarian intervention', *International Political Science Review* 18(1): 5–7.

Roberts, A. (1993) 'Humanitarian war: military intervention and human rights', *International Affairs* 69(3).

Robinson, P. (1999) 'The CNN effect: can the news media drive foreign policy?', *Review of International Studies* 25: 301–9.

9.6 Peace-building partnerships and human security

Timothy M. Shaw

Sub-Saharan Africa accounted for over half of all the armed conflicts taking place around the world in 1999, and some of the most costly in terms of human life. Three-quarters of the countries in the region are engaged in armed conflict, or confronted by a significant threat from armed groups with a mixture of political and economic motives

(IISS, 1999: 244)

BEYOND THE SPLENDID ISOLATION OF DEVELOPMENT STUDIES

Notwithstanding the historic antipathy between students/advocates of defence/security and development studies, the proliferation and containment of conflicts have become crucial aspects of the latter at the turn of the century. The dramatic escalation in both the frequency and intensity of conflicts in the South as the 1990s progressed – the reverse of the much-anticipated post-bipolarity 'peace dividend' – is a function of 10 interrelated factors which cannot be excluded from consideration within contemporary development policies and practices. This is so for not only states but also non-state actors such as companies and civil societies, whether or not they advocate human or national security/development. Similarly, any efficacious response has to not only take such diverse causes into account – which reflect distinct and divergent analytic assumptions and approaches – it also has to involve the full range of interests and institutions.

'Governance' among both state and non-state actors in both conflict and post-conflict contexts is challenging and problematic. Peacekeeping and post-conflict 'partnerships' necessarily include a heterogeneous range of non-governmental organizations and global to local companies as well as states, from local and national to regional and global organizations. The imperative yet elusiveness of such 'complex peace operations' is recognized in the welcome, enlightened millennium overview from the Secretary-General of the United Nations (UN, 2000: 48).

The literature on 'new' security issues and appropriate 'peace-building' responses is only beginning to develop (Mekenkamp *et al.*, 1999). Much of the most innovative analysis derives from international agencies, both state and non-state, and think-tanks. It constitutes a profound challenge to established assumptions and perspectives on 'development' as well as to orthodox disciplines such as international relations and political science along with conflict, peace and security studies, as indicated in the final paragraph of this entry. Such old 'solitudes' need to be transcended for reasons of both analysis and practice at the dawn of a new millennium.

CAUSES OF CONFLICT: WHAT IMPACTS ON DEVELOPMENT?

Among the factors identified as causes of contemporary conflict in this embryonic field are the following. (These all represent aspects of distinct analytic genres, so would be ranked differently depending on analytic assumptions/approaches. They are subdivided below in terms of less versus more strategic concerns/correlates.)

1   *Globalizations*, which are typically treated as neo-liberal policy imperatives and structural adjustment programme conditionalities, leading to exponential inequalities entailing intensified impoverishment for the majority; so the UNDP's (1999: 1) aspiration for 'globalization with a human face' may be excessively optimistic.

2   *Liberalizations, both economic and political*, with the former advancing globalizations and the latter facilitating the expression of hitherto constrained or repressed sentiments, such as ethnicities (Braathen, Boas and Saether, 2000), fundamentalisms, regionalisms, etc. In a belated effort to transcend such apparent incompatibilities and its association with notorious structural adjustment programmes, the World Bank (1999: 21) has proposed a Comprehensive Development Framework at the start of the new century.

3   The *proliferation of new states*, not just the familiar results of initial post-Second World War nationalist movements but as a function of the unfreezing of the Cold War, leading to a second wave of 'small' or 'micro' states in Central Asia, Southern Europe, etc., including Eritrea, Somaliland and others.

4   The *end of the Cold War* which had constituted a global regime which structured inter-bloc competition and served to limit it to more orthodox, inter-state forms of conflict characterized by bipolar patterns of alliance which, in turn, allowed for a classic style of peacekeeping as interposition between two regular military formations.

5   *Regional arms races* as reflections of both demand-side – new tensions between neighbours as in South Asia, the Horn and Southern Africa, Northeast Asia, etc. – as well as supply-side pressures – competition among the world's arms suppliers in a post-bipolar environment.

6   Controversially, the *privatization of security* along with other sectors (e.g. educational, financial, health, industrial, infrastructural, services) of several varieties: not only private guards/intelligence but also private soldiers/mercenaries (Cilliers and Mason, 1999; Musah and Fayemi, 2000) as well as the selling of statutory forces, such as African armies in UN peacekeeping operations, but also in morasses like Cambodia, the Congo or Sierra Leone, where their own private companies finance their presence through mining activities (as well as enrich their officers!) (e.g. Zimbabwean Osleg in Congo) (Shaw, 2000).

7   Relatedly, *complex and changeable patterns of regional 'alliances'* among a fluid, heterogeneous set of actors, both non-state and state, so that balances of forces can change rapidly as in Congo and Sierra Leone at the turn of the century, despite some erstwhile regional powers being expected to advance regional peacekeeping/confidence-building, etc. in highly problematic situations.

8   This leads to the *elusiveness of regional 'security communities'* (Adler and Barnett, 1998) so that recognized and predictable patterns of conflict and co-operation remain unlikely despite all the rhetoric about 'Asian values' or 'African renaissance'.

9   A relatively recent and novel development, the *criminalization of conflict*, in which gangs and mafias take advantage of unstable situations to escalate conflict for their own short-term financial and psychological reasons.

10 Finally, the *elusiveness of human security/development* given the nine previous points despite some progress on global norms/governance over related issues such as landmines, small arms and child soldiers: conflict is proliferating and escalating rather than the reverse (IISS, 1999).

TOWARDS A 'REAL' POLITICAL ECONOMY OF DEVELOPMENT

Given the above, there is an increasing realization that conflict may have real economic roots so its containment and reversal may thereby be quite problematic as orthodox peacekeeping responses only treat symptoms not causes. Thus, for example, a primary cause of protracted conflict on the Sierra Leone/Liberian border is the well-established informal diamond sector, which seeks to protect itself and can afford to buy weapons, child soldiers, neighbouring regimes, etc. (Smillie *et al.*, 2000). Oil in the Southern Sudan fuels conflicts in the Horn (Field, 2000). And the four-decade-old civil war in Angola is increasingly a function of fights over diamond fields (Unita) and oil fields (MPLA). Likewise, the war in Cambodia was about rights to tropical timber and drug routes (Lizee, 2000).

At the end of the twentieth century, in addition to the longstanding stand-offs between India and Pakistan, and between the two Koreas, the international community was preoccupied with conflicts in the former Yugoslavia and middle Africa, though it invested significantly greater resources in the former than the latter. The proliferation of states and struggles at Europe's back door generated a range of responses from willing partners around the OSCE. By contrast, around the Great Lakes and Horn, five interrelated conflicts received considerably less attention and investment: the smouldering civil war in the Sudan, longstanding battles within and around Angola, the fights over resources and territory throughout the Congo, flare-ups inside and around Sierra Leone, and the expensive and destructive classical war of position between Ethiopia and Eritrea (Anglin, 1999).

The ranking of the above set of causes depends not only on which of these several cases is being analysed, but also on the theoretical assumptions of the analyst; i.e. whether the approach is informed more by, say, anthropology than economics or constructivism rather than realism, political economy (i.e. diamonds and oil) rather than political culture (e.g. ethnicity or religion) (see Reno, 1998).

DEVELOPMENTAL IMPACTS OF CONFLICTS IN PRACTICE AND THEORY

A half-dozen correlates or consequences of this range of causes and cases are important for development studies and policies: what analysis and architecture for the twenty-first century?

First, peace-building has to involve flexible *partnerships among a set of state and non-state actors* building on established 'track-two' confidence-building processes and leading towards creative governance architectures for peace operations; blue-beret soldiers alone cannot effect peace let alone make it sustainable. However, such partnerships necessitate endless negotiations among all involved. And these divisions of labour evolve over time, so that the military–non-military balance will change along with the character of the non-state partners: more/less private business/relief and developmental NGOs, etc.

Second, '*civil–military relations*' in such complex circumstances also have to be redefined: the former need to be expanded to include not just states/parliaments/parties but also elements within civil societies such as NGOs and think-tanks, and the latter private militaries/guards as well as statutory soldiers and police.

Third, *sequencing* in such peace-building operations is rarely unilineal: there is no straight line from conflict prevention/confidence-building measures through peacekeeping/-building and on to post-conflict reconciliation/reconstruction, etc; rather setbacks are almost inevitable in which anarchies sometimes recur.

Fourth, sustainable post-conflict development necessitates identifying and taking advantage of particular *opportunities* in specific situations/periods, such as the redevelopment of the milk industry in Western Uganda or the tourist industry along the Maputo Corridor in (Southern) Mozambique in the 1990s.

Fifth, identifying the most *appropriate form of 'intervention'* is problematic given the 'complex' range of causes and interests involved. But it almost always necessitates the continuous assembling of 'coalitions' among willing partners at any particular time over any particular conflict – there is no standard formula to follow even in one continent (e.g. Africa) at any one decade – as well as the espousal of 'least harm' and 'best practices' principles.

Sixth, given the trans-border character of such conflicts, any sustainable peace-building activity also has to not only engage a heterogeneous range of actors but also be *regional in scope*. This is so whether extant inter-governmental regional organizations so admit/realize or not.

And finally, seventh, given the increasing recognition of the diversity of causes or catalysts of conflicts, including their real roots in the political economy of resources, inequalities, etc., *new forms of negative and positive sanctions* need to be identified and targeted, to be effected by a heterogeneous group of actors. Given the mix of state and non-state interests involved, such sanctions can be threatened and imposed by/on a range of states (from local to global), companies, civil societies, etc. (e.g. at any part of the diamond supply chain as increasingly advocated by the UN, capital and labour in the formal diamond industry, etc.).

The above overview of this burgeoning field has profound *implications for analysis, policy and practice in several interrelated disciplines/debates*. In particular, for development studies/policy, it suggests the imperative of a realistic evaluation of the causes of conflicts before any complex peace operations/interventions are considered let alone effected. In addition, it also indicates the profound limitations of orthodox approaches to international relations/political economy as they fail to recognize the structural bases of conflict and co-operation, which enable instability/destruction and production/accumulation to co-exist, at least within certain limits. This is so for both state and non-state actors; i.e. for both inter-state organizations and transnational companies and civil societies. And the broad implications of such a peace-building nexus are apparent when other parallel issues in this Companion as indicted in the editorial introductions.

GUIDE TO FURTHER READING

Ali, Taisier M. and Matthews, Robert O. (eds) (1999) *Civil Wars in Africa: Roots and Resolution*, Montreal: McGill-Queen's University Press. An informed overview of Africa's longstanding conflicts which emphasizes their complex causes, continuities and changes over time with some lessons derivable from the continent's few cases of resolution and reconstruction.

Chabal, Patrick and Daloz, Jean-Pascal (1999) *Africa Works: Disorder as Political Instrument*, Oxford: James Currey for IAI. A 'radical' critique of established African studies and related development policies which suggests that, because of the informalization of politics and retraditionalizing of society, the continent exhibits the intrumentalization of disorder.

Cilliers, Jakkie and Mason, Peggy (eds) (1999) *Peace, Profit or Plunder? The Privatisation of Security in Wartorn African Societies*, South Africa: Institute for Security Studies. A pioneering introduction to the variety of forms of 'private' 'security' on the continent, especially in Angola and Sierra Leone.

Reno, William (1998) *Warlord Politics and African States*, Boulder: Lynne Rienner. Seminal work which advanced the analysis of the privatization of the Africa state, leading to the rise of warlords who fight to control it to ensure access to scarce resources.

Uvin, Peter (1998) *Aiding Violence: The Development Enterprise in Rwanda*, West Hartford: Kumarian. Presents the controversial argument that the international community advanced the genocide in Rwanda through its support for the Kigale regime. Winner of the US African Studies Association Herskovitz Prize, 1999.

REFERENCES

Adler, Emmanuel and Barnett, Michael (eds) (1998) *Security Communities*, Cambridge: Cambridge University Press.

Anglin, Douglas G. (1999) 'Conflict in Sub-Saharan Africa, July 1998–July 1999', *Southern African Perspectives* 81, Bellville: CSAS, University of the Western Cape.

Braathen, Einar, Boas, Morten and Saether, Gjermund (eds) (2000) *Ethnicity Kills? The Politics of War, Peace and Ethnicity in Sub-Saharan Africa*, London: Macmillan.

Field, Shannon (2000) 'The civil war in Sudan: the role of the oil industry', Occasional Paper, No. 23, February, South Africa: Institute for Global Dialogue.

International Institute for Strategic Studies (IISS) (1999) *Military Balance 1999/2000*, Oxford: Oxford University Press.

Lizee, Pierre P. (2000) *Peace, Power and Resistance in Cambodia: global governance and the Failure of International Conflict Resolution*, London: Macmillan.

Mekenkamp, Monique *et al.* (eds) (1999) *Searching for Peace in Africa: an Overview of Conflict Prevention and Management Activities*, Utrecht: European Platform for Conflict Prevention and Transformation, with ACCORD.

Musah, Abdel-Fatau and J. 'Kayode, Fayemi, (eds) (2000) *Mercenaries: an African Security Dilemma*, London: Pluto for CDD.

Shaw, Timothy M. (2000) 'Conflicts in Africa at the turn of the century: more of the same?', in Albert Legault and Michel Fortmann (eds) *Les Conflits dans le Monde, 1999–2000/Rapport Annuel sur les Conflits Internationaux*, Quebec: IQHEI, Universite Laval.

Smillie, Ian, Gberie, Lansana and Hazelton, Ralph (2000) 'The heart of the matter: Sierra Leone, diamonds and human security', January, Ottawa: Partnership Africa Canada.

United Nations (UN) (2000) *We the Peoples: The Role of the UN in the 21st Century*, New York: UN.

UNDP (1999) *Human Development Report, 1999*, New York: Oxford University Press.

World Bank (1999/2000) *World Development Report, 1999/2000: Entering the 21st Century*, New York: Oxford University Press.

9.7 Risks analysis and reduction of involuntary resettlement: a theoretical and operational model

Michael M. Cernea

This chapter concisely describes a theoretical model of development-induced displacement and resettlement processes: the impoverishment risks and reconstruction (IRR) model. Using this model can help prevent, or at least mitigate and gradually reverse, the impoverishment risks embedded in development projects that involve forced population resettlement.

Theoretical modelling in resettlement research has been made possible by the vast body of empirical findings generated worldwide by numerous researchers about the adverse consequences of forced displacement. The accumulation of empirical data enables us to reveal basic regularities in a class of similar processes. In resettlement, the dominant regularity is the impoverishment of most resettlers. This impoverishment is captured, deconstructed and explained in the IRR model.

The IRR model was proposed in the early 1990s[1] and has been considerably refined since.[2] During recent years, the model has been widely discussed in the development literature[3] and is increasingly being adopted for practical application.

Basic concepts

At the core of the IRR model are three basic concepts: *risk, impoverishment* and *reconstruction*. The central issues of risks in development can be addressed with a set of more specific risk-related concepts such as risk exposure, risk prevention, risk reduction, risk reversal, risk coping and others. The theoretical underpinnings of the impoverishment risks and reconstruction model are informed by sociology, economics, anthropology and ethics. It reflects concerns for equity, human rights and social justice in development, rather than for economic efficiency alone.

Resettlement needs and trends

Involuntary population displacement results from the imperative need to build modern industrial and transportation infrastructure, expand power generation and irrigation, implement urban renewal and enhance social services – schools, hospitals, water supply. Increases in population density, tight land scarcities and growing socioeconomic needs will unfortunately maintain resettlement as a continuous companion of development. Nonetheless, by its adverse effects forced population resettlement remains a social pathology of development. During the last two decades of the twentieth century, the magnitude of forced population displacements entailed by development projects is estimated at about 10 million people annually, or some 200 million people over two decades. This clearly indicates the global dimension of this social pathology.

De-capitalization of resettlers

In developing countries (to which this chapter mainly refers), forced resettlement carries severe risks of impoverishing the uprooted people, many of whom are very poor even before displacement. Socio-anthropological research currently documents that resettlement operations tend to cause the de-capitalization and pauperization of vast numbers of resettlers. They lose capital in all its forms: natural capital, man-made capital, as well as human and social capital. Eliminating or mitigating such impoverishment risks and improving resettlers' livelihoods is incumbent upon governments, agencies and private entrepreneurs who initiate projects that cause displacement.

Poverty reduction policies

If development's fundamental objective is to reduce poverty and promote growth, than development policies must attempt, among other goals, to minimize resettlement occurrences and (when resettlement is unavoidable) to carry out impoverishment-free relocation.

This chapter argues that the orientation towards reducing existing poverty must go hand in hand with efforts for preventing the onset of new processes of impoverishment. Development itself is not free from risks and adverse impacts. Such risks of potential impoverishment regularly surface in development projects that require involuntary resettlement, and sometimes in other projects as well. If project planning and execution fail to anticipate the potential risks, and to prevent them from becoming reality, severe problems in resettlement operations will inevitably occur. This is why the socioeconomic and moral principles embedded in poverty reduction policies must be translated into targeted actions oriented against adverse impacts and against new impoverishment processes.

In project practice resettlement plans (RPs) are required as mandatory in most internationally assisted projects. However, they are far less frequently mandated by governments of developing countries in projects they finance from domestic sources alone. Therefore, the requirement for formal and sensitive RPs must be generalized.

The currently used analytical and planning tools are often not sharp and flexible enough to lead to differentiated responses to risks. Improving the analytical methodology for regular risk assessment is therefore indispensable and should result in the formulation of *specific* risks management actions.

METHODS FOR ANALYSING IMPOVERISHMENT RISKS

As a conceptual framework for risk analysis, the IRR model is able to perform the following functions:

- *a diagnostic and predictive function*, to anticipate risks in resettlement, assess their content and their expected intensity
- *a problem resolution and planning* function, to guide the incorporation of measures commensurate with each identified risk, for prevention or mitigation
- *a research function* to guide the scholarly analysis of impacts and of behaviours under risk, as well as operational monitoring studies.

Accumulated knowledge has forewarning power. The research utility of the IRR model results from using the knowledge about past processes, which is 'packaged' and synthesized in the model. This research utility also comes from its ability to guide data collection in the field and to coherently aggregate disparate empirical findings along key variables.

Applying the IRR conceptual template to the circumstances of each development project has several advantages:

- it ensures – most importantly – that no major risk to resettlers is overlooked during the feasibility analysis of planned developments
- it allows for the different intensity of each risk to be distinguished (high risks from low risks, in the given project context) rather than treating all risks uniformly
- it demands a pro-active risk-reversal orientation in project design and financing.

The deconstruction of the impoverishment process into a template of eight basic risks, which are predictable in most resettlement situations, permits the mobilization of proportionate resources for the highest risk or against the risks affecting larger numbers of people, while allocating less to risks with lower incidence or intensity in a certain context. In practice, this differential approach may vastly increase equity by rationalizing resource allocation. Early risk analysis may also conclude that in some projects one or another of the IRR model's risks is not likely to occur, or can reveal some locally specific risks that are not part of the template but need to be addressed.

The IRR model captures impoverishment not only in terms of 'income poverty', but also in terms of losing employment opportunities, shelter, health, nutrition or education, or disempowerment.

The modelling of main displacement risks results from deconstructing the syncretic multifaceted process of displacement into its essential and most widespread risks of:

- landlessness
- joblessness
- homelessness

- marginalization
- increased morbidity and mortality
- food insecurity
- loss of access to common property
- social disarticulation.

Each of these is briefly presented below. Further, we will point out how the IRR model is to be turned on its head to help derive counter-risk strategies and matching project measures against each of these eight basic risks.

- *Landlessness* Expropriation of land needed for the project's 'right of way' removes the main foundation on which many people build productive systems, commercial activities and livelihoods. Often land is lost forever, sometimes it is partially replaced, and only seldom fully replaced or fully compensated. This is the main form of de-capitalization and pauperization of the people who are displaced. Both natural and man-made capital are lost.
- *Joblessness* Loss of wage employment occurs both in rural and urban displacement. People losing jobs may be landless agricultural labourers, service workers or artisans. The unemployment or underemployment of resettlers may linger long after physical relocation. Creating new jobs for them is difficult and requires substantial investment, new creative approaches and relying also on the sharing of project benefits with resettlers.
- *Homelessness* Loss of housing and shelter may be only temporary for many people, but for some it remains a chronic condition and is felt as loss of identity and cultural impoverishment. Loss of dwelling may have consequences for family cohesion and mutual help patterns if neighbouring households of the same kinship group get scattered. Group relocation of related people and neighbours is therefore preferable over dispersed relocation.
- *Marginalization* Marginalization occurs when relocated families lose economic power and slide down towards lesser socioeconomic positions: middle-income farm households become small landholders; small shopkeepers and craftspeople lose business and fall below poverty thresholds. Economic marginalization is often accompanied by social and psychological marginalization, expressed in a drop in social status, in resettlers' loss of confidence in themselves and in society.
- *Increased morbidity and mortality* The vulnerability of the poorest people to illness is increased by forced relocation, as it tends to be associated with increased stress, psychological traumas, and the outbreak of parasitic and vector-borne diseases. Serious decreases in health levels result from unsafe water supply and sewerage systems that proliferate epidemic infections, diarrhoea, dysentery, etc., and may lead to higher mortality rates, particularly among children and the elderly.
- *Food insecurity* Forced uprooting diminishes self-sufficiency, dismantles local arrangements for food supply, and thus increases the risk that people will fall into chronic food insecurity. This is defined as calorie-protein intake levels below the minimum necessary for normal growth and work.
- *Loss of access to common property* Poor farmers lose access to the common property assets belonging to communities that are relocated (e.g., loss of access to forests, water bodies, grazing lands). This type of income loss and livelihood deterioration is usually overlooked by planners and therefore tends to remain uncompensated for.

- *Social disarticulation*   The dismantling of community structures and social organization, the dispersal of informal and formal networks, local associations, etc., is a massive loss of social capital. Such disarticulation undermines livelihoods in ways not recognized and not measured by planners, and results in disempowerment and further pauperization.

The risks discussed above affect non-uniformly various categories of people: rural and urban, tribal and non-tribal groups, children and the elderly or, in river-based projects, upstream and downstream people. Research findings show that women suffer the impacts of displacement more severely than men. Host populations are also subjected to new risks, resulting from increased population densities and competition for resources.

RISK REVERSALS AND RECONSTRUCTION

Before displacement actually begins, the social and economic risks of impoverishment are only impending risks. But if preventative counteractions are not initiated, these potential hazards convert into actual, dire impoverishment processes.

Robert K. Merton has insightfully observed that the prediction of an undesirable chain of events may become a 'self-destroying prophecy'[4] if people respond adequately to the prediction. It follows that a risk prediction model becomes maximally useful not when it is confirmed by adverse events, but rather when, as a result of its warnings being taken seriously and acted upon, the risks are pre-empted from becoming reality, or are minimized; the prophecy destroys itself, and the consequences announced by the model do not occur or occur in a limited way.

The internal logic of the IRR model as a planning tool suggests that in order to defeat its impoverishment prediction it is necessary to attack the looming risks *early on* during the preparation of a development project. In the same way in which it deconstructs the process of displacement into eight major risks of impoverishment, the IRR model also deconstructs the process of resettlement and reconstruction into a set of definable *risks-reversal activities*, able to lead:

- from landlessness to land-based resettlement
- from joblessness to re-employment
- from homelessness to house reconstruction
- from marginalization to social inclusion
- from increased morbidity to improved healthcare
- from food insecurity to adequate nutrition
- from loss of access to restoration of community assets and services
- from social disarticulation to rebuilding networks and communities.

These strategic directions for reconstruction indicate that the IRR model is not just a predictor of inescapable pauperization: on the contrary, it thus maps the way towards restoring and improving the livelihoods of the displaced. As with other models, the components of the IRR model can be acted upon and influenced through planning and resource allocation, in order to diminish the impact of one or several risks.

RISK REDUCTION THROUGH POLICY MEASURES

Development knowledge teaches us that measures to reduce risks can be taken both at the project level and at the policy level. For instance, policies that keep the costs of energy too low tend to encourage overconsumption and tolerate waste, thus leading to the construction of more dams or thermal plants, with entailed displacement risks. This suggests that the risks of resettlement can be diminished also through better demand-management policies. Ultimately, the interlocked risks inherent in displacement can be controlled when governments adopt broad national policies for safety nets and risk reversals. Single means – just cash compensation, say – cannot counterbalance all risks.

Maximum safeguarding is achieved when involuntary displacement is avoided altogether. This is the response to risks that should be considered first and foremost. Recognizing risks upfront and their financial implications is often a powerful stimulus to search for an alternative that will eliminate the need for displacement completely or cut down its size. This is technically possible, for instance, by changing the site of a projected dam, or by re-routing a highway around (rather than through) a village settlement; many other technical options can be found through creative search.

What can social research on resettlement tell us about the impacts of risk-reduction measures? Applied social research has indeed identified specific risk management strategies that can be employed against the common risks in resettlement, to prevent landlessness, joblessness, higher morbidity, etc. In turn, research on the effect of voluntary settlement schemes on patterns of self-management *after relocation*[5] has documented effective approaches, some replicable in involuntary resettlement, that can help those resettling to new lands to overcome the risks and difficulties of resettlement. (For empirical documentation on the impoverishment risks and pathological impacts defined above, as well as on experiences and results of risks reduction measures, please consult the guide to further reading below.)

NOTES

1. Cernea, Michael M. (1990) *Poverty Risks from Population Displacement in Water Resources Development*, Cambridge, MA: Harvard University, HIID. See also 'Involuntary resettlement: social research, policy and planning', in Michael M. Cernea (ed.) (1991) *Putting People First: Sociological Variables in Development*, New York and London: Oxford University Press.
2. For a detailed, up-to-date presentation and discussion of this IRR model, see Cernea, Michael M. and McDowell, C. (ed.) (2000) *Risks and Reconstruction: Experiences of Resettlers and Refugees*, Washington, DC: World Bank.
3. See, for example, Mathur, H.M. and Marsden, David (eds) (1998) *Development Projects and Impoverishment Risks: Resettling Projects Affected People*, Oxford: Oxford University Press. See also Mahapatra, L.K. (1999) *Resettlement, Impoverishment and Reconstruction in India*, New Delhi: Vikas.
4. Merton, Robert K. (1979) *The Sociology of Science: Theoretical and Empirical Investigations*, Chicago: University of Chicago Press.
5. Levi, Yair and Naveh, G. (1998) *Toward Self-Management in New Land Settlement Projects, A Cross National Study*, Boulder and London: Westview Press.

GUIDE TO FURTHER RECOMMENDED READING

Cernea. Michael M. (ed.) (1999) *The Economics of Involuntary Resettlement: Questions and Challenges*, Washington, DC: World Bank. This book sharply criticizes economic methodologies currently used for the analysis and financial provisioning of resettlement operations, particularly the cost–benefit analysis. See in particular Chapter 1 (by Michael M. Cernea) and Chapter 6 (by Warren van Wicklin) about economic fallacies in resettlement analysis and about sharing project benefits with displaced groups.

Cernea, Michael M. and McDowell, C. (eds) (2000) *Risks and Reconstruction: Experiences of Resettlers and Refugees*, Washington DC: World Bank. This volume includes 18 chapters documenting experiences from all continents with replicable approaches to risk prevention and risk management.

Levi, Yair and Naveh, G. (1988) *Toward Self-Management in New Land Settlement Projects: A Cross National Study*, Boulder and London: Westview Press. An excellent and informative review and analysis of management patterns and development processes in communities of resettlers.

Mathur, Hari Mohan (1998) 'The impoverishment risk model and its use as a planning tool', in H.M. Mathur and David Marsden (eds) *Development Projects and Impoverishment Risks*, Oxford and Delhi: Oxford University Press.

9.8 Ethnicity and development

Denis Dwyer

As Hettne (1996) asserts, ethnicity is an elusive concept. Although it has a primordial quality, ethnic identity may be shaped by historical experiences: it can also be manipulated for political purposes. So, for Hettne, ethnicity is both an objective and a subjective creation. 'That is why ethnic identity is, and has to be, a fluid concept: contextual, situational and rational' (Hettne, 1996: 17). Essentially, however, ethnicity is concerned with the idea of distinctiveness – a Them and Us dichotomy – frequently on a claimed basis of shared origins, a common culture and/or other communal characteristics. If there are no distinctions between insiders and outsiders, there can be no ethnicity.

The view that ethnicity was probably a transient phenomenon in the process of the formation of modern nations has been subject to radical revision during the last two or three decades. In new nations formed largely by immigration, for example the United States of America and Australia, the importance of ethnicity was for long seen as probably short-lived, since succeeding generations would be absorbed in the 'melting pot' of shared national identity and increasingly cohesive cultural characteristics. In the *Communist Manifesto*, moreover, Marx and Engels forecast that distinctive ethnic characteristics would disappear with the emergence of a worldwide industrial proletariat. Far from this happening, of course, the Soviet Union itself has fractured into a number of essentially ethnically based states.

The recent history of the Soviet Union calls attention to the fact that, globally, a conspicuous contemporary phenomenon is the increase in the number and intensity of ethnic conflicts: in fact it is plausible to claim that with the ending of the Cold War between the communist and non-communist worlds, internal conflict within states rather than international conflict has become the more significant of the two problems. The world is in a situation of prevalent ethnic discontent, agitation and, on occasion, violence. The Balkans, Rwanda, Nigeria, Sri Lanka and Lebanon are only a few of the cases in point.

Whilst there are many and varied reasons for the emergence of the present situation of prevalent ethnic discontent, it is undoubtedly true that one important reason is the persistence of global poverty. The building of the modern nation-state has usually been directed and accomplished by a minority of the peoples concerned, a minority which has frequently evolved into a privileged elite; and characteristically such elites have been constituted on an ethnic basis. In what, in all too many cases, are euphemistically called the 'developing' countries, development programmes are controlled and administered at the higher levels by members of the politically dominant ethnic group; and most of the economic fruits of such development flow into the pockets of a tiny ethnic elite or, at best, are distributed in a limited manner, largely within the same ethnic group. The overall development challenge in such circumstances is how to devise and implement equitable political and economic policies within states containing an often-bewildering variety of ethnic groups.

Hettne (1996: 40–2), predicting 'ethnocide' as the likely alternative, characterizes this developmental challenge as 'ethnodevelopment'. For Hettne, ethnodevelopment is a variety of the Another Development tradition (Hettne, 1995), not an alternative form of development but rather an essential precondition for harmonious development. Its principles are: (i) the acceptance in policy and planning of the fact of cultural pluralism rather than the adoption, as an indispensible basic, of the idea of a shared national cultural; (ii) measures towards internal self-determination within states, but within a situation of agreed compromise with state power, and the devolution of some powers to local communities; and (iii) sustainability, or the devising of strategies both of long-term worth and of acceptable environmental impact.

Where states have responded in terms of development policy towards the widespread problems of disadvantage based upon ethnicity in the world today, this has usually been on the basis of affirmative action programmes, or suites of policies specifically designed to benefit the members of those ethnic groups officially perceived to be lagging in the development process. The United States, for example, has developed many such policies, particularly towards the black sector of its population, whilst in Britain during the last decade such policies have become a political issue due to the increasing visibility on the national stage of its ethnic minorities. In some cases, however, the disadvantaged ethnic groups do not constitute minorities but rather the majorities within states. South Africa is a prominent case, with decades of economic appropriation to benefit a white minority now in the process of reversal through a series of affirmative action measures being undertaken by its post-apartheid government.

Another example is the case of Malaysia, which is significant because of the length of time affirmative action policies have been in operation. In Malaysia, during the colonial period, the indigenous population, largely Malay, came to be dominated economically by immigrant Chinese and Indians, even though it remained in the majority numerically. The idea of positive discrimination on an ethnic basis was actually first introduced in Britain by the colonial power, though only on a restricted basis and largely in terms of preserving certain land rights and access to jobs in government service for Malays. A much more comprehensive set of preferential policies, known as the New Economic Policy, was introduced in 1970, after serious ethnic rioting had taken place in the capital Kuala Lumpur the previous year.

Malaysia's affirmative action policies are directed both towards the rural Malays and towards those who have become urbanized and seek work in the manufacturing sector. However, a detailed study of manufacturing employment in Penang by Eyre and Dwyer (1996) has indicated that whilst the proportion of Malays employed in manufacturing has been increased, Malays overwhelmingly remain at, or near, the bottom of the industrial employment hierarchy, and skilled and managerial positions continue to be dominated by Chinese and Indians. These findings are indicative of the difficulty of implementing affirmative action policies effectively. In addition, in the case of Malaysia, it appears that the effect of restructuring under the New Economic Policy has been to produce a *rentier* class among the relatively few middle- and upper-class Malays rather than to foster true Malay entrepreneurship at a variety of levels. As a result, income disparities within the

Malay ethnic group as a whole remain conspicuously large whilst, at the same time, official corruption has increased significantly, even at the highest levels of government, and many cases of financial mismanagement have been exposed in recent years. The mirror-image of this situation was that, from a sample of small Chinese firms investigated by Eyre and Dwyer in their study, it was clear that one of the major objectives of such firms, far from seeking government assistance, was to limit contact with governmental organizations as far as possible. This was because of a fear of interference on ethnic grounds. Although many official agencies exist in Malaysia to direct and assist industrial development, the Chinese firms included in the survey exhibited a striking lack of contact with those agencies operating in Penang. There appeared to be a widespread feeling of distrust among smaller Chinese entrepreneurs of a national government perceived by them to have as a primary aim the promotion of Malay economic interests.

Clearly, in such circumstances, there are grounds for questioning the whole ethos of development policy if the ethnic aspects of this ethos are neither producing the economic advancement anticipated for the target ethnic group nor inspiring trust in other ethnic groups within the national territory, thus alienating some of the potential participants crucial for further national development. Such a situation draws attention to Brown's (1994: xii) perhaps over-cynical description of ethnicity, which was 'one of the several forms of association through which individuals pursue interests relating to economic and political advantage'. It also draws attention not only to the need for the careful analysis and evaluation of affirmative action policy towards disadvantaged ethnic groups but also to the need to reorient development theory to accommodate the realities of the global ethnic situation. Class, then gender and most recently environment have each in turn fallen under the developmental spotlight in the decades following the Second World War. Ethnicity has remained in the shadows, or at least was in the shadows until a global explosion of ethnic conflict forced this issue much nearer to centre-stage.

GUIDE TO FURTHER READING

Dwyer, Denis and Drakakis-Smith, David (eds) (1996) *Ethnicity and Development*, Chichester: Wiley. An analysis of concepts of ethnicity; ethnicity and development theory; and the political and economic policy contexts of ethnicity.

Hettne, Björn (1995) *Development Theory and the Three Worlds*, Harlow: Longman. An excellent summary and analysis of development theory.

Moynihan, Daniel Patrick (1993) *Pandemonium: Ethnicity in International Politics*, Oxford: Oxford Univeristy Press. A well-written and provocative examination of the forces of ethnicity, nationalism and self-determination.

REFERENCES

Brown, D. (1994) *The State and Ethnic Politics in South East Asia*, London: Routledge.

Eyre, Jill and Dwyer, Denis (1996) 'Ethnicity and industrial development in Penang, Malaysia', in Denis Dwyer and David Drakakis-Smith (eds) *Ethnicity and Development*, Chichester: Wiley, pp. 181–94.

Hettne, Björn (1995) *Development Theory and the Three Worlds*, Harlow: Longman.

Hettne, Björn (1996) 'Ethnicity and development: an elusive relationship', in Denis Dwyer and David Drakakis-Smith (eds) *Ethnicity and Development*, Chichester: Wiley, pp. 15–44.

9.9 Arms control and disarmament in the context of developing countries

Paul Rogers

Although the East–West confrontation of the Cold War years did not lead to a world war, or even to a direct conflict between NATO and Warsaw Pact forces, one of its main consequences was a series of proxy wars fought throughout the Third World. These, together with many regional and local conflicts, meant that the period from 1945 to 2000 saw substantial losses of life and serious injuries, together with repeated disruption to local and regional economies.

In all, over 25 million people were killed and 75 million seriously injured in over 120 conflicts during this period. Several individual wars resulted in more than one million deaths, including wars in Korea, Vietnam, Southern Africa and Afghanistan, and a feature of the whole period was the disproportionate effect on the Third World (Sivard, 1996). By the end of the century, the direct East–West confrontation was over, but many of the conflicts of the 1990s related to the consequences of the break-up of the Warsaw Pact in general and the Soviet Union in particular.

The latter part of the century was also a period in which intensive efforts were made to control armaments through a series of negotiated agreements. Some of these were bilateral, principally a series of nuclear arms control agreements between the United States and the Soviet Union, whereas others were multilateral, frequently involving the majority of the world's states. Most of the arms control activity until the 1990s involved nuclear armaments, together with the other weapons of mass destruction, chemical and biological agents, whereas most of the casualties of war were caused by conventional weapons, especially light arms. Even so, Third World states have been significant participants in many aspects of arms control.

NUCLEAR ARMS CONTROL

The United States used nuclear weapons against Japan in 1945 and began to build a substantial nuclear arsenal by the early 1950s. The Soviet Union tested its first nuclear device in 1949 and followed the United States in developing thermonuclear weapons and numerous delivery systems including long-range bombers and missiles. Britain, France, China and Israel all developed nuclear weapons in the following 20 years, South Africa maintained a small nuclear arsenal for several years until the early 1990s, and India and Pakistan were nuclear-capable by the end of the century.

Serious nuclear arms control negotiations began in 1963 following the dangerous Cuba Missile Crisis of 1962. A Limited Test Ban Treaty (LTBT) was agreed between the USA, USSR and the UK in 1963 and has since been signed by more than 100 countries. It had the effect of banning atmospheric testing of nuclear weapons, bringing under control the dangerous effects of radioactive fall-out that was prone to affect countries across the world.

From 1969 to 1992, a series of bilateral Soviet/American agreements brought limited control to the strategic nuclear arms race. These included the Strategic Arms Limitation Treaty I (SALT I) in 1972 and SALT II in 1979, setting high limits on nuclear delivery systems and warheads, but having little direct effect on the nuclear arms race. The Intermediate Nuclear Forces Treaty (INF) of 1987 involved the elimination of a class of modern missiles and was also significant in allowing a highly intrusive inspection system, and two Strategic Arms Reduction Treaties (START I and II) allowed tentative progress in actually reducing the size of strategic arsenals.

In terms of global developments of direct relevance to developing countries, three areas of arms control were significant. The Limited Test Ban Treaty (LTBT) was the starting point for protracted negotiations towards a Comprehensive Test Ban Treaty (CTBT), a multilateral agreement promoted, in particular in the 1990s, by a number of Southern states including South Africa and Mexico. Although finally open for signature towards the end of the decade, it was dealt a severe, if possibly temporary, blow by the refusal of the United States Senate to ratify the Treaty in 1999.

For 35 years from the mid-1960s, there was a series of regional negotiations to establish nuclear-free zones, beginning with the Latin American nuclear-free zone agreement, the Treaty of Tlatelolco, of 1967. This established the whole sub-continent as a nuclear-free zone, and was further boosted by the disengagement of Argentina and Brazil from a potential nuclear arms race in the late 1980s. During the 1990s, further major nuclear-free zone treaties were agreed for Africa, the Pacific and much of Southeast Asia. While all of these treaties received relatively little attention in Northern states, they were indicative of an essentially anti-nuclear attitude among many developing countries.

Finally, the Non-Proliferation Treaty (NPT) was agreed in 1968, came into force in 1970 and was subject to regular review at five-yearly intervals. The NPT bans the possession of nuclear weapons by signatories in return for the potential transfer of civil nuclear technologies to non-nuclear weapons states. Article Six allows certain existing nuclear states to be parties to the Treaty provided they engage in serious nuclear disarmament measures.

There are two distinct Third World views of the NPT. Some countries, notably India, regard it as a device by which powerful nuclear states control the spread of nuclear weapons without having to give up their own arsenals, essentially an exercise in political hypocrisy. A much larger number of states recognize this aspect of the Treaty, but regard progress towards a nuclear-free world as being of over-riding importance.

The refusal of the US to ratify the CTBT did some damage to prospects for further developing the NPT, not least because there had been a tacit agreement at the time of the 1995 NPT Review Conference to extend the treaty indefinitely in return for progress on the CTBT negotiations and a renewed commitment by nuclear weapons states to disarmament. At the 2000 NPT Review Conference in New York, the nuclear weapons states came under surprisingly heavy pressure to accept a commitment to a nuclear-free world. This they were prepared to do, in some cases with some reluctance, but a timetable was not established.

Furthermore, the NPT negotiations were overshadowed by a US interest in developing a National Missile Defence system. This, allied to the formidable US offensive nuclear systems, had the potential to cause a renewed nuclear arms race with both Russia and China. As such, it was deeply unpopular with many developing countries who saw the potential for the unravelling of a number of nuclear arms control agreements.

CHEMICAL WEAPONS

Attempts to negotiate a Chemical Weapons Convention (CWC) banning all chemical weapons were made over several decades but were boosted by the experience of the 1991 Gulf War and the ending of the Cold War. As a result, a Convention was agreed and opened for signature in 1993 and entered into force in 1997. By the end of the century 128 states were party to the treaty with a further 42 signed but still to ratify.

As the term 'convention' implies, the CWC imposes a complete ban on the development, production, acquisition, stockpiling or transfer of chemical weapons and obliges parties to the CWC to destroy all their CW stocks and the production facilities. It is thus a 'complete' treaty, widely welcomed by most states across the world, and includes an Organization for the Prohibition of Chemical Weapons (OPCW) with a professional inspectorate empowered to undertake a range of inspections of states that are party to the treaty (Kenyon, 2000).

Several key states, including Syria, Iraq and Egypt, have not signed the CWC, and Israel has signed but not ratified it. While this is considered a drawback, it is also the case that the CWC is a genuinely global treaty, with the protracted negotiations receiving consistent support from a number of developing countries.

BIOLOGICAL WEAPONS

A convention banning biological weapons (BWs) was one of the early multilateral arms control successes, the Biological and Toxin Weapons Convention (BTWC) being negotiated by 1972. It was, though, an agreement without any effective verification procedures, and there was evidence that the Soviet Union, South Africa and Iraq were among a number of states pursuing active BW programmes in the subsequent decades. Furthermore, developments in genetic engineering and biotechnology were making it technically possible to develop very much more potent BW agents (Dando, 1996).

After the end of the Cold War, and with the completion of the Chemical Weapons Convention, negotiations intended to refine the BTWC in a much more strengthened treaty commenced in Geneva. While good progress had been made by 2000, substantial problems remained, not least the concern of major biotechnology companies that an intrusive inspection regime would breach issues of commercial secrecy. At the same time, many states, not least from the Third World, were strongly committed to a strengthened treaty.

CONVENTIONAL WEAPONS

Most recent wars have taken place in developing countries, and almost all casualties are caused by conventional weapons. Furthermore, at the end of the Cold War, major conflicts in Africa and Central Asia resulted in huge quantities of light arms being shipped to areas in conflict, many of them later entering the 'grey' market, leading to what has been termed a 'Kalashnikov culture' in some regions.

Efforts to control the spread of conventional armaments were limited until the early 1990s, although some countries had legislation that controlled arms exports to regimes unacceptable to them, and there were some multilateral agreements such as the Missile Technology Control Regime, which involved a number of Western states. From 1993, a UN Arms Transfers Register has been under development, with its prime function being to make the transfer of items such as warplanes, ships and tanks more transparent. While it is a broad-based multilateral process with potential for further development, its impact on light arms transfers has so far been minimal.

There are a number of regional developments, some involving groups of Western states such as the European Union, and others relating to Third World regions. The EU adopted a Programme for Preventing and Combating Illicit Trafficking in Conventional Arms that has three aims: to strengthen collective efforts to prevent illicit arms transfers; to assist affected countries in controlling arms movements; and to promote light arms reduction by buy-back and other programmes (Benson, 1998).

The Organization of American States agreed an inter-state convention on illicit manufacturing and trafficking, the Organization for African Unity has undertaken some limited work on the issue, starting with a statement on light weapons at its 1998 Summit in Burkina Faso, and a group of West African states have sought a regional agreement on arms transfers. There has also been an increasing interest in arms transfers control by the Southern African Development Community including potential co-operation with the European Union.

At a more global level, three developments are relevant. The Wassenaar Agreement has developed from collaborative Western restrictions on arms transfers to Warsaw Pact countries during the Cold War, and involves a number of Southern and former Soviet-bloc countries. Interpol has established an International Weapons and Explosives Tracking System (IWETS) to try to track and recover stolen weapons, and the UN established a Panel of Government Experts on Small Arms in 1995 that has sought to promote a range of measures (Benson, 1998). One significant arms control success has been the intensive campaign, principally by citizen groups, to ban antipersonnel land-mines, leading to a 1997 agreement signed by over 100 countries.

While there has been a degree of progress over the control of conventional arms in recent years, it is still small in relation to the overall problem. In particular, there is no process for controlling most kinds of area-impact munitions, including cluster bombs, fuel-air explosives and multiple-launch rocket systems dispensing antipersonnel sub-munitions. Some of these systems are as damaging as small tactical nuclear weapons, yet they are proliferating to many countries.

CONCLUSION

Overall, the role of developing countries in arms control has had two significant elements. First, many countries have played a significant if largely unrecognized role in advocating the control of weapons of mass destruction, most notably with the Nuclear Non-Proliferation Treaty. Second, they are playing an increasingly important role in seeking to control conventional weapons. Given that these are the weapons responsible for almost all casualties in wars across the developing world, this is an area of arms control that is ripe for much greater attention and effort in the future.

GUIDE TO FURTHER READING

Alternative Nuclear Futures, edited by John Bayliss and Robert O'Neill (Oxford University Press, 2000) is a multi-author analysis of trends in nuclear weapons and strategy. The development of the Chemical Weapons Convention is succinctly summarized in *Controlling Chemical Weapons*, by Ian R. Kenyon (International Security Information Service, 2000). The increasingly important issues of biological weapons and their control are dealt with by Malcolm Dando in *Biological Warfare in the Twenty-first Century* (Brasseys, 1996). A wide-ranging analysis of light arms issues is in William Benson's *Light Weapons Controls and Security Assistance: A Review of Current Practice* (joint report by Saferworld and International Alerts, 1998). Wider issues of international security in the context of North–South relations are covered by *Losing Control: Global Security in the Early Twenty-first Century* by Paul Rogers (Pluto Press, 2000).

REFERENCES

Benson, William (1998) *Light Weapons Controls and Security Assistance: A Review of Current Practice*, London: Saferworld and International Alert (joint report).

Dando, Malcolm (1996) *Biological Warfare in the Twenty-first Century*, London: Brasseys.

Kenyon, Ian R. (2000) *Controlling Chemical Weapons,* London: International Security Information Service.
Sivard, Ruth Leger (1996) *World Military and Social Expenditure,* Washington DC: World Priorities Inc.

9.10 The role of the United Nations in developing countries

Jim Whitman

THE UNITED NATIONS AS A DEVELOPMENT ACTOR

Three factors inform and constrain the role of the United Nations in developing countries. The first is that the United Nations is a political organization, not a developmental one. Development is an intensely political and often highly contested matter and unlike dedicated development organizations or individual nation-states, the UN, its organs, agencies, funds and programmes have very little room for independent initiative. The UN's developmental roles are shaped directly and indirectly by the priorities of its more powerful member states.

The second factor is that beyond general statements about human betterment in the UN Charter and elsewhere, the ends and means of development have been subject to very considerable change since the founding of the UN – again, much of it politically determined. Decolonization more than tripled the number of UN member states and brought nearly all of humanity within its remit. As much of the 'underdeveloped' world became the 'Third World' of Cold War competition, development was subject to strategic considerations. More recently, globalization has begun to alter the perceptions and expectations of governments and peoples, rich and poor alike. In addition, development thinking on every scale is subject to economic trends and prevailing ideologies; the perceived needs of the poor; and factors once peripheral which take on considerable significance – human rights, gender, environment. The United Nations does not stand above or outside any of these currents.

Third, in development matters as in most other fields, the UN is not a single actor. In operational terms, there is a good case to be made for specialization in health (WHO), food (WFP), agriculture (FAO), education and culture (UNESCO) and the like, but there are more fundamental divisions at work. The Bretton Woods institutions (the World Bank and the International Monetary Fund) are part of the UN 'family' but not part of the UN 'system' – essentially, they have functional independence.[1] In practice, this means that the developing country initiatives of a number of UN agencies, even including the World Bank, can run counter to the structural adjustment programmes of the IMF. The debt burden of many developing countries has been exacerbated by structural adjustment programmes, while many of the UN's agencies work to mitigate the consequences. A more disturbing dysfunction has been visible in Iraq for more than a decade. While the UN acts under its Charter remit to maintain international peace and security through its sanctions regime against Iraq, UN development agencies struggle to deal with the resultant human suffering, including a dreadful surge in child malnutrition.

However, the role of the United Nations in developing countries is not merely a lowest common denominator of its more powerful member states – sometimes expressed as the notion that the UN is no more than the sum of its parts. The eradication of smallpox in the 1970s, led by WHO, is a case in point, as is the achievement of access to clean water for tens of millions of people. Food dependency has been eliminated from many regions and the UN also provides the technical expertise and administrative oversight for an impressive range of international regulation and global monitoring, from telecommunications to disease surveillance. Nor is the UN confined to operational matters. Development has no clear boundaries and since many of the most fundamental human needs also find expression in human rights laws and norms – clearly embodied in the UN Charter and the Universal Declaration of Human Rights as well as in extensive international law – the UN embodies powerful and near-universal ideals. The UNDP's annual *Human Development Report* is as important in normative terms as its rankings are in political terms. The eventual inclusion of 'human liberty' as a crucial indicator beside life expectancy, income and education is important in ensuring that measures of development are not confined to technical matters and aggregate statistics such as Gross Domestic Product. The United Nations also provides a focal point for new thinking, 'bottom-up' agenda-setting and the articulation and dissemination of norms. UN summits have been central to the inclusion of human rights, the claims of indigenous peoples, the needs of children, gender issues, population control and environmental considerations as part of development. Through a combination of norm-setting, data-gathering and monitoring, the UN and its various agencies have been instrumental in such substantial if undramatic advances as improvements in agriculture, literacy and infant mortality rates in many parts of the world.

CURRENT TRENDS

Yet as the gap between rich and poor continues to widen and as a spiral of poverty, environmental degradation and violent conflict become all but a way of life in some regions,[2] the difference between what the UN enshrines and what it is able to accomplish threatens its legitimacy. When the Cold War ended, much hope was invested in UN peacekeeping, occasionally to the detriment of development, as considerable resources were devoted to the demands of emergency humanitarianism. Even when peacekeeping or peace enforcement are relatively successful, the demands of post-conflict reconstruction and development are typically complex, politically volatile and indifferently funded. The operational budgets of those UN agencies most closely involved – UNDP, WFP, UNHCR – are donor-driven, which means that their ability to move from relief to development is conditioned not only by the immediate political interests of states, but also by the general trend in decreasing overseas aid budgets.

The decline in assistance to developing countries, in combination with unmet but growing emergency needs, are mutually reinforcing. Between 1996 and 1997, world aid declined from US$55.4 billion to US$47.6 billion; and aid to the poorest countries is at its lowest level for a decade.[3] Stretched UN capacity cannot address even the worst need; and capacity-short operational failures are not uncommon. While more populations sink from 'underdeveloped' to 'conflict-ridden', matters not commonly regarded as development issues, such as the global refugee crisis or the proliferation of landmines, impact on UN development initiatives and it becomes ever more difficult to address local manifestations of international iniquities and inequities in isolation. This trend is furthered by a variety of globalizing forces – most notably the harmonization of international trade being ushered in by the World Trade Organization; and also trans-boundary issues as diverse as the HIV/AIDS pandemic, regional water scarcity, resource depletion and the arms trade.

These trends make UN development initiatives all the more important, since the alleviation of human suffering, the empowerment of the dispossessed and the extension of universal norms to marginalized populations is what gives development its moral force. They are also a large part of what gives the UN its standing and legitimacy, which it will need to preserve and strengthen in order to address threats to human welfare, particularly in poorer states. The difficulty facing the UN and its operational agencies is how to deal with immediate and burgeoning need, while planning for a very different development future. In fact, the role of the UN in developing countries is becoming ever more difficult to separate from the role of the UN in framing an equitable and humane international order. In a rapidly globalizing world,[4] the interests of powerful states are no less subject to change than poorer ones, and reconsidered calculations of costs and benefits make plain the advantages of peace and stability over containment; the worth of vaccination and literacy programmes; the social and economic conditions that make and sustain export markets; and the importance of balancing trade and environment. It is plain that if the role of the United Nations in developing countries is to remain programmatic rather than events-driven, and if it is to sustain an inclusive and long-term approach to the welfare of humanity, then 'high-level' deliberations and country-level operations must come to be expressions of a single ethos. In other words, we must come to see the development of impoverished nations and peoples as the development of global society; and our own welfare as closely bound up with the welfare of humanity.

THE PROSPECT

At present, state-based fears about empowering the UN are coupled with fierce criticism of its operational deficiencies, while debate about UN reform is sidetracked into matters of bureaucratic streamlining. This pernicious cycle can only be broken by recognizing the worth of the UN's inclusiveness and standing, and its very considerable expertise, both strategically and operationally. The UN's role in developing countries properly begins with ensuring that the elimination of poverty is an inescapable requisite of international agreements that include or affect poor states, much as the UN has been instrumental in ensuring the same for human rights and for the environment. Macroeconomic strategy, currency stabilization, food production, trade regimes, employment and other large-scale considerations are not the backdrop against which 'development' can commence; if the former are not human-centred, culturally attuned and equitable, then UN agency involvement will be largely curative and, often, merely palliative.

There is no shortage of modernizing (as opposed to merely 'reform') proposals to ensure that the UN's existing organs and agencies further a 'culture of development', from a re-orientation of the Bretton Woods institutions, to the establishment of an Economic Security Council. Better coordinated programmes between various UN agencies and between the UN and various government and non-government bodies are also necessary. Concerted initiatives that capture the public imagination and garner official support – the anti-landmines campaign, or the progress made toward eliminating polio, for example – more easily dissolve barriers and open the door on political possibility than declarations. And at every level, the legacy of development as large-scale intervention must be replaced by the goal of human emancipation, which means forging working partnerships with those whom we would assist.

Conflicting interests, unrecognized difficulties and all manner of obstacles and dilemmas are the stuff of development work, but these will only become more entrenched when the aspirations of the United Nations Charter do not find expression in practical programmes. Article 55 of the Charter states that the United Nations 'shall promote solutions to international economic, social, health, and related problems'. Vision and commitment will be required to summon the necessary political engagement at a time when the restoration of war-torn societies, the majority of which are in the developing world, absorb so much political capital, often with disappointing results. A more strategic, regional approach to resolving impacted conflict holds open possibilities for combining relief with longer-term and more broadly conceived development, since so many violent conflicts range across borders. The role of the UN in these instances should extend well beyond familiar technical matters, into the restoration of justice systems, building or restoring civil administration, income generation and ensuring that the delicate fabric of social welfare provision is not left to the mercies of market forces. The sum of UN initiatives should nurture war-torn societies back into the community of states, not propel them as full players on to the 'level playing field' of the world political economy.

A more integrated, less sectoral approach to underdevelopment will be essential for development planners facing problems which are global in character as well as extent. HIV/AIDS, for example, now affects 24 million people in sub-Sarahan Africa,[5] driving a downward spiral of disease, impoverishment and social splintering. Development initiatives as conceived in previous decades cannot be undertaken in such circumstances, nor in places where violence has become entrenched or social stability and coherence has been under siege for a generation or more. Perhaps the biggest obstacle in the way of creative thinking and concerted political initiative would be an alarmist or defensive reaction on the part of governments in the developed world, which would further erode United Nations capacity.

CONCLUSION

In a world full of 'lessons' from recent events, one widely shared perception about the Gulf War should give us pause: it is that when the cause is sufficiently important, we – the international community – can move swiftly; can find in the United Nations the legal and political means to address a gross injustice; and can marshall the diplomatic, financial and logistical means few would have thought possible beforehand. A true culture of development can not grow out of charitable impulses, narrow self-interest or emergency provision. Nor, more importantly, is the way of life enjoyed by the developed world sustainable in a world of 800 million malnourished human beings. The role of the United Nations in developing countries is ultimately the work of uniting all nations in equality; facilitating this work will be the principal characteristic of enlightened self-interest in the twenty-first century.

NOTES

1. See ul Haq, Mahbub (ed.) (1995) *The UN and the Bretton Woods Institutions: New Challenges for the Twenty-First Century*, Basingstoke: Macmillan.
2. Suliman, Mohamed (ed.) (1999) *Ecology, Politics and Violent Conflict*, London: Zed Books.
3. Randel, Judith, German, Tony and Ewing, Deborah (eds) (1998) *The Reality of Aid, 1998/1999*, London: Earthscan, p. 4.
4. Thomas, Caroline and Wilkin, Peter (eds) (1997) *Globalization and the South*, Basingstoke: Macmillan.
5. Figures from UNAIDS.

GUIDE TO FURTHER READING

Klingebiel, Stephan (1999) *Effectiveness and Reform of the United Nations Development Programme*, London: Frank Cass.

Norgaard, Richard (1994) *Development Betrayed: The End of Progress and a Coevolutionary Revisioning of the Future*, London: Routledge.

Randel, Judith, German, Tony and Ewing, Deborah (eds) (1998) *The Reality of Aid, 1998/1999*, London: Earthscan.

ul Haq, Mahbub (1995) *Reflections on Human Development*, Oxford: Oxford University Press.

United Nations Development Programme (2000) *Human Development Report, 2000*, Oxford: Oxford University Press.

Agents of development

EDITORIAL INTRODUCTION

Development activity was for long virtually the monopoly of the state. However, the lack of alternatives did not mean the state was always a positive force for development. Moreover, in the late twentieth century, the state's claim to this monopoly weakened, while other agencies of development such as the World Bank, the IMF and non-governmental organizations (NGOs), gained a higher profile. Development has to be seen in the economic context of global capitalism, but also in the political context. The most crucial relationship is between the state and the economy: states participate directly in processes of productive capital formation (establishing a set of economic policies favourable to capitalist accumulation), provide infrastructure and affect private-sector resource allocation through monetary and fiscal policies. The state provides an enabling environment/structure for development by other agencies. The state is the network of government, quasi-government and non-government institutions that co-ordinates, regulates and monitors economic and social activities. The role of non-state actors seems destined to grow as the power of the nation-state declines and global economic activity intensifies.

Total official development assistance (ODA) allocated by all major donors is low and declining. Little is used directly to alleviate poverty. Even though some ODA appears altruistic, much is manifestly deployed to promote the political and economic concerns of donors. Increased emphasis on aid conditionality underlines this. Now not only the World Bank and the IMF but also many bilateral ODA programmes require recipients to adhere to certain policies. Aid is viewed as a means of promoting donors' perceptions of 'good governance' and 'sound' economic practices, leading many analysts and politicians to become very critical of aid. Good governance is defined as sound management of a country's economic and social resources for development. What is 'sound' for the World Bank and others holding the view that 'democratization stimulates development' is a range of management techniques that are believed to work well within a standardized liberal democratic model. Critics contend that there are, and ought to be, different paths for development; they are not opposed to 'good governance' but urge that this is compatible with alternatives to liberal democracy in poor countries with different institutional contexts.

The purpose of giving ODA and its deployment is more open to scrutiny. One response has been increased funding for NGOs, generally thought more able to reach the local grassroots level.

In the New Policy Agenda, combining market economics and liberal democratic politics, NGOs are simultaneously viewed as market-based actors and central components of civil society. NGOs fill gaps left by the privatization of state services as part of a structural adjustment or donor-promoted reform package.

There are various types of NGO. At the international level we can differentiate between campaigning and charitable or service-providing NGOs. Both of these are generally based in the North. International campaigning NGOs are epitomized by Greenpeace. Such NGOs will address development policy issues from a distance. Northern-based, service-providing NGOs include Save the Children, Oxfam, Christian Aid and so on. These generally have branches in the Southern countries in which they work. Often they will run their own projects, sometimes setting up their own bureaucracies, effectively by-passing those of the state. In other circumstances they will fund and monitor local service-providing NGOs or membership organizations.

At the national level many NGOs are public-interest research or campaigning organizations. Some are Western-style human rights or conservationist NGOs. Usually relatively few, they often represent the concerns of particular groups. Other types of NGO are indigenous, national (and provincial) service-providing NGOs – mostly concerned with welfare and development. Many international NGOs have moved from directly running projects to working through partnerships with such NGOs. Lastly, there are membership organizations, often called 'grassroots organizations', which exist to further their members' interests.

Recent findings have shown that NGOs are weak in contextual analysis of societies in which they work and that their approaches to monitoring and evaluation are rarely adequate. Further, certain key technical skills are frequently seen as lacking in their human resource base and many are more concerned with micro- than macro-context work. Finally, the practice of participation and innovation in project implementation can be poor.

10.1 Foreign aid in a changing world

Peter Burnell

Official development assistance (ODA) is at the heart of foreign aid. The Development Assistance Committee (DAC) of the Organization for Economic Co-operation and Development (OECD) defines ODA as resources transferred on concessional terms with the promotion of the economic development and welfare of the developing countries as the main objective. Over 150 countries and territories are recipients. In addition, the early 1990s witnessed a growth in 'official aid' to 'Part II' countries, which shares ODA's essential features but goes to 12 'transition' countries in the former communist world, primarily Russia, and advanced countries like Israel, both of which receive aid worth over US$1 billion annually. Concessionality ('softness') refers to grants or loans on especially favourable terms. Over time grants have become the dominant mode of bilateral aid to the least developed countries, many of whom experience difficulties in servicing their foreign debt including loans formerly acquired on concessional terms.

Aid takes several forms including transfers of finance, commodities and other goods, technical co-operation (around half of all bilateral aid) and debt relief. A conventional distinction is between development aid and humanitarian or disaster relief aid. Military assistance, which was substantial, especially from the United States and Soviet Union during the Cold War, is now relatively insignificant. Although the distinctions between different types of aid are theoretically coherent, in reality the boundaries sometimes break down; aid intended for one particular purpose may end up serving very different ends – the problem of 'fungibility'.

THE BIG PICTURE

Over 95 per cent of ODA now comes from DAC members comprising 22 countries and the European Commission, who in 1998 collectively increased their net ODA by almost 10 per cent, to nearly US$52 billion, following a five-year real-terms decline of 21 per cent. Total net 'official aid' receipts came to US$7 billion. ODA disbursements represented 0.24 per cent of combined Gross National Product, well below the 0.7 per cent target adopted by the United Nations General Assembly in 1970 and the 0.33 per cent typical of previous decades. While the United States before 1989 and Japan in most years since have been easily the largest donors (see Table 1), the European

Table 1 Net official development assistance, leading donors, 1998

By volume	Volume (US$ billion)	Percentage of GNP	By percentage of GNP	Percentage of GNP	Volume (US$ billion)
Japan	10.64	0.28	Denmark	0.99	1.70
United States	8.78	0.10	Norway	0.91	1.32
France	5.74	0.40	Netherlands	0.80	3.04
Germany	5.58	0.26	Sweden	0.72	1.57
United Kingdom	3.86	0.27	Luxembourg	0.65	0.11

Source: Organization for Economic Co-operation and Development, 2000: 168–9

Union (EU) member states together with the EU's own development co-operation budget (the fourth largest in the world, the largest multilateral budget, but heavily criticized for the dominance of EU politics in its administration) now account for around 55 per cent of all ODA. Approximately 30 per cent of ODA is managed by the multilateral donors including the World Bank Group's International Development Association, which makes interest-free loans to the least developed countries, and various United Nations agencies. Multilaterals account for over 40 per cent of Britain's aid of just over £3 billion and set to rise. Non-governmental agencies like CARE, Médecins Sans Frontières and Oxfam provide up to US$6 billion annually in private grants; official donors use them to channel several more billions, especially in humanitarian emergencies. Before 1989 the USSR was a leading provider of technical and economic assistance, and military aid. For several years after the 1973/4 oil price rise some oil petroleum exporting countries (OPEC), chiefly Saudi Arabia and small Gulf states, were also important donors – Saudi Arabia being in the top five until the 1990s. Kuwait is still generous in per capita terms. These countries are not members of the DAC, which was established in the 1960s to improve and help co-ordinate international aid efforts.

The United States' Marshall Plan (1948–51) aid to economic reconstruction in western Europe set a successful precedent of promoting development, which aid to other countries since has never really matched. But the pattern whereby US aid was strongly motivated by political reasons of national security and superpower rivalry has been an enduring feature. Other donors who became prominent later have also pursued multiple goals, although with individual characteristics. These range from economic objectives (Germany and Japan, for example), and a *mission civilisatrice* (France) to maintaining close historical relationships (around two-thirds of Britain's aid has traditionally gone to Commonwealth countries). The Netherlands, Canada and the Scandinavians are sometimes called 'like-minded' donors: they are presumed to share an attachment to goals of 'humane internationalism'.

Around one-quarter of ODA goes to the least developed countries; around 55 per cent goes to these and other low-income countries where annual per capita incomes are below US$760. Approximately 30 per cent of ODA goes to sub-Saharan Africa and a similar percentage to Asia including China. The most aid-dependent countries are not the major recipients (see Table 2); smaller countries are treated more favourably, on a per capita basis. Relief and reconstruction work in former Yugoslavia have been prominent in recent years. A small number of former aid recipients have 'graduated' to donor status, most spectacularly Japan, and on a small scale Taiwan, South Korea and Turkey.

Table 2 Net official development assistance, leading recipients

By volume			By percentage of GNP		
	Percentage of GNP 1997	Volume (US$ billion) 1998		Percentage of GNP 1997	Volume (US$ million) 1998
China	0.23	2.35	São Tomé and Príncipe	85.32	28
Egypt	2.53	1.91	Guinea-Bissau	48.86	96
India	0.39	1.59	Micronesia	44.90	80
Indonesia	0.40	1.25	Guyana	38.76	93
Bangladesh	2.31	1.25	Mozambique	29.07	1,039

Source: Organization for Economic Co-operation and Development, 2000: 214–17

A SHORT HISTORY OF AID

In the early decades development assistance was underpinned by an economic logic that stressed its contribution to filling two 'gaps' constraining development. Aid supplements savings and enhances investment, which makes possible the expansion of productive capacity. It furnishes foreign exchange for essential imports like machinery and, in many cases, fuel and food. Aid built large construction projects. Later, the remit was to lift the limits to the absorptive capacity for such capital inflows, for instance those deriving from technological backwardness.

By the 1970s heavy criticism was directed at most forms of aid, by dependency thinkers and other social scientists in the North and the South, many of whom believed aid is an instrument of domination and exploitation. They doubted that it could be an effective means for reducing Third World poverty, and noted that it benefited privileged elites in the South as well as in donor countries. In the 1980s ODA was challenged by the rise of the neo-liberal agenda in the West. Aid was now held to contribute to excessive government and harm economic markets. Both groups of critics see aid as part of the problem, not part of the solution to weak development. Neo-liberals especially claim it is also detrimental to donor countries, where it acts as a state subsidy to exports, so distorting resource allocation. This applies especially to tied aid (tying can be formal or informal), which binds some bilateral flows and which economists have long criticized. Donors vary greatly: for some (e.g. Japan) over 90 per cent of bilateral aid is formally untied; for others (e.g. the US) the figure is under a third.

The 1980s saw a dramatic expansion of conditional aid lending – quick-disbursing loans in the form of programme lending to help meet balance of payments and public-sector financing requirements, linked to recommendations for economic policy and institutional reform. The advice embraces neo-liberal tenets and embodies what became known as the 'Washington consensus' (after the International Monetary Fund and the World Bank). Structural adjustment loans (SALs) for structural adjustment programmes (SAPS) became a major feature. The 'conditionalities' incurred much resentment not least because they appeared to be coercive and offensive to sovereignty. However, they are difficult to enforce. Detailed examination by Mosley, Harrigan and Toye (1995) and Killick et al. (1998) showed such conditionalities to be often ineffective, notably where the governments reckon they threaten their particular interests. Accordingly the belief that it is essential to get the economics right has now been overtaken by the notion that, to improve the chances of sound economic management and make development aid effective, the political environment must also be addressed. This gave aid a new role.

Aid's agenda in the 1990s has included encouraging and assisting progress towards liberal democracy, 'good governance' and respect for human rights, in developing and post-communist states. The end of the Cold War and Soviet collapse made it possible for DAC donors to attach explicit political conditionalities to their aid, additional to economic, environmental and other conditionalities. Relatively modest sums of under US$5 billion annually are being spent on 'political development', especially by the US government's Agency for International Development and the publicly funded, non-governmental National Endowment for Democracy, and Germany's party foundations (*Stiftungen*). International bodies include the United Nations Electoral Assistance Division and the Soros Foundation (Open Society). The activities include supporting the electoral process, especially for 'reconciliation elections' in post-conflict situations, improving governance institutions, and even helping new political parties. Strengthening civil society is very fashionable. But as Carothers (1999) argues, devising suitable methodologies to evaluate the effectiveness and impact of democracy aid is just as problematic as it for more conventional forms of assistance.

FINAL OBSERVATIONS

Over the last 50 years aid has undergone significant changes in respect of what we understand about it and our expectations. By the 1990s some observers claimed aid was in crisis. Its achievements were questioned by many shades of opinion. There seemed to be minimal popular support for aid in the US, because its instrumental value for traditional foreign policy goals had obsolesced. A number of other donors manifested 'aid fatigue'.

Yet the post-Cold War disorder has seen the emergence of new kinds of security 'threats'. Sub-state violent conflict has the potential to cross borders. Issues like international migration, internationally organized crime, drugs trafficking, global environmental threats, and the challenge of mainstreaming gender, command attention. All these have greatly expanded aid's horizons. Moreover poverty is seen to be connected with all these issues, and aid agencies have rearticulated poverty reduction as the priority. The emphasis now is more on achieving results, especially social development, than maximizing aid funds. The British government's 1997 White Paper, *Eliminating World Poverty: a Challenge for the 21st Century*, exemplifies this (see Burnell, 1998). It prefers the language of development 'partnership' to the older terminology of 'overseas aid'. This change purports to place aid relations on a more equal basis. This new mantra also transfers increased responsibility for achieving aid's purposes to recipient constituencies.

It remains to be seen whether development co-operation can deliver the wide-ranging mandate that it has acquired, on the basis of relatively insignificant resources (ODA has reduced to just one-fifth of all net resource flows from DAC countries and multilateral agencies to aid recipients). An important lesson from the aid experience points to the magnitude of the problems it seeks to address – complex problems, requiring interdisciplinary approaches geared to 'holistic' solutions. 'Policy coherence', which means compatible policies in such matters as international trade, is also deemed to be crucial. The moral is that we should moderate our expectations that aid by itself will make a difference.

GUIDE TO FURTHER READING

Burnell, Peter (1997) *Foreign Aid in a Changing World*, Buckingham and Philadelphia: Open University Press. The philosophy, politics and economics of foreign aid; compares bilateral, multilateral and non-governmental dimensions, including developments following the collapse of the USSR. Accessible across all social science disciplines.

Burnell, Peter (ed.) (2000), *Democracy Assistance: International Co-operation for Democratization*, London: Frank Cass. Compares the main actors and examines strategic issues in democracy aid.

Lancaster, Carol (1999) *Aid to Africa. So Much to Do, So Little Done*, Chicago and London: University of Chicago Press. Political perspectives on aid's failings in Africa plus detailed policy recommendations.

Organization for Economic Co-operation and Development, *Development Co-operation Report*, Paris: OECD. Published around February each year, this comprehensive statistical 'bible' also carries extensive notes on selected major new themes and developments in development co-operation. Source of all data in this entry.

Randel, Judith, German, Tony and Ewing, Deborah (eds) (2000), *The Reality of Aid 2000*, the seventh revised annual edition, London: Earthscan Publications. Experts from non-governmental organizations compare the DAC performance against the challenge of eliminating absolute poverty.

REFERENCES

Burnell, Peter (1998) 'Britain's new government, new white paper, new aid?', *Third World Quarterly* 19(4): 787–802.

Carothers, Thomas (1996) *Aiding Democracy Abroad*, Washingon DC: Carnegie Endowment for International Peace.

Killick, Tony with Gunatilaka, Ramani and Mar, Ana (1998) *Aid and the Political Economy of Policy Change*, London and New York: Routledge.

Mosley, Paul, Harrigan, Jane and Toye, John (1995) *Aid and Power* (2nd edn), Vol. 1, London: Routledge.

Organization for Economic Co-operation and Development (2000) *Development Co-operation 1999 Report*, Paris: OECD.

10.2 Third World debt

Stuart Corbridge

It is now almost 20 years since Mexico defaulted on its external debt and the financial press announced the start of 'the debt crisis'. In the years that have followed, enormous sums of money have been recycled from low- and middle-income countries to their creditors in the North, and campaigning groups have arisen – such as the Jubilee 2000 coalition – which have called for a cancellation of the debts of the poorest countries. This demand has been made on the grounds that the original sums borrowed have been paid back many times over (because of the interest payments attached to the principal sum), but it has also been made with regard to the damage that is being done to human development. According to a report prepared recently for Oxfam, in Africa as a whole, 'where only one child in two goes to school, governments transfer four times more to northern creditors in debt payments than they spend on health and education' (United Nations Development Programme, 1999a: 14, citing Oxfam, 1998).

Why should this be? Why are the sins of one generation (if indeed they were sins) visited upon the next? And why is this happening today, after a long economic boom in the world's most important creditor (and indeed debtor) country, the USA? Part of the answer has to do with geography, or with where the debt crisis is assumed to have first broken out. Although countries as diverse as Zaire and Poland had defaulted on their external debts in 1975 and 1981 respectively, it was not until the Mexican default of 1982, and the defaults which followed in Brazil and some other South American countries in 1983, that the international financial community began to speak of a 'debt crisis'. The fact that they did so, of course – the fact that the front cover of *Time Magazine* in January 1983 featured the earth as a ticking debt bomb – was because large sums of money were owed by Latin American countries to a group of money-centre banks from the USA, Western Europe and Japan. It is estimated that the nine leading US money-centre banks (a group including Citibank, Chase Manhattan, Chemical Bank and Bank America) were owed US$48.6 billion in late 1984 by just five countries in Latin America (Mexico, Brazil, Venezuela, Argentina and Chile), a sum equivalent to 166.5 per cent of their shareholders' equity (after Kaletsky, 1985). These and other commercial banks had made large profits by recycling petro-dollars from OPEC to countries which found it hard to pay for higher oil bills, or which needed funds to finance their programmes of industrial development.

Most of these loans were made for a period of 5–7 years, were denominated in the US dollar, and were repayable at floating rates of interest. Real rates of interest were sometimes negative in the mid-1970s because of spiralling world inflation, but this changed when the new Chairman of the Federal Reserve, Paul Volcker, began to tighten the US money supply in 1979. In just three years the main index of the price of an international loan, the London Inter-Bank Offered Rate (LIBOR), climbed from an average of 9.20 per cent (in 1978) to 16.63 per cent (in 1981). As money became more expensive the world economy was thrown into depression, and many countries in Latin America were unable to service their debts. Faced with a 'scissors' crisis of declining exports to the US and Europe, and higher debt payments in a strengthening dollar, most of these countries sought to reschedule their debts (pay them back over a longer period, sometimes at higher rates of interest, and always for a fee) in the context of 'London Club' negotiations which brought debtors and creditors together with institutions like the World Bank and the International Monetary Fund (IMF). The IMF typically used these meetings to persuade the defaulting country to 'put its house in order' by agreeing to a structural adjustment programme. A standard programme involved currency devaluation, tax and public spending cuts, and incentives to support export-led growth. As such, it embodied the view that the debt crisis of any given country was caused by domestic economic mismanagement rather than by an uncontrollable change in external economic circumstances.

The USA encouraged the IMF to deal with the crisis in Latin America in a more pragmatic manner than some on the Right would have liked (see below). Neo-liberals have insisted that debt in itself is not a bad thing, nor is it in any way unnatural (Beenstock, 1984). Just as young people take out mortgages in their 20s and 30s (to be repaid over 15, 25 or 30 years), so too should 'young' countries expect to take out loans from the older or richer countries which had developed before them. But these loans have to be serviced. Just as a person in default on his or her mortgage must expect to lose that property to the mortgage company, so also should a country in default on its debt expect to be dealt with harshly. Failure to punish a defaulter would encourage what economists call 'moral hazard' – or the disposition to act badly again in the knowledge that one had got away with something the first time around. In addition, a policy which aimed to write-down some or all of the debts of a country in default on its external loans would impose a hidden cost on those countries which did not default on their debts (South Korea was often mentioned in this context), or which were too poor to attract large bank loans in the first place (for example, India or Bangladesh). Debt write-downs, while comforting to many liberals, could in this light be considered 'unfair' or even 'immoral' (Buiter and Srinivasan, 1987).

The Left has objected strenuously to these arguments, and has blamed US economic policy and an ideology of untamed 'developmentalism' for the plight in which many debtor countries find themselves (George, 1989). In making this critique it has enjoyed the support of the Latin American economist Carlos Diaz-Alejandro. In a much-cited paper, Diaz-Alejandro argued that almost all Latin American countries were forced to default on their debts in the 1980s, notwithstanding the fact that they had run very different trading, monetary and fiscal policies. The default was prompted by the unilateral decision taken by the USA to raise interest rates. He further suggested that commercial banks had acted unhelpfully when they refused to make new loans to Latin America in 1982–83, and that while some economic reforms were required in some Latin American countries, 'nothing in the situation [before 1982] called for traumatic depressions' (Diaz-Alejandro, 1984: 382).

In a curious way, this argument was echoed by some exporting groups in Florida, Texas and California which put pressure on the administration in Washington to treat the crisis in Latin America as a trade crisis as well as a banking crisis. The US was also keen to police the debt crisis in Latin America in such a way that the principle of repayment was consistently entrenched, but not so deeply that Latin countries would join together in a collective repudiation of their debts (as was proposed by Castro in Cuba and Garcia in Peru). There is evidence to suggest that the USA pushed for Mexico to be dealt with more leniently than some other countries, in order to dissuade Mexico from siding with Brazil against the USA. In time, too, the USA took a lead in making debt management proposals that promised better times ahead for countries faced with 'a lost decade of development'. These proposals included the Baker Plan of 1985 ('Adjustment with Growth') and the Brady initiative of 1989 (which promised financial support for those severely indebted middle-income countries [SIMICs] which agreed to avail themselves of debt write-downs in the secondary markets). In this manner, the USA demonstrated its willingness to temper a concern for 'moral hazard' with a measure of *realpolitik*. The IMF had to acknowledge these twin motives.

Positive net flows of money into Latin America in the 1990s encouraged the view that the banking crisis was over, and that sound economic management had laid the foundation for a group of 'emerging markets'. But if these claims were overstated, and ignored both the volatility of short-term money flows to Latin America (as witness the Mexican peso crisis in 1994–95) and the continuing depredations suffered by the poor or those dependent on public spending, the spotlight did at last turn to the debt crises which were affecting some parts of Asia and large parts of Africa. And these crises, which had been going on for at least as long as the crisis in Latin America, were sometimes of a hue different to those in Brazil or Mexico, and arguably were more traumatic for their debt-encumbered populations.

In Latin America, just over half of the external debt outstanding in 1982 was owed to private creditors. In sub-Saharan Africa, in contrast, and in some poorer countries in Asia (including Pakistan and the Philippines), loans had been taken out mainly from official creditors like the World Bank or the European Union (or from sovereign nations) and their renegotiation was discussed in the Paris Club. In Africa, too, the total dollar value of the loans outstanding in 1982 or 1997 was often quite small when compared with the total external debt stock of Brazil ($194 billion in 1997) or Mexico (US$150 billion) or the USA (more than US$1 trillion but with no hint of a default): in 1997 the total external debt of Mozambique stood at US$6.0 billion; Angola owed US$10.2 billion, Congo US$12.3 billion and Kenya US$6.5 billion. But when these sums are compared with the gross national products of these countries, we see that the crisis is more severe in sub-Saharan Africa: whereas in Brazil and Mexico the ratio of external debt to GNP stood at 24.1 and 38.4 per cent respectively in 1997, in Mozambique, Angola, Congo and Kenya, the respective figures were 232.9, 231.8, 232.3 and 64.7 per cent. It is true, of course, that not all countries in Africa had high debt-GNP ratios in the mid-1990s (Malawi, Chad and Burkina Faso were all below 50 per cent), and there were some very high ratios still in Latin America (notably in Nicaragua – over 600 per cent in 1993), but average debt–GNP ratios in Latin America fell from 62.2 per cent in 1985 to 37.1 per cent in 1994, while in sub-Saharan Africa they rose from an average of 75.9 per cent to 135.8 per cent over the same period (all data from UNDP, 1999b).

These figures, and the often crippling debt–export ratios under which some African countries labour, help to explain why it is that the 'debt crisis' has become a crisis of development in parts of that continent. But if African countries owe so little to their creditors why is this situation allowed to persist, and not least after a decade of unprecedentedly high growth in the USA? There is no simple answer to this question, and it is possible that pressure from the Jubilee 2000 coalition, amongst other groups, will encourage Western leaders to deal more generously with countries in Africa. But part of the answer has to do – again – with geography and geopolitics. The USA policed the debt-cum-banking crisis in Latin America in order to maintain the integrity of the international financial system, while at the same time recognizing the political and economic importance of Latin America to the USA. Sadly, there are few signs that African countries can exert a similar pull on their creditors. Africa's debts might not matter much in the overall scheme of things (except to the countries concerned), but with the ending of the Cold War there is little evidence to suggest that Africa 'itself' matters much today. Inaction is then a corollary of 'unimportance'.

GUIDE TO FURTHER READING

Buiter, W. and Srinivasan, T. (1987) 'Rewarding the profligate and punishing the prudent and poor: some recent proposals for debt relief', *World Development* 15: 411–17. A provocative critique of liberal proposals for debt relief.

Corbridge, S. (1993) *Debt and Development*, Oxford: Blackwell. A guide to competing interpretations of the debt crisis.

Diaz-Alejandro, C. (1984) 'Latin American debt: I don't think we are in Kansas anymore', *Brookings Papers on Economic Activity* 2: 335–89. Possibly the best single article on the crisis in Latin America.

Jubilee 2000 (1998) *Debt Education Package*, Washington DC: Jubilee, 2000 (see also its website, particularly the UK version – www.jubilee2000uk.org). Up to date, and useful as an antidote to 'creditor' accounts of the debt crisis.

Woodward, D. (1992) *Debt, Adjustment and Poverty in Developing Countries* (2 Volumes), London: Pinter/Save the Children. Still the best book on the debt crisis. Can be updated by reference to various publications of the World Bank or the United Nations Development Programme (UNDP).

REFERENCES

Beenstock, M. (1984) *The World Economy in Transition* (2nd edn), London: George Allen and Unwin.

George, S. (1989) *A Fate Worse Than Debt*, Harmondsworth: Penguin.

Kaletsky, A. (1985) *The Costs of Default*, New York: Twentieth Century Fund.

Oxfam (1998) *Making Debt Relief Work*, Washington DC: Oxfam.

UNDP (1999a) *Debt and Sustainable Human Development*, Technical Advisory Paper No. 4, New York: UNDP, Management Development and Governance Division.

UNDP (1999b) *Human Development Report, 1999*, Oxford: UNDP/Oxford University Press.

10.3 Aid conditionality

Tony Killick

MEANING AND SIGNIFICANCE

Much aid comes with strings attached specifying actions which recipient governments should undertake in return for the assistance. This practice of *conditionality* is particularly central to the operations of the International Monetary Fund (IMF), and conditional lending is also an important part of the work of the World Bank and of other development agencies. Bilateral donors – mainly the governments of Western industrial nations – also rely on conditionality, often by supporting the stipulations of the IMF and World Bank (the IFIs) but sometimes by laying down requirements of their own, most notably to promote human rights, improved governance and environmental protection.

We are here concerned with *policy* conditionality. We differentiate it from the financial and legal provisions – relating to the financial terms, and provisions for accounting and auditing – which are also written into agreements. We also differentiate from the non-controversial points of mutual agreement on policy which the parties often write into agreements, and from the manifold other ways in which donors seek to influence the governments they aid. According to *The Oxford English Dictionary*, a condition is 'something demanded or required as a prerequisite to the granting or performance of something else; a stipulation'. Applying this to the present case:

> conditionality consists of actions, or promises of actions, made by recipient governments only at the insistence of aid providers; measures that would not otherwise be undertaken, or not within the time frame desired by the providers.

Being widely practised, conditionality is important for the efficient use of aid monies, particularly the loans of the IFIs. Indeed, with questions being asked about the rationale for their continued existence, given the huge development of private international capital markets, some writers have defended these institutions by asserting that they have a superior ability to enforce conditionality, by comparison with private lenders (e.g. Hopkins *et al.*, 1997).

PURPOSES AND JUSTIFICATION

The practice of conditionality requires legitimation because it limits the freedom of action of governments internationally recognized as sovereign, and because the policies required often impose political and economic costs on these governments and their peoples. How might such legitimation be conferred?

- Conditionality can be viewed as *a substitute for the collateral assets* which private lenders would require as a safeguard against the danger of default by the borrower (see Mosley *et al.*, 1995). The IFIs, for example, need to assure themselves that borrowing governments will be in a position to repay. Conditionality can be seen as offering such a safeguard, ensuring that borrowing countries put policies in place that will raise their debt servicing capacities.
- Relatedly, conditionality can be viewed as *a safeguard against moral hazard*, i.e. against the danger that the provision of aid will actually weaken a government's will to undertake policy reforms. If conditionality can be enforced, moral hazard is ruled out.
- A related justification concerns *the influence of recipient-country policies on aid effectiveness*. Bilateral donors and IFIs are dispensing public monies paid by the taxpayers of the richer countries. Donor agencies thus have an obligation to ensure that these monies are effective in achieving the objectives for which they were provided. There is good evidence that the quality of a country's economic policies exerts a decisive influence on the developmental effectiveness of the aid it receives (e.g. Hadjimichael *et al.*, 1995; World Bank, 1998), at both the macro-economic and project levels. This link between policies and aid effectiveness gives donors a legitimate interest in the policies of recipient governments.
- Donors additionally argue that their support can be used as *a political resource by reformers* within a government and may tip the balance in favour of improvement by giving reformers additional clout when policy decisions are taken.
- Conditionality can further improve domestic economic policies by *inducing greater consistency over time* (e.g. Rodrik, 1996). This is important where a government's policies lack credibility among potential investors and others whose decision will impact on the economic results

obtained. People may suspect the government's sincerity or its staying power, fearing that today's policy signals will be reversed, particularly in countries which are in economic crisis and/or have a history of instability. Governments which lack credibility could gain from the possibility of using conditionality as a way of locking into policies which otherwise may not command much confidence (e.g. see Collier *et al.*, 1997).

Essentially, the above supporting arguments boil down to the claim that conditionality improves economic policies, promoting development and raising countries' abilities to repay the credits received. The corollary of this is that *the justification of conditionality stands or falls on its ability to change policies for the better.* However, whether it does this is questionable.

IMPACT ON POLICY

The evidence indicates that the high-conditionality adjustment programmes of the IFIs achieve their economic objectives only to a limited degree. It appears that programmes are instrumental in strengthening export and balance of payments performance but have little impact on inflation; they do not typically make much difference to the pace of economic growth; but they are consistently associated with reduced investment levels, which threatens economic progress in the longer term.[1]

Among the possible explanations of weak results, poor programme implementation is a large problem, manifested by programmes which break down or take far longer than originally planned, and a lot of pretending that conditions that have been met when the reality is otherwise. Neither the IMF nor the World Bank has been able to show a systematic connection between their own programmes and improvements in economic policies. The revealed leverage of programmes over various policy instruments is quite weak. It appears that they can make a decisive difference to policy instruments (like the exchange rate) which can readily be monitored, are directly controlled by the government, involve a few individuals and agencies, and are not easy to organize against. But the results are more problematical when it comes to complex structural, distributional or institutional measures.

This limited effectiveness of conditionality is regrettable because the evidence further shows that, when executed, the IFIs' approach to policy does result in improved economic performance. In the words of a World Bank report (1995: 1), 'generally adjustment lending has mostly promoted good policies, but got weak program results'. But if the policies are broadly sound, why might implementation be so imperfect? In the general case, domestic political imperatives appear to dominate the financial pressures of the donors. This appears also to extend to donor attempts to influence political reforms: in only two out of 29 cases examined by Crawford (1997) was donor pressure judged as significant in bringing about political change.

EXPLAINING WEAK IMPLEMENTATION

The *ownership* of policies is a key factor here. Government ownership is at its strongest when the political leadership, with broad support among agencies of state and civil society, decide of their own volition that policy changes are desirable, choose what these changes should be and when they should be introduced. There is substantial evidence that recipient-government ownership of policy reform programmes is crucial to their effective implementation (Johnson and Wasty, 1993; Killick *et al.*, 1998, Chapter 4). There is growing acceptance among aid practitioners that donor pressures by themselves cannot produce reform. Changes must have their local champions and domestic leadership is essential.

Ownership is important because of disagreements between recipient governments and aid agencies, whose objectives and interests rarely coincide. The two parties are conditioned by different historical and institutional backgrounds; they are answerable to different constituencies; they each have their own internal management imperatives; it is recipients rather than donors who bear the costs of reforms, which makes them more cautious about the desirable extent of change; and nationalistic resentment of donor 'interference' undermines the legitimacy of externally promoted policy reforms.

REWARDS, PUNISHMENTS AND DOMESTIC POLITICS

Interest conflicts could be overcome if incentives were in place that made it rewarding for recipients to comply with donor stipulations. This would require rewards for compliance *and the withholding of aid from non-compliers.* However, the evidence suggests that neither dimension of the incentive system is adequate. Programmes may be under-funded. Governments may have little incentive to accept unwanted policy stipulations because they can borrow elsewhere or because the domestic economy is strong enough without. There is also little evidence that, in practice, conditionality enhances the credibility of government policies, as suggested earlier. Reform programmes have proved too unreliable to have strong credibility effects.

Above all, governments often see that they have little to fear if they do not keep their side of the policy-for-money bargain. Killick *et al.* (1998: Chapter 6) find 'an overwhelming body of evidence' that non-implementation is rarely punished effectively and, therefore, that domestic politics override the requirements of conditionality. Other studies confirm this dominance of domestic influences (e.g. Haggard *et al.,* 1995). The appearance of punishment conveyed by programme cancellations (in the case of the IMF) or the withholding of payments (World Bank) is misleading because the costs to a government of waiting out a delay are usually not great and new credits can usually be negotiated.

Delinquency goes unpunished for various reasons. There are often external pressures on donor agencies to continue aid. The institutional interests of the aid agency often push in the same direction. Except in extreme cases, it is difficult to act strongly against sovereign governments (who are themselves shareholders of the IFIs). There are fears that withdrawal of aid will have destabilizing macroeconomic effects. Staff promotion criteria and accounting systems create powerful pressures to keep on spending, even when governments break their promises.

CONCLUSION

The chief study of this topic (Killick *et al.,* 1998: Chapter 7) concludes that, generally, conditionality has not been effective in improving economic policies in recipient countries; that it has failed to achieve its objectives and therefore lacks practical justification; that over-reliance on conditionality has wasted much public money; and that the obstacles to adequate improvement are probably intractable. There are, they suggest, exceptions to these generalizations but not too many.

Bilateral donors have, in fact, begun to downgrade reliance on conditionality. So has the World Bank, instead placing emphasis on the more selective support of governments with proven policy track records and experimenting with new ways of using its financial leverage to support policy reforms. There has been less response from the IMF. It, too, doubtless feels frustration with the limited impact of its programmes but has yet to demonstrate enough flexibility in its own modalities to overcome the problems described above.

NOTE

1. For citation of the relevant evidence in support of these results see Killick *et al.*, 1998, especially Chapters 2 and 3. See also Mosley *et al.*, 1995, on the World Bank; and Killick, 1995, on the IMF.

GUIDE TO FURTHER READING

The principal source on conditionality is Killick *et al.*, 1998. Killick, 1997 provides a more summary statement. Other useful studies include Mosley *et al.*'s study of World Bank structural adjustment programmes (1995), and Killick's 1995 examination of IMF programmes. Collier *et al.*, 1997, has proved a particularly influential critique of conditionality. For general studies of the economics of aid, which include some coverage of conditionality, see World Bank, 1998, and Tarp and Hjertholm, 2000.

REFERENCES

Collier, P., Guillaumont, P., Guillaumont, S. and Gunning, J.W. (1997) 'Redesigning conditionality', *World Development* 25(9), September.

Crawford, Gordon (1997) 'Foreign aid and political conditionality: issues of effectiveness and consistency', *Democratization* 4(3).

Hadjimichael, Michael T., Ghura, Daneshwar, Mühleisen, Martin, Nord, Roger and Murat Ucer, E. (1995) *Sub-Saharan Africa: Growth, Saving, and Investment, 1986–93*, Occasional Paper 118, Washington DC: International Monetary Fund.

Haggard, Stephan, Lafay, Jean-Dominique and Morrisson, Christian (1995) *Political Feasibility of Adjustment in Developing Countries*, Paris: OECD Development Centre.

Hopkins, R., Powell, A., Roy, A. and Gilbert, C.L. (1997) 'The World Bank and conditionality', *Journal of International Development* 9(4), June.

Johnson, John H. and Wasty, Sulaiman S. (1993) 'Borrower ownership of adjustment programs and the political economy of reform', *World Bank Discussion Paper* 199, Washington DC: World Bank.

Killick, Tony (1995) *IMF Programmes in Developing Countries: Design and Impact*, London and New York: Routledge and Overseas Development Institute.

Killick, Tony (1997) 'Principals, agents and the failings of conditionality', *Journal of International Development* 9(4), June.

Killick, Tony with Gunatilaka, Ramani and Marr, Ana (1998) *Aid and the Political Economy of Policy Change*, London: Routledge and Overseas Development Institute.

Mosley, Paul, Harrigan, Jane and Toye, John (1995) *Aid and Power: The World Bank and Policy-based Lending*, Vol. 1 (2nd edn), London: Routledge.

Rodrik, Dani (1996) 'Understanding economic policy reform', *Journal of Economic Literature* XXXIV, March.

Tarp, Finn and Hjertholm, Peter (eds) (2000) *Foreign Aid and Development*, London and New York: Routledge.

World Bank (1995) 'Higher impact adjustment lending', Report of a Working Group to SPA Plenary, Washington: World Bank, October.

World Bank (1998) *Assessing Aid: What Works, What Doesn't and Why*, Washington: World Bank.

10.4 The emergence of the governance agenda: sovereignty, neo-liberal bias and the politics of international development

Rob Jenkins

During the 1990s, governance emerged as a catch-all term in both the study and practice of development. It can be generically defined as the prevailing patterns by which public power is exercised in a given social context. Official and non-governmental development agencies have sought to operationalize the idea of *good* governance by restructuring state bureaucracies, reforming legal systems, supporting democratic decentralization and creating accountability-enhancing civil societies. The notion of good governance should, in principle, refer to any mode of public decision-making that helps to advance human welfare, *however conceived*. But because of the heavy influence of aid donors, governance has come to be associated with institutions designed to support market-led development.

This built-in ambiguity finds its parallel in the imprecision of the cognate terms on which has been built the 'D&G [Democracy and Governance] Sector', the term invented by the aid business for the set of programmatic initiatives funded by foreign assistance. Development consultants deployed to overhaul failing Third World states have seized upon two suitably plastic ideas in particular: participation and accountability. Improving both, while not undermining managerial efficiency, has been the focus of intensive development intervention (Carothers, 1999).

CLASSIFYING GOVERNANCE'S MANY MEANINGS

One of the most useful ways of classifying governance's many meanings is to begin with the rather fundamental division alluded to above: the difference between the concerns of theorists and practitioners. These are not, of course, air-tight categories: development agencies increasingly cultivate internal analytical capacities and contribute to governance debates; academic theorists engage more than ever in 'applied' advisory work on behalf of development agencies. Still, the distinction is valid. While academics can explore complicating factors that explain divergent patterns of governance, practitioners do not have this luxury: they cannot hope to replicate complex historical conditions.

As Hirst (2000) argues in his survey of governance, the study and practice of development is just one of several contexts in which the term has taken root. Hirst identifies five 'versions', corresponding to the fields of: (i) 'economic development'; (ii) international institutions and regimes; (iii) corporate governance; (iv) new public management; and (v) 'network governance', the increasingly popular deliberative forums found in (mainly) Western polities that address sets of related issues through a structured process of consultation and negotiation among relevant civil society and governmental actors.

It is worth noting that, among the five categories, the experience in the field of 'economic development' has been uniquely all-encompassing. Debates on how understandings of governance can be applied to development problems by aid-recipient governments and external agencies have drawn promiscuously on ideas contained in each of the other four fields. International institutions, for instance, are expected to constrain the performance-inhibiting instincts of Southern (and Northern) governments by subjecting them to multilateral policy 'disciplines'. And since the birth of new public management in the late 1980s, its proselytizers have been exported to the South as fast as consultancy contracts could be written. Corporate governance reforms were a later addition in many places, but the demand for them rose as access to private capital led internationally inclined Southern firms to clothe themselves in organizational forms, and present their accounts in formats, that globally roaming investors would find familiar. The resistance to 'network governance' by Southern bureaucracies, many of which still possess distinctly colonial characteristics, has not prevented a proliferation of consultative mechanisms and public–private management structures; indeed, these are a mainstay of the governance agenda.

ORIGINS AND THE SOVEREIGNTY CONTEXT

The idea that governance was central to official development assistance received one of its earliest manifestations in a 1990 speech by British Foreign Secretary Douglas Hurd. Over the next two years Hurd's statement was echoed by similar declarations from his counterparts in other rich countries. The shift towards governance thus coincided with the end of the Cold War. This was in fact no coincidence, as the governance agenda represented – whatever the merits of its conception or execution – a further intrusion on the sovereignty of aid-recipient states. Today, externally funded 'national' anti-corruption agencies probe the finances of key political elites in developing countries and are 'advised', often in fairly substantial detail, by foreign aid agencies and consultants. Even the courts that theoretically define the chief executive's authority are in many cases undergoing comprehensive organizational restructuring under the auspices of donor-funded governance programmes. These sorts of external intervention would have been unacceptable to Third World leaders during the Cold War when bipolarity placed more leverage in their hands by making it possible for the more capable among them to play off East against West.

In assessing the sovereignty implications of this level of external intervention, it is worth taking note of Hirst's observation that sovereignty consists *both* of states' ability to make decisions independently of external authorities *and* their capacity actually to govern – that is, to effect at least a respectable percentage of intended outcomes. This latter dimension of sovereignty had long been lacking in many countries that attained 'independence' in the great wave of decolonization from 1945–75. This has been analysed by Robert H. Jackson, whose work introduced a new term into the study of development: 'quasi-states' (1991). The term quasi-states is now routinely associated with the lost independence of action implied by foreign economic intervention in the form of World Bank and IMF policy conditionalities. But this obscures a key aspect of its theoretical relevance, which is that the advent of strings-attached structural adjustment lending was merely the second half of a larger story of sovereignty lost.

The first half was the dismal failure of Third World states at translating priorities into policies and executing them effectively – that is, at governing. Many states were not even fully in control of their territories, let alone able to regulate authoritatively, implying failure on an even less demanding definitional threshold for sovereignty. Thus, many Third World states had lost one dimension of sovereignty before the other was forfeited in exchange for continued access to international financing. The former helped to make possible the latter: the impositions of international financial institutions would have been more successfully resisted had developing countries possessed a more credible claim to having in practice exercised the governance aspect of sovereignty, defined in terms of minimal levels of societal penetration, not on the basis of how 'good' any such governance might have been.

When, from 1980, external agencies began using conditionality-based lending to pursue their policy agendas they initially controlled only policy-making, not the structures through which policies were enacted and applied. Thus the shift towards governance in the 1990s – including 'political conditionality', the conditioning of aid on the existence of liberal constitutionalism and multi-party electoral contestation – must be understood as the culmination of a larger process through which sovereignty slipped from the grasp of Southern states. By pursuing a governance agenda throughout the 1990s, development agencies were able to substantially enhance their hold over the functioning of aid-recipient states.

FEASIBILITY AND NECESSITY OF GOVERNANCE INTERVENTIONS

While the end of the Cold War made increased penetration of Southern states by development agencies more politically *feasible*, other trends seemed to make it *necessary*. Within multilateral organizations, one of the main justifications for conditioning aid on the reform of domestic agencies was that sub-optimally designed institutions were ruining otherwise sound policy initiatives. This view served several useful purposes for the beleaguered aid agencies. It helped to ward off criticism of structural adjustment's marked failure to bring results in most places it was tried: 'it wasn't the policies, but the governance framework', became part of the revised 'Washington Consensus'. At the same time, by speaking in terms of correcting perverse organizational incentives, unblocking institutional bottlenecks, diversifying civil society, reorienting the citizen–state interface, and other such 'technical' solutions, external agencies were able to disavow any interference in the 'domestic politics' of the states in which they operated. While the World Bank's Articles of Agreement prohibit such intrusive practices, they *do* permit the organization to address 'managerial' issues, to the extent that they are relevant to the effective discharge of the Bank's responsibilities as a creditor agency (World Bank, 1994). This, in effect, meant that the more technical-sounding the interventions, the more publicly justifiable they would be. Gradually, this gave way to less carefully camouflaged forms of intervention. A watershed of sorts was passed in 1997, when the World Bank, IMF, UNDP and other traditionally non-interfering institutions placed the issue of corruption firmly on their agendas, and even cut off aid to Kenya for a time, partly on grounds of the government's failure to tackle corruption.

The idea that fundamental governance reform was necessary found its way into academic writings on development around the same time that agencies took up the idea. These studies were based largely on detailed empirical investigations, rather than on abstract model-building. Atul Kohli's dissection of (1990) India's crisis of (un)governability was followed by a raft of popular articles, such as Robert D. Kaplan's 'The coming anarchy', which analysed the collapse of so-called 'failed' states in large parts of sub-Saharan Africa (Kaplan, 1994).

In short, several trends combined to facilitate the emergence of a composite notion known as governance: geo-strategic realignments, bureaucratic convenience, the legacy of previous policy failures. It would be wrong, however, to ignore the contribution of important ideological transformations. The vastly increased emphasis on market-based solutions naturally had its influence on the full range of ideas about governance. This 'neo-liberal bias' has undermined many otherwise useful insights about the nature of institutions in structuring dissent and, under some circumstances, promoting accountability (Kaufman *et al.*, 1999). Attempts to use foreign aid to build the sort of civil society that would check the power of government, without capturing it, were all but destined to fail. They did so spectacularly at times, such as when an NGO leader funded by American 'democracy assistance' programmes seized power in a coup in Burundi in 1996 (Jenkins, 2001).

GOVERNANCE IN PRACTICE: THE FEAR OF SUCCESS

Indeed, the manner in which governance objectives were pursued points to a larger pattern in the linkage between theory and practice. This is what might be called a fear of success. By seeking to recreate a badly flawed vision of how 'functional' civil societies in the West actually operate – or, even worse, operated at an earlier stage in their developmental trajectories – both social theorists and development practitioners have betrayed an instinctive reluctance to face up to civil society's inherently precarious condition and sometimes ugly character, or to let democracy do its unpredictable work (Gellner, 1994). Private associations that aid agencies for one reason or another found distasteful were excluded from their civil society 'strategic frameworks' and denied funding, just as civil society groups that upset the predictions of academic theorists were banished from their carefully constructed models. Usually, the problem concerned their contribution to undesired ends.

The same is true for other aspects of democratic governance in which both development theorists and practitioners have been involved – for instance, elections, where outcomes can be injurious to democracy's long-term health and yet still be democratic. In such instances, the international community has demonstrated a palpable fear of democracy – or at least a strong desire to retain control over what should, by definition, be a local process of conferring legitimacy. The incumbent government of Algeria was permitted by otherwise governance-conscious donor governments, and large sections of the associated development intelligentsia, to simply ignore the results of the 1992 elections, because the group widely believed to have won, an avowedly Islamist party, did not conform to the recipe for good government promoted by theorists and advanced by agency staff.

The institutional arena in which development policy is least elaborated is international and transnational governance. The fear of democracy partly explains this as well. Genuine governance reforms that would reduce the North–South disparities that characterize, for instance, *participation* within international organizations (to say nothing of the *accountability* deficit within even rule-based institutions of global governance such as the WTO) would represent a substantial challenge to the very governments that control development agencies. Even technical assistance to encourage poorer countries (and poorer groups within them) to participate more whole-heartedly in these organizations is heavily slanted away from programmes that might assist them in negotiating for such things as enhanced terms of trade, new rules for enforcing international agreements, and compensation for global environmental-protection measures.

The extreme versatility of the idea of governance will ensure its survival for the foreseeable future. But it will continue to be shaped by political constraints, including the interests of powerful actors, the changing nature of sovereignty, and the performance of development agencies and Southern states.

GUIDE TO FURTHER READING AND REFERENCES

The following text references provide the basis for further reading.

Carothers, Thomas (1999) *Aiding Democracy Abroad: The Learning Curve*, Washington DC: Carnegie Endowment for International Peace.

Gellner, Ernest (1994) *Conditions of Liberty: Civil Society and Its Rivals*, London: Hamish Hamilton.

Hirst, Paul (2000) 'Democracy and governance', in Jon Pierre (ed.) *Debating Governance*, Oxford: Oxford University Press.

Jackson, Robert H. (1991) *Quasi-States: Sovereignty, International Relations and the Third World*, Cambridge: Cambridge University Press.

Jenkins, Rob (1999) *Democratic Politics and Economic Reform in India*, Cambridge: Cambridge University Press.

Jenkins, Rob (2001) 'Mistaking governance for politics: foreign aid, democracy and the construction of civil society', in Sudipta Kaviraj and Sunil Khilnani (eds) *Civil Society: Histories and Possibilities*, Cambridge: Cambridge University Press.

Kaplan, Robert D. (1994) 'The coming anarchy', *The Atlantic Monthly* (February).

Kaufman, Daniel, Kraay, Aart and Zoida-Lobaton, Pablo (1999) 'Governance matters', World Bank Policy Research Working Paper 2196, Washington DC: World Bank.

Kohli, Atul (1990) *Democracy and Discontent: India's Growing Crisis of Governability*, Cambridge: Cambridge University Press.

World Bank (1994) *Governance: The World Bank's Experience*, Washington DC: World Bank.

10.5 Strengthening civil society in developing countries

Alison Van Rooy[1]

WHY BOTHER ABOUT CIVIL SOCIETY?

The answer is that talk about civil society is shaping the very way in which we 'do' international relations today. That conversation pulls together global ideas, values, institutions and dollars in a vibrant, and sometimes violent, fashion. In many ways, civil society is the Rome of today's internationalism; wherever we may begin, we will arrive at this debate sooner or later.

Certainly, writing about the role of civil society has grown in volume and depth in the past decade. From this sphere are to come agents of change to cure a range of social and economic ills left by failures in government or the marketplace: autocracy, poverty, oppression, social malaise. Cornucopian expectations for social change have been heaped on this idea and, indeed, for some Northern donors in particular, the 'discovery' of civil society has promised a solution to the enduring problems of development and democracy. Many have devoted official development assistance dollars to a range of civil society projects throughout the world, and the number and variety of those projects increases daily.

Yet serious questions remain about the whole enterprise. What are people talking about when they use the term 'civil society'? What are the issues and implications, both for good and for ill, of this growing debate in the international aid business? This chapter poses, and begins to answer, some of these vexing questions.

WHAT DOES 'CIVIL SOCIETY' MEAN?

What do we mean, *precisely*, when we use the term 'civil society'? The term has a long history in political philosophy, and its definition has altered with Roman, Lockean, Hegelian, Marxist and Gramscian interpretations long before it was resurrected in the 1990s. Out of that long debate, what messages have we brought forward today? I think that there are at least six different elements, and at least as many dangers in turning them into policy directions.

Civil society as values and norms

For some, the 'civil' in civil society is the operative word: the term describes the kind of well-behaved society that we want to live in, the goal for our political and social efforts. This ideal society is trustful, tolerant, co-operative – ambitions held to be universal and to be universally good.

Note the current conversation about 'social capital,' for instance, invigorated by Robert Putnam's *Making Democracy Work* and *Bowling Alone* (1993, 1995). Building on the work of others, Putnam illustrated – in Italy and the United States – that communities held together by overlapping memberships in neighbourhood associations were also more prosperous, healthy and livable. The bonds of trust and reciprocity created in these neighbourhood civil society organizations (CSOs) are what are called social capital.

Faced with such a normative and ideologically laden concept, the policy-maker's first task may be simply to recognize the ethical motors that shape the civil society (and social capital) debates.

Civil society as a collective noun

While the normative note is always present, civil society is most commonly defined as a collective noun: synonymous with the voluntary sector (or the Third Sector), and with advocacy groups, non-governmental organizations (NGOs), social movement agents, human rights organizations and others actors explicitly involved in change work. The definition most often excludes those groups belonging to the marketplace and the state, and further specifies that civil society organizations do not include those groups interested in acquiring political power, hence the usual exclusion of political parties.

The response from the academic community has been to start counting: just how many CSOs are there? The prominent and important work of Salamon and Anheier *et al.*, for example, shows variations in the shape and structure of the sector, and historical and cultural patterns (1999).

From a policy perspective, however, there are difficulties with the empirical focus alone. One is that the term is equated, in practice at least, with particular sectors or kinds of organization – those that we like – even if the definition is meant to encompass a larger population. In development circles, civil society is further reduced to 'NGO'. If we are trying to understand processes of social change, we must go beyond exercises in cataloguing.

Civil society as a space for action

Civil society has also been used to describe the sphere or arena in which civil organizations prosper (or wilt). The United Nations Development Programme's definition is typical: 'Civil society is, together with state and market, one of the three "spheres" that interface in the making of democratic societies' (1993: 1).

Throughout the policy literature, we see circles like the one in the figure opposite used to describe civil society, drawn with clear boundaries around the state, the market and a 'residual' category of non-state, non-market actors. One problem is that the circles are frequently drawn in even, egalitarian sizes. The intent is schematic, but the effect is to depict a vision of balance and segregation that may not exist in reality. Another problem is that this description divides the world by organizational type, hiding other aspects of an organization's role or function in society. Even if one allows overlapping identities (unions, for example, as part market, part civil society), the

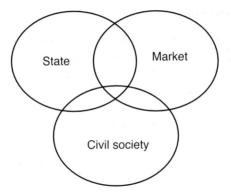

Modelling civil society

effect is nonetheless of sorting by organizational identity rather than by purpose, goal, vision, method, function or other more interesting distinctions.

Civil society as a historical moment

Others describe civil society as a historical moment, either a real or idealized description of society when a set of prerequisites was in place. Adam Seligman's prerequisites were the primacy of the individual, rights-bearing and autonomous, and a shared public space in which agreed rules and norms are sustained (1992). Blaney and Pasha, searching for civil society in India and Africa, similarly argue that 'the stabilization of a system of rights, constituting human beings as individuals, both as citizens in relation to the state and as legal persons in the economy and the sphere of free association' (1993: 4). They suggest that this mix of prerequisites cannot simply be assumed to exist in other countries.

The interesting thing about a historical view of civil society is that it raises questions about how civil society emerges and why it might disappear. The goal for policy-makers has subsequently been a quest for the foundations, the prerequisites of civil society. Can one create a system of rights? What about a culture of association? Obviously, the potential for intervention on such an enormous field becomes small – or, at best, very long term.

Civil society as anti-hegemony

One of the most radical optics on the debate argues that civil society is not conducive to modern liberalism (in politics or economics) but is instead its antithesis.

First, many CSOs are disengaged from formal political processes and work partly underground, outside conventional institutions of civil society and the state, or are mobilized in opposition to prevailing cultural norms. In positing alternate visions of society (about gender and power, sexual identity, anti-consumerism, anti-globalization or anti-Westernism), movements may not ever join in formal political action. If one defines civil society primarily in terms of its relationship with the state, one may well miss this aspect of civil organizing.

For policy-makers trying to work in other cultures or in sub-cultures within their own, the implication is that their intervention may be utterly unwanted – a symptom of the perceived cultural and economic dominance of 'hegemonic' institutions.

Civil society as an antidote to the state

The sixth overlapping optic describes civil society by its activities in opposition to a centralized or autocratic state. Promoting civil society has come to mean limiting the state.

Part of the reason is a loss of faith in both the abstraction and the physical manifestation of The State. Jessica Mathews, then with the Council of Foreign Relations, suggested that 'The end of the Cold War has brought no mere adjustment among states but a novel redistribution of power among states, markets, and civil society,' such that today, 'NGOs are able to push around even the largest governments' (1997: 50, 52). For Mathews, not only *should* states wield less power, they actually *are* less powerful in the face of the civil society onslaught.

Another concern focuses on the implications for sovereignty in a *globalizing* civil society. Lipschultz argues that we are seeing an increase in international activism *because* of a leaking away of sovereignty (1992). Environmental degradation, the universalization of human rights (and the notion that foreign actors can act upon the transgression of rights in other countries), civil wars, drug trafficking, and other transborder activities are no longer seen to belong to the governments that govern the territory upon which they take place.

The legitimacy of the state itself thus becomes less certain. In the world of international activism, there is a growing notion that true democracy may involve the circumvention of some governments altogether. That position presents a very serious challenge to policy-makers, indeed.

STRENGTHENING CIVIL SOCIETY IN DEVELOPING COUNTRIES?

The debates and rebuttals presented here do not mean, however, that there is no role for the international community in supporting CSOs and a broader civil society in the South. I think that there is a role, but one that must be taken with more self-criticism and public debate. Working with CSOs, after all, is both practically and politically complex. One set of guidelines, therefore, first asks donors to interrogate, and to seek help in interrogating, their own goals.

Interrogate goals

Because the debate on civil society is normatively convoluted, it is important that all players are aware of their own motivations. What is the aid agency doing? Why? Who wants the donor to be there? It is important that the philosophical underpinnings of programmes are described and understood; only then can they be debated.

Get the lie of the land

It is also important that one's own philosophies of change bear some relevance to the countries in which one works. Donors need to develop a knowledge about the dynamics of power among CSOs, the market and the state. For example, what level of political and financial support or resistance is put up by home governments? International agencies? Powerful domestic players?

Getting the big picture also implies an examination of the other forces that are working on civil society. Socially and culturally, one needs to learn about the informal or unregistered organizations of civil society – clan associations, extended family networks, church affiliations – that nonetheless carry tremendous weight in social change. One also needs to offer at least a passing consideration of international factors of debt; economic liberalization, protectionism and globalization; transborder flow of ideas, people and illicit and legal goods; and environmental problems.

Make political assessments

If anything, the debate on civil society has shown that political motivations for aid have come out from under the table. Can donor politics be justified in the context of local agendas? Whose agendas are those? What impact might intervention make on shaping political outcomes? Civil society organizations at the centre of much donor attention are often political (if not partisan) bodies at the centre of real conflicts, real debates. The question is not whether politics can be avoided, but whether one's particular choice of political stance and partnerships can be justified and to whom.

Plan strategically

Given these considerations, donor planning should consider at least three facets: on the organizations themselves, their relationships and the environments in which they work. A metaphor of civil society as a building of bricks, mortar and site is used to make the distinctions clearer.

Bricks

The bricks, the constituent parts of the building, are organized groups. They may be morally good, bad or neutral in function. Donor programmes could be designed to help the activities and influence of particular bricks in the civil society edifice.

Mortar

Relationships are the mortar that holds the building together. One needs to ask how are organizations related: are they disparate and atomized, or tightly woven into coalitions? What groups exist in opposition or in support of their work? Programmes to increase the strength of that mortar might fund umbrella organizations, meetings, training centres and networking travel.

Building site

But this building is not drawn from thin air; there are preconditions or enabling environments necessary for its existence. The metaphorical equivalents might be the building site and its zoning laws, union rules and bank practices. In political terms, these include a system of rights, a culture of association, legal protection, the role of the state and market, and the availability of financing among other factors – some of which an outside donor agency might affect.

MOVING FORWARD

What, then, to make of all this? Is there any point for development practitioners, North or South, to get on board the 'strengthening civil society' bandwagon?

This chapter suggests, after all, that the idea of civil society has become omnipresent in donor language today in large part because it rings many political, economic and social bells. The ideas packed into the two familiar words are rich, contradictory and in danger of being all things to all people. At the same time, both the ideas embedded in 'civil society' and the manifestation of CSOs themselves hold out tremendous inspiration for change. Indeed, in treading very carefully in the world of real politics, the task for a new generation of development activists, North and South, is not to throw babies out with bath water.

NOTE

1. This paper draws substantively from Van Rooy, 1998 (see under 'Civil society and donors', below).

GUIDE TO FURTHER READING AND REFERENCES

Theoretical history

Chandhoke, Neera (1995) *State and Civil Society: Explorations in Political Theory*, New Delhi, Thousand Oaks, California, and London: Sage Publications.

Cohen, Jean L. and Arato, Andrew (1992) *Civil Society and Political Theory,* Cambridge, MA and London: MIT Press.

Hall, John A. (ed) (1995) *Civil Society: Theory, History, Comparison,* Cambridge, UK and Cambridge, MA: Polity Press.

Seligman, Adam B. (1992) 'Trust and the Meaning of civil society', *International Journal of Politics, Culture and Society* 6(1): 5–21.

Critiques

Blaney, David L. and Pasha, Mustapha Kamal (1993) 'Civil society and democracy in the Third World: ambiguities and historical possibilities', *Studies in Comparative International Development* 28(1): 3–24.

Harbeson, John W., Rothchild, Donald and Chazan, Naomi (eds) (1994) *Civil Society and the State in Africa,* London and Boulder: Lynne Reinner.

Trends and issues

Lipschultz, Ronnie D. (1992) 'Reconstructing world politics: the emergence of global civil society', *Millennium* 21(3): 389–420.

Mathews, Jessica T. (1997) 'Power shift', *Foreign Affairs*, January/February.

Salamon, Lester M., Anheier, Helmut K. *et al.* (1999) *Global Civil Society: Dimensions of the Nonprofit Sector,* Baltimore: Johns Hopkins University Press.

Civil society and donors

Bernard, Amanda, Helmich, Henny and Lehning, Percy B. (eds) (1998) *Civil Society and International Development*, Paris: North–South Centre of the Council of Europe and Development Centre of the Organization for Economic Cooperation and Development.

Carothers, Thomas (1999) *Aiding Democracy Abroad: The Learning Curve,* Washington DC: Carnegie Endowment for International Peace.

Van Rooy, Alison (ed.) (1998) *Civil Society and the Aid Industry: The Politics and Promise,* London and the North–South Institute, Ottawa: Earthscan.

Other references

Putnam, Robert D. with Leonardi, Robert and Nanetti, Rafaella Y. (1993) *Making Democracy Work: Civic Traditions in Modern Italy*, Princeton: Princeton University Press.

Putnam, Robert D (1995) 'Bowling alone: America's declining social capital', *Journal of Democracy* 6(1): 65–78 (expanded in *Bowling Alone: The Collapse and Revival of American Community*, New York: Simon and Schuster (2000)).

UNDP (1993) *UNDP and Organizations of Civil Society*, New York, NY: UNDP.

10.6 Role of non-governmental organizations (NGOs)

Vandana Desai

THE GROWTH OF THE NGO SECTOR

The term NGO is applied to many kinds of organization, ranging from large Northern-based charities such as Oxfam to local self-help organizations in the South. They are mainly private initiatives, involved in development issues on a non-profit basis. The term 'NGO' is understood to refer to those autonomous, non-membership, relatively permanent or institutionalized, non-profit (but not always voluntary) intermediary organizations, staffed by professionals or the educated elite, which work with grassroots organizations in a supportive capacity. Grassroots organizations (GROs) on the other hand are issue-based, often ephemeral, membership organizations; they may coalesce around particular goals and interests, and dissipate once their immediate concerns have been addressed.

Since the 1950s, NGOs have come to play an increasingly important part in the formulation and implementation of development policy, becoming key actors in the political economy of development. There has been increased collaboration both with governments and aid agencies based on a growing belief over the period that the promotion of NGOs could offer an alternative model of development and play a key role in processes of democratization. Donor pressure towards structural reform and privatization underlies the increased interest in NGOs as 'service deliverers' – part of a wider and explicit objective to facilitate productive NGO–state partnership.

Growth in numbers of NGOs both in the North and South has been rapid. Edwards and Hulme (1992) report over 4,000 NGOs existing in 1989 in OECD member countries alone. Clark (1991) reports a doubling in their real resources over the decade from the mid-1970s to mid-1980s, though more as a consequence of increased official contributions than of increased private generosity. In 1989 Northern NGOs were responsible for shifting US$6.4 billion to the South. Across all countries Hulme and Edwards (1997) suggest a figure of 28,900 international NGOs existing in 1993.

The expansion in partnership between Northern and Southern NGOs originated in changing attitudes in the North in the 1960s and 1970s. A view took hold that merely transferring resources in the form of tools or funds was not an adequate response to poverty when that was rooted in structural problems. Indeed such transfers could just preserve the situation by creating financial dependency. The establishment of research departments and policy units in Northern NGOs marked this change in approach and contributed to its sustainment.

Southern NGOs have the basic responsibility among NGOs for leading the development process in Third World countries and the expertise to do so. Relationship between Northern and Southern NGOs must be based on an equal partnership incorporating transparency, mutual accountability and risk-sharing.

CHARACTERISTICS AND ROLES OF NGOS

NGOs are popular because they demonstrate unique characteristics and capabilities – they are perceived to be flexible, open to innovation and able to reach the poor through work at the grass-roots level.

NGOs play two main roles, either service delivery or policy advocacy. As service delivery agents, NGOs provide welfare, technical, legal and financial services to the poor or work with community organizations in basic service and infrastructure provision. This is frequently a matter of filling gaps left by the partial service delivery of governments withdrawing from involvement in provision. In the past, governments of developing countries were seen as spearheading the development process. However, such paternalism reached its limits when it became clear that government did not have the financial resources to pay for the essential services of the poor and lacked the organizational expertise to be effective. In such an environment, the important role for NGOs in the last two decades has been in mitigating the adverse costs of structural adjustment and promoting donor reform packages in offering insurance against a political backlash against harsh adjustment regimes. Such a role raises important questions. Patterns of service delivery through the voluntary sector may lack compatibility and co-ordination. In so far as such efforts rely on government funding, their ultimate durability may also be queried. At a deeper level, there are worries about the long-term impact of NGO service provision on the sustainability of national health and education systems (rather than programmes) and access to quality services for all. Robinson (1991, 1993) has argued, for instance, that large, influential and well-funded NGOs may be able to 'concentrate resources in regions and sectors that might not be most important for national development', with a 'patchwork quilt' of services of varying quality emerging without any overview of overall needs.

The other frequent role for NGOs is policy advocacy, seeking social change by influencing attitudes, policy and practice, seeking to reform state services on the basis of NGO experiences and to lobby directly for the policy changes. This is involvement in participatory, public-interest politics, and NGOs engaging in such activity realize the increasing importance of information (which they gather by doing extensive research and documentation) as they begin to utilize the power of ideas and information to promote positive change in the wider structures of government and the official aid community. These NGOs often play a catalytic or seeding role – demonstrating the efficacy of a new idea, publicizing it, perhaps persuading those with access to greater power and budgets to take notice, and then encouraging the widespread adoption by others of the idea.

Neither of these roles need exclude the other. Indeed Korten (1990) suggests a process of progression whereby an NGO established to fill a gap in service delivery can recognize the need to look outward to the wider context in which the need arises and find itself drawn, possibly through involvement in NGO networks, into national or global policy advocacy.

NGOs work with grassroots organizations which often comprise poor and marginalized groups. In this respect they both widen (in social and geographical terms) and deepen (in terms of personal and organizational capacity) possibilities for citizen participation. NGOs have been important in mobilizing large numbers of people against either entrenched elites or state interests, campaigning on their behalf and seeking to influence public policy. Several commentators have pointed to successful NGO efforts to support indigenous peoples' and environmental movements across Latin America and Asia (Clark, 1991; Fisher, 1998). Fisher in particular argues that this type of 'bottom-up democracy' has been so successful in many instances that it might eventually lead to 'top-down political change' (1998: 126). NGOs have become key actors in a process of transformatory development.

NGOS' ROLE IN STRENGTHENING CIVIL SOCIETY AND DEMOCRATIC DEVELOPMENT

The point that NGOs contribution to development might be more important for political rather than economic reasons was first made in the late 1980s by Michael Bratton (1989). There is an increasing interest in the role of NGOs in promoting democratic development. The perspective of 'security policy' democracy poses the threat of opening a Pandora's Box of ethnicity, conflict and instability.

Their role is emphasized in this context by virtue of their existence as autonomous actors, NGOs are said to pluralize and therefore to strengthen and expand the institutional arena and bring more democratic actors into the political sphere. More civic actors mean more opportunities for a wider range of interest groups to have a 'voice', more autonomous organizations to act in a 'watchdog' role *vis-à-vis* the state, and more opportunities for networking and creating alliances of civic actors to place pressure on the state. 'NGOs . . . enhance democracy by expanding the number and range of voices addressing government' (Silliman and Noble, 1998: 306). NGOs have a key role to play during and after democratic transitions. For example, in Chile, NGOs played a vital role in opposing the Pinochet regime throughout the late 1970s and 1980s, and their role has undergone some degree of change since the early 1990s (Lambrou, 1997).

NGOs have become inextricably implicated in civil society, democracy, good governance and social capital. Clarke (1998a), in one of the few studies which examines the role of NGOs in the politics of development across the developing world, opines that the failure to theorize the political impact of NGOs has led to an overly 'inadequate, explicitly normative interpretation of NGO ideology' (1998a: 40). This failure has encouraged a tendency to take NGOs' positive political role as natural/self-evident.

NETWORKING AND BUILDING MOVEMENTS

NGOs create alliances and networks to place pressure on the state. The Philippines provides some of the strongest evidence of NGOs' role in networking and building coalition movements, where the NGO sector is regarded as being among the most organized and effective within the developing world (Clarke, 1998b; Silliman and Noble, 1998). A variety of national, regional and issue-based coalitions are buoyed by the activities of prominent and politically active NGOs. For example, the Philippines Rural Reconstruction Movement (PRRM) and the Task Force Detainees of the Philippines (TDFP), two of the largest and best-organized NGOs across the country, have linked a broad range of political actors (from government officials and elites, to political parties and left-wing movements) in campaigning for an end to authoritarian rule and, more recently, for continued democratic reform, the right to participate in local and national governance, and human rights, among other issues (Clarke, 1998b).

Many Northern NGOs have moved away from the direct implementation of projects to a 'partnership approach' with Southern NGOs, but the precise nature and terms of such partnerships often remain unclear (Lewis, 1998).

NGOS AND THE STATE

NGOs provide expertise in 'development software' (participatory approaches, community organizing, stakeholder ownership strategies); NGOs are more innovative, adaptable, cost effective and aware of the local situation; and their grassroots representation brings legitimacy and community mobilization to the programme. NGOs strengthen the state through their participation in improving the efficiency in government services, acting as strategic partners for reform-oriented ministries, filling in gaps in service provision, and helping the government forge ties with the grassroots.

The impact of states upon NGOs is absolutely central in defining the role NGOs can play in national development, for it is governments which give NGOs the space and the autonomy to organize, network and campaign (Clarke, 1998a, 1998b; Fowler, 1991). Of course, it is difficult to generalize about state–NGO relations, as local political networks are always diverse.

CONCLUSION

The key issue for the future is whether and how NGOs will adapt to the global changes which are currently under way. NGOs will need to link both local and global agendas if they are to be effective, and they will increasingly be forced to learn from, and adapt to, changing demands and opportunities.

The increased availability of large-scale funding has been one of the primary factors driving NGO growth in the 1980s, encouraging the proliferation of social welfare organizations which often had little or no political agenda. The 'inherent' advantages of the NGOs themselves are gradually worn away by increased funding, professionalization, bureaucracy and the shifting of objectives away from 'social mobilization' (which might be less attractive to donors) towards service delivery. This process may lead to a widening rift between well-resourced service providers and poorly funded social mobilization organizations. This highlights that NGOs exhibit potentially illuminating contrasts in emphasis and packaging of activities, in client groups and organizational style. Considerable diversity exists in relation to how autonomous NGOs are from the influence of funding agencies or management influences of donors. Increasingly questions have been asked. Can NGOs deliver all that is expected from them? Is the glowing image realistic? How effective are NGOs? There seems to be more concentration on success stories such as the Grameen Bank and Seva, and there seems to be a gap emerging between rhetoric and practice, which raises issues of objective monitoring and evaluation of NGOs' projects, effectiveness, legitimacy, performance and accountability.

GUIDE TO FURTHER READING

Edwards, M. and Hulme, D. (eds) (1992) *Making A Difference: NGOs and Development in a Changing World*, London: Earthscan Publications.

Edwards, M. and Hulme, D. (eds) (1995) *Beyond the Magic Bullet: NGO Performance and Accountability in the Post-Cold War World*, London: Macmillan.

Hulme, D. and M. Edwards (1997) (eds) *Too Close for Comfort? NGOs, States and Donors*, London: Macmillan.

These three collections bring together a range of diverse authors and perspectives forming a useful starting point for someone approaching the subject of NGOs (and various issues related to them) for the first time.

REFERENCES

Bratton, M. (1989) 'The politics of government–NGO relations in Africa', *World Development* 17: 69–87.

Clark, J. (1991) *Democratizing Development: The Role of Voluntary Organizations*, London: Earthscan, and West Hartford: Kumarian Press.

Clarke, G. (1998a) *The politics of NGOs in South-East Asia: participation and protest in the Philippines*, London: Routledge.

Clarke, G. (1998b) 'Non-governmental organisations (NGOs) and politics in the developing world', *Political Studies* XLVI: 36–52.

Fisher, J. (1998) *Non Governments: NGOs and the Political Development of the Third World*, West Hartford: Kumarian Press.

Fowler, A. (1991) 'The role of NGOs in changing state–society relations: perspectives from Eastern and Southern Africa', *Development Policy Review* 9: 53–84.

Korten, D. (1990) *Getting to the 21st Century: Voluntary Action and the Global Agenda*, West Hartford: Kumarian Press.

Lambrou, Y. (1997) 'The changing role of NGOs in rural Chile after democracy', *Bulletin of Latin American Research* 16: 107–16.

Lewis, D. (1998) 'Development NGOs and the challenge of partnership: changing relations between North and South', *Social Policy and Administration* 32(5): 501–12.

Robinson, M. (1991) *Evaluating the Impact of NGOs in Rural Poverty Alleviation: India Country Study*, Working Paper 49, London: Overseas Development Institute.

Robinson, M. (1993) *Governance, Democracy and Conditionality: NGOs and the New Policy Agenda*, London: Overseas Development Institute.

Silliman, G.S. and Noble, L.G. (1998) 'Citizen movements and Philippine democracy', in G.S. Silliman and L.G. Noble (eds) *Organising for Democracy: NGOs, Civil Society and the Philippine State*, Honolulu: University of Hawaii Press, pp. 280–310.

10.7 The World Bank and NGOs

Paul J. Nelson

Thousands of demonstrators at the April 2000 meetings of the World Bank's and International Monetary Fund's governing boards made the World Bank's relations with non-governmental organizations (NGOs) front-page news. But while the demonstrations were perhaps the World Bank's most public encounter with NGOs, they were not its first. Although the world's largest lender for development is owned and governed by its 183 member governments, its contact with NGOs grew rapidly in the 1980s and 1990s, both in policy debates and in service delivery. A wide variety of NGOs, based in the industrial countries and in the World Bank's borrowing countries, were drawn into lending and policy processes that were long almost exclusively the province of national governments.

Three clear types of contact have emerged: NGO collaboration in World Bank-financed projects; invited consultation in policy discussions; and confrontations over projects or controversial policies. Both project collaboration and more confrontational critiques have helped make way for changes in the World Bank policy, forced a more open information disclosure policy, and, in a few cases, influenced its lending practice.

THREE FORMS OF INTERACTION

NGO involvement in World Bank-financed projects

The World Bank makes loans to governments to finance development projects and encourages policy changes by offering non-project 'structural adjustment' loans that require changes in national economic policy. NGO involvement in the implementation of WB-financed projects grew rapidly during the 1980s and 1990s, as some staff came to see NGOs as potential project imple-menters in a period when many governments' service delivery capacity was shrinking. Fewer than 10 per cent of projects between 1973 and 1988 were reported to involve an NGO, but the World Bank (1998a) reports that one-third of projects approved in the 1990s involved an NGO in some role.

These roles are variable, and NGO involvement does not necessarily signal a change in the char-acter of the project, or in decision-making about the project. The World Bank (1998a) acknowl-edges that the NGO roles are 'often quite minor', limited to implementing projects designed and negotiated by government and WB officials. Many projects in the early 1990s, for example, involved NGOs in a single project 'component', or as recipients of small grants through special social service funds known as Emergency Social Funds (ESFs) or Social Investment Funds (SIFs).

ESFs and SIFs are partial 'social safety nets' in countries undergoing structural adjustment. The World Bank invested more than US$3.7 billion to finance 108 funds in 57 countries between 1987 and 1995 (World Bank, 1999), and NGOs had a role in most. A fund, administered by a special unit of the central government, typically makes grants in response to proposals from local governments or NGOs for social service, job creation or other programmes.

'Consultation' in policy formation

'Consultation' is a buzzword at major development agencies, and the World Bank is no exception. In addition to project-level talks with NGOs or community organizations, the World Bank increas-ingly solicits opinions or sponsors formal consultations when designing new Bank-wide policy or publications. Formal meetings or electronic consultations have been held to elicit NGO input on Sector policy papers (forestry, water, energy, etc.), and on the themes of the annual *World Development Report.* The World Bank has co-sponsored conferences, groups and electronic consul-tations on social policy issues such as hunger alleviation, gender, participation, globalization and micro-enterprise lending. These consultations are frequent, relatively public, and do not have immediate implications for any particular loan or member state. Their impact is varied, and consultation is often a ritual that lends legitimacy to the policy process without creating binding commitments.

Confrontation: the NGO critique

While many NGOs seek co-operation and funding for projects, others have made the WB a target for policy advocacy. The World Bank has been a lightning rod for criticism of the international economic system and of development aid. NGOs have pressed the WB to become more generous, egalitarian, and responsive to gender and minority concerns; more transparent and open to effective civil soci-ety participation; and more sensitive to natural resource use and human rights standards.

Resistance to WB-financed infrastructure projects has been the most visible form of NGO crit-icism, and has forced the WB to give attention to environmental and social issues involved in major dam and energy projects. NGO critics have blocked one project, provoked amendments to others, and helped to motivate the creation of an independent inspection panel to which affected commu-nities can appeal (Umaña, 1998). They have also motivated the World Bank to carry out an unusu-ally thorough and self-critical review of its role in involuntary resettlement of communities for major infrastructure projects (World Bank, 1996; Fox, 1998).

The blocked project – a proposed loan for a major dam on Nepal's Arun River – illustrates the political tools that NGOs have used. The project, discussed since 1989 but formally proposed for WB funding in 1994, was opposed by some of the indigenous residents of the remote river valley, but their objections had little influence with the Nepalese government. NGOs lobbied the World Bank directly, pressuring member governments' representatives on the WB Board. In October 1994, before the project had been approved for funding, they filed a claim with the new Independent Inspection Panel. The claim, submitted by anonymous residents of the river valley and a national NGO, the 'Arun Concerned Group', was investigated by the Panel, which determined that the WB had violated its own policies in preparing the project. New WB President James Wolfensohn ended World Bank involvement in the project in June 1995.

Working through the US representation on the Board of Executive Directors, and lobbying the World Bank directly and through the media, NGOs have focused heavily, but not exclusively, on the early stages of the policy-making process, i.e., on putting issues on the agenda and framing the outlines of a policy. They have adopted a variety of strategic postures toward the World Bank – attacking, confronting, persuading and co-operating – and have formed coalitions with NGOs, and alliances with other agencies and researchers.

EFFECTS ON POLICY AND PRACTICE

The World Bank's activities are of interest to a wide range of actors in the international political economy. OECD governments, international organizations and borrowing country governments have strong interests in virtually all decisions at the World Bank. Within each government there may be distinct views among the Central Bank, Treasury, Development Ministry or Agency, or export agency. Other organizations in the UN system sometimes take an interest in World Bank policies that affect their mandates, and see the WB as an important potential source of co-financing for projects. UNICEF, for example, helped to mobilize NGO interest in structural adjustment in the 1980s. As the World Bank re-creates itself as the centre of a web of 'partnerships', a 'comprehensive development framework' (World Bank, 1998b), NGOs are not alone in trying to influence WB decision-makers.

Effects at the World Bank

What effect has all this attention had on the World Bank? The complex political environment makes it difficult to sort out causes of policy change, but NGOs have arguably had important roles in four trends at the World Bank, both intended and unintended. They have helped make greater space for innovators on staff, greater openness to external scrutiny, extensive changes in formal policy, and they have helped expand the World Bank's influence over many borrowing governments.

Space and support for internal innovators

Staff who want to use participatory methods, or innovate in other ways, have benefited from external pressure on the WB (Miller-Adams, 1999). Internal advocates for more participatory project design and implementation brought NGO advocates into the internal 'participation learning group' that documented participatory strategies, made policy recommendations and led to the creation of a widely distributed WB *Participation Sourcebook*. Internal working groups on micro-enterprise lending and gender issues also relate closely to interested NGOs.

Greater openness

NGO pressure also contributed directly to adoption of a new, more liberal information policy in 1993, under which the public can gain access to at least summaries of most project-related documents.

Formal policy changes

In a handful of environmental and social policy areas it is clear that NGOs have contributed to policy changes. More confrontational strategies have led to new environmental and rights policies in fields such as energy, forestry and involuntary resettlement related to major infrastructure projects (Fox and Brown, 1998). Involuntary resettlement, perhaps the area of most intense NGO advocacy and monitoring, is also the area where both internal and independent reviewers have found the clearest evidence of changes in practice.

NGO pressure has had other, unintended, effects on the World Bank as well. It is an increasingly agile institution, capable of policy change and of partial strategic reorientation when conditions require them. A spate of recent initiatives, including the partnership initiative, anti-corruption programmes, its somewhat heterodox position in the debate over the Asian financial crisis, and interest in corporate governance, are all examples. NGOs have also forced the WB to learn to manage external criticism, raising its threshold of sensitivity: an open letter or critical public statement that might have attracted much attention at the World Bank in 1985 was a routine matter in the year 2000.

Expanding influence over borrowers

In expanding its policy domain and the safeguards it applies to lending, the World Bank has also expanded its authority over its borrowers. Among the requirements of its borrowers, new since 1980, are environmental impact assessments, national environmental action plans, disclosure of certain documents, poverty assessments, and a variety of safeguards and reports regarding 'good governance' (Nelson, 1996).

Any new requirement or safeguard on WB projects lending translates into a requirement on borrowing government ministries. For example, the requirement that environmental impact assessments (EIAs) be completed and released to the public before approval of most projects, affects not just the WB but the borrowing government agency, which must undertake and release the EIA, even if normal practice includes no such freedom of information practice.

Effects on the NGOs

The World Bank, too, has an agenda in its work with NGOs. Like most development aid agencies, it treats NGOs as an important constituency in securing political support. The World Bank's economic policy framework of liberalization, privatization, export promotion and reshaping the welfare state also depends on NGOs to manage social programmes and emergency social funds during structural adjustment programmes and to implement components of social and environmental projects. This project collaboration parallels and reinforces the increasing reliance of many NGOs on national and international donors (Hulme and Edwards, 1997).

Network links built among the World Bank's NGO critics help to shape the structure, orientation and capacity of civil society organizations. Sustained NGO campaigns to influence World Bank projects and policy in involuntary resettlement and energy policy have built enduring networks. These links between civil society organizations in the global North and South can help build capacity for self-representation, an important addition to other capacity-building programmes among NGOs, which often focus on capacities for service delivery.

But NGO networks themselves will likely be asked to meet a standard of democracy and accountability, if they are to be considered legitimate political actors. International NGOs, particularly environmental advocates, have figured prominently in advocacy networks and coalitions, and the World Bank's borrowing governments and Southern NGOs themselves are increasingly demanding greater clarity about who represents whom, and on what agendas, in advocacy toward international organizations such as the World Bank (Nelson, 1997).

Prospects

NGOs have won a seat at the policy-making table at the World Bank, and the WB has established mechanisms that allow it to benefit from the service-delivery capacity and the knowledge of NGOs, including those in its borrowing countries. Both parties face challenges in building on these arrangements. The World Bank will need to devise ways to bring NGOs and its borrowing governments into more consistent effective contact if it is to continue to benefit from NGOs' co-operation while placing beleaguered governments 'firmly in the driver's seat' (World Bank, 1998b) of World Bank-financed programmes.

NGOs have built networks and won policy changes. They will increasingly need to build the local capacity to monitor and force implementation of these policy commitments won at WB headquarters, and devise ways to give increasing voice and control to NGOs based in the borrowing countries, without losing co-ordination and political effectiveness. As they give greater attention to trade, debt and other issues in international finance, NGOs will draw lessons from their successes and failures at the World Bank. In the process, they may find ways to make the World Bank a source of leverage for humane and accountable solutions to a new round of international finance and development issues.

GUIDE TO FURTHER READING

Fox, Jonathan and Brown, David L. (eds) (1998) *The Struggle for Accountability: The World Bank, NGOs and Grassroots Movements*, Cambridge: MIT Press.

Gibbs, C., Fumo, C. and Kuby, T. (1999) 'Nongovernmental organizations in World Bank supported projects', Washington DC: World Bank Operations Evaluation Department.

Miller-Adams, Michelle (1999) *The World Bank: New Agendas in a Changing World*. London: Routledge.

Nelson, Paul (2000) 'Heroism and ambiguity: NGO advocacy in international policy', *Development in Practice* 10 (3 and 4): 478–90.

REFERENCES

Fox, Jonathan (1998) 'When does reform policy influence practice? Lessons from the bankwide resettlement review', in Fox and Brown, pp. 303–44.

Fox, Jonathan and Brown, David L. (eds) (1998) *The Struggle for Accountability: The World Bank, NGOs and Grassroots Movements*, Cambridge: MIT Press.

Gibbs, C., Fumo, C. and Kuby, T. (1999) 'Nongovernmental organizations in World Bank supported projects', Washington DC: World Bank Operations Evaluation Department.

Hulme, David and Edwards, Michael (eds) (1997) *NGOs, States and Donors: Too Close for Comfort?*, New York: St Martin's in association with Save the Children.

Miller-Adams, Michelle (1999) *The World Bank: New Agendas in a Changing World*, London: Routledge.

Nelson, Paul J. (1996) 'Internationalising economic and environmental policy: transnational NGO networks and the World Bank's expanding influence', *Millennium* 25(3): 605–33.

Nelson, Paul J. (1997) 'Conflict, legitimacy and effectiveness: who speaks for whom in transnational NGO networks lobbying the World Bank?', *Nonprofit and Voluntary Sector Quarterly* 26(4): 421–41.

Umaña, Alvaro (ed.) (1998) *The World Bank Inspection Panel: The First Four Years (1994–1998)*, Washington, DC: World Bank.

World Bank (1996) *Resettlement and Development: The Bankwide Review of Projects Involving Involuntary Resettlement, 1986–1993*, Environment Department Paper 032, Washington DC: World Bank.

World Bank (1998a) 'Overview – NGO World Bank collaboration', Washington DC: World Bank.

World Bank (1998b) 'Partnership for development: from vision to action', September, Washington DC: World Bank.

World Bank (1999) 'World Bank briefing note on social funds', 27 October 1999, Washington DC: World Bank.

10.8 NGOs and the state

John D. Clark[1]

WHAT DO NGOS OFFER?

When I raised money for Oxfam at school I first heard the proverb: 'Give a man a fish and you feed him for a day; teach a man to fish and you feed him for a lifetime'; it seemed a profound statement on the need for development and self-reliance, not hand-outs. But I have come to see it as an eloquent parody of all that is wrong with so much that passes for 'development'. It begs important questions and is based on dubious assumptions.

Do the experts teach *everyone* to fish, or just the poor? Without targeting, there may be little left for the most deserving. If you teach the poor to fish, do they have the nets and boats they need; will they be able to buy or rent them? Do they have access to the fishing grounds, or are these monopolized by the local elite? If they catch fish, are they able to market them and get a fair price – or are they exploited by middle-men? Are they equipped to withstand the risks of fishing in dangerous waters? Are the waters polluted, either killing the fish or rendering them inedible? How environmentally sustainable is the trade? If you teach only the *man* to fish, will the benefits be shared within his family? These questions are unanswered. And, by the way, has anyone bothered to ask the poor whether they *like* fish? Is it a culturally appropriate skill to teach?

The proverb's assumptions insult the intelligence of the poor. It paints a picture of ignorant, hungry people sitting idly beside well-stocked waters, just waiting for the expert to arrive from outside and show them how it's done. Anyone who has come close to poor people knows how hardworking and resourceful they generally are. But the greatest false assumption is that the problem of hunger is reduced to a technical issue of production, when in reality it is largely a political issue of distribution and inclusion.

Keeping with the metaphor, there may be a compelling case for helping people catch fish, but unless the approach taken is founded on realistic assumptions and addresses the above questions, the programme will at best be irrelevant and could well be harmful. It is for these reasons that NGOs and other civil society actors have vital roles to play in development; hence governments and development agencies such as the World Bank are increasingly working with NGOs and promoting the growth of the sector.

NGOs can offer essential 'local knowledge' about local conditions and the poor. They can deliver services to vulnerable and difficult-to-reach population groups. Their parallel activities may make the programme much better for the poor (by providing credit for nets and boats, say, or by setting up a refrigeration plant so the catch can be frozen and sent to market, so ending the stranglehold of the one local merchant). Through social assessments and participatory research, NGOs can point out how the programme can better serve different communities, and be tailored differently for different ethnic groups. By sensitizing authorities about the ideas and preferences of the poor, they can help attune the project to their real needs. Through gender training and mobilizing the women, they can ensure equity within the family. And through social mobilization they can help the poor organize themselves, either to form co-operatives, demand changes, or ensure the accountability and probity of the programme's officers (Clark, 1995).

These are vitally important roles, best served by NGOs, community-based organizations and others in civil society who are close to the poor and enjoy their trust. Some argue that NGOs are *better* at development than government or official donors. This is a sterile line of argument. NGOs will never be able to do many things or acquire the scale of government programmes. Their value is that they do *different* things.

Generalizations are dangerous. Not all NGOs are effective; some talk a fine patter but do little for the vulnerable. In some countries, NGOs congregate close to big cities and don't reach into the poverty belts. There are important questions of accountability and legitimacy, regarding for example their claim to 'speak for the poor' (Edwards and Hulme, 1995). But the sector as a whole plays important and increasingly powerful roles. This may include challenging decisions of States, but in ways which shift governments to better serve their responsibilities *vis-à-vis* their populations, and therefore enhance their legitimacy. Legitimate governments, therefore, have no need to fear a well-functioning and responsible NGO sector.

WHY STATES NEED NGOS

Governments, therefore, need NGOs to help ensure their programmes are effective, well-targeted, socially responsible and well understood. The media likewise need NGOs because they trust the local knowledge and alternative perspectives they offer. The public need them because of their services and their mobilizing capacity – helping citizens express their voice, or challenge authority. Parliamentarians need them for policy guidance, for feedback on what people want, and as watchdogs in monitoring public programmes and enhancing the accountability of officials.

The legitimacy of individual NGOs rests not necessarily in their mass-membership or their budget, but in their *usefulness* to these constituencies. The NGO sector, therefore, is symbiotic with a well-functioning, democratic state, not parasitic or undermining.

Since the earliest days of tribal government, the keenest goal of leaders has been to hold on to the reins. This is achieved through wielding power over competitors (especially through military might), and cultivating popularity by allowing important population groups to do what they want as long as it doesn't undermine the leadership, and by making plausible promises of rewards to come (in this, and subsequent lives).

Cultivating popularity needs channels for eliciting what would be popular, for providing people with what they need, and for enabling people to do the things they want. Over the centuries civil society has evolved to provide these channels. Some states muzzle or do not permit free civil society; these risk being isolated from their populations. At times civil society pressure might be anti-social or reinforce appalling regimes. The vibrant citizens' organizations in Weimar Germany in the 1920s and 1930s, for example, demanded more and more from a weak government and, some argue, precipitated a shift towards the populist government form of the Nazi Party (Berman, 1997). But in general, civil society helps attune governments to their populations and strengthens mechanisms of democracy and accountability. This is more so where states have coherent and transparent mechanisms for policy-making. For example, vigorous environmental campaigning in USA drove the creation and expansion of government environmental agencies, laws and enforcement mechanisms (Carothers, 1999/2000).

Electoral democracy is valuable for assessing the main concerns of the majority. But everyone is a minority in one respect or another – due to our age, religion, location, ethnic group, physical attributes, employment status, sexual orientation, hobbies, convictions or passions. And we tend to see ourselves as defined more by these factors than our nationality, but national democratic processes are often blind to them. For thousands of years throughout the world, therefore, civil society has emerged in varying degrees to represent these interests. Some causes may be detested by others (such as those promoted by the National Rifle Association in the USA, and racist groups), but citizens' advocacy in general reinforces democracy and strengthens state capacity.

In summary, NGOs are important to states in that they can

- encourage governments to adopt innovations from the voluntary sector
- educate and sensitize the public about their rights and opportunities
- collaborate in making government programmes more effective
- attune programmes to public needs
- strengthen local institutions and make them more accountable
- act as conduits for citizen consultation and advocacy.

(Clark, 1991)

HOW STATES SHAPE CIVIL SOCIETY

Though civil society has become important in virtually every country, its magnitude, scope and influence – hence its contribution to society and to development – varies enormously. A number of factors account for this – including the tradition for philanthropy, exposure to Western ideas and education, national religions, etc. – but one factor is of paramount importance: the NGO–state relationship. NGOs sometimes prefer to keep their distance from government or side with the opposition. Sometimes governments resent and mistrust NGOs. Tandon (1991) describes a typology of state–NGO relations, according to whether the regime is autocratic, weak and unpredictable, or a mature democracy.

The relationship's kernel is usually the framework of laws and regulations which govern the formation and operation of NGOs. Ideally this framework is fully enabling while instilling some discipline. Laws which hamper the formation of independent NGOs, which deny citizens rights to join or support NGOs, or which subject NGO operations to strict government control and unpredictable intervention, fetter the NGO sector. Not only are citizens thereby denied the positive contributions NGOs offer, but they are denied the 'rights of association' guaranteed by most states (including China) who have signed the UN International Covenants on Civil and Political Rights.

Conversely, where laws are so lax that anyone can form an NGO, register it for tax and fundraising advantages, and where there are no rules for ensuring a modicum of transparency and account-ability, the public are unprotected from unscrupulous NGO operators.

Getting the balance right is not easy, and will depend on the legal tradition and other aspects of the country in question (ICNL/World Bank, 1997). Governments should not seek to manage NGOs – this would undermine NGOs and inappropriately stretch government capacity. Instead they should create conditions that encourage effective self-regulation of the sector. NGOs that seek benefits from the state or the public should be expected to be transparent and accountable, propor-tionate to the scale of these benefits.

HOW STATES CAN WORK WELL WITH NGOS

Governments' stance towards NGOs can be either non-interventionist, encouraging, offering part-nership, seeking co-option or controlling (Brown, 1990). In addition to promoting a healthy policy environment, there are five ways in which governments can ensure a positive NGO relationship (Clark, 1995).

First, governments can provide NGOs with information about state programmes and policies for dissemination to their constituencies and gathering feedback. NGOs can help governments strengthen citizen consultation and public awareness of rights and opportunities.

Second, governments can offer opportunities for operational collaboration, commissioning NGO activities that complement their programmes and strengthening the NGOs. This partnership approach is strongly encouraged by the World Bank and other donors. Even where governments are suspicious or hostile towards NGOs it may be that some line ministries are disposed towards partnership.

Third, governments can involve NGOs in policy debate and public consultations on new poli-cies or major government projects. For example, NGOs can help orchestrate effective public hear-ings about infrastructure projects. The World Bank now *requires* public hearings, including civil society, for all projects it funds that may have a significant environmental impact.

Fourth, governments can co-ordinate – or encourage co-ordination – between the various agencies (non-governmental, governmental, donors and private sector) who work in a common field. This is an important element of the 'Comprehensive Development Framework' approach currently being promoted and piloted by the World Bank (Wolfensohn, 1999).

And finally, governments can help finance NGOs, through grant funding, loans, contracts and opportunities to be conduits for government resources provided to communities. The World Bank, for example, supports 'Social Funds' in many countries in which funds are often provided through NGOs to poor communities for village infrastructure, community investments or micro-credit.

CONCLUSION

In all these areas there is potential for conflict and difficulties. NGOs may be at odds with govern-ments; collaboration by some may appear to undermine advocacy efforts of others. Government agencies may seek to co-opt (and possibly corrupt) the NGOs it works with, or NGOs may find that their own agendas get lost.

There are many reasons to promote close state–NGO relations. NGOs may be cost-effective, work in remote areas or be innovative. But their most important potential is for engaging citizens, particularly the poor, in shaping the decisions that affect them and in allocating associated resources. Popular participation is the main argument for improving state–NGO relations and fostering an enabling environment for NGOs, because ultimately 'development' is what is done *by* people, not *to* people.

NOTE

1. This chapter reflects the author's views and not necessarily those of the World Bank or affiliated organizations.

GUIDE TO FURTHER READING

Chambers, R. (1983) *Rural Development: Putting the Last First*, Harlow: Longman.

Clark, J. (1991) *Democratizing Development: The Role of Voluntary Organizations*, London: Earthscan, and West Hartford: Kumarian Press.

Edwards, M. (1999) *Future Positive: International Cooperation in the 21st Century*, London: Earthscan.

Fowler, A. (1997) *Striking a Balance: a Guide to Enhancing the Effectiveness of NGOs in International Development*, London: Earthscan.

Salamon, L. and Anheier, H. (1998) *The Emerging Sector Revisited*, Baltimore: Johns Hopkins University, Institute of Policy Studies.

REFERENCES

Berman, S. (1997) 'Civil society and the collapse of the Weimar Republic', *World Politics*, USA, April.

Brown, L.D. (1990) *Policy Impacts on the NGO Sector*, Mimeo, Washington DC: World Bank.

Carothers, T. (1999/2000) 'Civil society: think again', *Foreign Policy*, USA, Winter 1999–2000.

Clark, J. (1991) *Democratizing Development: The Role of Voluntary Organizations*, London: Earthscan, and West Hartford: Kumarian Press.

Clark, J. (1995) 'The state, popular participation and the voluntary sector', *World Development* 23(4).

Edwards, M. and Hulme, D. (eds) (1995) *NGO Performance and Accountability: Beyond the Magic Bullet*, London: Earthscan and West Hartford: Kumarian Press.

International Center for Not-for-Profit Law (ICNL) (1997) *Good Practices for Laws Relating to NGOs*, draft handbook prepared for the NGO Unit, World Bank, Washington DC.

Tandon, R. (1991) *NGO Government Relations: A Source of Life or a Kiss of Death*, New Delhi: Society for Participatory Research in Asia.

Wolfensohn, J. (1999) *A Proposal for a Comprehensive Development Framework*, Washington DC: World Bank.

10.9 NGDO–donor relationships: the use and abuse of partnership

Alan Fowler

THE STORY IN BRIEF

The story of relations between non-governmental development organizations (NGDOs) and official donors over the past 30 years is essentially one of a move from separation to convergence, and from mutual mistrust and antagonism to an asymmetric co-optive embrace.[1] Partnership has been chosen to describe the intended intensification of relations. This type of relationship is seen as an antidote to inadequate aid performance. It is also a defensive strategy against a decline in aid finance[2] and its eventual, albeit unevenly spread, replacement by foreign direct investment (FDI). The forces leading to these changes can be found in a post-Cold War shift to a 'new aid agenda' (OECD, 1996). Recent, rapid growth of NGDOs across the world is a product of, and increasingly reliant on, tax-derived finance. Consequently, NGDOs are more likely to relate to donors as (sub-) contractors (Fowler, 2000b).

CONVERGENCE

In the early decades of international aid, government was regarded as the motor of development in non-industrialized countries – the South. Economic growth, with a 'trickle-down' of wealth to the poor, dominated as the development model. NGDOs were few on the ground, predominantly self-financed and thought to be of negligible consequence in terms of the big picture of development. NGDOs in the industrialized world of donors – the North – with an international outreach were often allied to churches. Or, they had origins in humanitarian assistance provided in response to civil war (Spain, Korea), and the First and Second World Wars (Lissner, 1977). This imperative was to change in the 1970s when Northern NGDOs began to expand (often as role models) in newly independent countries (South Asia and sub-Saharan Africa) and where left-leaning intellectuals took refuge from military and civilian dictatorships (in much of Latin America). While growing in number, NGDO relations with donors were low key and episodic. There was also mutual mistrust and separation, fostered by NGDOs often adopting a *dependencia* analysis of underdevelopment (Lehmann, 1986), set against the official government-centred 'modernization' model propagated by donors. However, the advent of economic policies associated with Ronald Reagan and Margaret Thatcher was set to significantly change the relational framework.

In the 1980s, domestic policies in donor countries shifted attention from government to the market as the engine of growth and progress. In addition to freeing business from restrictive shackles, a push for 'less government' also meant more responsibility to citizens and their organizations. Domestic policies 'spilled over' into international aid through the Bretton Woods Institutions (BWIs) – the International Monetary Fund and the multilateral development banks. They did so by adopting a uniform set of conditions – known as structural adjustment – on which BWI finance would be given. These conditions were premised on an optimum institutional division of functions in society that started to recognize and open up space for non-state actors, giving added impetus to NGDO growth and interaction with government. Hence, the start of the rise in official finance to and number of NGDOs (Van Rooy, 2000) and production of guides for working with official agencies (Malena, 1995; NGLS, 1995).

Throughout the 1980s, 1990s and to this day, a second force for convergence was coming from NGDOs themselves. Experience of having their local development efforts undermined by ill-conceived policies and often poor, corrupt national public management, caused them to shift their horizons to policy formulation and its actors at home and abroad. The result has been growing NGDO advocacy pressure on and engagement with donors. The intention is not limited to dialogue about policy implementation but about policy choices themselves and the right of citizen participation and of rights-based development more generally (Nelson, 1995; Van Tuijl, 1999). Substantial NGDO presence and lobbying at the Rio summit on the environment and demonstrations at the meeting of the World Trade Organization in Seattle are examples of how far things have come. In addition, NGDOs were learning about 'participatory' development and poverty reduction, asserting that they were better at it than the official system. In other words, they argued that they had comparative advantages and something to offer that donors could learn from, and hence merited official support (Fowler, 1997). In other words, in seeking official funding NGDOs had a 'reverse agenda' of co-opting government into adopting people-centred practices (Riddell *et al.*, 1995).

Third, the implosion of the Soviet Union gave rise, in the 1990s, to the concept of civil society as a legitimate and necessary actor in development. Consequently, NGDOs and other civic actors came into their own as recognized players that must be associated with development goals, both as means and ends.[3] For the aid system, greater interaction with and dedicated efforts to enhance the growth of civil society were necessary for two reasons. One is to help deal with the institutional reconfiguration required by 'privatization' of supposedly over-extended government (social) services. Another is to accelerate the consolidation of democracy as the political dimension of aid, especially in 'transition' economies that are now implementing capitalist, free market economic systems (Clark, 1991; Van Rooy, 1998).

Overall, these forces have conspired to create new, complex arenas for more intensive and extensive interaction between NGOs and donors in the North and the South. The rules of the game are being made up on the spot but are largely guided by donor preferences, needs and procedures. One example is the donor priority for and practice of direct funding of NGDOs in the South (INTRAC, 1998).

PARTNERSHIP

In today's official aid system, only one type of relationship seems to count. It is called 'partnership'. Theoretically, the term relates to a 'social contract' between state and society derived from the thinking and writing of political philosophers such as Plato, Locke, Hobbes, Mill, Rousseau and de Tocqueville. It has been chosen as the preferred relational modality between NGDOs and donors (and others) today for a number of both sound and questionable reasons.

On the positive side, more than 30 years of experience in international aid has shown just how complex and indeterminate the process of development can be. No one party can be relied on to make growth or poverty reduction a reality. Moreover, aid is just one – sometimes small (India), sometimes large (Mozambique) – component of the process. More humility and realism has led the aid system to the reasonable conclusion that as many actors and forces as possible must be brought to bear on making a country more liveable in for the population as a whole and viable in a rapidly evolving world order. Hence the attraction of partnership as the guiding idea. However, it also has other attractions.

An ongoing decline in real aid levels signals a lessening of political will. Demotivation for aid in the North is fed, amongst others, by the perception that development assistance has not performed well enough. The causes, and partnership as a solution, are captured in the following quotation.

> The purpose of the 'partnership' framework is to address what recent diagnoses of the aid industry conclude are the critical gaps which accounted in the past for the ineffectiveness of aid. These are identified as: (1) the lack of local 'ownership' of policies and programmes, perceived as the key to good management; (2) inappropriate donor behaviour, including [insufficient] aid co-ordination and the ineffectiveness of conditionality as a surveillance and quality control mechanism and; (3) the underlying environment, including the nature

of policies, institutions and the political system. Consequently, partnership seeks to address inclusiveness, complementarity, dialogue and shared responsibility as the basis of managing the multiple relationships among stakeholders in the aid industry.

(Abugre, 1999: 2)

By 'partnering' with NGDOs and others, donors hope to widen and deepen the array of actors who will 'own' development in the South and be committed to aid finance and the success of its interventions. In addition, in support of the global introduction of neo-liberal economic policy, partnership can help align the efforts of government, business and civil society in a concerted effort at poverty reduction and redress the other dysfunctions and limits to competition in a capitalist market economy (Group of Lisbon, 1995). Finally, partnership should help set a 'consensus' framework within which different parties and their interests can be negotiated. In other words, partnership can generate constituencies for, and reinvigorate political confidence in, the value of aid, so protecting the system from further threat and decline.

Set against these positive features are some serious flaws in the theory and practice of partnership as the relational framework for development. First, it assumes that only harmony of interest moves society forward. But it can be argued that contention and its resolution between conflicting groups, forces, interests and power distribution has proven to be just as important for social stability and equitable progress in the past and will remain so in the future. For example, complex social contract arrangements to be found in countries of continental Europe are the product of over 200 years of internal struggle and their organic resolution. This fact seem to be glossed over in the quest for partnership in development with everyone, on everything, everywhere. The appropriateness of 'partnership' as the relational mode to be applied will depend on the context and moment in history of the country concerned. It cannot be assumed as appropriate *a priori*.

Second, partnership implies many features that the aid system must be able to deliver. For partnership to be 'authentic' requires, *inter alia*, a joint commitment to a long-term interaction, shared responsibility for achievement, reciprocal obligation, equality, mutuality and balance of power (Fowler, 1998). In most of these areas, the aid system is structurally weak. Three reasons illustrate aid's deep limitations. One is the inherent power difference between giver and recipient that always interferes with relational balance. It is and remains an asymmetric dependency-inducing arrangement where the piper usually calls the final tune (SIDA, 1996). Second, with limited exceptions of block funding (Smillie and Helmich, 1993, 1999), the vast majority of donor assistance to NGDOs is based on a sequence of discrete, time-bound projects. This transactional foundation seldom if ever evolves to a truly organization-to-organization relationship that real partnership requires (Fowler, 1997; Holloway, 1997). Finally, because projects are the relational currency, often on a contractual basis, there is no system for holding NGDOs and donors jointly to account for success or failure.

The final worrying aspect of partnership as currently envisaged by the aid system is the way in which the concept is being located in comprehensive development frameworks. These recent aid constructions seek to embrace and incorporate everyone in a developing country (Wolfensohn, 1999).[4] However, in this approach partnership can be (i) used to sideline alternative views about development and (ii) permit deeper and wider foreign penetration into the internal workings of the recipient country, inviting a backlash and charge of neo-colonialism (Mohammed, 1997).

Overall, partnership is not always a laudable, benign or appropriate aspiration. Its blanket use can simply hide abuse and mystify the deep structural problems of power imbalance that continue to plague the aid system and its many relationships, including between NGDO and donors.

PRESENT AND FUTURE PERSPECTIVES

Today, many if not most NGDO–donor relations pivot around willing buyer and willing seller of development or humanitarian services (Smillie *et al.*, 1996; Weiss, 1998). The past trend of donor direct financing of NGDOs in the South will continue. Unless the 'rules of the game' change substantially (Fowler, 2000a), these are likely to remain the major modalities in the years to come, leavened and complicated by increasing advocacy and policy assertiveness of a few. The few are likely to be part of a group of NGDOs that have or will successfully diversify their resource base away from international aid, but without simply knocking on the door of the domestic government in the South (Bennett *et al.*, 1996; Norton, 1996; Fox and Schearer, 1997). The future continues to hold out the prospect of more relational intensity and complexity between donors and NGDOs, but greater power balance, mutuality and partnership worthy of the name will probably remain politically correct but illusive.

NOTES

1. This chapter does not consider NGDO relations with private 'donors', i.e. funding from the general public (the gift economy – Fowler, 1992) or from foundations. The focus is limited to NGDOs and official aid.
2. Figures for official aid are: 1992, US$60.8 billion; 1998, US$51.5 Billion, an 18 per cent decrease in real terms (DI, 1999). Current estimate is that somewhat over 50 per cent of NGO finance derives directly or indirectly from the tax base in donor countries (Fowler, 2000a).
3. The other two sectors in society sectors are government and for-profit business. As predominantly defined (Salamon and Anheier, 1997) the non-profit Third Sector does not equate with civil society because, amongst others, it does not include non-formal associational life, giving preference to bodies with a legal personality. In this article, the more inclusive concept of civil society is employed.
4. See the World Bank website: <www.worldbank.org/cdf/>.

GUIDE TO FURTHER READING

Hulme, D. and Edwards, M. (eds) (1997) *NGO, States and Donors: Too Close for Comfort?*, London: Macmillan. Probably the most comprehensive volume on NGDO relations with donors seen from an NGDO perspective. The papers, presented at conference in 1994 describe the issues of co-operation and the danger of NGDO displacement from the poor and powerless to the more powerful. In other words, this volume also examines the impact of NGDO–donor interaction on performance and NGDOs' other relationships.

Smillie and Helmich (1993) and Smillie and Helmich (1999). These volumes provide a systematic country-by-country review of donor relations with their domestic NGDOs. The six-year time span between them allows longitudinal analysis of trends and changes in the issues, predominantly from a donor point of view. The synthesis chapters are particularly insightful and useful.

ODC/Synergos (1996) *Strengthening Civil Society's Contribution to Development: The Role of Official Development Assistance*, report of a conference organized by the Overseas Development Council and the Synergos Institute, Washington DC/New York. These papers result from commissioned studies detailing policy and practical issues donors face in their quest to engage with and support civil society organizations. It contains an array of recommendations to reform donor behaviour.

REFERENCES

Abugre, C. (1999) *Partners, Collaborators or Patron-Clients: Defining Relationships in the Aid Industry – A survey of the Issues*, background paper prepared for the CIDA/Canadian Partnership Branch, Accra: ISODEC.

Bennett, J., James, R. and Rider, P. (1996) *Guide to NGO Fundraising*, Geneva/Oxford: ICVA/International NGO Training and Research Centre.

Clark, J. (1991) *Democratizing Development: The Role of Voluntary Organizations*, London: Earthscan.

DI (1999) 'An end to the fall in global aid?', *Development Information Update* No. 1, July: 1, Evercreech: Development Initiatives.

Fowler, A. (1992) 'Distant obligations: speculations on NGO funding and the global market', *Review of African Political Economy* 55: 9–29.

Fowler, A. (1997) *Striking a Balance: A Guide to Enhancing the Effectiveness of Non-Governmental Organisations in International Development*, London: Earthscan.

Fowler, A. (1998) 'Authentic partnerships in the New Policy Agenda for international aid: dead end or light ahead?', *Development and Change* 29(1): 137–59.

Fowler, A. (2000a) 'NGOs, civil society and social development: changing the rules of the game', *Geneva 2000 Occasional Paper* No. 1, Geneva: United Nations Research Institute for Social Development.

Fowler, A. (ed.) (2000b) 'Beyond partnership: getting real about relationships in the aid system', *IDS Bulletin*, University of Sussex: Institute of Development Studies Vol. 31, No. 3, August.

Fox, L. and Schearer, B. (eds) (1997) *Sustaining Civil Society: Strategies for Resource Mobilisation*, Washington DC: CIVICUS.

Group of Lisbon (1995) *Limits to Competition*, Cambridge, MA: MIT Press.

Holloway, R. (1997) *The Unit of Development is the Organisation, Not the Project: Strategies and Structures for Sustaining the Work of Southern NGOs*, Washington DC: Paul H. Nitze School of Advanced International Studies.

INTRAC (1998) *Direct Funding from a Southern Perspective – Strengthening Civil Society?*, Oxford: International NGO Training and Research Centre.

Lehmann, D. (1986) 'Dependencia: an ideological history', *Discussion Paper*, No. 219, Brighton: University of Sussex, Institute of Development Studies.

Lissner, J. (1997) *The Politics of Altruism: A Study of the Political Behaviour of Voluntary Agencies*, Geneva: Lutheran World Federation.

Malena, C. (1995) *Working with NGOs: A Practical Guide to Operational Collaboration between the World Bank and Non-governmental Organizations*, Washington DC: World Bank.

Mohammed, A. (1997) 'Notes on MDB conditionality on governance', in *International Monetary and Financial Issues for the 1990s*, Research Papers for the Group of 24, Vol. III: 39–145, New York and Geneva: United Nations.

Nelson, P. (1995) *The World Bank and Non-Governmental Organisations: The Limits of Apolitical Development*, Basingstoke: Macmillan.

NGLS (1995) *The NGLS Handbook: A Handbook for NGOs of UN Agencies, Programmes and Funds Working for Economic and Social Development*, Geneva: Non-Governmental Liaison Service.

Norton, M. (1996) *The World-Wide Fundraiser's Handbook: A Guide to Fundraising for Southern NGOs and Voluntary Organisations*, London: Directory of Social Change.

OECD (1996) *Shaping the 21st Century: The Contribution of Development Co-operation*, Paris: Organization for Economic Co-operation and Development.

Riddel, R., Bebbington, A. and Davis, D. (1995) *Developing Country NGO and Donor Governments*, Report to the Overseas Development Administration, Overseas Development Institute, London, January.

Salamon, L. and Anheier, H. (1997) *Defining the Non-Profit Sector: A Cross-National Analysis*, Manchester: Manchester University Press.

SIDA (1996) *Aid Dependency: Causes, Symptoms and Remedies*, Stockholm: Swedish International Development Agency.

Smillie, I., Douxchamps, F. and Sholes-R/Covey, J. (1996) 'Partners or contractors? Official donor agencies and direct funding mechanisms: three Northern case studies – CIDA, EU and USAID', *Occasional Papers Series* No. 11, Oxford: International NGO Training and Research Centre.

Smillie, I. and Helmich, H. (eds.) (1993) *Non-Governmental Organisations and Governments: Stakeholders for Development*, Paris: OECD.

Smillie, I. and Helmich, H. (eds) (1999) *Stakeholders: Government–NGO Partnerships for Development*, London: Earthscan.

Sogge, D. (ed.) (1996) *Compassion and Calculation: The Business of Private Aid Agencies*, London: Pluto Press.

Van Rooy, A. (ed.) (1998) *Civil Society and the Aid Industry*, London: Earthscan.

Van Rooy, A. (2000) 'Good news! You may be out of a job: reflections on the past and future 50 years for Northern NGOs', *Development in Practice* 10(3/4), Oxford: Oxfam.

Van Tuijl, P. (1999) 'NGOs and human rights: sources of justice and democracy', *Journal of International Affairs* (52)2: 493–512.

Weiss, T. (ed.) (1998) *Beyond UN Subcontracting: Task-Sharing with Regional Security Arrangements and Service Providing NGOs*, Basingstoke: Macmillan.

Wolfensohn, J. (1999) *A Proposal for a Comprehensive Development Framework*, Washington DC: World Bank, 21 January.

10.10 The role of the Northern development NGO (Christian Aid)

Leo Bashyam

INTRODUCTION

This chapter focuses on the role of Northern non-governmental organizations (NNGOs) engaged in development work in the South. It gives a brief overview of the main types of activity that have been undertaken by NNGOs. It then looks specifically at the work of one NNGO, Christian Aid, exploring its work in supporting both development in the South and in campaigns, advocacy and development education in the North.

AN OVERVIEW OF THE ROLE OF NORTHERN NGOS

The roles of the Northern NGOs fall under six main categories:

1 responding to *emergencies*, short-term relief and long-term rehabilitation, such as the victims of war and of natural disasters or man-made disasters
2 delivering *welfare services* like healthcare, education and clean water
3 *raising money* in the North, from the general public, private sector and governments to pay for their work, and to share as much as possible with their Southern counterparts
4 supporting *long-term development* projects overseas for empowerment process and poverty eradication
5 helping in building the *capacity of Southern NGOs (SNGOs)*, people's movements, churches and other networks, so that they are in a better position to plan and manage their work
6 *educating their own constituencies* in the North about the underlying causes of poverty, and drawing people into active lobbying and campaigning for change.

These six categories are not mutually exclusive. For example, in a major emergency, relief is followed by rehabilitation leading to long-term development with built-in advocacy work. Some NNGOs have a particular focus, such as the Red Cross on emergencies, WaterAid on water and sanitation, and Save the Children on promoting children's rights. Other large NGOs, such as Oxfam and Christian Aid, have a broader mandate. In general most NNGOs work through local organizations rather than directly implementing their own programmes. They provide resources and technical advice in order to assist local organizations to implement development interventions. But there are some exemptions, especially in emergencies.

NGOs in general are regarded as having a number of distinct advantages over official aid agencies and governments for the following reasons: they work closely with poor people, promote participatory approaches, advocate on behalf of poor people in the North, understand the local culture and context in the South, foster democracy through awareness-raising capacity building, and strengthening of civil society, they are cost-effective, flexible and innovative, trying new approaches and taking risks.

However, while most NNGOs may strive to work according to these principles, in reality the track record of NNGOs is mixed. The huge number of NNGOs makes it very difficult to make general conclusions about their overall performance, and of their advantages and disadvantages. A number of donors have commissioned impact studies of NGOs in recent years (e.g. SIDA, OECD, DANIDA); these studies have all found that NNGOs make very important and unique contributions to development in the South, but have also pointed to the continued need for NNGOs to improve their effectiveness.

CHRISTIAN AID

Established in the mid-1940s in response to the post-war situation in Europe, Christian Aid is the official relief and development agency of 40 church denominations in the UK and Ireland. It is the third biggest overseas development aid agency in the UK/Ireland. It works where the need is greatest, in over 60 countries, helping communities regardless of religion, through local organizations to enable people living in poverty to find their own solutions to the problems they face. Christian Aid is non-operational in its work overseas. It supports local organizations. It does not support poverty projects in the UK/Ireland but engages in challenging the root causes of poverty through education, advocacy and campaigning. In 1999/00 its income was about £55 million, of which about 70 per cent is donated from the public and the rest from the government or EU sources. It has four distinctive fundamental roles that make it different from other NNGOs in the UK/Ireland. First, it is a church-based ecumenical organization where its influence and commitment to the poor are rooted in the tapestry of biblical and gospel values; second, CA's approach to 'partnership' with Southern NGOs is a unique feature (see below); third, it is non-operational in the field as it supports and works through local NGOs who are closer to the people on the ground and who know the local situation; finally, CA supports a number of projects jointly with other NNGOs, mainly with ecumenical organizations in the North.

Essential purpose

Supported and sustained by the churches, driven by the Gospel, Christian Aid is inspired by the dream of a new earth where all people can secure a better and more just future. Christian Aid's purpose is to expose the scandal of poverty, contribute to its eradication, and be prophetic in challenging the systems, structures and processes that work against the interests of those who have been made poor or marginalized. The organization recognizes that such change will only come about as a movement is built, of people who are committed to a better world for all, bringing their faith and talents, their energy, their influence, their gifts and their actions, to achieve what should surely be possible.

Role of Christian Aid

Christian Aid has two main roles to play: development and humanitarian work in the South; education, advocacy and campaign work in the North.

Development and humanitarian work

The first of these is *poverty and poverty eradication*. Christian Aid exists not merely to help poor people but to work to eradicate poverty. This involves identifying who the poor are, understanding the way poverty is manifested, its nature and its causes, especially the gender dimensions of poverty, exposing the 'scandals of poverty', and working to eliminate it. In many ways, our humanitarian work can also be seen from the poverty perspective: by responding to a particular and often, though not always temporary, manifestation of poverty. In recent years, too, growing problems of conflict in some parts of the world – from Colombia in Latin America, the Great Lakes region of Africa, Afghanistan in central Asia, and closer to home in the Balkans – have led us to focus more on helping people affected by conflict and working to try to reduce conflict.

The question of 'how to eliminate' poverty is one that has challenged Christian Aid for many decades. Approaches have differed and continue to differ. We do not now try to engage with, 'touch' and help everyone who is poor – currently over 1.3 billion people worldwide – to believe we could would be extremely arrogant. We try to focus on where we can 'make a difference', building upon who we are, our own history, skills and experiences. We increasingly try to adopt an approach which is broader than one solely addressing immediate welfare needs – supplying food and medicines, water and sanitation. Our view of development has widened to embrace the social and political dimensions: we believe that there is a critical link between development, participation and democracy. As a result, our work has tended to look 'beyond the immediate needs of the project' and to focus additionally on areas of empowerment, on efforts to increase the voice and participation of the poor (particularly poor women and others who are discriminated against) in the development process, and to examine the status of minorities and other excluded groups. It is because poverty is manifested in different ways in different parts of the world that we do not have a 'one size fits all' blueprint for 'doing' development. We examine each situation and work out how best we can use the resources we have to help the poor people we have identified as particularly needy.

The second pillar of Christian Aid's approach to its work is the notion of *partnership*. With very rare exceptions, Christian Aid's development and emergency work is undertaken with and through its different partners, to use the jargon, Christian Aid is a non-operational agency – you will not find Christian Aid projects and programmes in poor countries, but rather the projects and programmes of the partners which Christian Aid chooses to support. It is because Christian Aid believes that eradicating poverty involves letting poor people take greater control of their lives that the thrust of our development work is built on the view that the best way to help is to assist and strengthen local groups. But partnership means even more than this: it means involving poor people, and those who work with them, in the analysis of poverty, its different manifestations and its causes, and hence in its reduction and, hopefully, elimination. Sometimes these groups are themselves poor people, living in rural or urban areas; sometimes they are intermediary or support organizations working to help poor people, sometimes they are involved in assisting development indirectly through advocacy, lobbying, research, campaigning or media work. Currently, Christian Aid works directly to assist the work of some 700 partners in over 60 countries across the world – often providing funds to support their projects and programmes, sometimes to build and strengthen their own capacities, or to link them up to other groups working in the same or similar fields.

Education, advocacy and campaign work

- *Public education*   CA believes in projecting positive images of the poor. Christian Aid has many thousands of active volunteers playing their part in becoming part of a worldwide movement that strives for justice. CA regularly facilitates exchange visits to and from the UK/Ireland and linking up communities in the UK/Ireland with the South.
- *Fundraising*   Fundraising entails working to raise money from churches, UK and Irish governments, European Union, the general public and corporate bodies to support the poor. The total income of CA is around £55m per annum, of which about £12m is raised during Christian Aid Week.
- *Advocacy and campaigning*   The Global Advocacy department researches, analyses and promotes agreed advocacy positions related to the experience and concerns of its partners, its corporate goals and campaigns. It takes a lead in influencing policy-makers at the British, Irish, European and global levels on international economic and social justice, working with others internationally and in the UK/Ireland. The best example is the Jubilee 2000 debt initiative where CA is a major player.
- *Research, documentation and publications*   Christian Aid communicates its concerns in ways that make its key issues matter, and make an impact in the wider world, so as to encourage widespread support and action from decision-makers, the media, individuals and from the youth. CA produces provocative, timely, tactical and empowering public education campaigns, media stories and advertising campaigns.
- *Theological reflection*   Christian Aid does this by giving theological reflection to its development work through its publications, stories, talks and work overseas.
- *Networking*   co-operation and strengthening the NGO sector in the UK/Ireland is another role CA plays in the North. Examples include BOND (British Overseas NGOs for Development) and DEC (Disaster Emergency Committee). Christian Aid contributes to the wider debate on the role of civil society, voluntary organizations, development agencies and development issues.
- *Global advocacy*   CA responds to emergencies and sociopolitical concerns with involvement in media initiatives during the year and develops strategic alliances, partnerships and contacts to promote CA as a global advocacy agency working especially with ecumenical partners. Its concerns are poverty eradication, debt relief, trade, gender, human rights and civil society participation. It will have particular focus on the World Trade Organization, World Bank, International Monetary Fund, the UN, European Union, government departments and the private sector.
- *Ecumenical movement*   As a church agency it has close connections with ecumenical development agencies in Europe and with sister churches and other regional, national and international ecumenical councils. Today it is specially linked with the World Council of Churches and ACT (Action by Churches Together) for emergency relief based in Geneva.

- *Networking and coordination* CA is part of world ecumenical bodies (WCC, APRODEV, ACT) and part of other networks such as Jubilee 2000), CA helps co-ordinate on issues such as food security or in joint advocacy with governments, such as supporting the Global March Against Child Labour. Christian Aid brings *ethics and values* into the discussions on development at various levels, through engaging with the private sector and multilateral agencies such as the UN and World Bank.

THE FUTURE

What of the future? What will be the future of our relationship with our partners, with our ecumenical partners, and with the development and humanitarian work of our sponsoring churches?

Our work will continue to be informed and profoundly influenced by areas such as the focus on poverty, the importance of partnerships, and the Christian roots of the organization. In the near term, we are planning for a steady expansion of our international work, especially our development work, made possible by an anticipated increase in our core income; our humanitarian work, as now, will continue to be funded largely by special income sources, from the churches, from special appeals to the British public and by tapping funds made available by government and governmental agencies.

GUIDE TO FURTHER READING

Ball, C. and Dunn, L. (1995) *Non-governmental Organisations: Guidelines for Good Policy and Practice*, Commonwealth Foundation.

Edwards, M. and Hulme, D. (1997) *NGOs, States and Donors: Too close for comfort?* and *NGO Performance and Accountability: Beyond the Magic Bullet*, London: Earthscan.

Flowler, A. (1997) *Striking a Balance: A Guide to Enhancing the Effectiveness of NGOS in International Development*, London: Earthscan.

Hancock, G. (1992) *Lords of Poverty: The Power, Prestige and Corruption of the International Aid Business*, New York: Atlantic Monthly Press.

INTRAC (1998) *Strengthening Civil Society: Direct Funding from a Southern Perspective*, Oxford: INTRAC.

Lewis, D. (1999) *International Perspectives on Voluntary action*, London: Earthscan.

Oakley, P. (1999) *Overview Report: The Danish NGO Impact Study*, a review of Danish NGO activities in Developing countries, Oxford: INTRAC. Full text at www.um.dk/udenrigspolitik/udviklingspolitik/ngosamarbejde/impact/syntese_eng/.

Riddell, R. (1992) 'Judging success: evaluating NGO approaches to alleviating poverty in developing countries', ODI working paper 37, London: ODI.

Riddell, R.C., Kruse, S-E., Kyollen, T., Ojanpera, S. and Vielajus, J-L. (1997) *Searching for Impact and Methods*, NGO evaluation synthesis study for OECD/DAC, Department for International Development Co-operation, Ministry of Foreign Affairs, Helsinki. www.valt.helsinnki.fi/ids/ngo.

Tvedt, T. (1998) *Angels of Mercy or Development Diplomats?: NGOS and Foreign Aid*, Africa World Press Inc.

Uphoff, N. (1996) 'Why NGOs are not a third sector: some thoughts on accountability, sustainability and evaluations', in Edwards and Hulme (1997).

CHRISTIAN AID MATERIALS

Christian Aid policy documents for 2000–2004, 'Towards a New Earth', Corporate Plan.

Christain Aid 2000 resources catalogue, books, videos, tapes, games, church material, teaching packs, posters.

Christian Aid website: www.christian-aid.org.uk.

Christian Aid, 35 Lower Marsh, Waterloo SE1 7RT, Tel: +44(0)20 620 4444.

Taylor, Michael H. (1997) 'Past their sell-by date? The role of NGOs in the future of development', Bradford annual development lecture, London: Christian Aid.

Riddell, R.C. (2000) 'The state and NGOs: overview of present and future roles', presented in Copenhagen.

10.11 Non-governmental organizations: questions of performance and accountability

David Lewis

INTRODUCTION

Non-governmental organizations (NGOs) can be defined as 'self-governing, private, not-for-profit organizations that are geared to improving the quality of life for disadvantaged people' (Vakil, 1997: 2060). There has been a rapid growth in the numbers and profile of NGOs in the past decade, both in the industrialized 'North', where NGOs are concerned with poverty and social justice at home and abroad, and in the aid-recipient countries of 'the South', where NGOs old and new have been identified as potential 'partners' by governments and international aid agencies (Salamon, 1994; Smillie, 1995). The term NGO includes many different types of organization, from small local groups operating on a largely voluntary and informal basis, such as Educare Trust in Nigeria, to large private development agencies with multi-million-dollar budgets and thousands of paid, professional staff, such as the Bangladesh Rural Advancement Committee (BRAC).

There are three main interrelated reasons for the rise of development NGOs. First was the disillusionment in the 1980s of international development donors with the ability of governments to tackle successfully problems of poverty. NGOs were seen as more administratively flexible, closer to the poor, innovative in problem-solving and more cost-effective than corresponding state partners (Cernea, 1988). Second was the fact that working with NGOs had important ideological attractions to donors and governments at a time when privatization policies were dominant – in the form of efforts to 'roll back' the state by governments in the North, and in the design and imposition of 'structural adjustment' in the South by the World Bank and the IMF. Third has been the new interest in 'civil society' – an institutional space between state, market and household in which citizens can organize and represent their interests. NGOs have come to be seen as one form of 'civil society organization' – in addition to trade unions, religious groups, the media and others – which has the capacity to strengthen democratic processes, widen citizen-participation civic life and contribute to the formation of wider 'social capital' (Putnam, 1993).

During the past decade or so, NGOs have become established organizational actors within development policy and practice, but more critical questions are now increasingly being asked of their performance and accountability (Edwards and Hulme, 1995; Lewis and Wallace, 2000).

THE COMPLEXITY OF NGO ACCOUNTABILITY

Drawing upon the work of the US sociologist A. Etzioni, three broad families of organizations have been identified: government agencies, for-profit businesses and a diverse group of 'third sector' organizations which have been variously termed non-profit, voluntary or non-governmental (Najam, 1996). In theory, private companies are accountable for their actions to shareholders and democratic governments are accountable through the electoral process to their public, but there are no such basic accountability mechanisms which exist for NGOs. Critics have observed that while many NGOs may claim accountability to the poor, unless they are membership 'organizations *of* the poor' operating at the grassroots, they may find themselves in practice more accountable to donors or to the government with which they may contract to provide services.

The problem of too much accountability 'upwards' to funders and too little 'downwards' to people has led Smillie (1995) to characterize the problem of accountability as the 'Achilles heel' of the NGO movement. It has also contributed to the use of rather narrow definitions of NGO accountability in terms of the proper use of financial resources rather than a broader idea of accountability as the carrying out of effective, appropriate work which stays true to the needs of clients and the values of the organization itself. A useful distinction can be drawn between *functional* accountability, concerned with accounting for resources and their immediate impacts, and *strategic* accountability, which refers to the wider implications of an NGO's actions in terms of impacts on other organizations and on the wider environment in which the NGO operates (Edwards and Hulme, 1995).

There are two main strands in the literature in the analysis of NGO accountability. The first approach, following from M. Weber's analysis of bureaucratic structures, sees accountability primarily in terms of rule-bound responses by organizations and individuals who must report to recognized authorities such as government agencies or donor organizations in order to ensure that the resources they receive are used properly and that the work they undertake is done effectively. Accountability may therefore be conceptualized in institutional terms as a 'principal–agent' relationship in which a government agency or donor contracts an NGO in order to provide a specified service (Brett, 1993). This requires checks and balances to be put in place – such as mechanisms for monitoring and evaluation – in order to ensure that the NGO provides in a trustworthy manner and that a service is provided properly in terms of cost-effectiveness, quality and targeting.

The second strand of thinking is more open-ended and draws upon the idea that organizations are socially constructed entities. In this view, accountability can be understood as the maintenance of organizational integrity through dialogues among and between different stake-holders – such as staff, clients, governors or funders – which seek to enhance the effectiveness of the NGO. Rather than accountability as an issue which becomes important only when things go wrong, accountability can be seen instead as a process which is part of the daily organizational life of an NGO (Fry, 1995). Such a view stresses the ethical dimension of organizational accountability: it is not simply a set of controls to be imposed upon an organization from the outside, but a set of 'felt responsibilities' derived from an organization's own values, mission and culture.

Most writers on NGO accountability now emphasize its complex, multi-directional character. Najam (1996) shows how an NGO is simultaneously accountable to its *patrons* such as donors (whose concerns are usually centred upon whether funds are used for designated purposes), to *clients* such as its users in the community (who are concerned with ensuring that the NGO acts in their interests, but have no clear means of ensuring this) or the government (which may contract an NGO to carry out a particular task) and finally to *itself* (in the sense that each NGO has a vision which it seeks to actualize, and staff for whom it is responsible). Najam argues that NGO accountability is often skewed heavily towards patrons.

A symptom of this unbalanced accountability is goal displacement, when for example an NGO drifts away from its original emphasis on education work towards credit delivery, due to the availability of donor funds for this purpose rather than any special competence. For example, one small local NGO known to the author in Nepal, which was undertaking environmental conservation work based mainly on local resources, changed direction dramatically when large sums of money became available from a foreign donor for national HIV/AIDS awareness-raising work. Another symptom is unplanned growth, where a 'successful' small-scale NGO may quickly evolve into a large, hierarchical organization which then faces many of the bureaucratic problems associated with traditional government agencies – such as a slowness to respond to problems, loss of contact with a certain part of the community, or the disappearance of a flexibility which made it possible to learn from experience.

An important accountability problem concerns the unequal relationships between donors, Northern NGOs and Southern NGOs. Many Northern NGOs have moved away from the direct implementation of projects in developing countries towards a 'partnership approach' with Southern NGOs, part of which includes efforts to undertake 'capacity building' work with local organizational partners in order to build greater levels of effectiveness and self-reliance, but the precise nature and terms of such partnerships often remain unclear (Lewis, 1998). Concerns have also been raised as to whether some NGOs may be co-opted by states and donors into fulfilling the larger geo-political objectives of 'containing disorder' in parts of the post-Cold War world rather than the response to humanitarian needs (Fowler, 1994).

NGO PERFORMANCE – JUDGING 'SUCCESS'

The issue of NGO performance is closely linked to that of accountability. It has become a controversial area because, after the initial 'discovery' of NGOs as development actors in the 1980s, hard evidence of effective NGO performance has proved elusive. Earlier assumptions that were made about the comparative advantages of NGOs over other kinds of organization in poverty reduction work have increasingly been challenged by critics. Concerns have arisen because despite the existence of some remarkable NGOs around the world, many organizations are in practice hindered by confused vision, weak administrative systems and domineering leadership (Dichter, 1989). In some contexts, the term 'NGO' has become synonymous with such opportunistic activities as building political patronage, or accumulating resources for leaders or staff. Finally, while there is evidence that many NGOs can achieve impact locally on a small scale, some have argued that there is an urgent need to increase impact through 'scaling up' NGO work (Edwards and Hulme, 1992).

A recent evaluation of Danish NGOs in Bangladesh, Nicaragua and Tanzania presented findings that echo many of those which have emerged from similar studies undertaken over the past decade (Oakley, 1999). Results showed that NGOs have particular strengths in maintaining a poverty focus in their work, that they can build reasonably effective partnerships with local community organizations and that they can often provide basic health and education services effectively. But the findings also showed that NGOs are generally weak at contextual analysis of the societies in which they work, that their approaches to monitoring and evaluation are rarely adequate, that certain key technical skills are lacking in their human resource base, that many are more concerned with micro- than macro- context work, and that the practice of participation and innovation in project implementation does not always live up to the stated claims. In a comparison of four local NGOs in South Asia, Edwards (1999) suggests that the most effective NGO was characterized by independent thinking, clear goals, personal qualities of commitment among staff and volunteers, and a close working relationship built up with clients over time.

Efforts to evaluate systematically the development impact of NGOs have generally therefore produced mixed results. Some NGOs have received large amounts of resources but have been unable to demonstrate convincingly that they have 'made a difference', while others have shown that relatively small levels of funding can produce innovative, challenging solutions to problems of development. As a result, there is little general agreement on whether or not NGOs are 'effective' at what they do.

CONCLUSION

The record of NGOs is therefore a mixed one. While some positive changes in development practice can be associated with the rise of development NGOs – such as more participatory planning techniques and the integration of gender concerns into mainstream development policy (ODI, 1995) – concerns about NGO accountability and performance remain. An ability to confront these issues may be the key to the survival of the NGO movement.

The role of non-state actors of one form or another seems destined to grow as the power of the state is increasingly called into question and the pace of global economic activity intensifies (Giddens, 1998). NGOs will need to link both local and global agendas if they are to be effective. Global changes may bring more complex accountability pressures, and there may be a 'trend towards more diverse and seemingly unconnected voices making requests or demands of the nonprofit organisation to be accountable for different things' (Fry, 1995: 191).

GUIDE TO FURTHER READING

Najam, A. (1996) 'Understanding the third sector: revisiting the Prince, the Merchant and the Citizen', *Nonprofit Management and Leadership* 7(2): 203–19, is an excellent critical introduction. A good practical overview is Fowler, A. (1997) *Striking a Balance: A Guide to Enhancing the Effectiveness of NGOs in International Development*, London: Earthscan. For a general introduction, see Lewis, D. (2001) *The Management of Non-governmental Development Organisations: An Introduction*, London: Routledge.

REFERENCES

Brett, E.A. (1993) 'Voluntary agencies as development organisations: theorising the problem of efficiency and accountability', *Development and Change* 24: 269–303.

Cernea, M. (1988) *Non-Governmental Organisations and Local Development*, Washington DC: World Bank.

Dichter, T.W. (1989) 'Development management: plain or fancy? Sorting out some muddles', *Public Administration and Development* 9: 381–93.

Edwards, M. (1999) 'NGO performance – what breeds success?', *World Development* 27(2): 361–74.

Edwards, M. and Hulme, D. (eds) (1992) *Making a Difference: NGOs and Development in a Changing World*, London: Earthscan Publications.

Edwards, M. and Hulme, D. (eds) (1995) *Beyond the Magic Bullet: NGO Performance and Accountability in the Post-Cold War World*, London: Macmillan.

Fowler, A. (1994) 'Capacity building and NGOs: a case of strengthening ladles for the global soup kitchen?' *Institutional Development* 1(1): 18–24.

Fry, R. (1995) 'Accountability in organizational life: problem or opportunity', *Nonprofit Management and Leadership* 6(2): 181–95.

Giddens, A. (1998) *The Third Way: The Renewal of Social Democracy*, Cambridge: Polity Press.

Lewis, D. (1998) 'Development NGOs and the challenge of partnership: changing relations between North and South', *Social Policy and Administration* 32(5): 501–12.

Lewis, D. and Wallace, T. (eds) (2000) *New Roles and Relevance: Development NGOs and the Challenge of Change*, West Hartford: Kumarian Press.

Najam, A. (1996) 'NGO accountability: a conceptual framework', *Development Policy Review* 14: 339–53.

Oakley, P. (1999) *The Danish NGO Impact Study: A Review of Danish NGO Activities in Developing Countries*, Oxford: International NGO Training and Research Centre (INTRAC).

ODI (1995) 'NGOs and official donors', *Briefing Paper* 4, London: Overseas Development Institute.

Putnam, R.D. (1993) *Making Democracy Work: Civic Traditions in Modern Italy*, Princeton: Princeton University Press.

Salamon, L. (1994) *Partners in Public Service: Government–Nonprofit Relations in the Modern Welfare State*, Baltimore: Johns Hopkins University Press.

Smillie, I. (1995) *The Alms Bazaar: Altruism Under Fire Non-Profit Organisations and International Development*, London: Intermediate Technology Publications.

Vakil, A. (1997) 'Confronting the classification problem: towards a taxonomy of NGOs', *World Development* 25(12): 2057–71.

10.12 Monitoring and evaluating NGO achievements

Rick Davies

CHANGING PERSPECTIVES

Over the last decade there has been a dramatic growth in the number of NGOs involved in development aid, in both developed and developing countries. Associated with this growth has been a growing concern about identifying the achievements of NGOs, evident in the burgeoning literature on the monitoring and evaluation of NGO activities.

There has been a steady stream of experimentation with specific methods, especially those focusing on participatory approaches to monitoring and evaluation (M&E) and impact assessment (e.g. IIRR, 1997). On a smaller scale, a number of NGOs have produced their own guides on monitoring and evaluation (Broughton and Hampshire, 1997). Recent books on NGO management are giving specific attention to assessing performance (Fowler, 1997) and the management of information. As well as doing their own evaluations, some NGOs are now doing meta-evaluations (of methods) and syntheses (of results) of their evaluations to date. Similar but larger-scale studies have been commissioned by bilateral funding agencies (Riddell *et al.*, 1997; Oakley, 1999). Both sets of studies have attempted to develop a wider perspective on NGO effectiveness, looking beyond individual projects, across sectors and country programmes. Overall, NGOs have become much more aware of the need for evaluation, compared to the 1980s when there was some outright hostility.

WHAT DO THEY KNOW?

The DAC (Riddell *et al.*, 1997) study *Searching for Impact and Methods: NGO Evaluation Synthesis Study* is the most comprehensive overview of NGO impact, and impact evaluation methods to date. This study looked at evidence from 60 separate reports of 240 projects undertaken in 26 developing countries. On the first page the authors report that:

> A first, overarching, conclusion – confirmed by data and interviews in *all* the different case study countries – is that in spite of growing interest in evaluation, there is still a lack of reliable evidence on the impact of NGO development projects and programmes.

They go on to say:

> a repeated and consistent conclusion drawn across countries and in relation to all clusters of studies is that the data are exceptionally poor. There is a paucity of data and information from which to draw firm conclusions about the impact of projects, about efficiency and effectiveness, about sustainability, the gender and environmental impact of projects and their contribution to strengthening democratic forces, institutions and organizations and building civil society.
>
> (Riddell *et al.*, 1997: 99)

Similar conclusions were reached by the recent Danida-funded study of 45 Danish NGO projects in four countries (Oakley, 1999: 94).

These two multi-country studies raise serious doubts as to whether many NGOs *know* what they are doing, in the sense of their overall impact on people's lives. NGOs may or may not be having a positive impact, but their ability to scale up that impact must be limited by their inability to provide evidence of those achievements (and their limitations) and communicate this information to others with more resources and/or influence.

WHAT IS THE PROBLEM?

Given the many millions of pounds that have been spent by NGOs over the last decade why has it been so difficult to come to persuasive conclusions about the results of their work? Several different reasons are examined below.

Ambitious expectations

In the DAC review, Riddell *et al.* (1997: 66) noted that almost all

> the Terms of Reference [for evaluations] set the scene for anticipating exceedingly high expectations of what can be achieved, particularly what can be said about development impact. In quite sharp contrast, the tone of the conclusions is usually cautious and tentative, arguing that it is difficult to come to firm and decisive conclusions.

Both the DAC and Danish NGO studies used *nine* different performance criteria to compare NGO projects. The proposed SPHERE (2000) Training Module on Monitoring and Accountability lists 10 different criteria. Most of these are in addition to what are often a quite ambitious set of objectives defined within a project's Logical Framework.[1] However, unlike the contents of these Logical Frameworks there must be some doubt as to whether many NGOs knowingly sign up to all of these additional ambitious expectations at the time when they seek funding for the project.

Complexity caused by scale

Expectations of project performance are raised even further by the hierarchical structure of large NGOs, and their position in a larger hierarchy of associated partner organizations (including both implementing partners and back-donors). Large international NGOs can have country, regional and international strategies. Each of these strategies has its own set of objectives. Donors, such as DFID, will in turn have their own international objectives and targets. This plethora of objectives is only manageable if objectives are clearly nested, such that local objectives are detailed versions of more macro-level objectives. In these circumstances judgements about the smallest units can be used as raw material for judgements of larger units that they belong to (Fowler, 1997: 169). In practice, doing so is complicated by the heterarchical nature of aid supply chains. Individual NGOs often belong, through their donors, to more than one hierarchy of organizations, each with differing strategic objectives and priorities. In the UK, the largest NGOs are still struggling with the complex issues associated with aggregating their experience on a large scale.

Diversity of activities

The majority of the largest NGOs tend to be generalists, being involved in a wide range of development activities, across a number of sectors (Oakley, 1999). This must make the task of comparing and aggregating performance information more difficult. The problems of diversity are accentuated by growth in organizational scale. One response to diversity of practice within many NGOs has been to initiate more thematic studies, which focus on one type of activity (e.g. micro-finance, health, water, etc.), but across a number of countries. Another response has been to develop assessment methodologies tailored to specific types of intervention (e.g. MEASURE and SPHERE). Both responses manage diversity through specialization. A less common response has been to reduce the scale of the task, but to maintain a more holistic focus, by undertaking within-country cross-activity studies. Each option carries with it an implied judgement about the type of knowledge that matters (sectoral versus country based), and whose judgement matters.

Vague objectives

It is widely recognized that the achievements of many development objectives, such as empowerment, institutional strengthening and the development of civil society, are difficult to define in advance. Evidence of their achievement is not easy to agree on, and there is no one single path to their realization. The value of what is achieved often depends on local context and history. Establishing pre-defined near-universal indicators for such changes is inherently difficult. This is a problem if *measurability* is over-emphasized, as it seems to be in the case of many evaluations (Thin, 1999: 26).

The tools being used

Fowler has argued that the 'limitations of the instruments that NGOs use to monitor, evaluate and review' (1997: 160) are one reason why NGOs have not been able to substantiate their achievements. Logical Frameworks have been useful in encouraging the identification of indicators at the planning stage, but much less so in ensuring their actual use during project monitoring or evaluation. In practice, the widespread focus on *identification* of indicators reflects a bias towards planning, rather than monitoring and evaluating, that is built into most NGOs, and other agencies.

Outside of the Logical Framework many NGOs have been actively searching for appropriate methods, especially in ways of enabling people's participation in the monitoring and evaluation of projects (IIRR, 1997). The problem here has been how to aggregate the complex and large volume of information and analysis generated by these methods.

Methodological developments have been less noticeable with analysis of performance above field and project level. At the country programme level and higher, Logical Frameworks have been pre-empted by strategic planning frameworks, suggesting that Logical Frameworks are not scalable solutions to planning and monitoring. With some applications of strategic planning NGOs have found they need to assess their country programmes according to multiple strategic objectives, rather than one goal-level statement (Oxfam, ActionAid). While this plurality allows some variation in strategic emphasis between different countries it does complicate the task of inter-country comparisons and coming to high-level generalizations about achievements.

The absence of baseline information and adequate monitoring systems

The absence of adequate baseline information is an almost universal complaint found in both NGO and donor meta-evaluations/synthesis studies (Riddell *et al.*, 1997; Oakley *et al.*, 1998) Another common phenomenon is base-line survey data being lost or forgotten, and unavailable to evaluation teams. Although most organizations have monitoring systems of some sort, many writers (Fowler, 1997: 169; Riddell *et al.*, 1997; Roche, 1999) have noted the pervasive problem of organizations monitoring expenditure, activities and outputs, but not effects and impacts. All of these phenomena are really symptoms rather than explanations of why NGOs do not seem to know what impact their work is having. If some types of information are not being produced then we need to ask why is there no demand for that information.

Alternative explanations

Organizational structure and relationships may be a more significant factor than the absence of appropriate M&E concepts or methods. Inside most organizations proximate rationality rules. Activities are measured against activity plans, expenditure against budget. These are immediate tasks where delays are visible and have consequences for those responsible. Staff have to cope with the short term before they can worry about the long term. On the other hand there are external demands for information about performance, arising primarily from donors and governments. Financial reporting is required most often, then implementation relative to plans, then, much less frequently, achievement in terms of changes in people's lives (purpose and goal-level type statements). Not being dependent on their clients for their financial survival, NGOs' incentives to attend to clients' judgements about effects and impact are dependent on organizational culture and values.

Variations do exist between NGOs in terms of their dependence on bilateral and multilateral donors versus individual members of the public. The nature of this dependence is likely to affect the information demands being made on those NGOs, and their motivation and capacity to assess their achievements. Individual members of the public donate to charities on the basis of trust, and that relationship is managed by marketing departments, not M&E units. There is some anecdotal evidence to suggest that the NGOs with the most financial independence from official donors have invested the least in monitoring and evaluation (e.g. World Vision versus CARE International). Similar contrasts can be found amongst UK agencies.

WHERE TO NEXT?

Many of the problems discussed above relate to the scale and structural features of individual organizations, and their place in the wider ecology of aid organizations. The structure of information flows between those organizations is now open to the possibility of radical change, because of the increasing accessibility of the internet.

Most of the large bilateral aid agencies are now making their evaluation reports publicly accessible on a global scale, via the web (See www.mande.co.uk/sources.htm). A small number of NGOs have done the same. The next step forward in transparency, and more immediate public accountability, would be for those organizations to place their annual progress reports in the public domain as well, via the web. Another step forward, already take by organizations such as Christian Aid, is to provide hypertext links to their own Southern partner NGO websites, allowing outsiders more direct access to documented accounts of aid-funded activities written by those closer to the action.

In effect the internet is opening up the possibility of direct progress reporting to the public (Northern and Southern) being devolved to organizations much further down the aid supply chain. Associated with this is the possibility of those organizations gaining more direct and global access to public funds. This dis-intermediation process, already seen in the private sector, may require Northern NGOs to rethink how they add value in the aid supply chain. One option will be for Northern NGOs to focus on building partners' capacity to report this way, and on monitoring public interaction and reaction to the information provided. In future, development education and public accountability concerns could be addressed at the same time, while also providing greater opportunities for lateral learning between NGOs. Value could be unlocked from today's NGO 'conglomerates'.

NOTE

1. A summary representation of a project in table form, describing project activities, outputs, purpose and goal in four rows, and a narrative summary, measurable indicators, means of verification and assumptions for each row, listed in four columns.

GUIDE TO FURTHER READING

Monitoring and Evaluation NEWS at www.mande.co.uk/news.htm. Funded by six NGOs: a news service focusing on developments in monitoring and evaluation methods relevant to development projects with social development objectives.

Riddell, R.C., Kruse, S-E., Kyollen, T., Ojanpera, S. and Vielajus, J-L. (1997) *Searching for Impact and Methods: NGO Evaluation Synthesis Study. A Report produced for the OECD/DAC Expert Group on Evaluation*, Helsinki: Department for International Development Cooperation, Ministry of Foreign Affairs. This is the most definitive study of NGO impact to date, primarily because of the breadth of its coverage and detailed analysis.

Roche, C. (1999) *Impact Assessment for Development Agencies: Learning to Value Change*, Oxford: Oxfam. Based on original research undertaken by Oxfam GB, this book draws on in-depth case studies undertaken in a range of settings, from large-scale integrated development programmes to small-scale community development initiatives.

Thin, N. (1999) *Methods and Approaches for Evaluation of Development Assistance for Poverty Reduction: A Literature Review*, Edinburgh: University of Edinburgh. This very comprehensive review was prepared as a background paper for the OECD/DAC Working Party on Aid Evaluation Workshop on Evaluation of Poverty Reduction, Edinburgh 12–14 October.

Additional extensive references can be found at http://www.mande.co.uk/docs/arnold.htm

REFERENCES

Broughton, B. and Hampshire, J. (1997) *Bridging the Gap: A Guide to Monitoring and Evaluating Development Projects*, Canberra: Australian Council for Overseas Aid.

Carlsson, J., Kohlin, G. and Ekbom, A. (1994) *The Political Economy of Evaluation: International Aid Agencies and the Effectiveness of Aid*, London: St Martin's Press.

Davies, R.J. (1998) 'An evolutionary approach to facilitating organizational learning: an experiment by the Christian Commission For Development in Bangladesh', *Impact Assessment and Project Appraisal* 1(1): 243–50.

de Waal, A. (1998) *Famine Crimes: Politics and the Disaster Relief Industry in Africa*, Bloomington, IN: Indiana University Press.

Fowler, A. (1997) *Striking a Balance: A Guide to Enhancing the Effectiveness of Non-Governmental Organisations in International Development*, London: Earthscan.

IIRR (1997) *Participatory Monitoring and Evaluation: Experiences and Lessons.* Workshop Proceedings 24–29 November, Cavite: International Institute of Rural Reconstruction.

Oakley, P. (1999) *Overview Report. The Danish NGO Impact Study. A Review of Danish NGO Activities in Developing Countries*, Oxford: INTRAC.

Additional extensive references can be found at http://www.mande.co.uk/docs/arnold.htm

10.13 The relevance of strategic planning for UK aid agencies

Elsa L. Dawson

INTRODUCTION

Since 1980, many British aid agencies have undertaken strategic planning to professionalize their activities at both programme and global levels. Instead of focusing on individual isolated projects, different forms of long-term planning are being used to develop a broader framework for decisions about resource allocation to improve the impact of their work.

This chapter addresses the questions of whether impact was actually improved, and what significant improvements are produced in the lives of intended beneficiaries. Oxfam GB's experience is reviewed, and references are made to that of Save the Children (SCF-UK), ActionAid, CAFOD and Children's Aid Direct (CAD).

Definition of strategic planning

Johnson and Scholes (1999: 51), writing mainly for the commercial sector, describe strategic planning as 'a sequence of analytical and evaluative procedures to formulate an intended strategy and the means of implementing it'. They define 'strategy' as 'the direction and scope of an organization over the long term which achieves advantage for the organization through its configuration of resources within a changing environment, to meet the needs of markets and to fulfil stakeholder expectations'.

WHY AID AGENCIES ADOPTED STRATEGIC PLANNING

UK aid agencies grew fast in the 1980s and 1990s, and needed to gain greater organizational coherence to become more effective and improve impact. Growth led to rapid staff increases, less clarity regarding overall direction, and tensions emerged between staff involved in different functions such as fundraising, development and advocacy (Wallace *et al.*, 1997: 36).

Strategic planning was introduced to move away from isolated projects decided upon by individual staff concerns. Attempts were made to develop a strategic sense to country programmes, to ensure initiatives funded would contribute to a sustainable development and optimum use of resources.

Some organizations had outgrown their founder's original vision and needed new ideas to guide them, especially given uncertainties about how to promote development (Wallace *et al.*, 1997: 36). Despite years of trying, poverty had not been eradicated, while the world was going through rapid changes such as globalization and the emergence of complex conflict situations. The introduction of strategic planning was also due to greater emphasis by universities, management advisers and agency trustees on sound management practices. Organizations hoped to improve their performance, stimulate forward thinking, clarify future directions and solve major organizational problems (Barry, 1994: 9, 13). They hoped that participative strategic planning processes would improve team building and staff clarity on how their work helped the organization achieve its purpose.

In 1990 Korten related the move to strategic management to a conceptualization of poverty as resulting from institutional and policy constraints. He contrasts this with the view that poverty results from shortages or local inertia, which lies behind the isolated project approach. Oxfam GB and SCF-UK now express objectives as changes in policy and practice which they wish to bring about, for example international finance institutions pledge to adopt the principles of ethical investment.

MODEL USED

Agencies developed strategic planning processes based on the figure below:

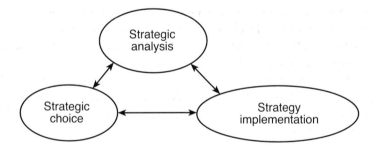

Private-sector model of strategic management
Source: Johnson and Scholes, 1999: 18

Many agencies used John Bryson's adaptation of private sector methods for non-profit organizations (1988) consisting of the stages shown in Table 1.

Table 1

Model	Stages
Strategic analysis	• Analysis of needs to be addressed, mandate, internal capacity and comparative advantage
Strategic choice	• Identification of strategic issues (Oxfam GB used this stage to help staff focus on and prioritize key issues) • Design of strategic objectives
Strategy implementation	• Action/business planning, management of strategic change

Some staff also developed strategic visions of the future organization and the external world they hoped to build. This process, given scant attention by Johnson and Scholes (1999), is lent greater importance by Bryson (1988: 61), who cites Martin Luther King's famous 'I have a dream' speech as an example of an inspiring vision based in heartfelt conviction. Within these organisations, strategic planning is carried out at different levels, i.e. centrally for the organisations as a whole, regionally for different areas of the world, e.g. East Asia, and at country level.

HAVE STRATEGIC PLANNING PROCESSES HELPED ACHIEVE GREATER IMPACT?

Oxfam GB defines impact as 'where significant changes have been brought about in the lives of poor women and men', and not just the immediate effects of interventions. To rigorously evaluate impact of this kind requires detailed research, and it is generally too early to say whether the introduction of strategic planning has actually improved impact. However, the following would enhance impact:

a) focus, prioritization and organizational coherence to ensure that resources are targeted effectively;
b) a clear concept of organizational comparative advantage to exploit to the full distinctive competencies, i.e. knowledge and skills
c) activities firmly embedded in sound contextual analysis, ensuring these respond to real needs and exploit opportunities
d) capable staff teams committed to their workplans
e) effective partner networks to engage with implementing plans
f) strong micro–macro linkages in addressing the structural causes of poverty.

To what extent has strategic planning helped enhance these factors?

a) Focus, prioritization and organizational coherence

Agencies generally consider strategic planning has helped achieve greater focus, but not necessarily prioritize their work. For example, strategic planning helped CAFOD become more rational and coherent, thereby increasing capacity and skills. It improved internal discussions about priorities, opportunities and choices, and focused work more effectively. An Oxfam GB field manager noted that a useful process of identifying unifying programme themes emerged from an extensive analysis of problems facing poor people. The resulting programmes enhanced the impact of their programme by providing a holistic framework for working synergistically through local partner organizations, with improved linkages between Oxfam GB's lobbying activities and its research and documentation. This process enabled the design of programmes that were more presentable to large donor agencies, hence scaling up Oxfam GB's investment. However, the number of issues being addressed by the programmes was still felt to be too great in relation to organizational capacity.

Oxfam GB's organizational-level strategic planning process led to the definition of eight strategic objectives to work towards with others, with which all activities had to be aligned (see box). Regional-level strategic planning was adapted into 'business planning' to include the human resources, funding and other management and organizational development elements required for implementing the corporate plan. Although this process provided greater organizational clarity around purpose, it also opened up new areas previously not central to the organization's activities, such as education and health. The workload for programme staff remains high, but some work no longer corresponding to these objectives has been phased out.

For each strategic change objective (SCO), Oxfam GB is developing a number of 'policy and practice' change objectives on which efforts will be targeted, such as:

- better paced and sequenced trade liberalization, with protection for vulnerable sectors and assistance for losers
- creditors provide increased debt relief and ensure the integration of debt relief savings into national poverty reduction strategies for improving access, quality and equity in basic health and education.

These are then being further prioritized by the identification of priority issues, such as war economies and the arms trade for Objective 3 (see box), to form the main elements for Oxfam GB's global programme.

Oxfam GB's strategic change objectives (SCOs)

(The word 'change' indicates the actual change Oxfam GB hoped to produce.)

SCO 1 Right to secure livelihoods
Each SCO has more detailed objectives, e.g. for SCO 1:
        SCO 1.1 People living in poverty will achieve food and income security
        SCO 1.2 People living in poverty will have access to secure paid employment, labour
                rights and improved working conditions
SCO 2 Right to health and education
SCO 3 Right to life and security
SCO 4 Right to a say
SCO 5 Right to gender equity

---

b)   A clear idea of an organization's comparative advantage

Strategic planning can be useful if it helps reorient agencies to doing what they are good at (Fowler, 1997: 47). Both SCF-UK and CAD developed more child-focused plans. Oxfam GB's 1998 Fundamental Strategic Review identified more clearly the organization's strength as an advocacy organization with a local knowledge base acquired through grassroots work. Large investments were then made in developing advocacy potential, e.g. increases in lobbying staff. This potentially increases its impact in terms of beneficiary numbers reached.

c)   Activities clearly embedded in sound contextual analysis

Some excellent country analyses were produced, and agencies were able to identify new opportunities and threats leading to more effective action. However, it was difficult to know when sufficient time had been spent on contextual analysis. The time required for country analysis left staff feeling they lacked time to operationalize plans. Working in volatile situations and within ever-changing organizations made it hard for planning to keep pace, especially in emergency contexts.

Regional analyses showed up commonalties between different developing countries useful for organizational planning. However, they also led to country-level understanding being watered down to 'common denominator' levels. For advocacy purposes, one of the most influential sets of institutions remains the state, making national-level analysis key.

Both country and regional analysis are important, but agencies have to balance the need for formal analysis with that for programme implementation. Fowler comments that agencies have to achieve the right balance between organizational coherence and maximum impact with sufficient flexibility for local interpretation and application (1997: 48).

Nevertheless, the systematic production of country and regional strategic plans is a significant advance on previous practice, and makes greater impact more likely.

d) Capable teams of staff, committed to their workplans

Strategic planning processes contributed significantly to team building. Oxfam GB's programme staff learnt much about their context, and gained analytical capacity and confidence in their own ideas. For years after their production, some staff still quoted their strategic plans. However, in other cases busy staff lacked sufficient time to refer back to lengthy documents.

e) Capable and effective partner networks

Oxfam GB found its partners became more able to scale up their competencies, supported by its strategic planning process, particularly in lobbying. They worked more effectively together, as a result of participating in Oxfam's strategic planning process. Oxfam GB also gained a clearer idea through its process of objectives as the basis for future partnerships and alliances.

f) Strong micro–macro linkages in addressing the structural causes of poverty

Strategic planning processes helped organizations to focus on key lobbying leverage points and to connect up grassroots development work, research and documentation with advocacy goals.

Because SCF-UK staff had to produce Country Strategic Plans, they made connections between macro-level issues and those encountered at grassroots level, for example, around child labour. The understanding gained of this issue's complexity, i.e. that a simplistic ban would not help poor children, allowed the organization to develop a better informed campaign to improve multinational company employment practice. The organization now draws together its wide experience of the reality of children's lives to influence policy.

RECOMMENDATIONS FOR FUTURE PLANNING

What recommendations flow from this analysis for future planning processes in UK aid agencies? Oxfam considers that strategy needs to evolve and adapt, and that developing strategic leadership qualities in its staff is important. It is working on organizational development to develop the behavioural competencies its staff require to ensure maximum effectiveness.

However, time and resources spent on strategic planning may be wasted to the extent that organizations are unable to focus or change. It is difficult for NGOs to prioritize with the overwhelming demands made of them, especially given their concern to respond to felt needs. This leads to a tendency to overstretch capacities and consequent poor performance. Processes can even be counter-productive by encouraging organizations to encompass yet more new issues.

The key question is to what extent organizations undertaking strategic planning changed as a result and thereby increased their impact. Oxfam GB's increased emphasis on advocacy, mirrored by

ActionAid's latest strategic plan (1999), would logically lead to increased impact. However, the impact of advocacy work is particularly difficult to measure, given the difficulties in establishing causal links between specific lobbying activities, changes in policies achieved with changes in people's lives.

If strategic planning is to be used, less complex systems are required and unintelligible jargon needs to be minimized. Making strategic choices amongst options identified would be a more understandable method for prioritizing between demands than identifying strategic issues and resolving them as proposed by Bryson (1988: 56). With regard to the time country analysis takes, there will always be a need for more knowledge about countries worked in. Agencies should maximize their use of secondary data and ways of managing acquired knowledge. They should seek and respect staff capable of sound judgements regarding situations encountered. Only external informants without a vested interest in agency funding should be consulted.

More space should be made for evaluation, i.e. plans should run their course without additional organizational changes which mean performance can never be judged. The opinions of major stakeholders, i.e. beneficiaries, regarding impact should be sought in this process.

Finally, is strategic planning actually a substitute for inspirational, intuitive leadership (Barry, 1994)? My final recommendation is that UK aid agencies put the visioning back into strategic thinking – visions of success, visions of their organizations, but most importantly visions of a more humane world. This may lead to more heartfelt plans which staff would have no trouble in remembering, without retrieving those dusty volumes from their shelves.

NOTES

Although Oxfam GB employs the author, the views expressed are purely her own and do not represent an organizational view.

Persons interviewed: Ashvin Dayal and Heather Grady (Oxfam), Mike Aaronson (Save the Children), Pat Jones (CAFOD), Stephen Bell (Children's Aid Direct) and David Waller (Acord, ex-Oxfam).

GUIDE TO FURTHER READING

Mintzberg, Henry, Ahlstrand, Bruce and Lampel, Joseph (1998) *Strategy Safari: A Guided Tour Through the Wilds of Strategic Management*, London: Prentice Hall, contains a tour through the main fields of strategic management, 10 different approaches are shaped into a coherent school of strategy formation.

Bryson, John M. (1988) *Strategic Planning for Public and Non-profit Organisations – A Guide to Strengthening and Sustaining Organisational Achievement*, San Francisco: Jossey-Bass, provides a useful adaptation of commercial-sector strategic planning models for use in the public and non-profit sector.

Fowler, Alan (1997) *Striking a Balance: A Guide to Enhancing the Effectiveness of Non-Governmental Organisations in International Development*, London: Earthscan, provides an overview of how NGDOs can scale up their impact and improve their performance on all fronts, and includes a useful section on strategic planning implementation in NGDOs.

Johnson, Gerry, Scholes, Kevin (1999) *Exploring Corporate Strategy* (5th edn), London: Prentice Hall, provides a comprehensive overview of strategic management and organizational development with real-life examples and case studies.

REFERENCES

ActionAid (1999) *Fighting Poverty Together – ActionAid's Strategy 1999–2003*, London: ActionAid.

Barry, Brian (1994) *Strategic Planning Workbook for Non-profit Organisations* (9th edn), New York: Amherst H. Wilder Foundation.

Korten, David C. (1990) *Getting to the 21st Century, Voluntary Action and the Global Agenda*, West Hartford: Kumarian Press.

Wallace, Tina, Crowther, Sara and Shepherd, Andrew (1997) *Standardising Development: Influences on UK Aid Agencies Policies and Procedure*, Oxford: WorldView Publications.

10.14 Challenges for NGOs

Janet G. Townsend, Emma Mawdsley and Gina Porter

A TRANSNATIONAL COMMUNITY

NGOs working directly with the poor in the South face two great challenges to sustaining their own missions: the power of Northern fashion in 'development' (Esteva, 1992), and the speed of change in communications. NGOs around the world share ideas and practices across frontiers and across languages: they have become a transnational community, knit together by face-to-face encounters, a shared NGO language (Tvedt, 1998), flows of money (probably more than US$10 billion a year: Smillie, 1993) and the transmission of information, through newsletters, manuals, faxes, letters, and emails. Like the transnational business community, NGOs have been brought closer together by new speeds and lower prices of communication, by fax, telephone, cyberspace and cheap air travel. For NGOs, the spark-points of communication and change are in personal contact.

The geography of this transnational community of NGOs has been transformed. In 1980, the community was hierarchical and strongly controlled from the North, in both funding and knowledge. Then, with the rise of neo-liberal policies, multilateral agencies and other donors began to route funds to SNGOs (Southern NGOs) rather than the state, and many Southern governments began to sub-contract work to them. SNGOs burgeoned across most lower-income countries (outside China) in response to new funds from donors and government (Tvedt, 1998). In 1980, NNGOs (Northern NGOs) raised money to work directly in the South, on their own projects. Now, most support 'partner' SNGOs and few work direct.

SNGO access to outside knowledge has grown enormously. In the 1990s, a flood of manuals was published, while thousands of development workers from the South took short courses or master's degrees in the North, learning above all how the development industry operates. Many SNGOs have become 'professionalized'. Now, the big SNGOs which act as gatekeepers of knowledge and funding are often able to by-pass NNGOs and go straight to the donors; they have their own, smaller Southern 'partners'. Many roles once restricted to NNGOs are now also filled in the South, and some Northern workers feel that they have become managers, not activists or development workers, and doubt their future position.

Many knowledges

At the same time, many SNGOs feel excluded, cut off from access to knowledge and funding. In order to work and to survive, an SNGO needs many knowledges.

- Without *local knowledge*, no project or other intervention can succeed. Yet leaders of SNGOs will often startle a Northern visitor by saying, 'We are so ignorant. Tell us what to do/how to do it.' They underestimate what they know, and feel disqualified by those who command the latest language of 'development'. (This exclusion is compounded when their first language is not English.)
- Committed SNGOs are keen to find better ways to do what they do and better means of reaching their goals, whether they work in microfinance or environmental improvement. Networks which really exchange *information* can be invaluable to each member, but are rare.
- To work at all, NGOs need funding, and success is often measured much more in money secured than in achievements. To be able to submit an acceptable proposal to a donor breeds success, which breeds more success. Success breeds knowledge: how to write a 'log frame', whom to approach, and what language and what concepts to employ, and knowledge then breeds further success. For NGOs working directly with the poor, it now seems far more critical to 'success' *to access an information loop* than to '*make a difference*' with their clients. All these knowledges confer power, so that the hazards facing NGOs alter by the day.

'Partnership' between NNGOs and SNGOs was itself seen as a solution to inequalities in knowledge. Most partnerships, however, are a façade only, concealing highly asymmetrical power relations. Worse, they may act to exclude knowledge, by concentrating thought on issues known to appeal to the Northern partner, while other forms of possible change lie forgotten. A new and insidious form of external domination follows, even harder to resist (Fowler, 2000).

Cyberspace

In the North, the 'digital divide' cuts off the poor, the old or the ignorant from the skilled and prosperous who have access to computers and particularly to the internet, email and the World Wide Web. A whole new world of (relatively) cheap, very fast communication is open to some. Arguably, the internet makes NGOs more effective, whether in campaigns and advocacy or in fast response to disasters. Opportunities may be enormous. Within a decade, we may hear of a disaster in Orissa, India, go to the web, find a listing of all NGOs working in Orissa, all graded on their past performance, and with details not only of their past and present activities and finance but their plans for the immediate emergency, and we may send money direct by credit card to the NGO we fancy. So far, very few SNGOs use the web, because of its demands on their scarcest commodities: staff time and core funding. There is too much 'noise', too much useless and wrong information; finding what you need is far too time-consuming and too skilled; unless your equipment is state-of-the-art, everything takes too long; you may simply not have reliable electricity, and the telephone charges can be very prohibitive.

Email tends to strengthen inclusion in information loops and exclusion from them, but new 'virtual NGOs' may soon change the geography again. NNGOs already exist to supply SNGOs with knowledge and information: the IIED, the ITDG, INTRAC and others.[1] NGOs are now appearing which do all their work in cyberspace, setting up websites to share knowledge more cheaply (to those in cyberspace). SNGOs working in urban poverty can learn or teach through http://www.urbandevelopmentforum.org, or those seeking academic findings can go to http://www.eldis.org.[2] NGOs must face wholly new demands to explore worlds which may offer them much, or nothing, depending on both technical and social change.

CHANGING ROLES OF NGOS

Accountability and performance

Many donors have come to measure projects and programmes in terms of 'performance indicators', 'results' or 'outputs' rather than by evaluation of the difference which they make. Particularly in the longer term, this 'difference' is hard to identify and many writers are critical of the current framework. Accountability is normally upwards, to donors, not to the poor who are the most intimately concerned. Reporting mechanisms often seek to establish that money is not being misappropriated and that the approved activities are completed rather than that the desired changes are achieved, let alone that they are sustainable. 'Capacity building', seen as an important service to SNGOs, tends to be more about management and accountancy than about, say, legal literacy or dry latrines. 'If you can't count it, it doesn't count.' Microfinance yields 'performance indicators' rapidly, and has grown enormously as an activity. Perhaps the dominant knowledge is now about how an NGO and its jobs can survive, not about how the NGO may succeed in achieving its goals. 'Many [NGOs] have been created as survival strategies for a professional middle class' (Bebbington and Riddell, 1997: 111); many others, however committed, must first survive if they are to continue to work for their goals.

Sub-contracting services

SNGOs have grown immensely by sub-contracting services from the state. In India, they contract to care for a remarkable amount of mother-and-child health. They may work more cheaply than the state. In Bangladesh, for instance, while the civil service is heavily unionized, NGOs, despite being leading promoters of democracy, do not permit trade unions. Many think that such non-profit service providers should no longer call themselves NGOs, and their future is not at all clear. Several Bangladeshi NGOs, for instance, are enormous and provide services to millions. Donors are beginning to ask, 'What next?' Will donors have to hand back to the state? How? Will the state take over their education, health and training activities, and pay for them from taxes? Or will it keep them in the private sector, with more regulation? Will microfinance be taken over by banks? Become mutual institutions? Become banks, like the Grameen Bank and the SEWA bank? We may already have a large number of non-profit service providers, and a small number of thinking NGOs. Can thinking NGOs survive in such a world?

Bearers of social change

In the 1990s, new roles in mainstream development were conferred on NGOs by, for instance, the World Bank. NGOs are to strengthen civil society (Hulme and Edwards, 1997), to build social capital, to inform policy and to engage in advocacy and empowerment. Each presents a new challenge, for it can be an empty term for an empty activity or can bring radical change. Empowerment, for instance, could be merely learning how to vote. Self-empowerment, deciding how to use a vote and feeling able to take such a decision, although far more important, is extremely difficult both for the individual to achieve and the NGO to measure (Townsend *et al.*, 2000).

Future challenges to NGOs

The old struggles to secure funding while, perhaps, holding to a mission are rendered even more difficult by the sheer speed of change. There is talk of a world 'beyond aid', and NGOs have been advised to find new sources of funding, from their clients, from the local public or from business or both, which demands yet more new expertise. Sub-contracting, partnership, accountability and performance will continue to be contested. New communications technologies, particularly the web, may bring appalling digital divides and/or very positive changes around networking and/or new virtual NGOs which work only on the web. Many NGO workers at all levels feel that in this 'all change' world they keep leaping new hurdles and running desperately to stay in the same place. We hope that they will be able to use and create technical and social change to make greater contributions to positive change for the poor, for justice, for human rights and capabilities, through both practice and advocacy; but the demands could clearly overwhelm any sense of mission.

ACKNOWLEDGEMENTS

Acknowledgements are due to ESCOR (DFID) which is funding our research on knowledge in the transnational NGO community, and to Peter Oakley and Brian Pratt (from INTRAC, Oxford). The UK Department for International Development (DFID) supports policies, programmes and projects to promote international development. DFID provided funds for this study as part of that objective but the views and opinions expressed are those of the authors alone.

NOTES

1. IIED: International Institute for Environment and Development.
   ITDG: Intermediate Technology Development Group.
   INTRAC: Institute for Training, Research and Consultancy.
2. See also www.oneworld.org (for information by and about European NGOs working in low-income countries), www.mande.co.uk/news.htm (for monitoring and evaluation methods for social development), and www.id21.org (for European academic research on development).

GUIDE TO FURTHER READING

Fowler, A. (1997) *Striking a Balance: A Guide to Enhancing the Effectiveness of Non-governmental Organisations in International Development*, London: Earthscan.

Hulme, D. and Edwards, M. (eds) (1997) *NGOs, States and Donors: Too Close for Comfort?*, London: Macmillan.

Lewis, D. and Wallace, T. (eds) (2001) *New Roles, New Relevance: Development NGOs and the Challenge of Change*, Oxford: WorldView Publications.

Mawdsley, E., Townsend, J.G., Porter, G. and Oakley, P. (2001) *Knowledge, Power and Development Agendas: NGOs North and South*, Oxford: INTRAC.

Townsend, J.G., Zapata, E., Rowlands, J.M., Alberti, P. and Mercado, M. (2000) *Women and Power: Fighting Patriarchies and Poverty*, London: Zed Books.

REFERENCES

Bebbington, A. and Riddell, R. (1997) 'Heavy hands, hidden hands, holding hands? Donors, intermediary NGOs and civil society organisations', in D. Hulme and M. Edwards (eds) (see above).

Esteva, G. (1992) 'Development', in W. Sachs (ed.) *The Development Dictionary: A Guide to Knowledge as Power*, London: Zed Books.

Fowler, A. (2000) 'Introduction: Beyond partnership. Getting real about NGO relationships in the aid system', *IDS Bulletin* 31(3): 1–13.

Hulme, D. and Edwards, M. (1997) 'Conclusion: Too close to the powerful, too far from the powerless?', in D. Hulme and M. Edwards (eds) (see above).

Smillie, I. (1993) 'Introduction', in Ian Smillie and Henny Helmich (eds) *Non-Governmental Organisations and Governments: Stakeholders for Development*, Paris: Development Centre of the OECD.

Tvedt, T. (1998) *Angels of Mercy or Development Diplomats: NGOs and Foreign Aid*, Oxford: James Currey.

Index

Note: page numbers in *italics* refer to tables, page numbers in **bold** refer to figures.